T0270916

SVERIGES RIKSBANK AND THE HISTORY OF CENTRAL BANKING

Written in celebration of its 350th anniversary in 2018, this book details the history of the central bank of Sweden, Sveriges Riksbank, as presented by Klas Fregert. It relates the bank's history to the development of other major central banks around the world. Chapters are written by some of the more prominent scholars in the field of monetary economics and economic history. These chapters include an analysis of the Bank of England written by Charles Goodhart; the evolution of banking in America, written by Barry Eichengreen; a first account of the People's Bank of China, written by Franklin Allen, Xian Gu, and Jun Qian; as well as a chapter about the brief but important history of the European Central Bank, written by Otmar Issing.

Rodney Edvinsson is Associate Professor and Senior Lecturer in Economic History at the Stockholm University, where he also received his PhD, in 2005. He is also Pro Futura Fellow at the Swedish Collegium of Advanced Study. His main research interests include long-term economic growth, historical national accounts and monetary history.

Tor Jacobson is an economist with the central bank of Sweden, Sveriges Riksbank. He received a PhD in statistics at Uppsala University. Tor Jacobson's research interests include econometrics, empirical macro, banking, and empirical micro applications.

Daniel Waldenström is Professor of Economics at the Research Institute of Industrial Economics, IFN, and visiting professor at the Paris School of Economics. He received a PhD in economics from the Stockholm School of Economics and a PhD in economic history from Lund University.

STUDIES IN MACROECONOMIC HISTORY

Series Editor: Michael D. Bordo, *Rutgers University*

Editors
Owen F. Humpage, *Federal Reserve Bank of Cleveland*
Christopher M. Meissner, *University of California, Davis*
Kris James Mitchener, *Santa Clara University*
David C. Wheelock, *Federal Reserve Bank of St. Louis*

The titles in this series investigate themes of interest to economists and economic historians in the rapidly developing field of macroeconomic history. The four areas covered include the application of monetary and finance theory, international economics, and quantitative methods to historical problems; the historical application of growth and development theory and theories of business fluctuations; the history of domestic and international monetary, financial, and other macroeconomic institutions; and the history of international monetary and financial systems. The series amalgamates the former Cambridge University Press series *Studies in Monetary and Financial History* and *Studies in Quantitative Economic History.*

Other books in the series

Laurence M. Ball, *The Fed and Lehman Brothers* (2018)

Peter L. Rousseau and Paul Wachtel, Editors, *Financial Systems and Economic Growth* (2017)

Ernst Baltensperger and Peter Kugler, *Swiss Monetary History since the Early 19th Century* (2017)

Øyvind Eitrheim, Jan Tore Klovland, and Lars Fredrik Øksendal, *A Monetary History of Norway, 1816–2016* (2016)

Jan Fredrik Qvigstad, *On Central Banking* (2016)

Michael D. Bordo, Øyvind Eitrheim, Marc Flandreau, and Jan F. Qvigstad, Editors, *Central Banks at a Crossroads: What Can We Learn from History?* (2016)

Michael D. Bordo and Mark A. Wynne, Editors, *The Federal Reserve's Role in the Global Economy: A Historical Perspective* (2016)

Owen F. Humpage, Editor, *Current Federal Reserve Policy Under the Lens of Economic History: Essays to Commemorate the Federal Reserve System's Centennial* (2015)

Michael D. Bordo and William Roberds, Editors, *The Origins, History, and Future of the Federal Reserve: A Return to Jekyll Island* (2013)

Michael D. Bordo and Ronald MacDonald, Editors, *Credibility and the International Monetary Regime: A Historical Perspective* (2012)

Robert L. Hetzel, *The Great Recession: Market Failure or Policy Failure?* (2012)

Tobias Straumann, *Fixed Ideas of Money: Small States and Exchange Rate Regimes in Twentieth-Century Europe* (2010)

Forrest Capie, *The Bank of England: 1950s to 1979* (2010)

Aldo Musacchio, *Experiments in Financial Democracy: Corporate Governance and Financial Development in Brazil, 1882–1950* (2009)

Claudio Borio, Gianni Toniolo, and Piet Clement, Editors, *The Past and Future of Central Bank Cooperation* (2008)

Robert L. Hetzel, *The Monetary Policy of the Federal Reserve: A History* (2008)

Caroline Fohlin, *Finance Capitalism and Germany's Rise to Industrial Power* (2007)

John H. Wood, *A History of Central Banking in Great Britain and the United States* (2005)

Gianni Toniolo (with the assistance of Piet Clement), *Central Bank Cooperation at the Bank for International Settlements, 1930–1973* (2005)

Richard Burdekin and Pierre Siklos, Editors, *Deflation: Current and Historical Perspectives* (2004)

Pierre Siklos, *The Changing Face of Central Banking: Evolutionary Trends since World War II* (2002)

Michael D. Bordo and Roberto Cortés-Conde, Editors, *Transferring Wealth and Power from the Old to the New World: Monetary and Fiscal Institutions in the 17th through the 19th Centuries* (2001)

Howard Bodenhorn, *A History of Banking in Antebellum America: Financial Markets and Economic Development in an Era of Nation-Building* (2000)

Mark Harrison, Editor, *The Economics of World War II: Six Great Powers in International Comparison* (2000)

Angela Redish, *Bimetallism: An Economic and Historical Analysis* (2000)

Elmus Wicker, *Banking Panics of the Gilded Age* (2000)

Sveriges Riksbank and the History of Central Banking

Edited by

RODNEY EDVINSSON
Stockholm University

TOR JACOBSON
Sveriges Riksbank

DANIEL WALDENSTRÖM
Research Institute of Industrial Economics and
Paris School of Economics

CAMBRIDGE
UNIVERSITY PRESS

CAMBRIDGE
UNIVERSITY PRESS

University Printing House, Cambridge CB2 8BS, United Kingdom

One Liberty Plaza, 20th Floor, New York, NY 10006, USA

477 Williamstown Road, Port Melbourne, VIC 3207, Australia

314-321, 3rd Floor, Plot 3, Splendor Forum, Jasola District Centre, New Delhi - 110025, India

79 Anson Road, #06-04/06, Singapore 079906

Cambridge University Press is part of the University of Cambridge.

It furthers the University's mission by disseminating knowledge in the pursuit of
education, learning and research at the highest international levels of excellence.

www.cambridge.org
Information on this title: www.cambridge.org/9781107193109
DOI: 10.1017/9781108140430

© Sveriges Riksbank 2018

First published 2018

A catalogue record for this publication is available from the British Library

Library of Congress Cataloging in Publication data
Names: Jacobson, Tor, editor. | Edvinsson, Rodney, editor. |Waldenström, Daniel, 1974– editor.
Title: Sveriges Riksbank and the history of central banking / edited by Tor Jacobson, Sveriges
Riksbank, Rodney Edvinsson, Stockholm University, Daniel Waldenstrom, Uppsala
University.
Description: Cambridge, United Kingdom ; New York, NY : Cambridge University Press, 2018. |
Series: Studies in macroeconomic history | Includes bibliographical references and index.
Identifiers: LCCN 2018009851 | ISBN 9781107193109 (alk. paper)
Subjects: LCSH: Sveriges riksbank. | Banks and banking, Central – Sweden – History.
Classification: LCC HG3176 .S975 2018 | DDC 332.1/109485–dc23
LC record available at https://lccn.loc.gov/2018009851

ISBN 978-1-107-19310-9 Hardback

Contents

Figures

Tables

Contributors

Franklin Allen is Professor of Finance and Economics and Director of the Brevan Howard Centre at Imperial College London and has held these positions since July 2014. He was on the faculty of the Wharton School of the University of Pennsylvania from July 1980 to June 2016. He now has Emeritus status there.

Vincent Bignon is a Senior Expert Economist and Deputy Head of the Microeconomic Analysis Unit of the Banque de France, where his research deals with economic history and monetary theory and his policy work analyses the collateral framework of central banks and the regulation of central clearing counterparties. He received his PhD from Ecole Polytechnique in Paris, and has held various academic positions in Paris, Philadelphia and Geneva.

Michael D. Bordo is a Board of Governors Professor of Economics and director of the Center for Monetary and Financial History at Rutgers University, New Brunswick, New Jersey. He has held previous academic positions at the University of South Carolina and Carleton University in Ottawa, Canada. He is a Research Associate of the National Bureau of Economic Research, Cambridge, Massachusetts, and a member of the Shadow Open Market Committee. He has a BA degree from McGill University, an MSc in Economics from the London School of Economics and received a PhD in 1972 from the University of Chicago. He has published many articles in leading journals and thirteen books on monetary economics and monetary history. He is editor of a series of books for Cambridge University Press: Studies in Macroeconomic History.

Jakob De Haan is Professor of Political Economy, University of Groningen, the Netherlands and Head of Research of De Nederlandsche Bank. He graduated at the University of Groningen, where he also got his PhD. He has published extensively on issues like public debt, monetary policy, central bank independence, political and economic freedom and European integration.

Rodney Edvinsson is Associate Professor and Senior Lecturer in Economic History at the Stockholm University, where he also received his PhD in 2005. He is also Pro Futura Fellow at the Swedish Collegium of Advanced Study. His main research interests include long-term economic growth, historical national accounts and monetary history.

Barry Eichengreen is George C. Pardee and Helen N. Pardee Professor of Economics and Political Science at the University of California, Berkeley; Research Associate of the National Bureau of Economic Research; and Research Fellow of the Centre for Economic Policy Research.

Øyvind Eitrheim is a director at General Secretariat, Norges Bank. He served as Director of the Research Department at Norges Bank from 2001 to 2009 and has been coordinating projects related to Norges Bank's bicentenary project 1816–2016 and Norges Bank's projects on historical monetary statistics for Norway. He is a co-editor of *Central Banks at a Crossroads: What Can We Learn from History?* (Cambridge University Press, 2016, with M. D. Bordo, M. Flandreau and J. F. Qvigstad) and a co-author of *A Monetary History of Norway, 1816–2016* (Cambridge University Press, 2016, with J. T. Klovland and L. F. Øksendal).

Marc Flandreau holds the Howard Marks Chair of Economic History at the University of Pennsylvania. He received his PhD in Economics from the Ecole des Hautes Études en Sciences Sociales, Paris, in 1993 and is also a former graduate from the Ecole Normale Supérieure in Paris. Flandreau has published extensively on the history of the international monetary system, central banking, exchange-rate regimes, public finance, monetary unions, rating agencies, financial journalism, white-collar criminality, investment banking and the dynamics of financial crises.

Klas Fregert is Associate Professor of Economics at Lund University. His research interest is the interaction between macroeconomic regimes and the institutional structure of the economy in its organisation of labour and financial markets, and the degree of monetisation.

Charles A.E. Goodhart was trained as an economist at Cambridge (undergraduate) and Harvard (PhD). He then entered a career that alternated between academia (Cambridge, 1963–1965; London School of Economics, 1967/1968; again 1985–date), and worked in the official sector, mostly in the Bank of England (Department of Economic Affairs, 1965/1966; Bank of England, 1968–1985; Monetary Policy Committee, 1997–2000). He has worked throughout as a specialist monetary economist, focusing on policy issues and on financial regulation, both as an academic and in the Bank. He devised 'the Corset' in 1974, advised Hong Kong on 'the Link' in 1983, and Royal Bank of New Zealand on inflation targetry in 1988. He has written more books and articles on these subjects throughout the last 50 or 60 years than any sane person would want to read.

Xian Gu is an Assistant Professor of Finance at the School of Finance, Central University of Finance and Economics, Beijing. Her research interests are empirical banking and corporate finance. She received her PhD from Beijing Normal University and was a post-doctoral fellow at the Wharton School, University of Pennsylvania. She also served as an economist at CITIC Securities.

Otmar Issing is President of the Center for Financial Studies – Goethe University, Frankfurt, Germany. He was a member of the Executive Board of the Deutsche Bundesbank and thereafter a member of the Executive Board of the European Central Bank. Before becoming a central banker, he was Professor of Economics at the universities Erlangen-Nuremberg and Wuerzburg.

Tor Jacobson is an economist with the central bank of Sweden, Sveriges Riksbank. He received a PhD in statistics at Uppsala University, Sweden. Tor Jacobson's research interests include econometrics, banking and empirical micro applications.

Jan Tore Klovland is a Professor of Economics at the Norwegian School of Economics in Bergen, Norway. He is also affiliated with Norges Bank's bicentenary project, which comprises the construction of a database on historical monetary statistics and the publication of *A Monetary History of Norway, 1816–2016* (Cambridge University Press, 2016). His main research fields are business cycle history and price history as well as the development of ocean freight rates.

Pablo Martín-Aceña is Professor of Economics and Economic History at the University of Alcalá, Madrid. His research interests are Spanish and European financial and monetary history. Presently his main area of investigation is central banking. He has also done research in entrepreneurial history. He received a PhD in Economics from the Universidad Complutense de Madrid.

Jun "QJ" Qian is Professor of Finance and Executive Dean at Fanhai International School of Finance, Fudan University, Shanghai. His research interests span many topics of corporate finance, financial institutions and markets. He also examines the relationship between financial system development and economic growth in China, India and other emerging markets. He received his PhD in financial economics from University of Pennsylvania.

Masato Shizume is Professor of Economics at the Faculty of Political Science and Economics, Waseda University, Tokyo. Currently, his main research interests are in the Japanese economy in the modern world, the emergence of central banking, and origins and evolutions of money and monetary systems. He received a PhD in economics from Kobe University, Japan.

Pierre L. Siklos is based at Wilfrid Laurier University and Balsillie School of International Affairs, Ontario, specialises in macroeconomics with an emphasis on the study of inflation, central banks and financial markets. His research has been published in a variety of institutions and central banks.

Gianni Toniolo is a Senior Fellow at the LUISS School of European Political Economy, Rome; a Research Fellow at the Centre for Economic Policy Research, London; a Research professor emeritus of Economics and History at Duke University, North Carolina; and a Member of the European Academy. His main research areas are Europe's economic development since 1800, Monetary and banking history, the history of central banking and the economic policy of the European Union.

Daniel Waldenström is a Professor of Economics at the Research Institute of Industrial Economics, IFN, and Visiting Professor at the Paris School of Economics. He received a PhD in economics from the Stockholm School of Economics and a PhD in economic history from Lund University, Sweden. Daniel Waldenström's main research interests concern income and wealth inequality, taxation, intergenerational mobility and economic history.

Gerarda Westerhuis is Assistant Professor at the Department of History and Art History, Utrecht University. Her research focuses in particular on corporate governance, CEOs and boards, entrepreneurship, elites and financial history. She is co-author of the book on corporate governance and financing of Dutch business in the 20th century (Boom Publisher 2015) and project coordinator and co-editor of the volume *The Power of Corporate Networks: A Comparative and Historical Perspective* (Abingdon: Routledge 2014).

Jan Luiten van Zanden is Professor of Global Economic History at Utrecht University and is also affiliated with the University of Stellenbosch. He is the author of many publications on economic growth, inequality and gender relations. His publications include *The Long Road to the Industrial Revolution. The European Economy in a Global Perspective, 1000–1800* (Leiden: Brill Publishers, 2009); *How Was Life? Global Well-Being since 1820*, with Joerg Baten, Marco Mira d'Ercole, Auke Rijpma, Conal Smith and Marcel Timmer (eds) (Paris: OECD, 2014).

Introduction

Rodney Edvinsson, Tor Jacobson and Daniel Waldenström

In 2018 Sveriges Riksbank celebrates its 350-year anniversary. This volume outlines the Riksbank's historical development, along with the histories of some of the more important and dominating central banks worldwide.

The Riksbank was established in 1668, after the collapse of Stockholms Banco. It is thereby the world's oldest central bank, at least among the currently existing central banks.[1] Even if Sweden is a small country, and the Riksbank a small central bank, its unique historical continuity offers an international point of reference for studying the evolution of central banking in the international monetary system.

One ambition with this book is to place the history of the Riksbank in an international context of the development of central banking. For this reason, it assembles historical presentations of major central banks in the world, and presents comparisons between these. Each chapter on central banks in various countries – one chapter per bank – has a common theme, centred on their history of central banking practice and the various functions of money and central banking in different periods.

By attempting comparative historical analyses, this collective volume aims to clarify our understanding regarding some of the main lessons to be learned from the evolution of central bank institutions around the world. The tasks of central banks have evolved over a long period and are therefore, to a considerable extent, historically contingent. As shown in this book, many of the functions performed – or potentially performed – by central banks could well be undertaken by other organisations or institutions in society; for example, the private financial system, or other

---

[1] Which bank was the first acting central bank is, however, another, and still debated matter. For example, Quinn and Roberds (2006) claim that the early Bank of Amsterdam acted as central bank in the early sixteenth century.

governmental authorities. A recent example is the responsibility for micro-prudential bank supervision now re-allocated to the Bank of England. The question remains, what features characterise a central bank? Many of today's central banks were established after episodes of financial panic. Economic crises as stimuli for financial innovation are a fascinating phenomenon, still far from fully understood. In some countries, most notably in the USA and in Brazil, central banks were not called for until the twentieth century. Whereas in other countries they have been in place for centuries. Through a better understanding of regularities and irregularities in the past of central banks, we may be in a better position to foresee their future development.

1.1 Overview of the Book

The book contains 13 chapters – excluding this Introduction – written by some of the world's more prominent and renowned scholars on central bank history. The next chapter is intended to provide the readership with an international overview for the evolution of monetary policy regimes and central banking throughout four centuries, and is written by Michael Bordo and Pierre Siklos. They argue that the shifts from one monetary regime to another, for example from the Classical Gold standard to the gold exchange standard, have not always been smooth. Financial crises and the desire to maintain price stability contributed considerably in the transformation towards modern central banking. The chapter combines a narrative and econometric approach and investigates how the timing of the establishment of a central bank impacted on various economic variables, and poses the important counterfactual question of how aggregate economic activity would have developed had not a centralised monetary institution been in place. The authors show that the gold standard delivers the lowest inflation rate, while the Bretton Woods system the higher economic growth. The role models for central banking were the Bank of England in the eighteenth and nineteenth centuries, and the Federal Reserve in the twentieth century. However, in the late twentieth century, it was small open economies that were more prone to adopt new policy regimes, when the old ones no longer served their purpose.

Chapter 3, written by Klas Fregert, presents a history of the Riksbank – or Sveriges Riksbank – from an international perspective. One of the central questions raised is how the Riksbank has performed relative to its mandates, and the chapter finds a great deal of continuity in this respect. During the first 260 years, the convertibility of the

Riksbank deposits and notes into metal, and into foreign currencies until 1992, have been its overriding mandate. Already in the charter from 1668 it is stated that one purpose of the bank is to uphold the value of domestic coins. However, on several occasions the bank had to suspend convertibility, many times due to a crisis, such as warfare. Another mandate has been to take a responsibility for the financial system, which in its first century entailed that the Riksbank was the only financial intermediary. Although Stockholms Banco in 1661 was the first bank to issue paper notes in Europe, its subsequent failure delayed a further expansion of paper notes to the eighteenth century. While the King's attempt to use the Riksbank to finance the war with Russia in 1788 failed, the King nonetheless established a parallel currency issued by Riksgäldskontoret – The Swedish National Debt Office – which made the Riksbank irrelevant up to 1803. During the course of the nineteenth century, the Riksbank transformed from *the* (only) bank to *a* bank (among other banks), as a consequence of the expansion of private banking, and finally took the role of a central bank in the early twentieth century. In 1895 all interest-bearing deposits were closed, and the Riksbank obtained monopoly of issue in 1904. The Riksbank suspended convertibility in 1914 and 1931, and Sweden joined the Bretton Woods system in 1951. The banking sector was deregulated in the 1980s, which was followed by two major financial crises: 1991–1994, which was largely domestic, and 2008–2009, which was arguably mostly internationally caused. Inflation targeting was declared in 1993, after the abandonment of the fixed exchange rate in 1992.

In Chapter 4, Charles Goodhart offers a novel account of the history of the Bank of England. Given the considerable number of books written about this bank, the chapter is not yet another chronological overview. Instead, it describes the various functional activities and responsibilities of the bank separately – the relationships to the government, the people and other commercial banks – and explores how they have evolved over time. The Bank of England was established in 1694, and is thus the second oldest central bank in the world. It was originally established by the government to finance warfare, and continued to play that role later as well. For the main part of its history, up to the fall of the Bretton Woods system, the objective has been to maintain an external standard. At its inception, the bank received deposits from the general public, but their importance declined over time relative to notes. The bank ceased its activities as a commercial bank in 1914, enabling a focus on its role as a banker's bank. The main connection the bank has had with the general public is through its role as note issuer, and from 1844 it became the sole note issuer in England and Wales.

Chapter 5 covers the central bank of Spain, Banca de España, and is written by Pablo Martín-Aceña. Spain's central bank has old roots. Banco Nacional de San Carlos was established in 1782 by Charles III. The chapter argues that this was the same bank as Banca de España, on account of an institutional continuity. It was renamed as the Bank of San Fernando in 1829. The bank began issuing banknotes in the 1840s and in 1856 the bank was again renamed Banca de España. However, from an early stage the bank engaged actively in the government's monetary and fiscal policies, and gained monopoly of issue in the late nineteenth century. During the Spanish Civil War the Bank of Spain was divided, and a national and republican peseta circulated in parallel for three years. During the Franco regime, the Bank of Spain became an appendix to the Treasury, while after 1975 it regained its role as a monetary authority.

Chapter 6 deals with Banque de France, and is written by Vincent Bignon and Marc Flandreau. The French central bank was founded in 1800 by Napoleon Bonaparte and controlled by bankers, gaining monopoly of note issue in 1803. The bank was not formed to refinance sovereign debt, as in the case of the Bank of England and Norges Bank, and, in its ambition to stabilise the system of payment, was closer to the Bank of Amsterdam and the Riksbank. The bank also served the financial system by discounting bills of exchange. While the second half of the nineteenth century was characterised by a resilient financial system, in France accompanied by a low long-term inflation rate, the two world wars were a game changer. France was part of the gold bloc, and missed the recovery after the Great Depression because it was last to devalue. The Bank of France lost its independence in 1936, and was finally nationalised in 1945. After the Second World War the franc was regularly hit by exchange rate crises, and the euro could be seen as an institutional fix to that problem.

Chapter 7 describes the Dutch history of central banking, and is written by Gerarda Westerhuis and Jan Luiten van Zanden. The chapter takes a very long-term perspective and begins with the Amsterdam bank, which was founded in 1609 and functioned as a role model for Stockholm Banco and the Riksbank. For a very long period the bank money of Amsterdam bank was very stable, but confidence in the bank eroded in the late eighteenth century, and it was liquidated in 1821. The current De Nederlandsche Bank was founded in 1814, but served initially both public and private actors with ordinary retail functions. In this way, the activities resembled those of the Riksbank, which at this time had not taken on the full role of a central bank, and was essentially also a publicly-owned commercial bank. In the nineteenth century most shares of DNB were in private hands, and could distribute quite high dividends. At the end of the nineteenth century and beginning of the twentieth century the bank developed into a banker's bank. With the Bank Act of 1948, it became focused mostly on public, rather than private functions.

In Chapter 8, Øyvind Eitrheim and Jan Tore Klovland write the history of Norges Bank, the central bank of Norway, which was established in 1816, after Norway was separated from Denmark. Although Norway and Sweden formed a political union which lasted over most of the nineteenth century, Norges Bank nevertheless functioned independently, performing central bank services to the Norwegian economy. The chapter compares the developments in Norway and Sweden, and shows some striking similarities, for example in the development of consumer and real estate prices, but also points to important differences. In 1875, Norway, Sweden and Denmark formed the Scandinavian Monetary Union, and the krona was introduced as the common currency, but the union collapsed in 1914. During the Second World War there was a *de jure* Norges Bank in London, and a *de facto* Norges Bank in Oslo. As is the case for Sweden and the UK, Norway has not joined the euro.

Chapter 9 deals with the Italian central bank, Banca d'Italia, and is written by Gianni Toniolo. He discusses the specific circumstances of the evolution of Italian central banking: the political unification, the backwardness of the economy, the bank-oriented financial system and a relatively inefficient public administration. While the Italian financial system had once been the most advanced in Europe, by the time of the political unification in 1861 it was backward. The first decades of the Kingdom of Italy were characterised by the operation of several monetary authorities. The Bank of Italy was formed as a merger of several banks of issue in 1893, after the bankruptcy of the Banca Romana. According to Toniolo, Banca d'Italia graduated as a modern central bank after the crisis of 1907, when it became responsible for both monetary policy and the stability of the financial system. However, it did not gain monopoly of issue until 1926.

In Chapter 10, Masato Shizume deals with the Bank of Japan. After the Meiji Restoration in 1868, the government moved to establish a modern monetary and financial system. However, this turned out to be a process characterised by many trials and many errors. The Bank of Japan was formed in 1882, and was granted the right to issue banknotes alone. The primary objective of the bank was initially to reduce the quantity of notes in circulation, but also to consolidate the banking system. The gold standard was adopted in 1897, although suspension of convertibility occurred in 1917. Convertibility was briefly resumed in 1930, and then abandoned in 1931. The bank was reorganised in 1942. After Japan had lost the war, the bank faced ballooning government debt and high inflation. The bank provided liquidity for economic growth up to the 1970s, when a refocus was made towards stabilising the domestic economy.

In Chapter 11, Barry Eichengreen writes about the evolution of central banking in the United States. He divides its history into two eras: one before 1935, characterised by decentralisation due to opposition to the formation of a central bank system; and a second era after 1935, when the Federal Reserve became more centralised. The hostility towards central banking in the US goes back to the tension between the rights of the states and the federal government. There were two earlier, failed, attempts to introduce central banking in the country, the last one ending in 1836. The period 1837–1862 is sometimes described as the free banking period, since in these years only state-chartered banks existed, issuing their own notes which were convertible into specie. In the 1860s the union established federally-chartered banks, and nationwide banks were required to back their notes with federal government bonds. The Federal Reserve was established in 1913 as a consequence of the financial panic in 1907, which had demonstrated that the lender of last resort function could not be fully performed by private agents. The early Fed had a hybrid design, where different reserve banks asserted their independence, which inhibited expansionary open market operations. It was the Great Depression that exposed the weakness of the decentralised approach, when the Fed failed to act as lender of last resort. The chapter also describes the post-war episodes, such as the high levels of inflation during the 1970s and the Subprime crisis in the 2000s, and the unorthodox policies that the Fed developed in its aftermath.

Chapter 12 covers the history of the Bundesbank, and is written by Jakob de Haan. Germany's post-war central bank, the Bundesbank, was Europe's largest central bank at the time of the introduction of the euro. The Bundesbank continued to exercise the central bank functions that had already been performed by its predecessor, the Reichsbank, which existed between 1876 and 1945 and had a very volatile history. The financing of the budget deficit by the Reichstag from 1916 led to the well-known German hyperinflation period. In 1924, the new Reichsmark was set equal to one trillion (old) marks. After the Second World War the monetary system in Germany was in disarray for a second time, and the

Reichsmark became virtually worthless. In 1948 the allied forces created the Bank Deutcher Länder, and the D-mark replaced the Reichsmark. In 1957 the Bundesbank Act was passed, and the Bundesbank succeeded the Bank Deutcher Länder in 1958. Whereas the Bundesbank Act left it open to prioritise the internal or external value of the D-mark, the bank had to choose exchange rate stability over price stability. After the fall of the Bretton Woods System, the fight against inflation became the main goal of monetary policy. In the 1980s the Bundesbank was the most independent central bank in the world. In the 1990s, the Bundesbank oversaw two monetary unifications. Upon joining the euro, the Bundesbank became the largest central bank in the European System of Central Banks and it is probably fair to say that the monetary policy of the European Central Bank bears some resemblance to that of the Bundesbank.

Chapter 13 is written by Franklin Allen, Xian Gu, and Jun "QJ" Qian and is an historic account of the People's Bank of China, and is to the best of our knowledge the first one, thus quite the opposite of the case of the Bank of England. China had long experimented with paper currency and financial institutions, but it was not until 1897 that the first modern bank was formed – The Imperial Bank of China. The Nanjing-based Republican government established the Central Bank of China in the late 1920s; in the 1940s its excessive note issue led to hyperinflation. The People's Bank was formed in 1948, right before the foundation of the People's Republic of China. Despite being the world's largest central bank, its conduct of monetary policy is still not completely understood. The chapter shows how the People's Bank of China has evolved from initially a mixture of a commercial bank and a central bank, to what can be thought of as a modern central bank. The chapter further discusses the various policy instruments used by the People's Bank and how various financial reforms have promoted the development of the financial system and fostered economic growth.

In the final chapter, Otmar Issing outlines the evolution of the youngest amongst our selection of central banks, namely the European Central Bank, established in 1999. Issing shows that the European Central Bank has historically unique features in that monetary policy pertaining to the euro area has been ceded to a supranational institution. While the convergence criteria all involve nominal variables, real criteria – as given by theories of optimal currency areas, which emphasise real aspects – have been ignored. Its short history is filled with experiences providing various lessons for crisis management. During the recent financial crisis, the European Central Bank

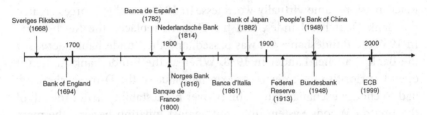

Figure 1.1 Timeline of central banks based on founding years (* denotes predecessor's founding year)

relied on a battery of measures, which contained the downside risks to price stability. Issing also discusses future challenges, for example the problems with the present low interest rate policy, which arguably may increase the risk of a future crisis, and the *de facto* deviations from the non-bailout clause.

The timeline of the central banks covered in this volume, ranked according to their founding years, is shown in Figure 1.1.

1.2 What is a Central Bank?

The evolution of the functions in central banking can be linked to the evolution of three important functions of money: as a medium of exchange, a unit of account, and a store of value. Following Stanley Jevons, one can also add the monetary function of a standard of deferred payment to this list.[2] The most important of these functions is money being a medium of exchange. Historically, establishing a common unit of account and standard of deferred payment has at times been a difficult process, and it was not fully accomplished until the Classical Gold standard of the late nineteenth century. It was during the Classical Gold standard that many central banks adopted functions that today are viewed as the defining features of central banking, although, as Eichengreen argues, a metallic standard itself provided the means to accomplish price and economic stability, without a central bank.

A precondition for a standard of deferred payment is a unit of account whose value is stable over time, i.e., that the debt money fulfils its role as a store of value. If there is great uncertainty concerning the future value of the means of payments that are used to repay debts, transaction costs increase, and may undermine financial intermediation altogether. The role of central banking is to reduce those risks and increase social trust, which

---

[2] Jevons (1875, p. 13).

also lowers the interest rate. If the private banking system is at risk of collapsing, central banks must act as lenders of last resort, i.e., as the defenders of convertibility of bank accounts.

As in the case of money, the definition of central banking is multi-faceted and there does not seem to exist any one definition of central banking that is accepted by all. For this reason, it is not trivial to judge which was the first central bank, and, more importantly, exactly when a bank becomes a central bank. The functions performed by central banks have also evolved over time, and sometimes central banks have retaken some of the functions they have previously performed, while abandoning others.

The IMF's (2016, p. 33–34) manual on monetary and financial statistics provides the following definition of a central bank, followed by a list of various functions usually performed:

The central bank is the domestic financial institution that exercises control over key aspects of the financial system ... The central bank functions generally comprise the following: (1) issuing currency; (2) conducting monetary policy, including by regulating money supply and credit; (3) managing international reserves; (4) transacting with the IMF; (5) providing credit to ODCs [Other Depository Corporations]; and (6) usually acting as banker to government in holding central government deposits and in providing credit in the form of overdrafts, advances, and purchases of debt securities.

Obviously, not all these functions were performed at all times by the banks discussed in this book. The term proto-central banking may be used to describe central banks that do not perform fully all functions of a modern central bank. Eichengreen suggests that since the Bank of United States in its capacity to redeem notes could be seen as a kind of monetary discipline, it assumed a proto-central bank role. The Second Bank assumed further proto-central bank functions, such as acting as a fiscal agent, performing open market operations, and intervening to stabilise the value of the dollar. Similarly, Westerhuis and van Zanden describe the Amsterdam Bank as a proto-central bank. The IMF definition is quite broad, and could be applied on the early proto-central banks established in the seventeenth, eighteenth and nineteenth centuries, including Stockholms Banco, the predecessor to the Riksbank. As mentioned by Bordo and Siklos, some of these banks were termed 'bank of issue', while the term 'central bank' first came into usage in the nineteenth century. Many of the early central banks were in fact the only banks, for example the Riksbank in 1668, or Norges Bank in 1816. As shown by Allen, Gu and Qian, the People's Bank of China was, although under a completely different economic system, initially also such a 'super bank'. Most of the banks discussed in this book assumed modern central bank functions in the early twentieth century, although Allen, Gu and Qian argue that the People's Bank of China did not start to function as a central bank until 1984.

The main function of a central bank is to provide and defend the value of the currency. The most important instrument to maintain that function consists in the control of the monetary base, with the backing of a state authority. According to the IMF, a currency 'consists of notes and coins that are of fixed nominal values and are issued or authorized by central banks or governments', while the domestic currency 'is the one that is legal tender in the economy' (IMF, 2016, p. 58). The monetary base 'comprises central bank liabilities that support the expansion of credit and broad money' and 'is defined as currency in circulation, ODCs' deposit holdings at the central bank, and those deposits of money-holding sectors at the central bank that are also included in broad money' (IMF, 2016, p. 197). The last quote also entails that deposits at a central bank from non-financial corporations or households are also included in the monetary base. For example, the bank money of Amsterdam Bank and all the deposits in the early Riksbank could be classified as a monetary base, if the two banks are classified as central banks. As shown by Westerhuis and van Zanden, the Amsterdam Bank enforced the use of its bank money by suppressing alternative uses; furthermore, private banking was not allowed – in this way the Amsterdam Bank functioned as a proto-central bank. If the unit of account of a currency always follows the issued currency that functions as a means of payment in its role as legal tender, the latter cannot lose its fixed nominal value. In contrast, private banknotes – and accounts in private banks – that are not legal tender can lose their nominal value, or even become worthless, and are therefore neither part of the domestic currency, nor the monetary base. Private note issuing banks during the free banking period were unable to perform central bank functions, since they did not control the monetary base. Their ability to perform the role of lender of last resort and government's bank in times of emergency was limited, since they could not issue a theoretically unlimited amount of notes that would be generally accepted, and backed by a state authority. Interestingly, the paper notes of a central bank may, similar to private notes, not be legal tender, as was the case with the banknotes of Bank of France in the nineteenth century. However, that limits the role of the bank as a central bank. As discussed by Bignon and Flandreau, this entailed that any doubts concerning the convertibility of notes could have led to the refusal of those notes in payment, which would have threatened the bank's ability to issue more banknotes to mitigate a liquidity crisis, one of the most important functions of a central bank.

Neither issuance of domestic currency, nor financial supervision, are necessary or sufficient conditions for central banking. Central bank functions can also be performed by other institutions. According to the IMF, a central bank can be distinguished from government, other depository corporations and other financial corporations; however, all four may perform central bank functions. Institutional sectorisation must be distinguished from functional sectorisation (IMF, 2016). Minting of commodity money did not necessarily involve a central bank, or even a depository corporation. As shown in this volume, government-backed paper money was issued in many countries without the backing of a central bank; in the US, for example, by Congress during the War of Independence and by the Treasury in the nineteenth century. When the Riksbank refused to act as the government's bank to finance the war of Gustav III, the king simply and swiftly established a competing money issuing institution.

Still today, in a few territories – Hong Kong, Scotland and Northern Ireland – private banks have been authorised to issue currency, but it is fully backed by reserves held at the central bank (IMF, 2016, p. 33). Although the early Swedish Riksbank did not issue domestic currency (since all currency consisted of coins issued by the mint) or provide credit to other depository corporations (since there were no other banks), from the start it exercised control over key aspects of the financial system. It was also a depository corporation, since it has always issued broad money. As discussed by Fregert, the early Riksbank defended the value of this broad money, even if it did not issue currency.

1.3 The Evolution of Central Banking: A Historical Overview

For the early modern period, the monetary standard in most countries can be described as bimetallism. Coins were minted in silver and gold, and circulated at a face value slightly above their intrinsic values. A generic problem was that bimetallism tended to revert into the circulation of separate currencies. Bimetallism allowed the circulation of different kinds of coins for both small and large transactions, but the circulation of different units of accounts increased transaction costs. As Charles Kindleberger notes: 'The medium-of-exchange function can tolerate more than one money without too much trouble; the unit-of-account function cannot.'[3] Because of the problems of debasement, the function as a standard of deferred payment was only partially accomplished. There

---

[3] Kindleberger (1984, p. 55).

were large problems in that newly minted coins were clipped from the sides, and the cut-off pieces sold as bullion. This increased transaction costs and in some periods a shortage of bullion occurred, which hampered further trade development. The use of bills of exchange spread in this period, and there was an incentive to pay the creditor in debased coins (Quinn and Roberds, 2006). Finding a solution to the problem of metallic money in its various monetary functions was a driving force in the early development of proto-central banking during the course of the eighteenth century. However, the development of non-commodity-based money generated new challenges, which further spurred the development of central banking.

Westerhuis and van Zanden describe how the Amsterdam Bank was originally founded as an exchange bank by the city. The Wisselbank valued coins according to their actual silver content and not their nominal value, which eliminated the rationale for debasement and explains why bank money circulated at a higher value than current money. Government-owned exchange banks had previously been developed in Mediterranean countries, which were not fractional reserve banks, to provide a stable base for the system of payments based on bills of exchange. Quinn and Roberds (2006) argue that their purpose was, however, not to stabilise the banking system, but the coinage.

As discussed in this volume, in early modern Sweden and Japan copper coins circulated as well (both countries were large copper producers), forming in effect trimetallic systems. In Sweden, the high transaction costs in using copper money led to an early development of paper money. Stockholms Banco was the first bank in Europe to issue paper notes even if it later collapsed due to a bank run, and was subsequently reorganised as the Riksbank in 1668. The rise of paper money introduced new contradictions into the monetary system. On the one hand, a paper currency strengthened the function of money as an abstract unit of account. On the other hand, the link between this abstract unit of account and precious metal was weakened.

Reduction of transactions costs is a fundamental feature of financial system development, and especially risk reduction. Before the Stockholms Banco was established in Sweden, a commonly applied interest rate was 12 per cent, but there is an example of a rate as high as 42 per cent. Towards the end of the century, the rates in Sweden were typically 5 to 12 per cent.[4] As described by Klas Fregert in this volume, one of the purposes of the

----

[4] Heckscher (1936, vol. I:2, pp. 577–581).

Riksbank was to act as financial intermediator in order to reduce interest rates. Bank money entailed that agents no longer had the direct guarantee for the value of money in the form of the earlier metal content of the coin. That presupposed a higher level of trust, which was accomplished through institutional innovation.[5]

Many of the functions today associated with central banking were not fulfilled by earlier proto-central banks. The Riksbank was not the main provider of the means of payment. In contrast to the Amsterdam Bank, the Riksbank in this period did not provide a common standard of deferred payment in the form of bank money. It had to operate different accounting systems for the four different currencies in circulation.[6]

The last decades of the eighteenth century and the first decades of the nineteenth century saw great political and monetary instability. Many countries experienced very high inflation rates. For example, the Danish-Norwegian monetary unit, the Riksdaler courant, was devalued by 90 per cent in 1813 against silver. This instability, however, also generated great political and monetary innovations. It was during this period that many of the central banks were established; for example, Banco Nacional de San Carlos in 1782, Banque de France in 1800, Finlands Bank in 1811, De Nederlandsche Bank in 1814, Norges Bank and the Österreichische Nationalbank in 1816 and Danmarks Nationalbank in 1818. In the US, the First Bank of the United States was established in 1791, and the Second Bank of the United States in 1816. The establishment of national banks fulfilling certain central bank functions was an important part of the process of establishing modern institutions.

During the 1820s the monetary system started to stabilise, and it remained stable for nearly a century, up to 1914. While in the early nineteenth century most countries were on a bimetallic standard, many of them switched to a gold standard in the 1870s. In 1873 Sweden switched to the gold standard, and formed the Scandinavian Monetary Union together with Denmark and Norway. The spread of industrialisation to countries outside the UK and the Netherlands was followed by a transformation of the international monetary and financial system. This process was accompanied by another wave of national, or central, bank creations among the great powers, for example, in Italy, Japan and the US. The gold standard finally established a common unit of account and standard of deferred payment, and there was no return to parallel domestic currencies after that.

---

[5] See also Bordo, Eitrheim, Flandreau, and Qvigstad (2016, p. 1).
[6] Heckscher (1936, vol. I:2, p. 607) and Davidson (1919, pp. 117–120).

The gold standard was made possible because of the spread of other means of payment, such as notes and bank accounts, and the minting of silver coins as a kind of coin token according to the so-called standard formula. However, there were also exceptions. For example, as discussed by Martín-Aceña, Spain never adopted the gold standard, and convertibility of notes into gold and silver was eventually suspended in 1883.

As discussed in this volume, the rapid growth of commercial banking in the second half of the nineteenth century posed new challenges for central banking. In Norway, the first savings bank was established in 1822, and the first commercial bank in 1848. The US ceased to have a proto-central bank after 1836. However, the free banking era in the nineteenth-century US had its counterpart in Europe as well. The note issue of proto-central banks, such as the Riksbank, was later challenged by the issuance of private notes. As discussed by Fregert, private banks issued their own notes, constituting a large part of the money supply. And as shown by Martín-Aceña, the monopoly of the Bank of San Fernando was broken by the formation of new commercial banks in the 1840s and hostility developed between these banks. Free banking practices thus had consequences for the functioning of economies. In the US, free banking led to recurrent banking panics, whereas none of the private note issuing banks in Sweden ever went bankrupt.

During the course of the nineteenth century, the development of the financial system ultimately led to the monopolisation of note issue and to a lender of last resort function – two parallel and interconnected processes. It was in this period that central banking was formed in a stricter sense. Goodhart notes that as long as the central bank also competed with commercial banks, it was restricted in its ability to act as a direct supervisor of other banks, and to act as lender of last resort. The London Clearing Bank viewed the role of the Bank of England as a central bank as being inconsistent with its residual role as a competitor with those same banks; the inconsistency was resolved in 1914, when the Bank of England ceased to be a commercial bank. During the nineteenth century, the role of financial intermediator for the central banks, towards the general public and non-financial firms, was taken over by private banks. The Norges Bank was granted monopoly of note issue already in 1818, even before the Bank of England became the sole note issuer in England and Wales in 1844. Although the Banque de France was granted monopoly of issue in 1803, it was only granted for 15 years. In 1874, the Banca de España, obtained monopoly of issue, which, according to Martín-Aceña, was a true milestone in Spanish financial history. As described by Masato Shizume, when the Bank of Japan was formed in 1882, the purpose initially was just to reduce the stock of private banknotes, but soon regulations were altered and the bank monopolised note issuing in 1883. Sweden was late, and did not gain monopoly until 1903.

It was largely the banking crisis of 1907 that forced many central banks to adopt the function of lender of last resort; in the US, this crisis led to the formation of the Federal Reserve in 1913. Hence, by 1914, central banking had been established as a practice among most of the richest countries in the world.

During the world wars and in the interwar period, the monetary system fell into disarray, reflecting the overall economic and political turmoil of the time. The gold standard was abandoned by most countries at the outbreak of the First World War, and its return in the 1920s was often accompanied by deflationary policies. Sweden did not participate in any of these wars, and could benefit from that. Generally, countries belonging to the sterling bloc, Britain and Scandinavia, experienced better economic development during the Great Depression than did countries retaining the gold standard. As discussed by Eichengreen, the decentralised system of the Federal Reserve prevented this institution from acting effectively during the Great Depression.

In the post-war period, Sweden was among the countries that joined the Bretton Woods system, in 1951. Like many other countries in the West, Sweden introduced heavy regulations of the financial system. The Federal Reserve adopted the dual mandate of full employment and price stability. Many central banks were nationalised in the 1940s – for example, Banque de France by 1945, Bank of England in 1947, and De Nederlandsche Bank in 1948. With the 1936 Bank Act, the Banca de España was *de facto* nationalised. As shown by Bordo and Siklos, this changed the mandate of central banks, initiating a process whereby central banks gained greater independence. Although the Banca de España became an appendix of the Treasury during Franco's regime (similar to the Reichsbank under Hitler), after his death in 1975, the bank's independence was re-established. Fixed exchange rates, free capital movements and independent monetary policy constituted the well-known impossible trinity, and, for example, the D-mark was revalued on several occasions against the dollar.

After the fall of the Bretton Woods system, the last vestiges of commodity money disappeared. There was no longer a link between the value of money and precious metal. This takes the function of money as an abstract unit of account to its extreme. The role of central banks changed from monopolisation of the main means of payment, to upholding the value of the unit of account and the standard of deferred payment. However, it was necessary to establish another type of anchor. The high inflation rates in the 1970s were followed by the fight to curb inflation. As described in this book, in various countries, including Sweden, the first anchor was initially a basket of exchange rates. As argued by Goodhart, the Bank of England initially became a 'pragmatic monetarist', with targets for broad money. Inflation targeting has characterised the last two or three decades of monetary policy. Inflation targeting has a similar function to convertibility into a precious metal. It involves a kind of convertibility, but in a bundle of commodities constituting the Consumer Price Index instead of gold, which, however, depreciates over time. Monetary policy evolved in response, and must be placed in a historical context to be understood. Although central banks always had the goal of defending the value of money, stability in terms of convertability into precious metal value, exchange rates or prices are different goals. While in the pre-industrial period the main concern was to defend convertibility into precious metal, short-term price stability could not be the main goal due to sharp fluctuations in harvests. While in the last 20 years, consumer prices have been stable in Sweden, exchange rates and the price of gold have not, and certainly not house prices.

In Sweden, one consequence of financial deregulation in the 1980s was the eruption of a financial crisis. As argued by Klas Fregert, Sweden has experienced two deep financial crises in the last 25 years, while no such crisis occurred after the Great Depression up to the 1980s. The return of financial crises entails that the role of the central bank as the lender of last resort has become more emphasized. As discussed by Eichengreen, the Subprime crisis posed new challenges for the Federal Reserve, which made the fateful decision not to rescue Lehman Brothers, but later exercised an unconventional monetary policy in order to avoid risking a new great depression. Nevertheless, Bordo and Siklos argue that monetary policy has not changed much following the recent financial crisis.

1.4 Comparing the Central Bank Histories: Commonalities and Dissimilarities

Comparing experiences from history across various central banks shows both commonalities and dissimilarities. As Bordo and Siklos argue, the search for common features may also be problematic; given, for example, that each financial crisis is different, it is unlikely that the business cycle can be regulated, and that imperatives of central banks are still linked to the government and domestic needs. Good results may also be due to good luck rather than good policies. Nevertheless, comparisons may provide grounds for important lessons on the restrictions imposed on central banking, as well as the scope for improvements of the functions associated with central banking, in various contexts. In the next chapter Bordo and Siklos quantify these similarities and idiosyncrasies, and discuss to what extent central banks can learn from each other.

As shown in this book, the relation between central banking and economic development is not straightforward – there has been much path dependence. Sweden has the oldest central bank, but nineteenth-century Sweden has been described as an impoverished sophisticate, with more advanced institutions than countries with a higher GDP per capita. Kindleberger argues that the advanced Swedish financial institutions in a context of economic backwardness provide a good counter-example to the Coase theorem, which states that an institutional outcome dances to the tune of economic reality.[7] However, the root to the advanced Swedish institutions is path dependence, going back to the Great Power period of the seventeenth century, when the Riksbank was formed. Nineteenth-century US was quite developed, surpassing the UK in terms of GDP per capita towards the end of the century, but, as discussed by Eichengreen, the Federal Reserve was not established until 1913. As shown by Bignon and Flandreau, in France there were several attempts to establish a bank of issue before the Banque de France was established in 1800: the Banque Générale Privée established by John Law in 1716, which crashed in 1720 (the bursting of the Mississippi Bubble), the establishment of Caisse d'Escompte in 1767, which never had any significant operation, and the formation of Caisse d'Escompte (again) in 1776 by a coalition of Parisian merchant bankers, only to disappear in 1793. Similar to the First and Second Bank of the USA, the Banque de France was not granted an infinite charter. However, in contrast to the Banque de France, the charters of the American banks were not prolonged, as discussed by Eichengreen.

In terms of upholding long-term price stability, the successes of central banks and their precursors have varied. Upholding the stability of the value of the currency has always been a concern for monetary authorities, but this was expressed differently in different countries under various periods. The instruments have varied over time: bimetallism and trimetallism, the gold standard, the gold exchange standard, the Bretton Woods system, money supply targeting and inflation targeting. The establishment of

---

[7] Kindleberger (1984, p. 74).

central banks has been important for the stability of the currency. In Holland, England and Sweden proto-central banks were established already in the seventeenth century – all three countries have later also avoided hyperinflation, even if prices in Sweden increased more than in Holland and England. Many countries with central banks experienced hyperinflation during and after the two world wars, most notably in Germany after the First World War, but these two wars were exceptional events. Today, inflation targeting seems to be the norm, with some small differences in targeted levels. While Sweden has an inflation target of 2 per cent, the Bank of Norway has set the target to 2.5 per cent, and the ECB below 2 per cent. The Federal Reserve did not introduce a formal target until 2012, when it was set at 2 per cent.

The nature of the relationship between the central bank and government has greatly varied over time and across countries. Until its nationalisation, the main objective of the Banca de España as a private joint-stock company was profit maximisation. Amsterdam Bank was established to provide a stable bank currency, not primarily as the government's bank, but was a public institution without a profit motive. The Banque de France was operationally independent from the government, while the enterprise of John Law more than 80 years earlier was an attempt to restructure the King's debt – however, both banks were private. The main function of the Riksbank was as a financial intermediator to the general public. The Riksbank was owned by the parliament, but various restrictions were imposed on it to ensure its role as the government's bank. Although many of the early central banks were private, they were *de facto* forced to take a public role. The Bank of England was established as the bank of the government, but was a private joint-stock company. However, as Goodhart notes, the Court of Directors never saw it as a profit-maximising institution, and the shareholders ceased to play any significant role in selecting the management of the bank after the first few years. According to the Bank of Japan Act of 1882, the governor was appointed by the Emperor, and the vice governor by government, and not by the shareholders. As Bordo and Siklos note, with a few exceptions private ownership of central banks has been eliminated. Today, most central banks are owned by governments, but also enjoy a large measure of independence. Decision-making, earlier often exercised by one individual, has also changed tremendously over time.

An important commonality in the developments of central banks occurred in the late nineteenth and early twentieth centuries, when most central banks monopolised the issuance of currency, and assumed the role of the banker's bank, or lender of last resort – two of the most prominent functions that we today associate with central banking. This seems to have followed in the wake of the massive expansion of deposit banking in the second half of the nineteenth century, and a free banking period.

Another important commonality is the impact of monetary instability and financial crises on the development of central bank functions. Many central banks were formed as a response to a crisis. Crises could be both enabling and disenabling. While the collapse of Stockholms Banco led to the formation of the Riksbank, the collapse of Banque Générale led to the postponement of a French public bank for almost a century. The Bank of England was given special privileges by the government, such as being the only joint-stock company in England, in exchange for providing finance to conduct war with France. Many banks were formed during the Napoleonic wars, or their aftermath. The Bank of Japan was formed after the Meiji Restoration. As discussed by Toniolo, the Banca d'Italia was formed in 1893 as a response to a bank crisis that swept away a number of banks, including one bank of issue. The financial crisis in 1907 had a huge impact on various central banks. For example, the Banca d'Italia then acquired some of the key features of a central bank, while in the US the crisis led to the establishment of the Fed. Westerhuis and van Zanden note that the financial crisis of 1921–1923 was a turning point for De Nederlandsche Bank, as it was then that the bank, for the first time, was forced to act as a lender of last resort. The People's Bank of China was established at the end of the Chinese Civil War. As discussed by Eichengreen, countries that moved towards having a formal inflation target early on often did so as a response to crisis, for example in Sweden in the early 1990s. After the Global Financial Crisis in 2007–2009, many central banks developed unconventional monetary policies to avoid deflation traps and the prospect of a new depression. The maintenance of financial stability rose to prominence.

An important dimension in central banking concerns the degree of centralisation and decentralisation. Central banking in itself reflects a development towards centralisation, but some central banks have been more decentralised than others. At one extreme is mono-banking, for example the early Riksbank, or the early People's Bank of China; at the other extreme is free banking without any central bank, for example the US in the nineteenth century. As argued by Eichengreen, the question of centralisation versus decentralisation has run throughout the history of the US, and the criticism pointed to the Federal Reserve's extraordinary measure during the Subprime crisis, and the opposition to government intervention in the economy, can be traced back to Andrew Jackson and Nicholas Biddle. Similarly, the decentralised structure of the early Italian central bank system, and its late monopolisation of note issue, as discussed by Toniolo, goes back to the political divide before unification in 1861. More recently, although the European Central Bank centralises monetary policy in the euro area, fiscal policy and political sovereignty belong to individual states, which puts the no-bailout clause in jeopardy, as discussed by Issing. This book also documents the interesting phenomenon of parallel central banking, for example, the competition between the Riksgälds and Riksbank notes in Sweden around 1800, and the splitting of the central banks in Spain during the Spanish Civil War and in Norway during the Second World War. As noted by Goodhart, the London Clearing Banks considered establishing a rival central bank in the years around 1910, before an agreement was reached, and the Bank of England ceased to operate as a commercial bank.

As shown in this book, throughout history the formats of monetary institutions have spread from country to country. In this respect, the evolution of central banking has been truly international. As mentioned by Westerhuis and van Zanden, the Amsterdam Exchange Bank was modelled after the Venetian Banco della Piazza di Rialto from 1587. The Amsterdam Bank, in turn, served as a model for Stockholms Banco, the precursor of Sveriges Riksbank, the Bank of England, and other proto-central banks, for example the Bank of Hamburg. Both Stockholms Banco and Sveriges Riksbank were divided into two departments, the lending bank and the exchange bank, a divide based on the secret cooperation between two Amsterdam banks. Hamilton's vision of the Bank of United States was modelled on the Bank of England. As discussed by Shizume, before establishing a central bank, Matsukata went abroad and studied the central bank system in Europe, and received the advice to use the National Bank of Belgium as a model for Japan. Various monetary unions and exchange rate regimes have also spread internationally. For example, the Banque de France was active in the formation of the Latin monetary union in the middle of the nineteenth century, a union which later inspired the formation of the Scandinavian currency union in 1873.

As shown in this book, the monetary policy instruments available to central banks, mainly through the control of the monetary base, have evolved tremendously over time, and there have been considerable differences across countries. The policy rules and recommended policy measures have to be related to their specific historical contexts. As argued by Bordo and Siklos, successful monetary policy only needs one instrument, the interest rate. As described by Fregert, the role of the seventeenth-century Riksbank as a financial intermediator was limited, since the interest rates of its operations were fixed and limited its ability to conduct monetary policy. During the nineteenth century, with free capital movement and convertibility of notes into gold or silver, the Mundell trilemma entailed that there was no monetary policy autonomy for the central bank. However, Bignon and Flandreau argue that the 'gold devices', which made it more costly to convert notes into precious metal, gave some autonomy to the Banque de France. As discussed by Goodhart, as guardian of the gold standard the Bank of England had to raise interest rates following panic (although Thornton and Bagehot argued that this measure should also be combined with ample lending). The Riksbank was a latecomer in this respect, and it was not until the 1890s that the bank started to influence short-term interest rates through the discounting of bills. As put forward by Eichengreen, the disinflation period during Paul Volcker showed that when inflation rates increase, the federal fund rates have to be raised proportionally more than the increase in inflation. This regularity later became known as the Taylor rule. Allen, Gu and Qian argue that in contrast to central banks in many advanced countries, no policy instruments represent a good proxy for China's monetary policy. In recent decades, central bank communication skills have been vastly improved worldwide, recognising the importance of transparency for the management of expectations.

1.5 The Future of Central Banking

Can history teach us something about the future of central banking? As shown in this book, changes in the functions performed by the Riksbank and other central banks have been both very gradual and very sudden. Gradual changes often reflect underlying economic transformation processes, such as the expansion of markets and industrialisation, while sudden changes have often been the consequences of economic or political crises, but could also happen due to political decisions taken. Roberds and Velde (2016) apply a Darwinian model to describe how central banks have evolved from the successes and failures of past institutions. There is no absorbing steady state, and the present conditions are also bound to evolve.

A striking feature of the last decade of central banking is that an ever-growing share of payments are performed electronically. It is conceivable that future central banks may no longer function as providers of means of payment, but undergo changes in ways similar to many of the current central banks' retreats from their functions as commercial banks in the nineteenth and early twentieth centuries. In a very long-term perspective, such changes in the functions performed by the central or national banks are by no means unique. In fact, some of the central banks presented in this volume were not the main providers of means of exchange throughout several periods in history; for example, the Riksbank up to the 1730s, in the 1790s, and in the mid-nineteenth century.

Another question is whether central banks could retreat from their functions as providers of a unit of account and standard of deferred payment, and lenders of last resort. Will the spread of crypto-currencies and financial innovations addressing bank risk-taking make central banking obsolete and irrelevant? Historically, it has usually been a state – or a state-like authority – that provided a unit of account. Even during the free banking era in the US, private banks did not invent their own unit of account. The use of several parallel currencies, fulfilling different roles in different settings, is hardly new historically, and was the characteristic feature of commodity money before the gold standard was adopted. The question is whether crypto-currencies could replace the standards of deferred payment currently upheld by central banks. Such standards would have to be legally binding, which in the final instance presupposes a state authority. In early seventeenth-century Holland, private agents were unable to develop instruments that would settle debts in a unit with a stable precious metal content; it was the city-sponsored Amsterdam Bank that created a new unit of account in the form of the banco florin. Legal measures can also be used to counterbalance the spread of electronic money. For example, Issing points out that reserve requirements create a structural demand for central bank money, forcing the financial institutions to come to the central bank.

However, when pondering the threats from crypto-currencies on central banks' functions as of today, there is reason to also consider the possibility that central banks may not resort to passively observing the ongoing transformation of payment systems. Very recently considerable efforts are being devoted by central banks around the globe to investigating if and how a central bank digital currency can be introduced – in parallel, or even as a replacement of paper currency – in light of future dwindling demand for cash in society. Thus, for example, projects in more or less advanced stages are currently, in 2017, pursued by the Bank of Canada, the Bank of England, and not least by the Riksbank. In Sweden the use of cash has rather dramatically declined recently, which has spurred an interest in a central bank digital currency. The Riksbank effort – known as the E-Krona project – aims at investigating this issue broadly from a host of perspectives including monetary policy, financial markets and their functioning and stability, consumers, and IT-technology, to mention just a few.

Since the financial crisis in 2007–2009, discussion has been raised about whether central banks should also take on additional tasks; for example, to once again become financial intermediators outside of the banking system (use the printing press), or take on a more active role in combatting unemployment. Furthermore, what position would central banks take in the short term, should there be a complete melt-down in the international financial system, and could they be superseded by other political institutions? Many of the authors in this book discuss to what extent usage of the unorthodox instruments developed after the recent financial crisis will continue into the future. As argued by Goodhart in relation to the Bank of England, 'the more severe the crisis, and the less successful the Central Bank in defusing that, the more likely will it be that the Government will take back into its own hands the conduct of monetary policy'. This specific phenomenon has been observed for Sweden on numerous occasions throughout history: at the end of the Great Nordic Wars; the circulation of a parallel currency by the King in the 1790s; and in the immediate post-war period. More recently, one repercussion of the failure of the European Central Bank to address the euro crisis fully has been the Brexit outcome and a growing opinion against the European Union. Goodhart argues in this book that when time comes, there will be a need to re-impose direct control of the banks, given that an increase in the interest rate would be too disruptive for the economy at large. A similar development occurred after the Great Depression.

1.6 Final Remarks

Given that the Riksbank is the world's oldest central bank, and Sweden was the first country to issue paper money in Europe, just how unique is the history of the Swedish central bank and its predecessor? We think this book demonstrates the many similarities between the history of Swedish central banking and those of central banking in other countries. Although Sweden is by no means universially unique, it was at the forefront as an institutional innovator. The Stockholms Banco was based on the model of the Amsterdam Bank, but in the specific setting of the Swedish copper standard. Sweden was among the first countries in the eighteenth century in which money supply was dominated by paper notes, but the development was similar in countries such as Denmark and England.

One of the important tasks of a central bank is to defend the long-term value of the unit of account and the standard of deferred payment. Historically this has been implemented by convertibility into precious metal, into other more stable currencies and by pursuing inflation targeting. As Klas Fregert discusses, England has historically been more successful in avoiding long-term inflation. However, compared with other countries, such as Germany, France, Japan and China, Sweden has been able to avoid spells of hyperinflation.

What the study of history enables us to do is not necessarily to predict the future more accrurately, but rather to become more open to different possibilities. By recognising historic patterns in changes as they occur, we may be able to better identify appropriate measures and reactions. An interesting feature of the formation of central banks is that shifts have often followed crises – the mother of many institutional innovations. Another lesson from this book is that what central banking ultimately entails, and which monetary policies are more efficient, will depend on the historical and geographical context. The very same functions are differently related to the role of central banking in different historical periods and countries. There has been some discussion of whether the Amsterdam Bank, the Riksbank, and the Bank of England were actually central banks when they were first formed. For example, none of these banks monopolised the issuing of coins and notes, and none acted as a lender of last resort. The monopolisation of note issue around 1900 in many countries has rightly been seen as a fundamental feature establishing central bank functionality. In contrast, in Sweden in the late seventeenth century, all money consisted of commodity money, while in the near future electronic payments may completely replace notes and coins. If the central bank is the only bank, as was the Riksbank during its first century and the People's Bank of China between 1950 and 1978, it does not need to act as lender of last resort. The function of managing the system of payment using debt money can then be fulfilled, even if the lender of last resort function is not in place. A central bank operating as a commercial bank, when there are many other commercial banks, introduces a conflict of interest with the basic features of central banking; it causes competition with the other banks and undermines the function of lender of last resort.

References

Bordo, M., Eitrheim, Ø., Flandreau, M., and Qvigstad, J. (2016) 'Introduction', in Bordo, M., Eitrheim, Ø., Flandreau, M. and Qvigstad, J. (eds), *Central Banks at a Crossroads: What Can We Learn from History?*, 1–17. Cambridge: Cambridge University Press.

Davidson, D. (1919) 'Sveriges Riksbank 1668–1918, I. Den Palmstruchska banken och Riksens Ständers bank under karolinska tiden'. Af Sven Brisman, *Ekonomisk Tidskrift*, vol. 21, pp. 115–146.

Heckscher, E. (1935–1949) *Sveriges ekonomiska historia från Gustav Vasa*, vol. I:1, I:2, II:1 and II:2. Stockholm: Bonnier.

IMF (2000) *Monetary and Financial Statistics Manual*, www.imf.org/external/pubs/ft/mfs/manual/pdf/mmfsFT.pdf.

IMF (2016) *Monetary and Financial Statistics Manual and Compilation Guide: Prepublication Draft*, www.imf.org/en/~/media/BA1EEFCA3BAD47F291BBFDF A8D99F05D.ashx.

Jevons, S. (1875) *Money and the Mechanism of Exchange*. London: Henry S. King & Co.

Kindleberger, C. (1984) *A Financial History of Western Europe*. London and New York: Routledge.

Quinn, S. and Roberds, W. (2006) 'An Economic Explanation of the Early Bank of Amsterdam, Debasement, Bills of Exchange, and the Emergence of the First Central Bank', www.frbatlanta.org/-/media/Documents/research/publications/wp/2006/w p0613.pdf.

Roberds, W. and Velde, F. (2016) 'The Descent of Central Banks (1400–1815)', in Bordo, M., Eitrheim, Ø., Flandreau, M. and Qvigstad, J. (eds), *Central Banks at a Crossroads: What Can We Learn from History?*, 1–17. Cambridge: Cambridge University Press.

Central Banks: Evolution and Innovation in Historical Perspective

Michael D. Bordo and Pierre L. Siklos[*]

2.1 Introduction

Central banks have evolved for close to four centuries. Their evolution was initially tied up with meeting the fiscal needs of nascent states to finance government expenditures in wars and to market the government's debt. This was certainly true of the Riksbank, originally named the Bank of the Estates of the Realm and created in 1668 and often referred to as the first central bank[1], and even the Bank of England created in 1694, in the midst of King William III's war with France.[2]

They were not initially called central banks but rather banks of issue. The term central bank only came into use in the late nineteenth century. Henry Thornton (1802) was arguably one of the first to lay down concepts of central banking, including the role of autonomy.[3] Later in the nineteenth century, central banks played a key role in managing the Gold Standard (i.e., following the "rules of the game").

The era of the Gold Standard, which in one form or another was to last until the 1920s, also saw the publication of Bagehot's *Lombard Street* (1873

---

[*] The authors are grateful to Maria Sole Pagliari for research assistance in collecting the data for this study. Comments on earlier drafts by the late Allan Meltzer, our discussant, Jan-Egbert Sturm, the editors, and participants at the April 2017 Riksbank Conference are gratefully acknowledged.

[1] The Riksbank was formed as a successor to its predecessor Stockholms Banco. It didn't immediately fund the government but did so later. See Fregert (2017).

[2] As Bagehot (1873) famously remarked: "It was founded by a Whig government because it was in desperate need of money ... "

[3] "To suffer the solicitations of merchants or the wishes of government to determine the measure of bank issues is unquestionably to adopt a very false principle of conduct" (Thornton 1802).

[1962]), which suggested that a central bank should be seen as a guarantor of financial stability by being a lender of last resort.[4]

The definition of financial stability has changed significantly over time. In the eighteenth and nineteenth centuries it meant avoiding or managing banking panics, that is, serving as a lender of last resort to the banking system and the payments system. This changed in the twentieth century with the adoption of the real bills doctrine, followed by the Federal Reserve in its early years. The real bills doctrine urged a central bank to head off an asset price boom because it would lead to inflation, then depression and deflation (Meltzer 2003, chapter 1). More recently, financial stability encompasses both being a lender of last resort and preventing imbalances that will lead to asset price booms and busts. Also the role of lender of last resort has expanded to include the entire financial system, not just the banking system.

The pace of central bank creation intensified in the nineteenth century reflecting a number of forces including the fiscal motive, the maintenance of specie convertibility and managing financial crises, especially towards the end of the century. The banks founded included the Banque de France (1800), the Norges Bank (1816)[5], the First and Second Banks of the United States (1791 and 1816), the Bank of Japan (1882), the Banca d'Italia (1893), and eventually the US Federal Reserve (1913). A few other central banks (e.g., the Reichsbank (1873), and the Swiss National Bank (1907)) reflected attempts to centralize the currency issue and facilitate financial transactions.

Central banks, because of their special status of having government charters and because of their size, evolved into bankers' banks and later into lenders of last resort. The Bank of England is generally viewed as the first central bank to successfully develop as a lender of last resort, as discussed in the Narrative Appendix in the NBER Working Paper version of this chapter. However, other early central banks such as the Riksbank, and the Banque de France, engaged in rescue operations in the nineteenth century. Indeed, the Banque de France in 1889 arranged a lifeboat operation of the Comptoir D'Escompte involving other commercial banks to provide the resources to keep the bank afloat before a recapitalization could be arranged. The Banque used very little of its own resources in the rescue but guaranteed the participants in the event of losses (Hautcoeur, Riva, and White 2014). According to the authors, the idea

---

[4] Perhaps best captured by Bagehot's view that "money would not manage itself."
[5] A political element played a role here as well because of the failed finances of Denmark which at the time had jurisdiction over Norway. See, for example, Qvigstad (2016).

for the famous lifeboat rescue by the Bank of England of Barings Bank in 1890 in London came from the French operation the year before. In the late twentieth century the Federal Reserve adopted the Too Big to Fail doctrine (Bordo 2014) but its first use goes back to several big bailouts in Germany in 1931 (Bordo and James 2015). Thus, as we show below, with the LLR function, as with other central bank functions, there was considerable learning among the central banking community. Indeed, we provide some suggestive evidence of a relationship among ten central banks that has all the markings of a network of a kind. In addition, along with the lender of last resort function, they evolved as both providers and protectors of the payments system.

In the twentieth century central banks took on the role of stabilizing the macroeconomy (i.e., maintaining price stability), stabilizing the business cycle and maintaining full employment. Since the 2007–2008 crisis, central banks have also been given responsibility for financial stability, namely, defusing financial imbalances and asset price booms before they destabilize the economy. In so doing central banks have only reprised a variant of a role that explains why many were created in the first place (e.g., see De Kock 1974).

The dual requirements of a monetary policy geared towards stable economic outcomes and a financial stability remit have always created challenges and this is nowhere more evident than in recent years, with central banks greatly expanding their interventions in the financial system while struggling to meet inflation objectives.

We consider the role of central banks in designing economic policy strategy and regime choices. Table 2.1 from Siklos (2002, Table 1.2) lists the year of origin and the primary motivation for the creation of 21 central banks in what are now referred to as advanced economies (AE). That table is updated to provide a few more details about the ten central banks that are the focus of the present study. If we exclude the European Central Bank (ECB), we find that the gap between the first central bank created (Sweden in 1668) and the last one (Canada in 1934) is 266 years. As noted above, in most cases, there was a fiscal motivation (e.g., war finance) or an attempt to stem the incidence of financial crises, that is, a financial stability imperative that largely explains the creation of several central banks. The lender of last resort function, often thought of as the *raison d'être* of central banking, grew in importance in the late nineteenth and twentieth centuries.

Our study blends quantitative with narrative explanations of the evolution of central banks. Our quantitative analysis covers the period from

Table 2.1 *The origins of central banks*

Year	Country	Name	Motivation
1668	Sweden	Bank of the Estates of the Realm. Forerunner of the Riksbank	Finance war and the consequences of excessive inflation
1694	UK	Bank of England	Finance war, debt management and banker to the government
1800	France	Banque de France	Manage public debt, issue notes, improve state revenue (seigniorage)
1816	Norway	Bank of Norway	Economic crisis in neighboring Denmark prompts monetary reform (note issue, lending)
1876	Germany	Reichsbank. Forerunner of Bundesbank	Consolidation of previous note issuing authorities following unification, upholds Gold Standard, under government management
1882	Japan	Bank of Japan	Part of modernization of Meiji regime, reserves management, vehicle to promote industrialization
1893	Italy	Banca d'Italia	Consolidation of previous note issuing authorities following unification and a banking crisis
1907	Switzerland	Swiss National Bank	Centralization and standardization of note issue, banker for the government and custodian of reserves
1913	USA	Federal Reserve System	Creation of lender of last resort and other banking-related functions
1934	Canada	Bank of Canada	Lender of last resort

Source: Adapted, updated, and expanded from Siklos (2002), Table 1.2. Several of the central banks in our sample have posted historical time series but they do not always include prices or real economic information (e.g., the Swiss National Bank's Historical time series: www.snb.ch/en/iabout/stat/statrep/statpubdis/id/statpub_histz_arch#t3).

1870 to 2015. The chosen sample reflects data limitations as well as the fact that central banks before that period did not resemble the institutions we know today. Nevertheless, where appropriate, we also examine data since the seventeenth century.

In Sections 2.2 and 2.3 we provide an overview of the evolution of monetary policy regimes, taking note of the changing role of different meanings of financial stability over time. In Section 2.4, we then provide some background to an analysis that aims, via econometric means, to quantify the similarities and idiosyncrasies of the ten central banks and the extent to which they represent a network of sorts where, in effect, some central banks learn from others. The empirical evidence is presented in Section 2.5. We examine a wide variety of evidence focusing on the behavior of inflation differentials of various kinds, their determinants in a panel setting. We also consider some counterfactuals that ask what inflation and real GDP performance might have looked like in select economies in our data set had central banks appeared on the scene earlier than was actually the case. Additional counterfactuals also consider how inflation and economic growth might have evolved had inflation targeting not been introduced in some of the countries that eventually adopted this monetary policy strategy.

Small open economies are especially useful harbingers of reform and change in central banking, most clearly during the second half of the twentieth century, particularly in the aftermath of the Bretton Woods system which arguably represents the last gasp of large economies dictating the monetary policy strategy of smaller and more open economies. The small open economies evince greater responsiveness to shocks emanating from the global and dominant economies over time. They also often experience crises whose duration is less persistent but happen frequently enough to prompt changes in how monetary policy is carried out. The combination of these two findings suggests a greater willingness to change course when it is needed.

Overall, however, the economies considered remain crisis prone in spite of the introduction and greater sophistication of monetary policy and central banking. Financial crises impose considerable economic costs even if these may have declined with improvements in central banking. Also, because of, or in spite of, exchange rate systems the influence of central banks is global. Finally, Section 2.6 concludes by summarizing lessons learned and the current prospects for central banks.

In spite of notable developments in our understanding of how macro-economies function and how they respond to shocks, policy makers continue to search for common features and hence a basis for cooperation across the many financial crises that have plagued the global economy over the centuries. Unfortunately, this kind of strategy does not bode well for the future of central banking for at least four reasons. First, financial crises are not alike except in so far as they all, to a greater or lesser extent, create significant to severe economic costs. Second, the central bank remains a critical institution within government. Autonomy or independence cannot prevent governments from eventually getting the monetary policy they want. Third, unless the pendulum swings back to greater sharing of sovereignty across countries, an unlikely scenario as this is written, domestic imperatives will ultimately dictate central banks' behavior. As a result, they will cooperate but only if it is beneficial for them to do so. Finally, even if financial crises of the kind experienced in 2007–2008 (Global Finiancial Crisis) and 2010–2012 (Eurozone sovereign debt crisis) are a thing of the past, political economy considerations are unlikely to relegate to history booms and busts in financial and business cycles.

As the current recovery in the real economy continues and the stance of monetary policy tightens, the likelihood that central banks will face a litmus test rises. And it is quite possible that the next time will be different and central banks will lose their prominence among the institutions responsible for carrying out stabilization policies. Early indications are that this is already happening (e.g., see Geithner 2016).

2.2 The Ebb and Flow of Policy Regimes

As is the case with many other institutions that evolve over time, certain features come to dominate before receding into the background as other more important forces emerge. The same is true of central banks. While the supporting role in the fiscal realm dominated the early history of many central banks this receded into the background as financial crises and real shocks led to larger and more volatile business cycle movements than governments were willing to tolerate. To be sure, there were fiscal implications from a change in the role of the central bank but the shift implied that monetary authorities would henceforth stand squarely between financial markets and other major economic stakeholders.

Business cycle volatility combined with the ever-present desire to maintain some form of price stability have also played a critical role in the evolution of central banking. As Paul Volcker, former FOMC (Federal Open Market Committee) Chairman, once pointed out: "No doubt several factors have contributed to enhancing the reputation of central banks. However, given the responsibility for monetary policy, shifting perceptions with respect to the importance of price stability must have been the most important" (Volcker 1990).

Once governments began to intervene more heavily to reduce the amplitude of business cycle movements, central banks moved from being subservient in the face of fiscal demands to eventually becoming a bulwark against fiscal pressures for monetary accommodation that would threaten to spill over into intolerably high inflation rates. Of course, recent successes in limiting excessive inflation need not imply that a permanent solution has been found, as we shall see. Indeed, any conquest of inflation must be weighed against the current fashion in government of maintaining a stable and sustainable fiscal policy. Were this view to change it is difficult, again based on the historical experience, to see how central banks can stand in the way of eventually accommodating the fiscal stance the politicians want.[6]

Beginning approximately in the 1950s, and culminating in the 1990s, central banks around the world became more autonomous. After World War II many countries adopted a full employment objective or nationalized their central banks so that they could serve as a tool of macroeconomic policy (e.g., the US in 1945). This significantly changed the mandate of central banks. Some, like the Fed, were required by legislation to follow a dual mandate – to maintain both price stability and full employment. In the US in the 1950s the Fed, under its Chairman William McChesney Martin, attached primary importance to price stability. He believed that price stability would encourage economic growth and high employment (e.g., see Bremner 2004).

By the mid-1960s, however, with the ascent of Keynesian thinking in the economics profession in the US administration and inside the Federal Reserve, the goal of price stability was made subservient to that of full employment. Similar shifts in thinking occurred in the UK, Canada, and the continent of Europe (with Germany and Switzerland being notable exceptions). Many argue that the belief in the ability to exploit the Phillips Curve trade-off was a key force leading to the Great Inflation from 1965 to 1983. Other factors such as political pressure (e.g., in the US to finance the Vietnam war and the Great Society), accommodating two oil price shocks, the consistent misreading of economic activity, and faulty analytics about

---

[6] Even the German Bundesbank, celebrated as the model of central bank autonomy, was, as article 12 of the 1957 Law states (since replaced when the Bundesbank joined the European System of Central Banks): "The Deutsche Bundesbank shall be bound, in so far as is consistent with its functions, to support the general economic policy of the Federal government" (Deutsche Bundesbank 1957, p. 120). Needless to say, when the government's and the central bank's policies are inconsistent, conflicts emerge and the Bundesbank is no stranger to these.

what drives business cycle activity, also contributed to the Great Inflation (see Bordo and Orphanides 2013). The Great Inflation ended in the period 1979 to 1982, thanks to the pursuit of credible anti-inflation policies, especially by Paul Volcker in the US and Margaret Thatcher in the UK, with similar actions in other countries later in the decade. This helped cement the importance of central bank independence and facilitated the wave of legislative changes that gave the monetary authorities the authority to carry out their policies according to their assigned mandate. However, this strategy needed to be balanced with the requirement of democratic accountability which, simultaneously, created the pressure to promote greater transparency.

Moreover, independence never meant that the central banks were free to engage in a monetary policy strategy of their own choosing. Rather, the monetary authorities, at least in advanced economies, were given or negotiated a remit received from the political authorities. Within the limitations of the tasks set out in legislation they were free to choose the manner in which that remit was carried out. This is the principle that came to be called instrument independence as distinct from goal independence. The latter is normally set by the government (see Debelle and Fischer 1994).[7]

These developments since the mid-1980s represented a sea change in the conduct of monetary policy as central banks had previously been proudly secretive. Indeed, central banks in the advanced world began a race to determine which one was most transparent or could provide the clearest forward guidance. This is the so-called "... long march toward greater transparency ..." (Blinder et al. 2008, p. 911) that has defined central banking since the early 1990s.[8]

The global financial crisis of 2007–2009 saw a reversal in all of these developments. Central banks were seen as less independent of government and more willing to provide fiscal support, even if only indirectly. Some also saw some advantage in becoming more "artful" and less forthcoming about their plans and policies. The days of the monetary authority standing by unless inflation and real economic activity showed signs of being excessively high or low quickly vanished. Central banks would do "whatever it takes" and intervene heavily and across a wide spectrum of economic activity.

Central bank governance has also evolved over time although, along this dimension, there are few indications today of any momentous reversals in

---

[7] The one notable modern exception being the European Central Bank.

[8] This development is reflected in indicators of central bank transparency. See Siklos (2002, 2011, 2017), and Dincer and Eichengreen (2014).

the offing. This is surprising, since the global financial crisis has revealed a number of flaws in the decision-making strategy adopted by some central banks and the reliability of their economic outlook.

Early in their history most central banks were dominated by a single decision-maker. While staff no doubt provide support to the Governor, central banking was seen as a top-down institution with extraordinary authority vested in the Governor. Even if Governors largely remain *primus inter pares* there is now recognition and perhaps even an expectation that decisions cannot be taken without the advice of a committee of experts whose accountability to the government varies. Moreover, it is now *de rigueur* to see central banks with technical and research support as a further indication of the professionalization of the central banking profession (e.g., see Adolph 2013). Paralleling this development has been the growth in the number of academics and economists as central bankers that have increasingly replaced the bankers and bureaucrats who originally ran most central banks. Moreover, in recent years, there is an impression that Central Bank Governors are once again playing a seemingly outsized role in public policy discussions. The media hangs on their every word. Meanwhile, political pressure on central banks is also on the rise. Surprisingly, perhaps, there have been fewer indications of policy makers questioning whether there is sufficient diversity of opinions represented in policy-making committees. Indeed, using the US case as an example, the slightest indication of greater Fed dissent attracts the immediate attention of financial markets.[9] To the extent there exists dissent it is reflected in monetary policy committee members' economic outlook. A recent example, of course, is the so-called Fed "dot plot."[10]

One area of central banking that has been left untouched by fads or fashion is the virtual elimination of a private sector ownership role in central banks. With a few notable exceptions (e.g., Switzerland), central banks were eventually nationalized and there is no hint that this phenomenon will ever be reversed. Indeed, whereas private ownership was part and parcel of the oldest central banks, after World War II, the central bank became an institution entirely within government.

At this juncture in monetary and economic history what has come to dominate the current debate is the policy strategy of central banking.

---

[9] Thornton and Wheelock (2014) review the history of dissents inside the FOMC. These peaked under Volcker and declined under Greenspan only to rise under Bernanke and Yellen's chairmanship.

[10] These are found in the projections contained in the Monetary Policy Reports of the US Federal Reserve. See www.federalreserve.gov/monetarypolicy/mpr_default.htm. Accessed September 2017.

Indeed, in order to understand where we might go from here there is a need to re-examine the evolution of monetary strategies since their creation in Sweden almost three and a half centuries ago.

From about the early 1990s until around 2007 monetary policy was increasingly viewed in narrow terms as concerned with inflation control. Prior to the most recent era, however, there was a never-ending struggle between central banks and governments that were thought to behave in a manner captured by the famous time-inconsistency hypothesis of Kydland and Prescott (1977). The hypothesis suggests that central bank independence (or "conservatism" in the language of Barro and Gordon (1983) and Rogoff (1985)) is a mechanism that can avoid inflation rising above what is deemed socially optimal by pushing back against the desire of the political authorities to exploit the Phillips Curve trade-off. By implication, this implies that the central bank can protect or even enhance its reputation by committing itself to a policy that is successful at preventing the discretion that may originate from political pressure on the monetary authorities.

Finally, a successful monetary policy requires only a single instrument, an interest rate, to ensure low and stable inflation. Indeed, ever since central banks became a tool for macroeconomic stabilization, especially after World War II, until the late 1980s and early 1990s, the strategy that consisted of aiming for adequate economic growth while limiting inflation (captured in the famous Taylor Principle) came to dominate the consensus about how best to conduct monetary policy. Moreover, these developments took place in parallel with acceptance that fiscal discipline is essential to allow the central bank to meet its objective.

The foregoing sentiments were also given credence by central bankers. As Mervyn King, former Governor of the Bank of England, once said (King 1995): "*Central banks are often accused of being obsessed with inflation. This is untrue. If they are obsessed with anything, it is with fiscal policy.*"Although this is arguably an exaggeration it does highlight the potential threat of fiscal dominance.

Events in recent years have not changed the consensus. Indeed, most governments and their central banks have not changed their numerical targets at all since the 2007–2009 global financial crisis. An outside observer would be hard-pressed to conclude that monetary policy changed as a result of the momentous events of the past few years. Yet, the strategy of monetary policy has changed and many central banks now have to balance the need to maintain financial system stability defined as preventing imbalances, in addition to achieving an inflation objective. The resort to a multiplicity of instruments to carry out a strategy that has yet to be made clear also suggests a regime shift in monetary policy.[11]

Equally important, the turmoil in global financial markets since 2007, followed by the admittedly slow return to a state that approaches pre-crisis conditions, led more central banks to invoke "data dependence" as a guide to monetary policy. The problem is that, even in the heyday of the Great Moderation, when central banks were fond of saying that they looked at everything before setting the stance of monetary policy, post-crisis this was seen by some as an inability, if not an unwillingness, to return to more rule-like behavior (e.g., see Siklos 2017).

Other than the breadth and scope of the interventions by central banks in recent years, there is some irony in that central banks are being encouraged, implicitly or explicitly, to adopt a strategy that defined the mandate of some of the oldest central banks, namely, a concern about preventing financial instability together with allowances for the possibility of fiscal dominance. Finally, the continued resort to various forms of quantitative easing (QE)- type policies in systemically important economies over an extended period of time also creates the possibility of a return of fiscal dominance through a back door.

Unlike our pre-crisis understanding of inflation, central bankers are not yet able to convince the public that their forays into financial market intervention are as effective as they have claimed or have consequences that they fully understand. Part of the problem is that so-called Unconventional Monetary Policies (UMP) are intended to deal with short-term difficulties in the financial system. Not surprisingly, much of the recent literature focuses on how QE affects asset prices. Demonstrating that UMP can help boost economic growth, return inflation to a normal level, or even convincing the public that output growth would have been even lower without it (a counterfactual) is much more difficult.

No wonder then, when faced with "pushing on a string," the response of central banks is to "push harder," but without a convincing reason to persist with such a strategy. A look back at the history of central banking, however, suggests that policy makers are attempting to define a new monetary policy strategy but one which has yet to be fully debated, let alone well understood.

---

[11] We define a monetary policy strategy in terms of the goals of monetary policy. In contrast, a monetary policy regime is characterized by the instruments used to achieve the stated strategy.

Central banks, it is sometimes forgotten, are creatures of sovereign states. As a result, while they are geared towards domestic objectives these are rarely removed from international concerns. Obviously, the prime symbol of the transmission of international shocks is via the exchange rate.

Other than flexible inflation targeting there have been three other monetary policy regimes that have, in one way or another, implicitly or explicitly taken a stand on the behavior of the exchange rate. Stated differently, declaring a policy regime aimed at some price stability objective, especially when this is combined with other goals (e.g., employment, another economic or political objective), should have implications for exchange rate behavior. Examples are the gold and the gold exchange standards, the Bretton Woods system of pegged but adjustable exchange rates, and the European Monetary Union which created a common currency by setting an irrevocable exchange rate between sovereign nations. Moreover, the strategy has generally always been the same across all regimes, namely, to achieve a form of price stability.

Financial system stability was generally believed to be the collateral benefit from any strategy that aims to keep inflation low and stable. At the risk of over-simplification, policy makers have always sought to, but did not always succeed, define a monetary policy regime that could rely on a minimum of policy instruments. One of the great appeals of flexible inflation targeting is that a single instrument is capable of meeting the strategic objectives of monetary policy. One only has to look at most central banks' depictions of the monetary policy transmission mechanism prior to the global financial crisis to get confirmation of this view.

Beyond these questions is the age-old role of exchange rates that has also re-emerged as a fallout from large swings in currency values as central banks follow non-traditional policies and deviate from the simple rules-based policies that appeared to have worked so well during the Great Moderation (Bordo and Schenk 2016). Some central banks have also returned to using the older tools of exchange market intervention to short circuit the market's view of the currency's appropriate value.

This development is also a reflection of another perennial concern of policy makers, namely, exchange rate stability. In contrast to the attempt to return to the pegged rates of the gold standard after World War I, the post-Bretton Woods era has favored greater exchange rate flexibility. Nevertheless, one cannot entirely dismiss the possibility of a return to some attempt to moderate exchange rate movements especially if inflation targeting, with its reliance on a floating exchange rate, is threatened. Since the latest global financial crisis there are signs, so far unsuccessful, that this movement towards formal exchange rate management could take place.[12]

What remains unclear is the form in which this might take place. A great deal of the difficulty is that the trade channel of exchange rate changes differs from the financial channel. In the former a depreciation improves the balance of trade but has negative effects on financial flows. Complicating matters is that these channels have a different impact depending on the sophistication of the financial system (e.g., see Kearns and Patel 2016).

Now is a propitious time to examine whether certain kinds of economies are more prone than others to adopting new strategies and to leave the past behind.[13] Moreover, it is also germane to ask whether certain types of events, such as a financial crisis, are likely to push an economy to a tipping point leading to a change in the monetary policy strategy in place.

Historically, large systemically important economies were at the forefront of creating central banks and vesting them with the authority and tools to influence economic outcomes. By the late twentieth century, however, it was the small open economies that were seen as relatively more innovative in developing best practices in monetary policy and coherent policy strategies. We provide some suggestive supporting evidence for this insight.

This chapter also argues that, by the late twentieth century, small open economies were more prone to adopting a new policy regime when the old one no longer served its purpose whereas large, less open, and systemically important economies were more reluctant to embrace new approaches to monetary policy.[14] Small open economies are more flexible[15] and as trade and financial globalization have progressed over time, especially after

---

[12] Ilzetzki, Reinhart, and Rogoff (2017), reprising an earlier study (Reinhart and Rogoff 2004), dispute the view held, for example, by the International Monetary Fund, that exchange rate regimes have typically become more flexible over the past couple of decades. Many inflation targeting economies are said to have adopted a variant of managed floating. One can, of course, quibble with their identification strategy. For example, Canadian officials would likely object to Canada's regime being labelled a managed float. Nevertheless their results remind us that policy makers scrutinize exchange rate movements as an indicator of exchange rate management.

[13] In what follows we focus on historical and economic reasons for the choice of regimes and not on the nexus between monetary thought and the adoption or rejection of particular forms of monetary policy. Interested readers should consult Laidler (2015), and references therein.

[14] In our data set these economies are: Canada, Norway, Sweden, and Switzerland.

[15] And are, in the words of Capie, Wood, and Castañeda (2016), perhaps more likely to be "high trust" societies.

World War II, more aware of the importance of global shocks. In contrast, large and systemically important countries have tended to rely on a pre-conceived notion that they were more immune to global influences, that is, that their policies potentially influence the rest of the world but not the other way around. It has taken the aftermath of the global crisis of 2007–2008 for even the Fed to begin publicly acknowledging that global conditions do matter. Assuming, as Milton Friedman once wrote, that in the aftermath of a crisis policy makers tend to be more receptive to the "ideas that are lying around"[16] there are at least two sets of results that can be informative about whether and what central banks learn from each other. First, the policy response and reforms in the aftermath of a financial crisis. Second, if the good ideas include the demonstration effect from the experience in other economies, then the extent to which global factors influence inflation in particular may well be to provide another indication of the likelihood of learning from others.

The combination of a flexible exchange rate regime, a concern for ensuring a form of price stability, and more effective prudential requirements rendered small open economies more nimble to policy shocks from various sources. Hence, innovations in the area of deciding when to reform an existing monetary policy regime may well originate in small open economies.[17]

A significant challenge in explaining the evolution of central banks across several economies lies in part with limitations on the scope and availability of data over a long span of time combined with what appear to be frequent breaks or interruptions in the conduct of monetary policy. Accordingly, this chapter combines a narrative approach with some empirical evidence that is intended to support some of the claims being made. While the empirical evidence may not be definitive, it does point in the direction of clear connections across economies in the policy regimes adopted over time. Our work is also assisted by the recent empirical

---

[16] In the Preface to the 1982 edition (p. xiv) of *Capitalism and Freedom* (2002) Milton Friedman argued: "Only a crisis – actual or perceived – produces real change. When that crisis occurs, the actions that are taken depend on the ideas that are lying around. That, I believe, is our basic function: to develop alternatives to existing policies, to keep them alive and available until the politically impossible becomes politically inevitable."

[17] There are, of course, some exceptions such as the UK, an early adopter of many innovations in the conduct of monetary policy that persist to this day. Similarly, in other important cases, such as in Europe, politics overwhelms economics leaving the tension between the desire to have a common currency, while relying on monetary policy to deliver economic outcomes its members aspire to, largely unresolved. See, for example, James (2012).

macroeconomic literature that has led to the view that a few common factors can explain the bulk of the variance of macroeconomic data. If this is the case, then there is considerable useful information in cross-country estimates of the drivers of inflation and economic growth.

As we shall see below, we can also potentially exploit correlations among cross-sectional units to consider a series of counterfactuals. Several central banks have existed for a long time although, in historical terms, the institution is comparatively young. Hence, one way to ascertain their influence is to ask "what if " kinds of questions to better understand their economic impact as policy regimes and strategies have evolved over time.

One asks whether countries that did not have a central bank while others did would have ended up with better macroeconomic performance had they created a central bank earlier. Relying on panel data since at least 1870, or before, for at least ten economies, we can generate hypothetical estimates of inflation and real GDP growth under a counterfactual scenario such as the one just described. Until the 1990s, major changes in policy regimes were often adopted more or less simultaneously by several countries. However, regimes often ended as a result of examples from the smaller economies. It is, therefore, worth asking whether the data are suggestive of a learning mechanism whereby a change in the policy regime originates first from smaller, more open economies instead of from the dominant economies in the international monetary system.

2.3 Policy Regimes in Historical Perspective

Convenience dictates that exchange rate regimes should be sub-divided into the fixed or floating varieties. Of course, fixed exchange rate regimes come in different guises while floating rate regimes are ill-defined unless an anchor for policy is chosen. In the case of fixed exchange rates we have seen the Gold Standard, through Bretton Woods, followed by the limited exchange rate systems that eventually gave birth to the European Exchange Rate Mechanism (ERM) and, finally, a monetary union of the kind that resulted in the creation of the euro. Floating regimes have generally targeted either a monetary aggregate or, in recent decades, inflation.

Since central banks represent one of the most potent symbols of sovereignty their ability to respond to both domestic and foreign shocks is an appropriate way to think about policy regimes. Clearly, how the exchange rate regime is understood is one way to identify how the balance between these two shocks defines the regime in place.

All told, it is fair to say that the world economy has seen five major monetary policy regimes adopted over the past two centuries.[18] They are: the gold and gold exchange standards of pre-World War II. Then, shortly after World War II ended, the Bretton Woods system was put in place though it took several years to fully take effect. Like its pre-war counterpart the regime remained anchored to the notion that exchange rate fluctuations should be limited. For a policy regime that has been outlived by all the other major monetary arrangements, save one, it is surprising how the Bretton Woods arrangement continues to appeal to the imagination of some policy makers. Perhaps, as Dooley et al. (2009) have argued, it is because the system survived in a different form after its presumed collapse in the early 1970s. Alternatively, as the global financial crisis reached its peak in 2008 and 2009, there were calls from many quarters for a "new Bretton Woods," culminating with the London Summit of the G20 leaders.[19]

Once Bretton Woods ended, the search for an anchor of monetary policy led, in quick succession, to variants of the Bretton Woods system, chiefly in Europe. It also led to the adoption of money growth targeting in a number of countries. The money growth targeting regime survived for less time than did Bretton Woods. In the case of Europe, the volatile transition from the end of the Bretton Woods system and the pegged exchange rate systems of the 1970s and 1980s hastened the adoption of a common currency (the euro) and a common central bank (the ECB) among several sovereign states, a monetary regime that had never before in history been implemented in this manner. Yet, the drive to create a single currency in Europe was primarily driven by political motives. Hence, while politics eventually enabled the creation of the euro, it also left the enterprise bereft of the necessary institutional structures and policy instruments necessary for its long-term survival which, as this is written, may be in doubt (e.g., see James 2012; Sinn 2014; Brunnermeier, James, and Landau 2016). Nevertheless, this regime has so far still managed to outlive Bretton Woods.

While loose forms of exchange rate targeting persisted in various parts of the world, it is the spread of inflation targeting that came to define the last two or three decades of monetary history. Indeed, on the eve of the global financial crisis, ten advanced economies had adopted an explicit

---

[18] Six regimes if we add the creation of central banks. See below.
[19] The desire for a new Bretton Woods was, like the aim for a monetary union in Europe, more enthusiastically supported by politicians than academic economists.

numerical inflation target (IT) as well as 23 emerging market economies. Four other economies (i.e., the US, the Eurozone, Switzerland, and Japan), although unwilling to acknowledge the IT label, do formally recognize the need to aim for some inflation objective and have made public a numerical value associated with some notion of price stability (e.g., see Siklos 2017).

Two other striking features about the foregoing brief history of policy regimes are worth noting. First, it is often the case that the transition from one type of regime to another, regardless of the type, has not always been a smooth one. The end of the Gold Standard during the interwar era and the Great Inflation that spelled the end of Bretton Woods immediately come to mind. Second, whereas there was less of a tendency for different policy regimes to overlap each other before World War II, following Bretton Woods there is seemingly more overlap in the adoption date of policy regimes ranging from inflation targeting to the most binding form of a fixed exchange rate regime, namely, the Eurozone single currency area. Nevertheless, with the exception of the UK, the adoption of IT is largely driven by small open economies while the larger, more systemically important economies have either resisted embracing the IT moniker or eschewed the label entirely. Table 2.2 provides a summary chronology of the principal monetary regimes since central banks examined in our sample were created.

If we focus on inflation performance only, the Gold Standard always delivers the lowest mean inflation rate followed by inflation targeting in those countries where it was adopted. Note, however, that inflation volatility is relatively higher than in any of the other policy regimes considered. Where IT is not adopted the period since the euro enters into circulation provides the next best inflation outcome.[20] In contrast, Bretton Woods always delivers the highest rate of economic growth. No wonder then that some of the G20 leaders at the 2008 Washington Summit summoned the memory of Bretton Woods (Winnett 2008). The Gold Standard comes in second place everywhere except for the UK, France, and Norway. Similarly, the relatively brief era of monetary targeting often performed worse than the other policy regimes, other than for the UK.

Comparisons such as these are hazardous for several reasons. First, performance in a particular era reflects a delay in problems that only emerge in the next era. Second, economic growth performance cannot entirely be associated with the monetary policy regime in place. Structural

---

[20] Except for France where ERM has a trivially lower average inflation rate (1.52 percent versus 1.54 percent during ERM).

Table 2.2 *Principal monetary regimes in select economies since the early nineteenth century*

Economy	Gold Standard	Bretton Woods	Monetary targeting	Inflation targeting	Exchange rate targeting/monetary union
Sweden	1873–1914 & 1922–1931	1959–1973		1993–	1993–1999 (MU)–2001
Inflation	-0.20 (3.75)	4.47 (1.98)		1.30 (1.24)	1.52 (0.61)
real GDP growth	2.63 (5.70)	3.97 (1.55)		2.20 (2.65)	1.37 (1.42)
United Kingdom	1821–1914 & 1925–1931	1959–1972	1976–1992	1992–	
Inflation	-0.38 (5.91)	4.26 (2.40)	7.79 (4.16)	2.65 (1.17)	
real GDP growth	0.94 (2.59)	2.49 (1.31)	1.82 (2.09)	1.72 (1.83)	
France	1878–1914 & 1926–1936	1959–1973			
Inflation	-0.94 (8.44)	4.50 (1.49)			1.54 (0.83)
real GDP growth	0.91 (4.09)	4.20 (1.02)			0.74 (1.43)

(cont.)

Table 2.2 (cont.)

Economy	Gold Standard	Bretton Woods	Monetary targeting	Inflation targeting	Exchange rate targeting/monetary union
Norway	1875–1914 & 1928–1931	1959–1971		2001–	1971–2000
Inflation	-0.17 (3.63)	4.08 (3.03)		1.82 (0.90)	5.82 (3.28)
real GDP growth	2.13 (2.70)	4.24 (1.34)		1.32 (1.41)	3.55 (1.64)
Germany	1871–1914 & 1924–1931	1959–1971	1975–1991		1993–1999 (MU)–2001
Inflation	0.70 (3.18)	2.54 (1.12)	3.23 (1.79)		1.89 (1.31)
real GDP growth	2.75 (4.40)	4.67 (2.10)	2.62 (1.84)		1.51 (1.13)
Japan	1897–1917 & 1930–1931	1964–1972		2013–	1973–2012§
Inflation	3.50 (8.93)	5.30 (1.16)			1.64 (2.84)
real GDP growth	3.05 (6.56)	9.11 (3.40)			1.04 (2.34)
Italy	1884–1917 & 1927–1934	1959–1973			1993–1999 (MU)–2001
Inflation					2.52 (4.35)
real GDP growth					2.52 (2.66)

(cont.)

	1878–1914	1964–1971	1980–1999	2000*–
Inflation	0.83 (7.23)	3.50 (2.00)	3.26 (1.40)	1.95 (1.00)
real GDP growth	2.57 (4.45)	5.44 (1.80)	1.42 (1.17)	−0.08 (2.09)

Switzerland

	1878–1914	1964–1971	1980–1999	2000*–
Inflation	−0.57 (4.30)	3.72 (1.31)	2.75 (1.92)	0.52 (0.89)
real GDP growth	2.66 (4.01)	4.07 (1.55)	1.70 (1.73)	1.82 (1.57)

USA

	1880–1917 & 1922–1933	1959–1971	1975–1991	2012**–
Inflation	0.73 (4.29)	2.71 (1.74)	5.75 (3.07)	
real GDP growth	3.00 (7.17)	4.23 (2.11)	2.94 (2.49)	

Canada

	1854–1914 & 1926–1929	1962–1970	1975–1981	1991–
Inflation	0.47 (3.78)	2.89 (1.14)	9.13 (1.56)	1.90 (1.11)
real GDP growth	4.08 (5.24)	5.36 (1.65)	3.41 (1.14)	2.41 (1.95)

*Inflation forecast targeting; **Medium-term inflation objective.

Source: Siklos (2002), Bordo and Siklos (2016), and references therein. Annual data are used. See the text for additional details. The first set of figures gives mean inflation; the second gives real GDP growth for the samples listed. The last column occasionally provides two sets of figures because two separate regimes are considered.

factors, often slow moving, emerge in the aftermath of wars or technological developments that are independent of the monetary policy in place. Finally, Stock and Watson (2004) noted some time ago that inflation performance during the Great Moderation reflected a healthy dose of "good luck" and not "good policy." The former was facilitated by relatively small shocks to the US economy. The same type of phenomenon may well have explained inflation performance elsewhere.

The recent financial crisis, however, has also reminded policy makers about another important distinction that has the potential of shifting the singular focus on the role of the exchange rate regime which has dominated the discourse about the influence of monetary policy regimes throughout history at least until 2008. The events of the past eight years have led to a rediscovery of the critical distinction between shocks that originate from the real and financial sectors of the economy. The interdependence referred to above, ostensibly guaranteed by a pure float, can be upended when financial flows enter the picture. In particular, the subsequent global impact of the financial shock that originated in the US in 2007 transcended how existing exchange rate regimes operated. Indeed, the highly synchronized downturn in economic activity and inflation was felt around the world irrespective of how flexible exchange rate regimes were.[21]

Instead, it was a coherent policy strategy which included commitment to an inflation objective at its core, a resilient and effective financial regulatory regime, together with the flexibility and willingness to use the available fiscal space, that proved to be the defining characteristic of economies that suffered relatively less economically, especially during the worst moments of the global and subsequent Eurozone sovereign debt crises in 2008 to 2010. Another important factor in the success of these countries was the financial structure and regulatory oversight. Before the crisis, Canada, Australia, and New Zealand had nationwide universal banks and one regulator in contrast to the US. Of course, these countries were not global financial centers unlike the UK which had a similar banking and regulatory structure (see Bordo, Redish, and Rockoff 2015). Finally, given

---

[21] Rey (2013), for example, is another study that emphasizes the importance of a global financial cycle since the 1990s, that is, a reflection of the monetary policy of a dominant or "centre country" (namely, the US). This has the implication of reducing the trilemma conditions for an independent monetary policy, where a floating exchange rate plays a critical role, to a dilemma. Hence, capital account management is necessary to preserve policy independence. Aizenman, Chinn, and Ito (2016) conclude, however, that the trilemma is alive and well, at least in emerging market economies.

the preference in some economies for a policy strategy that includes less than perfect exchange rate flexibility, a preference for anchoring expectations to an inflation objective proves relatively more important than the *de facto* exchange rate regime in place, especially in some emerging market economies. Indeed, IT regimes have been sufficiently successful at anchoring inflation expectations to the target that, years after the GFC, below target inflation rates are raising questions about whether central banks have become complacent, leading to calls to raise the inflation target substantially (e.g., see Ball 2014, and references therein). It seems that proponents of higher inflation want fewer opportunities to hit the ZLB (zero lower bound), which can create problems for central banks in search of still looser policies. But those who favor a tactic of raising inflation targets cannot provide a convincing argument that higher inflation will also improve aggregate economic performance. Estimating a threshold beyond which inflation produces a deterioration in economic growth has proved elusive (e.g., Bruno and Easterly 1998; Vaona 2012) Instead, the essence of their argument is that central banks must want to avoid the ZLB and negative interest rates as much as possible even though there is little evidence that these developments have proved difficult for central banks to implement

2.4 Methodological Approaches

The preceding section suggests that evaluating the impact of central banks throughout history is full of challenges requiring the interested observer to ask several "what if" questions. Even under ideal circumstances engaging in counterfactuals is difficult. For example, we ask what aggregate economic activity would look like if an institution expected to intervene in the economy to meet a particular objective, or set of objectives, did not exist. However, as noted above, central banks have been a pervasive feature of the economic landscape for a century or more. We have very few examples, or the necessary data, to evaluate what might happen if the monetary authority did not exist. Additionally, monetary history teaches us that it is difficult to neatly separate policy regimes from other events that are very likely to also have macroeconomic effects. To illustrate, it can be hazardous to contemplate what inflation and real economic growth might have been if a central bank had been created earlier, especially during an era when rules such as the Gold Standard were in place. Two reasons immediately come to mind. First, central banks under the Gold Standard were less interventionist than today's monetary authorities. Second, the Gold

Standard is squarely focused on price-level developments not inflation per se. Nevertheless, depending on the statistical properties of the price level, one may still be able to explore central bank performance in terms of inflation.[22]

However, there is considerable value in conducting counterfactual experiments if only to get an impression of some of the potential impacts of institutional changes such as the creation of a central bank. In part this is because rules are rarely followed exactly as intended. This is especially true when these institutions must also consider the international environment in which the rules are intended to be applied.

Counterfactuals, while useful, cannot entirely replace inference based on the observed behavior of time series. Accordingly, we also perform a set of econometric tests to help us understand not only when central bank policies may have changed but also the extent to which these changes are transmitted from one country to another over time.

2.4.1 Breaks, Gaps and Their Significance: Combining History and Econometrics

From a practical perspective the choice of a monetary policy regime is likely the result of a shift in the behavior of one or more key economic performance indicators. Of course, a regime change may create additional forces that may also produce changes in one or more of these indicators. For example, one can imagine that the creation of a central bank, the abandonment of one exchange rate regime and the adoption of another, or even an explicit commitment to achieving a form of price stability, at least statistically, is identified by a structural break. Given the particular importance of inflation in assessing central bank performance, an obvious choice then is to focus on the behavior of this variable. Output growth is another equally valid candidate for analysis. After all, an ostensible reason for inflation control is to create an environment for mitigating business cycle fluctuations, at least when interpreted through the prism of modern macroeconomic thought.

Whereas monetary policy was geared towards inflation control post-World War II, the gold and gold exchange standards involved strategies that focus on achieving a form of price-level stability by maintaining gold

---

[22] "Under the Gold Standard the price level has a stochastic trend because real shocks to the demand and supply of gold caused changes in the money supply and, over the long-term, the price level" (Bordo and Schwartz 1999). The stochastic trend nature of price movements implies that the stationary component of prices can be expressed in first differences of the (log) of prices.

convertibility through the setting of the fixed nominal price of gold. In more modern parlance, the price of gold served as the instrument that translated into achieving price-level stability.

There exist, of course, several statistical time series-based tests for structural breaks. Since the countries in our data set may well have undergone more than one regime shift, it is natural to consider first a test that allows for multiple structural breaks. The Bai and Perron (1998) test is likely the best-known test under the circumstances and we also adopt it here. It has the advantage that it is model-based as opposed to the standard univariate approaches to testing for breaks. Of course, if the model is mis-specified the advantage disappears.

All structural break tests, and many have been proposed, have their drawbacks (e.g., see Perron 2005). For example, Perron (1989) pointed out that the behavior of US real GDP is best described as a trend stationary process with a structural break around the time of the Great Depression, but that the result is partly dependent on the choice of the year of the break. As a result, unit root testing from structural break testing cannot be easily separated. Moreover, one must also consider the possibility that the break is akin to a one-time shock or can occur gradually.[23]

A retrospective historical analysis may well have led to selecting a year that differs from the statistical testing. It is precisely differences between these two methodologies that require further analysis.[24] Moreover, as we shall see below, a narrative approach often leads to a range of years over which a break takes place as opposed to a single year. And when a gradual change is allowed the statistical procedure leaves little choice but to adopt a somewhat ad hoc function or model to capture such changes. History can provide more flexible timing for breaks, but this does not mean that there is unanimity in pinpointing, for example, when financial crises take place and for how long.[25]

In one set of calculations, we assume that before the creation of the US Federal Reserve the Bank of England serves as the benchmark for global

[23] An innovation (innovation outlier, or IO) model which assumes that the break occurs gradually, with the breaks following the same dynamic path as the innovations, while the additive model (or additive outlier, AO) model assumes the breaks occur immediately.

[24] There is occasionally the tendency to ignore history and rely instead on statistical testing alone. This ignores that the specification of the null and alternative hypotheses, not to mention the power of available tests, invites caution in relying too heavily on this kind of strategy. Similarly, historical analyses are also subject to selectivity bias. Presenting both forms of evidence at least has the advantage of prompting the researcher to look for some explanation for any discrepancy between the timing adopted by historians and the one generated via econometric means

[25] An illustration is the Reinhart and Rogoff (2009) dating of various types of financial crises. Bordo and Meissner (2016) find fault with some of the banking and currency crises identified by Reinhart and Rogoff. In what follows we adopt the Bordo and Meissner (2016) chronology.

price stability. After 1913 the Federal Reserve is then assumed to serve as the standard sought by the economies in our sample. The two are chosen because of the systemic importance of both economies. Clearly, other benchmarks are possible (see below). A difficulty here is that, under the traditional Gold Standard and successive regimes tied to gold, the instrument of policy, as previously noted, translates into a regime geared towards the maintenance of price-*level* stability. Once the Gold Standard ended in the middle of the twentieth century, the objective of policy evolved into a focus on inflation performance. In what follows the discussion is in terms of inflation performance strictly for convenience. For the Gold Standard era we derive the estimates of interest in terms of the price level (or, rather, the log of the price level) and then take the rate of change to ensure comparability with the post-Gold Standard era.[26]

Define

$$d_{it} = \pi_{it} - \pi_t^B \qquad (1)$$

where π is inflation and π^B is inflation in the benchmark economy. Each economy is indexed by i at time t. Notice that the benchmark economies are, by modern standards, large systemically important economies. If smaller, more open, economies adopt similar regimes over time and, as a result, deliver comparable inflation rates then d in equation (1) is expected to be stationary. If, however, stationarity is rejected then so is convergence of sorts between economy i and the benchmark economy. A possibility then is that adopting a new monetary regime is conditioned on the development, persistence, and size of any gap in inflation performance between economy i and the benchmark economy in question.[27] In other words, we treat equation (1) as serving as a proxy for the level of dissatisfaction with the existing policy strategy.[28] Dissatisfaction with the preferred or best-performing existing international strategy may reflect a domestic failure to follow best practice in monetary policy. Alternatively,

---

[26] For the Gold Standard (and related regimes) period we also present and provide cross-country comparisons in terms of the price level. Not all results are presented below.

[27] A similar argument can be made in terms of another key economic indicator such as real GDP growth. Arguably, economic development is influenced by structural factors that are not easily quantified. Hence, for reasons already stated, we prefer to focus on inflation performance.

[28] For the benchmark economies the level of unhappiness with the existing regime would be its own historical experience for one or more key economic indicator or continued discrepancies vis-à-vis expectations for the particular economic indicator in question. This brings up the question of credibility in monetary policy. See Bordo and Siklos (2016) for an historical examination relying on a similar data set as the one used in the present study. The current study is more comparative in nature.

if the benchmark economy no longer serves as the lodestar for how to conduct monetary policy then the source of unhappiness with the current regime lies with the economy that is seen as the standard for others to follow.

As noted above, other benchmarks are contemplated. For example, if the ten central banks in our study can, in fact, be treated as a global network of central banks that learn from each other then perhaps an international measure of inflation is a more suitable benchmark.[29] Unfortunately, no universally accepted measure of global inflation exists. Therefore, we construct three proxies. The simplest is an arithmetic average across the ten economies in our data set. Next, we extract the first principal component in a factor model of inflation, again including data from all ten countries in the sample.[30] Finally, many researchers extract a trend or equilibrium measure of a time series by applying the Hodrick-Prescott (H-P) filter. Hamilton (2017) not only reminds us of the drawbacks and distortions induced by this filter but recommends a simple new alternative. In what follows, we implement Hamilton's replacement for the H-P filter to proxy for π_t^B in equation (1).

2.4.2 Counterfactuals

At the simplest level counterfactuals are an attempt to answer "what if" kinds of questions. As a result, quantitative methods to obtain counterfactual results are varied. In what follows, we apply Hsiao et al.'s (2012) method.

To illustrate their methodology consider the following four central banks. They are, in order of the dating of their creation (years in parenthesis; see Table 2.1): the Bank of Italy (1893), the Swiss National Bank (1907), the US Federal Reserve (1913), and the Bank of Canada (1934). Ideally, we would like some data when these institutions did not exist in order to determine what macroeconomic performance would have been like if a central bank had been created earlier. The treatment or intervention then refers to the year when a central bank is created.

Next, consider Figure 2.1. The plot shows when central banks were created relative to when these economies became nation or sovereign states in the modern sense of the word.[31] A positive bar means that the central bank came into existence before statehood or independence, while a

[29] Alternatively, the real price of gold is also a suitable benchmark.
[30] Again, in the Gold Standard era, we can examine these same relationships in terms of the (log) of the price level although the conclusions did not change.
[31] The traditional definition relies on a date of independence or the introduction of a Constitution.

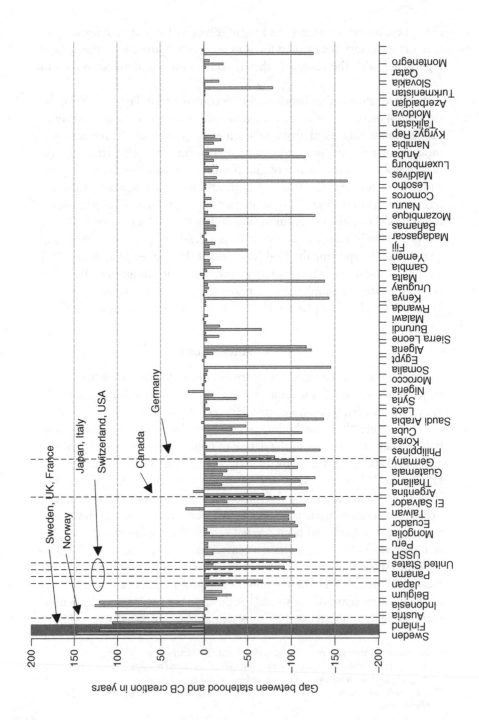

negative bar indicates how many years it took once statehood was achieved until the monetary authority was created. The central banks that are identified by the vertical dashed lines are the subject of the empirical analysis. The choices are dictated by data availability and quality over a long time span. Details are left to the following section.

Almost half the central banks in our sample were in existence before statehood. As discussed above they were, at least for a time, banks of issue and their functions would evolve over time. However, statehood generally comes first followed by the creation of a central bank. Indeed, in many cases, the gap between the two events is small, a reflection of the almost symbiotic link between the concepts of sovereignty and central banking.

Figure 2.2 plots the number of central banks created since the Riksbank, the world's first central bank, opened its doors in 1668. It is seen that central banks are largely a creature of the twentieth century. Indeed, the pace of central bank creation speeds up after the 1950s. Hence, central banks are comparatively young institutions. However, because so many central banks came into existence after World War II, when data availability increases dramatically, the experimental way of conducting a counterfactual experiment is simply not available or practical in the present context. Therefore, an alternative approach is required and this is where a long span of historical data is especially helpful.

Returning to the four central banks in our example, we have a substantial amount of data about how economies performed in several economies when monetary authorities did not exist in Italy, Switzerland, the US, and Canada. While data availability is adequate statistical challenges remain, as we shall see.

The approach proposed and implemented by Hsiao et al. (2012) exploits information in a cross-section of data. Hsiao et al. (2012) ask what economic growth in Hong Kong would have been like if sovereignty had not

---

Figure 2.1   Years of central bank formation and statehood (previous page)
Note: Vertical dashed lines indicate the central banks used in this study. The bars represent the difference between the year a central bank was established, less the year of statehood or independence.
Source: Data are from *Central Bank Directory* 2014 (London: Central Bank Publications) and the CIA World Factbook. The central banks explicitly labelled in the figure are the subject of the empirical and narrative analysis in the present study.

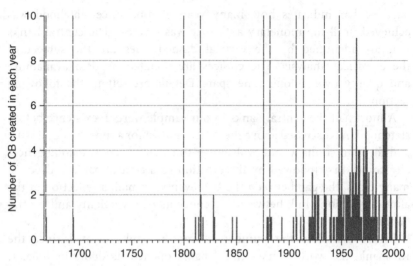

Figure 2.2 Number of central banks established
Note: See note to Figure 2.1.

changed hands from Britain to China in July 1997.[32] The basic premise of
the counterfactual is that there exist common factors that drive economic
variables of interest whether or not there is some treatment or intervention. In the present context, once a central bank is created there is the
presumption that an institution is created that has some discretion.
Granted, the scope of that discretion will be limited by the exchange rate
regime in place, the remit given to the institution, and its autonomy from
government influence, to name three important factors. Similarly, there is
not quite a comparable institutional mechanism that is able to fully take
the place of the central bank.[33] Yet, economic performance, as summarized, say, by the price level, inflation and output growth performance, in

[32] They also ask what economic performance would have been if the 2003 economic
partnership agreement with mainland China had not been signed.
[33] Before the creation of central banks there were, however, alternative institutional
mechanisms that effectively played some of the role later assigned to a central bank
(e. g., as the US Treasury did in the case of financial crises in the National banking era
when it shifted deposits from the Independent Treasury to key commercial banks or the
role of clearing houses in issuing emergency currency (Timberlake 1984; Gorton 1985)).
Also in the case of some dominant nationwide commercial banks in Australia, Canada,
and New Zealand. In some cases, the government would also intervene from time to time
in a manner reminiscent of what central banks would later do (e.g., as in the Finance Act
of 1914 in Canada; see Siklos 2006).

two countries respectively with or without central banks will still respond to some common factors.[34]

Therefore, we can use information in the cross-section of inflation and real economic growth performance in countries that had a central bank to ask how these two variables would have behaved had a central bank been created in a country that did not have a monetary authority over the same period.

More formally, suppose we observe a time series for country i, at time t, denoted y_{it}^N for the case where there is no central bank. The counterfactual assumes that there exist (common) factors that explain y. Hence, we can write

$$y_{it}^N = \alpha_i + \beta_i^* F_t + \varepsilon_{it} \, , \ i = 1, ..., N; \ t = 1, ...T \tag{2}$$

where β^* is a vector of coefficients that is constant over time but varies across the i cross-sections, F are the K common factors that vary over time, and ε is a residual that represents the random idiosyncratic component for i, such that $E(\varepsilon_{it}) = 0$. It is assumed, among other things, that the idiosyncratic components are uncorrelated across i. Therefore, $E(\varepsilon_t F_t') = 0$.[35]

Next, denote y_{it}^{CB} as the time series of interest when a central bank is in place. Therefore, the expression

$$\Delta_{it} = y_{it}^{CB} - y_{it}^N \tag{3}$$

is the treatment effect of i at time t. Since, in our example, we don't observe the right-hand side variables simultaneously, the observed data can be thought as being expressed in the linear combination form

$$y_{it} = \mu_{it} y_{it}^{CB} + (1 - \mu) y_{it}^N, \ \mu_{it} = \begin{cases} 1, \text{if } i \text{ is under treatment at time } t \\ 0, \qquad\qquad \text{otherwise} \end{cases} \tag{4}$$

Under the various assumptions made by Hsiao et al. (2012) y_{1t}^N can be predicted from $\hat{y}_{1t}^N$ obtained from estimating (4). With $i = 1$, and the remaining i assumed to be unaffected in the presence of intervention,[36] the foregoing expressions suggest that we can estimate what the price level,

---

[34] Productivity, demographics, geographical location, even historical events may link these economies even if they adopt different institutional frameworks. As we shall see, statistically speaking, the details of the common drivers of economic performance are less critical than the mere fact that some of these common factors are believed to exist.

[35] There are other assumptions that are less critical for the discussion that follows but should be borne in mind. See, however, Hsiao et al. (2012, p. 707).

[36] In the case of the Hsiao et al. (2012) application, Hong Kong may well have been affected by the change in sovereignty but the comparator economies (e.g., neighbor economies with similar economic characteristics; see Hsiao et al. (2012, p. 717–718) would not be similarly affected. In the present context, the creation of the US Fed may have affected US

inflation, or real GDP growth would have been in Italy, Switzerland, Canada, or the US, each of the $i = 1$ in the above illustration, using data from the countries where central banks were already in existence. The only additional piece of information required is knowledge of $T^{\#}$, that is, the year when the central bank is created. From $T^{\#}$ until the data ends (i.e., T) $\mathbf{y}_t = \mathbf{y}_t^N$, $t = 1, ..., T, T^{+1}, ..., T$. In other words, we observe a central bank in all economies examined. Hsiao et al. (2012) also show that one can fit time series models to Δ_{1t} (e.g., AR-type specifications) to determine the evolution of the treatment effect over time and in the long run.

For the illustration considered so far, the empirical strategy based on the counterfactuals proposed by Hisaio et al. (2012) imply that, in the case of the US, we can use data from all available countries before $T^{\#} = 1913$, with the exception of Canada which did not have a central bank at the time. Similarly, in the case of the Swiss National Bank, we can use all available data except for US and Canadian data since a monetary authority did not exist in these countries at $T^{\#} = 1907$. And so on for other available cases, assuming we have sufficient data (see below).

One potential criticism is that if the size of the other economies used to generate the counterfactuals is too large or too small, then estimates might be biased. This can be taken into consideration by adding a weight for the relative size of each economy in question. The difficulty is that if these weights change over time such an adjustment is ad hoc. We do not pursue this extension. Similarly, if location is thought to matter then, in principle, equation (2) could be expanded to include regional dummies (e.g., Europe versus North America).[37]

A more significant drawback perhaps is that for at least six economies in our data set (see the next section) we cannot ask what would have happened if a central bank existed because, with the exception of a few series, we have insufficient data.

Finally, we can use Hsiao et al. (2012) to determine what would have happened if, for example, targeting had not been adopted. Other counterfactuals can be imagined, but the combination of data limitations and

economic activity but it is less likely that these same variables would be impacted in the countries that already had central banks.

[37] Hsiao et al. (2012) examine the statistical benefits of relying on the factor model approach to generating the counterfactual series (i.e., equation (2)) and find a significant deterioration relative to the simplest case of, say, relying only on growth rates in countries with no treatment to estimate what would have happened in the treatment economy (i.e., Hong Kong in their example). In the estimates presented below, we report results using the simpler approach since, empirically at least, the performance of equation (2) was superior.

significant changes in economic structure in the economies considered here limit their usefulness. We briefly return to this issue later.

2.4.3 The Determinants of Inflation Differentials

The specification of equation (1) implies that, in a cross-section setting, there are likely economic and institutional determinants of inflation (or price-level) differentials across countries (and time). In the case of institutional determinants our narratives suggest that a financial crisis, either of the global or banking varieties especially, are likely critical determinants of these differentials and, hence, might spur the adoption of a different monetary policy strategy. Other candidates include the potential for fiscal dominance via the debt to GDP ratio.[38] We provide a variety of estimates of the following panel-type regression written as:

$$d_{it}^j = \theta_i^j + \lambda_t^j + \mathbf{x}_{it}'\beta^j + \epsilon_{it}^j \tag{5}$$

where equation (5) is a standard fixed effects model (country and time effects, if necessary) with $\mathbf{x}$ capturing the economic and crisis determinants of d. The index j is added to recognize that a variety of benchmarks were considered.[39]

2.4.4 A Network of Central Banks?

Billio et al. (2012) have proposed a measure of "connectedness" based on principal components analysis and Granger-causality. If the performance of central banks, measured in terms of the price level (prior to World War II), inflation, or real economic growth, is more similar, then this should be reflected in the number of orthogonal factors and their explanatory power. Define N as the total number of principal components in the ten-country data set used in this study. If central banks are highly interconnected then this should be reflected as a small number, n, of principal components that can explain most of the variation in the system of central banks considered.

---

[38] A world war or a major political conflict could be other candidate variables. These can sometimes represent harbingers of economic changes (e.g., following World War I the Gold Exchange standard was introduced; Bretton Woods can be traced as a fallout from World War II). Hence, it is difficult to identify these events as separate from other economic forces that produce regime changes.

[39] We specify (5) in terms of inflation for simplicity. In so doing we convert the price-level data to inflation during the Gold Standard period even if some of the tests described above are evaluated in terms of the (log) level of prices. This complication does not affect the real economic growth specification.

Alternatively, causality testing provides an indication of whether a particular time series j "Granger-causes" (GC) a time series i where past values of j contain information that help predict i. The test can be carried out in a bivariate or multivariate (i.e., as in a vector autoregression) settings. For example, continuing with equation (1), which measures the inflation differential vis-à-vis a particular benchmark in the bivariate setting, a Granger-causality test between d^j_{it} and d^j_{kt} with $i \neq k$, would be carried out by estimating the following two regressions, namely

$$d^j_{it+1} = a^j d^j_{it} + b^j_{ik} d^j_{kt} + e^j_{it+1}$$
$$d^j_{kt+1} = a^j d^j_{kt} + b^j_{ki} d^j_{it} + e^j_{kt+1}$$

$$(6)$$

where a rejection of the null hypothesis that $b_{ik} \neq 0$ implies that k Granger-causes i. We can augment equation (6) with other determinants to allow for the possibility that there are additional factors, such as the type of exchange rate regime, or the incidence of financial crises, to give two examples that can influence the Granger-causality test which have no direct association with the notion that central banks learn from each other. Billio et al. (2012) propose an indicator of connectedness they call the "degree of Granger-causality" (DGC) defined as follows:

$$DGC = \frac{1}{N(N-1)} \sum_{i=1}^{N} \sum_{k \neq i} (k \rightarrow i)$$

$$(7)$$

where $k \rightarrow i$ signifies that k GC i. A value of DGC that exceeds a certain threshold indicates a systemic relationship between the various measures of d.

2.5 Data and Empirical Evidence

2.5.1 Data

Annual data, originally collected for ten economies until 2008 by Bordo and Siklos (2016), were updated where possible to 2015. The data used in their study represent the accumulation of data collected and disseminated over the years by many scholars, including Reinhart and Rogoff (2009), Bordo and Landon-Lane (2013), and Schularik and Taylor (2012), with additional historical data from some individual central banks (namely,

Norway, Sweden, USA) who have made available historical data covering a long span of time.[40]

Other original sources that were used to construct the series used in Bordo and Siklos (2016) are found at the NBER (www.nber.org/data/). Global financial data, and Historical Financial Statistics of the Center for Financial Stability (www.centerforfinancialstability.org/hfs.php), are other data sources where some of the series used in this study can be found.

The ten economies examined are: Canada, France, Germany, Italy, Japan, Norway, Sweden, Switzerland, the United Kingdom and the United States. An appendix provides the list of available time series and the samples over which they are available. Additional data were collected from various issues of the Central Bank Directory (Central Banking Publications) (Siklos 2002 2017). A file containing a list of original sources and the sources of updates to the Bordo and Sikos (2016) data is available.

2.5.2 Empirical Results

Figures 2.3 and 2.4 plot inflation rates, where sufficient data are available, around the time of regime changes identified by our historical narratives. Inflation five years before and after the creation of eight of the ten central banks in the data set is shown. Figure 2.3, for example, shows that it is unlikely that the prime motivating factor to create a central bank in Sweden or the UK was a desire to control inflation. Indeed, history clearly shows there were other factors at play. The same appears true for all the other cases shown with the exception of Norway where inflation becomes far less volatile after the Norges Bank opened for business in 1816. Indeed, the volatility in inflation is related to the fact that, in most instances, the Gold Standard was in place. Hence, the focus was on the behavior of the price level and not inflation.

The top portion of Figure 2.4 highlights the evolution of inflation in all ten countries in our data set around the time of the breakdown of Bretton Woods. Whereas inflation differentials were fairly small by the mid-1960s, a divergence begins to emerge as we approach the decade of the 1970s. The

---

[40] Many of the links are provided in Bordo and Siklos (2016). Our data set also overlaps the recently published Jordà-Schularik and Taylor data set (JST; www.macrohistory.net/) which was also partially constructed based on some of the earlier work of, for example, Bordo and Jonung (1995). One slight difference between their data set and ours is the Canadian price level. We use data since 1910, not 1870, to maintain consistency in the measurement of the price level. JST have data since 1870.

Central Banks

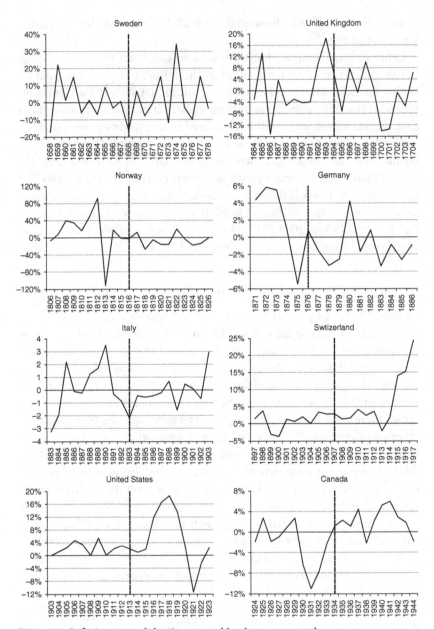

Figure 2.3 Inflation around the time central banks were created
Note: Inflation is 100 times the first log difference in the CPI. The vertical dashed lines mark the year when the central banks shown were created.

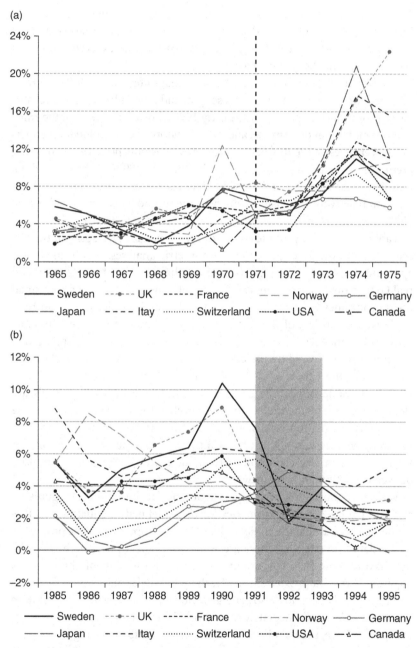

Figure 2.4 Inflation around the time of change in monetary policy strategy: inflation targeting and Bretton Woods

Note: The shaded area in the bottom figure highlights the years when Inflation Targeting (IT) was introduced in Canada, Sweden, the UK, and Norway. The vertical line in the top figure approximately dates the end of the Bretton Woods regime.

"unanchoring" or drift in inflation that emerges following the end of Bretton Woods, underscored perhaps by the Smithsonian agreement of 1971, produced the great divergence in inflation rates exacerbated by the two oil price shocks of the 1970s.

The bottom portion of Figure 2.4 reveals that differences in inflation rates persisted for some time as countries sought, and then failed, to find a reliable anchor for monetary policy. By the early 1990s, however, several of the small open economies in our sample, and the UK, adopted explicit inflation targeting. Nevertheless, all central banks, in their own fashion, placed a much higher premium on inflation control. Hence, by the mid-1990s we began to see a return to much smaller inflation differentials. Indeed, the convergence in inflation rates would intensify throughout the second half of the decade of the 1990s and the first decade of the new millennium (not shown).

Tables 2.3 and 2.4 provide some summary statistics for some of the key series used in the descriptive and econometric analyses. It is immediately apparent that the choice of the benchmark has an impact on inflation and real GDP growth performance. It is generally the case, however, that small open economies in our data set (i.e., Canada and Sweden) perform relatively well regardless of the metric employed while a few others, notably Italy and France, consistently under-perform. Also note that inflation is not noticeably affected by the exclusion of financial crises but only when the UK and the US serve as the benchmark. Otherwise, there is a much more noticeable impact. In contrast, real GDP growth differentials are strongly affected by the exclusion of years when there is a GFC. Indeed, the asymmetry in inflation versus output growth performance is striking. This has some bearing on notions of how much central banks ought to concern themselves with real economic performance or the strength of any link between inflation and real growth.

We can obtain a few more insights about the data by looking at Figures 2.5 and 2.6. Figure 2.5 displays proxies for d_{it} as defined in equation (1). It is immediately clear that the choice of benchmarks impacts the time properties of the data. Nevertheless, there are some common features both pre- and post-World War II.[41] For example, the Great Inflation of the 1970s is apparent across all proxies. Similarly, the great deflation of the early 1920s and the Great Depression also generally show up in all variants of d_{it} as does the rise in inflation immediately after World War II. Note that parts A and B of Figure 2.5 are, unless otherwise noted, cross-sectional averages.

---

[41] The sub-samples were partly chosen to facilitate visual comparisons across filters and across time.

Table 2.3 *Summary statistics – inflation adjusted for benchmarks: UK & US, global inflation, global financial crises*

Country	Benchmarks: I: UK & US	Benchmark I excluding financial crises	Benchmark II: global inflation	Global inflation excluding global financial crises	Benchmark II excluding financial crises	Global inflation excluding financial crises
(1)	(2)	(3)	(4)	(5)	(6)	(7)
Canada (CAN)	-0.11 (2.49)	-0.15 (2.37)	-1.10 (3.32)	-1.12 (0.34)	-0.22 (0.26)	-1.25 (0.34)
Switzerland (CHE)	-0.47 (4.36)	-0.57 (0.38)	-1.46 (3.64)	-1.55 (0.32)	-0.46 (0.38)	-1.45 (0.31)
Germany (DEU)	0.38 (4.56)	0.42 (0.40)	-0.67 (3.57)	-0.65 (0.32)	0.35 (0.41)	-0.67 (0.32)
France (FRA)	1.41 (7.37)	1.68 (0.71)	0.79 (5.91)	1.08 (0.56)	0.61 (0.77)	0.12 (0.61)
United Kingdom (GBR)	0.72 (4.36)	0.68 (0.38)	-0.24 (4.10)	-0.28 (0.36)	4.69 (1.37)	3.53 (1.21)
Italy (ITA)	4.20 (14.97)	4.13 (1.30)	3.22 (13.20)	3.15 (1.15)	1.30 (0.59)	0.50 (0.52)
Japan (JPN)	1.35 (5.94)	1.37 (5.85)	0.50 (5.19)	0.54 (0.50)	0.82 (0.47)	-0.21 (0.35)
Norway (NOR)	0.87 (5.38)	0.76 (0.47)	-0.09 (3.95)	-0.20 (0.34)	0.63 (0.45)	-0.34 (0.33)
Sweden (SWE)	0.70 (5.03)	0.74 (0.44)	-0.26 (3.78)	-0.22 (0.33)	0.25 (0.37)	-0.57 (0.36)
United States (USA)	0.18 (2.61)	0.20 (0.23)	-0.78 (3.48)	-0.75 (0.30)	0.08 (0.23)	-0.85 (0.31)

Note: Inflation is 100 times the log difference of the price level. Deviations from the US and UK benchmark and global inflation. A negative value implies below the benchmark. Standard deviations in parentheses. Standard errors in columns (3), (5), (6), and (7). For the US, the level of inflation is defined in the text and in the note to Figure 2.6. Global inflation is defined in column (2). Global financial crises are the ones identified by Bordo and Landon-Lane (2010). Financial crises are as defined in Bordo and Meissner (2016).

Table 2.4 *Selected summary statistics output growth relative to benchmarks: UK & US, and global mean*

Country	Benchmark: UK & US			Global mean		
	Full	Full – Adj.	Full ex crises	Full	Full – Adj.	Full ex crises
CAN	0.14 (4.03)	1.16 (4.37)	1.06 (4.49)	0.90 (4.10)	0.60 (3.72)	2.15 (4.02)
CHE	0.04 (6.29)	0.26 (4.88)	-0.21 (6.36)	-0.14 (4.47)	-0.34 (3.41)	-0.17 (4.57)
DEU	0.08 (7.34)	0.99 (5.69)	-0.21 (7.44)	-0.07 (6.61)	0.42 (4.32)	-0.13 (6.69)
FRA	-0.84 (8.53)	-0.31 (5.36)	-1.15 (8.73)	-0.98 (5.73)	-0.87 (3.85)	-1.06 (5.85)
GBR	-1.19 (3.96)	-1.23 (3.98)	-2.03 (4.39)	-1.33 (2.75)	-1.40 (2.53)	-1.35 (2.70)
ITA	-0.14 (7.26)	0.43 (4.82)	-0.52 (7.25)	-0.28 (4.63)	-0.14 (3.49)	-0.43 (4.59)
JPN	1.03 (7.49)	1.74 (5.38)	0.71 (7.42)	0.89 (5.60)	1.19 (4.11)	0.80 (5.550)
NOR	0.22 (5.75)	0.65 (4.33)	-0.11 (5.59)	0.07 (3.21)	0.07 (2.72)	-0.03 (3.11)
SWE	0.18 (5.80)	0.47 (5.14)	-0.10 (5.78)	0.15 (4.39)	0.03 (4.25)	0.11 (4.41)
USA	3.51 (5.62)	3.25 (5.19)	4.06 (5.23)	0.79 (5.06)	0.43 (4.42)	1.09 (4.97)

Legend: CAN: Canada, **CHE:** Switzerland, **DEU:** Germany, **FRA:** France, **GBR:** United Kingdom, **ITA:** Italy, **JPN:** Japan, **NOR:** Norway, **SWE:** Sweden, **USA:** United States.

Note: The benchmark means that the UK serves as the benchmark until 1912; thereafter the benchmark is the US. For the US, the first three columns are growth rates and not in deviation form. Hence, the values are in italics. Full means data since 1870, data permitting. See the Appendix. Adj. means that the war years 1939–1946 are excluded as data are missing for some of the economies in the data set. Standard deviations in parentheses. 100 times the first log difference in real GDP is output growth. See the text for the definition of the global mean. Crises are the global financial crises identified by Bordo and Landon-Lane (2010).

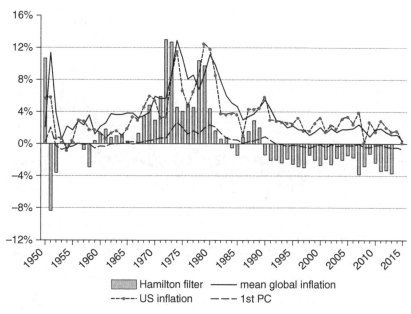

A. 1950–2015

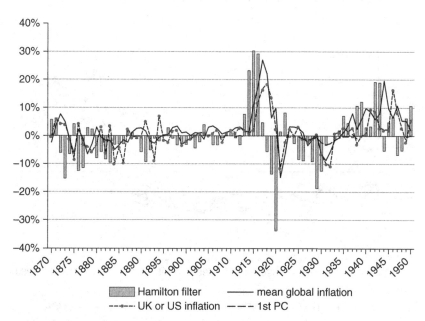

B. 1870–1949

Figure 2.5   Varieties of inflation rate differentials
Note: See equation (1) for the definition and the text for estimation details. Part C
shows the (log) price level less the Hamilton (2017) applied to the log of prices. Part D
shows the (log) of prices normalized to 1 on 1885 in each country. See Table 2.4 for
country name legends.

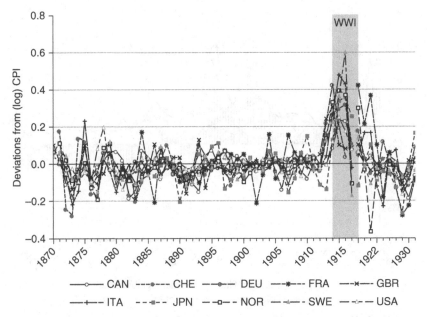

C. The Gold Standard: deviations from equilibrium (log) price level

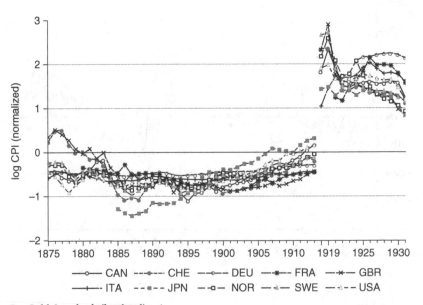

D. Gold Standard: (log level) prices

Figure 2.5 (*cont.*)

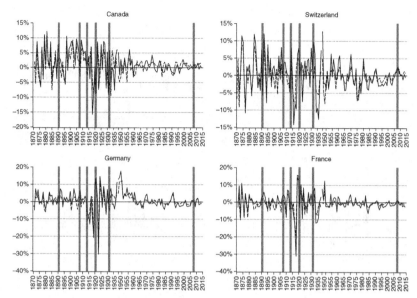

Figure 2.6 Observed inflation versus deviations from global mean inflation
Note: Observed inflation is 100 times the first log difference in the CPI. Global mean inflation is the overall arithmetic mean inflation rate in an unbalanced sample (1870–2015). The dashed line is d_{it} (see equation (1)). The shaded areas represent the years when there was a global financial crisis as defined in Bordo and Landon-Lane (2013).

Parts C and D of Figure 2.5 display the behavior of deviations in the price level or a normalized indicator of the price level covering the Gold Standard period. Deviations from the equilibrium price level, as proxied by Hamilton's (2017) filter, are stationary, as noted earlier (also see Table 2.6). The contrast between the deviation form and the original (log) levels of the series are shown in part D, for comparison.

Figure 2.6 plots the deviations in domestic inflation from the global mean.[42] Although inflation is generally stationary the plots reveal sharp departures, often around the time of financial crises of the global variety (highlighted by the shaded areas in the figure). Note that, from this perspective, the GFC of 2008–2009 pales in comparison with earlier GFCs. Volatility across the ten economies also varies greatly. This may well have implications for understanding the dynamics of inflation from a cross-sectional standpoint (see below).

Next, we turn to some comparisons between the narrative and statistical approaches to dating crises. Tables 2.5 and 2.6 present a selection of results,

---

[42] That is, the arithmetic mean for all ten countries in the data set.

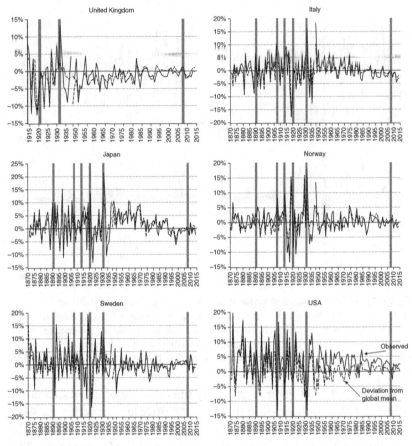

Figure 2.6 (*cont.*)

while Table 2.7 provides a general summary. Table 2.5 distinguishes between financial crises that have been deemed global in nature, according to Bordo and Landon-Lane (2010), while the last two columns rely on the country-specific chronology from Bordo and Meissner (2016). In addition, Table 2.5 identifies the joint occurrence of banking and currency crises.

If crises are associated with a break in the time series properties of the data then Table 2.6 provides some indications of when these were most likely to occur. The manner in which the tests were applied is such that the first date shown represents the most likely occurrence of a statistical break in the time series in question. The last date then represents the least likely timing of a break. Interestingly, the most recent GFC is often, though not always, one of the least likely sources of a break, at least in the time series

Table 2.5 *Dating crises: narrative schemes*

Country	Global financial crises	Alternative chronologies Banking crises	Currency crises
CAN	1890–1891[1] 1907–1908[1] 1913–1914[1] 1920–1921 1931–1932 2007–2008	1923 2008	1891, 1893, 1908, 1914, 1921, 1929, 1931, 1950, 1962, 1981[4]–1983, 1986
CHE	1890–1891[1] 1907–1908[1] 1913–1914[1] 1920–1921 1931–1932 2007–2008	1931, 1933–1936, 2008	1914, 1939, 1971, 1977
DEU	1890–1891[1] 1907–1908[1] 1913–1914[1] 1920–1921 1931–1932 2007–2008	1901–1902, **1931–1932**, 2008	1893–1894, 1907–1910, 1914, **1931–1932**, 1934, 1949
FRA	1890–1891[1] 1907–1908[1] 1913–1914[1] 1920–1921 1931–1932 2007–2008	1882, **1888**, 1889, 1907– 1910, 1994–1995, 2008	**1888**, 1914, 1923–1929, 1936–1937, 1948, 1957– 1959, 1968, 1992–1993[2]
GBR	1890–1891[1] 1907–1908[1] 1913–1914[1] 1920–1921 1931–1932 2007–2008	1890–1893, **1974–1976**, 2007	1914, 1931–1932, 1947, 1949, 1961–1962, 1964– 1967, **1974–1976**[4], 1992[3]
ITA	1890–1891[1] 1907–1908[1] 1913–1914[1] 1920–1921 1931–1932 2007–2008	1891–1892, **1893–1894**, **1907–1908**, 1914, 1921, 1930–1933, **1935–1936**, **1990–1995**, 2008	1893–1894, 1907–1908, 1935–1936, 1964–1969, 1976, 1981, **1990, 1992, 1995**[2]

(cont.)

Table 2.5 (*cont.*)

Country	Global financial crises	Alternative chronologies Banking crises	Currency crises
JPN	1890–1891 1907–1908[1] 1913–1914[1] 1920–1921 1931–1932 2007–2008	**1900–1901, 1917,** 1927–1929, 1992–1997	**1900–1901**, 1904–1908, **1917**, 1921, 1931–1934, 1979–1980
NOR	1890–1891[1] 1907–1908[1] 1913–1914[1] 1920–1921 1931–1932 2007–2008	1921, 1931–1935, **1986–1993**	1914, 1931–1935, 1949, 1971–1972,[2] **1986– 1993**[2]
SWE	1890–1891[1] 1907–1908[1] 1913–1914[1] 1920–1921 1931–1932 2007–2008	1897–1899, 1907–1909, 1921–1922, **1931–1932, 1991–1994**, 2008	1914, **1931–1933**, 1949, 1971–1972, **1991–1994**[3]
USA	1890–1891[1] 1907–1908[1] 1913–1914[1] 1920–1921 1931–1932 2007–2008	1884–1886, **1891–1893,** 1907–1908, 1914, **1930– 1933**, 2007–2008	**1891–1893, 1930–1933**, 1960–1961, 1971

Note: Dates for global financial crises are from Bordo and Landon-Lane (2010). Dates for the other crises are from Bordo and Meissner (2016). **Bold** numbers identify the simultaneous occurrence of banking and currency crises. The superscript numbers indicate the occurrence of a crisis under the regimes identified in Table 2.2,[1] for the Gold Standard,[2] for exchange rate targeting or a monetary union,[3] for monetary targeting, and[4] for Bretton Woods.

property of inflation.[43] Similarly, the most prominent location of breaks in the data often take place before World War II. The rank of breaks post-World War II is often fairly low. Of course, this is only indicative of the

---

[43] Not shown are results for output growth where the prominence of the 2008 GFC is higher relative to inflation.

Table 2.6 *Unit root and break-point properties of univariate inflation time series*

Country	Benchmark: UK & US		Global mean inflation		Hamilton filter		Factor model	
	ADF	Breaks	ADF	Breaks	ADF	Breaks	ADF	Breaks
CAN	−9.62*	1919, 1938, 1948, 1981, 1987	−6.54*	1919, 1942, 1946, 1951, 1977, 1983, 1999	−5.51*	1917, 1931, 1980	−3.68*	1965, 1983, 1992, 1999
CHE	−5.37*	1918, 1937, 1945, 1951,1979, 1984, 1994	−9.05*	1878, 1916, 1974, 1989, 1994	−7.81*	1911, 1916, 1921, 1981	−3.69*	1931, 1936, 1994, 2009
DEU	−1.01	1891, 1915, 1932, 1973, 1987, 1991, 1995	−6.92*	1932, 1915, 1893, 1946, 1974, 1991, 1995	−7.85*	1912, 1917, 1931, 1944, 1990	−4.49*	1930, 1951, 1984, 1989, 1995
FRA	−1.85	1904, 1927, 1936, 1987, 1991, 2008	−6.00*	1908, 1927, 1936, 1954, 1986, 1994	−5.93*	1887, 1923, 1932, 1953, 1974, 1986, 1990	−1.37	1927, 1936, 1954, 1986, 2013
GBR	−3.73*	1917, 1941, 1948, 1991, 1975, 2006	−3.64*	1879, 1912, 1917, 1931, 1941, 1952, 1968, 1981, 1986, 1991, 1995	−10.26*	1878, 1915, 1921, 1974, 1982, 2010	−3.36*	1925, 1935, 1949, 1991, 2013
ITA	−4.59*	1891, 1915, 1948, 1974, 1987, 1996	−5.02*	1895, 1916, 1948, 1973, 1986, 1997	−5.10*	1878, 1912, 1917, 1949, 1974, 1986, 1990, 1997	−3.57*	1927, 1936, 1996, 2014
JPN	−1.52 (9)	1908, 1978, 1983, 2012	−9.67*	1908, 1932, 1950, 1977, 1989, 2013	−7.67*	1917, 1921, 1978, 1990, 1998	−8.78*	1930, 1932, 1982, 1999

(*cont.*)

Table 2.6 (cont.)

Country	Benchmark: UK & US		Global mean inflation		Hamilton filter		Factor model	
	ADF	Breaks	ADF	Breaks	ADF	Breaks	ADF	Breaks
NOR	−10.98*	1914, 1919, 1930, 1941, 1950, 1989, 2003, 2013	−9.21*	1876, 1912, 1921, 1930, 1950, 1942, 1957, 1989, 1994, 2013	−10.03*	1878, 1915, 1921, 1987, 1991	−5.00*	1878, 1915, 1921, 1980, 1987, 1991, 2007
SWE	−6.83*	1914, 1919, 1930, 1941, 1992, 1996	−7.54*	1876, 1914, 1919, 1942, 1950, 1992, 1996	−8.37*	1878, 1915, 1909, 1921, 1980, 1992, 1996	−4.56*	1931, 1934, 1950, 1992, 1996, 2013
USA	NA	1879, 1920, 1941, 1991, 1973, 1982, 2008	9.55*	1878, 1915, 1987, 1994, 2008	−8.87*	1879, 1912, 1917, 1931, 1980, 1990, 2011	−4.03*	1966, 1982, 2008

Note: ADF refers to the Augmented Dickey-Fuller statistic. Perron (1989) test with only an intercept break, an additive outlier for the break, with the lagged dependent variable selected according to the Schwarz criterion, and a 10 percent trimmed estimate. The breaks are found sequentially starting with the full sample (usually 1870–2015, depending on data availability). In italics are estimates of the breaks before the central bank in question was established. * signifies rejection of the unit root null at least at the 5 percent level. NA means not applicable. Note that estimation samples are affected by the filter used as well as data availability. This is especially the case for the factor model.

Table 2.7 *The anatomy of financial crises*

Country	(1) Total number of crises	(2) Rank order	(3) Number of statistical breaks crises (% pre-WWII)	(4) Overlap of narra-tive & statistical (%)	(5) GFC as a share (%)	(6) Crises that exceed a year, consecutive (%)
CAN	13	3	3 (66.7)	23	46.1	7.7
CHE	7	10	4 (75)	14.3	28.6	46.7
DEU	9	8	5 (80)	40	55.6	55.6
FRA	15	2	8 (37.5)	77.8	26.7	55.6
GBR	11	4	6 (50)	72.7	36.4	70
ITA	18	1	8 (37.5)	27.8	33.3	62.5
JPN	10	6	5 (40)	30	30	72.7
NOR	8	9	6 (50)	87.5	50	14.3
SWE	11	4	7 (57.1)	36.4	54.5	54.5
USA	10	6	7 (57.1)	20	60	80

Note: See Table 2.4 for country name legends. The total number of financial crises is the sum of banking and currency crises according to the Bordo and Meissner (2016) chronology. The rank order is from largest to smallest number of financial crises. Column (3) is the number of statistical breaks relying on the application of the Perron (1989) break test. See Table 2.6 for details about the estimation strategy. Column (4) indicates the fraction of financial crises whose dates overlap with the ones obtained from a purely statistical analysis. Column (5) represents the fraction of financial crises that are global in nature according to the Bordo and Landon-Lane (2010) chronology. Column (6) indicates the fraction of financial crises (see column (11)) with a duration of more than one consecutive year.

possibility that developments in central banking contributed to this outcome since other factors were also clearly at play (see below).

Table 2.7 provides some overall perspective on the importance of financial crises based on both the narrative and statistical approaches. The small open economies in the sample do comparatively well across the various indicators of crisis conditions, especially Norway and Switzerland (e.g., see column (3)). Although this result does not exclusively reflect the quality of monetary policy in these economies, it is likely one of the factors at play in explaining the relatively small number of statistical breaks found in the behavior of inflation. Most of the breaks in the small open economies are observed before World War II.

The extent to which global financial crises, based on the narrative approach, dominate the landscape of crises in the individual countries sampled varies of course. GFCs are least frequent in Switzerland (two of seven crises identified) while half, or a slightly higher proportion of the total, accounts for crises in four of the ten economies examined (US, Germany, Norway, and Sweden). There is also considerable variation in the fraction of crises that exceed a year in duration. It is also notable that there are differences in the degree of agreement between the statistical and narrative dating of financial crises. It is somewhat reassuring that, other than perhaps Switzerland, the overlap between the quantitative and narrative interpretations of history is not small. Nevertheless, the results also suggest that both approaches are essential for a proper understanding of the determinants of financial crises and the potential role of the central bank to which we now turn.

Tables 2.8 through 2.10 present a selection of panel regressions that seek to quantify the importance of some determinants of inflation in the ten economies in the sample. Although the results are, broadly speaking, robust across the various filters applied to the data, the most consistently reliable results, across various specifications and samples, were obtained when Hamilton's filter or global inflation were used as proxies to generate deviations from country-specific inflation rates.

Tables 2.8 and 2.9 differ only according to the proxy for financial crises. Bordo and Landon- Lane's (2010) definition of GFCs is used as a determinant while, in Table 2.9, Bordo and Meissner's (2016) combined banking and currency crises serve as a proxy for the impact of crises on inflation.[44]

---

[44] Combining both types of crises seem to produce better results than separately including banking and currency crises.

Table 2.8 *Panel regression estimates of the determinants of inflation differentials*

Dependent Variable: Deviation from Hamilton Filter
Method: Pooled Least Squares
Sample (adjusted): 1872 2013
Included observations: 142 after adjustments
Cross-sections included: 10
Total pool (unbalanced) observations: 1111
Convergence achieved after 13 iterations

Variable	Coefficient	Std. Error	t-Statistic	Prob.
Constant	1.16	0.72	1.60	0.11
Oil price inflation	0.07	0.01	6.89	0.00
Exchange Rate change	0.03	0.02	1.42	0.16
Real GDP growth(−1)	0.29	0.05	5.70	0.00
Debt/GDP ratio(−1)	0.02	0.01	2.30	0.02
GFC	−2.31	1.12	−2.07	0.04
AR(1)	0.37	0.03	12.72	0.00
Fixed effects?	NO			
Time Fixed Effects?	NO			
R-squared	0.19	Mean dependent var.		3.24
Adjusted R-squared	0.18	S.D. dependent var.		9.99
Log likelihood	−4018.95			
F-statistic	41.82			
Prob(F-statistic)	0.00			

Note: See Table 2.5 for the dating of the GFC variable which is the Bordo and Landon-Lane (2010) chronology. Sample reflects adjustment for data availability and the filter used. The absence of fixed effects follows the application of a redundant fixed effects test (F-based statistic; results available on request). The mean of the dependent variable is different from zero because the precise samples over which individual filtered estimates are computed can differ from the unbalanced sample used in estimation. This also explains that the total number of observations is not number of years times number of cross-sections.

Finally, Table 2.10 estimates the same relationship for the Gold Standard period only based on the dates provided in Table 2.2.

We focus on the common features found in these results and their implications. Financial crises, whether of the global or domestic variety, affect inflation performance negatively. However, the impact is quantitatively largest when the crisis is global. In contrast, crises are found to have a much smaller impact on deviations in inflation from a benchmark during the Gold Standard era. Output growth is also seen, on average, as raising

Table 2.9 *Panel regression estimates of the determinants of inflation differentials*

Cross-section fixed effects test equation:
Dependent Variable: Deviation from Hamilton Filter
Method: Panel Least Squares
Sample (adjusted): 1872 2013
Included observations: 142 after adjustments
Cross-sections included: 10
Total pool (unbalanced) observations: 1214
Convergence achieved after 5 iterations

Variable	Coefficient	Std. Error	t-Statistic	Prob.
Constant	1.08	0.71	1.53	0.13
Oil price inflation	0.06	0.01	6.89	0.00
Exchange Rate change	0.00	0.00	0.62	0.54
Real GDP growth (−1)	0.27	0.05	5.84	0.00
Debt/GDP ratio (−1)	0.03	0.01	2.63	0.01
Financial Crises	−1.60	0.62	−2.58	0.01
AR(1)	0.39	0.03	14.43	0.00
Fixed effects?	NO			
Time Fixed effects?	NO			
R-squared	0.19	Mean dependent var.		3.09
Adjusted R-squared	0.18	S.D. dependent var.		9.68
Log likelihood	−4352.66			
F-statistic	46.30			
Prob(F-statistic)	0.00			

Note: See note to Table 2.8. The Bordo and Meissner (2016) chronology is used to measure financial crises by summing banking and currency crises (see Table 2.5). The absence of fixed effects follows the application of a redundant fixed effects test (F-based statistic; not shown).

inflation relative to any of the benchmarks considered, other than for the Gold Standard period. These results merely confirm that inflation and aggregate economic activity links are severed during the Gold Standard but are a feature of the full sample.

If fiscal dominance is proxied by the debt to GDP ratio then this too is a feature of central banking outside the Gold Standard era. Nevertheless, even if this variable is statistically significant, it does not appear to be economically significant as it is dwarfed by the real and financial crises variables. Equally interesting is the finding that deviations in inflation from some benchmarks are highly persistent in the Gold Standard era while there is much less persistence in the full sample estimates. Hence, once domestic

Table 2.10 *Panel regression estimates of the determinants of inflation differentials: the Gold Standard period*

Dependent Variable: Deviation from Global Inflation
Method: Pooled Least Squares
Sample (adjusted): 1871 1917 1923 1931
Included observations: 56 after adjustments
Cross-sections included: 10
Total pool (unbalanced) observations: 458
Convergence achieved after 7 iterations

Variable	Coefficient	Std. Error	t-Statistic	Prob.
Constant	0.42	0.23	1.86	0.06
Oil price inflation	−0.00	0.00	−2.74	0.01
Exchange rate change	0.00	0.00	1.47	0.14
Real GDP growth (-1)	−0.00	0.00	−0.11	0.91
Debt/GDP ratio (-1)	−0.00	0.00	−0.47	0.64
Financial Crises	−0.19	0.05	−3.94	0.00
AR(1)	0.83	0.03	28.08	0.00
Fixed Effects?	YES			
Time Fixed effects?	NO			
R-squared	0.96	Mean dependent var.		0.09
Adjusted R-squared	0.96	S.D. dependent var.		2.38
Log likelihood	−291.73			
F-statistic	766.47			
Prob(F-statistic)	0.00			

Note: See note to Table 2.8. Deviations are derived from the log level of the CPI series less the mean log levels globally (all ten economies in the data set). See the text for more details. Sample is based on the dating of the Gold Standard in different countries. See Table 2.2.

inflation moves away from the benchmark, there is a relatively fast return to the benchmark. In other words, to the extent that this represents a global factor not captured by the benchmark it exerts less impact since the end of the Gold Standard. One way of thinking about the results is that there is potentially greater variation in inflation regimes after World War II ended relative to some global benchmarks (e.g., the US).

Three other results are notable from Tables 2.8 through 2.10. First, the exchange rate variable does not exert any significant influence on inflation relative to the benchmark. This suggests that the benchmark captures the global component. Second, although oil price inflation raises inflation relative to the benchmark in all regressions, the coefficient is economically

Table 2.11 *The first principal component: inflation and output growth*

Sample	# of principal components	Inflation	# of principal components	Output growth
1911–1930	3	0.56	3	0.45
1916–1935	3	0.56	3	0.48
1921–1940	3	0.67	4	0.55
1926–1945	3	0.73	3	0.48
1931–1950	2	0.81	3	0.46
1936–1955	3	0.61	2	0.65
1941–1960	3	0.62	2	0.56
1946–1965	3	0.60	3	0.62
1951–1970	1	1.00	4	0.42
1956–1975	1	1.00	3	0.73
1961–1980	2	0.84	3	0.71
1966–1975	2	0.82	3	0.68
1971–1990	2	0.85	4	0.60
1976–1995	2	0.85	4	0.54
1981–2000	2	0.88	3	0.59
1986–2005	2	0.76	3	0.59
1991–2010	3	0.64	2	0.86
1996–2014	3	0.58	1	1.00
Other Samples				
1871–1914	1	0.39	4	0.31
1886–1913, 1925–1933	2	0.59	3	0.53

Note: See text for the details. The columns give the number of principal components estimated via maximum likelihood and the proportion of the total variation explained by the first principal component in a factor model for inflation or real GDP growth for the ten countries in the data set (unbalanced panel).

small. Finally, once we omit fixed effects, the determinants combine to explain a relatively small fraction of the variation in inflation relative to some benchmarks. Consistent with some of the other results, there may be sufficient idiosyncrasies in inflation performance that cannot be adequately captured in the panel framework. Alternatively, as Bernanke (2010) and Yellen (2015), among other central bankers, have pointed out we still have much to learn about what drives inflation dynamics.

Next, we turn to network effects in inflation performance. Tables 2.11 and 2.12 evaluate the degree of connectedness in inflation and real output growth performance. There is clearly considerable variation in the degree of connectedness based on the principal components analysis. Indeed, the latest "wave"

Table 2.12 *Degree of Granger-causality*

Variable	Full sample	1870–1925	1950–2015
INF	21.0%	23.3%	17.8%
HAM	15.6%	17.8%	21.0%
FACTOR	22.2%	NA	23.3%
GLOBAL	27.8%	14.4%	26.6%
DEVIATION FROM BENCHMARK	16.7%	15.6%	13.3%
Conditioned on GFC	17.8%	NA	NA
Conditioned on RR	16.7%	NA	NA

Note: See text for the definition and estimation details.

of globalization is clearly seen in the data for the last two or three decades, with brief spurts beginning in the 1950s and falling by the 1970s while the reduced importance of the first principal component in the first decades of the twentieth century is also evident. In contrast, there is considerably more connectedness and persistently more so in inflation throughout history. Nevertheless, the strong connection in inflation performance is clearly a feature of the post-World War II era. There is no indication that inflation targeting per se has raised the degree of connectedness over the last two decades. However, as noted earlier, first Bretton Woods followed by a stronger commitment to lower inflation, together with more exchange rate flexibility, implies that the exchange rate regime as it is defined here plays a smaller role than we think in explaining inflation differentials.

The measure of connectedness based on GC tests (see Table 2.12) also suggests that central banks behave as if they are part of a related network, at least in so far as inflation differentials are concerned. Note that networks permit relationships to be indirect.[45] Hence, the existence of a network does not imply how integrated economies are, only that there are links, some stronger, some weaker, that tie the inflation fortunes of the economies in question.[46] Moreover, other than for d_{it}^{Global}, there is little empirical indication that this has changed markedly over almost a century and a half of data used here.

Finally, we turn to some counterfactual experiments. These are shown in Figures 2.7 through 2.9. Figure 2.7 shows what inflation would have

[45] This is most readily seen by visualizing networks as a collection of nodes that are linked with varying degrees of strength. A typical application is the identification of bank networks. See, for example, Rönnqvist and Sarlin (2016).

[46] Indeed, the existence of network effects implies that economies need not be integrated for a shock to have systemic or global effects.

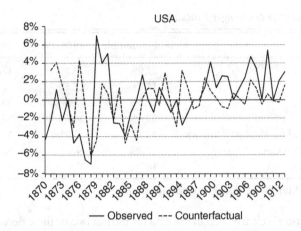

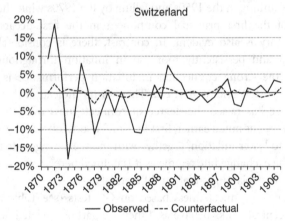

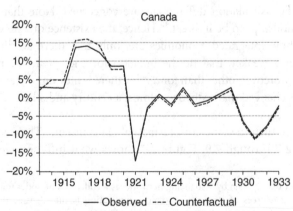

Figure 2.7 Counterfactual experiment: inflation had the SNB, Fed, and BoC been created earlier
Note: The top figure is for the US, the middle is Switzerland, and the bottom plot is for Canada. Details of the counterfactuals are in the text.

been like if the Swiss National Bank (middle), the US Federal Reserve (top), and the Bank of Canada (bottom) had been in existence before they were actually created.[47] Data limitations imply that we can only go back to 1870 for the SNB and the Fed and 1913 for the BoC. The smallest impact from the late introduction of central banking is observed for Canada. The observed and counterfactual lines are almost on top of each other. It is worth noting, however, that thanks to the Finance Act of 1907, Canada arguably had a quasi-central bank before the Bank of Canada's creation (e.g., see Rich 1989).

In the case of Switzerland, had the SNB been created in 1870 instead of 1907 inflation would have been not much different, on average, but considerably less volatile. Finally, in the US case, it is difficult to see any impact on inflation and inflation volatility had the Fed been in place in 1870. It should be pointed out, as explained above, that the *raison d'être* of the Fed lies in the search for financial stability not inflation stability and the series of financial crises that hit the US throughout the period shown testifies to the real problem with the monetary regime in the US. Indeed, as shown in the next figure (Figure 2.8) which shows the counterfactuals for real GDP growth, the chief benefit of an earlier central bank in the US would have been observed through a substantial decline in the volatility of real GDP growth.[48] The reduction in real GDP volatility is plain to see in all three cases shown with the impact least dramatic for Canada, likely for the reason cited earlier.

Finally, we examine one more counterfactual, this time in the more recent era of central banking. While some central banks are accountable via a numerical inflation target (Canada, Norway, Sweden, the UK), others maintain they are equally accountable in achieving low and stable inflation (the remaining countries listed in Table 2.1) but not at the expense of an explicit recognition that real economic performance is also part of their objective function.[49] Figure 2.9 then considers the inflation and real economic growth consequences of inflation targeting

[47] Under the classical Gold Standard a central bank can only have a small impact on the price level except in the sense that a credible central bank could temporarily use its policy rate to affect domestic variables within the gold points which served as a target zone. See Bordo and Macdonald (2010).

[48] This result is also consistent with Miron's (1989) finding that the founders of the Fed did not believe their mission was to stabilize output. Instead, their role was to influence asset prices, as also reflected in the drop in the seasonal variation of interest rates (also, see Mankiw, Miron, and Weil 1994, and Mankiw and Miron 1991).

[49] Since Norway adopted inflation targeting only in 2001 we opted not to consider this case since this leaves us with relatively few (annual) observations.

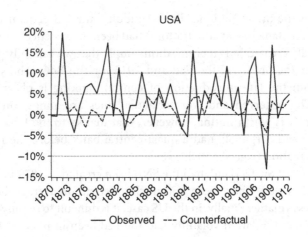

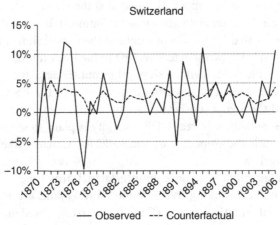

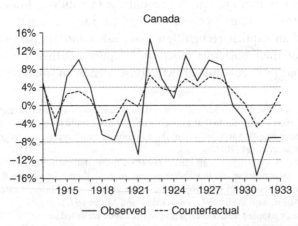

Figure 2.8 Counterfactual experiments: real GDP growth had the SNB, Fed, and BoC been created earlier
Note: See note to Figure 2.7.

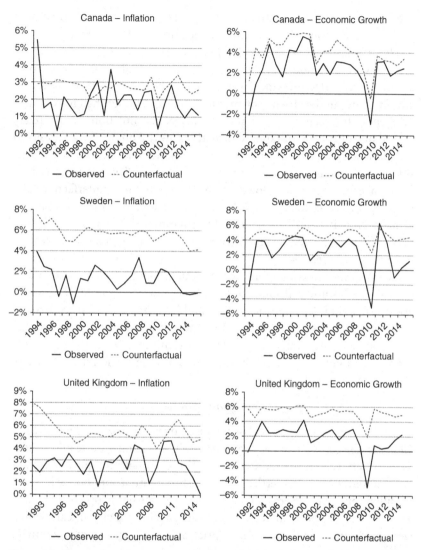

Figure 2.9 Counterfactual experiments: inflation and real economic growth with and without inflation targeting

Note: See notes to Figures 2.7 and 2.8 and the text for a description.

(IT). We ask what inflation and growth would have been if Canada (1991), Sweden (1993), and the UK (1992) had not adopted an IT strategy. Adoption years of IT are in parentheses. The USA, Japan, and Switzerland did not adopt IT. Hence, these economies act as the controls used to estimate the treatment effect of IT. We define the treatment period as the period since Bretton Woods until IT is adopted.[50]

The left-hand side of Figure 2.9 plots the observed and counterfactual estimates for inflation while the right-hand set of plots display the outcomes for real GDP growth. It is immediately clear that inflation is almost always higher in the absence of an inflation target. Other than for Canada, differences between observed and counterfactual inflation rates actually exceed one or even two standard deviations away from the mean observed inflation rates. Hence, the improvement in inflation performance is considerable. Turning to real economic growth the evidence is more mixed, with real economic growth lower under IT than in the counterfactual case. Once again the differences are larger for Sweden and the UK than for Canada. Note that, among the three IT economies, Canada has the reputation of having adhered most closely to its inflation target since the regime was introduced (e.g., see Siklos 2014).

Clearly, one can contemplate other counterfactuals but the methodology followed is not well suited to carry them out. For example, one might ask what might have happened if the Gold Standard had persisted beyond the 1930s, or if a central bank had not been created after World War II. Unfortunately, the available data do not permit the creation of a sensible set of common factors where the treatment or intervention does not exist.

2.6 Conclusions

Central banks have evolved considerably over the past three centuries. Globally, the central bank is a comparatively young institution and its role as a primary vehicle for economic stabilization is both unique and also of fairly recent vintage. Nevertheless, the history of monetary policy is also a turbulent one with several changes in policy strategies adopted over time. There has clearly been an evolution of sorts, again on a global scale, with a clear preference for some form of price stability even if many countries eschew adopting a formal numerical target.

Just when a consensus of sorts developed that convinced policy makers that best practice consisted of giving a central bank a clear mandate,

---

[50] We considered other control periods with little impact on the conclusions. We also tried to include France, Germany, and Italy, as part of the control group and our conclusions are unchanged. It should be noted, however, that since these three economies adopted a common currency as well as transitional arrangements in the lead up to the introduction of the euro, it was deemed preferable to exclude them from the control group.

narrowly focused on attaining some inflationary outcome that would promote stable economic growth, two major financial crises, beginning in 2007 until about 2012, that is, the so-called global financial crisis and the Eurozone sovereign debt crisis, led to some sober second thinking.

Although there are few indications that price stability is no longer a desirable objective, central banks are being asked, or are adopting by default, to widen the scope of their mandate to include evincing a concern for financial stability. Historically, we have seen this. Indeed, long before some central banks were given a macroeconomic stability mandate, their task was for a time largely centered on the maintenance of financial stability. However, this took place at a time when little thought was given to whether the monetary authority should be autonomous from government. As we have now come to accept central bank autonomy as useful, if not appropriate, it is less clear how this principle is squared with an expectation that financial stability and monetary stability are both tasks that a central bank ought to carry out. Moreover, for central banks in large economies or ones that have a systemic impact on the global economy, this development may further restrict their ability to improve how policy is conducted and to innovate. In the early days of central banking this was not the case partly because these countries were the first and also due to the greater frequency of financial crises necessitating change and adaptation to new circumstances.

In contrast, small open economies have long been buffeted by the complications of navigating the occasional conflict between domestic objectives and the impact of external shocks, regardless of the exchange rate regime in place. As a result, there is some evidence that there is more of a willingness to adopt different monetary policy strategies than in many, but not all, of the systematically important economies, at least based on observed choices made in recent decades. It remains to be seen whether this finding will extend to how the maintenance of financial system stability is managed.

The only thing that is certain is that we have not seen the last of attempts to improve how monetary policy is conducted nor in how central banks are governed. It is equally possible that just as the pendulum has swung back to the monetary authorities evincing a concern for financial stability, the same forces will lead to a rewriting of the "contract" between the central bank and the government. Whether this means a loss of autonomy or the development of a contingent contract between the central bank and government remains to be seen. Clearly, crisis times require a different approach to policy than normal times.

References

Adolph, C. (2013), *Bankers, Bureaucrats, and Central Bank Politics* (Cambridge: Cambridge University Press).

Aizenman, J., M. Chinn, and H. Ito (2016), "Monetary Policy Spillovers and the Trilemma in the New Normal: Periphery Country Sensitivity to Core Country Conditions," *Journal of International Money and Finance* 68 (November): 298–330.

Bagehot, W. (1873) [1962], *Lombard Street: A Description of the Money Market* (Homewood, Ill.: Richard Irwin).

Bai, J. and P. Perron (1998), "Estimating and Testing Linear Models with Multiple Structural Changes," *Econometrica* 66: 47–78.

Ball, L. (2014), "The Case for a Long-Run Inflation Target of Four Percent," IMF working paper 14/92, June.

Barro, R.J. and D.B. Gordon (1983), "Rules, Discretion and Reputation in a Model of Monetary Policy," *Journal of Monetary Economics* 12 (July): 101–121.

Bernanke, B. (2010), "Monetary Policy and Tools in a Low-Inflation Environment," speech given at the Revisiting Monetary Policy in a Low-Inflation Environment Conference, Federal Reserve Bank of Boston, Boston, Massachusetts, October 15.

Billio, M., M. Germansky, A.W. Lo, and L. Pelizzon (2012), "Econometric Measures of Connectedness and Systemic Risk in the Finance and Insurance Sectors," *Journal of Financial Economics* 104: 535–559.

Blinder, A.S., M. Ehrmann, M. Fratzscher, J. De Haan, and D. J. Jansen (2008), "Central Bank Communication and Monetary Policy: A Survey of Theory and Evidence," *Journal of Economic Literature* 46: 91–945.

Bordo, M.D. and H. James (2015), "Capital Flows and Domestic and International Order: Trilemmas From Macroeconomics to Political Economy and International Relations," NBER working paper 21017, March.

Bordo, M. and L. Jonung (1995), "Monetary Regimes, Inflation and Monetary Reform: An Essay in Honor of Axel Leijonhufvud," in D.E. Vaz and K. Vellupillai (eds.) *Inflation, Institutions and Information: Essays in Honor of Axel Leijonhufvud* (London: Macmillan).

Bordo, M. and J. Landon-Lane (2010), "The Global Financial Crisis of 2007–08: Is it Unprecendented?" NBER working paper 16589, December.

Bordo, M.D. and J. Landon-Lane (2013), "Does Expansionary Monetary Policy Cause Asset Price Boom?" *Journal Economia Chilena (The Chilean Economy)*, Central Bank of Chile, 16 (August): 4–52.

Bordo, M. and MacDonald, R. (2010), *Credibility and the International Monetary Regime* (New York: Cambridge University Press).

Bordo, M.D. and C.M. Meissner (2016), "Fiscal Crises and Financial Crises," in J.B. Taylor and H. Uhlig (eds.) *North Holland Handbook of Macroeconomics* (Amsterdam: North Holland Publishers).

Bordo, M.D. and A. Orphanides (eds.) (2013), *The Great Inflation: The Rebirth of Modern Central Banking* (Chicago, Ill.: Chicago University Press).

Bordo, M.D., A. Redish, and H. Rockoff (2015), "Why Didn't Canada Have a Banking Crisis in 2008 (or in 1930, or 1907, or …)?" *The Economic History Review* 68 (February): 218–243.

Bordo, M.D. and C. Schenck (2016), "Monetary Policy Cooperation and Coordination: An Historical Perspective on the Importance of Rules," Hoover Institution working paper.

Bordo, M. and A. Schwartz (1999), "Monetary Policy Regimes and Economic Performance: The Historical Record," in John B. Taylor and Michael Woodford (eds.) *Handbook of Macroeconomics* (Amsterdam: North Holland Publishers).

Bordo, M.D. and P.L. Siklos (2016), "Central Bank Credibility: An Historical and Quantitative Exploration," in M.D. Bordo, Ø. Eitrheim, M. Flandreau, and J. Qvigstad (eds.) *Central Banks at a Crossroads* (Cambridge, Cambridge University Press), pp. 62–144.

Bremner, R. (2004), *Chairman of the Fed: William McChesney Martin* (New Haven, Conn.: Yale University Press).

Brunnermeier, M., H. James, and J.P. Landau (2016), *The Euro and the Battle of Ideas* (Princeton, NJ: Princeton University Press).

Bruno, M. and W. Easterly (1998), "Inflation Crises and Long-Run Growth," *Journal of Monetary Economics* 41: 3–26.

Capie, F.H., G. Wood, and J. Castañeda (2016), "Central Bank Independence in Small Open Economies," in M.D. Bordo, Ø. Eitrheim, M. Flandreau, and J. Qvigstad (eds.) *Central Banks at a Crossroads* (Cambridge Cambridge University Press), pp. 195–230.

CIA https://www.cia.gov/library/publications/the-world-factbook/

De Kock, M.H. (1974), *Central Banking* (New York: St Martin's Press).

Debelle, G. and S. Fischer (1994), "How Independent Should a Central Bank Be?" in J. C. Fuhrer (ed.) *Goals, Guidelines and Constraints Facing Monetary Policymakers* (Boston, Mass.: Federal Reserve Bank of Boston), pp. 195–221.

Deutsche Bundesbank (1957), *Annual Report* (Frankfurt).

Dincer, N. and B. Eichengreen (2014), "Central Bank Transparency and Independence: Updates and New Measures," *International Journal of Central Banking* (March): 189–253.

Dooley, M.P., D. Folkerts-Landau, and P.M. Garber (2009), "Bretton Woods Still Defines the International Monetary System", NBER working paper 14371, February.

Fregert, K. (2017), "Sveriges Riksbank: 350 years in the Making," Lund University, mimeo.

Friedman, M. (2002), *Capitalism and Freedom: Fortieth Anniversary Edition* (Chicago, Ill.: University of Chicago Press).

Geithner, T. (2016), "Are We Safer? The Case for Updating Bagehot," Per Jacobsson Lecture, October 8, Washington, DC, available from http://www.perjacobsson.org/lectures.htm. Accessed August 2017.

Gorton, G. (1985), "Clearing Houses and the Origin of Central Banking in the United States," *Journal of Economic History* 45: 277–283.

Hamilton, J.D. (2017), "Why You Should Never Use the Hodrick-Prescott Filter," *Review of Economics and Statistics* (forthcoming).

Hautcoeur, Pierre Cyrille, Angelo Riva, and Eugene N. White (2014), "Floating a Lifeboat: The Banque de France and the Crisis of 1889," NBER working paper 20083, May.

Hsiao, C., H.S. Ching, and S.K. Wan (2012), "A Panel Data Approach for Program Evaluation: Measuring the Benefits of Political and Economic Integration of Hong Kong with Mainland China," *Journal of Applied Econometrics* 27: 705–740.

Ilzetzki, I., C. Reinhart, and K. Rogoff (2017), "Exchange Rate Arrangements Entering the 21st Century: Which Anchor will Hold?" NBER working paper 23134, February.

James, H. (2012), *Making the European Monetary Union* (Cambridge, Mass.: The Belknap Press of Harvard University Press).

Kearns, J. and K. Patel (2016), "Does the Financial Channel of Exchange Rates Offset the Trade Channel?" *BIS Quarterly Review* (December): 95–113.

King, M. (1995), "Commentary Monetary Implications of Greater Fiscal Discipline," in *Budget Deficits and Debt: Issues and Options, Proceedings of the 1995 Jackson Hole Symposium* (Kansas City: Kansas City Federal Reserve), pp. 171–183.

Kydland, F.E. and E.C. Prescott (1977), "Rules Rather than Discretion: The Inconsistency of Optimal Plans," *Journal of Political Economy* 85 (June): 473–492.

Mankiw, N. Gregory and Jeffrey A. Miron (1991), "Should the Fed Smooth Interest Rates? The Case of Seasonal Monetary Policy," *Carnegie-Rochester Conference Series on Public Policy*, Elsevier, vol. 34 (1) January, (pp. 41–69).

Mankiw, N. Gregory, J. Miron, and D. Weil (1987), "The Adjustment of Expectations to a Change in Regime: A Study of the Founding of the Federal Reserve," *American Economic Review* 77 (June): 358–374.

Miron, J. and Romer, C. (1989), "A New Monthly Index of Industrial Production, 1884–1940," *Journal of Economic History* 50 (June): 321–337.

Perron, P. (1989), "The Great Crash, the Oil Price Shock, and the Unit Root Hypothesis," *Econometrica* 57 (November): 1361–1401.

Perron. P. (2005), "Dealing with Structural Breaks," working paper, Boston University, April.

Qvigstad, J. (2016), *On Central Banking* (Cambridge: Cambridge University Press).

Reinhart, C. and K. Rogoff (2009), *This Time is Different: Eight Centuries of Financial Folly* (Princeton, NJ: Princeton University Press).

Rey, H. (2013), "Dilemma not Trilemma: The Global Financial Cycle and Monetary Policy Interdependence," in *Proceedings – Federal Reserve Bank of Kansas City Economic Policy Symposium* (Karsas city), pp. 285–333.

Rogoff, K. (1985), "The Optimal Degree of Commitment to an Intermediate Monetary Target," *Quarterly Journal of Economics* (November): 1169–1189.

Rönnqvist, S. and P. Sarlin (2016), "Bank Networks from Text: Interrelations, Centrality and Determinant," ECB working paper 1876, January.

Schularik, M. and A.M. Taylor (2012), "Credit Booms Gone Bust: Monetary Policy, Leverage Cycles, and Financial Crises, 1870–2008," *American Economic Review* 102 (2): 1029–1061.

Siklos, P.L. (2002), *The Changing Face of Central Banking* (Cambridge: Cambridge University Press).

Siklos, P.L. (2006), *Money, Banking, and Financial Institutions: Canada in the Global Environment*, Fifth Edition (Toronto: McGraw-Hill Ryerson Ltd.).

Siklos, P.L. (2011), "Central Bank Transparency: Another Look," *Applied Economics Letters* 18 (10): 929–933.

Siklos, P.L. (2017), *Central Banks into the Breach* (Oxford: Oxford University Press).

Sinn, H.-W. (2014), *The Euro Trap* (Oxford: Oxford University Press).

Stock, J. and M. Watson (2004), "Has the Business Cycle Changed? Evidence and Explanations," in *Monetary Policy and Unicertainty: Adapting to a Changing*

Economy, Economic Symposium (Kansas City: Federal Reserve Bank of Kansas City), pp. 9–56.

Thornton, D.L. and D.C. Wheelock (2014), "Making Sense of Dissents: A History of FOMC Dissents," *Review of the Federal Reserve Bank of St. Louis* (Third Quarter): 213–227.

Thornton, H. (1802) [1939], *An Enquiry into the Nature and Effects of the Paper Credit of Great Britain* (London: George Allen and Unwin).

Timberlake, R. (1984), "The Central Banking Role of Clearing House Associations," *Journal of Money, Credit and Banking* 1691: 1–15.

Vaona, A. (2012), "Inflation and Growth in the Long-Run: A New Keynesian Theory and Further Semiparametric Evidence," *Macroeconomic Dynamics* 16: 94–132.

Volcker, P.A. (1990), *The Triumph of Central Banking?*, The 1990 Per Jacobsson Lecture, International Monetary Fund, Washington, DC, September 23.

Winnett, R. (2008), "Financial Crisis: Gordon Brown Calls for 'New Bretton Woods'," *Daily Telegraph*, October 13.

Yellen, J. (2015), "Inflation Dynamics and Monetary Policy," speech delivered at the Philip Gamble Memorial Lecture, University of Massachusetts, Amherst, Massachusetts, September 24.

3

Sveriges Riksbank: 350 Years in the Making

Klas Fregert*

3.1 Introduction

While the legal mandates of the Riksbank[1] have changed slowly over its 350-year history, the degree of fulfillment of them has changed a great deal. For most of its 350-year history, convertibility of Riksbank deposits and notes has been the overriding mandate, first into metals from 1668 to 1931 and then into foreign currencies between 1933 and 1992. During the periods of inconvertibility before 1931 (1745–1776, 1809–1834, 1914–1924), the restoration of convertibility was the key concern.

A general explanation for poor goal fulfillment is insufficiency of means relative to goals. Goals in the form of war finance, subsidized loans to favored borrowers, and business cycle stabilization have at times overridden the convertibility goal. A Swedish peculiarity is that some of these goals have been imposed as a result of changes in the political balance between the executive government and the parliament due to the Riksbank's status as an authority under the parliament. Other forces of change emanate from the financial sector with new services, instruments, and markets, and from the academic sector with new ideas.

I first describe the relatively stable legal framework of the Riksbank, which defines its constitutional status, governance, and legal mandates. The subsequent history is divided into periods, which follow the changes between metallic standards or fixed exchange rates, and fiat standards with flexible exchange rates.[2]

* I am grateful for helpful comments from Lars Jonung, Juha Tarkka, and the editors.

[1] I use "the Riksbank" to stand for "*Riksens Ständers Bank*" (The Nation's Estates' Bank) and its current name used since 1866 "*Sveriges Riksbank.*"
[2] The history until 1900 is based largely on the five-volume Riksbank history in Swedish published between 1918 and 1931 to celebrate the 250-year jubilee of the Riksbank. I refer to the contributions by individual authors. This is also the main source in the surveys in English by Heckscher (1934) and Wetterberg (2009). An early survey of Swedish banking,

3.2 The Constitutional Status, Governance, and Legal Mandates of the Riksbank

3.2.1 Constitutional Status

The constitutional status of the Riksbank as an authority under the Swedish parliament, the Riksdag, originally *Riksens ständer* (the nation's [four] estates), has been unchanged since its founding in 1668. This feature is almost unique among central banks, which normally are authorities under the executive government. It explains some traits in the development of the Riksbank, which may appear peculiar in an international context. The Riksbank's charter and a royal decree from 1668 established the Riksdag as the owner of the Riksbank, which was announced in its name *Riksens Ständers Bank*. The Instruments of government (*regeringsformen*, part of the constitution) of 1772 (§55), 1809 (§72), and 1974 (§13) guarantee the Riksbank's status as an authority under the Riksdag. This status was seen in 1668 as a guarantee for the independence of the Riksbank from the government. How to regulate and at times circumscribe this independence has been a leitmotif of the life of the Riksbank during all of its history.

3.2.2 Governance

The Riksbank was led by a non-professional board from 1668 until 1999, the General Council, *Riksbanksfullmäktige*, appointed by the parliament among its own members. The Riksdag directed the General Council by written instructions from a subcommittee, the so-called Secret Committee until 1772. Thereafter the parliamentary Banking Committee, subsumed in the Finance Committee in 1971, issued instructions until 1975. The nobility, the burghers, and the clergy were represented, but the fourth peasant's estate, was excluded from the Banking Committee until 1800.

From the end of the nineteenth century, the instructions from the Banking Committee have decreased in importance as the government's influence has increased. Part of this influence emanated from the new constitution in 1809, which was valid until 1975. The 1809 constitution was based on the division of power between the parliament and the government. The division went further than the division between legislative and executive power in that most legislation was to be taken jointly by the government and the parliament, such that they could veto each other.

including the Riksbank, is Flux (1910) written for the National Monetary Commission in the United States.

This was the case with coin laws, which determine the convertibility rate under a metal standard.

A strengthening of the government's role occurred with the Riksbank Act of 1897, a law jointly voted for by the government and the parliament, which replaced the Riksbank charter from 1668. The chairman of the General Council was to be elected by the government. In addition, the Riksbank Act specified the so-called note-cover rules, previously set in the Banking Committee's instructions. A further strengthening was the new constitutional provision in 1915, which gave the right to the government and the parliament jointly to revoke convertibility.

The joint responsibility for convertibility created tensions between the two state organs during periods of inconvertibility. The return of convertibility in 1834 after 25 years of inconvertibility was delayed due to different opinions between the government (the King) and the parliament over whether the new coin parity should be the original or a devalued parity. During World War I, the determination of both goals and means for monetary policy was largely left to the governor and his deputies at the Riksbank. In the 1930s, a debate among economists and policy makers led to a consensus of cooperation between the government and parliament regarding means, but with the government given the last word of the goal formulation.[3]

An underlying force behind the reduced independence of the Riksbank from the government from the end of the nineteenth century was the shift to parliamentarism. The government became gradually more dependent on the parliament after the change to a two-chamber parliament in 1865, and fully so in connection with the introduction of full franchise in 1918, when the parliament gained the right to oust the government. The fact that the executive and the General Council both are elected by the Riksdag creates an indirect source of control by the government of the Banking Committee and the General Council. The new constitution, valid from 1975, revoked the parliamentary Finance Committee's right to give instructions to the Riksbank and the General Council was thus given full formal discretion over monetary policy.

The Riksbank Act was amended in 1999 by the creation of an Executive Board, consisting of six directors employed by the Riksbank, which decides monetary policy. The governor has the deciding vote in case of a tie (Riksbank Act 3.2). The independence of the Riksbank and its legal mandate (see below) follows the Maastricht Treaty. The General Council appoints new directors. The parliamentary Finance Committee is

---

[3] See Kock (1961, 112–116).

responsible for evaluations of the Riksbank, which it performs through regular hearings of the Riksbank governor. It has also commissioned evaluations by foreign academics in 2006, 2011, and 2015.

A source of tension and confusion between the government and the General Council has at times been the prohibition of the government to instruct the members of the General Council according to the constitutional laws governing the Riksdag – Regeringsformen 1809, §72 and Riksdagsordningen 1810, §70 – and the Riksbank laws of 1897, §34 and 1934, §32. The new law of 1988 scrapped the prohibition against instruction from the government and replaced it with compulsory joint deliberations (*samråd*) before major monetary policy decisions. The change was proposed by the government inquiry (SOU 1986:22) to better reflect actual practice.[4] When the Riksbank Act of 1988 was amended in 1999 to create an independent and professional Executive Board, the directors were forbidden to take instructions:

Members of the Executive Board may neither seek nor take instructions when fulfilling their monetary policy duties. (The Sveriges Riksbank Act (1988: 1385), Chapter 3, Article 2)

Such an independence paragraph is a requirement for EU central banks according to the Maastricht Treaty of 1992, but also a resurrection of the provision in the 1809 constitution.

3.2.3 Legal Mandates

The Riksbank Act from 1988 was amended in 1999 to include: "The objective of the Riksbank's activities shall be to maintain *price stability*," which is complemented in the next sentence with: "The Riksbank shall also promote a *safe* and *efficient* payments system." Analogous mandates appear in the charter for the Riksbank given in 1668. The Riksbank should:

... facilitate trade, such that the *rightful and reasonable value* of our domestic coin thereby will be upheld and prevent all unjust increases in the value of foreign coin, and [make sure] that the *commodiousness for the country's inhabitants* may grow, by getting rid off the plentiful counting, dragging and other discomforts that occur from the handling of the coin; And also, as far as possible, ... that the inhabitants' means and property will be much *safer* against fire, thieves and other inconveniences than at their own abodes.[5]

---

[4] See SOU (1986:22, 85–86) on clashes between practice and law.
[5] Sveriges Rijkes Beslut och Förordning om Banken [Sweden's decision and statutes for the Riksbank] i Stockholm, September 22, 1668, reproduced in Brisman (1918, 82). My translation from the preamble.

The three italicized mandates in the current law correspond to the three italicized mandates in the 1668 statutes (my italics).[6] The preamble was quoted in the instructions of the parliamentary Banking Committee to the General Council from 1668 until the Riksbank Act of 1897.[7] The charter guaranteed the convertibility of the deposits in the Riksbank:

[The depositor] should without exception command his money at his own pleasure, no different from him having the same money in his house, office, or store ... (Article 1)

Convertibility of the Riksbank notes was written into the Riksbank law of 1830, with the conversion rate set in the coin law of the same year. Convertibility was added to the Instrument of Government in 1851. In 1915, an escape clause was added to this paragraph, codifying an unconstitutional suspension of convertibility in 1914:

These notes shall on request be converted to gold according to their inscription; *but that the exception, when the consideration of war, danger of war or a severe money crises make it without doubt necessary, may for a certain time be allowed the King and the Parliament together, or if the Parliament is not convened, by the King on the request of the General Council of the Riksbank and after consultation with the National Debt office.* (§72 Regeringsformen, 1851–1974 with the 1915 escape clause amendment in italics by myself)[8]

Between 1915 and 1924 and from 1931, the government (the King) and the Riksdag together waived the conversion requirement on a yearly basis until the Instrument of Government from 1809 was replaced in 1975. The provision that the government and the parliament together invoke the escape clause led the government to take the lead in the formulation of monetary policy in connection with these decisions. This began in 1920 when the government declared its intention to return to the gold standard at the pre-war parity after the redeemability of notes was revoked by the government and the Riksdag in 1920. The Banking Committee thereafter generally accepted the proposals of the government on the goals of monetary policy. A statement by the Banking Committee in 1937 states the right of the

---

[6] Price stability and stability of the metal content of the currency are not identical goals, but closely related. Price stability, interpreted as inflation stability, stabilizes prices over the medium run, but allows for drift in the price level over the long run. Metal convertibility likewise stabilizes prices over the medium run, but typically leads to drift in the price level in the long run as the relative price of the metal to goods changes over time.

[7] Simonsson (1934, 104).

[8] Current and former Instruments of Government (Regeringsformen) are collected in Sveriges konstitutionella urkunder (1999). The Instrument of Government of 1974 is available in English at riksdagen.se.

government to formulate the goal of monetary policy.[9] The government inquiry SOU (1986: 22, p. 86) pointed to statements to the same effect in 1958 and 1973.[10] In 1975, the Riksbank Finance Committee lost its constitutional right to give instructions to the Riksbank General Council.

After the abandonment of gold convertibility in 1931, the parliament and government yearly invoked the escape clause until 1975. Thus from 1931 until the amended Riksbank Act of 1999, no legal mandate for the Riksbank existed.

The Riksbank had an additional legal mandate to function as an intermediary between lenders and borrowers according to the charter of 1668:[11]

We have, in consideration of the great abuse through usury and exorbitant interest rates, that by a well-organized lending bank these abuses may be abrogated, so that otherwise fruitless capitals with good security may for the owner's benefit ... be more usefully employed.

The Riksbank thus took responsibility for the financial system by becoming the first and only financial intermediary for the next century and remained an important intermediary until the second half of the nineteenth century.

3.3 1668–1718: The Quasi-independent Riksbank as Lender and Deposit Institution[12]

The immediate cause for the creation of the Riksbank was the failure of its predecessor the *Stockholms Banco* founded 1658 by the merchant Johan Palmstruch. He was granted a royal monopoly with the government owning half the shares. *Stockholms Banco* consisted of two departments – an exchange bank and a lending bank. Palmstruch had learned how the two municipal Amsterdam banks, the exchange bank, the *Wisselbank*, and the lending bank, the *Lehnebank*, collaborated in secret by letting the lending bank use reserves of the exchange bank. Officially the exchange bank had 100 percent reserves, and the lending bank limited reserves, being a pure intermediary. Together the two banks worked as a fractional reserve bank, which Palmstruch described in a written application to the government as a safe and profitable

---

[9] "This formulation [the goal of monetary policy] is of course the prerogative of the government, who has decided to suspend the redeemability of the notes" (Bankoutsksottet 1937).

[10] Bankoutskottet utlåtande (1958)and the statements with regard to the proposition to the parliament for the new constitution of 1974.

[11] Statute 44, Brisman (1918, 94).

[12] The major reference to this section is Brisman (1918).

business.[13] *Stockholms Banco* did not hide that it was a fractional reserve bank and was trusted by the public. Remarkably, Palmstruch was the first one, at least officially, to operate a bank as a fractional reserve bank. He also pioneered funding the Riksbank with notes in given denominations, *kreditivsedlar*. The purpose of the *Stockholms Banco* was to improve the payment system and to act as an intermediary. By the goal of increasing the efficiency of the national payment system and the government's involvement, *Stockholms Banco* can be regarded as an early central bank.

Stockholms Banco closed in 1666 after a panic due to an over-issue of notes and consequential losses. The government asked the parliament to investigate how it could be reconstituted. The investigators identified three flaws of *Stockholms Banco*: (1) its governance by a private owner, (2) its note issue, and (3) its lending on unsafe personal collateral.[14] The solution was the new Riksbank owned by the Riksdag with a charter prohibiting note issue and lending based on safe collateral. These features should preserve the "credit" of the Riksbank and guarantee the convertibility of its deposits. Early in the Riksdag's investigation, the idea that the parliament would be a better guarantor than the government arose from the realization that the government may have strong incentives to abuse the Riksbank through borrowing. One inspiration was the municipal ownership of the Amsterdam *Wisselbank* and *Lehnebank*. Convincing the government was a delicate issue, but the timing was fortuitous as the executive was a weak regency. The Riksbank's independence from the government and the motive for it is clearly stated in the royal decree of 1668:

The means of the Riksbank ... should neither, not by us or anybody else, in one way or the other be taken; nor at war, by one King or the other or the Government, be confiscated, nor (despite the necessity and distress be ever so large) there take advances and credit. (Brisman 1918, bilagor, p. 80, §8)

According to the charter of 1668, the Riksbank was divided into two departments: the lending bank (*Lähne-banken*) and the exchange bank (*Wexle-banken*). Both *Stockholms Banco* and the Riksbank thus took inspiration from the two Amsterdam banks, but the combination of the two functions in one institution was new. The Riksbank introduced one significant innovation: interest-bearing deposits at the lending bank, which may be the first time for a bank. It was also to be the state's bank by the instruction to let the government deposit its monetary revenues in

[13] The application is reproduced in Brisman (1918) and discussed in Heckscher (1934).
[14] The government the borrowed a small amount 1663–1664, which was promptly repaid. Thus government abuse was not a cause for the panic, Brisman (1918, 50).

the exchange bank, in particular its custom duties. It was, however, not allowed to lend to the government, and is in this respect different from many later central banks, which were founded to serve the government's lending needs, such as the Bank of England in 1694.

The mandates quoted above clearly state the Riksbank's aims. The exchange bank should facilitate payments, which had its cause in the cumbersome monetary standard with silver coins circulating in parallel with unwieldy copper coins and plates. The lending bank should make "fruitless capital" work by letting it be used as collateral for lending. This formed the basis for the Riksbank as a mortgage-based bank, as opposed to a bank for trade finance based on real bills. The Riksbank was an early version for a type of central bank in northern Europe described by Tarkka (2009) as land-based proto central banks.

The exchange bank needed to have a reserve ratio of 100 percent, while the lending bank needed only small reserves as it was set up for intermediation of coins with matched six-month maturities for loans and deposits. From the beginning, however, the banking instruction allowed, against the charter, for temporary borrowing by the lending bank of funds at the exchange bank, such that the 100 percent reserve ratio of the exchange bank could be reduced. The possibility was used for sudden deposit outflows threatening the normal reserve at the lending bank.

The lending bank's deposits turned out to be more attractive than the exchange bank's deposits as they paid interest, and they unintentionally also came to provide better liquidity. The checking services provided by the exchange bank turned out to be exceedingly complicated and appear to have been used only to a limited extent (Brisman 1918, 131–143). One reason was that accounts were separated according to four types of coin, so a check was cashed according to the coin specified in the account. A spontaneous use began, against the statutes, of using receipts of deposits at the exchange bank in payments. Similarly, the receipts of deposits at the lending bank became means of payment (Brisman 1918, 145). The receipts of the lending bank deposits represent an increase in the money supply to the degree that they circulated, though they did not appear on the Riksbank balance sheet. The receipts of the exchange bank did not imply an increase in the money supply as long as the reserve ratio was 100 percent. From 1701, the exchange bank issued notes, *transportsedlar*, which appear as a liability on the balance sheet from 1710, constituting money, though of negligible amounts before 1726.

An overview of the period for the consolidated Riksbank's first 50 years is given in Figures 3.1 and 3.2 of the assets and liabilities 1668–1718 with war periods shaded. The lending bank was a success for the first decades, measured

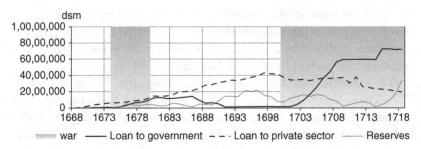

Figure 3.1 Riksbank assets 1668–1718.
Note: Unit of account is *Daler silvermynt* (dsm).
Source: Fregert (2014).

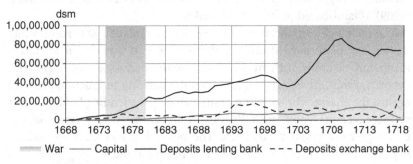

Figure 3.2 Riksbank liabilities 1668–1718.
Note: Unit of account is *Daler silvermynt* (dsm).
Source: Fregert (2014).

by its deposits, which grew to eight times the exchange bank deposits by 1708. For the Riksbank to cover its costs and generate profits, it had to generate an income from a positive interest margin over longer periods for the lending bank, which turned out to be difficult. The Riksbank could at the start set the lending rate up to 8 percent, but was from 1668 prohibited to set it higher than 6 percent. It had little power to change the interest rate, which created two kinds of difficulties. On the one hand, too large deposits relative to lending would result in losses as interest was paid on the deposit at the lending bank and deposits piled up as reserves, which yielded no interest. On the other hand, too small deposits relative to lending required the use of reserves if it were to keep up lending, since note issue was forbidden as a source for lending and capital was low.

Due to the fixed interest rate set by law, the lending bank had trouble matching loans with deposits. With too few depositors it had to decline new loans and terminate outstanding loans. With too few borrowers, it had to decline new deposits.

Before 1709, the lending bank was closed to new deposits for lack of suitable lending on three occasions 1684–1685, 1691–1699, and 1704. The causes were strong deposit *inflows* rather than the drying up of lending opportunities. The lending was, however, more difficult than anticipated. Most of it was based on mortgages, though collateral in the form of silver, gold, or copper also was possible. The charter stipulated a loan maturity of 18 months, but also gave the right to prolong the loan, unless the Riksbank lacked deposits. In addition, the charter only required the borrower to pay interest; amortization was voluntary. These features made for long maturities. A key problem for the Riksbank was how to ascertain that the collateral rules were followed by the borrowers. Borrowers could have used the same collateral for other lenders or may have hypothecated their property more than the required proportion (1/2 for town properties, 2/3 for country properties).

In 1709 a deposit outflow at the lending bank forced the Riksbank to suspend convertibility of the lending bank deposits. The cause was the Swedish loss in 1708 at the battle against the Russians at Poltava in present-day Ukraine. A limited conversion of deposits occurred through rationing for public institutions. The lending bank deposit certificates continued to circulate at a discount between 10 and 20 percent until 1721 when the deposits became available for conversion to coins. The smaller exchange bank survived without any suspension of convertibility of its deposits.

A bad omen was that the Riksbank had been pressured to lend to the government. Loans to the government were made during the war against Denmark between 1674 and 1679, and then during the Great Nordic War between 1701 and 1718. The source of the pressure was the reduced power of the parliament under the reigns of the despotic kings Karl XI 1671–1697 and Karl XII 1697–1718. The first period of war finance was actually a success in that the loans were paid back by 1692.

3.4 1718–1776: The Dependent Riksbank as Lender, Note Issuer, and Monetary Policy Maker[15]

The death of King Karl XII in 1718 ushered in the Age of Freedom with a new constitution in 1719, revised in 1720.[16] Sweden was run by the parliament controlling the executive with the king as a ceremonial

---

[15] The main references are Hallendorff (1920) and Montgomery (1920).

[16] Karl XI (King, 1672–1697) and his son Karl XII (King, 1698–1718) ruled largely without consulting the parliament.

figurehead until 1772. The Riksbank's status thereby shifted from being independent of the executive to an authority controlled by the executive. The Riksbank became a tool for carrying out the government's goals for foreign and fiscal policy.

3.4.1 Restoration of the Riksbank Balance Sheet under the Old Cap Party 1718–1738

Large loans from the Great Nordic War 1700–1718 were bequeathed to the new parliamentary regime. The parliamentary Banking Committee began directly under the parliamentary meeting 1718 to make an inventory of the government debt, including its debt to the Riksbank, with the intention to pay back according to priority. In 1720, the Riksbank was virtually bankrupt, with a small amount of capital. Its largest asset by far was the loans to the government. The largest item on the liability side was the deposits at the lending bank, frozen since 1709.

At the parliamentary meeting in 1723, the decision was taken to write off some of the government's debts to the Riksbank and pay off the remaining loans gradually. As long as these loans remained, the General Council did not dare make the lending bank deposits convertible for fear of a run, for which there would not be enough reserves. The lending bank continued to be virtually closed to new deposits as well as to lending. The exchange bank continued, now mainly used by government authorities and public charities.

While the charter prohibited the issue of notes, the Banking Committee authorized in 1701 the issue of notes to be used as money, thus overruling the charter. In 1726, the notes became accepted for tax payments. The growth in notes was limited before 1739; there was little outlet for them as new lending was virtually closed.

3.4.2 Expansion, Fiat Money and Inflation under the Hat Party 1738–1765

The parliamentary meeting of 1738–1739 is a watershed in the history of the Riksbank. The newly formed Hat party elected a new Executive Council (*Riksråd*) and put leading members on the Banking Committee. The Hat party represented a change from post-war consolidation to an expansionist stance. In domestic policy they propagated mercantilist policy with support to domestic industry and in foreign policy they wished to recoup land lost in the Great Nordic War. A new program for opening the Riksbank to lending was

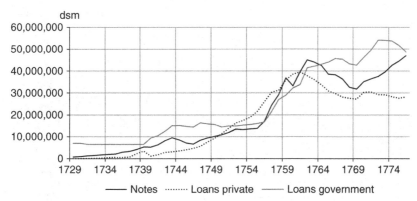

Figure 3.3 Private loans, government loans, and notes 1729–1776
Note: Private loans consist mainly of mortgages on real estate. Unit of account is *Daler silvermynt* (dsm).
Source: Fregert (2014).

implemented in the Banking instruction of 1739. Loans paid in notes would be given against mortgages of property, including industrial properties.

New government borrowing at the Riksbank started in 1740 in preparation for a war with Russia, which began in 1741 and ended in 1743 (see Figure 3.3). The Riksbank experienced a slow drain of reserves from 1740, as notes began to depreciate against copper. The lending bank was opened for deposits in 1743 in the hope that some metal would be deposited. The hope was in vain. In 1745, the Riksbank had to suspend convertibility for notes and copper deposits at the exchange bank, when reserves were almost depleted. While the Secret Committee encouraged lending to manufacturing (iron ores), the cautious General Council only let private lending increase slowly until 1747 (Figure 3.3), when mortgage lending began to take off. The Secret Committee continued to press for increased lending, in particular to those of its members who were among the borrowers.[17]

Between 1757 and 1762 the note issue tripled as a result of the large primary budget deficits financed at the Riksbank incurred due to Sweden's involvement in the Seven Years' War, and the continued increase in private mortgage lending (see Figure 3.3).[18]

The increase in lending was most drastic at the end of the war between 1760 and 1762, when the parliament met. The exchange rate had slowly

---

[17] See Hallendorff (1920, 283).
[18] The note supply did not increase to the same extent as the loans, reflecting interest payments which increased capital substantially.

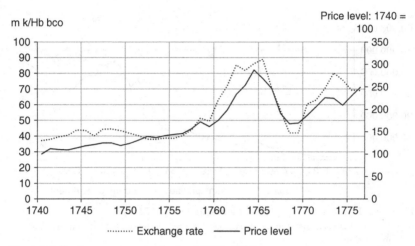

Figure 3.4 Exchange rate and price level 1740–1776
Note: m k is the Swedish currency unit mark kopparmynt, and *Hb bco* is Hamburger banco.
Source: Edvinsson (2010), and Edvinsson and Söderberg (2010).

depreciated from 1757, and then precipitously from 1760 to 1762, so that the notes had lost half of their value compared to 1745 (Figure 3.4). It became clear that the increase in note issue was a principal cause behind the depreciation.[19] The Banking Committee instructed the Riksbank in 1762 to stop all new private loans and to require amortization by 4 percent per year to reduce the note issue.

3.4.3 Restoration of Convertibility 1765–1776

The chaotic consequences of the Hat's policies led to their opponents, the Cap party, winning a majority in 1765. They began an inquiry into the management of the Riksbank back to 1738 and the government budget. The inquiry made the financial situation of the Riksbank and the state public knowledge. The Secret Committee decided on a plan to restore convertibility at the old parity. The General Council was ordered to withdraw loans and thereby reduce the note issue with the aim of making the notes redeemable in silver at the old parity. The plan contained a pre-set gradual reduction of the note issue, based on strict proportionality between the money supply (notes, coins, and deposits) and the exchange rate.[20]

---

[19] A clear analysis based on the quantity theory was presented by the Uppsala Professor Pehr Niclas Christiernin in 1761, see Eagly (1971).
[20] Fregert and Jonung (1996) discuss and show in graphs the monetary plans 1765-1776.

When the secret plan became known in 1765, the expectation of an appreciation led to an instantaneous actual appreciation. A deflation followed with some delay so that the nominal appreciation led to a real appreciation and a fall in exports. Domestic industry suffered through an increasing real value of loans hurting many borrowing firms.[21] Widespread bankruptcies in the small manufacturing sector followed. The restoration plan was, however, followed until the next parliamentary meeting in 1769 with a Hat majority when it was abandoned.[22] The experience represents an early lesson of the short-run Phillips curve.

A *coup d'état* in 1772 by King Gustav III circumscribed the independence of the Riksbank. The Riksbank General Council was forced to follow the King's instructions, which were to be in accord with the Riksbank charter. The Minister of Finance Liljencrants ordered the Riksbank to increase the specie reserve of the Riksbank through foreign loans. Government loans at the Riksbank were written off in 1776 with an immediate loss of Riksbank capital. The King declared notes denominated in copper to be convertible to silver at a rate corresponding to a devalued rate relative to 1745 beginning on January 1, 1777.

The social loss of the access to easy credit for the government in 1740–1762 and the failed restoration after 1765 is essentially imponderable, but would include several effects, including the costs from enabling the expensive and fruitless wars and the business downturn after 1765 (see Hallendorff 1920, 278).

3.5 1777–1808: The Riksbank's Return to Convertibility, Demotion to Insignificance, and back to Convertibility[23]

The overarching goal of the Riksbank from 1776 was securing convertibility. The General Council's resolve to maintain convertibility was backed by the Banking Committee's instruction of 1779, which set the goal of a 75 percent reserve ratio to be achieved by a gradual reduction of notes by requiring 2 percent amortization per year of its mortgage lending. The experience with land-backed and tax-backed notes in 1745–1776 had converted the

---

[21] The contractionary effects of a deflation forced by restoration of the old convertibility rate were predicted by Christiernin in 1761, who argued against going back to the old parity. The members of parliament were also reminded of the dangerous effects by one of their members, Anders Chydenius (1766/2012).

[22] The depth of the recession is discussed by Montgomery (1920, 63).

[23] The main references for this section are Hallendorff (1920), Brisman (1931a), Heckscher (1949), and Fritz (1967).

government and the General Council to the original idea of notes and deposits being representatives of coins needing substantial metal backing. The reserve ratio increased slowly until 1788 when a new war with Russia began. Attempts were made by the King to obtain loans from the Riksbank. The General Council granted a loan reluctantly, initially, but successfully refuted further loans. The Riksbank's determination to protect its independence from the executive to protect convertibility, however, turned out to make it virtually irrelevant for the next decade. The reason was a new parallel currency issued by the newly established National Debt Office (NDO), *Riksgäldskontoret*, under the Riksdag, so-called *Riksgäldssedlar* (Treasury notes).

The NDO notes were issued with the promise of being converted to Riksbank notes at a one-to-one ratio. In less than a year it became clear that NDO notes would not be converted any time soon and they were traded at a depreciated rate relative to the Riksbank notes (see Figure 3.6). Thus two parallel currencies and units of account were born: the NDO notes in *Riksdaler Riksgäld* and the Riksbank notes in *Riksdaler banco*. The NDO notes quickly became the dominant medium of exchange and unit of account, being accepted in tax payments (see Figure 3.5). The Riksbank note issue and reserves dwindled. While convertibility of the Riksbank notes remained, the Riksbank was demoted to irrelevance from 1789 until 1803.

The King convened an extraordinary parliamentary meeting in 1803 for the purpose of making the Treasury notes convertible. It was decided that the Riksgäld notes would became convertible to Riksbank notes, such that one *Riksdaler Riksgäld* could be exchanged for 2/3 *Riksdaler banco*, a Riksbank note convertible to specie at the Riksbank (see Figure 3.6). To secure the convertibility, the silver reserve was increased by a capital levy paid in silver and by the sale of the Swedish colony Wismar in Pomerania.

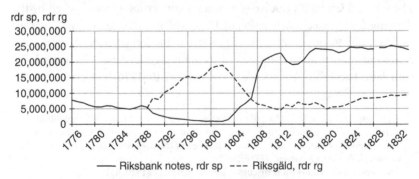

Figure 3.5 Riksbank and Riksgäld (NDO) note issue components 1776–1834
Source: Edvinsson and Ögren (2014).

3.6 1808–1834: The Return of War Finance, Subsidized Lending and Fiat Money

3.6.1 The Suspension of Convertibility 1809 and the Return of Convertibility 1834[24]

The financing of the war of 1808–1809 against Russia with loans paid in notes began the second long period of inconvertibility of Riksbank notes, which lasted until 1834. Russia attacked Finland, a part of Sweden, in 1808, and incorporated it into Russia as a Grand-duchy in 1809. The threat of a drain of silver led to the suspension of convertibility in 1809. The fiat regime lasted until 1834, with a stable note supply, price level, and exchange rate after the initial increase in the note supply, price level, and exchange rate.

The long delay in restoring convertibility had its roots in the political developments set off by the war. The King was dethroned in a *coup d'état* in 1809, which resulted in the new Instrument of Government of (*Regeringsformen*) 1809. The constitutional change implied that laws were to be decided jointly by the government and parliament.[25] Hence both the executive and parliament had veto power over the other. Plans to restore convertibility were discussed at every parliamentary meeting. While there were hopes for a restoration of the original parity for the first years, the general opinion swung in favor of devaluation from 1815 and definitely by 1823.

The issue was delayed due to divisions in the Riksdag, and between the King and the Riksdag over how to secure convertibility. A common opinion in the Riksdag meeting of 1823 was that history had shown that the Riksdag

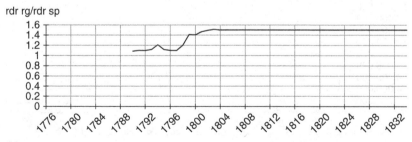

Figure 3.6 The exchange rate *riksdaler riksgälds* (rdr rg) per riksdaler specie (rdr sp)
Source: Edvinsson (2010).

---

[24] The main references are Brisman (1931a) and Andreen (1958, 1961).
[25] The French Marshal Jean Baptiste Bernadotte was made Crown Prince of Sweden 1810 and King in 1818. Karl XIII, the uncle of the dethroned Gustav IV, adopted Bernadotte and was King until his death in 1818.

alone was not able to safeguard convertibility. A proposal was prepared, but failed to get support, to privatize the Riksbank in order to create a personal responsibility for the planned convertibility. Instead, a proposal to safeguard the convertibility by letting the King share the responsibility by promulgating a coin law gained support. By making convertibility a law under the constitution of 1809, it was guaranteed jointly by the King and the Riksdag. A complication was that King Karl XIV initially was opposed to a devaluation. A new coin law was decided by the parliament and the King in 1830 implying a devaluation relative to the old parity of the size of the initial depreciation. A further delay was the decision in 1830 that convertibility was not to be implemented until the reserve ratio had increased to 5/8. Finally, the King called an extraordinary parliamentary meeting in 1834, which decided to implement convertibility immediately despite the reserve ratio not having reached the goal of 5/8.

3.6.2   The Riksbank as lender[26]

At the return of convertibility in 1803, the Riksbank made a return both as provider of the main medium of exchange and as a lender, from a position of irrelevance in both these activities. Figure 3.7 shows the increase in private lending beginning in 1803, particularly discount lending and other lending. The lending reflected a desire in parliament to use the Riksbank for improvements in infrastructure and land.

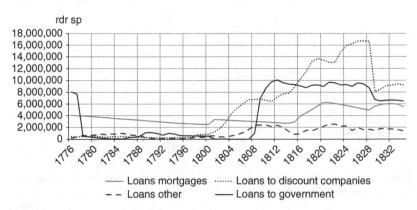

Figure 3.7 The major Riksbank loan categories 1776–1834
Source: Fregert (2014).

---

[26] The Riksbank lending 1803–1830 is treated by Pettersson (1989).

Regarding discount lending, the Riksbank in 1803 took over two so-called discount companies which lent short term against trade bills. One had begun in the 1770s and the other had been run by the National Debt Office using *riksdaler riksgäld*. The new entity was named *Riksdiskonten*. The increase from 1815 (Figure 3.7) was an unintended consequence of the large government loans taken in the war of 1808–1809. The Riksdag decided that the Riksbank should be paid interest on the loans and that amortization should begin. These payments implied that notes were returned to the Riksbank and the note supply declined between 1810 and 1814 (Figure 3.5). The Riksdag in 1815 decided to increase lending for infrastructure projects to private discount companies and thereby undo the reduction in the note supply. During the period 1815–1823, the Riksbank also paid out direct subsidies to canal projects from its profits and offered interest-free loans. Thus the Riksbank again became a source for modernization of the economy, but unlike, during the Age of Freedom, without the use of inflation finance.

In 1830 a new discount company owned fully and financed by the Riksbank began, *Handels och näringsdiskonten*, replacing *Riksdiskonten*. Effectively it was a Riksbank operation, though not included in its balance sheet until the 1860s.

3.7 1834–1913: The Transition from *the* Bank to *the* Central Bank[27]

Sweden changed between 1834 and 1914 from a poor and isolated agricultural country to an industrialized country embedded in the global economy through trade and borrowing in international capital markets. An outward sign of the transformation was the switch from a North-European silver standard to the international gold standard in 1873. At the same time, Sweden adopted the krona as its currency unit, together with Norway and Denmark forming the Scandinavian Currency Union. The progress was conditioned on the long period of international peace, which also contributed to the preservation of convertibility at a constant conversion rate for the longest period in the Riksbank's history. I analyze the Riksbank development in three parts as: bank, the banks' bank, and defender of convertibility and lender of last resort. Finally, I discuss the Riksbank's late transition to a modern central bank compared to other central banks.

---

[27] The main references are Davidson (1931) and Brisman (1931b).

3.7.1   From *the* Bank to *a* Bank to the Note-issuing Bank

The Riksbank always faced competition from private bankers and bill brokers. From 1831 it also faced competiton from private banks, which by the end of the nineteenth century had reduced the Riksbank's role as provider of deposits and loans to insignificance as shown in Figure 3.8. The Riksbank was also threatened as a note issuer by private note-issuing banks. Its share of the note issue stabilized at around 45 percent in the 1860s where it stayed until the Riksbank regained its note monopoly by the Riksbank Act of 1897, a process finished in 1904.

The development of banking emanated from bank laws and charters issued by the government.[28] Bank legislation did not require the consent of the Riksdag as other legislation would, based on the provision in the Instrument of Government of 1809 that the government could promulgate "economic laws."

A first wave of banking growth was based on the bank law of 1824, which stipulated that banks could be chartered with joint unlimited liability for ten-year periods. They were called "enskilda" (personal [liability]) banks. The first – *Skånska Privatbanken* – opened in 1831, inspired by note-

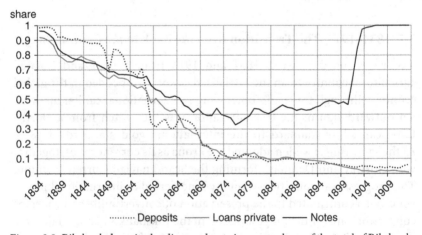

Figure 3.8 Riksbank deposits, lending, and note issue as a share of the total of Riksbank and private (joint-stock and limited liability) banks 1834–1914
Source: Sveriges Riksbank 1668–1924 (1931). Del A. Bankens tillgångar och skulder 1668–1924 and Del A. Privatbankerna. Tillgångar och skulder 1834–1924.

---

[28] The key reference for the development of Swedish banking is Brisman (1924, 1934). Sandberg (1978), Grossman (2010, chapter 8), and Ögren (2013) cover Swedish banking evolution in English.

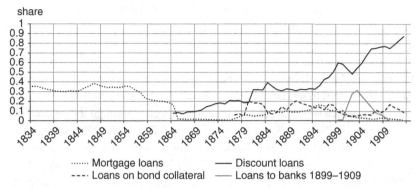

Figure 3.9 Major Riksbank loan types 1834–1914
Note: Discount loans against bills appear in the Riksbank balance sheet from 1864, but existed before as part of the Riksbank loans intermediated by *Handels- och Näringsdiskonten*, owned by the Riksbank.
Source: Fregert (2014).

issuing Scottish joint-stock banks. The law was silent on the right to issue notes: notes were neither illegal, nor were they legal tender. Five more note-issuing banks started in the 1830s, two in the 1840s, and 15 in the 1850s. They were scattered in the provinces and were de facto local monopolies until the end of the 1850s. Almost all of their lending was based on note issue as opposed to deposits (and capital). From 1835, the size of private note issue was regulated in the charters by relating the note issue to the equity stipulated in the charter. The bank law of 1846 set common rules for the note issue for all banks. Reserves were held in Riksbank notes and were voluntary until the next bank law in 1864 which required reserves in Riksbank notes. The bank law of 1874 required the enskilda banks to keep reserves in gold.

A second wave of banking began in 1856 with the first private bank in Stockholm –*Stockholms Enskilda Bank*. It used interest-bearing deposits as the main source of credit. It competed with the note-issuing banks and bill brokers by offering better services, like postal bills for payments across the country, improved check payments, and a clearing service for the note-issuing banks. The change to deposit banking took off in earnest in 1863 with the first limited-liability bank, *Skandinaviska Kreditaktiebolaget*. The new deposit-based banks were chartered based on the limited-liability corporate law of 1848, which did not allow note issuing. A key supplementary reform was the scrapping of usury laws in 1864. This opened up competitive interest setting on deposits and lending of the banks, which now could compete fully with the unregulated bill brokers.

The limited-liability banks quickly grew in numbers and size and soon dominated over the enskilda banks. Deposits grew to eight times the note issue by the end of the nineteenth century.

Financial supervision of the banks was undertaken by the Ministry of Finance, first by supervising their chartering, then by inspections. From 1864 banks were forced to send in quarterly balance sheet statements to the Ministry of Finance, which were published. The inspection grew through the creation of the formal position of Bank Inspector in 1877, and in 1907 it became a government authority, the Bank Inspection Board (*Bankinspektionen*). The Bank Inspection Board merged with the Insurance Inspection Board in 1991 into the Swedish Financial Supervisory Authority (*Finansinspektionen*) under the Ministry of Finance.[29]

The parliament was not a passive bystander to the diminishing Riksbank market shares of deposits and loans. In 1852 it initated a system of privately owned, so-called *filialbanker*, regional banks financed by subsidized loans from the Riksbank. They were not successful as lenders and were abolished between 1863 and 1877. The Riksbank's own lending practices also changed from the 1860s towards shorter loans and away from mortgage lending. The evolution had begun already at the end of the eighteenth century, with support of the discount banks. Short-term discount lending had from around 1815 constituted almost half of lending with the other half composed of mortgages and government borrowing. In the 1860s, the Riksbank managed to increase its funding by offering interest-bearing deposits. Initially a success, the interest-bearing deposits were abolished in 1895.

The rise of private note issuing early on became a contentious issue. From the 1840s the opposition in parliament to enskilda banks grew. The note-issuing banks were seen to appropriate the limited but growing seigniorage provided by a growing and monetizing economy.[30] Their profits were regarded as subsidies to the rich, who could afford the capital requirements. The parliament, however, could do little, having no direct power over bank legislation. The two-chamber parliament, replacing the old four-estate one in 1865, was divided on the private note issue. The first chamber, dominated by the nobility, demanded government control over the Riksbank to safeguard convertibility. The second chamber, dominated by the agricultural interest, demanded the end of the private note issue. The issue was

---

[29] Wendschlag (2012) provides a history of Swedish banking supervision.

[30] The enskilda banks were supported by a coalition of owners and borrowers, which both typically were landowners and industrialists (Brisman 1924, 141). The coalition was supported by the government, which issued the charters (Brisman 1934, 20–22).

eventually forced with the decision of the second chamber to tax the private note issue. The first chamber demanded, and received in exchange for giving up the note issue, the government's right to appoint the chairman of the General Council.[31] The result was the Riksbank Act of 1897 which replaced the 1668 charter. Private notes were taken out of circulation by 1904.

3.7.2   From *a* Central Bank to *the* Central Bank

The two essential tasks of a modern central bank are the control of the interest rate to conduct monetary policy – the macro function, and the maintenance of the safety and efficiency of the payment system – the micro function. The micro functions were provided by the private sector until the Riksbank took over the liquidity provision gradually from the 1880s and then clearing in 1899.

The need for clearing of private bank notes increased as the number of enskilda banks increased and their activities spread across larger areas. The enskilda banks tried to spread their notes beyond their local area, thereby lengthening their time of circulation. This required that they redeem private notes into Riksbank notes at other locations for which they used local agents.[32] The need for a more efficient system was realized by *Stockholms Enskilda Bank*. Within a year of its founding in 1856, it had signed contracts with a majority of the enskilda banks for a clearing service. It lost its clearing position in 1864 to *Skandinaviska Kreditaktiebolaget*. As a bank without note issue, in contrast to *Stockholms Enskilda bank*, it did not compete with its customers in the spreading of notes (Söderlund 1964, 116). It continued as the clearing bank until the Riksbank took over clearing in 1899.

Skandinaviska Kreditaktiebolaget also provided liquidity services to banks with deposit facilities as well as loans in the form of credit lines and rediscounting, services which were complementary to clearing. Söderlund (1964) surmised that the *Skandinaviska Kreditaktiebolaget* was able to provide larger credits to the enskilda banks than *Stockholms Enskilda Bank*, which was limited in its capital, had. When a severe crisis hit Sweden in 1877, both the Riksbank and *Skandinaviska Kreditaktiebolaget* increased their loans to the banks (Figure 3.10).

[31] §72 in the Instrument of Government of 1809 amended 1897.
[32] Local tax officials received private bank notes for tax payments against a fee from the issuing bank (Brisman 1934, 23–26). The expenses for spreading and redeeming the notes are rent-seeking costs with no social value as they only redistribute seigniorage.

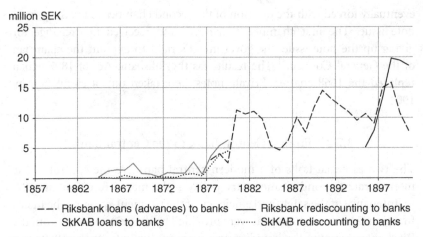

Figure 3.10 Banks' borrowing at the Riksbank and at *Skandinaviska Kreditaktiebolaget* (SkKAB) 1857–1900

Source: Riksbanken: End-of-year data from Fregert (2014) and *Bankoutskottets memorial* 1895–1904; Skandinaviska Kreditaktiebolaget: Total year data from Gasslander (1962, 122).

The Riksbank was allowed to open credit lines for banks from 1872 (from 1873 for the limited-liability banks). Rediscounting by the Riksbank first occurred in 1885 to some enskilda banks to compensate for limitations of their small-denomination note issue in connection with new charters. Riksbank lending increasingly consisted of rediscounting trade bills originated by the private banks. They were discounted at a rebate of half of 1 percent – the rediscount rate. Regular rediscounting to banks was offered to banks from 1893, note-issuing as well as limited-liability banks. The rediscounting was based on individual contracts with the banks until 1901, when the General Council declared that all bills of prime quality could be discounted by any bank. Short-term interest rates charged by the banks had been equalized since 1879. At first the Riksbank followed the private banks, while it took the lead in the early 1890s (Brisman 1934, 212). By the end of the period, virtually all Riksbank lending consisted of discounting bills, most of it rediscounting to banks.

The evolution of banking paralleled the evolution of Sweden's engagement in the international capital markets as a borrower. The two largest borrowers were the National Debt Office (NDO)(*Riksgäldskontoret*), which borrowed mainly to finance the state railway trunk lines, and the National Mortgage Association, *Allmänna Hypoteksbanken*, which borrowed for large-scale land improvement projects. Typically, the foreign exchange raised abroad from international bond issues was not used

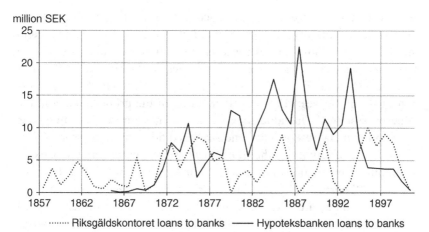

Figure 3.11 Banks' borrowing of foreign exchange at the *Riksgäldskontoret* (NDO), and *Allmänna Hypoteksbanken* 1857–1900
Source: Riksgäldskontoret (NDO) and Allmänna Hypoteksbanken: Total year data from Nygren (1989, tables 2 and 4).

immediately but lent short term in Sweden, as shown by Nygren (1989). In times of crisis their lending of foreign exchange increased, especially to the banks, which in turn lent to firms which often were dependent on short-term foreign credit (Figure 3.11). Nygren (1989) described the two institutions as complementary lenders of last resort to the Riksbank.

3.7.3 The Riksbank as Defender of Convertibility and Lender of Last Resort[33]

The Banking Committee's instruction of 1835 contained detailed rules to safeguard the convertibility restored in 1834. There were two types of rules: *proactive* for the long run and *reactive* for crises. The proactive rules determined the long-run positive co-evolution of notes and reserves. The reactive rules were invoked in response to a "sustained reduction" of reserves, which might lead to a violation of the proactive rules and, in the end, pose a threat to convertibility.

Three types of *proactive rules* set limits to the note supply through: (1) maximum limits on lending according to type of loan, (2) minimum

---

[33] This section builds mainly on Davidson (1931) and Brisman (1931a, b). Overviews of the classical gold standard 1873–1914 are provided by Flux (1910), Heckscher (1926/1930 127–136), and Jonung (1984).

absolute level of reserves, and (3) note-cover rules relating the note issue to the amount of reserves. The maximum limits on lending were scrapped in the 1880s, while minimum reserve levels and note-cover rules existed until 1948. The period contains three different rules for the note cover. Between 1835 and 1845 the note cover was *proportional*, between 1845 and 1901 *fiduciary*, and between 1901 and 1948 a mix of the proportional and the fiduciary system.[34] The fiduciary system stipulates a maximum note issue equal to the metal reserve plus a non-covered fiduciary note issue.

Two types of actions for the *reactive rules* were identified in the Banking Committee's instructions between 1835 and 1874: (1) reducing the note issue and (2) borrowing reserves. In a crisis, notes and reserves decrease one for one, as notes are exchanged for reserves. The first option implied a further reduction of notes through the reduction of domestic assets (loans or bonds), that is, acting according to "the rules of the game" (see below). This option would contract new lending in the bill market directly and would also indirectly contract bank lending, since the private banks used Riksbank notes as reserves. Borrowing reserves did not have this effect.

The proactive and the reactive rules, determined by the Banking Committee, together with the rules of convertibility, safeguarded from 1851 in the constitution, made up the monetary regime. The convertibility rate was set by the coin law of 1830. The new coin law of 1873 changed the reserve metal to gold and the currency unit to krona. The currency switch was a consequence of the Scandinavian Currency Union (SCU) agreement between Sweden, Denmark, and Norway to accept each other's coins, denominated in the common currency unit krona, as legal tender. The SCU did not constitute a full-blown monetary union, since it did not rest on mutual guarantees to redeem each other's currencies in gold.[35] The nominal anchor was the Riksbank's legal obligation to gold convertibility.

How did this regime handle reserve drains? The source of reserve changes in Sweden emanated from the balance of payment, "external drains," as opposed to bank panics, "internal drains."[36] The major crises were of

---

[34] See Eichengreen (1996, 23–24) for an international overview of these rules during the classical gold standard.

[35] The agreement was complemented by a non-binding voluntary practice of accepting Danish and Norwegian notes by the Riksbank. In 1885 the three central banks made an agreement to accept drafts on each other for larger amounts, which was abandoned in 1905 by the Riksbank, when Norway gained independence from Sweden. See Heckscher (1926/1930, 129–131), Jonung (2007), and Eitrheim et al. (2016, 182–185) for overviews.

[36] Brisman (1931b) and Davidson (1931) analyze the sources of shocks and reaction to them in great detail. There was only one minor bank panic, which occurred in 1856 (Brisman 1934, 98–107).

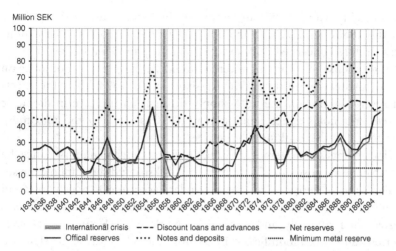

Figure 3.12 Notes, official reserves, net reserves, minimum reserves, and discount and advances lending 1834–1895
Note: Net reserves: Official reserves minus foreign debt at the Riksbank.
Source: Fregert (2014).

foreign origin. Reserve reductions finance by definition a shortfall between the current account and the financial account. The current account and the financial account thus constitute two sources of reserve shocks. Swedish exporters were until the end of the nineteenth century dependent on short-term financing for working capital. These foreign credits were intermediated by trading companies before banks took on this function. A foreign crisis typically led to a decrease in both exports and foreign finance.

The yearly outcome of the monetary regime is shown in Figure 3.12 for the period 1834 to 1895. The international crises of 1847, 1856/1857, and 1873 dominate the outcome. Reserve reductions led to decreases in notes of equal size in the crises.[37] The Riksbank did not reduce the note issue by a reduction of domestic assets in these crises. Some borrowing of reserves, seen as the difference between total and net reserves in Figure 3.12, took place to a limited extent in 1856 to 1858, during the 1870s, and in 1889/1890. Only once did the General Council order a reduction in discount lending to reduce the note supply, namely, in 1879 when reserves were close to the minimum level (Brisman 1931b, 178–179).

Brisman (1931b, 85–93) described the monetary regime between 1835 and 1874 as a "direct deflation regime" and contrasted it

---

[37] The international financial crisis 1857 was preceded by a crisis in 1856 in Sweden due to a decrease in exports after the end of the Crimean War.

unfavorably with the discount policy of the Bank of England beginning in the 1860s. In his view, the Banking Committee in its instructions was unduly concerned with external liquidity to defend convertibility, at the expense of providing internal liquidity, the provision of loans on good collateral at all times. The Riksbank could not sterilize the effects of reserve drains on the note supply through an increase in domestic assets and notes, since lending typically was close to the maximum limits set by the Banking Committee.

Two points should temper Brisman's critical judgement. First, since the Riksbank was mostly passive in crises, the Riksbank did not follow the so-called "rules of the game" of a metal standard according to which notes and domestic assets should move in the same direction at all times. This was tested internationally and rejected by Nurkse (1944) for the interwar period and by Bloomfield (1959) for the classical gold standard 1880–1913.[38] Instead their tests indicated that the central bank actively attempted to undo the reduction of the note supply ("internal liquidity") from reserve drains, a policy of sterilization of reserve flows. The Riksbank passive policy before 1890 meant neither following the "rules of the game," nor the sterilization of reserve fluctuations.

Second, the large reserve reductions in Sweden in 1847, 1856/1857, and 1873 represent returns to normal reserve levels. In all these instances, reserves had increased during an international boom before the reserve crises as seen in Figure 3.12. A policy for a small country like Sweden to even out domestic liquidity would entail reducing domestic assets in the upturn and increasing domestic assets in the downturn. A policy of sterilizing only in the downturns and not in the upturns would soon conflict with the note-cover rules and threaten convertibility.

As the Riksbank gradually took over the role as the banks' bank and took command of the money market, it moved closer to a modern central bank by taking responsibility for stabilizing internal liquidity. The period from 1880 to 1914 contains two international financial crises, the Baring crisis 1890 and the US crisis 1907. The international crisis 1907 affected Sweden mainly through the drying up of short-term foreign capital. Figure 3.13 shows the same variables 1905–1913 as for the period 1834–1895 in Figure 3.12. The striking difference is that the note issue in 1907 hardly changed, while net reserves declined and domestic assets increased. Thus the external liquidity shock did not translate into an internal liquidity shock.

---

[38] See Eichengreen (1996) and McKinnon (1993).

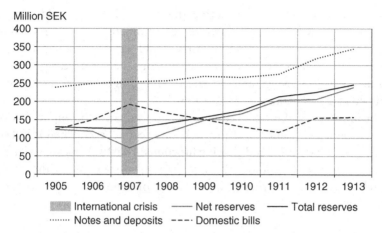

Figure 3.13 Total and net reserves; notes and discount lending 1905–1913 at the Riksbank

Note: Net reserves = Reserves – Foreign debt – Loans of FEX from NDO (Other liabilities).

Source: Fregert (2014).

The reason is that the Riksbank extended its discount lending to foreign currency. Foreign short-term lending at this time went through private banks. The banks covered the shortfall by borrowing foreign credits at the Riksbank, which registered in the Riksbank balance sheet as an increase in domestic bills denominated in foreign currency. The same amount was deposited by the National Debt Office (NDO) at the Riksbank, so the Riksbank's total reserve was unchanged. In essence, the Riksbank acted as an intermediary between the NDO and the banks with the NDO as the lender of last resort. The Riksbank's response was praised by Cassel (1908) as the proper response to a temporary reserve loss, though he scolded it for not acknowledging that this was its duty, but rather indicating it was an act of discretionary benevolence on its part.

Finally it should be noted that a complementary insulating mechanism to reserve drains was stabilizing private capital flows, as stressed by Heckscher (1926/1930, 36):

The factor which played the main role was in all likelihood the *knowledge itself of the existence of fixed exchange rates and the faith in their continuance.* The person with a claim on another country which exchange rate is temporarily below its usual level would have an interest in not immediately withdrawing the amount, since he then would receive a smaller sum in his own currency than usual and the counterpart would normally not wish anything else. (Italics in original)

The point is proven by considering the miniscule yearly gold reserve changes at the Riksbank, which make up the difference between current accounts and private capital imports. Gold reserves changed by a few million kronors, while the current account showed yearly current account deficits varying between 20 and 100 million on a yearly basis (Lindahl et al., 1937, tables 174 and 175).[39]

The importance of the gold commitment underscores the importance of the Riksbank as the anchor of the monetary regime, even when it lacked the lender-of-last-resort and clearing functions. The Riksbank kept a larger gold reserve than the combined private banking system during the whole period, and more importantly, a reputation of commitment to convertibility built up since 1834.

3.7.4   The Riksbank's Evolution to a Central Bank Compared to Other Central Banks

The Riksbank' s evolution to a modern central bank was slow compared to other European countries. Capie et al. (1994, table 1.1) used discount policy and note monopoly as defining characteristics of a central bank. Only Banca D'Italia was later in giving the central bank a note monopoly, and only Banka de Espana later in using discount policy. Only in Portugal and Sweden was note monopoly granted after discount policy began. Sweden's neighbors, Finlands Bank and Norges Bank, were contemporaries also starting discount policy around 1890. This was a long delay compared to the Bank of England which began in connection with the international 1857 crisis, followed shortly after by Banque de France and Danmarks Nationalbank.

The late note monopoly was due to the long-standing stalemate between the government, protecting the private note-issuing banks' interests, and the parliament, protecting the Riksbank interests until the Riksbank Act of 1897. The exceptional delay was rooted in exceptional features of the Riksbank's constitutional status and the constitutional division of power.

The late introduction of discount policy emanated from within the Riksbank's leadership, for which there is little documentation. Since the policy developed gradually, it is natural to tie its slow evolution to the competing   elements   of   private   clearing   and   rediscounting. The combination of stringent capital requirements and an increasingly

---

[39] The credibility-induced mechanism is also stressed in modern treatments of the gold standard, see e.g. Eichengreen (1996, 31–32).

effective banking inspection made for a safe banking system. The safety of the banking system in turn made it possible for the banks to use the central bank function of clearing and a limited lender-of-last-resort function created by the private bank *Skandinaviska Kreditaktiebolaget*. Thus it appears that Sweden's early start in private banking legislation and inspection contributed to a late start in central banking.

The evolution of the Swedish Riksbank into a modern central bank does not fit either of the two main stylized hypotheses of central bank evolution. The appearance of discount policy and the Riksbank adopting the role of lender of last resort arrived without any political prompting and thus goes against the hypothesis of a central bank wholly being a creature of government suggested by Smith (1936, 167). The note monopoly, on the other hand, was the outcome of a political process. It was not a necessity for discount policy or lender-of-last-resort function, neither did the private note issue create any problems of moral hazard leading to over-issue and bank panics. The note monopoly was thus not part of a natural evolution emanating from clearing and discounting being natural monopolies as suggested by Goodhart (1988, 5), since these functions appeared before the note monopoly.

3.8 1914–1929: From Inconvertibility to Convertibility

World War I broke the 80-year period of convertibility. It is the most volatile period in modern Swedish monetary history, with yearly inflation reaching 30 percent in 1918 and a deflation during 1921–1922, which reduced the price level by 40 percent. The outcome was the result of large shocks and a mostly passive Riksbank.[40]

Decreasing reserves during the summer of 1914 and the outbreak of World War I in August led the General Council to ask the Banking Committee for permission to suspend the convertibility of notes into gold, which was granted. The suspension was unconstitutional, but no one protested. The motive was to preemptively "preserve the financial backbone of the country" as metal reserves were far from exhausted.[41]

The change to fiat money eventually led to the doubling of the note supply between 1914 and 1918. It was made possible by a doubling of the fiduciary (uncovered by gold) note issue in 1914 and large gold inflows due to a surge in export demand. A contributing factor was loans to the government.

---

[40] A detailed treatment of Sweden's monetary history 1914–1924 is Heckscher (1926/1930).
[41] Heckscher (1926/1930, 139).

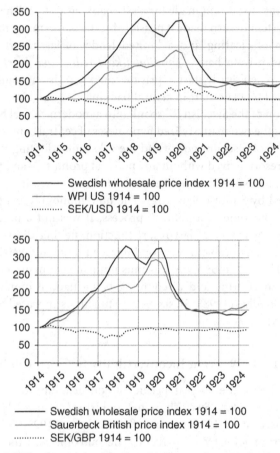

Figure 3.14 Wholesale price levels and exchange rates between Sweden and the UK (bottom) and Sweden and the US (top), 1914–1924, quarterly data, 1914 = 100

Sweden experienced a higher inflation than its main trading partners (see Figure 3.14), despite a similar monetary policy, as evidenced by its discount rate being equal and sometimes above the Bank of England (see Figure 3.15). The cause was an increased demand for exports, which resulted in a real appreciation of about 50 percent between 1914 and 1918 and a large current account surplus. Half of the real appreciation took place through a nominal appreciation of about 25 percent from early 1917 relative to the gold countries, Great Britain and the United States, and half through higher domestic inflation than foreign inflation (see Figure 3.14).

The nominal appreciation was an effect of a unique policy beginning in the spring of 1916 by ending the right to convert gold to notes at the

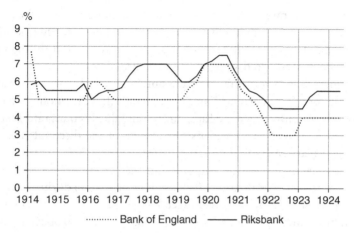

Figure 3.15 Discount rates of the Riksbank and the Bank of England 1914–1924, quarterly data

Riksbank (a "gold embargo").[42] The immediate cause was an inflow of gold to the Riksbank in the spring of 1916. The Riksbank considered the inflow an expensive way of acquiring gold and a cause of concern due to the increase in the note supply. The idea of ending the right to convert gold to notes was picked up by the Riksbank governor from an article by David Davidson.[43] Such a policy could stabilize the Swedish price level by avoiding the two causes of Swedish inflation: the real appreciation effect of increasing import prices in kronor and the international decrease of the value of gold relative to goods. Davidson was asked in 1916 by the Riksbank to give advice. This may be the first time the Riksbank asked for the opinion of an outside economist.[44] The impact in 1916 was limited since the Riksbank was obliged to convert gold coins from Norway and Denmark to Swedish currency according to the SCU (a link which could also be used by other countries). An agreement in early 1917 between the SCU members prohibited gold exports including all Scandinavian legal tender gold coins. The agreement de facto ended the SCU as the one-to-one parity between the Swedish, Danish, and Norwegian krona disappeared due to the different monetary policies and the import and export restrictions on gold in all the member countries.

The Riksbank raised the discount rate to 7 percent from 1916 to 1917, which was 2 percent above the rate at the Bank of England. In principle

[42] According to Heckscher (1926/1930, 189).
[43] Professor of Economics at Uppsala University.   [44] Heckscher (1926/1930, 190).

a higher discount rate could have dampened inflation more, in which case the real appreciation would have come about through a further nominal appreciation. The possibility of complete price stabilization through the abandonment of the gold standard and the use of the discount rate had been argued long before the war by Knut Wicksell. The gold embargo opened up for a "free currency" and price stabilization. Economists led by Wicksell consistently urged the Riksbank to raise the discount rate. Instead the Riksbank governor claimed its inefficiency of the discount rate and urged the private banks to ration their loans.

The international deflation beginning in the summer of 1920 affected Sweden from the fall of 1920 and decreased the price level during 1921 and the first part of 1922 by 40 percent (see Figure 3.14). The Riksbank contributed by an increase in the discount rate in March 1920 above Bank of England in response to a run for gold (Figure 3.15). This led to a suspension of convertibility of the notes into gold. The deflation was reinforced from August 1920 by declarations by the government and the Banking Committee of a return to the gold standard at the pre-war parity. Expectations of an appreciation of gold, and hence the US dollar (convertible to gold) exchange rate, led to a nominal and real appreciation of the krona (as in 1766). The krona had from 1919 depreciated to the degree that it was depreciated relative to the pre-war parity (see Figure 3.14). The process was over by November 1922 when the exchange rate reached the pre-war parity, which led the Riksbank to peg the krona–dollar exchange rate at the old parity level in preparation for the return to the gold standard. An outflow of foreign exchange and gold during 1923 led the Riksbank to borrow US dollars in New York through the NDO. Sweden became the first country to restore convertibility of notes to gold in April 1924. It was reinstated at the pre-war parity.[45]

The sharp deflation led to a deep financial and real crisis with unemployment reaching almost 30 percent in 1922. Still, there was no banking panic. One explanation is that the government took over a few banks together with other banks in the government-sponsored *Aktiebolaget Kreditkassan*. The Riksbank helped initially with a short-term loan (see Hagberg 2007).

The 1923–1929 period was calm. During the war Sweden became a capital exporter by buying back Swedish bonds from abroad sold before the war, which continued after the war (Franzén 1989). The note supply was virtually constant, but increased in real terms due to a mild deflation.

---

[45] An analysis of the forces behind the deflation 1920–1922 compared to 1931–1933, and their effects is given in Fregert and Jonung (2004).

3.9 1929–1939: The Riksbank as Price Stabilizer[46]

The Great Depression was first experienced by an inflow of foreign capital during 1930 as Sweden was considered a safe haven. In the summer of 1931, the capital inflow turned to an outflow. The Riksbank suspended convertibility in September 1931 one week after the Bank of England after a run on foreign exchange reserves. The defense failed after attempts to borrow in New York and Paris failed and the foreign exchange reserves were almost exhausted.

The suspension was followed by a depreciation of the exchange rate of about 10 percent. The suspension was followed by a declaration by the Minister of Finance at the end of September 1931 stated that the Riksbank should aim for stable prices for the foreseeable future. The statement had been prepared in discussions with the economists Hammarskjöld, Cassel, Davidson, and Heckscher. The latter three were given a questionnaire on how to fulfill the goal, which was delivered in October 1931, described in Jonung (1979).

The price stabilization goal was discussed by the Banking Committee in the spring of 1932. It supported the goal with the addition that it would be desirable to increase wholesale prices to their level before deflation set in 1931. The issue was further discussed in the spring of 1933 on the basis of an inquiry of a committee of experts, *valutasakkunniga*.[47] The inquiry was ordered by the Social Democratic government elected in the fall of 1932. There was a continued broad agreement that price level stabilization should be the overriding goal. There was also agreement that the executive government should take the overarching responsibility to make sure monetary and fiscal policy cooperated. The committee included the professors Cassel, Davidson, Heckscher, and Myrdal, the latter two publishing pamphlets supporting these positions in late 1931 and early 1932.

The Riksbank pegged the exchange rate to the British pound in July of 1933 (with notes still inconvertible to gold). The fixed exchange rate worked as an intermediary goal with low inflation until 1937. Following an increase in inflation in 1937 in the United Kingdom, the Swedish inflation began to increase towards 3 percent (Figure 3.16). Heckscher and Cassel urged the Riksbank to appreciate the krona to avoid importing the rising British inflation, citing the need to fulfill the commitment to the price level goal. The Finance Minister was reluctant on the ground that the

---

[46] Kock (1961) and Jonung and Berg (1999) are the main references.

[47] Kock (1961, 112–115) summarizes the discussions of the relation between the government and the Riksbank in the 1930s, including the economists' opinions.

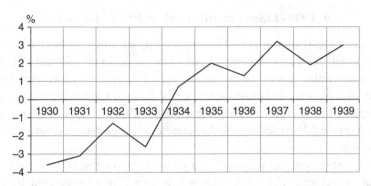

Figure 3.16 Yearly CPI inflation 1930 to 1939

inflation increase was minor and would help a further decrease in unemployment. He also referred to the fixed exchange rate as a goal in itself. The Finance Minister Ernst Wigforss thus saw a trade-off between price, exchange rate, and unemployment stabilization, which was not part of the initial announcements. Wigforss's viewpoint prevailed with the support of the Banking Committee, which also acknowledged the government's right to formulate the goal of monetary policy when convertibility was revoked.[48] The inflation outcome 1930 to 1939 is shown in Figure 3.16.

Regarding its actions, two features stand out in the balance sheet of the Riksbank. First, discounted bills disappeared in 1932. The reason was the increase in exports earnings after the gold suspension, which was deposited at the banks. The commercial banks in turn deposited the proceeds of the foreign exchange at the Riksbank and wound down their rediscounted bills at the Riksbank. Thus the banks' liquidity position switched from a deficit to a surplus and the discount rate lost its function (Figure 3.17). Since the banks' deposits at the Riksbank did not pay interest, the market short-term interest rates were free to fluctuate between zero and the discount rate announced at 3 percent for the rest of the 1930s. The continuing high and increasing liquidity surplus seen in Figure 3.17, led to falling market interest rates until 1939.[49]

The second feature is the substantial acquisition of Swedish government bonds in 1932, which were sold in 1934. The purchase was made to provide funds to the National Debt Office for a rescue operation of *Skandinaviska kreditaktiebolaget*, which had lent to Swedish financier Ivar Kreuger, who committed suicide in March 1932. It should also be pointed out that the

---

[48] See footnote 8.   [49] See Kock (1961, 161–164).

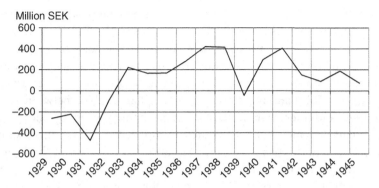

Figure 3.17 The structural liquidity position of the banks vis-à-vis the Riksbank
1929–1945

Riksbank did not buy any of the government bond issues which were
issued from 1932 to finance a budget deficit to help fight the depression.

3.10 1939–1971: The Riksbank as Regulator[50]

The outbreak of World War II led to a temporary import surge in antici-
pation of reduced trade due to the war, which led to a loss of foreign
exchange. The Riksbank met the liquidity contraction by a combination of
open market purchases of Swedish government bonds and reopening of
the discount window. For the rest of the war, the Riksbank was affected by
the purchase of bonds to finance the budget deficits which increased
domestic assets, and a surplus in the current account which increased
reserves. These two sources of asset increases were of the same magnitude
and both increased the amount of high-powered money (notes and banks'
deposits at the Riksbank). A substantial part of the current account surplus
showed up as an increase in foreign exchange reserves until 1942, while the
gold reserve continued to increase until 1945, most of it coming from
Germany.

The goals for stabilization policy in the post-war period were formulated by the Social Democratic government and ratified by the
Riksdag in 1944. As in many other countries the goal of low long-
term interest rates was added to the goals of low inflation and high
employment. The 1944 program also added the goal that inflation

---

[50] Overviews are given in Werin et al. (1993), Eklöf (1990a, b), SOU (1982:52 and 1982:53).
kock (1962) covers the period 1939 to 1958 in detail.

should move in the opposite direction to the general productivity level, but it quickly lost relevance.[51] The goal forced the Riksbank to buy government bonds to prevent an increase in the long-term interest rate. The private banks had acquired bonds during the war and now sold them to build cash reserves in order to be able to increase private lending. The Riksbank bond holdings more than doubled between 1946 and 1947 and then stabilized. An export boom fueled by increased investment demand in the devastated Europe led to a large increase in foreign exchange reserves. To forestall a post-war inflation, the krona was revalued in 1946. The revalued krona and a weakened export boom soon led to a reversal with dwindling foreign reserves. When Great Britain devalued the pound in 1949, Sweden followed suit and kept the fixed exchange rate with Great Britain, thereby devaluing against other countries by the same amount as Great Britain.

Sweden joined the Bretton Woods agreement in 1951. Sweden thus switched form pound sterling to dollar convertibility and became part of a system of international capital controls. The capital controls allowed an independent monetary policy. At the same time, the capital controls, together with the unwritten rule that the government should not borrow abroad, laid a restriction on the overall impact of stabilization policy and aggregate demand growth. Any increase in aggregate demand above GDP, implying a current account deficit, would lead to an outflow of foreign reserves, which could not be covered by capital imports. The required coordination of monetary and fiscal policy worked through the government's indirect control of the General Council, which reflected the same parliamentary majority as the government.

The years after World War II and the devaluation in 1949 made it clear that low interest rates could not be preserved with convertibility, unless aggregate demand was checked, to avoid balance of payments crises. Attempts to control the credit market began in 1947 with exhortations from the Riksbank to the banks to restrict lending while keeping interest rates low. The attempts failed and a new credit market law in 1952 gave the Riksbank the means to directly control the credit market. The law was an enabling act (fullmaktslag), by which the Riksbank could impose controls by decree. The means used to control the banks were minimum liquidity ratios, lending ceilings, and minimum cash ratios. In addition, the Riksbank controlled private bond emissions.

---

[51] The inverse productivity norm for the price level is akin to the modern idea of nominal GDP stabilization. It had previously been advocated by David Davidson and Erik Lindahl, see Fregert (1993).

The enabling feature implied that the Riksbank could regulate bank lending without issuing decrees through mere threats. Liquidity ratios and emission controls were continuously used to channel lending into housing and industry. Lending ceilings were imposed by moral suasion in 1955–1956 and 1969 (backed up by threats of decrees). Cash reserve ratios were only used in 1968–1969. The main purpose of the low-interest goal was to provide low-cost loanable funds to industrial investments and housing investment. The result was a mixture of detailed regulations and controls of the credit market coupled with discretionary controls of the banks through monthly meetings between the central bank governor and the CEOs of the private banks. The Riksbank gradually complemented the quantitative controls by changing the discount rate for bank lending at the Riksbank. A new feature was the appearance of so-called investment deposits. They were tax-favored deposit accounts for firms who could deposit profits at the Riksbank in upturns. The purpose was to drain liquidity from the banks in upturns, and withdraw them in downturns.[52]

This regime of financial repression worked well until 1971 with low and stable inflation and unemployment and no financial crisis. The control of aggregate demand was consistent with stabilization of the business cycle (internal balance) and the current account (external balance). Fiscal and monetary policy, working on aggregate demand, could stabilize the economy as shocks emanated from the demand side. Because of capital controls, the limited foreign exchange reserve position forced the policy makers to avoid persistent current account deficits so that domestic demand had to adjust to GDP.

The need to coordinate monetary and fiscal policy to obey the external balance naturally pressured the Riksbank and the government to closer cooperation. The practice of the government taking the upper hand in the coordination to reach additional goals, in particular a low interest rate, was not, however, without conflicts. The first time was when the Riksbank governor Ivar Rooth protested against the low-interest policy after the war

---

[52] Jonung (1993, 353–360) chronicles the rise and fall of the credit controls, including the monthly meetings between the CEOs of the banks and the Riksbank governor. The complex mix of regulations, market measures, and moral suasion appears to be matched by the complex mix of underlying causes listed by Jonung as: "the monetary program of 1944, the experience of the second world war, the legitimacy of government intervention and economic planning, political forces: the dominance of the Social Democratic party, the effect of the AP fund, the dominance of Keynesianism and the low-interest-rate doctrine, the role of housing policy and the 'million [apartment] program', the role of organized interest groups, and international demonstration effect."

which forced the Riksbank to accumulate bonds and increase high-powered money.[53] He resigned in 1948.

The second time was in 1957 when the General Council raised the discount rate by 1 percent without informing the government. The action was seen as a move away from the low-interest policy and a demonstration of independence from the Riksbank. The chairman of the Council, appointed by the government, was forced to resign. An intense debate ensued involving politicians and economists about the constitutional status of the Riksbank and the (il-)legality of the government's pressure on the General Council members.[54]

The third conflict occurred in 1969. The Riksbank noted a steady decline of foreign reserves during an upturn and asked the government for a fiscal contraction. When it was not forthcoming, the Riksbank imposed a lending ceiling and ordered the banks to cut their check credits by 20 percent. This drastic contraction caused a downturn, which moved the current account into a surplus, reversing the outflow of foreign reserves.[55]

3.11 1971–1989: The Riksbank under Pressure[56]

Inflation and unemployment were far more volatile in the two decades from 1971 to 1989 than in the two decades before or after. The period begins with the end of the Bretton Woods agreement, and ends with the abandonment of external capital controls in 1989. Aggregate supply shocks, in particular the oil price shocks 1973 (OPEC I) and 1979 (OPEC II), presented new challenges, by creating a tension between the goals of external balance (zero current account) and internal balance (full employment).

The tension was relieved by government foreign borrowing beginning after the OPEC I oil shock in 1974. An expansionary fiscal policy to avoid the international downturn was begun by supporting industry through subsidizing inventories to be sold when the downturn ended. The policy began several years of current account deficits caused by the combination of high prices and wage inflation, and fixed exchange rates, which reduced the international competitiveness of Swedish industry. Current account deficits together with rising unemployment were met by a devaluation in 1977 of 10 percent, one in 1981 of 10 percent, and one in 1982 of 16 percent.[57] The period also saw increased used of credit market regulations to stem

---

[53] Rooth (1988).   [54] Carlson (1993).   [55] Eklöf (1990b).

[56] See Werin et al. (1993). An overview is given in the government inquiry SOU 1993:16, summarized in English in Lindbeck et al. (1993).

[57] See Jonung (1991) for analyses of the 1982 devaluation from many perspectives.

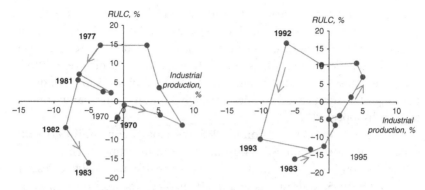

Figure 3.18 Two devaluation-price-wage cycles: 1970–1983 and 1983–1993
Note: RULC = relative unit labor cost. RULC and industrial production measured as percentage deviations from log-linear trends.
Source: Jakobsson (1997).

inflation and current account deficits financed by government foreign borrowing. The devaluations fed future inflation and, thereby, expected inflation and wages creating the wage-price-devaluation cycles seen in Figure 3.18. Underlying causes of the cycles were the combination of a lower weight put on the external balance goal (current account balance) by foreign borrowing and a higher weight on the internal balance goal (lower unemployment) by expansive fiscal policy compared to the Bretton Woods period.[58]

Policy makers and economists realized the inherent time consistency problem of repeated devaluations. The Finance Minister, Kjell-Olof Feldt, in charge of the 16 percent devaluation in 1982, described it as a one-time devaluation to restore the lost competetiveness of the export industry. He warned the labor market parties that excessive wage increases would not be accomodated by new devaluations. Several Swedish economists urged the need for a strong commitment to the fixed exchange rate as the nominal anchor (Hansson et al. 1985). How to make the commitment credible was less clear. A group of Brookings economists (Bosworth and Rivlin 1987), on the other hand, urged Sweden to adopt a a flexible exchange rate since a high nominal wage increase rate was built into the negotiating system.

The increasing importance of private capital flows during the 1980s, despite the exchange controls, made the external balance the overriding goal for interest rate setting, leaving little room for the internal goals. At the same time the leakage of the credit market controls became apparent, which were described in the government inquiry SOU

---

[58] For a theoretical analysis, see Horn and Persson (1988).

1982:52. More market-oriented measures had begun in 1980 with an emergent money market in bank certificates and from 1982 a market in Treasury bills and bonds. The credit market was deregulated in 1985 when banks' lending ceilings and interest rate controls were lifted. Likewise emission controls and the placement of building bonds at banks and insurance companies through liquidity ratios and similar means disappeared.

The result of the deregulation in 1985 was a long boom until 1991 with a steady increase in domestic consumption and investment. Thereby the burden fell on fiscal policy to stabilize aggregate demand, fueled by easier credit after 1985, and especially after 1989 when the exchange controls were scrapped. A contractionary fiscal policy was, however, not forthcoming. In the end the fixed exchange rate could not hold with the combination of loose fiscal policy and free capital mobility.

3.12 1989–2016: The Riksbank as Inflation Targeter

The period is unusual in that two financial crises affected Sweden, the first one beginning 1991 and the second one beginning 2008. The first crisis precipitated the switch from a fixed to a floating exchange rate regime with inflation targeting. The erratic outcome of the 1970s and 1980s and the abandonment of capital controls in 1989 had laid the ground for the new regime. The two financial crises are compared after the next section.

3.12.1 The Inflation-Targeting Regime

The inflation-targeting regime was declared in January 1993, two months after the forced abandonment of fixed exchange rates of November 19, 1992, after a speculative attack. The goal of low inflation was written into the amended Riksbank Act in 1999. At the same time the monetary policy decisions were transferred from the General Council to the new six-member Executive Board.

The proximate cause of the new regime was the financial crisis of 1991–1992, which led to speculative attacks on the krona during 1992. The attacks appeared during a turbulent period in Europe with exchange rate volatility and rising interest rates culminating in the November attack when the Riksbank raised the policy rate to 500 percent and then abandoned the fixed exchange rate.

Figure 3.19 CPI inflation and the inflation target, January 1995–December 2015
Source: The Riksbank.

The inflation target of 2 percent was set to be reached by January 1995 and did so (Figure 3.19). From the beginning, the regime was in practice a flexible inflation-targeting regime taking into account variability in real GDP and unemployment.[59] This implied that changes in the policy rate were smoothed and delayed to minimize fluctuations in GDP growth. In addition, supply shocks were allowed to temporarily affect consumer price inflation. This formulation was, however, not declared officially until 2006, when a statement appeared in the Riksbank Inflation Report. The change to inflation targeting was supported by the amended Riksbank Act 1999 which increased the Riksbank's independence and mandated a price-stability goal.[60]

The macroeconomic outcome under the inflation-targeting regime has been significantly better than in the 1970s and 1980s. How much is due to the inflation-targeting regime and how much is due to the calmer international environment before 2008 ("the Great Moderation") is uncertain. The inflation outcome has been somewhat low: around 1.5 percent for the 1995–2012 period (see Anderson et al. 2012).

---

[59] See Heikensten (1999).
[60] The legal changes had been suggested earlier by the government inquiries SOU 1993:16 and SOU 1993:20.

Could a better goal fulfillment have been reached? The Riksbank has been evaluated by foreign academics at the request of the Finance Committee of the Riksdag: Giavazzi and Mishkin (2006), 1995–2005; Goodhart and Rochet (2011), 2005–2010; and Goodfriend and King (2015, 2010–2015).

Giavazzi and Mishkin (2006) noted that the policy rate remained high until 1995 when it was lowered from 9 percent to reach 4 percent at the end of 1997. As inflation went down quickly, actual real interest rates remained high and may have delayed the fall in unemployment. They also raised concerns over the period 2002 to 2005, when policy rates were increased and unemployment remained high with low inflation. While acknowledging the difficulty of inflation forecasting, they suggested two possible mistakes by the Riksbank. First, better forecast methods may have better predicted productivity growth in this period (which was underestimated) and, second, exaggerated concerns by the directors for a high rate of house price inflation coupled with increases in household debt (Figure 3.20) led to a too-high policy rate. On the whole, the Riksbank received high marks for its serious efforts to implement inflation targeting and learn from mistakes.

The period 2005 to 2010, evaluated by Goodhart and Rochet (2011), includes the Riksbank reaction to the global financial crisis discussed below. They stress the atypical character of the period, which makes it difficult to assess if mistakes were made. The Riksbank's choice of policy

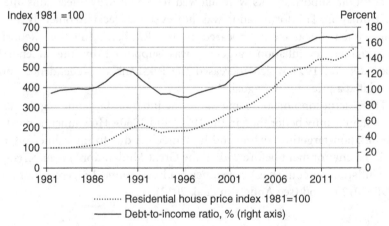

Figure 3.20 Residential house price index and the households' debt-to-disposable income ratio 1981–2014
Source: The Riksbank.

rates and its extraordinary support to banks were similar to that of other central banks in timing and size. They noted growing discrepancies between the market's expectations imputed from the yield curve and the Riksbank's own forecast of the future repo rates, which indicates a reduced credibility in the ability to affect the economy. With regard to the unusual circumstances, they considered it difficult to assess the change.

Goodfriend and King (2015) also noted a discrepancy between the forecasted policy rate and the markets expectations policy and expressed a concern about an erosion of the Riksbank's credibility. They also pointed out that during the period, a schism between the minority (Svensson and Ekholm), who wanted a lower policy rate, and the majority complicated the interpretation of the Riksbank's intentions according to its published policy rate path. They noted forecasting mistakes of the world economy in 2010 when they Riksbank decided to begin to raise the policy rate from 0.25 to 2 percent. They suggested that more resources should be spent on forecasting the future of the world economy.

3.12.2   The Riksbank and Financial Crises

The Swedish financial crisis beginning in 1991 was the worst in Europe after World War II (Englund 1999). It was the outcome of a boom–bust process started by financial deregulation in 1985 with fixed exchange rates. It was part of a Nordic crisis, in particular Finland and Norway, with the same underlying causes.[61] The krona was strongly overvalued after a long boom with high prices and wage inflation eroding competitiveness. The credit-financed boom was exacerbated by the high marginal tax rates coupled with generous deductibility of interest rate against tax payments, which led households to participate in the credit expansion. The price of stocks and real estate increased to record level before they collapsed in 1992.

In hindsight, the fixed exchange rate was doomed when international capital movements were deregulated in 1989. Among the proximate causes turning the boom to a bust was the drastic reduction of tax deductibility for households in 1991. This, together with the international downturn and the ERM crisis in Europe, triggered a collapse of domestic and foreign demand, leading to a financial crisis and an explosion of government debt.

The Riksbank countered the speculative attacks beginning in 1991 with increases in the policy rate to defend the exchange rate, unilaterally fixed to

---

[61] See Jonung et al. (2009) for analyses of the Nordic crises in the early 1990s.

the precursor of the euro, the ecu. The attacks became more virulent in the summer of 1992 as did the Riksbank interest rate response. The attacks culminated in November 1992 and were met by a 500 percent policy rate, shortly before the Riksbank gave up the defense of the exchange rate on November 19.

The Riksbank did not pursue any lender-of-last-resort actions, since there was no general liquidity crisis among the banks. The government introduced a deposit insurance scheme when there were signs of banking panic at one small bank (HSB Bank). A few insolvent banks were bailed out by the National Debt Office. An immediate and long-lasting depreciated krona of around 20 percent contributed to the recovery made possible by a strong resurgence in exports for the rest of the 1990s.

The global financial crisis 2008 hit Swedish GDP and exports hard in 2009, but Sweden rebounded quickly, helped by a substantial depreciation of the floating krona. There was no collapse in real estate prices or insolvent banks as in 1991–1992. On the other hand, the 2008 crisis created a liquidity crisis as the interbank market froze, with massive intervention by the Riksbank. The interest spreads in the overnight interbank market grew quickly as uncertainty over indivudal banks' exposure to toxic assets increased. The Riksbank intervened to avoid a financial crisis in the banking sector by supplying the banks with monetary base and foreign exchange. The monetary base in Sweden tripled in 2008 and had quadrupled by 2009 at its peak relative to its level in 2007. Most of the increase took place through a new Riksbank facility, which provided lending for up to a year's maturity to reduce the spreads in the interbank market.[62]

Virtually all of the increase in the lending to banks was in effect returned to the Riksbank through fine-tuning operations and the purchase of short-term certificates issued by the Riksbank. The Riksbank also increased lending in dollars to banks by about 200 million kronors in 2008. To cover this lending without depleting its existing reserves, the Riksbank borrowed dollars from the Federal Reserve and euros from the ECB by swap agreements, which were automatically extinguished at the end of their maturity. The reason was the large reliance on foreign financing of the Swedish banks. The situation revealed a weakness which has led the Riksbank to increase its foreign exchange reserves.[63]

---

[62] See Nessén et al. (2011).

[63] The Riksbank's involvement in the financial crisis 2008–2009 prompted a government inquiry into its need for equity and foreign exchange reserves with regard to its financial independence and preparedness for future crises, SOU 2013:9.

The legal mandate for a safe and efficient payment system has been clarified by the Riksbank after the global financial crisis to mean "financial stability" generally. The broadening of the mandate has been motivated by a clarification of the law, similar to the previous clarification of inflation targeting to mean flexible inflation targeting. How to interpret the relation between the financial stability goal and the inflation goal has proven to be the most challenging for the Riksbank. It has generated disagreements within the Executive Board and been a main concern in the three external evaluations of the Riksbank. The key question has been: Should monetary policy take into account the risk of financial crisis caused by the increase in household debt?

Giavazzi and Mishkin (2006) criticized the Executive Board for taking into account house prices in their policy rate decisions as a separate objective. The two subsequent external reviews by Goodhart and Rochet (2011) and Goodfriend and King (2015) argued that high house prices and high household debts could forebode a collapse, which would have repercussions on inflation and real GDP and therefore should have some influence. They did not make any specific recommendation, but worried over too much reliance on forecast-based computer simulations of large-scale models with scant attention to "long-tail risks."

Goodfriend and King (2015) found the division of responsibility between the Riksbank, the National Debt Office, and the Financial Supervisory Authority unclear. In 2015 the government decided that the Swedish Financial Supervisory Authority is responsible for macroprudential supervision, in addition to its original task of microprudential supervision. The three authorities discuss and coordinate activities through the Financial Stability Council created in 2013. The issue of boundaries of the three institutions' mandates must be regarded as unsettled, with further institutional development to be expected as argued by Georgsson et al. (2015). The issue remains topical as house prices and debts continue to increase.

3.13 Conclusions

Figure 3.21 illustrates the Riksbank (chartered 1668) record relative to that of the Bank of England (chartered 1694) using the Swedish and British price levels in 1668–2014. The price level developments are virtually identical between 1850 and 1970. After a higher inflation in the 1970s in the United Kingdom, the developments have been similar again.

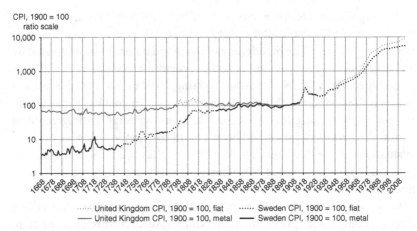

CPI, 1900 = 100
ratio scale

········ United Kingdom CPI, 1900 = 100, fiat   ······ Sweden CPI, 1900 = 100, fiat
—— United Kingdom CPI, 1900 = 100, metal   —— Sweden CPI, 1900 = 100, metal

Figure 3.21 The price level in Sweden and the United Kingdom 1668–2014 during metal convertibility and fiat periods, ratio scale
Source: Sweden: Edvinsson and Söderberg (2010), United Kingdom: Thomas and Dimsdale (2017).

The difference before 1850 is dominated by the three inconvertibility periods 1745–1776, 1788–1803, and 1809–1834 in Sweden. The Swedish price level increased permanently as the currency was devalued at each return to metal convertibility. The evolution stands in contrast to the Bank of England, with the only period of inconvertibility in 1798–1821 when convertibility was restored in 1821 at the old gold parity.

The proximate cause of non-convertibility and inflation before the post-World War II period has been wars financed in part by borrowing at the Riksbank. This happened despite legal safeguards for convertibility defined in the original charter and in the constitutional provision from 1851 to 1914. The experiences of inconvertibility and inflation during the three inconvertibility periods before 1834 led to debates about the desirability of the Riksbank as an authority under the Riksdag on several occasions in the nineteenth century.[64] Government inquiries in the twentieth century have discussed the legal regulation of the relation between the government and the Riksdag.[65] Still, the legislative changes have been few over the 350 years. It is a remarkable fact that the Riksbank's status as an authority under the parliament has stood firm for 350 years.

---

[64] Montgomery (1934) describes the proposals presented in the inquiries by *Finanskommittéerna* 1822, 1860, and 1883.
[65] See SOU 1955:43, SOU 1986:22, and SOU 1993:20.

The history of the Riksbank gives reasons to believe that the discussion of its legal framework will continue, while the Riksbank's constitutional status remains. One reason for the substantial degree of institutional continuity may be due to a fundamental difficulty of designing a legal framework for the central bank, which was pointed out by the member of parliament Erik Gustaf Geijer at the parliamentary meeting 1828–1830:

> The estates have at this parliamentary meeting used a not minor effort regarding their bank and the return of convertibility to invent a kind of self-commitment machine . . . A self-commitment machine for a being with free will, for a people, for a legislative body, cannot exist other than in this will. (Cited in Montgomery 1934, 27)[66]

References

Andersson, Björn, Stefan Palmqvist and Pär Österholm (2012), "The Riksbank's attainment of its inflation target over a longer period of time," *Economic Commentary* no. 4.

Bankoutskottet (1937), Utlåtande No. 67.

Andreen, Per G. (1958), "Retrospect and survey" in Politik och finansväsen. Från 1815 års riksdag till 1830 års realisationsbeslut. Del I: 1815–1818, Stockholm Studies in History. Stockholm: Almqvist & Wiksell, 577–613.

Andreen, Per G. (1961), "Summary" in Politik och finansväsen. Från 1815 års riksdag till 1830 års realisationsbeslut. Del II:2 1823–1830, Stockholm Studies in History. Stockholm: Almqvist & Wiksell, 363–375.

Bankoutskottet (1958), Utlåtande No. 6.

Bloomfield, Arthur (1959), *Monetary Policy under the International Gold Standard*, New York: Federal Reserve Bank of New York.

Bosworth, Barry P. and Alice M Rivlin (eds.) (1987), *The Swedish Economy*, Washington, DC: Brookings Institution Press.

Brisman, Sven (1918), "Den Palmstruchska banken och Riksens Ständers bank under den karolinska tiden" (The bank of Palmstruch and the parliament's bank under the Karls, in *Sveriges Riksbank 1668–1918*, Vol. I1.

Brisman, Sven (1924), *Sveriges affärsbanker. Grundläggningstiden* (Sweden's commercial banks. The founding period), Stockholm: Svenska bankföreningen.

Brisman, Sven (1931a), "Tiden 1803–1834," in *Sveriges Riksbank 1668–1918*, Vol. IV.

Brisman, Sven (1931b), "Den stora reformperioden 1860–1904," in *Sveriges Riksbank 1668–1918*, Vol. IV.

---

[66] McCallum (1995, 210) made the same point: "Indeed, if the absence of any pre-commitment technology is actually a problem, then it must apply to the consolidated central-bank-government entity just as it would to an entirely independent central bank. If the technology does not exist, then it does not exist."

Brisman, Sven (1934), *Sveriges affärsbanker. Utvecklingstiden* (Sweden's commercial banks. The development period), Stockholm: Svenska bankföreningen.

Capie, Forrest, Charles Goodhart and Norbert Schnadt (1994), "The development of central banking," in Capie, Forrest et al (eds.) *The Future of Central Banking. The Tercentary Symposium of the Bank of England*, Cambridge: Cambridge University Press, 1–231.

Carlson, Benny (1993), "Den enprocentiga revolutionen. Debatten om riksbankens ställning i samband med räntekuppen 1957" (The one-per cent revolution. The debate of the Riksbank's status in response to the interest rate coup 1957), Lund Papers in Economic History No. 26.

Cassel, Gustav (1908), *Riksbanken under krisen 1907–1908*, Stockholm: Hugo Gebers förlag.

Chydenius, Anders (1766/2012), *Rikets hjälp genom en naturlig finance-system* (A remedy for the country by means of a natural system of finance), translated in P. Hyttinen and M. Jonasson (eds.) (2012), *Anticipating the Wealth of Nations. The Selected Works of Anders Chydenius*, London: Routledge.

Davidson, David (1931), "Tiden 1834–1860," in *Sveriges Riksbank 1668–1918*, Vol. IV.

Eagly, Robert V. (1971), *The Swedish Bullionist Controversy. P.N. Chistiernin's Lectures on the High Price of Foreign Exchange in Sweden*, Philadelphia: American Philosophical Society.

Edvinsson, Rodney (2010), "Foreign exchange rates in Sweden 1658–1803," in R. Edvinsson et al. (eds.) *Historical Monetary and Financial Statistics for Sweden, Volume I: Exchange Rates, Prices, and Wages, 1277–2008*, Stockholm: Sveriges Riksbank and Ekerlids.

Edvinsson, Rodney and Anders Ögren (2014), "Swedish money supply 1620–2012," in R. Edvinsson et al. (eds) *Historical Monetary and Financial Statistics for Sweden, Volume 2: House Prices, Stock Returns, National Accounts, and the Riksbank Balance Sheet, 1620–2012*, Stockholm: Sveriges Riksbank and Ekerlids.

Edvinsson, Rodney and Johan Söderberg (2010), "The evolution of Swedish consumer prices 1290–2008," in R. Edvinsson et al. (eds.) *Historical Monetary and Financial Statistics for Sweden, Volume I: Exchange Rates, Prices, and Wages, 1277–2008*, Stockholm: Sveriges Riksbank and Ekerlids.

Eichengreen, Barry (1996), *Globalizing Capital*, Princeton, NJ: Princeton University Press.

Eitrheim, Öyvind, Jan Tore Klovland and Lars Fredrik Öksendal (2016), *A Monetary History of Norway 1816–2016*, Cambridge: Cambridge University Press.

Eklöf, Kurt (1990a), "Penningpolitikens mål och medel 1955–1967" (The goals and means of monetary policy 1955–1967), Occasional Paper 8, Sveriges Riksbank.

Eklöf, Kurt (1990b), "Tre valutakriser 1967–1977" (Three currency crisis 1967–1977), Occasional Paper 7, Sveriges Riksbank.

Englund, Peter (1999), "The Swedish banking crisis: Roots and consequences," *Oxford Review of Economic Policy* 15, 80–97.

Flux, A.W. (1910), *The Swedish Banking System*, Senate Document No. 586, National Monetary Commission, Vol. XVII, Washington, DC: Government Printing Office.

Franzén, Christer (1989), "När utländsk statsskuld blev inhemsk" (When foreign government debt became domestic), in Erik Dahmén (ed.) *Upplåning och utveckling. Riksgäldskontoret 1789–1989*, Stockholm: Allmänna förlaget.

Fregert, Klas (1993), "Erik Lindahl's norm for monetary policy," in L. Jonung (ed.) *Swedish Economic Thought*, London: Routledge.

Fregert, Klas (2014), "The Riksbank balance sheet 1668–2012." in R. Edvinsson et al. (eds.) *Historical Monetary and Financial Statistics for Sweden*, Vol. 2 House Prices, Stock Returns, National Accounts, and the Riksbank Balance Sheet, 1620–2012: Stockholm: Sveriges Riksbank and Ekerlids förlag.

Fregert, Klas and Lars Jonung (1996),"Inflation and switches between species and paper standards in Sweden 1668–1931: A public finance interpretation," *Scottish Journal of Political Economy* 43, 419–443.

Fregert, Klas and Lars Jonung (2004), "Deflation dynamics in Sweden: Perceptions, expectations, and adjustment during the deflations of 1921–1922 and 1931–1933," in C.K. Burdekin and P.L. Siklos (eds.) *Deflation. Current and Historical Perspectives*, Cambridge: Cambridge University Press, 91–128.

Fritz, Sven (1967), "Summary," in *Studier i svenskt bankväsen 1772–1789*, Skrifter utgivna av Ekonomisk-historiska institutet i Stockholm, 273–281.

Gasslander, Olle (1962), *History of Stockholm enskilda bank to 1914*, Stockholm: Stockholms enskilda bank.

Georgsson, Magnus, Anders Vredin and Per Åsberg Sommar (2015), "The modern central bank's mandate and the discussion following the financial crisis," *Sveriges Riksbank Economic Review* 2015:1.

Giavazzi, Francesco and Frederic Mishkin (2006), *An Evaluation of Swedish Monetary Policy between 1995 and 2005*, Rapport från riksdagen 2006/07:RFR1.

Goodfriend, Marvin and Mervyn King (2015), *Review of the Riksbank's Monetary Policy 2010–2015*, Rapport från riksdagen 2015/16: RFR7.

Goodhart, Charles (1988), *The Evolution of Central Banks*, Cambridge, MA: The MIT Press.

Goodhart, Charles and Jean-Charles Rochet (2011), *Evaluation of the Riksbank's Monetary Policy and Work with Financial Stability 2005–2010*, Rapport från riksdagen 2010/11:RFR5.

Grossman, Richard S. (2010), *Unsettled Account. The Evolution of Banking in the Industrialized World since 1800*, Princeton, NJ: Princeton University Press.

Hagberg, Axel (2007), *Bankkrishantering. Aktörer, marknad och stat* (Bank crisis management. Actors, markets, and state), Stockholm: Ekonomiska forskningsinstitutet vid Handelshögskolan i Stockholm.

Hallendorff, C. (1919), "Bankens öden från mössväldet till den andra realisationen 1766–1803" (The history of the Riksbank from the reign of the Caps until the second devaluation 1766–1803), in *Sveriges Riksbank 1668–1918*, Vol. III.

Hansson, Ingemar, Lars Jonung, Johan Myhrman and Hans Tson Söderström (1985), *Vägen till ett stabilare Sverige. Konjunkturrådets rapport* (The road to a more stable Sweden), Stockholm: SNS förlag.

Heckscher, E., (1926/1930), "Sweden. Part III. Monetary history, in its relation to foreign trade and shipping," in J.T. Shotwell (ed.) *Sweden, Norway, Denmark and Iceland in the World War*, New Haven: Yale University Press. Translation from Swedish in 1930.

Heckscher, Eli F. (1934), "The Riksbank of Sweden in its connection with the Bank of Amsterdam," in J. G. van Dillen (ed.) *History of the principal public banks*, The Hague: Martinus Nijhoff, reprinted by A.M. Kelley, USA, 1964.

Heckscher, E., (1949), "Riksgälds. En unik fas i det svenska penningväsendets historia" (Riksgälds. A unique phase in the history of the Swedish monetary system), *Ekonomisk Tidskrift* 51, 235–257.

Heikensten, Lars (1999), "The Riksbank's inflation target – clarifications and evaluation," *Sveriges Riksbank Quarterly Review* 1999:1, 5–17.

Horn, Henrik and Torsten Persson (1988), "Exchange rate policy, wage formation and credibility," *European Economic Review* 32, 1621–1636.

Jakobsson, Ulf (1997), "Den svenska devalveringscykeln" (The Swedish devaluation cycle), *Ekonomisk Debatt* 25:3.

Jonung, Lars (1979), "Cassel, Davidson and Heckscher on Swedish Monetary Policy. A Confidential Report to the Riksbank in 1931," *Economy and History* 22, 85–101.

Jonung, Lars (1984), "Swedish experience under the classical gold standard, 1873–1914," in Michael D. Bordo and Anna J. Schwartz (eds.) *A Retrospective on the Classical Gold Standard, 1821–1931*, Chicago: University of Chicago Press.

Jonung, Lars (ed.) (1991), *Devalveringen 1982 -rivstart eller snedtändning* (The devaluation 1982 – flying start or backfire?), Stockholm: SNS förlag.

Jonung, Lars (1993), "The rise and fall of credit controls: The case of Sweden, 1939–89," in M.D. Bordo and F. Capie (eds.) *Monetary Regimes in Transition*, Cambridge: Cambridge University Press, 346–372.

Jonung, Lars (2007), "The Scandinavian Currency Union 1873–1924", in P. Cotrell, G. Notaras and G. Tortella (eds.) *From the Athenian Tetradrachm to the Euro. Studies in European Monetary Integration*, Ashgate: Aldershot.

Jonung, Lars and Claes Berg (1999), "Pioneering price level targeting: The Swedish experience 1931–1937," *Journal of Monetary Economics* 43: 525–551.

Jonung, Lars, Jaakko Kiander and Pentti Vartia (eds.) (2009), *The Great Financial Crisis in Finland and Sweden. The Nordic Experience of Finanical Liberalization*, Cheltenham: Edward Elgar.

Kock, Karin (1961), *Kreditmarknad och räntepolitik*, Första delen Del I och II, Uppsala: Sveriges Allmänna Hypoteksbank.

Kock, Karin (1962), *Kreditmarknad och räntepolitik, Andra delen*, Uppsala: Sveriges Allmänna Hypoteksbank.

Lindahl, Erik, Einar Dahlgren and Karin Kock (1937), *National Income of Sweden 1861–1930. Part Two*, Stockholm: Norstedt & Söner.

Lindbeck, Assar, Per Molander, Torsten Persson, Olof Petersen, Agnar Sandmo, Birgitta Swedenborg and Niels Thygesen (1993), "Options for economic and political reform in Sweden," *Economic Policy*, October. Summary of SOU 1993:16.

McCallum, Bennett T. (1995), "Two fallacies concerning central-bank independence," *The American Economic Review* 85, 207–211.

McKinnon, Ronald I. (1993), "The rules of the game: International money in historical perspective," *Journal of Economic Literature* 31, 1–44.

Montgomery, Arthur, (1920), "Riksbanken och de valutapolitiska problemen 1719–1778" (The Riksbank and the problems of exchange rate policy 1719–1778), in *Sveriges Riksbank 1668–1918*, Vol. III.

Montgomery, Arthur (1934), "Riksdagen och Riksbanken efter 1809," in *Sveriges Riksdag. Historisk och statsvetenskaplig framställning*, Vol. 13.

Nessén Marianne, Peter Sellin and Per Åsberg Sommar (2011), "The framework for the implementation of monetary policy, the Riksbank's balance sheet and the financial crisis," Economic Commentary No. 1, The Riksbank.

Nurkse, Ragnar (1944), International Currency Experience. Lessons of the Inter-war Period, Geneva League of Nations.

Nygren, Ingemar (1989), "När lång upplåning blev korta krediter 1840–1905" (When long borrowing became short credits), in Erik Dahmén, (ed.) Upplåning och utveckling. Riksgäldskontoret 1789–1989, Stockholm: Allmänna Förlaget.

Ögren, Anders (2013), "The financial revolution in Sweden 1650–1900," in G. Caprio (ed.) Handbook of Global Financial Markets, Institutions, and Infrastructure, Oxford: Elsevier, 270–280.

Pettersson, Lars (1989), "Riksgäldskontoret, penningpolitiken och statsstödssystemet under tidigt 1800-tal" (The National Debt Office, monetary policy and the state support system in the early 1800s), in Upplåning och utveckling. Riksgäldskontoret 1789–1989, Stockholm: Allmänna förlaget.

Rooth, Ivar (1988), Ivar Rooth. Riksbankschef 1929–1948. En autobiografi intalad för och utskriven av Gösta Rooth.

Sandberg, Lars G. (1978), "Banking and economic growth in Sweden before World War I," The Journal of Economic History 38, 650–680.

Simonsson, K.G. (1934), "Riksdagen som Riksbankens principal," in Sveriges Riksdag. Historisk och statsvetenskaplig framställning, Vol 13.

Smith, Vera (1936), The Rationale of Central Banking and the Free Banking Alternative, Westminster: P.S. King Ltd.

Söderlund, Ernst (1964), Skandinaviska banken i det svenska bankväsendets historia 1864–1913, Uppsala: Almqvist och Wiksell.

SOU 1955:43, Om sedelutgivningsrätten och därmed sammanhängande penningpolitiska frågor (The right to note issue and connected questions), Stockholm: Finansdepartementet.

SOU 1982:52, Kreditpolitiken. Fakta, teorier och erfarenheter (Credit policy. Facts, theories, and experiences), Stockholm: Finansdepartementet.

SOU 1982:53, Kreditpolitiken. Fakta, teorier och erfarenheter, Expertrapporter, Stockholm: Ekonomidepartementet.

SOU 1986:22, Riksbanken och Riksgäldskontoret. Förslag till ny riksbankslag och ändrat huvudmannaskap för riksgäldskontoret (The Riksbank and the National Debt Office. A proposal for a new Riksbank Act and a new principal for the National Debt Office), Stockholm: Finansdepartementet.

SOU 1993:16, Nya villkor för ekonomi och politik (New requirements for economy and politics), Stockholm: Finansdepartementet.

SOU 1993:20, Riksbanken och prisstabiliteten, Stockholm: Finansdepartementet.

SOU 2013:9, Riksbankens finansiella oberoende och balansräkning, Stockholm: Finansdepartementet.

Sveriges konstitutionella urkunder (1999), Stockholm: SNS Förlag.

Sveriges Riksbank 1668–1924 (1931), Statistiska tabeller 1668–1924, Vol. V, Stockholm: Norstedt och Söner.

Sveriges Riksbank Act (1988:1385), riksbank.se.

Tarkka, Juha (2009), "The North European model of early central banking," in David Mayes and Geoffrey Wood (eds.) *Designing Central Banks*, London: Routledge.

Thomas, R. and N. Dimsdale (2017) "A Millennium of UK Data," Bank of England OBRA dataset, www.bankofengland.co.uk/research/Pages/onebank/threecenturies .aspx. Accessed August 2017.

Wendschlag, Mikael (2012), *Theoretical and Empirical Accounts of Swedish Financial Supervision in the Twentieth Century*, Linköping Studies in Arts and Sciences 555, Linköping: Linköping University.

Werin, Lars, Peter Englund, Lars Jonung and Clas Wihlborg (eds.) (1993), *Från räntereglering till inflationsnorm, Det finansiella systemet och Riksbankens politik 1945-1990* (From interest-rate regulation to inflation target. The financial system and the policy of the Riksbank 1945-1990), Stockholm: SNS förlag.

Wetterberg, Gunnar (2009), *Money and Fower. From Stockholm Banco 1656 to Sveriges Riksbank Today*, Stockholm: Atlantis.

4

The Bank of England, 1694–2017

C.A.E. Goodhart*

4.1 Introduction

There have been four, officially commissioned, histories of the Bank of England, covering different, but overlapping, historical periods, by Sir John Clapham, 1694–1914 (2 Volumes), Professor Richard Sayers, 1891–1944 (3 Volumes), John Fforde, 1941–1958, and, most recently, Forrest Capie, 1950s to 1979. For a review of the latter and a brief comparison with the earlier three histories, see Goodhart (2011a). A further official history, covering the period from the 1970s to 1998 has now been commissioned; Harold James will be its author. Moreover, there are 20, or so, books, besides these official histories, with Bank of England in their title available on Amazon. So there is no lack of historical coverage.

So what can additionally be done now both briefly and of some potential interest, one might hope, for both reader and author? The twist adopted here is not to take the story of the Bank chronologically, but to take each of the functional relationships and activities of the Bank separately and to explore how each of these relationships has developed over time, though giving most attention to their evolution since 1945, a 70-year period during much of which (1968–2000) I was myself directly involved with the Bank.

We start with the crucial relationship between the Bank of England and the Government. Like most other Central Banks, the Bank of England was, and has remained, a creation of Government. It was founded in 1694 on the basis of a *quid pro quo*; in exchange for providing finance, in the shape of bond purchases, to conduct war with France, the Bank of England was given

* The author would like to thank the following for their constructive comments: Susan Howson, Mervyn King, David Learmonth, Ben Norman, Brian Quinn, Paul Tempest, Ryland Thomas, Marilyne Tolle, and Geoffrey Wood, and a special mention for Forrest Capie, my discussant at the earlier Stockholm Conference, who saved me from numerous errors.

certain special advantages; it was the only joint stock bank then allowed in England (unlike Scotland), and it was, very clearly, the Government's preferred bank. As Capie and Wood note (2015), 'When the Bank of England was founded in 1694 it was not founded as a central bank. The concept of a central bank did not exist in the seventeenth century.' It was established by a Parliamentary Charter, which had to be reconsidered and renewed at discrete intervals, e.g. 21 years in the 1742 Act (Clapham, 1970, pp. 95/96); such occasions of renegotiation of the Bank's privileges naturally led the Bank to focus on its continuing relationship with the Government.

We shall divide up analysis and discussion of the Bank's ongoing relationship with Government (Section 4.2.1) into three main parts, these are:

(4.2.1) Governance;
(4.2.2) Debt and Cash Flow Management;
(4.2.3) Macro-Monetary Policy.

Then we shall turn to the Bank's relationship with people (Section 4.3.1), under four headings:

(3.1.1) The Public as Clients of the Bank as a Commercial Bank;
(3.1.2) The Bank as Chief Note Issuer;
(3.1.3) The Bank's Proprietors, Shareholders;
(3.1.4) The Bank's Directors, Governors, Court and Staff.

Finally, we review the Bank's relationship with the other commercial banks, under the headings:

(4.1.1) Managing the Payment System;
(4.1.2) Lender of Last Resort;
(4.1.3) Supervising the Banks;
(4.1.4) Bank Resolution.

Since there are no less than 11 functional sub-headings to review, over a period in each case of some 322 years, the attention and detail given to each is, perforce, quite limited.

4.2 Relationships with Government

4.2.1 Governance

The Bank of England was established in 1694, by Act of Parliament, as a private joint stock, limited liability, company, with a Charter subject to

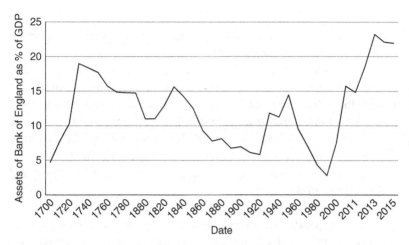

Figure 4.1 Assets of Bank of England as percentage of GDP
Source: www.bankofengland.co.uk/research/Pages/onebank/threecenturies.aspx.

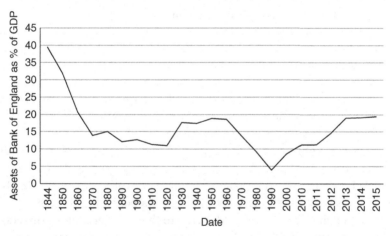

Figure 4.2 Assets of Bank of England as percentage of broad money supply
Source: www.bankofengland.co.uk/research/Pages/onebank/threecenturies.aspx.

periodic renewal and renegotiation. Each such occasion provided an opportunity for the Government of the day to try to extort further favourable financing. On the other hand the Bank's privileges and its role as the Government's preferred bank gave it a pre-eminent position amongst all other commercial banks in England and Wales, and its note circulation and deposits soon became large, prior to the second half of the nineteenth century, both as a proportion of GDP and in relation to the broad money stock (see Figures 4.1 and 4.2).

It was the large profits that the Bank made on the seignorage from its note issue that raised the ire of David Ricardo in his long pamphlet on 'Proposals for an Economical and Secure Currency' (1816), see later Section 4.31. Ricardo believed that the provision of the banknote circulation and the seignorage profits thereby arising should be a public, not a private, function. Although his analysis of the cause and extent of the depreciation of the pound from gold during the suspension of gold specie payments from 1797 to 1821 (during the Napoleonic Wars) differed from that of the Banking School (see Fetter, 1978, Chapter 1), Ricardo thought that the Bank had *not* taken undue advantage of the suspension to expand its balance sheet unduly.

But there was always a danger that a privately run Bank might do so. Ricardo then expanded his previously extremely brief comments on the appropriate institutional arrangements for note issue, into a later pamphlet, his 'Plan for the Establishment of a National Bank' (1824), published posthumously. In this he argued for a separate public sector Currency Board to control the note issue, expanding in line with the availability of gold-backing at a fixed conversion price. Since most commentators then would have defined 'money' as synonymous with notes and coin, and since Ricardo's Currency Board would have had a monopoly of note issue, this was akin to proposing that transactions balances, i.e. notes, should be issued by a 'narrow bank', while other bank assets, e.g. loans and securities, should be backed by non-strictly-monetary bank liabilities.

After Ricardo's death (1823), proposals to concentrate note issue in England were continued by his supporters, e.g. Colonel Torrens and his brother, Samson Ricardo, amongst what became known as the Currency School. Following on some macro-economic disturbances in the 1830s, and dissatisfaction with the Bank of England's policies at the time (plus agreement that seignorage should accrue to the taxpayer, not to bankers), it did seem then possible that Ricardo's idea for an independent Currency Board might get adopted (see Fetter, 1978, Chapter VI).

Fetter attributes the fact that this did not happen almost entirely to one man, Sir Robert Peel, the Prime Minister at the time. Peel wrote a paper to his Cabinet colleagues offering three alternatives:

a. Leave everything as it was.
b. A Ricardian independent Currency Board.
c. Divide the Bank of England into two parts, with the Issue Department being, in effect, a Currency Board, and a separate Banking Department on top of that.

Not surprisingly his Cabinet colleagues voted, virtually unanimously, for the compromise option (c). It had the virtue of avoiding unsettling institutional disruption, and of being more acceptable to the Bank.[1] It also seemed to go sufficiently far to meet the demands of the Currency School.

What is much less clear is whether Peel, or anybody else at the time, realised the crucial difference between having an independent Currency Board and imbedding the Issue Department within the Bank. This was that the cash reserves of the whole British banking system would continue to be centralised in the Bank of England under the Bank Charter Act of 1844, whereas they would have been (much more likely) dissipated more widely amongst the individual banks, including the Bank of England, under an independent Currency Board.

The key was that the unissued notes held in the Banking Department provided the margin of flexibility which allowed the Bank, under normal circumstances, both to maintain the Gold Standard and to manage the regular workings of the financial system (see Sayers, op. cit.). In practice the Bank had a reaction function, much the same as the Taylor reaction function under an inflation target. Thus if the 'Proportion' (of unused bank notes to liabilities) fell, it would start being restrictive and seek to raise the Bank rate, and vice versa (see the papers by Dutton, 1984; and Goodhart, 1984; Pippenger, 1984).

Thus, just as the inflation target has been applied flexibly, so was the Gold Standard in the UK. But despite such flexibility, there were, and remain, abnormal occasions when a panic ensued, and there is a rush for cash. After 1844 this led to the need to suspend the Bank Act; in the context of an inflation target, it led to unconventional monetary policy; again rather similar.

So, under normal circumstances the conduct of monetary policy could be delegated to the Bank, but in a crisis, e.g. when the available cash reserves at the Bank were near exhaustion, the Bank had to seek support from the Government, and both Bank and Government had to work closely together, with the Government taking the lead. The biggest crisis, by far, was the outbreak of war in 1914, in some large part because it was unexpected, right up to the last week, or so, and thus the financial system was caught unprepared. This has now been well documented by Roberts

---

[1] According to Fetter, Peel had had prior talks with Cotton and Heath, the Governor and Deputy Governor of the Bank of England (1978, p. 183), 'Out of their discussions came a memorandum from Cotton and Heath that was in effect an outline of the act that finally emerged, plus a provision not in the final act that would have permitted the fiduciary issue to be exceeded on the authorization of three Ministers of the Crown.'

(2013). The ramifications of this crisis were so extensive and threatening that the Government had largely to take over the conduct of the monetary response, even going so far as to print and issue its own note liabilities,[2] (known as a Bradbury, who was the Permanent Secretary of the Treasury), partly because the lowest denomination bank note was £5, and, to conserve gold, the public needed lower denomination notes).

During the war, 1914–18, the conduct of monetary policy, e.g. interest rates, exchange rates, borrowing both abroad (i.e. in the USA) and at home, became matters of Government policy, with the Bank acting as agent and adviser. A problem then arose that the then Governor, Walter Cunliffe (described by Sayers (1976) as autocratic (Vol. 1, p. 67), and a bully (p. 101), refused to accept that he would have to act under the direction of the Treasury, and in 1917 tried to countermand some Treasury orders about the use of gold reserves held in Canada. That led Lloyd George, then Prime Minister, to threaten to 'take over the Bank' and to present a statement for Cunliffe to sign[3] (Sayers, 1976, pp. 101–109)

10 July 1917
That during the War the Bank must in all things act on the directions of the Chancellor of the Exchequer whenever in the opinion of the Chancellor National interests are concerned and must not take any action likely to affect credit without previous consultation with the Chancellor.

So, it had now become clear that in any crisis situation, and throughout any major war, the Bank was strictly subservient to the Government in general, and to the Chancellor and HM Treasury (HMT) in particular. But quite what represented a crisis? In particular the 1931 foreign exchange crisis, and its aftermath of international disturbances and then rearmament, did. Increasingly through this inter-war period, pushed on by the collapse of the Gold Standard, the locus for decisions on all the major strategic issues of monetary policy shifted from the Bank to the Treasury; the Bank was becoming the agent and adviser to Government, rather than the decision maker on monetary policy, either domestically or externally. This process was, of course, greatly reinforced by the exigencies of World War II, so by the end of 1945 the Bank was agent and adviser on all policies such as exchange control, exchange rate management, interest rates, quantitative controls over banks, etc., but the strategic decisions were taken by the Chancellor. On the main issues of the day, the Bank had

---

[2] The Bank could have done this itself, but the Treasury insisted that it took the lead.
[3] Cunliffe refused to sign, but subsequently wrote a letter of apology in which he agreed that he 'must not attempt to impose my own views on you'.

become, in effect, subservient to the Government, though on the tactical implementation of such strategic policies the Bank usually made most of the running.

When the Labour Party took over the reins of Government in 1945, it then proceeded to nationalise the Bank in March 1946. In practice this was a purely symbolic gesture; this is exemplified by the fact that the Act said absolutely nothing about the purposes and objectives of the Bank; working relationships between Bank and the Chancellor/Treasury remained exactly as before, with the Bank acting as key agent and adviser, but subservient to the Chancellor/Government in respect of all key decisions.

That continued, largely unchanged, until 1997. The Bank occasionally chafed at such subservience, and its influence depended on its knowledge of the workings of financial markets, since the Chancellor was inevitably closer to the advice of HMT economists than to Bank economists. In some large part, the working interactions depended on the personal relationships amongst those at the top in the Bank and in HMT, which were notably good between Governor Richardson and Chancellor Healey, and bad between Richardson and Thatcher and Lawson.

Macro-economic outcomes were bad in the 1970s, a decade of stagflation, as bad, or worse, than in the years after 2008/9, the Great Financial Crisis (GFC). The attempt to apply monetarist theory, in the guise of monetary targets, did largely succeed, during the 1980s, in reducing inflation, but the targetry itself appeared fallible, and was succeeded (after a brief flirtation first with shadowing the DM and then with joining the ERM, 1990–92), in the early 1990s by the adoption of (flexible) inflation targets.

In principle such inflation targets could be pursued by a Ministry of Finance, advised by a subservient Central Bank. But the general perception, transformed by academic economists into the technical language of 'time inconsistency', was that the political authorities would regularly be tempted to adopt excessively expansionary policies, most likely in advance of elections. Although the empirical evidence for this syndrome is, in the UK at least, weak, it panders to the public's general distrust of politicians. So, expectations of future inflation would, indeed, fall if governments, especially left-wing governments, gave operational independence to Central Banks, subject to an inflation target set by Government. And this is what happened in 1997 in the UK.

From 1997 until 2007 this new regime worked perfectly. The GFC (2008/9) then forced the Bank to take unconventional policy measures, as the official short-term interest rate fell towards the zero lower bound

(ZLB). Such measures, such as Quantitative Easing and various asset swaps with commercial banks, had implications for CB profitability, for debt management and for the workings of financial markets that seemed to lie on the boundary between monetary and fiscal policies. Consequently the prior clear separation of policy space between Bank and Treasury has become fuzzier.

Nevertheless, not only was disaster averted in 2008/9 by the strong actions of Central Banks, but also the inflation target objective has remained intact (although inflation dipped below target, it was not by much, with no deflationary spiral occurring). But the experience of the GFC has led to a second objective, of achieving financial stability, coming back into prominence.

More generally, the more severe the crisis, and the less successful the Central Bank in defusing that, the more likely will it be that the Government will take back into its own hands the conduct of monetary policy. For the time being the Bank of England, like most other CBs, has done well enough to maintain operational independence. Whether that can continue is yet to be determined.

4.2.2 Debt and Cash Flow Management

Since the Bank of England was the creature of the Government, the Government naturally used it as its usual bank, with the Bank doing for this client what it would do for other clients, that is, to manage its cash flow, receipts and expenditures, in the most economical fashion, and to advise on financing, especially debt management. Although debt issuance was always the ultimate responsibility of the principal, the UK Government, nevertheless the Bank, with its market savvy and close connections to markets and market players, was from the outset the key agent and adviser to the Government on debt management.

Indeed, it was essential for the Bank's wider monetary management that it did have this central role in debt management. The Bank was created initially to finance war, and the series of subsequent wars dominated the time series of the ratio of debt to GDP, with peaks of around, or over, 200 per cent after each of the major wars (Napoleonic 1797–1815, World War I 1914–18, World War II 1939–45), as shown in Figure 4.3. below:

This massive (post-war) scale of debt had several direct monetary consequences. First, the occasions of debt issuance, debt redemptions and dividend (interest) payment became the main seasonal factors influencing cash injections, and, in the case of new issues, cash withdrawals from the

Figure 4.3 Public sector debt outstanding in the United Kingdom
Source: https://fred.stlouisfed.org/series/PSDOTUKA.

market. The Bank had to develop mechanisms for smoothing such discrete, and relatively huge, (seasonal) cash flow factors in order to keep control of money market rates; Sayers (1936) is particularly good on this.

Second, the Bank was always acutely aware that an arising inability to roll-over the debt, even for relatively short periods, as it became due, could flood the system with money, and lead to a combined collapse of the Gold Standard (foreign exchange market) and domestic inflation. Preserving the health of the gilt-edged market was, hence, always a priority for the Bank, even if that could lead at times to temporary monetary control problems.

When debt ratios rise over 100 per cent (or thereabouts; there are no key trigger points), debt and monetary management become absolutely inseparable and intertwined. There have been periods when the debt ratio fell sufficiently for this close link to be relaxed. Mid nineteenth century until 1914 was one such, with most of the debt held in undated Consols. The unexpected inflation of the 1970s extinguished much of the debt burden of World War II, so the period 1980–2008/9 has been another. Nevertheless the removal of debt management from the Bank to a separate, Treasury controlled, Debt Management Office (DMO) in 1997 was a hostage to fortune. In thinking about the consequences of Quantitative Easing (QE), it proved problematic to have an independent DMO. The separation would seem to assume the continuance of a debt ratio that would remain low relative to the market's funding capacity. Should the debt ratio continue its current steady rise, previously unparalleled in peace-time, this institutional re-arrangement would need reconsideration.

Normally, in peace-time, the scale of the public sector borrowing requirement has, on average, been quite low, though the automatic stabilisers push it up during recessions. Thus concern about inflation has related more to the problems of rolling over the existing debt (especially in the immediate aftermath of wars), and of lengthening the duration of that debt, than about avoiding any monetary finance of the current deficit. Indeed, the Bank has always been prepared to finance unexpected public sector shortages through Ways and Means Advances. But these have been meant to be temporary.

Over the centuries, the Bank has smoothed out medium-term fluctuations in the Government's cash requirements, from the end of the nineteenth century onwards largely via variations in Treasury Bill (TB) issue, and it encouraged structural changes, such as its support for the London Discount Market, from the 1870s to the 1990s, to achieve that. Major movements in the ratio of TBs to the monetary base and to the broad money supply were, however, a signal and a warning that the underlying liquidity of the monetary system was changing. It was just this kind of analysis that led Sayers, in the later editions of *Modern Banking* (e.g. 1967), and in the Radcliffe Report, to put more weight on a fuzzier concept of liquidity than on a (or the) monetary aggregate.

Currently, with interest now being paid on commercial bank deposits at the BoE, the distinction between bank holdings of TBs and bank cash reserves has narrowed considerably, and the overall liquidity of the banking system, and of the wider economy, has rocketed upwards. The only comparable occasion was in the immediate aftermath of World War II. Now, as then, when the time comes to reverse engines, there may be a need to re-impose direct controls on banks, since sizeable increases in interest rates would be too disruptive (in present over-indebted conditions).

4.2.3 Macro-Monetary Policy

For the greater part of the Bank's first 300 years, the macro-monetary policy objective of the Bank was to maintain an external standard. From 1694 until 1919, apart from the Suspension, 1797–1821, this was maintenance of the Gold Standard (GS);[4] from World War I until 1925, it was to return to the GS, and then from 1925 to 1931 to maintain the GS; and from

---

[4] Strictly speaking, it was supposed to be a 'bimetallic standard' initially, with a de facto Gold Standard emerging in the early eighteenth century.

1945 until 1971, it was to hold the exchange rate pegged against the dollar (and gold). The periods when the GS was in suspension, 1797–1821, 1919–25, 1931–45, were treated as abnormal, due to exceptional war-time (or depression) pressures. Each of these periods led to intense soul-searching, about how we got into this unnatural and undesirable state; and how best we could get out of it, especially the exchange rate at which the UK should re-peg.

In this context, with an external objective, the standard reaction function was straightforward; raise interest rates to protect the peg when the Proportion (available fx reserves) was falling, and lower interest rates, in support of the domestic economy, when the reverse was happening. Perhaps for historians, the more interesting question was what else the Bank, and the Government (because here, even more than with Debt Management, the Government was, and remains, the principal and the Bank the agent) could do to prop up the pound at times of pressure.

The two standard measures to do so were exchange controls over capital movements and borrowing in foreign currency to augment the reserves. Both measures became increasingly used over time, hardly at all before 1900, some foreign currency borrowing in the disturbed period between 1914 and 1939; and then from 1939 until 1979 exchange controls were comprehensively and continuously in place (the Exchange Control Department had more staff than any other Department of the Bank in the 1960s), while the efforts of successive Governors of the Bank to arrange temporary fx financing from their colleagues at the BIS fill up several of the chapters in both Fforde and Capie.

All this changed after the Bretton Woods (BW) system collapsed in the early 1970s, ushering in a 'non-system' of floating (but sometimes mana-ged) rates between major zones, and pegged, or fixed, rates within zones, such as the Eurozone. In this latter context, how was a 'floater', such as the UK, to manage macro-monetary policy?

After a confused, and disturbed, few years, 1972–77, the answer in the UK was to become a 'pragmatic monetarist' with targets for broad money, £M3. The Government switched from unwilling acceptance (Labour 1977–79) of such a monetarist approach to zealous adherence (Thatcherite Conservative 1979–85), whereas the Bank remained prag-matic and sceptical throughout. While the effects on policy outcomes, 1981–85, were much as desired, i.e. falling inflation and a strong recovery from the deep recession of 1980–82, monetary targetry itself performed poorly, with velocity proving to be unstable and an inability either to forecast or to control £M3. Doubts were cast over which was the 'best' aggregate to track, and subsequent targets for multiple aggregates were not conducive to credibility. This led Lawson, when Chancellor, to return to a form of pegging, first shadowing the DM and then joining the Exchange Rate Mechanism.

Fortunately, when the UK was ejected from the ERM in September 1992, a much more robust monetary control mechanism had become available, in the guise of a (flexible) Inflation Target. This was successfully introduced in 1992 and from then onwards became the touchstone of monetary policy. This new macro-monetary regime played a significant part (quite how much is debatable) in making the years 1992–2007 into a NICE (non-inflationary continuous expansion, to use Mervyn King's phrase) period.

Since 2008/9 the Bank has, however, struggled, like many other Central Banks, despite unparalleled expansionary policies, including a four-fold expansion in its own liabilities (i.e. the monetary base) to bring about a strong recovery or to return inflation to its 2 per cent target. Since the problem has been an inability of instruments to hit the target, it is not clear why this might indicate that the target itself needed reconsideration. Nevertheless some unhappiness with current macro-economic outcomes has been leading to some (but not yet much) questioning both of monetary mechanisms and targetry; though there has been much greater discussion about the appropriate conduct of fiscal policies.

4.3 The Bank of England and People

4.3.1 The Bank of England as a Commercial Bank, and its Connections with the Public

The Bank began as a commercial bank, albeit with some special privileges and the advantages of being the Government's preferred bank. It extended normal (for its day) services of a bank to all clients, whether Government (as already discussed), other (country) banks (to be discussed in the next section) or non-bank private clients. Given this status, it rapidly built up a comparatively large balance sheet. In Table 4.1 below, we show data taken from the Bank of England for each twentieth year from 1700 to 2000. Unfortunately we cannot split either deposits, or obviously notes in circulation, into the sectoral holdings by government, other banks and non-bank private sector, until 1833, when we could use estimates from Huffman and Lothian, JMCB (1980). But even these are of limited value since they cannot split deposits at the Bank into bank and non-bank categories, and make no allowance for bank notes, or specie held within

Table 4.1 *Liabilities*

	Liabilities, £ Notes in circulation	Capital	Rest	Deposits
1700	1,616,839	2,201,172	94,767	118,030
1720	2,493,968	5,559,996	145,062	1,638,821
1740	4,349,366	8,959,996	307,652	3,906,527
1760	4,809,102	10,780,000	297,447	3,104,315
1780	8,032,060	10,780,000	1,347,409	3,154,893
1800	16,122,102	11,642,400	3,661,150	4,265,575
1820	22,082,909	14,553,000	3,520,879	3,347,555
1840	15,720,413	14,553,000	2,878,073	7,801,320
1860	20,645,310	14,553,000	3,680,876	21,401,325
1880	26,305,410	14,553,000	3,365,771	33,808,763
1900	28,437,985	14,553,000	3,752,158	55,550,312
1920	96,526,440	14,553,000	3,509,269	190,146,815
1940	531,215,913	14,553,000	3,582,920	184,009,879
1960	2,111,915,274	14,553,000	3,898,192	340,800,115
1980	9,651,000,000	14,553,000	0	1,376,447,000
2000	24,918,000,000	14,553,000	0	55,811,447,000

Source: www.bankofengland.co.uk/research/Pages/onebank/balancesheet.aspx.

other banks rather than by the public. Thus their estimated fall in velocity of high-powered money could have been mainly due to a relative fall in non-bank deposits at the Bank.

Deposits from the general public always represented a small proportion of Bank liabilities, and they became smaller over time, both relative to notes in circulation, and to the aggregate money stock. There were a variety of reasons for this. First, as Clapham noted (1970, Vol. 1, p. 215), the Bank traditionally focussed its private business and operations in London; thus 'In the conduct of its private business the Bank . . . lived up to its old nickname of the Bank of London. Only a London resident could have a discount account, and very few non-Londoners . . . deposited money with it.' As the amalgamation movement (see Sykes, 1926) among small country banks took place in the latter half of the nineteenth century, the Bank of England stood aside. This resulted in the establishment of comparatively huge joint stock, limited liability, commercial banks, whose individual size ultimately came to dwarf that of the Bank of England.[5]

---

[5] Though, with the advent of QE, the Bank's balance sheet has ballooned recently, while that of some of the Clearing Banks, e.g. RBS, has declined.

As they all had their headquarters in London (apart from the Scottish banks, the Royal Bank of Scotland, the Bank of Scotland and Clydesdale), they became known generically as the London Clearing Banks.

Second, those who managed the Bank, the Court of Directors, never saw it as a profit-maximising institution, particularly after Ricardo's attack on its seignorage profits in 1816. It had special responsibilities and obligations, e.g. to maintain the Gold Standard and to support and to advise the Government. So long as the conduct of these duties was consistent with a sufficient return to satisfy the shareholders, there was no drive to maximise returns or to expand business. So few conscious steps were taken to drum up new deposit business.

Third, and most important, the role of the Bank as a Central Bank (e.g. in setting money market rates and quality standards in bill markets, and in seeking to maintain financial stability, as in the first Baring crisis (1891)) was considered by the increasingly (self) important London Clearing Banks from about 1900 onwards to be inconsistent with the Bank's residual role as competitor with those same banks for commercial business (see Goodhart, 1972, pp. 100–117). Indeed, the London Clearing Banks even considered establishing a rival Central Banking body in the years around 1910. In the event, however, an unpublished concordat was reached whereby the Bank would allow its existing commercial business to run off, and not tender for any such new business, while the Clearing Banks in return would accept the Bank of England's leadership as Central Bank. Thus, from 1914 onwards the Bank effectively ceased to be a commercial bank, though vestiges of its prior commercial business hung on for several decades.

4.3.2 The Bank as Chief Note Issuer

The main connection that the Bank has always had with the general public has been in its role as note issuer. From the start, almost all other London bankers ceased issuing their own notes (see Clapham, 1970, Vol. 1, p. 162; 'they found that the Bank note and the cheque met their needs'). But outside London the Country Bankers continued to issue notes, with notes and coins rather than deposits being then treated as 'money'. Although the greater prestige and solidity of the Bank will have meant, almost certainly, that BoE notes will have gained share, possibly considerably so, of total bank note issue in England and Wales prior to 1844 (but not in Scotland and probably not in Ireland), even so the procyclicality tendency of country bank note issue in England remained a continuing concern (Thornton, 1802).

Naturally the Currency School, aiming to control monetary growth (which in this case was assumed to be synonymous with note issue), wished to halt such country bank note issue. This was done in the 1844 Bank Charter Act. As Clapham notes (1970 Vol 1, p. 183):

No one but a banker who issued notes on 6 May 1844 may issue in future, and Parliament may at any time stop such issue entirely: no bank's notes may exceed their average in the twelve weeks ending 26 April 1844; a lapsed issue cannot be resumed; and a partnership the number of whose partners rises above six may no longer issue.

Effectively from 1844 onwards, with the exception of the Treasury (Bradbury) issue in World War I (already noted) the note issue of England and Wales was concentrated solely in the hands of the Bank of England. But the Bank's lowest denomination note was £5, so for the ordinary working family money took the form of coins.

Bank note issue remains entirely passive, meeting demand (now mainly from banks to fill ATMs) from the store of available, but unissued, notes in the Banking Department of the Bank. The main concern with note issue nowadays is the prevention of counterfeiting (e.g. by holograms), durability (e.g. by now substituting polymer for paper), and symbolism (e.g. in the choice of portraits). Also the Bank has been careful to restrict the value of the top denomination to £50, in order to make the use of currency in facilitating black and grey economy less easy, see Rogoff (2016).

Currency usage surges during war-time, owing to dislocation and the inability to establish repeat use credit and trust relationships. Figure 4.4 below shows the ratio of currency to deposits (C/D ratio) from 1921 to 2016. Unlike the USA, where there was widespread concern about the solvency and safety of US banks, the C/D ratio did not increase sharply during the 1930s in the UK. For a brief period in 2008/9 there was a surge in the demand for £50 notes that was probably related to nervousness about UK bank solvency. From 1945 until about 1995 the C/D ratio declined steadily, under the influence of technological improvements in payments transactions, starting with greater usage of banks and cheque payments, followed by plastic (debit and credit) cards, and later electronic payment mechanisms. More recently, however, the C/D ratio has been rising again, under the influence of sharply falling interest rates and the growing use of cash in the grey economy to evade higher levels of taxation, see Ashworth and Goodhart (2018, forthcoming).

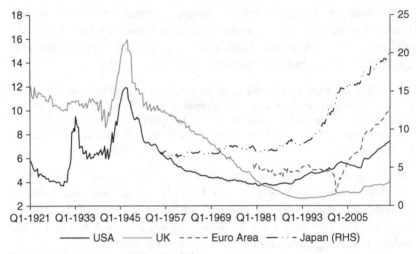

Figure 4.4 Currency-to-GDP ratios (%)
Source: Ashworth and Goodhart (2018), Friedman and Schwartz (1963), US Bureau of Economic Analysis, US Federal Reserve Board, Bank of England, Bank of England Three centuries of macroeconomic data – version 2.2, July 2015 (UK GDP data annual prior to 1955), UK Office for National Statistics, European Central Bank, OEF, Bank of Japan, Cabinet Office of Japan. For Japan we use Gross Domestic Expenditure until the end of 1979 and Gross Domestic Product subsequently.

4.3.3 The Bank's Proprietors (Shareholders)

In his Appendix presenting the dividends on Bank of England stock, Clapham (1970, Appendix A, p. 428). notes at the bottom that 'Steady dividends aimed at before 1847 and from 1897: the intervening half-century is that of maximum competitive activity and fluctuating dividends.' Perhaps in the early period, pre- 1847, the Bank kept dividends steady, partly to counter criticism about seignorage being siphoned off to the benefit of wealthy insiders and, in the good years, to build up the strength of the Bank. But after 1847 the Bank Charter Act forced it to hold a high proportion of non-interest bearing notes in the Banking Department, where its profits could mostly be made. After 1844 most, and after 1928 all, of the seignorage income arising in the Issue Department went straight to the Treasury. Meanwhile, its macro-monetary policy role led it to push up interest rates during dangerous periods, when fewer clients wished to borrow, except as a Last Resort, and to lower rates when funds were flowing into the UK. On such occasions the Bank often had difficulty in keeping money market rates in line with Bank rate (Sayers, 1936), so the Bank would lose business to the joint stock banks. So, its most profitable periods tended to be in crisis years.

I had always thought from my reading of the literature (e.g. Sayers, 1936, Vol. 1, p. 11) that there were some general problems involved in *both* managing the financial system *and* maintaining the dividend in the decades prior to 1914. Certainly the commercial banks and the Treasury would have liked the Bank then to hold more gold reserves, in order to avoid sharp movements in interest rates as external conditions altered (i.e. to be more like the Banque de France). But that would have meant that the Bank would have needed a larger balance sheet to maintain its profits, and that would have led to more competition with those same commercial banks. Moreover, how did the Bank reconcile its dual duty to the country and to its proprietors? An Inspector of Branches, Edye (see Clapham, 1970, Vol. 1, p. 372) wondered,

whether the Bank's dual position could be maintained. Was it to be 'duty to the public' and care of gold, or duty to the proprietors – mostly 'trustees, spinsters and clergymen' – and the dividend? If the former, the Bank might as well be nationalized and its stock turned into Consols; to him a drab prospect. To what the latter might lead he did not stay to consider.

In effect, I had believed that it was the former choice that was adopted around that time; so that Bank stock became treated as a (riskless) bond with a quasi-constant dividend, and nationalisation in 1946 led, in practice, to the transformation of one version of riskless debt into another. But some recent research by my discussant, Forrest Capie, with his co-author, Mike Anson, the Bank's archivist (2017), shows that the profitability of the Bank, and with that the returns and dividends on Bank stock in the years up until 1946, were a good deal greater than I had appreciated.

4.3.4 The Bank's Directors, Governors, Court and Staff

The proprietors, i.e. the shareholders, of the Bank ceased, after the first few years of its existence, to play any significant role in the selection of management of the Bank. Instead, the management, in the form of the Court of Directors, was a self-selecting body, choosing candidates from amongst the financial aristocracy of the City (with the exception of commercial bankers, who were excluded since they competed with the Bank and were also held to be, prior to about 1890, of lower status). The Directors generally held full-time roles in their main jobs, e.g. in the Accepting Houses, and worked only part-time at the Bank. Once they had served long enough as Directors, and both wanted to do so, and were viewed as sufficiently capable, they would become first Deputy Governor, and then immediately the next Governor, each for two-year full-time stints. Prior Governors, having 'passed the Chair' would often remain on the Court for quite a few years to provide experienced advice.

All things considered, this system worked better than might have been expected. It lasted until 1914. Then the problems of war-time finance became so complex that it was felt right to continue with Cunliffe, until his personal shortcoming became too great. Shortly thereafter he was followed by Montagu Norman. In the difficult financial conditions of the post-war period, his expertise and command of the issue was viewed as irreplaceable, and he became a fixture (Sayers, 1976). After his departure, and nationalisation, the Governor and the Deputy Governor(s) became appointed by the Government, normally for a five-year period, once renewable. This has now changed once again with the arrangements made for the present Governor, Mark Carney, involving a single period of office, potentially lasting eight years.

Until the inter-war years, there was a huge gulf between the Court, the managing body, made up of (mostly part-time) upper-class gentlemen[6] (no ladies, of course), and the staff of the Bank, the clerks, usually from a middle-class background. Members of staff could rise to leadership roles, rather like non-commissioned officers (NCOs) in the army, such as Chief Cashier, Secretary, etc., but no further. Perhaps the best-known Bank official ever to work there was Kenneth Grahame, author of *The Wind in the Willows*, who became the Bank's Secretary, but he left under a cloud for daring to express some criticism of Cunliffe.[7]

During the inter-war period this gulf between the Court and the Directors on the one hand, and the Bank's Staff narrowed considerably. About a decade after World War II, the relationship reversed. There had been a claim that a Bank rate change had been leaked, and used for insider dealing, by a member(s) of the Court, who, of course, mostly had other City jobs. Although nothing was ever proven in the Bank Rate Tribunal (1955), it was agreed that the Court could no longer be consulted in *advance* of policy changes. So the Court became a somewhat honorific body, a 'sounding board', and a means of checking on the Governors and on the efficiency and structure of the Bank, but largely divorced from policy making. In recent years, however, the growing emphasis on financial stability and prudential issues, where the procedural structure was less

---

[6] Though Ricardo dismissed them as a group of traders, and Bagehot described them as 'merchants'.

[7] There is an apocryphal story that Grahame got his own back by modelling the character of Mr. Toad on Cunliffe.

clearly defined, has led to a revised role for the Court as an independent arbiter of the process, alongside the Treasury Select Committee (TSC) of Parliament.

Even with such a narrowing gulf, the first Governor to be appointed who had worked his way up through the Bank's staff was L.K. O'Brien (1968–73), to be followed in this by Eddie George (1993–2003). King (2003–13) went into the Bank, as Chief Economist, in 1991. Several of the recent Deputy Governors have previously come from the Staff, but the majority of the current Deputies have been outside appointments, many from the Civil Service, especially the Treasury. The staff are now professionals, rather than clerks, with a sizeable proportion of them being trained economists.

4.4 The Bank and the Banking System

4.4.1 Managing the Payment System

Once the Bank of England had been established, its privileged position soon made it into the dominant (commercial) bank in London. So, a pyramid of inter-bank relationships then developed, with the other London banks holding deposits with the Bank of England, and the myriad of small country banks in turn holding correspondent relationships with their own London bank contact, in each case to provide for them what they did for their own clients in their own locality, for example to hold deposits with the Bank (or London correspondent bank) and to borrow from it at times of need. Perhaps the most important aspect of such banking services was to facilitate payments. Rather than transport gold specie, at great cost and some risk, around the country, a country bank, or indeed any depositor, at the Bank could arrange for a payment to be made by drawing on (their deposit at) the Bank or their correspondent. Economies of network scale rapidly led almost all the major financial intermediaries in the UK (including in this case the major Scottish and Irish banks) to establish correspondent relationships with London, so payments could be effected over the books of the Bank.

So the Bank became the manager of the UK's payment system, and has remained such throughout its history (see Norman, Shaw and Speight, 2011). From time to time it has introduced various technical improvements, such as Real Time Gross Settlement (RTGS), but these have been essentially methods of speeding up, and/or reducing settlement risk, in a process which remains one of clearing payments over the ledger pages (once on paper, now electronic) of the Central Bank. Now, however, there is a possibility that, rather than clearing payments over a *central* ledger (at the Central Bank), this could be done over a *distributed* ledger, using blockchain technology. Whether this latter would still need a trusted Central Party to run, and what role a Central Bank, such as the BoE, would have in that process, assuming that it does go ahead, are questions whose answer lies in the future.

4.4.2 Lender of Last Resort

In some ways it is a pity that the term 'Lender of Last Resort' (LOLR) has become so universally used. Country banks, and other commercial banks, would in the early days apply to the Bank, as their London correspondent, for a loan, just as any client would go to their own bank to borrow. Under normal circumstances such a correspondent would choose alternative sources of funding, e.g. from the Bank, the money market, discounting Bills, etc., depending on terms and conditions.

The phrase Lender of Last Resort, coined by Sir Francis Baring (1797), referred to panic conditions, when other usual (market) sources of liquid funds had dried up, and the Bank was (as the strongest bank in the country) the sole remaining source of additional cash and liquidity. The initial and proper meaning of LOLR related to occasions when the whole banking and financial system might become dysfunctional, as in 2008/9. Unfortunately its meaning has become misinterpreted, so that a bank seen to be borrowing from a Central Bank is often assessed to be only doing so as a Last Resort, which naturally has carried with it the danger of massive reputational loss, i.e. serious stigma, and has become a self-reinforcing equilibrium.

The role that the Bank *should* play in panic conditions was, however, problematical. Most often the panic would lead *both* to an external (over the foreign exchanges) and to an internal drain of gold from the Bank. As guardian of the Gold Standard, the natural response of the Bank would be both to raise interest rates *and* either to refuse, or to toughen the terms on, requests for loans. Instead, both Thornton (1802) and Bagehot (1873)[8] argued that the Bank must seek to stem the panic by combining increased interest rates with ample lending (though after 1844 this might involve suspension of the Bank Charter Act).

---

[8] Thornton's book on *The Paper Credit of Great Britain* not only precedes Bagehot's *Lombard Street*, but it also is more profound. It is a minor scandal that Bagehot fails to cite his predecessor.

But at a time of panic, when asset prices in markets were tumbling and everyone was struggling to increase liquidity, how was the Bank to avoid risking its own solvency and to prevent those who did not really need extra liquidity from borrowing? The answer that Bagehot gave was to combine high interest rates (he *never* uses the word 'penalty') with the requirement that such lending only be done on the basis of first-class collateral, basically government debt or best bank bills.

In their study of the 'Political Foundations of the Lender of Last Resort', Calomiris, Flandreau and Laeven (2016) state that 'the 1833 Act was a watershed'. Prior to that, notably in 1825, the Bank had failed to act as an effective LOLR, partly because of the usury ceiling on interest rates, partly because it may have been trying to maximise profits. They further note that 'The parliamentary discussion of the decision to make the Bank's notes legal tender made it clear that legal tender status was intended to empower the Bank to act as an effective LOLR' (ibid., p. 22).

With the Bank being competitive with other banks for commercial business in the nineteenth century, there was no question of it acting as a direct supervisor of other banks, either on or off site. So the Bank then had no direct evidence of the solvency of those approaching it for loans, and in any case, then and now, solvency is a fuzzy concept, depending, *inter alia*, on the actions taken by the Bank to stem the panic. So the idea that the Bank should only lend to solvent, but illiquid, borrowers is a misconstruction. What determined whether it would lend was the quality of the collateral on offer.

Of course, the Bank, being a major player in the money market, especially in rediscounting bills of exchange, had access to some generalised appreciation, and the normal gossip, about the business of the financial institutions with whom it was dealing. So, if it had reason to believe that a financial institution seeking assistance was in really bad shape, then it could, and would, as in the case of Overend Gurney in 1866, refuse to lend. Equally a financial intermediary, subject to adverse rumours, preventing it from borrowing in the market, could, at its own initiative, open its books to the Bank, to enable the Bank to mount a rescue, as with Barings in 1891. Also note that almost all the participants in the London money market, and many participants in other London financial markets, were technically insolvent after the outbreak of war in 1914. The idea of shutting them down, and with them much of the City, was never seriously considered.

Subsequent history, of the inter-war and post-World War II years, is filled with accounts of rescues, some overt, some covert, of financial intermediaries in trouble (see Sayers, Fforde and Capie). Often this involved the thinly capitalised discount houses; again it often involved a considerable degree of forebearance. The life-boat rescue of financial institutions involved in the Fringe Bank crisis, 1973/74, is one of the wider, and better known, events (Reid, 1983).

There is no simple dividing line to draw between deciding whether to rescue or to close down a bank in severe difficulties. It depends on circumstances, and weighing up the relative dangers of moral hazard and contagion. In part, perhaps, because this latter is such a difficult exercise, King in his book, *The End of Alchemy* (2017, Chapter 7), has suggested reverting back to the original Bagehot position, that Bank of England lending should be done *solely* on the basis of pre-positioned collateral on pre-arranged terms, thereby abstracting completely from the difficult questions about whether the bank/intermediary is currently solvent and would deserve help.

4.4.3 Supervising the Banks

In the field of macro-monetary policy, the aim of achieving price stability has been a constant. What changed was the intermediate means (the target) for doing so, from Gold Standard, to Bretton Woods peg, to monetary target, to inflation target. In pursuit of financial stability, however, ideas about (and following on from that the structure of) regulation and supervision have changed dramatically over the centuries and in recent decades.

Until quite recently, large-scale government deficits have almost always been connected with war-time. Since war destroyed, rather than created, productive capacity, it was inflationary. So monetary finance of government deficits was anathema to Central Banks.[9,10] Instead, banks should finance (self-liquidating) bills of exchange, and loans, relating to trade and production; under the quantity theory of money financing such 'real' bills could neither be inflationary, nor dangerous to stability, since the proceeds of trade/output would pay them off. The 'real' bills theory, particularly beloved by the Banking School, reigned supreme until the 1930s.

Under this theory the key to supervision lay in monitoring the quality of the bills of exchange passing through the money market in London, and in

---

[9] Though the need to finance such wars was often the trigger that led the government to establish a 'central' bank in the first place, as in the case both of the Bank of England and the Banque de France.

[10] The editors of this book noted in private correspondence that 'the Swedish Riksbank was superseded by the Riksgäldskonstoret in the 1990s due to war with Russia'.

discouraging speculative, or 'finance' bills. Meanwhile the institutions that needed most direct, hands-on, supervision were the London Accepting Houses, whose acceptances of bills transformed them into the marketable two-name bills (Nishimura, 1971), and the Discount Houses, who made the prime market for such bills. The London Discount Houses had been fostered by the Bank in the second half of the nineteenth century to provide a buffer between the Bank and the increasingly large London Clearing Banks. Neither the Bank nor these banks were keen to deal face-to-face. So the banks lent short-term to the Discount Houses. When base money became tight, the banks would withdraw such funds, and the Discount Houses would borrow from the Bank. Later on, in the twentieth century, the Discount Houses also organised themselves always to cover the Treasury Bill tender. Later in the 1990s the arrival of many foreign banks in the City and the development of much more developed wholesale money markets made the need for the Discount House buffer redundant and they disappeared.

Even so, still in 1974, at the outset of the Fringe Bank crisis, the *only* financial intermediaries directly supervised by the Bank, in the person of the Principal of the Discount Office, were the Discount and Accepting Houses! Commercial banks were not directly supervised by the Bank before 1979. Initially this was because the Bank and the banks were competitors, but from the 1930s, when the 'real bills' theory broke down during the Depression, until 1971, another theory and structural arrangement took pride of place.

This latter theory was that the root cause of the (US financial and UK industrial) crisis in the 1930s was excessive competition, driving down profitability and making financial institutions reach for yield by taking on riskier assets. And the way to counteract this was to encourage cartels, where pricing competition would be prevented, and interest rates set by some formula or by the cartel. Rather than encouraging small 'challenger' entrants, smaller and/or weaker participants were persuaded to merge with bigger (and safer) members. Montagu Norman followed this general line enthusiastically with all kinds of industry (see Sayers).

But it was in finance that such cartelisation was most marked. The Building Societies, Finance Houses, London Discount Market were all regimented into Associations, and the London Clearing Banks had their own cartel. Rates were all pegged (relative to Bank rate) at net interest margins that guaranteed reasonable (not far off average), but unexciting, profit margins. Capital ratios and solvency were not seen as a problem. If, at the official interest rate chosen for other macro-economic purposes, credit expansion was too fast, then direct controls, e.g. on hire purchase terms, would be applied. One of the side effects of this system was to make housing finance counter-cyclical. The BSA's authorised interest rate changes would lag behind money market rates, so when such rates were moving up, funds would flow out of the building societies, and there would be a mortgage famine.

There is more truth to this theory that it is the ultra-competitive challenger banks that represent the main danger to financial stability than current received wisdom allows, as Northern Rock and Anglo-Irish Bank exemplify. Nevertheless the old cartelised, controlled system had serious weaknesses. It restrained innovation, raised costs, benefited the 'fringe' institutions not subject to a cartel and to direct controls (at the expense of the core), and anyhow was increasingly breaking down by the end of the 1960s under the influence of international competition and technology (that facilitated globalisation), of which the euro-dollar market was the most tangible feature (Johnston, 1982). Such was the context in which the old system was abandoned in 1971 with the introduction of Competition and Credit Control (C&CC).

Neither the Bank nor the banks in the UK had had prior experience of unfettered competition; C&CC opened a financial Pandora's Box. The big UK banks opted to go for expansion in 1971–73, for market share and glory, rather than profit maximisation and safety. In the early 1970s, as in the years before 2007, there are almost always sufficient bank CEOs like Fred Goodwin (of RBS) to force staider bank managers to go along with the dance, and the result can be an exaggerated boom/bust cycle.

Although the application of the 'Corset' in the 1970s represented a partial reversion to the prior regime of direct control, the experience of the Fringe Bank crisis 1974/75 led to direct supervision of the banks. With the trend being away from direct controls to market mechanisms, the experience of banks failing to control themselves in a socially satisfactory fashion implied that there would need to be external supervision from the authorities.[11]

There was already a patchwork of supervision in place in the early 1970s. Existing large banks had to abide by certain Bank of England rules, especially regarding exchange controls; new and smaller banks were

---

[11] There is a school of thought, mainly in the USA, that attributes the excessive urge by bank managers for expansion to deposit insurance. This was not the case in the UK, where (limited) deposit insurance was not introduced until the mid 1970s, and was not made more general until 2007.

authorised, and supposedly looked after, by the Department of Trade; building societies and finance houses had their own oversight bodies. But the main functions of such supervision related to consumer protection, prevention of fraud and adherence to the rules of the relevant association. There had been little, or no, concept that supervision was needed to achieve overall financial stability.

All this changed in the 1970s. The Bank set up a new department, Banks and Money Market Supervision (BAMMS) in 1974 under George Blunden (Capie, 2010, Chapter 12), to supervise UK banks. The legal basis for this came later in the 1979 Act. Meanwhile Governor Richardson encouraged the establishment of an equivalent international Basel Committee on Banking Supervision in 1974, initially chaired by Bank officials, Blunden and then Peter Cooke, and often described as the Blunden/Cooke Committee (Goodhart, 2011). The Bank played a pioneering role in the establishment of international regulation and supervision.

There was very little theoretical (nor empirical) underpinning for such new supervisory practices. The general, pragmatic, approach then was to try to identify what were generally accepted to be best practices, often how the most admired banks operated in the industry, and then to seek to bring all other participants to behave in the same way. It was a micro-prudential exercise to try to raise the standard of behaviour of each individual bank. The idea that enhancing self-similarity might have macro-prudential dangers was not entertained until much later.

It was the 1980–82 Less Developed (Mexico, Argentina, Brazil) crisis (LDC/MAB crisis) that focussed the attention of regulators/supervisors on capital adequacy. The potential loss from international loans to MAB borrowers then seriously threatened the solvency of the main City Centre banks in New York and some large international banks in Europe. So the Basel I and Basel II Accords focussed on capital adequacy. Prior to the 1970s, concern about systemic stability focussed mainly on cash and liquidity adequacy, with capital largely taken for granted; after the 1970s that reversed, with liquidity, increasingly available in wholesale markets, largely taken for granted.

Governor Richardson had hoped to limit the Bank's direct supervisory involvement to the big banks, with his distinction between banks as a first tier, and licensed deposit-takers, the second tier, in the 1979 Act. That proved unsuccessful, and the Bank was increasingly forced, for example, by the problems of JMB (Johnson Matthey Bankers) and BCCI (Bank of Credit and Commerce International) to expand its supervision to all banks. Also with the arrival of foreign banks in London and the ability of

Building Societies to become, or be taken over by, banks, both in the 1980s, the remit of the Bank to act as supervisor to banks in the UK, having been almost non-existent up until 1974, suddenly exploded to being one of the main functions of the Bank, in terms of use of staff and attention.

Then suddenly, and without any prior warning (or subsequent justification), this whole function (and most of the relevant prior staff) was removed by the incoming Chancellor of the Exchequer, Gordon Brown, in May 1997 to a new Financial Services Authority (FSA), which was to cover all prudential and conduct of business issues for the *whole* financial system, including all non-bank financial intermediaries, as well as banks, such as insurance companies.

But the FSA could not handle a crisis by itself. In any such crisis the Bank would be needed to provide liquidity and the Treasury to cover losses and inject extra capital. So a Troika of all these three parties was established (HMT, Bank, FSA), to monitor and to maintain systemic stability. But when a crisis did arrive, in 2007/8, the Troika did not appear to work well. The FSA seemed fixated on ensuring Basel II capital ratio compliance for banks, and failed to anticipate, or to check, other developing causes of financial fragility, such as excessive leverage, shortages of liquidity, the property boom (and inappropriate LTV (loan to value) and LTI (loan to income) ratios) and RBS' ill-fated purchase of ABN-Amro. The crisis caught the FSA unaware. When it first arrived, in the guise of Northern Rock's difficulties, Governor King cited moral hazard as a reason for limiting assistance. Whether the resulting delay played much of a role in the affair is moot, and the assessment of responsibilities for that whole saga remains contentious.

Be that as it may, the working of the Troika in the crisis was held to have failed, at least in the eyes of the Conservative opposition and their supporting press. So when the Conservatives returned to power in 2010, they decided, once again, to revamp the structure of bank supervision. Under their new Financial Services Act 2012, prudential regulation, both micro and macro, again for the whole financial system not just for the banks, was returned to the Bank, initially in the form of its wholly owned subsidiary (but now part of the Bank), the Prudential Regulation Authority (PRA), while all conduct of business issues were hived off into a separate body, the Financial Conduct Authority (FCA). The PRA (and FCA) in turn answer to the Financial Policy Committee (FPC), with external members, which sets the strategy and makes the key policy decisions for the PRA, in the sense that the FPC can issue Directions and Recommendations to them.

Since 2009, bank regulation, especially for capital, but also for liquidity, and for business structure (the Vickers Report), has been tightened, at a time of sluggish recovery and minimal inflation. In this context banks have been casting off leverage and struggling to remain profitable. Banking in the UK remained closer to 'bust' than to 'boom', so the FPC has so far had a relatively easy ride. The need, perhaps, is to succour rather than to constrain the banks. And the immediate concern will be how to cope with Brexit.

Basically, there is no consensus, yet, on how best to manage the problems of maintaining financial stability.

4.4.4 Bank Resolution

Prior to the Great Financial Crisis, the last *major* bank failures in the UK had been in the third quarter of the nineteenth century: Overend Gurney in 1866 and City of Glasgow Bank in 1873. Proponents of a 'moral hazard' viewpoint claim that allowing such failures warned banks thereafter to be more careful. Opponents argued that the Bank and HMT became cleverer in discovering ways of rescuing banks (and Discount Houses) running into difficulties, not only in 1914 but on numerous other occasions, such as the 1974/5 life-boat.

Be that as it may, Northern Rock in 2007 was followed by RBS and HBOS in 2008, when the latter were bailed out by the injection of public funds. This led to a political storm, not so much because the banks were saved, but more because the *bankers'* bonuses and pensions continued to be paid. So, there was a general revulsion at the use of public funds to support banks in difficulties. The new idea is that a wider range of (bond-holding) creditors will be bailed in to meet bank losses.

Whether this switch of loss-bearing from taxpayers to a narrower segment of bank creditors will prove any more successful, either economically or politically, has yet to be seen. But this new resolution process has to be managed. Under the law as it stood up to the GFC, banks that failed were subject to the standard general bankruptcy law. In the crisis, that was seen to be too slow and inappropriate for banks. So the law, applying to banks, has been changed. The Bank has now also been given the responsibility of handling any, and all, instances requiring Resolution, but there was little, or no, prior public discussion in the UK of whether it was better to place the 'Resolution Authority' within, or outside, the Central Bank.

We will have to wait and see how it works.

End-Note

The years of the 'Great Moderation' (1992–2007) were very successful, almost triumphant, for most Central Banks, notably including the Bank of England, which largely escaped from decades of subservience to HMT and to the Government. But the Great Financial Crisis, 2007–9, has led to change in, and uncertainty about, the proper functions of the Bank. Such change has been most marked for giving Central Banks a further major objective – that of achieving financial stability besides their primarily objective of price stability – but has also led to questions both about the definition of such price stability and the instruments for achieving it. Meanwhile, and quite remarkably, such Central Banks have mostly proved, as yet, unable to bring back inflation to target (usually 2 per cent per annum), despite the most expansionary policy measures ever adopted.

Bibliography

Anson, M., and F. Capie, (2017), 'Over 300 years of Bank of England profits: financial crises, wars and distribution', Work in progress.

Ashworth, J., and C.A.E. Goodhart, (2018), 'The surprising recovery of currency usage' (forthcoming available from the authors).

Bagehot, W., (1873), *Lombard Street: A Description of the Money Market*, New York: John Wiley & Sons, Inc. [1999].

Baring, F., (1797), *Observations on the Establishment of the Bank of England and on the Paper Circulation of the Country*, from the 1967 facsimile reprint by Augustus Kelly, pp. 19–23.

Bordo, M.D., and A.J. Schwartz (Editors), (1984), *A Retrospective on the Classical Gold Standard, 1821–1931*, National Bureau of Economic Research, University of Chicago Press.

Calomiris, C., M. Flandreau, and L. Laeven, (2016), 'Political foundations of the Lender of Last Resort: a global historical narrative', Centre for Economic Policy Research Discussion Paper DP11448, July.

Capie, F., (2010), *The Bank of England, 1950s to 1979*, Cambridge University Press.

Capie, F., and G. Wood, (2015), 'The development of the Bank of England's objectives: evolution, instruction, or reaction?', Chapter 10 in *Central Banking and Monetary Policy: What will be the Post-crisis New Normal?*, edited by. E. Gnan and D. Masciandaro, BAFFI CAREFIN Centre, Bocconi University and SUERF: Vienna and Milan, pp. 124–140.

Clapham, J., (1970), *The Bank of England: A History, Volume One, 1694–1797*, Cambridge University Press.

Dutton, J., (1984), 'The Bank of England and the rules of the game under the International Gold Standard: new evidence', Chapter 3 in *A Retrospective on the Classical Gold Standard, 1821–1931*, edited by M.D. Bordo and A.J. Schwartz, National Bureau of Economic Research, University of Chicago Press, pp 173–202.

Fetter, F.W., (1978), *Development of British Monetary Orthodoxy, 1797–1875*, Fairfield, NJ: Augustus M. Kelley.

Fforde, J., (1992), *The Bank of England, and Public Policy, 1941–1958*, Cambridge University Press.

Goodhart, C.A.E., (1972), *The Business of Banking, 1891–1914*, London School of Economics and Political Science.

Goodhart, C., (1984), 'General discussion of Dutton and Pippenger papers', Chapters 3 and 4 in *A Retrospective on the Classical Gold Standard, 1821–1931*, edited by M.D.

Bordo and A.J. Schwartz, National Bureau of Economic Research, University of Chicago Press, pp 227–232.

Goodhart, C.A.E., (2011a), 'The commissioned historians of the Bank of England', Chapter 1 in *Monetary and Banking History: Essays in Honour of Forrest Capie*, edited by G. Wood, T.C. Mills, and N. Crafts, New York: Routledge, pp 13–26.

Goodhart, C.A.E., (2011b), *The Basel Committee on Banking Supervision: A History of the Early Years, 1974–1997*, Cambridge University Press.

Johnston, R.B., (1982), *The Economics of the Euro-market: History, Theory and Policy*, London: Palgrave Macmillan.

King, M., (2017), *The End of Alchemy: Money, Banking, and the Future of the Global Economy*, London: W.W. Norton & Company.

Nishimura, S., (1971), *The Decline in Inland Bills of Exchange in the London Money Market, 1855–1913*, Cambridge University Press.

Norman, B., Shaw, R., and G. Speight, (2011), 'The history of interbank settlement arrangements: exploring Central Banks' role in the payment system', Bank of England Working Paper No. 412, June.

Pippenger, J., (1984), 'Bank of England operations, 1893–1913', Chapter 4 in *A Retrospective on the Classical Gold Standard, 1821–1931*, edited by M.D. Bordo and A.J. Schwartz, National Bureau of Economic Research, University of Chicago Press, pp. 203–227.

Radcliffe Report, (1959), *Committee on the Working of the Monetary System: Report*, London: Her Majesty's Stationery Office.

Reid, M., (1983), *The Secondary Banking Crisis, 1973–75: Its Causes and Course*, London: Palgrave Macmillan.

Ricardo, D., (1816), 'Proposals for an Economical and Secure Currency', pamphlet (London: John Murray), reproduced in P. Sraffa (1951), pp. 43–142.

Ricardo, D., (1824), 'Plan for the Establishment of a National Bank', pamphlet (London: John Murray), reproduced in P. Sraffa (ed.) *The Works and Correspondence of David Ricardo*, Volume IV Pamphlets and Papers, 1815–1823, Cambridge University Press (1951), pp. 271–300.

Roberts, R., (2013), *Saving the City: The Great Financial Crisis of 1914*, Oxford University Press.

Rogoff, K.S., (2016), *The Curse of Cash*, Princeton University Press.

Sayers, R.S., (1936), *Bank of England Operations, 1890–1914*, London: P.S. King and Son.

Sayers, R.S., (1956), *Financial Policy 1939–45* (History of the Second World War, UK, civil series), HMSO and Longman.

Sayers, R.S., (1967), *Modern Banking*, Seventh Edition, London: Oxford University Press.

Sayers, R.S., (1976), *The Bank of England, 1891–1944, Volume 1*, Cambridge University Press.

Sykes, J., (1926), *The Amalgamation Movement in English Banking, 1825–1924*, London: P.S. King & Son Limited.

Thornton, H., (1802), *An Enquiry into the Nature and Effects of the Paper Credit of Great Britain* (with an introduction by F.A. von Hayek, 1939), New Jersey: A.M. Kelley [1978].

5

The Bank of Spain, 1782–2017: A History

Pablo Martín-Aceña*

5.1 Introduction

The Bank of Spain is one of the oldest European central banks. It was founded under the name of Bank of San Carlos in 1782, renamed Bank of San Fernando in 1829, and finally became known as Bank of Spain in 1856. It was formed as a private joint-stock company which held the privilege of issuing banknotes. In 1946 the Bank was *de facto* nationalized and its banknotes became legal tender. It was *de jure* nationalized in 1962. The Law of Autonomy of the Bank of Spain passed in 1994 established its independence from the government and conferred full responsibility for monetary policy on the institution. Also in 1994, the Bank of Spain joined the European System of Central Banks.

Until its nationalization, the Bank of Spain's paramount objective as a private joint-stock company was profit maximization. This involved managing the Bank so as to distribute the highest possible annual dividend to the shareholders, to ensure the highest market prices for its stock and to guarantee the convertibility of its notes into cash at all times. The board of directors was far from concerned about the Bank's duties as a "central bank" (lender of last resort, and monetary stability, whether exchange rate or price stability).

* The author is a member of the Research Group ECO-2015-66782-P: Economic crises: changes and challenges. A historical perspective. I would like to thank all participants of the conference "Sveriges Riksbank 350 years: a central bank in a world of central banks" (Sveriges Riksbank, Stockholm, April 6–7, 2017), for heir helpful comments and insights. In particular, I have received extremely useful comments from Olivier Feiertag, Rodney Edvinsson, Tor Jacobson, and Daniel Waldenström. Two Spanish colleagues, Elena Martinez-Ruiz and Maria A. Pons have also contributed to ameliorate the chapter. All missing issues and errors are exclusively mine.

After 1939, this state of affairs changed. The Bank was placed under State control and subject to the close supervision of the Ministry of Finance. Indeed it became a mere appendix of the Treasury. Some independence was regained in the mid-1970s, after the death of Franco. The economic reforms undertaken during the political transition to democracy and the entrance into the European Economic Community allowed a new generation of Bank officials to transform the institution from within and to assume central bank policy objectives. In 1994 it finally gained the full autonomy it had never had and was given a unique and complex mandate: price stability.

The aim of this chapter is to provide an overview of the history of the Bank of Spain from its foundation up to the present day. The main issues to be addressed include identifying the forces that had driven the life of the institution, how and when the Bank has assumed functions as central bank, which were the relations of the Bank with the Treasury, and the degrees of autonomy or independence enjoyed by the institution. The text has been divided into periods which reflect changes in the Spanish banking legal framework, monetary regimes, and domestic and world politics that affected the life of the Bank (international and civil wars, the fall of the monarchy, the proclamation of two Republics, the long Franco dictatorship, the restoration of democracy, joining the EEC and the EU).

5.2 The Foundation: The Bank of San Carlos, 1782–1829

The origin of the Bank of Spain dates back to 1782, when it was founded under the name of Bank of San Carlos. Like its forerunners it was established to meet the financial needs of the Treasury. The Crown, unwilling to raise taxes and unable to borrow, authorized the issue of *vales reales* (a special sovereign debt). The main task of the Bank was to redeem the *vales* in specie at par. A second goal was to be in charge of the Crown's payments abroad. The Bank was created as a private joint-stock company under the protection of the State, with a capital of 300 million reales.[1] The charter had no time limit whatsoever. The San Carlos was granted the privilege of issuing banknotes, known as *cédulas*, bearing no interest and redeemable in cash. From its birth it was identified as a national institution and was known as the Bank of Spain both at home and abroad.

---

[1] The real was Spain's unit of account until its replacement by the peseta in 1868. The peseta was equivalent to four reales. The peseta remained the Spanish currency until the introduction of the euro in 1999. The euro-peseta exchange rate was fixed at 1:166.386.

The first decade of the Bank of San Carlos was one of prosperity. Despite the increase in the outstanding quantity of *vales reales*, their market value held steady, and the Bank was able to redeem all the paper presented at par. During the Bank's second decade, Spain was involved in uninterrupted armed conflicts against revolutionary France and against England up to 1808. The military conflicts required the continuous issue of new *vales*. As a result the market value of the securities fell sharply. In 1798 the Bank suspended the payment of the *vales* in cash, and their discount reached a low of 30 percent. At the turn of the century the San Carlos was unable to fulfill the principal purpose for which it was founded.

The wars' financial exigencies tied the future of the San Carlos to the government's needs. By 1808 the Treasury indebtedness with the Bank reached 70 percent of its overall balance sheet, and 90 percent of its paid-up capital. The government had absorbed the institution's entire resources. The San Carlos was on the verge of bankruptcy, with largely non-performing assets, since the Treasury was financially exhausted. Nor could any relief be expected from the colonies, as the British naval blockade had severe trading links between the metropolis and the American territories still under Spanish sovereignty.

The invasion of Napoleonic troops in 1808 marked the beginning of the Spanish War of Independence that was to last six years. The institution was split in two, one part remaining in Madrid under the control of the French authorities, the other reorganized in 1810 in the city of Cádiz where the Spanish Revolutionary Committee established its headquarters. All ordinary activities came to a halt. Both institutions were seized by the authorities to ensure that they channeled their scant resources to finance the corresponding treasuries. The end of the conflict in 1814 brought the reunification of the San Carlos. The comparison of the balance sheet of the Bank in 1808 and that of 1814 revealed that the indebtedness of the Royal Treasury with the Bank had substantially increased. The likelihood that the government would meet its financial commitments with the Bank was nil. If the institution was paralyzed before the war, in 1814 it was near to collapse. The ailing body of the San Carlos, with hardly any activity, lingered for another 15 years. It did not close its doors, but its life as a credit and issuing institution was plagued with difficulties. In 1820 it was close to being dismantled, when the Minister of Finance offered the shareholders the opportunity to exchange their stocks in the Bank for a new issue of Treasury bonds. The proposal was rejected.

The solution came in 1829 when the government prepared a project to rescue the Bank. The Treasury offered the institution fresh money in exchange for writing off the unpaid loans and credits on the balance sheet. The shareholders, with no other alternative, accepted the plan whereby the Bank would receive 40 million reales in cash in exchange for the 316 million reales of non-performing State assets. The government's plan included a restructuring of the institution, a new charter and a new name for the Bank. Its starting capital would be precisely the 40 million reales apportioned by the Treasury. The near collapse of the Bank was a consequence of its close relationship with a broke Treasury, but curiously enough its survival was the result of a rescue operation orchestrated by the Treasury itself.

5.3 The Successor: The Bank of San Fernando, 1829–1855

The Bank of San Fernando, established in 1829, after the agreement reached between the Crown and the owners of the San Carlos, was the immediate successor of the latter. Its time span was fixed at 30 years. The Bank was authorized to embark in all sorts of financial operations. It remained the financial agent of the government in charge of the payments operations abroad. It was granted the monopoly of issuing banknotes in Madrid that ought to be convertible into metallic (gold or silver reserves) on demand, but it did not fix any issue limit.

During its first years of life, the San Fernando tried to make the best use of its large capital, while maintaining the financial respectability that its predecessor had lost. The board of directors restricted lending, limited the issue of banknotes, and assured high liquidity ratios. The management also tried to keep its financial relationships with the Treasury under strict surveillance in order to avoid the problems that brought down the San Carlos.

When in 1833 the first of a series of nineteenth-century civil wars broke out between the supporters of liberalism and the parties in favor of maintaining the absolutist regime, the period of calm for the Bank ended. Moreover, the wars coincided with the collapse of Spain's empire in the Americas, whose silver wealth had been the financial pillar of the metropolitan State since the sixteenth century. The conflict lasted until 1839, and the San Fernando was called upon to cover the financial needs of the Treasury. In 1833, Treasury assets accounted for a mere 10 percent of the Bank's overall balance, while in 1839 this figure soared to 57 percent. Less than five years after its foundation, the San Fernando was in a fragile situation, heading toward the financial state that had provoked the dire troubles of the San Carlos.

The civil war ended in 1839 with the victory of the liberal army. The peace created a new environment for business activities which led to a period of intense, albeit short-lived, economic expansion, accompanied by a parallel expansion in banking. In 1844 two commercial and issue banks were founded: the Bank of Isabel II in Madrid and the Bank of Barcelona, putting an end to the *de facto* monopoly of the Bank of San Fernando. For the San Fernando, the Bank of Isabel II, in particular, was both a competitor and a threat. To face the challenge posed by its rival, the San Fernando changed its conservative policy.

The good times ended in 1846. At the end of the year the economic cycle had definitely turned. The crisis that broke out in London in January 1847 spread to other European financial centers with devastating effects. Panic was widespread in Madrid as tension in the money market intensified because of the acute shortage of metal, the deterioration in the balance of payments, and the sharp decline in government bond prices. The crisis unveiled the weak financial position of the Bank of Isabel II. Holders of banknotes and current accounts demanded their conversion into cash, to which the Bank, short of liquidity, responded by restricting its operations while desperately seeking for metallic reinforcement. To avoid bankruptcy the directors of the Isabel II turned to the Ministry of Finance for help. The financial position of the Bank of San Fernando, although less critical, was not free of difficulties. The San Fernando's immediate financial future depended on its main debtor – the Treasury – which was also in serious financial troubles and unable to pay off its debts. A solution to avoid the collapse of both institutions was sought in their consolidation.

After the merger the Bank of San Fernando was reorganized. However, the Bank's financial troubles did not vanish. In 1848 the economic and political situation throughout Europe took a turn for the worst, and the effects were felt in Spain. Laden with deteriorated assets inherited from the Isabel II, and forced to continue providing financial support to the Treasury, the San Fernando found it extremely difficult to maintain the convertibility of its notes. Panic spread, with holders gathering in front of the Bank's gates and demanding the conversion of their notes into cash. The Bank did not suspend payments, but limited opening hours and restricted the per capita quantity of notes to be converted daily. Eventually the government had to intervene, a second time, to rescue the institution. A decree was passed, making the San Fernando's banknotes partially legal tender and the Treasury accepted them in payment of taxes and customs duties. The government also arranged a domestic loan to obtain fresh metallic to be transferred to the Bank's vault.

Two Acts were passed in 1849 and 1851 to restructure the Bank and strengthen its financial position. The paid-up capital was reduced, non-performing loans were written-off, the banknotes issuance restricted, and the distribution of dividends limited. Nonetheless, it took the Bank seven years (seven years during which its activities and operations came to a standstill) to recover and only in 1855 was it ready for new undertakings.

5.4 The Bank of Spain during the Period of Plurality of Issue, 1856–1873

The modern history of Spanish banking began in 1856, with the approval of the Law on Banks of Issue and the Law on Credit Companies. The former established the principle of plurality of issue, while renaming the Bank of San Fernando as the Bank of Spain. An immediate consequence of the Act was the establishment of banks of issue throughout the country. From only three, their number jumped to 20 by 1866. The enactment of the Credit Companies Law also led to the emergence of a larger number of credit banks.

The issuing law established a twofold limit on the banks' issuing capacity: notes in an amounts equivalent to three times their paid-up capital and a specie (gold and/or silver) reserve equivalent to one-third of the notes in circulation. Banks had to be chartered by government decree, had to be incorporated and their capital fully paid-up. The Act required the Bank of Spain to open branches within a year in at least eight cities, government supervision was to be exercised by a governor appointed by the Ministry of Finance, and the Bank's privilege of issue was fixed for 25 years. The Bank of Spain inherited the capital of the San Fernando. Another element of continuity was the permanence of the same board of directors, including the governor. The continuity is also confirmed by the fact that the Bank of Spain occupied the premises of the San Fernando in Madrid.

The Bank of Spain was far bigger than the others. Its paid-up capital was more than six times greater than that of the Bank of Barcelona, Spain's second largest credit company, and the volume of its notes in circulation greater than that of all the provincial banks combined. By the middle of the century the Bank of Spain was already a national financial institution, not only in terms of its name but because of its size. Its bills were beginning to be used as reserves and it maintained a close relationship with the Treasury, which included providing tax collection services and acting as the government's lender and cashier. Although the Bank defended its independence as a private credit institution, contemporary observers acknowledged that the government had a great deal of influence over the decisions taken by the institution's board members, since it not only appointed the governor but also used the Bank's resources to meet the Treasury's financial needs.

Despite its initial worries, plurality of issue hindered neither its growth nor its profit and loss account. Between 1856 and 1863 total assets increased by a non-negligible 30 percent. Both commercial bills and loans to the private sector and advances and loans to the government contributed to the expansion. Net benefits increased substantially, and the institution's share price in the Madrid Stock Exchange nearly doubled. The Bank's notes in circulation and current accounts grew rapidly (see Figures 5.1 and 5.2)

The financial expansion that began in 1856 came to a halt in 1864, when the economy faltered. The crisis erupted in May 1866, the same month in which Overend and Gurney collapsed in London. In Madrid the market,

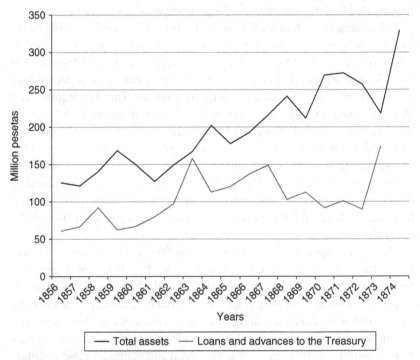

Figure 5.1 Bank of Spain assets, 1856–1874

Source: Banco de España (1970), *Ensayos sobre la economía española mediados del siglo XIX,* appendix 1; Tedde de Lorca (2015).

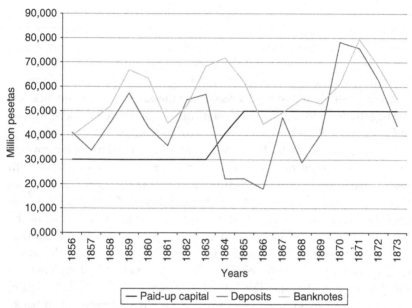

Figure 5.2 Bank of Spain liabilities, 1856–1873
Source: Banco de España (1970), *Ensayos sobre la economía española mediados del siglo XIX,* appendix 1; Tedde de Lorca (2015).

was shaken and in the following weeks there was a chain of bankruptcies. The panic was particularly pronounced in Barcelona. Two big financial firms suspended payments. A significant number of industrial and commercial firms also went bankrupt. The Stock Market closed and many banks closed their doors temporarily. From Madrid and Barcelona the crisis spread to the rest of the peninsula.

The 1866 crisis was deep and damaging. Financial and non-financial companies alike went into liquidation. The number of joint-stock banks fell and many private bankers and merchant houses disappeared. Of the 37 financial institutions funded after 1856, only 22 survived the crisis. Of the 82 bankers and private finance houses officially registered in 1866, just 43 were still in operation by 1870. Only savings banks, with no risky assets, remained untouched by the financial turmoil.

The Bank of Spain felt the crisis early in 1864, when depositors and notes holders began to demand their conversion into metallic. They feared that the Bank's excessive involvement with a broken Treasury would lead to the *corso forzoso* of the notes. The indebtedness of the Treasury with the Bank had reached a maximum in September 1864. There were widespread doubts about the institution's solvency. The Bank raised its interest rate two times, but the measures served to attract little metallic to the vaults, since the Bank of France and the Bank of England raised them as well. Moreover, the Bank increased its capital in an attempt to reinforce its financial position and to send a reassuring message to the public. Besides, the negotiations opened by the Bank with various foreign banking houses in London and Paris to obtain credits proved fruitless.

To make things worst, the Bank's position weakened when the government announced the creation, in April 1866, of a new National Bank, with the participation of foreign investors, with a nominal capital three times that of the Bank of Spain, and with the monopoly of issue for the whole country. The project was, in part, a response to a previous refusal of the Bank, which was already burdened with a large portfolio of dubious government debt, to advance additional funds to the Treasury. In return for the privilege of issue the National Bank was to extend a large credit to the Treasury far beyond the financial capacity of the Bank of Spain. Naturally, the new establishment implied the disappearance of all banks of issue, including the Bank of Spain, which would have to either merge with the new institution or become transformed into mere deposit and discount credit companies. However, the project failed because the crisis in London led to the collapse of Overend and Gurney, the main financial firm in the syndicate of London bankers behind the project.

Despite the failure of the National Bank project, the Bank's financial difficulties persisted. The run on deposits accelerated and in July cash reserves fell to a low of 17 percent of the banknotes in circulation – well below the statutory requirement of one-third. The 1866 scramble for liquidity placed the Bank of Spain on the verge of suspending cash payments. Convertibility was maintained at the cost of restricting the volume that could be exchanged daily and the quantity each note holder could present for conversion. The Bank also restricted its loans to its customers in order to reduce its notes in circulation. Relief came when the Bank was able to negotiate a large credit with Rothschild to buy silver to replenish the metallic reserve. This enabled the Bank to reduce its rates to normal levels.

The Bank of Spain survived the crisis, but not unscathed. Economic and political events delayed a rapid return to normalcy, indeed, prosperity never returned. The revolution of 1868 that overthrew the Bourbon monarchy and the proclamation of the First Spanish Republic in 1873 heightened uncertainty in the financial sphere. Reforms introduced by the revolutionary governments to modernize the structure of the economy and make it more market oriented also fomented an atmosphere of hesitation because the results would take time to materialize.

5.5 The Bank of Spain: A National Financial Institution, 1874–1913

On March 19, 1874 the Bank of Spain obtained the monopoly of issue. The decree radically changed the Spanish financial system. The end of the plurality of issue saw the disappearance of 15 institutions, which were given the choice between merging with the Bank of Spain or continuing as credit companies. The majority chose to merge. The granting of the monopoly was the result of the dire circumstances of the Treasury. Three simultaneous wars (civil, regional, and colonial) had led to a considerable rise in military spending. The stagnation of public revenues resulted in an increase of the budget deficit and the public debt in circulation. Salvation was sought from the Bank of Spain: an urgent loan in exchange for the monopoly of issue. The monopoly was granted for 30 years, and later extended to 1921.

For the Bank of Spain, the monopoly was similar to being founded anew, and the privilege to issue notes in the entire country transformed it into a genuine national bank and an unequalled financial power. In 1900, the issuer's assets accounted for 68 percent of the country's entire credit system. It also made the Bank one of the country's most successful trading companies. The Bank became the most important public–private institution, and the only one present all over Spain by means of its branches and banknotes. It was a kind of (financial) State within the State.

The monopoly of issue not only changed the structure of the banking system. The centralization of issue in a single credit institution contributed to the integration of the financial market. This process was based on three pillars: the expansion of the branch network, the adoption of a unified banknote throughout the country, and the establishment of a service between the Bank's current accounts free of charge. A fourth pillar that consolidated the position of the Bank as a national institution was its final conversion into the Bank of the State.

Figures 5.3 and 5.4 provide a cursory overview of the evolution of the Bank's balance sheet total assets and banknotes multiplied by a factor of 12 and nearly 30 respectively between 1874 and 1913. The main factor behind the increase in the Bank's total assets was the public portfolio, government debt purchases and loans, and advances to the Treasury. This is particularly clear in the period after 1895, when a huge amount of funds was required first to combat the colonial rebellion in Cuba, and later in 1898 to wage war against the United States on both the Caribbean and the Pacific seaboards. When the conflicts ended, the Treasury was able to balance the budget and reduce its indebtedness. By 1914, the Bank's public portfolio was barely 20 percent of total assets, compared with the record level of 75 percent in 1898. Conversely, loans and credits to the private sector were a minor part in the overall balance of the Bank, although they increased after 1900 to compensate for the fall in the volume of Treasury assets. A further factor that contributed to the expansion of the Bank's assets was the continuous increase in metallic reserves; first the silver component and then, after 1883, the gold reserves as a consequence of a gold purchase policy designed to maintain public confidence in the banknotes in circulation and to ensure their convertibility.

5.5.1 The Bank of Spain and Monetary Policy

The last quarter of the nineteenth century saw the spread of an international monetary system based on gold, linking the economy of the major countries of the world with fixed exchange rates for their domestic currencies. The adherence of almost all countries of the international economy could be taken as the most apparent proof that the system had considerable virtues. To be off the gold standard meant implicitly to opt for economic isolation and loose integration with the international economy.

The Spanish case appears in striking contrast with the international experience. Spain never adopted the gold standard. Convertibility of paper money into gold and silver was maintained until 1883, when eventually it was suspended. Resumption never took place, neither before 1913, nor after. Contrary to most European currencies, the Spanish currency thus remained inconvertible into gold and its exchange rate fluctuated throughout.

The Spanish economic authorities (the Treasury) never defined precise monetary goals except for a vague desire to adopt the gold standard at the official parity established in 1868. The stability of the currency was always a concern but an explicit policy was never formulated to assure it. The Ministers of Finance were aware of the fall in the international price of silver, but seem to have been unable to respond. They adopted an expectant policy, waiting to see how other nations responded. They eventually realized that most of the countries in Europe and elsewhere abandoned bimetallism and adopted a *de facto* or *de jure* gold standard. Nonetheless, Spain remained anchored to the bimetallic standard, and suffered from a fluctuating exchange rate.

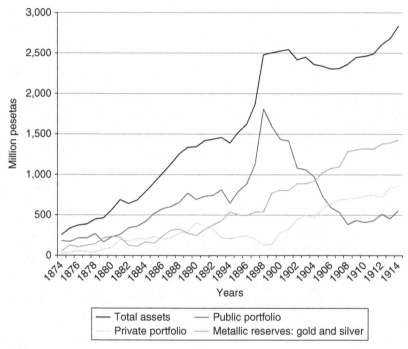

Figure 5.3 Bank of Spain assets, 1874–1914
Source: Banco de España, *Memorias anuales* (1874–1914).

An attempt was made to follow the example of the LMU (Latin Monetary Union). In 1876 the government discontinued the free coinage of silver on private accounts and gold coinage was resumed (having been suspended in 1873). Furthermore, a Committee on Currency Reform recommended the adoption of the gold standard, but the government ignored the recommendation. As the market price of silver fell, the unaltered official ratio undervalued gold relative to the market and, as predicted by Gresham's Law, silver eventually drove gold out of circulation and the Bank of Spain's gold reserves dwindled. Convertibility was suspended in the summer of 1883, following a contraction in foreign investment associated with the Paris stock market crash of January 1882. The measure was taken, so the argument goes, to defend the Bank of Spain's metallic reserves and halt the disappearance of gold from circulation and the export of gold. After the suspension of convertibility, the Spanish currency floated freely on the foreign exchange market.

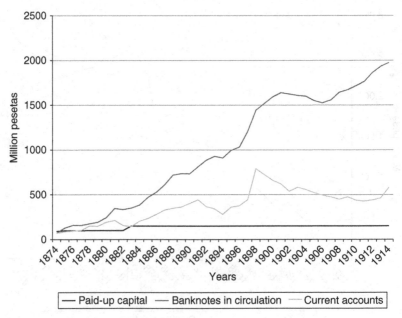

Figure 5.4 Bank of Spain liabilities, 1874–1914
Source: Banco de España, *Memorias anuales* (1874–1914).

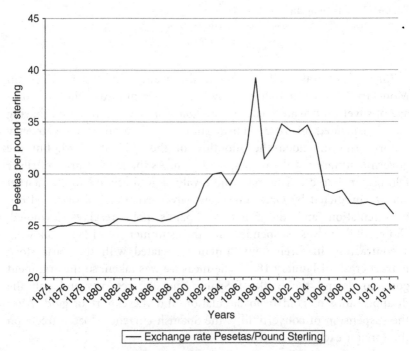

Figure 5.5 Exchange rate pesetas/pound sterling
Source: Banco de España, *Memorias anuales* (1874–1914); Martín-Aceña (2000).

Between 1890 and 1895 the value of the peseta fell, moderately but continuously, and the exchange rate to the pound depreciated from 25.6 to 28.9 pesetas. Subsequently, in 1896, the exchange rate began to rise sharply, peaking in 1898 at almost 40 pesetas, which represented 50 percent depreciation relative to parity. The end of the Spanish American War, in which Spain lost its last overseas colonies, permitted the return to financial orthodoxy and monetary stability and signaled a marked downward pattern in the exchange rate. At first it fell quickly, followed by a temporary rise and eventually, between 1900 and 1914, a continuous appreciation. In those 14 years, the peseta managed to recover almost all of its previous value, reaching a rate of 26.1 pesetas to the pound in 1914, a mere 4.6 percent below its 1880 value.

After 1900 there were some changes in Treasury policy objectives. The adoption of a successful stabilization program put an end to the depreciation of the peseta, and an array of projects to adopt the gold standard were discussed. Nevertheless, all failed because of governments' instability, a lack of faith in the projects, or weak political impetus, and most of all because of the lack of cooperation and in some cases even the tenacious opposition of the Bank of Spain.

The members of the board of directors of the Bank of Spain, as representatives of the shareholders, had two preoccupations. To maintain the public confidence in the banknotes, on the one hand, and, on the other, to ensure, as any other private financial company, the profitability of the Bank. The first concern entailed keeping in the Bank's vaults the largest possible stock of silver and gold to assure convertibility in either metal, at the convenience of the Bank. Silver and gold were considered as owned by the Bank and not as instruments of monetary policy to be used to defend the exchange rate. The Bank's board did not consider monetary policy its responsibility, and the discount rate was managed according to its private interest as a private company. It neither accepted the role of lender of last resort, or banker's bank, arguing that the other credit institutions were simply competitors. For the Bank's members of the board the issue of banknotes and its role as the Treasury's financial agent were the two only public responsibilities entrusted to them, both of which they assumed willingly because they were compatible with the overall goal of profit maximization.

5.6 A Reluctant Central Bank and Lender of Last Resort, 1914–1939

Neutrality during the First World War placed the Spanish economy in an advantageous position to meet the needs arising from the war: goods and services exports burgeoned, producing a balance of

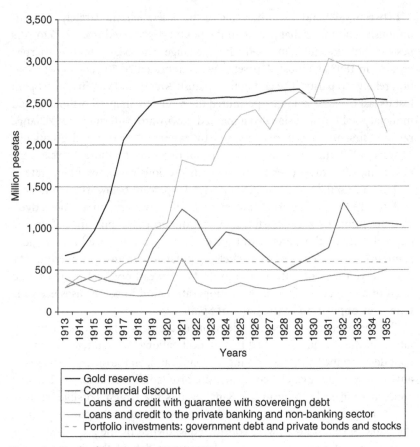

Figure 5.6 Bank of Spain assets, 1914–1935
Source: Banco de España, *Memorias anuales* (1913–1935).

payments surplus and an inflow of gold and foreign currency while the peseta appreciated. For the Bank of Spain the European war brought an extraordinary increase in its balance sheet, and in its gold reserves, as well as rising profits and dividends. Figures 5.6 and 5.7 offer a general overview of the evolution of the Bank's balance sheet during the interwar period.

Economic prosperity came to an abrupt close when the armed conflict ended, and it was followed, as elsewhere in the Continent, by a profound crisis. Credit institutions began experiencing liquidity and solvency difficulties, followed by some resounding crises. Fears that bankruptcies would spread, along with the conviction that due to their special nature credit

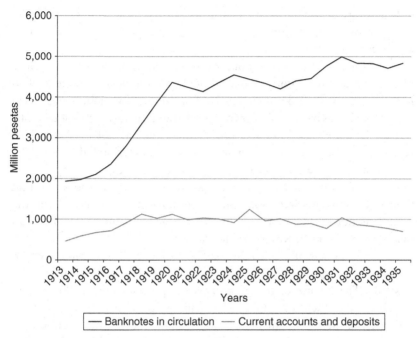

Figure 5.7 Bank of Spain liabilities, 1914–1935
Source: Banco de España, *Memorias anuales* (1913–1935).

companies should be subject to some form of control, argued in favor of a reorganization of the financial system.

A comprehensive Banking Law was approved in 1921. Its main purpose was to transform the Bank of Spain into a true central bank and to increase control of the State over the institution. The authorities believed that the postwar crisis could have been avoided had the Bank behaved as a real lender of last resort. The law extended its issuing privilege for another 25 years. In addition the law provided for the Treasury to have a share in the institution's profits. The discount rate was left in the hands of the Bank's board, while the rate of interest on loans and credits with the guarantee of sovereign bonds and debt had to be determined jointly by the Bank and the Treasury. The Act limited the amount of advances that the Treasury could obtain from the bank and fixed the quantity of banknotes in circulation. In order to strengthen the links between the banking community and the Bank of Spain, the law established that financial institutions could discount paper at a preferential rate. The Act did not prevent the Bank of Spain from operating with the non-banking private sector, but it set a ceiling on the outstanding amount of private securities in its portfolio. Moreover, the Act aimed to make the institution the executor of the government's monetary and exchange policies.

The 1921 Banking Act did not prevent the reappearance of a new wave of banking failures. Poorly managed banks were unable to write-off bad loans and dispose of devalued stocks. For a limited period, banks could carry large losses by running down reserves built up during previous years. But as the recession deepened and share prices did not rise, industrial recovery was delayed and the financial situation deteriorated. Eventually, the difficulties re-emerged after the summer of 1924. Once again, the stance of the Bank of Spain was to ignore the situation and argue that the banks' problems were not their concern. Its directors alleged that the Bank was not the guardian of poorly managed institutions; if they had made unwise loans, it was logical for them to fail.

Although the Great Depression was less severe in Spain than elsewhere in Europe, the spring of 1931 was politically complicated and financially unstable. The demise of the monarchy, the proclamation of the Second Republic, and the formation of a coalition government with various socialist ministers brought anxiety and fear to the business community and to the public at large. News of the failure of the Creditanstalt and the difficulties of central European institutions also contributed to the climate of gloom. The crisis erupted in April 1931. The run on banks was intense between April and June. The withdrawal of funds continued during the summer and up to the end of September. In the meantime the total volume of deposits had declined to 20 percent of the total outstanding in March 1931. Banks did not fail because they were able to obtain all the cash they needed to convert deposits into currency.

Two reasons may help to understand what made this possible. The Bank of Spain, for the first time in its long history, was prepared to behave as a lender of last resort and facilitate all the cash banks discounting bills on demand and accepting unhesitatingly eligible paper as collateral for credit. Moreover, the government authorized an increase in the limit of bank-notes in circulation. The other reason that contributed to preventing banks from collapsing was the fact that Spanish banks had a plentiful supply of gilt-edged Treasury securities; they simply pledged their unused portion of government paper in their balance sheet to obtain cash. Thus, the banks' holdings of public securities, used as collateral, acted as an automatic built-in stabilizer. So the rapid and unexpected intervention of the Bank, plus the ability of banks to monetize their holdings of government paper, explains why only a few financial institutions collapsed in 1931.

5.6.1 The Bank and Monetary Policy

The Spanish authorities were well aware of the worldwide re-establishment of the gold standard after the 1914 war. They too aimed at a prompt stabilization of the peseta. The opportunity came after the return to gold in Britain, France and Italy. At the same time a short-lived episode of appreciation of the peseta raised officials' expectations that currency would soon reach the parity of 1868 (25 pesetas to the pound). Plans to join the gold standard began in 1927, and lasted until 1932. The attempt, however, failed. Stabilization required two complementary measures. First, a decisive policy by the Treasury to impose financial discipline to balance the budget. Second, the Bank of Spain's cooperation to increase interest rates when needed, and being willing to defend the exchange rate with its metallic reserves, if necessary. However, neither of these two requirements were met. Despite statements to the contrary, the Treasury was never willing to enforce the necessary financial discipline, either before or after 1929, although it did manage to reduce the budget deficit. But specially, the Bank of Spain was not prepared to employ its huge gold reserves to sustain the exchange rate, when a continuous and unstoppable depreciation began in 1928, intensifying in 1929 when the pound sterling exchange rate rose to 33 pesetas. The depreciation became even more marked in 1930 and up to early September 1931, when the price of the pound reached a historical high of almost 60 pesetas.

The Bank's board maintained, as it had done systematically, that the exchange rate stability was not among its responsibilities and that the gold deposited in its vaults belonged to the shareholders, not to the Treasury, and was there to back the value and prestige of the banknotes in circulation. Since the Bank of Spain stubbornly upheld this view no matter who led the Ministry of Finance and no matter what political regime was in place, whether the Dictatorship or the Second Republic, the government eventually decided to amend the Banking Law of 1921. The reform was a response to the non-collaborative stance of the Bank of Spain in the government's attempt to defend the peseta exchange rate. The Bank refused to side with the Treasury and commit its huge gold reserves to contain the depreciation of the currency. No matter how inappropriate and untimely the intention, the spring of 1931, to stabilize the peseta and to adopt the gold standard, the Minister of Finance believed that the Bank ought to have supported official policy. But the owners and directors of the Bank considered that defending the exchange rate was not among its responsibilities.

5.6.2 The Bank and the Financing of the Civil War, 1936–1939

The military uprising that began in July 1936 split the country into two opposing factions. The Bank of Spain was divided, the official institution remaining under the authority of the Republican government while a parallel administration was created in the territory controlled by the so-called nationalist faction. The monetary unit also collapsed and for three years two different and opposing currencies were in circulation: the Republican peseta and the nationalist one.

The war was financed by both sides using internal and external resources. The main source of internal financing of both sides was money creation. The Republic raised more than 24,000 million pesetas through advances and credits from the Bank of Spain. The deficit of the so-called Nationals during the war amounted to 8,260 million pesetas. Foreign funding to pay for the war was especially relevant. The Franco military administration was able to purchase his military equipment with German and Italian "aid" and with loans from private banks in Portugal, Switzerland, and the United Kingdom up to 729 million dollars. Although the Republican government did not resort to external borrowing, it was not short of international means of payment, as it controlled most of the gold and silver reserves of the Bank of Spain that amounted to about 635 tons of fine gold, equivalent to 715 million dollars. The gold reserves were sold in two stages. First, the Bank of France acquired 175 tons, for which the Republican government obtained 196 million dollars. The remaining gold, 460 tons of fine gold valued at 519 million dollars, was sent to the USSR and deposited in Moscow in the vaults of the Gosbank, the Soviet central bank. When the conflict was over, the entire gold reserves of the Bank of Spain had been exhausted. Moreover, when most of the gold had gone, the Bank's silver holdings (1,225 tons) were put up for sale and bought by the United States Treasury and the Bank of France. In exchange, the Republican government received around 15 million dollars. All in all both sides spent roughly the same amount of foreign funds, although the lenders and the origin of the funds were different.

5.7 Under State Control: From the End of the Civil War to Nationalization, 1939–1962

After the Second World War and until the demise of the Bretton Woods accords, financial regulation became widespread throughout to avoid the chaos that had characterized international economic relations in the 1930s. During most of the 1950s and 1960s, the authorities determined and constrained both the total and the direction of lending. The commercial banks became in some senses co-opted into the public sector, rather like public utilities.

Spain was not an exception to this general trend. The autarkic and interventionist orientation of the early years of the Franco regime prompted the imposition of structural controls and a shift in bank supervision away from market discipline towards government discretion. Policy makers were convinced that financial institutions should be subject to strict controls and reoriented to supply whatever funds the "national economy" would require. As elsewhere in Europe, the financial market was suppressed and banks became the agents of government industrial policy.

For Spain, the two extreme years of this period are marked by the financial liquidation of the civil war and the law of nationalization of the Bank. For most of these years the Bank of Spain played a secondary role. It remained a private credit institution but it completely lost its autonomy. After 1939 the Bank lacked independency and had no objectives different from that established and defined by the Ministry of Finance. All monetary powers were assumed by the government, making the Bank a mere appendix and instrument of the Treasury. Foreign exchange policy was transferred in 1939 to a newly created organism, the Spanish Institute for Foreign Exchange, and put under the control of the Ministry of Industry and Commerce. A separation emerged between the internal and the external sides of monetary policy that lasted until 1971, when the Institute was dissolved. Moreover, Spain was excluded from the Bretton Woods conference, and hence kept out of the International Monetary Fund and the World Bank until 1958.

The financial framework after the civil war was set first in 1939 through a ministerial order declaring a *banking status quo* that forbade the opening of new banks, and second by a special Act of 1942, which *de facto* nationalized the Bank of Spain. Postwar legislation was completed by a new Banking Law in 1946 which included all the litany of regulations. The Ministry of Finance received discretionary powers to grant or to deny bank charters. Entry was at the discretion of the Ministry of Finance that used its authority rather arbitrarily. The banks' capital structure, its potential earnings, its management and the convenience and needs of the community were elements the new regulators considered before approving the establishment of a new bank. Branching expansion depended on the financial density of each region or the existence of unattended financial demand. The Ministry of Finance set maximum and minimum interest rates on deposits and on loans. It also set in preferential rates for the so-called "priority industrial sectors." Quantitative credit ceilings were imposed according to the industrial policy of the government. The Ministry of Finance also fixed the minimum capital requirements and the proportionality between assets and liabilities. Variations in nominal or paid-up capital, reserve provisions, and dividend distribution were all subject to ministerial approval.

It can be safely said that 1940 to 1957 were the worst years in the Bank of Spain's history. There was a complete absence of monetary policy. The Bank of Spain lacked autonomy and did not use instruments to regulate the quantity or the cost of money. Monetary management policy in those years led to the continuous creation of domestic resources at low interest rates. The Bank passively supplied liquidity to the system in magnitudes determined by the Treasury. Interest rates were kept low in order to facilitate the placement of public debt at the lowest possible cost.

This state of affairs continued until 1962 when the regulatory framework created after the civil war was partially altered. Changes in the European financial environment and the exhaustion of the domestic expansionary cycle that began in 1951 convinced the government that the autarkic and interventionist strategy ought to be dismantled. The Spanish economy grew fast during most of the 1950s, but at the same time it accumulated a series of fiscal and monetary imbalances that threatened to halt the past economic gains, and even to reverse what had been achieved in terms of income per capita. Protectionism and interventionism also had led to gross industrial inefficiencies and misallocation of resources. In 1959 a Stabilization Plan, modeled after a similar French plan, was adopted to correct the inflationary process and the mounting disequilibrium in the balance of payments.

Negotiations to join the International Monetary Fund and the International Bank of Reconstruction and Development began in 1958 at the same time that an agreement to enter the OECD was reached. The admission in both organizations led to the abandonment of autarky and a change in the orientation of its economic policy in order to align it with that of other European countries. Immediately measures were taken to correct the imbalances: a tax reform to raise revenues, the cessation of issuing government debt with the clause being automatically pledged in the Bank, and steps to limit budget expenditures. The Stabilization Program was approved in the summer of 1959. Monetary policy conducted by the Bank of Spain was paramount in the success of the elimination of the economic and financial disequilibria.

The Stabilization Program, and in particular the success of the measures taken in the field of monetary policy and the role played by the Bank of Spain, brought to the fore the need for a reform of the financial framework. It took three years, however, before the government decided to undertake the task. Eventually, a new Banking Law was prepared and approved in 1962. The law nationalized the Bank and put the basis for transforming the institution into a genuine central bank. Like in 1921 the authorities recognized that the Bank of Spain had not been, and was not yet, a real central bank. The 1962 law was aimed to correct this state of affairs. However, its content did so only halfway.

The Bank was not given full autonomy. Monetary policy remained in the hands of the Finance Ministry. The formulation of monetary targets, if any, was not the Bank's responsibility. Moreover, although the Ministry ceded the instrumentation of the corresponding policy to the Bank, it was not given the mechanisms to carry out its functions. No cash or liquidity coefficients were established; neither the framework to undertake open market operations; and most of all changes in the rate of discount were kept in the hands of the Ministry of Finance. Foreign exchange policy and the management of foreign reserves were not assigned to the Bank until the end of 1969, when the operative functions of the IEME (Spanish Institute of Foreign Exchange) were transferred to it. The 1962 law entrusted the Bank with the mission of inspection and supervision of the financial system. But in this field also it had to share these functions with other organisms. In fact, the Ministry of Finance maintained its fully comprehensive powers over the financial system. The Bank of Spain, lacking autonomy, continued to implement monetary policy, if any, as a mere instrument of the government.

Figure 5.8 shows the evolution of both total assets and banknotes in circulation. In these two decades the balance of the Bank multiplied ninefold, and banknotes in circulation by nearly eight times. It is apparent that in the 1950s, monetary expansion outpaced that recorded for the 1940s. The factors that explain the increase in the Bank's balance and account for the rapid increase in paper circulation can be gauged from Figure 5.9. First of all, rediscounting and loans and credits to the financial system. This hides, however, the fact that a large part of the rediscounting consisted of bills belonging to semi-public institutions and firms subscribed previously by the banks and saving banks. It, too, hides the already mentioned fact that a large volume of the outstanding credit of the financial system was obtained by placing in the Bank as collateral Treasury bonds and sovereign debt previously issued and subscribed by the private credit institutions.

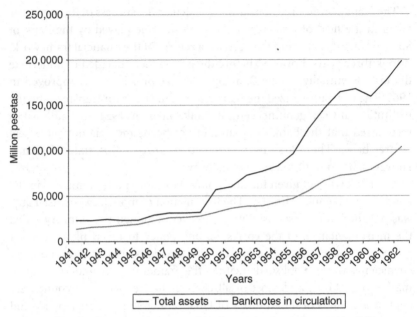

Figure 5.8 Bank of Spain total assets and banknotes in circulation, 1941–1962
Source: Bank of Spain, *Annual reports* (1942–1962).

5.8 From Nationalization to the Economic and Monetary Union, 1962–1999

The European economic golden age was shared by Spain. Growth was particularly rapid between 1962 and 1973, and Spanish GDP moved closer to the levels of the most developed countries of the Continent. There were also economic and financial reforms, albeit they proceeded at a slow pace and, as in the previous period, imbalances built up. Interventionism did not disappear entirely. Monetary policy, still under the control of the Ministry of Finance, was used sporadically. The nationalization of the Bank in 1962 did not lead to a modern monetary policy; instead, monetary instruments were used to resolve occasional problems.

Franco died in November 1975, and the transition to democracy that began immediately afterwards coincided with a deep industrial and banking crisis. The resolution of the crisis took time and radical measures had to be adopted to modernize the economic fabric of the country. The role of the Bank of Spain in the process was paramount, since it became, *de facto*, the monetary authority. Once the political transition was completed and

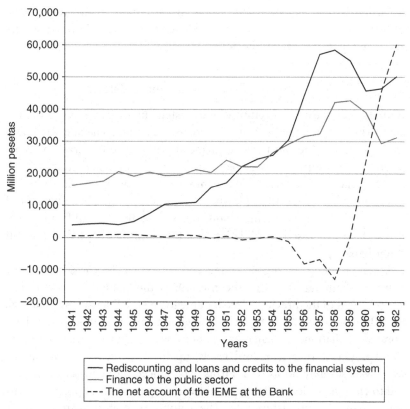

Figure 5.9 Bank of Spain main assets, 1941–1962
Source: Bance de España, informes anulaes (1942–1962).

the crisis surmounted, Spain joined the then European Economic Community (EEC) in June 1985. The ensuing years were characterized by growth, structural reforms and adjustment to EEC regulations. Spain signed the Maastricht Treaty in 1992, adhered to the European Monetary System in 1994 and joined the European Economic and Monetary Union (EMU) in 1999.

The Bank of Spain's role changed profoundly over the last four decades of the twentieth century. In 1971 the Bank's inspection duties were expanded. In 1973 the Institute of Foreign Exchange was closed and its functions transferred to the Bank. In 1980 the Law on the Governing Bodies of the Bank of Spain conferred upon the institution a substantial degree of autonomy. The Law of Discipline and Intervention of Credit Institutions of 1988 set out the supervisory function of the Bank.

A particular landmark was the Law of Autonomy in 1994, which finally made the Bank of Spain fully responsible for monetary policy, guaranteeing its independence from the government.

5.8.1 Banking Crisis and Financial Reforms

With the collapse of the Bretton Woods system, financial crises returned to the world scenario. Spain again was not an exception. The late 1970s and early 1980s saw the most severe financial crisis since the crash of 1866. Twenty-four institutions were rescued, four were liquidated, four merged, and 20 small and medium-sized banks were nationalized. All in all, 52 banks out of 110 were affected, which accounted for nearly 25 percent of the system's deposits. Savings banks also went through difficult times, although in this case consolidation was the solution adopted to prevent major bankruptcies.

A combination of exogenous and endogenous factors was behind the causes of banking crisis. In the mid-1970s the stable macroeconomic environment of the previous decade came to an end. Energy, raw material, and labor costs rose. The balance of payments on current accounts deteriorated, inflation escalated and nominal interest rates increased. Unemployment rose to record levels, up to 25 percent. The industrial sector was severely hit as well. Firms experienced heavy losses and many had to close their doors. Banks caught with large industrial portfolios saw their balance sheets deteriorate. The volume of non-performing assets rose. Banks profits were reduced and in some cases losses were recorded. Equity prices fell sharply, as did housing and commercial real estate prices after several years of a pronounced upward trend supported by high borrowing levels. Deregulation and competitive pressures were other causes of the banking crisis. Many of the previous restricted banking operations were lifted, and interest rates deregulated. Competition from foreign-owned banks after 1978, credit companies, and insurance companies also intensified the competitive environment.

As the banking crisis erupted almost unexpectedly, the Ministry of Finance and the Bank of Spain were caught unprepared. Deregulation had not been accompanied with the establishment of an efficient system of banking supervision. The authorities had neither the legal instruments, nor the institutional mechanisms to face the turmoil caused by the large-scale insolvencies. Although since 1971 the Bank of Spain had assumed all supervision of functions of credit institutions, its inspection division lacked the human resources to carry out adequate banking examination.

Disclosure requirements for financial holdings were not in place, auditing of banks was not at the time a widespread custom, and many firms resisted inspection by outsiders. Procedure and rules to impose sanctions on managers or to remove the administrators of banks in trouble were legally complicated, outdated, or non-existent. To avoid a catastrophe, the Bank had to implement emergency measures to prevent bank runs and a contagion effect from unsound to essentially solvent institutions. Containment included lender of last resort assistance to banks with temporary liquidity problems and intervention for failed banks.

To provide limited guarantees to depositors, two Deposit Guarantee Funds (one for banks and another for savings banks) were established in November 1977. Rescue operations began in 1978 and continued well until 1983. A new institution was set up: the Banking Corporation, a private joint-stock company, managed by the Bank of Spain. It proved to be a speedy and adequate mechanism to take control of troubled banks. In 1980 the Deposit Guarantee Funds were reorganized and replaced the Banking Corporation. The Fund took over 29 institutions. Only one was liquidated, while the rest were restructured before being sold on to other banks.

5.8.2 The Bank of Spain and the Return of Monetary Policy

The crisis of the early 1970s, with the sharp increase in oil prices and the collapse of the Bretton Woods agreements, marked the return of monetary policy to the forefront. Governments in Western Europe and elsewhere, although with delays, stood ready to combat inflation and rising unemployment with all the macroeconomic instruments at their disposal. Monetary policy relegated, for a long time, was called to head the response. Nor was Spain an exception.

For the Bank the crisis was an opportunity to regain autonomy and take control of monetary policy. Officials at the Bank realized that they could replace the old passive monetary stance for an active approach to economic management. The first step was to develop a macroeconomic model to observe the relations of the main macromagnitudes (or macrovariables). The second step was to design a scheme of monetary management. GDP and inflation were the two ultimate monetary targets. The monetary scheme designed had two levels, each with a goal to be attained. For the first level, the monetary aggregate chosen was M3, that is, a broad definition of money supply, presumably closely related to GDP and prices. For the second, the Bank selected an intermediate monetary goal, the so-called "liquidity assets in the hands of the public" (a variety of high-powered money), also assumed to be linked in this case to M3. By managing the intermediate or instrumental magnitude they expected to control M3 and eventually GDP and prices.

This scheme of monetary control worked well for nearly two decades. The major threat to its operation came from the continuous budget deficits that the Treasury was unable to finance save by resorting to the Bank. To avoid the interference with monetary policy the Bank and the Treasury introduced reforms to create a monetary market – until then non-existent. A second challenge to the scheme emerged in the mid-1980s, with the increasing variability of interest rates as a consequence of the strict control exercised over M3. The increasing volatility of the exchange rate was also a matter of concern. The Bank decided to pay attention to both variables in order to smooth their fluctuations. Indeed, when Spain joined the European Exchange Rate Mechanism in 1989, the peseta exchange rate became paramount. This coincided with a change in policy thinking that led to the belief that exchange discipline, more than domestic fiscal or monetary policy, was sufficient to guarantee price stability. The monetary storm of 1992 undermined this belief. The peseta was devalued along with the pound sterling, the Irish pound, and the lira, and the obsolete scheme based on instrumental monetary variables had to be adjusted and replaced with one based on direct inflation goals. In this instance, the opportunity came with the Maastricht Treaty of February 1992 and the establishment of the criteria for joining the future European Economic and Monetary Union.

The Law of Autonomy of the Bank of Spain was passed in 1994. Consistent with the Maastricht Treaty, the institution was granted full autonomy in the field of monetary policy with the goal of maintaining price stability. Hence, beginning in 1995, the Bank abandoned its traditional scheme of monetary policy, swapping it for an inflation targeting strategy. Besides the direction of the Bank's policy over the following five years was to ensure that the country fulfilled the inflation and the exchange rate criteria to join the EMU from the outset.

Figure 5.10 shows the annual percentage variations of the evolution of GDP and prices. Prices rose faster than total output after 1973, a time in which the Bank had not yet attained monetary control. In the 1980s and 1990s, the picture is the reverse. The yearly fluctuations of GDP were on occasion violent, but prices fell throughout. Encouraged by this indicator, the Bank of Spain policy aim of reducing inflation has been successful. The full assumption of the central bank's functions, and full autonomy since 1994, has been worthwhile.

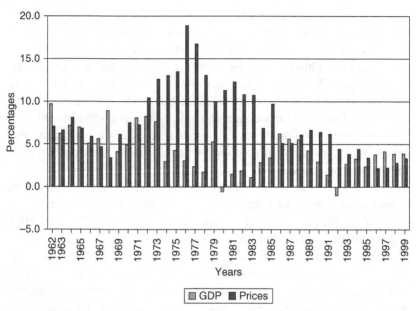

Figure 5.10 GDP and prices: annual variations, 1962–1999
Source: Banco de España, *Informes anuales* (1962–1999).

5.9 The Bank of Spain in the EMU, 1999–2017

The European Monetary Union (EMU) came into being in December 1999. Having fulfilled the conversion criteria laid down in the Maastricht Treaty, Spain became part of the euro area along with ten other EU member states. Joining the euro brought about fundamental changes in the institutional framework in which monetary policy decisions were made, meaning that the Bank of Spain also had to redefine its duties. Participation in the Eurosystem led to changes but not necessarily to a reduction in tasks. Hence, since January 1, 1999, the Bank has assumed two basic functions, one as member of the ECB and the other as a national central bank.

The first function includes: defining and implementing the Eurosystem's monetary policy, with the principal aim of maintaining price stability across the euro area; carrying out foreign exchange transactions consistent with provision of the EU Treaty, and holding and managing the State's official currency reserves; promoting the proper working payment system of the euro area; conducting emergency liquidity assistance operations and issuing legal tender banknotes. The functions of a national central bank encompass holding and managing currency and precious metal reserves not transferred to the ECB; promoting the proper working and stability of the financial system and, without prejudice to the functions of the ECB, of the national payment system; supervising solvency and compliance with the specific rules of credit institutions and assisting the ECB in the compilation of statistical information; and providing Treasury services and acting as financial agent for government debt.

The Spanish economy was among those that reaped most benefit from EMU membership. During the first seven years after the inauguration of the monetary union, Spain's economy enjoyed a phase of sustained growth in which real convergence with the core EMU member countries advanced: GDP per capita relative to the EMU average increased by more that 15 percentage points (pp), from 79 percent to 95 percent.

However, the growth of the Spanish economy in the 1999–2007 period was based on foundations that could not be maintained indefinitely. The demand stimulus provided by the adherence to EMU was only partially accommodated by the expansion in domestic output, based on an exceptional increase in the rate of employment. This was not adequately matched by an improvement in productivity. A series of imbalances thus began to emerge during the period, undermining the dynamism of the expansion. Three main imbalances accumulated: an inflation differential; an increasing trade deficit due to a pronounced loss of external competitiveness; and an increase in household and corporate debt.

The disequilibria emerged when the international economic atmosphere changed in 2007. The trigger was the financial crisis that erupted in the United States and Europe. The crisis did not take long to affect the Spanish economy, although the authorities failed to recognize it. Initially, Spanish banks were relatively unscathed by the first wave of the financial crisis, as they had no exposure to toxic assets. Spanish banks were able to confront the beginning of the crisis from an initially solid position also because they had built significant safety buffers during the years of expansion, thanks to the regulatory innovations that were introduced with the establishment of dynamic provisions. But after the bankruptcy of Lehman Brothers, these buffers were progressively exhausted. Although the problems were confined to a set of specific institutions (the saving banks), they had a systemic facet due to their influence on the reputation of the system as a whole.

The financial difficulties made their appearance in March 2009, when for the first time in nearly 15 years the Bank of Spain had to rescue a savings bank. From that date on, many other savings banks required the Bank's intervention, or had to be bailed-out or forced to merge, while at the same time they needed to be restructured, all with a high cost for the public purse. Nevertheless, the financial authorities' reaction in avoiding a financial catastrophe was belated and not clearly defined. The first step was to create (September 2009) a new resolution body, the Fund for the Orderly Restructuring of the Banking Sector (FROB), which complemented the existing mechanism provide by the Deposit Guarantee Funds. In 2010 a second set of regulatory measures affected the Bank of Spain's rules for credit risk provisions. In 2011 a royal decree introduced stricter measures to reinforce the solvency and liquidity of banks and savings banks. Capital requirement ratios were increased, the composition of capital redefined, and a new risk-based standard for provisioning assets was adopted. A major regulatory change was the merger of the two existing Guarantee Deposit Funds; the competences and responsibilities of the new Fund were enlarged and its financial capability increased.

The year 2012 also featured new regulatory measures. Two royal decrees of February introduced a new round of modifications concerning banks' capital requirements and credit risk provisions. A major issue was the so-called Memorandum of Understanding (MOU), signed by the Spanish authorities and the European Financial Stability Facility (now the European Stability Mechanism) whereby Spain received financial assistance of 100,000 million euros to cover losses and to capitalize viable banking institutions. As a consequence of the MOU, Spain was required to introduce new change in the law regulating the savings banks. The MOU also required that the objectives, procedures, and operations of the FROB were reformed, and that a new body was established – a joint public–private company to manage banks' toxic assets and non-performing loans: the Managing Society of Assets from Bank Restructuring. The Society was created in December 2012 and it has been in full operation since.

5.10 Conclusions

Three main historical forces have driven the history of the Bank of Spain. First, wars because they meant temporary increases in government expenditure that the Bank, as the official or semi-official issue institution, was called to finance. A second force modeling the life of the Bank has been its link with the Treasury. Even in peacetime, the Bank has been called to cover the fiscal needs of the government. Treasury policy and objectives have also shaped the historical trajectory of the Bank. There has always been a permanent tension between the Bank's objectives as a private maximizing commercial institution and its function as banker of the government. Third, because institutions and their functions do not develop in a vacuum, the

Bank has been profoundly influenced by ideas, theories, and perceptions about its proper role.

The monopoly of issue in 1874 did not mark the beginning of the Bank of Spain as a true or genuine central bank. The main objective of the Bank was profit maximization. Banknote convertibility into gold or silver was seen as essential to guarantee the financial respectability of the Bank; until its nationalization, monetary policy was not a major concern. The maintenance of the (domestic or international) value of the currency was considered a government responsibility. The fact that Spain was off the gold standard during its long time of domination was due, among other causes, to the non-collaborative stance of the Bank.

The stability of the financial system was not a responsibility that the Bank of Spain assumed while it was a private commercial company. The assumption of the lender of last resort function was delayed at least until the beginning of the twentieth century, if not later. First operations in this regard were undertaken under the pressure of the government, and unwillingly. Only in 1931, when the combination of the European banking crisis and the political crisis (the demise of the monarchy and the proclamation of the Second Republic) threatened the financial fabric of the country did the Bank intervene as lender of last resort, jointly with the Treasury, to avoid a complete breakdown.

After its *de facto* nationalization in 1939, and for more than three decades, the Bank of Spain lost its autonomy and became an agent or branch of the Treasury. It changed its "profit maximizing" objective for whatever goal the government decided: cheap and abundant money to foster economic growth, low interest rates to reduce the public debt burden, aid to rescue individual banks. On a few occasions, such as the Stabilization Plan of 1959, monetary policy was used to combat inflation or any other economic imbalances.

Despite its long history as an issue institution, the Bank of Spain did not assume the roles of a real central bank until late in the twentieth century. From 1977 onward, it regained its lost institutional autonomy and took full responsibility (of the duties) for monetary policy. In fact the transformation of the Bank of Spain into a modern, full-fledged central bank occurred just as it became part of the Eurosystem in 1999.

Further Reading

Anes Alvarez, Rafael (1974), "El Banco de España (1874–1914): Un banco nacional", *La banca española en la Restauración*. Madrid: Banco de España.

Banco de España (1874–1935), *Memorias anuales*. Madrid: Banco de España.

Banco de España (1962–1999), *Informes anuales*. Madrid: Banco de España.

Banco de España (1970), *Ensayos sobre la economía española mediados del siglo XIX*. Madrid: Banco de España.

Banco de España (1997), *La política monetaria y la inflación en España*. Madrid: Alianza Editorial.

Banco de España (2001), *El camino hacia el euro. El real, el escudo y la peseta*. Madrid: Banco de España.

Banco de España (2017), *Informe sobre la crisis financiera y bancaria en España, 2008–2014*. Madrid: Banco de España.

Castañeda, Lluis (2001), *El Banco de España, 1874–1900. La red de sucursales y los nuevos servicios financieros*. Madrid: Banco de España. Estudios de Historia Económica, p. 41.

Fernández Pulgar, Carlos and Rafael Anes Álvarez (1970), "La creación de la peseta en la evolución del sistema monetario de 1847 a 1868," in *Ensayos sobre la economía española a mediados del siglo XIX*. Madrid: Servicios de Estudios del Banco de España.

Galvarriato, Juan-Antonio (1932), *El Banco de España. Su historia en la centuria 1829–1929*. Madrid: Gráficas reunidas.

Gil, Gonzalo (2006), "The Bank of Spain, 2000–2006. Modernization and internationalization," in *150 years in the History of the Bank of Spain, 1856–2006*. Madrid: Banco de España.

Hamilton, Earl J. (1945), "The foundation of the Bank of Spain," *Journal of Political Economy*, 53, 2: 97–114.

Hamilton, Earl J. (1946), "The first twenty years of the Bank of Spain," *Journal of Political Economy*, 54, 2, 116–140.

Malo de Molina, José Luis (2012), "The macroeconomic basis of the recent development of the Spanish financial system," in José Luis Malo de Molina and Pablo Martín-Aceña (eds.), *The Spanish Financial System. Growth and Development since 1900*. London: Palgrave Macmillan.

Malo de Molina, José Luis and José Pérez (1990), "La política monetaria española en la transición hacia la unión monetaria europea," *Papeles de Economía Española*, 43: 31–51.

Martín-Aceña, Pablo (1984), *La política monetaria en España, 1919–1935*. Madrid: Instituto de Estudios Fiscales.

Martín-Aceña, Pablo (1994), "Spain during the classical gold standard years, 1880–1914," in Michael D. Bordo and Forrest Capie (eds.), *Monetary Regimes in Transition*. Cambridge: Cambridge University Press.

Martín-Aceña, Pablo (2000), "The Spanish monetary experience, 1848–1914," in Pablo Martín-Aceña and Jaime Reis (eds.), *Monetary Standards in the Periphery: Paper, Silver, and Gold, 1854–1933*. Houndmills: Palgrave Macmillan.

Martín-Aceña, Pablo (2006), "The Bank of Spain and the financial system, 1914–1962," in *150 years in the History of the Bank of Spain*. Madrid: Banco de España

Martín-Aceña, Pablo (2013), "Crisis bancarias. Nada nuevo bajo el sol," in Pablo Martín-Aceña, Elena Martínez-Ruiz, and M. Angeles Pons (eds.), *La crisis financieras en la España contemporánea, 1850–2012*. Barcelona: Crítica.

Martín-Aceña, Pablo and Olivier Feiertag (1999), "The delayed modernization of the central banks of France and Spain in the twentieth century," in Carl-L. Holtfrerich, Jaime Reis, and Gianni Toniolo (eds.), *The Emergence of Modern Central Banking from 1918 to the Present*. Aldershot: Ashgate.

Martín-Aceña, Pablo, Elena Martínez-Ruiz, and Pilar Nogues-Marco (2011), "Floating against the tide: Spanish monetary policy, 1870–1931," in A. Ögren and L.F. Øksendal (eds.), *The Gold Standard Peripheries: Monetary Policy, Adjustment and Flexibility in a Global Setting*. Basingstoke: Palgrave Macmillan, pp. 145–173.

Martín-Aceña, Pablo, Elena Martínez-Ruiz, and M. Angeles Pons (2012), "War and economics: Spanish Civil War finances revisited," *European Review of Economic History*, 16, 2: 144–165.

Martín-Aceña, Pablo, Elena Martínez-Ruiz, and Pilar Nogués Marco (2013), "The Bank of Spain. A national financial institution," *Journal of European Economic History*, XIII, 1: 11–45.

Martín-Aceña, Pablo, M. Angeles Pons, and Concha Betrán (2014), "150 years of financial regulation in Spain. What can be learned?," *Journal of European Economic History*, XLIII, 1–2: 35–81.

Martínez Méndez, Pedro (1981), *El control monetario a través de la base monetaria: la experiencia española*. Banco de España. Servicio de Estudios. Estudios Económicos, no. 20.

Martínez Méndez, P. (2005): *Trabajos de Historia Económica: Tesoro y Banco de España, 1900–1936*. Madrid: Banco de España.

Martínez Pérez, Eleuterio (1922), *Banco de España. Su régimen, operaciones y situación*. Madrid: Gráficas Reunidas.

Martínez-Ruiz, Elena and Pilar Nogués-Marco (2017), "The political economy of exchange rate. Stability during the gold standard. The case of Spain, 1874–1914." Université de Genève. Faculté des Sciences de la Societé. Economic History History Working Papers, no. 1.

Moro, Alesio, Galo Nuño, and Pedro Tedder de Lorca (2015), "A twin crisis with multiple banks of issue in Spain in the 1860s," *European Review of Economic History*, 19, 2, 171–194.

Olariaga, Luis (1933), *La política monetaria en España*. Madrid: Biblioteca Nueva.

Pons Brias, María A. (2002), *Regulating Spanish Banking, 1939–1975*. Aldershot: Ashgate.

Poveda, Raimundo (2012), "Banking supervision and regulation over the past 40 years," in José Luis Malo de Molina and Pablo Martín-Aceña (eds.), *The Spanish Financial System. Growth and Development since 1900*. London: Palgrave Macmillan.

Rodríguez Romero, José (1890), *El Banco nacional de España. Reseña histórico-estad ística de sus principales operaciones*. Madrid: Tipografía de Ricardo Alvarez y Pascual.

Rojo, Luis Angel (2002), "El largo camino de la política monetaria española hacia el euro," in *El camino hacia el euro. El real, el escudo y la peseta*. Madrid: Banco de España.

Rojo, Luis Angel and José Pérez (1977), *La política monetaria en España: objetivos e instrumentos*. Banco de España. Servicio de Estudios. Estudios Económicos, no. 10.

Santillán, Ramón (1865), *Memoria histórica sobre los Bancos Nacional de San Carlos, Español de San Fernando, Isabel II, nuevo de San Fernando, y de España*. Madrid: Establecimiento Tipográfico de T. Fortanet.

Sardá Dexeus, Juan (1948), *La política monetaria y las fluctuaciones de la economía española en el siglo XIX*. Madrid: CSIC.

Sardá Dexeus, Juan (1970), "El Banco de España, 1931–1962," *El Banco de España. Una historia económica*. Madrid: Banco de España

Serrano Sanz, J.M. (2004), *El oro en la Restauración*. Madrid: Real Academia Ciencias Morales y Políticas.

Sudrià, Carles and Yolanda Blasco (eds.) (2016), *La pluralidad de emisión en España, 1844–1874*. Madrid: Fundación BBVA.

Tedde de Lorca, Pedro (1982), "El Banco de España desde 1782 a 1982," *Banco de España. Dos siglos de historia, 1782–1982*. Madrid: Banco de España.

Tedde de Lorca, Pedro (1988), *El Banco de San Carlos, 1782–1829*. Madrid: Alianza Editorial y Banco de España.

Tedde de Lorca, Pedro (1999), *El Banco de San Fernando, 1829–1856*. Madrid: Alianza Editorial y Banco de España.

Tedde de Lorca, Pedro (2006), "The Bank of Spain, 1856–1874," in *150 Years in the History of the Bank of Spain*. Madrid, Banco de España, pp. 69–108.

Tedde de Lorca, Pedro (2015), *El Banco España y el Estado liberal, 1847–1874*. Madrid: Gadir Editorial.

Tortella Casares, Gabriel (1970), "El Banco de España entre 1829–1929. La formación de un banco central," in *Banco de España. Una historia económica*. Madrid: Banco de España.

Tortella Casares, Gabriel (1970), "La evolución del sistema financiero español de 1856 a 1868," in *Ensayos de la economía española a mediados del siglo XIX*. Madrid, Editorial Ariel.

Tortella Casares, Gabriel (2006), "The Bank of Spain: a new financial power, 1874–1914," in *150 Years in the History of the Bank of Spain*. Madrid: Banco de España, pp. 109–134.

Viver, Edualdo (1899), *El Banco de España considerado en sí mismo y en su relación con el Estado y la circulación monetaria del país*. Sabadell: Imprenta de Mariano Torner.

6

The Other Way: A Narrative History of the Bank of France

Vincent Bignon and Marc Flandreau*

At inception in 1800 the Bank of France was a central bank created by Parisian merchant bankers for Parisian traders. Its shareholders belonged mostly to the Parisian banking establishment, who were associated with previous attempts to create a central bank (Courtois, 1875; Bergeron, 1978). The founders of the Bank cherished the idea of an independent central bank, which makes the French history of central banking very different from the conventional narrative informed by the English experience. This does not mean that the government was absent from the picture. Quite the contrary, as the Bank was a chartered bank and the banker of the government. But the story is not one of support of fiscal policy or of refinancing of sovereign debt, contrary to the origin of the Bank of England or the Norges Bank. This does not mean, either, that politics did not play any role in the creation or management of the Bank. It is only that the *raison d'être* for the creation of the Bank of France followed an alternative path than that of England. France was, however, not the first to follow this path. Indeed, the Bank of Amsterdam, or the *Riksbank*, had also been created with the aim of conducting monetary policy to stabilize the payment system and/or the economy.

It was only with World War I that the Bank of France became permanently involved in the management of sovereign debt, and hence converged towards the English definition of a central bank. It does not come as a surprise that English economic history literature had judged that the Bank of France became central *by the English definition* only in the

---

* For their comments and suggestions, we thank Patrice Baubeau, Tor Jacobson, Daniel Waldenstrom, Eugen White, and the participants to the conference of the 350th anniversary of the *Rikskbank*. The views expressed in this chapter are those of the authors and shall not be interpreted as reflecting those of the Banque de France or the Eurosystem.

interwar period, when both banks faced the same policy issues (see, e.g., Capie and Goodhart, 1994). Yet, from the beginning, the Bank of France had all the attributes of a central bank: it organized the payment system, managed the government account, and provided lending of last resort services to private agents during crises and to public agents during wars or extreme political events. If not the Bank, which organization would have managed the sovereign debt overhang before 1914? Contrary to many other countries, this management was done by specific organization – sinking funds as they are known in economic history – such as the *Caisse d'Amortissement de la Dette Publique* – and later the *Caisse des Dépôts et Consignation* (Priouret, 1966).

World War I created a de facto dual mandate, as the Bank had to hold a massive amount of sovereign debt without disrupting its policy of accommodating private agents' liquidity shock. Conflicts of objectives followed, and it took some time before the operational framework could be adapted to the new situation, triggering tensions and tempers within the executive branch. The interwar period deeply changed the Bank, as the long struggle with the executive branch ended in the formal loss of independence in 1936 that was only to be recovered in 1992 with the prospect of the creation of the Euro.

This chapter views the history of the Bank of France from the point of view of how its operational framework addresses the loopholes of the French financial system. It shows that it took some time for the Bank to find a framework that enabled the financial and payment system to be made. This framework was influenced by negotiations for the periodic renewal of the Bank's charter, though before 1936 monetary policy decisions were in the hands of a council in which shareholders' representatives had the majority over government-nominated representatives. It was only with the nationalization of the Bank of France at the end of World War II that a new chapter of the Bank's history could be written. The Bank became actively involved in the regulation of the banking system, in the formulation of an active credit and monetary policy, but completely lost its independence in terms of policy rate decisions.

This chapter is organized as follows. The first part describes how contemporaries viewed the design of the central bank and its influence on the Bank charter. The second part describes the Bank's history in the long nineteenth century and proposes an assessment of its achievements, both in terms of financial and monetary stability. The third part focuses on the twentieth century, beginning with the outbreak of war in 1914.

6.1 Designing the Bank of France: Independence and Threats to the Payment System

It took three attempts and three failures before the creation of the Bank of France to create a bank that could monetize the debts of the other agents that could have been either banks, financial intermediaries or any non-financial firms except farmers. The lessons drawn explain both the governance of the Bank of France and a degree of independence from the government, similar to most central banks today. In this section, we explain how the creation of the Bank could have helped to stabilize the payment system in crisis time.

6.1.1 At Origin: Lessons from the Forerunners of Bank of France in Terms of Independence

The Bank of France was created in 1800 at the dawn of the Napoleonic Empire. Although Napoleon was one of the largest shareholders (Dauphin-Meunier, 1936; Bergeron, 1978), the Bank of France charter reflected the legacy of the troubled history of the French monetary system during the eighteenth century on two dimensions. First, it took three failures of note-issuing banks to establish the principle of independence of the Bank of France from any medium- to long-term government financing. Second, the Bank was created to fix the periodic threats to the smooth working of the payment system created by the use of two very different types of payment instrument: coins and bills of exchange. The high degree of independence from the government makes the charter of the Bank differ sharply from the charters of contemporary banks of issue like the Bank of England or the Bank of Austria in Vienna (Courtois, 1875). The Bank of France was not modeled on the Bank of Amsterdam either, because it secured the right to issue bearer notes.

In France, the first dramatic experience of a bank issuing bearer notes was the bank created by John Law in 1716. A Scot by birth but a European by choice (and maybe by chance, since he fled London to avoid a death sentence), John Law settled in Paris in 1714 and managed, in 1716, to convince the regent of King Louis XV to grant him the privilege of creating a bank endowed with the right to issue bearer notes. In 1718, he was also allowed to start a company managing the collection of government taxes and trade with Louisiana (Courtois, 1875). Various political and financial engineering arrangements transformed the enterprise into a gigantic attempt at restructuring the King's debt overhang away from the traditional mix of tax increases, partial defaults and monetary devaluation (Velde, 2007). The solution, it was thought, was to issue equity shares of a bank in order to finance the purchase of as much government debt as possible (Velde, 2003). In the meantime, the bank issued bearer notes that could be used in lieu of specie. Law never proved able to stabilize the price of banknotes. The experiment culminated in the crash of the system in 1720, with hyperinflation and demonetization of banknotes (Velde, 2009). The lesson learned was the separation of the management of sovereign debt from the management of the payment system (Du Pont de Nemours, 1806). Debt holding and amortization were later assigned to various forms of sinking funds (Lutfalla, 2006).

Various attempts were made to re-establish a note-issuing bank. In 1767 the *Caisse d'Escompte* was created with the aim of financing the King's court, but it was dissolved before any significant operations were implemented (Courtois, 1875, p. 69). A second attempt occurred in 1776, with the creation of the *Caisse d'Escompte* (again) by a coalition of Parisian merchant bankers. The *Caisse* discounted traders' bills but was also involved in the financing of the state. Interestingly, and contrary to other discounters, the *Caisse* could not be involved in the trade of any commodities, which insulated it from the ups-and-downs of this cyclical activity and reinforced its ability to discount in last resort in times of commodity price drops. It was only in 1783 that the government started to ask for support for short-term loans. During the Revolution, excessive government borrowing affected the *Caisse* very negatively, causing it to be dissolved in August 1793 (Courtois, 1875).

The free-market principles enshrined in the legislation of the Revolutionary regime left their imprint on banking regulation post-1793. The government did not want to choose its champion, and so it allowed several banks to be created. In Paris, at least four banks discounting bills against bearer notes were created in the aftermath of the stabilization of the hyperinflationary episode of the Assignats: the *Caisse des comptes courants* in 1796, the *Caisse d'escompte de commerce* in 1797, the *Comptoir Commercial* in 1800, but Courtois (1875) and Jacoud (1996) mentioned the existence of a few smaller banks, including the *Factorerie*. A similar bank was created in Rouen in 1798, with the *Societé générale du commerce de Rouen*. The Bank of France merged with the *Caisse des Comptes Courants* in January 1800. It secured the monopoly of notes issuance in Paris only in April 1803, when it merged with all other Parisian issuing banks.

It took a last round of dramatic events during the fall of 1805 to shape public belief in the contour of the Bank's independence vis-à-vis the government. The financial crisis then smashed many Parisian merchant bankers involved in financing the battles of the War of the Third Coalition, in which France was opposed to England, Austria and Russia. While Napoleon was defeating his opponents in Ulm and Austerlitz during the fall, the scheme used to finance his military campaign was crushed due to the failures of many suppliers of the army, including Ouvrard (Bergeron, 1978). The directors of the Bank, who had financed the supply of the army, relied on the discount of the Bank of France to roll over their liabilities. The implied crowding out on discounting to other traders triggered a public outcry against the Bank, while uncertainty over its ability to maintain convertibility triggered a run on the Bank and the first suspension of convertibility of notes into specie. Bank director Récamier resigned and the Bank's charter was rewritten. With the law of April 22, 1806, the shareholders lost their privileged access to the discount window, and renounced their right to choose the Bank's president.

The demise of the Napoleonic Empire did not impact the Bank's independence, despite the debt burden inherited by the monarchy and sizable reparations imposed by the victors (White, 2001). The sinking fund, and an appropriate management of public finance, allowed the smooth manipulation of the interest rate and sovereign debt consolidation (Oosterlinck, Ureche-Rangau, and Vaslin, 2014), insulating the Bank from the management of sovereign debt and making France an outlier in post-1815 central banking (Jobst and Ugolini, 2016).

The long-lasting lesson was that the Bank was endowed with a governance allowing a high degree of operational independence from fiscal authority. Here, we follow the current understanding of central bank independence in the day-to-day practice of central banks, which is that fiscal authorities do not influence monetary policy decisions, and, conversely, that monetary policy does not influence fiscal policy. Put differently, monetary policy is not designed to relax the long-term borrowing constraint of the government or to actively manage the interest rate of government debt. Money doctors of the times were well aware of this definition, as Dupont de Nemours (1806) was when he wrote about the need for strict independence from government financing, which nevertheless allowed the government to benefit from a reduction of its borrowing rate. As a result, the Bank had a "government" of three persons nominated by the executive branch. But it was still the shareholders, through the Bank's directors, who decided on which bills were discounted and those decisions had to be signed by the governor (Courtois, 1875).

6.1.2 At Origin: Rationale for the Founding of a Central Bank

What type of public benefit was expected from a privileged bank? What were the frictions that the Bank could solve that the market was not able to solve? There is no historical account of the intentions of the founding bankers of the Bank of France. Anyway, intentions may not reveal the function assigned by founders to the Bank of France. Monetary theory remained then in the realm of day-to-day banking and payment business. There are also few articulated monetary theories in pre-modern France that may have explained how the creation of a bank issuing banknotes might have helped to stabilize the payment system. We're left with hypothesizing the (theoretical) reason for which the Bank could have stopped the regular panics that plagued eighteenth-century French financial history.

Understanding the reason why banknotes could have tamed financial crises requires an understanding of the eighteenth-century payment system. In a context of limited use of checks, the bill of exchange was the main payment instrument (Gautier, 1839; Marsal, 1930). Discount banks traded bearer notes payable on demand at the bank of issue – in gold or silver coins – against bills of exchanges – a note payable at a specific location of an individual on a given date. When accepted in circulation, banknotes and bills of exchanges[1] were an effective, cost-saving payment instrument compared to coins. But banknotes and bills have different properties in terms of payment.

Issuing banknotes increased opportunities of risk sharing, compared to bills, for the following reason: when accepted by the payer, a bill could easily be sold to someone else. Each transfer of a bill (i.e. each discount) left the previous owners with a joint liability vis-à-vis the purchaser of the bill (the discounter), which was an acknowledgement of his commitment to pay the bill in case of default of the payer. Exercising the joint-liability clause was quick and easy. Cheating or defaulting on bill payment at maturity was harshly punished in the courts. This incentivized the careful screening and monitoring of counterparty risk, but limited bill endorsement within the confines of personal networks and financial intermediaries with an ability to monitor the debtors thus restricted risk sharing. The discounting of bills increased risk-sharing opportunities.

But banknotes were mostly thought of as a mechanism to stabilize the economy in times of commercial crisis (Juglar, 1862 [1889]). During these

---

[1] A bill is an order to pay addressed to an identified person (the payer) who has to pay some amount of money on a given day.

periods, the credit risk of some traders increased when commodity prices dropped. The pervasiveness of discount and endorsement in an economy that relied on bills as payment instruments transformed commodity price reversal into a correlated increase of the default probability of the endorsers. Coins were in short supply when the acceptability of bills in payment dropped. But minting coins was costly and time-consuming and the supply of gold and silver inelastic. The discount of bills was a substitution of a debt on a specific group of individuals against an "anonymous" banknote that had value as long as the credibility of the issuer was not questioned.

There is a clear analogy with the model of Gorton and Ordoñez (2014). During non-crisis times, when everybody is thought solvent, bills of exchanges are information-insensitive, as agents do not need to screen the quality of debtors or endorsers. Bills can circulate as means of payment and, hence, can be endorsed many times before maturity. But in periods of commercial crisis – to be precise, of drops in the prices of some commodities – the quality of some merchants' signatures starts being questioned, as everybody starts to worry about the impact of the commercial event on each merchant's credit risk. Bills become information-sensitive and people start screening the quality of endorsers, which reduces their liquidity on the market. A banknote, on the contrary, is information-insensitive also in times of commercial crisis if the bank is not involved in regular commercial business, as the value of banknotes is not correlated with commodity price movement in times of commercial tension. This relates to Gorton and Penacchi's (1990) idea that bank debt is liquid because it protects uninformed agents from the costs of information asymmetries.

6.2 The Quest for a Stable Payment and Financial System: The Long Nineteenth Century (1800–1914)

Cooling down panics triggered by commercial crises requires a clear and predictable framework to implement the Bank's policy. This explains how the operational policy framework was designed to address the loopholes of the contemporary payment system. The Bank faced two constraints. First, it had to decide which types of bills it wanted to purchase and against which guarantee, which amounted to choosing the share of the population with access to the discount window. Second, to secure the funding of its activity, the Bank had to reassure banknote holders of the credibility (viability) of its lending strategy. In nineteenth-century France, this meant ensuring the banknotes' convertibility into gold or silver coins.

6.2.1 The Monetary Regime

Banknotes represented a large share of the liabilities of the Bank. They were not interest-bearing, and their main advantage was their payment services – notably the fact that they saved on the risk of theft compared to specie, and their acceptability as a means of payment. In 1810, banknotes financed 44 percent of the Bank's total assets. In 1913, their share grew to 83 percent. In the meantime, demand deposits, which represented 18 percent of total assets in 1810, decreased to 8 percent in 1913. As a share of French GDP, Bank liabilities plateaued at about 2 percent in the 1820s–1840s before reaching 12–14 percent in the 1870s–1900s (see Figure 6.1).

Convertibility of banknotes in to gold and silver French coins was the norm. Post-1815, suspensions were explained by political events such as wars or revolutions. Absent any separation between an issuing and a banking department at the Bank of France, the suspension of banknote convertibility was seldom used as a management tool of crisis to allow a sharp increase of the discount activity. As with other banks who cannot force investors to hold their liabilities, the ability of the Bank of France to finance its discount activity rested on the stability of its funding model. Three important features of banknote convertibility could have impeded the ability of the Bank to deal with financial turmoil.

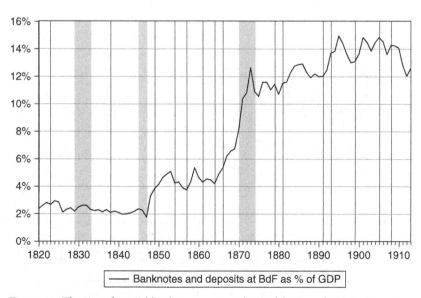

Figure 6.1 The size of central bank reserves as a share of the French GDP
Source: BoF (various years) annual reports and Toutain (1987) for GDP, Thorp (1926) for crisis years.

First, banknotes were not legal tender. The risk of a run on banknotes did not materialize except in 1805–06, but predecessors of the Bank of France were run due to fear of mismanagement of bank assets (Courtois, 1875) in a classic mechanism *à la* Diamond and Dybvig (1983). This provided an incentive for the Bank to preserve the quality of its balance sheet by purchasing only bills that could be paid at maturity.

Second, convertibility at agents' will was a commitment allowing agents to monitor the performance of the Bank in anchoring expectations on banknotes' purchasing power. In a context of little production of macro information, and because the stock of gold and silver was limited, it signaled the Bank's commitment to maintaining the banknotes' value through time and ultimately to not deviate from a non-inflationary path (Flandreau, 2008). As a result, the ratio of gold and silver reserves to banknotes was closely monitored by the public.

Third, variations in gold or silver prices abroad or in interest rates in offshore markets could have attracted coins abroad, which may have constrained banknote issuance (see Flandreau (1995, 2004) for a history of specie movement between London and Paris in mid-nineteenth century).

As shown in Figure 6.2, convertibility constraint was very high for much of the time. The value of the Bank's gold and silver reserves increased twenty times between 1820 and 1913.

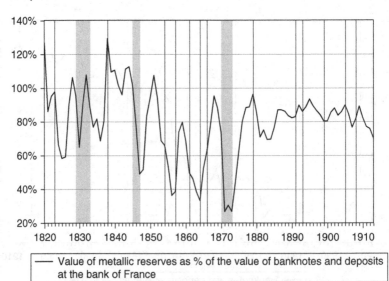

Figure 6.2 The convertibility ratio of the Bank of France (1820–1913)
Source: Authors using Bank of France balance sheet data.
Note: Vertical lines are years of stress on the money market according to Thorp-Business Annals.

Numerous papers explain how the peculiarities of the procedures used by the Bank to convert banknotes into gold or silver made it more costly for arbitrageurs to convert banknotes into specie. This is known as "gold devices" in the literature. These devices aimed to make it more complicated to exchange banknotes against coins at the Bank's offices. Flandreau (1996a) has shown that in a bimetallic system, the availability of two metals to reimburse banknotes allows the Bank to choose the metal that is in excess supply, thus adding a layer of arbitrage cost. The Bank used various tools to discourage the outflow of metallic reserves during bad times, such as reimbursing banknotes in silver rather than in gold when France was legally only using gold (Contamin and Denise, 1999).

Part of the recent historical literature studies the monetary policy autonomy that the Bank enjoyed. The issue has been framed as attempting to answer how the convertibility of notes into gold and silver (the gold standard rule) constrained the Bank's policy and how gold devices helped to relax the constraint. Bloomfield (1959) has (re)introduced the idea that free convertibility may have constrained central bank monetary policy autonomy during the gold standard. Economists have framed this issue as the Mundell trilemma, which said that in a world of free capital movements and fixed exchange rates caused by convertibility into gold, there is no monetary policy autonomy for a central bank. Within this context, gold devices have been thought of as a tool used by the Bank of France to gain some policy autonomy. Notice also that the monetary regime could have rendered arbitrage stickier. Friedman (1990a) and Flandreau (2002) argue that bimetallism also created space for monetary policy autonomy by enlarging the band inside which the exchange rate fluctuated compared to a gold standard only regime. This explains why Friedman saw the decision by France to leave the gold standard in 1873 as a crime: the reduction of the band of fluctuations induced by the move to gold must have reduced monetary policy autonomy (Friedman, 1990b; Flandreau, 1996b). Contamin (2003) describes how the "politics of species" contributed to monetary policy autonomy during the gold standard period of 1880–1913. Bordo and McDonald (2005) use an econometric model to estimate that the Bank was thus able to reduce its policy rate by about 100 base points compared to foreign interest rates (see also Tullio and Wolters, 2003; Bazot, Bordo, and Monnet 2016).

6.2.2 The Discount Operations and Lending of Last Resort:
Learning to Cope with Crises

Agents could also resort to the Bank for discount or for Lombard credit, which is a repo agreement in which a loan is granted against the guarantee of marketable securities with an agreement that those securities will be repurchased in a fixed period of time (usually three months). Discounting was by far a much more important activity than collateralized lending. It represented on average 91 percent of central bank operations during the period 1826–1913. The operation involved agents in need of cash asking for the discount of a bill by the Bank of France, which meant that the Bank bought the claim at its nominal value deduction made of a discount that was determined by the residual maturity of the bill and the discount rate. The discount rate was set by the Bank and applied, according to the 1808 decree that organized the statute of the Bank, indiscriminately in any of the places where the Bank had an office. This provision forbade the Bank to adjust the discount rate to local conditions.

The Bank implemented its monetary policy as a standing facility (it was the traders that asked for refinancing not the Bank) and through a floor system (the Bank rate was the floor compared to the market rate). The main advantage was that the Bank did not have to calibrate its reaction to the liquidity or credit situation, but only needed to accommodate any demand from solvent traders as long as the convertibility of its banknotes in to gold or silver was not questioned. This "as long as" was of course a big "if," and it took a while before the Bank managed to free itself from the convertibility issue. Much of the history of the success and failure of the lending of last resort function during the first half of the nineteenth century is tied to the Bank's ability to manage the credibility of its lending of last resort function while maintaining the credibility of the convertibility of its banknotes.

Because the discount is an outright purchase and may reduce the Bank's profit, the Bank charter aligned risk management incentives with shareholders' interests. Assessing the credit quality of bills was delegated to a discount committee using information collected by the Bank and verified by supervisors (Nishimura, 2015; Avaro and Bignon, 2017). The discount committee comprised three individuals chosen from the shareholders of the Bank. It was monitored by the portfolio committee, composed of board members. Finally the selection of the discount committee was made by three shareholders (*censeurs*) who were elected by the shareholders. A special body of supervisors – the *inspecteur* – monitored the collection of information on counterparties to the discount. This system of monitoring the operational risk associated with discounting came to an end only when discounting was stopped in the early 1990s.

Risk management was eased by three levels of guarantee. First, each bill was payable not only by the debtor but also by any agent who had endorsed it. Second, both the endorsers and the debtor pledged their wealth and their right to manage an independent business as a guarantee for the good end of the transaction. Third, the Bank was, by law, required to only accept discount bills that were endorsed by at least three individuals who were notoriously solvent.

The discount policy of the Bank went through three different phases before 1914. The first period spans 1815 to 1850. The Bank followed the policy advocated by Du Pont de Nemours, of rationing discounts when too many banknotes flew back to be converted (Ramon, 1929). In the 1850s, the Bank implemented a continental equivalent of Bagehot's (1873) dictum by lending freely against good collateral during normal times and increasing interest rates during crises (Bignon, Flandreau, and Ugolini, 2012). The last phase opened in the 1870s, when the Bank continued this policy but avoided increasing the policy rate in times of crisis.

Before 1850, the Bank's crisis management was criticized by many. During the crises of 1806, 1830 and 1847–48, public outcry grew louder against the Bank's policy of rationing discount when convertibility was at risk. Economists and politicians discussed two main solutions to this issue. Some blamed the monopoly position of the Bank, making France an active spot of free banking theories (Fazy, 1830; Coquelin, 1859; see Domin, 2007 for a survey). Others advocated increasing either the Bank capital to increase the Bank loss absorption capacity or the gold and silver reserves to relax the convertibility constraint. The failure of the Bank to accommodate more discount also led to the founding of new institutions such as the municipal "discount houses" (*Comptoirs d'escompte*).[2]

Yet the problem was not one of inaction (see Ramon (1929) for a history of the management of financial crises by the Banque de France). Quantitative proof is given by Figure 6.3, which plots the size of the increase of the Bank discount volume in times of crisis. The top panel shows that it was usual for the Bank to increase its volume of refinancing by 20 percent. The bottom panel shows that this pattern unraveled a huge increase of the permanent volume of discount, underlining a regime change in the 1870s.

The Bank also changed its operational framework to make it more inclusive (Leclerq, 2010). For example, in 1834 the Bank started additional discounting during the last two days of the month (Beaubeau, 2004). In

---

[2] See Delamathe (1848). The foundation of the Comptoir National d'Escompte in 1848 is said to have been inspired by the role assigned to the various *Comptoirs d'escompte* during the 1830 crisis.

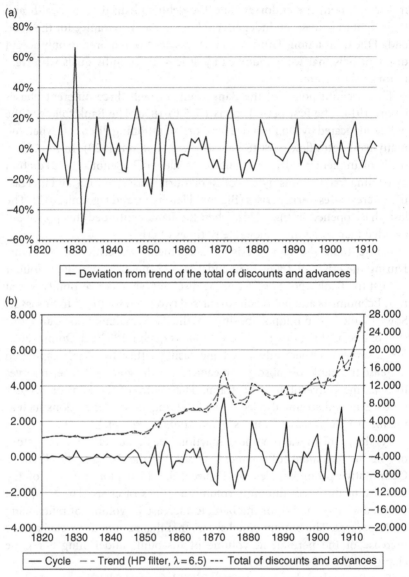

Figure 6.3 Deviation from trend of discounted bills and advances on securities at the Bank of France (top) and trend and cycle of CB discounts and advances (bottom)
Source: INSEE statistical yearbook (1946), retrospective part (pp. 143*–144*).

1837, it offered daily services at discount windows and started opening branches outside Paris (in reaction to growing pressure by local business communities to benefit from the services of a local bank of issue).

Access to the lender of last resort broadened after 1836, when the Bank started opening branches outside Paris.[3] The policy of branch opening translated into an increase of eligible collateral and a massive broadening of the proportion of agents eligible for the discount window (Bignon and Jobst, 2017). The Bank policy of geographic expansion intensified in the 1850s when the Periere tried to compete with the Bank of France in issuing banknotes.[4] By 1913, the inhabitants of 218 cities and their surrounding areas were allowed to open an account at the Bank to access the discount window. In 1913, 86,200 people had taken this opportunity (Lescure, 2003, p. 139). According to Courcelle-Seneuil (1840), this reduced the "exorbitant" interest rate that some had to pay in stressed times in cities where the Bank was not present and that could have reached 24 percent per annum, according to Gille (1970).

6.2.3 Measuring the Achievements in Terms of Financial Stability

Schwartz (1986) argues in favor of central bank active monetary policy management when the payment system is threatened, with the goal of avoiding a liquidity squeeze. Many structural changes in the financial sector make it impossible to construct comprehensive and century-long indices of financial (in)stability. No single price or interest rate provided a common metric to measure instability.

The structural transformation of the financial system – from private, short-term finance to a mix of public and long-term securities-cum-bank-intermediated bills of exchange – forbade any attempt to consider a class of financial intermediaries (such as banks or the stock exchanges) as representative of a century-long history. Finally, the absence of a legal regulation of the entry into banking before 1941 explains why we lack comprehensive quantitative information on banks.

To assess century-long measures of financial stability in a changing environment, we rely on three sets of statistics: (1) the number of financial crises per decade; (2) the gross default rate of financial intermediaries; (3) the delinquency rate on the most used financial instrument. Table 6.1

---

[3] The extension of the network of branches by the Banque de France followed a first attempt made during the Napoleonic period (see Pruneaux, 2009 for details).

[4] On the daily discount and the Periere, see Leclerq (2010). On the local issuing banks, see Gille (1970).

Table 6.1 *The number of crises per decade in France 1820–1910*

Decade	(1) Thorp's "Business annals"	(2) Juglar's criteria	(3) Peaks of 3-months' implicit interest rate	(4) Drops in stock index	Very large drop of stock index
1820s	2	1	3	2	1
1830s	2	3	3	2	1
1840s	2	1	3	1	2
1850s	2	1	3	2	1
1860s	3	1	3	2	0
1870s	3	1	3	3	0
1880s	2	1	3	1	1
1890s	2	1	1	1	0
1900s	2	2	3	2	0

Note: Authors' compilation using Table 6A.1 in the Appendix.

shows that the number of crises did not vary widely during the century, except in the 1890s, with about two to three per decade.

The number of financial crises is identified using four criteria. We first rely on the informed judgment of contemporary observers or academics, notably the synthesis of the mentions of financial crises in business annals compiled by former NBER director William Thorp (1926)[5] and the dating of financial crises by economists Clément Juglar (1862 [1889]) and Siegfried (1906).[6] We also identify crises by the years during which the three-month offshore interest rate of monetary conditions in Paris is so high that it lies one standard deviation above its secular average.[7] Indeed, when liquidity disappeared in Paris, traders relied more on offshore markets to borrow. Finally, we measure the number of large drops

[5] The accounts used were official documents, reports by contemporary observers and students of economic history, periodicals, pamphlets, and books. The date corresponds to years for which there is a mention that "Money was tight," or "Money very tight," or "Financial panic," or "Money tightens."

[6] Juglar was praised for his forecast in a newspaper article of the 1857 crisis, evidencing his claim that the study of the evolution of the key items of the balance sheet of the Banque de France enable the crises to be anticipated (Niehans, 1992, p. 548). He labeled those crises commercial, since the main financial instrument was the bills of exchange and the main financial activity was the discount of those bills by the banks.

[7] The method for computing those implicit interest rates relied on the use of the prices in British pounds of spot (three-days sight) and forward (three months) bills of exchange on Paris in London. There are two components in these prices: an exchange rate component

of the Paris stock market index either by drops of detrended index that followed a steady increase, or by drops larger than one standard deviation.[8] According to this last criterion, the severity of financial crises decreased over time as no crisis, apart from one in the 1870–1913 period, was larger than one standard deviation.

The default rate of financial intermediaries allows us to assess the magnitude of financial crises. There are very few records of systemic banking panic, partly due to the lack of development of deposit banking – Frenchmen kept their wealth in cash or in savings banks (François-Marsal, 1928) – but also because panics are endogenous to the broadness of lending of last resort and the Bank asset/liability management. We know from historian Gille (1959, pp. 324, 370) that the banking system collapsed both during the 1830 and the 1847–48 crises. We know from White (2007, p. 115) that the crash of 1882 "presented the Bourse with its worst crisis of the nineteenth century."

Figure 6.4, which plots the default rate of financial intermediaries, exhibits an upward trend between 1820 and 1847, which echoes Cameron's (1967) account the failure of systemic financial intermediaries such as Jacques Laffite in the 1830s–1840s. Starting in the 1870s, the default rate dropped, which suggests that the financial system became more stable in the last part of the century. Therefore, although the financial market crashed when some big banks failed in 1882 and 1889 (Bouvier, 1961; Bonin, 2006; Hautcoeur, Riva, and White, 2014), those failures occurred in a financially more stable economy.

This diagnosis is confirmed by the evolution of the delinquency rate on the bills, plotted on Figure 6.5 as the share of stamped bills (Roulleau, 1914).[9] The level declines from 5 percent in the 1840s to about 2 percent in the 1850s, before decreasing to 0.8 percent in 1912. On average, excluding

and an interest rate component. Following Flandreau et al. (2009) and assuming that exchange rate expectations are constant, the ratio of the spot over the forward prices is an estimate of the short-term (implicit) interest rate on Paris.

[8] We use Arbulu's (2006) index of stock prices and derive the deviations from the trend using a Hodrick-Prescott filter with λ set equal to 6.25.

[9] The number of bills unpaid at maturity is known as the protestation data (*protêt*), which was the only legal action that allowed the creditor to activate the guarantee created by the joint-liability clause. The protestation also allowed the bills bearer to go to court in an attempt to recuperate the amount due, provided the characteristics of the bill fulfilled legal requirements. For Articles 162 and 173 of the commercial code, see Bravard-Veyrières and Demangeat (1862, p. 421) and Dalloz (1825, p. 179). For a protest to be heard in court, a bill had to contain the following information: the location and the identity of the borrower, the amount to be paid, the date of the payment, the place at which payment would occur, and the means of payment.

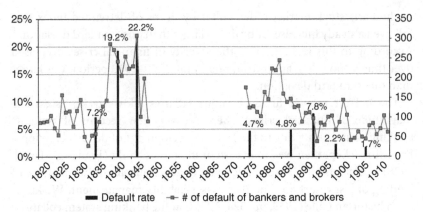

Figure 6.4 Number of and rate of default of financial intermediaries, France (1820–1913)

Source: Defaults between 1820 and 1849 are from National Archives (F20 720–1/2) and between 1875 and 1913 are from *Compte général de la justice civile et commerciale*. The number of financial intermediaries are from Hoffman et al. (2015) using Annuaire Didot-Bottin except 1856 (French census), 1892 (Plessis, 1999, p. 205) and 1906 (Nishimura and Yago, 2006, p. 200).

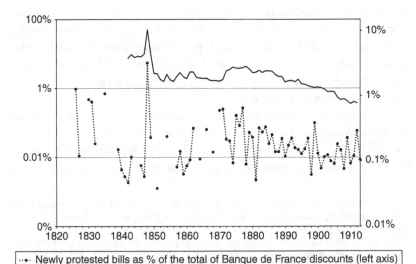

Figure 6.5 Delinquency rate of bills as percent of stamped bills of exchanges in France (1850–1912)

Source: Author's computation using Roulleau (1914).

1847–48, there was a 1.8 percent chance of unpaid bills at maturity, which is two times lower than, e.g., the average delinquency on consumer US credit card loans between 1985 and 2011.[10] This low level suggests that discounters made fewer errors when screening bills, in line with the major improvements of the organization of the banking and payment system (Vidal, 1910; Cameron, 1961; Leclerq, 2010).

6.2.4 Measuring Achievements in Terms of Monetary Stability

Before 1914, the Bank did not have an explicit inflation target, but the convertibility of banknotes into gold and silver effectively acted as an anchor to price expectations. No statistical office produced a price index that could act as an observable measure of the achievement of the central bank in terms of price stability. This complicates an assessment of the Bank's achievement in terms of price stability. Any conclusion is therefore highly speculative and always disputable. We used the cost of living index computed by Levy-Leboyer and Bourguignon (1985). Figure 6.6 reveals a

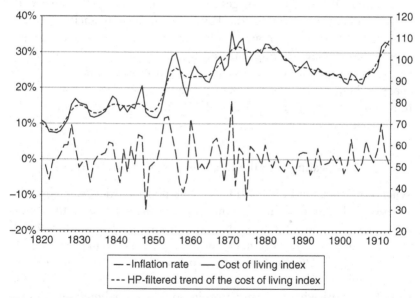

Figure 6.6 The French price index, 1820–1913, its trend and the inflation rate
Source: Trend is HP filtered with parameter Lambda equal to 6.5, inflation is computed as the first difference of the cost of living index.

---

[10] See www.federalreserve.gov/releases/chargeoff/delallsa.htm. Accessed January 9, 2018.

continuous increase of the cost of living during the 1820–70 period. During the forty years that followed 1870, it decreased quite continuously before increasing again during the 1906–13 decade.

The average inflation rate – computed as the year-on-year price difference of the cost of living index is positive and leveled at 0.55 percent during the 1821–1913 period. This level is lower than the contemporary target of modern central banks, but it reveals that the Bank of France delivers on achieving monetary stability. The median inflation rate is negative at –0.2 percent. Inflation is quite volatile, with an average of –3 percent in years of negative inflation and 4.3 percent in years of positive inflation. The average inflation of the 1820–70 period is, however, more volatile than during the latter part of the century. The cost of this quite high volatility is difficult to assess, as we know little about the degree of price rigidity in those economies.

6.3 1914–2001: The Tumultuous Road to the Loss of Independence and Its Recovery: World Wars and Post-war Debt Overhangs

So far, the available evidence suggests that the second half of the nineteenth century in France was characterized by a more resilient financial system in a situation of (relative) monetary stability. We have suggested that the operational framework implemented by the Bank was a contributing factor. In this section, we discuss how the two World Wars were a game changer, both by forcing the Bank to radically change its operational framework and because they led to the Bank losing its operational independence from the government.

6.3.1 Dealing with the Debt Overhang of World War I

When war broke out in July 1914, the Bank policy quickly adapted as the situation only required the implementation of the policy used to address financial crises. Indeed, because the war froze international transactions, payments could no longer be made and the balance sheets of private agents became illiquid. The closure of the stock exchanges – which were re-opened only during the winter of 1914 – was another reason for the Bank to propose what the market could no longer do: liquifying balance sheets by exchanging illiquid assets against banknotes. Massive lending of last resort support was the solution to avoid a wave of massive failures. As a further step, various legislations were enacted to suspend indefinitely the payments due.

The war also led the Bank to be more involved in government financing. The first changes were benign. The Bank extended emergency liquidity advances to the government and launched public campaigns to repatriate gold and silver back to the Bank coffers in order to finance the purchase of foreign materials. But soon the situation became complicated, as the government chose to delay the tax increases necessary to finance war expenses into the post-war period (Mouré, 2002). Most expenses were financed by monetary creation and, to a lesser extent, by long-term borrowing, which led to a massive increase of the money supply and the inflation rate (Blancheton, 2001).

When the war ended in 1918, the Bank's main policy goal was to organize the return to pre-war monetary stability. This required restoring the convertibility of banknotes into gold, and hence modifying the Bank balance sheet which was loaded by short-term government debt. Using the threat of not renewing the advances made, the Bank secured an agreement with the government in 1920 in which the government committed to a gradual reimbursment of the war debt to the Bank. But the government had hard fiscal choices to make, since it not only had to reimburse the Bank but also to compensate wounded soldiers and widows for the consequences of their loss, and, since most of the battles happened on French territory, to finance the reconstruction of numerous areas in the north and east of the country that had been devastated by four years of war.

No government found a majority in parliament to prioritize reimbursement of the debt owed to the Bank over the costs of reconstruction. More than that, the reconstruction involved an increase of government expenses and hence an increased reliance on borrowing from the Bank. In such a situation of deep fiscal crisis, the government had to choose between defaulting on its debt and devaluing the currency vis-à-vis gold or using some institutional scheme to consolidate the public debt and increase taxation to repay it gradually. The Bank campaigned publicly in the press against any devaluation of francs into gold. Between 1918 and 1926, all governments, from the left or the right, aligned with the Bank in refusing to default and devalue.

The interwar years were not years of institutional creativity in terms of operational framework. The main innovation was the creation of a trading desk to intervene on the forex market. Before 1926, no serious attempt was made either to consolidate the floating debt into long-term bonds or to create or endow a public institution with the goal of holding the debt in surplus. Everybody denied the severity of the situation, and repeated like a mantra that the French franc had to be convertible into gold again, and that the fiscal crisis would be solved by the payment of the reparations enacted by the Treaty of Versailles.[11] The reparations became the excuse used to avoid confronting the fiscal crisis. The debt was not consolidated, which weakened the government by exposing it to hard fiscal choices in times of crisis, to the goodwill of its financiers and, notably, to the Bank of France. In the meantime, various political crises precipitated regular debt and exchange rate crises were characterized by the threat of default of the government, caused by concern that the floating debt would not be rolled over and, hence, by the threat of depreciation of the exchange rate vis-à-vis the pound and the dollar.

With a balance sheet loaded by a significant (and growing) amount of public debt, the Bank had to navigate in unknown territory. It was not helped by the existence of a clear monetary theory on how to deal with situations of fiscal dominance. The lessons of how all central banks had managed the sovereign debt overhang of the post-Napoleonic period were not remembered. The Bank was not aided by the view, among the community of central bankers, that the exit strategy from debt overhang had to be implemented very quickly, and that it involved a quick restoration of fiscal discipline. History had been forgotten. Against this background, it is not unfair to write that the Bank's policy was, more often than not, characterized by a denial of the policy issues posed by the new situation and by some political infighting in an attempt to impose the Bank's view on the public.

The directors felt uncomfortable with the changes in the Bank's policy that this debt load must have involved in order to efficiently smooth the adverse consequences of the fiscal crisis. The debt crisis crystallized regularly in the periodic conflict between the Bank directors and the government, involving renegotiations on the level of the ceiling of Bank debt holding. The Bank resisted all increases as it aimed at restoring the pre-war discount system, in which credit lines to the government were limited and

---

[11] World War I was also a game changer in terms of post-war management. The Treaty of Versailles revisited the old idea that the defeated had to pay a tribute to the victors but with two twists. First, that this was reparation for the prejudice suffered and not a tribute to the victors. Second, that the international community, and not the victors, was the broker of the treaty, in charge of making sure that the treaty was enforced. Those two moves proved hard to implement for two reasons. First, disputes arose as to the evaluation of the level of destruction suffered and of the defeated power's ability to pay. Endless international discussions followed, which led to the enactment of two main amendments to the initial amount of money to be paid in reparation. Second, in a world that required international cooperation, diverging interests created a very divisive international community.

seldom used. More than that, before 1914 the Bank had seldom intervened on the sovereign debt market to support interest rates. In the interwar period, it resisted fiercely the implementation of any intervention in the foreign exchange market (before 1925) and any open market operations, even after 1928 when the Bank was under mounting international pressure from the Bank of England and the New York Fed to reduce the interest rate differential between their currencies and the franc (Mouré, 2002; Barbaroux, 2014).

Between 1920 and 1926, the Bank wanted the return of the franc to the gold convertibility rate, and made this the ultimate goal of its policy. But the public interpreted the Bank's policy by looking at the evolution of the monetization of public debt shown in the weekly press's disclosure of the main items of the Bank balance sheet. More than once, this disclosure fueled political struggles and pressure to rebalance of some budget. This, in turn, forced the Bank to push even further in the public debate for fiscal consolidation, which was supported with calls by politicians for the payment of reparations.

For lack of a clear conceptual framework on how to deal with debt overhang without imposing deflation, hence stabilizing the public debt yield and encouraging the rolling over of floating debt, the Bank began to publicly voice its concern with fiscal policy. This was an attempt to restore its pre-war monetary policy and protect the exchange rate. It became heavily involved in the political debate on the need for fiscal and debt consolidation. It insisted on the need for deflation to adjust for France's lack of competitiveness. It took stances in the debates between the left and the right, and tried to shape public opinion by regularly subsidizing the press to publish articles favoring the need for fiscal discipline and a quick return to gold (Jeanneney, 1984; Mouré, 2002). Some of the Bank's directors, who were also active lawmakers, were especially active in the public debate, and were sometimes influential in securing the dismissal of finance ministers or even force the resignation of the government leader (Jeanneney, 1976).

Many searched for a scapegoat to blame. Some blamed the franc depreciation on capital flight, but, as shown by Hautcoeur and Sicsic (1999), it was the threat of a capital levy that mattered most. Exchange rate crises were also blamed on foreign speculators (Mouré, 2002), and everybody blamed Germany for defaulting on its sovereign debt. The growing political crisis led to acrimonious relations with the Bank and a governor was even dismissed for lack of support of the government. Yet the regular conflict of the Bank with government officials became public, which led critics to voice their concerns in newspaper headlines. In 1924/25, with a government unwilling to increase the ceiling, the Bank even went as far as publishing faked balance sheets, to hide the fact that its support to the government exceeded the ceiling. The Bank's credibility was hit, even though most of the blame was directed at the center-left government, which ultimately resigned.

It was not until 1926 that French politicians stopped relying on the idea that the financial costs of the war would be covered by reparations. The exchange rate crisis had become so severe that a consensus formed on the need for a government of national unity in order to vote in tax increases and secure the cooperation of the Bank of France by adopting an agenda consistent with that of the Bank's directors. The franc started to appreciate against the pound. During the two years between 1926 and 1928, the debate raged within the media and the Bank with regard to the level at which the franc must be stabilized. Some argued in favor of returning to pre-war parity, while others underlined the depressing effect of the appreciation on the competitiveness of French exports. In 1928 the franc was devalued by 80 percent and made convertible into gold. Sicsic (1992) has shown that at this level, the franc was clearly undervalued.

6.3.2 The Great Depression and the Loss of Independence

Following the stabilization of 1926–28, the economy started booming and foreign reserves flew in massively, mostly because of the repatriation of capital that had fled during the inflationary period (Sicsic and Villeneuve, 1993). The Bank sterilized part of its reserves. Some UK and US contemporaneous critics had blamed the Bank of France for sterilizing capital inflows rather than expanding the money supply, thus relieving the pressures exerted by capital outflows on the pound and the dollar. Eichengreen (1996) explains that this led many developed countries to devalue in the early 1930s, and ultimately led to the collapse of the international monetary system. He explains that the interwar period was rigged by a lack of cooperation between the central banks of the Gold Bloc (Switzerland, Belgium, France, and the Netherlands) and those of countries with a deficit of balance of payments. Flandreau (1995, 1997) and Mouré (2002), however, argued that central bank cooperation was a myth already in the nineteenth century, and hence offered a skeptical view on the idea that a lack of international cooperation was instrumental during the Great Depression when compared with previous financial crises.

Between 1930 and 1933, France suffered from a massive banking crisis that unfolded in three waves of banking panic (Lacoue-Labarthe, 2005). During the fall and winter of 1930–31, and following the failure of the Oustric bank, many major regional banks were hit by a run on deposits (Bonin, 2000). Then, in the fall of 1931, the fourth national deposit bank was hit by a run that depleted it of 50 percent of its deposits in three months and ultimately led to its liquidation. Following this run, many other regional banks failed. Finally, the third wave started in February 1932 and again hit many regional deposit banks. As a result, the aggregate number of bank branches decreased by 15 percent in 1932 compared to 1931. The Bank of France offered support to the banks in liquidity stress but also directly to the economy by accommodating many of the direct discounts, which in the context of the 1930s consisted of discounts made by the central bank to non-bank agents. Already in the nineteenth century, direct discounts were the main instrument used by the Bank of France to inject money during periods of credit contraction, as direct discounts allow for neutralizing of the adverse impact on the money supply of a wave of massive bank failures (Friedman and Schwartz, 1963; Bernanke, 1983). Consistent with the role of direct discount in the transmission of an accommodative policy, Bridji (2013) has shown against Sauvy (1984) that the banking crisis had a depressing effect on the economy mainly through the increasing cost of financial intermediation *à la Bernanke* and not through a contraction of the money supply.

During the banking crisis, the monetary policy remained tight in the sense that interest rates were still used to manage the exchange rate. The Bank wanted to protect convertibility from the franc in a world in which all currencies had gone off-gold and had massively depreciated. The reaction of the Bank to devaluation abroad was to publicly and fiercely oppose any devaluation and, hence, the deflation occurring in foreign countries was ultimately imported. The rationales of this stubbornness are still debated, but it is hard to overlook the fact that the willingness to preserve the Bank's credibility may have played a role. After all, the discourse on gold was the main argument used by the Bank in its public intervention to force fiscal and debt consolidation. After 1932, and the devaluation of the dollar and the pound, pressure on the Bank grew in the press and among politicians to devalue and de-anchor the franc from gold. But again the Bank managed to convince politicians to stick to a policy of strong currency. It formed, with Belgium, Switzerland, and the Netherlands, the Gold Bloc, though the Bloc was not endowed with any tool that would have allowed it to defend the gold conversion. In the end, the economies of the Gold Bloc did not resist the relative overvaluation of their currencies and deflation kicked off. All countries moved off-gold, devalued, and imposed capital controls. France was the last to devalue in early October 1936. As a result, France entered the Great Depression in the mid-1930s when all other countries that had moved off-gold were on the road to the recovery.

During the interwar period, on two major policy issues, the Bank had taken a public policy stance against a government on a topic that was partly foreign to monetary policy and financial stability and had defended it fiercely in the media (Jeanneney, 1976; Mouré, 2002). As noticed by Mouré (2002), this had made the Bank a target for criticism. Columnists started arguing that the Bank was trying to influence the vote in favor of some political parties (Dauphin-Meunier, 1936). In the meantime, deflation had taken hold, partly because of foreign currency devaluation and partly because of the banking crisis. Bankers who had failed started voicing criticism of the Bank's policy of direct discount, accusing the lender of last resort of having participated in the weakening of the banking system (see, for example, Charpenay, 1939).

The failure to deliver on the economy and the regular intervention of the Bank in the political debate backfired on the Bank's directors with the law of July 24, 1936. The defense of the politics of internal deflation and of gold parity in the media had left the Bank exposed to public anger. Following the election of a coalition of left parties in 1936, the governor was dismissed and the governance of the Bank modified. The 1936 change of statute did not nationalize the Bank – the capital was still in the hands of the shareholders – but (1) it forbade the Bank's directors to be elected as lawmakers in order to increase their ability to form a coalition in parliament, and (2) it changed the composition of the board by removing bankers from it and replacing them with representatives of the economic and social interests of the country, as well as government officials from the Treasury. As Gonjo (2011) noticed, the change of governance was the beginning of an era of lost operational independence. Government officials and the Bank's governors (nominated by the government) now had the majority in the main council that decided on monetary policy. As a result, interest rate decisions were taken at the Treasury rather than at the Bank board as before. The choice of governors also became more political, with evidence of greater correlation between changes of government and changes of governors. Margairaz (2011) noted that in the decade between 1935 and 1947, five different governors ruled the Bank. He also remarked on the greater political acquaintances of governors with the color of the government.

6.3.3 The Road to Modernity: Inflation and Monetary Policy in Post-World War II France

After the 1936 change of governance, and under the pressure caused by the general atmosphere of rearmament in Europe, both monetary and fiscal policy became more accommodative, starting in 1938 (Mouré, 2002). Open market operations were allowed by a 1938 law (Saint-Marc, 1983). After the outbreak of war in 1939, and the Occupation that followed the capitulation of June 1940, France had to pay each year, between 1940 and 1944, the equivalent of 35 percent of its GDP to Germany (Occhino, Oosterlinck, and White, 2008). This and the blow on productive capacity triggered by the burden of many war prisoners weighed heavily on the budget: the fiscal deficit jumped from 21 percent of the GDP in 1939 to 57 percent in 1943. As a result, and despite active price and wage controls, and a very active black market for consumer goods (Debu-Bridel, 1947; Mouré, 2010) fueled by inflation, the price level increased by 155 percent between 1940 and 1944 (Patat and Luftalla, 1986).

In terms of the management of debt overhang, the political lessons of the post-World War I situation were learned. The government chose to not default on its debt, but consolidated it in January 1945. The Treasury organized a closed circuit in which deposit banks were incentivized to use deposits to hold the sovereign debt. The main advantage was the avoidance of discussion in the media on the opportunity of increasing the ceiling on sovereign debt held by the Bank. Finally, price controls had created forced saving that agents kept in overly liquid portfolios (Saint-Marc, 1983). Contrary to other countries, the government did not cut liquid holdings by forcing deflation through a conversion of banknotes (Gurley, 1953). Inflation reached 50 percent in the late 1940s, reducing massively the interest rate burden.

The financial system was entirely reorganized to prevent a fiscal crisis degenerating into a debt crisis. In December 1945, the Bank of France and all deposit banks were nationalized. The regulation of the banking system was written such that the government-owned banks and other financial intermediaries had an incentive to subscribe and hold Treasury bills. A National Credit Council, presided over by the minister of finance, decided the aggregated volume of credit and its allocation to each bank.

Monetary policy fell into a regime of fiscal dominance. The interest rate paid on the public debt became the main constraint in the determination of monetary policy until well into the 1960s (Gonzo, 2011). More than half of the deficit was financed by the monetization of public debt by the Bank. In

1944, all assets held by the Bank were claims on the Treasury. The Bank was still in charge of determining monetary policy to limit inflation, but the organization of the financial system converged toward the ministry of finance. Hence, in the few conflicts over objectives that popped up in the immediate aftermath of the war between monetary policy and credit or fiscal policies, the Bank lost (see Gonzo, 2011).

The operational framework of monetary policy was changed on two dimensions. First, the instruments of refinancing were actively used as an instrument of industrial policy, notably to boost construction activity and to encourage external trade (Koch, 1983). The balance sheet of the Bank changed massively. Medium-term claims became important in the Bank balance sheet, and short-term rediscounting leveled at 8 percent only in 1968. The Bank defined two main (but impaired) policy rates. The main rate was the discount rate on bills of exchanges, but with a lower upper volume limit defined at the bank level and fixed below the money market rate.

Second, the segmentation of the banking system radically changed the way the Bank implemented its monetary policy. The Bank applied bank-specific ceilings on the various discount facilities to influence the behavior of the banking system (Patat and Luftalla, 1986), thus making quantitative instruments an important instrument of the transmission of monetary policy (Monnet, 2014). To manage the liquidity of the banking sector, the Bank set fifteen different refinancing and preferential rates. There were three preferential discount rates on construction activity, two preferential rates on export, and the pension on private bills was potentially compelled to a "super-hell" rate, equal to the discount rate plus 2.5 percent.

The consequence, in terms of the organization of the financing of the economy, were long lasting (Patat and Luftalla, 1986). The level of interest rate was so low that French people switched their savings from bonds and stocks to very liquid instruments such as banknotes (that were very useful to pay for black market trade) or inflation-protected assets such as gold or gold-indexed government bonds. The French economy became bank-based. There was more public intervention, more regulation, and more segmentation. The banking license was introduced in 1941. Banks were specialized in the financing of a specific sector or a specific activity (e.g. mortgages, consumption loans, loans to the small and medium-sized enterprises). Many distortions followed in the allocation of savings (Saint-Marc, 1983).

During the 1960s, the Bank's policy started being heavily criticized for its complexity and for creating inefficient market segmentation that limited price discovery on the money market (Saint-Marc, 1983). Episodes of quantitative tightening were often bypassed by banks, notably by using the preferential rediscounting facilities dedicated to construction and export activities. But mostly, this system was hardly compatible with a policy aimed at fostering the free movement of capital flows that trade liberalization and the European project fostered. Various amendments to the post-war policy were implemented, all with the aim of making the system less regulated and more market based (Patat and Luftalla, 1986). The publication of the report written by Marjolin, Sadrin, and Wormser (1968) marked a "monetarist" turn of the Bank (Monnet, 2015). Written by a Bank official, a university professor, and a representative of the Treasury, this report reads as a market-driven proposal aimed at: (1) simplifying and reviving a genuine money market, (2) setting the discount rate above the fine-tuned money market rate to insulate retail and business interest rates from variations in monetary policy, and (3) focusing on Treasury bills and bankers' promissory notes to transmit the monetary policy. Many of those reforms were implemented in the 1970s, which ultimately led to the financial "big bang" of the mid-1980s, characterized by de-segmentation and a lower grasp of regulation on the functioning of the banking system.

The regime of fiscal dominance and regular deficits of the balance of payment meant that the franc was repeatedly exposed to exchange rate crises. In the Bretton Woods system of fixed exchange rates, this translated into devaluations or official changes of parity. The main currency that appreciated was the Deutsche mark of West Germany. Popular outcry accompanied those devaluations, whose long-term consequences in terms of economic efficiency are still to be assessed. In reaction to the demise of the Bretton Woods system in 1971, the Bank and the Treasury aimed at fostering cooperation among European countries and building a fixed but adjustable exchange rate system (James, 2012). Known as the European "currency snake" in the 1970s and reformed under the label of the European Monetary System in 1979 (Mourlon-Druol, 2012), this fixed exchange rate system seldom changed the periodic state of exchange rate crises triggered by the combination of German current account surpluses and lack of competitiveness of the French economy.

Against this background, the creation of the Euro can be interpreted as an institutional fix to the periodic exchange rate crises. In the late 1980s, the committee of experts chaired by Jacques Delors and mandated by European governments wrote a proposal to jump one step forward and created a single currency. As shown by James (2012), the proposal came with two main caveats. First, that fiscal rules must limit the ability of countries to vote fiscal deficit. Second, that the to-be-created central bank must be endowed with the required supervisory power of the banking system. Various interests coalesced to exclude banking supervision from the treaty signed in Maastricht in 1992 that enacts the process of European monetary integration. In 1999, the European Central Bank was responsible for conducting monetary policy for the Euro area and the Euro was introduced in 2001. As part of this process, the various national central banks had gained their independence from government intervention – the Bank of France achieved this in 1992.

6.4 Conclusions

France followed its own path to central banking, a path that was paved by its past and contemporary political and financial system. If anything, what this history of the Bank illustrates is that there are two regularities when it comes to the organization of central banking. First, the relation of the Bank to the state figures prominently. This brings in the discussion of the organization of its independence to ensure a fair balance between the urgent needs of the day and the wish to preserve the value of resources through time. The other regularity is that the efficacy with which a central bank stabilizes payment and credit systems is partly pinned down by how the operational framework of refinancing operations reduces financial frictions. In France, financial imperfections were partly caused by market frictions and passions (sometimes labeled "animal spirits"). But most of all, it is useful to think of them as created by loopholes of the legislation, aimed at defining creditors' rights and the trade of debts and credits. As a central bank, the Bank of France was created to fill in those loopholes, after financiers and politicians agreed that the costs of eighteenth-century monetary crises were too large. Yet these loopholes must not be understood as something that could easily have been fixed by changes in legislation. Rather, they must be thought of as the equivalent of creepage, but in the domain of finance.

APPENDIX. CRISES YEARS DURING THE NINETEENTH CENTURY ACCORDING TO VARIOUS CRITERIA

Column (1) of Table 6A.1 gives the years of financial tension identified by former NBER director William L. Thorp (1926), using accounts of business news. The accounts were official documents, reports by contemporary observers and students of economic history, periodicals, pamphlets, and books. The selected dates correspond to years for which

Thorp mentioned that "Money was tight," or that "Money very tight," or that "Money tightens," or that "Financial panic" happened.

Column (2) reports the years of financial crises according to Clément Juglar (1862 [1889]), who used items of balance sheets of the Bank of France to assess the occurrence of a crisis. He scrutinized two items: the total of circulating banknotes and the ratio of Bank discounts to its metallic holdings. The former measures the size of money creation and the latter

Table 6A.1

(1)	(2)	(3)	(4)	(5)
Thorp "Business annals"	Juglar's criteria	Short-term implicit interest rate, peaks of the HP-filtered cyclical series	Short-term implicit interest rate, deviation greater than 1 st. dev.)	Negative variations of the stock index
		1821		1821–23
1823	1825	1824		
		1826		1827–29
1829–34	1830	1831		1831–35
	1836	1837	1837	
1838–39	1839	1839	1839	1839–43
		1842		
1845–46		1846	1846	
1847–51	1847	1848	1848	1848–51
		1851		
1854		1854	1854	1854–55
1857	1857	1857	1857	1858–59
1860–61		1861	1864	
1864	1864	1864		1864
1866–67		1866		1866–67
1870–71		1870	1870–71	1870–71
1873–74	1873	1873		1873–74
1879		1875		1877–80
1881–83	1882	1882		1883–89
		1884		
1889–91	1891	1888–91		
1893		1893		1894–96
1898–99	1900	1900		1901–04
1904–05		1903		
1907	1907	1907		1907–09
1911–13	1913	1910		1911, 1913

the Bank convertibility constraint. Siegfried (1906) added the 1890s. We extend the dating to the 1900s.

Columns (3) and (4) used the information on the implicit three-month interest rate, annualized by taking for each year between 1820 and 1913 the maximal monthly value. Since monetary tensions could only occur during a few weeks, this is the only possible method of isolating years of funding tensions on the money market. Column (3) reports the local peak in the filtered interest rate series, thus allowing a medium-run trend in the data. Column (4) reports the crises years when the cyclical component of the local interest rate was greater than one standard deviation around the mean.

Column (5) used Arbulu's (2006) stock index to compute variations of the Paris stock price index greater than one standard deviation.

References

Arbulu Pedro, 2006, Le marché parisien des actions au XIXe siècle, in *Le marché financier français au XIXè siècle*, vol. 2, ed., G. Gallais-Hamono. Paris: Publications de la Sorbonne.

Annuaire-almanach du commerce, 1857–1908, de l'industrie, de la magistrature et de l'administration: ou almanach des 500.000 adresses de Paris, des départements et des pays étrangers: Firmin Didot et Bottin réunis, Paris.

Avaro, Maylis and Vincent Bignon, 2017, Monetary Policy and Counterparty Risk Management in Late Nineteenth-century France, mimeo.

Bagehot, Walter, 1873, *Lombard Street: A Description of the Money Market* (5th edition). London: Henry S. King and Co.

Bank of France, various years, *Compte rendu au nom du conseil général de la Banque et rapport de MM. Les censeurs*. Paris: Imprimerie Paul Dupont.

Barbaroux, Nicolas, 2014, The Bank of France and the Open-Market Instrument: An Impossible Wedding? University of Lyons GATE, Working Paper 1423.

Baubeau, Patrice, 2004, Les cathédrales de papiers: Naissance et subversion du systéme de l'escompte en France, XVIIIe–Premier XXe siècle. PhD thesis, University of Paris Nanterre.

Bazot, Guillaume, Michael, Bordo and Eric Monnet, 2016, International Shocks and the Balance Sheet of the Bank of France under the Classical Gold Standard. *Explorations in Economic History* 62: 87–107.

Blancheton, Bertrand, 2001, *Le Pape et l'empereur*. Paris: Albin Michel.

Bergeron, Louis, 1978, *Banquiers, négociants et manufacturiers parisiens du Directoire à l'Empire*. Paris: EHESS and New York: Mouton.

Bernanke, Ben, 1983. Non-monetary Effects of the Financial Crisis in the Propagation of the Great Depression. *American Economic Review* 73(3): 257–276.

Bignon, Vincent, Marc Flandreau, and Stefano Ugolini, 2012, Bagehot for Beginners: The Making of Lender of Last Resort Operations in the Mid-19th Century. *Economic History Review* 65: 580–608.

Bignon, Vincent and Clemens Jobst, 2017, Economic Crises and the Eligiblity for the Lender of Last Resort: Evidence from 19th-century France, Working Paper CEPR.

Bloomfield, Arthur I., 1959, *Monetary Policy under the International Gold Standard: 1880-1915*. New York: Federal Reserve Bank of New York, p. 62.

Bordo, Michael and Ron McDonald, 2005, Interest Rate Interactions in the Classical Gold Standard, 1880-1914. *Journal of Monetary Economics* 52: 307-327.

Bonin, Hubert, 2000, *Les banques françaises dans l'entre-deux-guerre: L'apogée de l'économie libérale bancaire française*. Paris: Editions Plage.

Bonin, Hubert, 2006, *Histoire de la Société Générale*. Geneva: Droz.

Bouvier, J., 1961, *Le Crédit Lyonnais de 1863 à 1882*. Paris: SEVPEN.

Bouvier, J., 1973, *Un siècle de banque Française*. Paris: Hachette littérature.

Bouvier, J., 1979, *L'extension des réseaux de circulation de la monnaie et de l'épargne*, in *Histoire économique et sociale de la France 1880-1950*, Volumes 1-2. Paris: PUF, pp. 161-198.

Bravard-Veyrières, M. and Demangeat Ch., 1862, *Traité de droit commercial, Volume III*. Paris: A. Marescq Aîné.

Bridji, Slim, 2013, The French Great Depression: A Business Cycle Accounting Analysis. *Explorations in Economic History* 50(3): 427-445.

Cameron, Rondo, 1961, *France and the Economic Development of Europe 1800-1914*. Princeton: Princeton University Press.

Cameron, Rondo, 1967, *Banking in the Early Stage of Industrialization*. Oxford: Oxford University Press.

Capie, Forest and Charles Goodhart, 1994, *The Future of Central Banking*. Cambridge: Cambridge University Press.

Charpenay, Georges, 1939, *Les banques regionalistes*. Paris: Nouvelle Revue Critique.

Compte général de la justice civile et commerciale, 1875-1913. Paris: Imprimerie Royale, Impériale or Nationale.

Contamin, Rémy, 2003, Interdépendances financières et dilemme de politique monétaire. La Banque de France entre 1880 et 1913. *Revue économique* 54(1): 157-179.

Contamin, Rémy and Caroline Denise, 1999, Quelle autonomie pour les politiques monétaires sous l'étalon-or, 1880-1913? *Économie internationale* 78: 59-84

Coquelin, 1859, *Le crédit et les banque*, (2nd edition). Paris: Guillaumin et Cie.

Courcelle-Seneuil, 1840, Le credit et la banque, p. 68.

Courtois, Alphonse, 1875, *Histoire de la Banque de France et des principales institutions de crédit depuis 1716*. Paris: Guillaumin.

Dalloz, Victor and Armand, Tournemine, 1825, *Jurisprudence générale du Royaume en matière civile, commerciale, criminelle et administrative*. Paris: Journal des audiences.

Dauphin-Meunier, A., 1936, *La banque de France*. Paris: Gallimard.

Debu-Bridel, J., 1947, *Histoire du marché noir 1939-1947*. Paris: Lagrande Parque.

Delamathe, J., 1848, *Réflexions sur la crise actuelle adressées au commerce de Paris*. Paris: Imprimerie Centrale des Chemins de Fer, de Chaix et Cie.

Diamond, Douglas and Philip Dybvig, 1983, Bank Runs, Deposit Insurance, and Liquidity, *Journal of Political Economy* 91(3): 401-419.

Domin, Jean-Pierre, 2007, La question du monopole d'émission de la monnaie: le débat banque banque centrale contre banque libre chez les économistes français. *European Journal of Social Sciences* XLV(137): 185-202.

Du Pont de Nemours, 1806, *Sur la Banque de France, les causes de la crise qu'elle a éprouvée, les tristes effets qui en sont résultés et les moyens d'en prévenir le retour. Avec une théorie des banques, Rapport fait à la Chambre de commerce*. Paris: Hatchard.

Eichengreen, Barry, 1996, *Golden Fetters: The Gold Standard and the Great Depression, 1919–1939*. Oxford: Oxford University Press.

Fazy, James, 1830, *Principes d'organisation industrielle pour le développement des richesses en France*. Paris: Malher.

Flandreau, Marc, 1995, *L'or du monde*. Paris: L'Harmattan.

Flandreau, Marc, 1996a, Les règles de la pratique. La Banque de France, le marché des métaux précieux et la naissance de l'étalon-or, 1848–1876. *Annales, Histoire, Sciences Sociales* 51(4): 849–871.

Flandreau, Marc, 1996b, The French Crime of 1873: An Essay on the Emergence of the International Gold Standard, 1870–1880. *Journal of Economic History* 56(4): 862–897.

Flandreau, Marc, 1997, Central Bank Cooperation in Historical Perspective: A Sceptical View. *Economic History Review* 50(4): 735–763.

Flandreau, Marc, 2002, "Water Seeks a Level": Modeling Bimetallic Exchange Rates and the Bimetallic Band. *Journal of Money, Credit and Banking* 34(2): 491–519.

Flandreau, Marc, 2004, *The Glitter of Gold. France, Bimetallism and the Emergence of the International Gold Standard, 1848–1873*. Oxford: Oxford University Press.

Flandreau, Marc, 2008, A History of Monetary Policy Targets, 1797–1997, in *The Role of Money: Money and Monetary Policy in the Twenty-first Century*: ECB Central Banking Conference 2006. Frankfurt am Main: European Central Bank, pp. 208–243.

Flandreau, Marc, Christophe Galimard, Clemens Jobst, and Marco Pilar Nogues, 2009, The Bell Jar: Commercial Interest Rates Between Two Revolutions, 1688–1789, in J. Atack and L. Neal, eds., *The Origin and Development of Financial Markets and Institutions from the Seventeenth to Twenty-first Century*. Cambridge: Cambridge University Press.

François-Marsal, 1930, Escompte des effets de commerce, in *Encyclopédie de Banque et de Bourse*. Paris: Crété.

Friedman, Milton and Anna Schwartz, 1963, *A Monetary History of the United States*. Princeton: Princeton University Press.

Friedman, Milton, 1990a, Bimetallism Revisited. *Journal of Economic Perspectives* 4: 85–104.

Friedman, Milton, 1990b, The Crime of 1873. *Journal of Political Economy* 98(6): 1159–1194.

Gautier, J.E., 1839, *article Banque, Encyclopédie du droit*. Paris.

Gille, Bertrand, 1959, *La banque et le crédit en France de 1815 à 1848*. Paris: Presses Universitaires de France.

Gille, Bertrand, 1970, *La Banque en France au 19ème siècle*. Geneva: Droz.

Gonzo, Yasuo, 2011, *Qui a gouverné la Banque de France (1870–1980)?* In O. Feiertag and I. Lespinet-Moret. eds. *L'économie faite homme – hommage à Alain Plessis*. Geneva: Droz, chapter 6, pp. 91–111.

Gorton, Gary and George Pennacchi, 1990, Financial Intermediaries and Liquidity Creation. *Journal of Finance* 45: 49–71.

Gorton, Gary and Guillermo Ordoñez, 2014, Collateral Crises. *American Economic Review* 104(2): 343–378.

Gurley, John G., 1953, Excess Liquidity and European Monetary Reforms, 1944–1952. *American Economic Review* 43(1): 76–100.

Hautcoeur, Pierre-Cyrille and Pierre Sicsic, 1999, Threat of a Capital Levy, Expected Devaluation and Interest Rates in France during the Interwar Period. *European Review of Economic History* 3: 25–56.

Hautcoeur, Pierre-Cyrille, Angelo Riva, and Eugene White, 2014, Floating a Lifeboat: The Banque de France and the Crisis of 1889. *Journal of Monetary Economics* 65: 104–199.

Hoffman, Philip, Gilles Postel-Vinay, and Jean-Laurent Rosenthal, 2015, Entry, Information, and Financial Development: A Century of Competition between French Banks and Notaries. *Explorations in Economic History* 55: 39–57.

INSEE, 1946, *Annuaire statistique*. Paris: Imprimerie Nationale

Jacoud, Gilles, 1996, *Le billet de banque en France (1796–1803)*. Paris: L'Harmattan.

James, Harold, 2012, *Making the European Monetary Union*. Cambridge, MA: The Bellknap Press.

Jeanneney, Jean-Noël, 1976, *François de Wendel en république. L'argent et le pouvoir (1914–1940)*. Paris: Le Seuil Univers Historique.

Jeanneney, Jean-Noël, 1984, *L'Argent caché: milieux d'affaires et pouvoirs politiques dans la France du XXe siècle*. Paris: Le Seuil-Fayard Points-histoire.

Jobst, Clemens and Stefano Ugolini, 2016, The Coevolution of Money Markets and Monetary Policy, 1815–2008, in Michael D. Bordo, Øyvind Eitrheim, Marc Flandreau, and Jan F. Qvigstad, eds., *Central Banks at a Crossroads: What Can We Learn from History?* Cambridge: Cambridge University Press, pp. 145–194.

Jones, Matthew and Maurice Obstfeld, 2004, Savings, Investment and Gold, in Money: A Reassessment of Historical Current Account Data, in Guillermo A. Calvo and Rudiger Dornbusch, eds., *Capital Mobility, and Trade: Essays in Honor of Robert A. Mundell*. Cambridge, MA: MIT Press, pp. 303–363.

Juglar, Clément, 1862 [1889], *Des Crises Commerciales et de leur retour périodique en France, en Angleterre et aux États-Unis*. Paris: Guillaumin.

Koch, Henri, 1983, Histoire de la Banque de France et de la Monnaie sous la Quatrième république. Paris: Dunod.

Lacoue-Labarthe, Dominique, 2005, La France a-t-elle connu des paniques bancaires inefficientes? *Revue d'économie politique* 115(5): 633–656.

Leclercq, Yves, 2010, *La Banque supérieure. La Banque de France de 1800 à 1914. Bibliothèque de l'économiste*. Paris: Classiques Garnier.

Lescure, Michel, 2003, La formation d'un système de crédit en France et le rôle de la banque d'émission (1850–1914), in O. Feirtag and M. Margairaz, eds., *Politiques et pratiques des banques d'émission en Europe (XVIIe–XXe siècle)*. Paris: Albin Michel, pp. 131–148.

Levy-Leboyer Maurice and François Bourguignon, 1985, *L'économie Française au XIXe siècle*. Paris: Economica.

Lutfalla, Michel, 2006, Economistes britanniques et français face à la question de l'amortissement, in A. Aglan, M. Margairaz, and P. Verheyde, eds., 1816 ou la genèse de la foi publique. chapter 1, pp. 23–42.

Margairaz, Michel, 2011, *Les gouverneurs dans la tourmente, in L'économie faite homme*, ed., O. Feiertag and I. Lespinet-Moret. Geneva: Droz, chapter 7, pp. 113–133.

Marjolin, R., J. Sandrine, and O. Wormser, 1968, *Rapport sur le marché monétaire et les conditions de crédit*. Paris: la documentation française.

Monnet, Eric, 2014, Monetary Policy Without Interest Rates: Evidence from France's Golden Age (1948 to 1973) Using a Narrative Approach. *AEJ: Macroeconomics* 6(4): 137–169.

Monnet, Eric, 2015, La politique de la Banque de France au sortir des Trente Glorieuses: un tournant monétariste? *Revue d'Histoire Moderne et Contemporaine* 62–1: 147–174.

Mouré, Kenneth, 1991, *Managing the Franc Poincaré.* Cambridge: Cambridge University Press.

Mouré, Kenneth, 2002, *The Gold Standard Illusion: France, the Bank of France and the International Gold Standard 1914–1939.* Oxford: Oxford University Press.

Mouré, Kenneth, 2010, Food Rationing and the Black Market in France, 1940–1944. *French History* 24(2): 262–282.

Mourlon-Druol, Emmanuel, 2012, *A Europe Made of Money: The Emergence of the European Monetary System.* Series: *Cornell Studies in Money.* Ithaca: Cornell University Press.

National Archives, 1820–1849, Paris-Pierrefitte. F 20 720 – 1/2 (Bankruptcies for each year).

Niehans, Jürg, 1992, Juglar's Credit Cycle. *History of Political Economy* 24(3): 545–569.

Nishimura, Shiyuza, 1995, The French Provincial Banks, the Banque de France, and Bill Finance, 1890–1913. *Economic History Review* 48: 536–554.

Nishimura, Shizuya and Yago Kazuhiko, 2006, La masse monétaire en France, 1890–1913. *Histoire, économie et société* 25(2): 195–211.

Occhino, F., K. Oosterlinck, and E.N. White, 2008, How Much Can a Victor Force the Vanquished to Pay? France under the Nazi Boot. *Journal of Economic History* 68: 1–45.

Oosterlinck, K., L. Ureche-Rangau, and J.-M. Vaslin, 2014, Baring, Wellington and the Resurrection of French Public Finances Following Waterloo. *Journal of Economic History* 74(4): 1072–1102.

Patat, Jean-Pierre and Michel Lutfalla, 1986, *Histoire monétaire de la France au XXe siècle.* Paris: Economica.

Plessis, Alain, 1999, *Banques locales et banques régionales en France au XIXe siècle*, ed., Alain Plessis and Michel Lescure. Paris: Albin Michel.

Priouret, Roger, 1966, *La Caisse des Dépôts et Consignations, 150 ans d'histoire financière.* Paris: PUF.

Prunaux, Emmanuel, 2009, Les comptoirs d'escompte de la Banque de France. *Napoleonica* 5: 14–146.

Ramon, Gabriel, 1929, *Histoire de la Banque de France d'après les sources originales.* Paris: Grasset, 503 pp.

Roulleau, Gaston, 1914, *Les règlements par effets de commerce.* Paris: Dubreuil et Frèrebeau.

Saint-Marc, M., 1983, Michèle, *Histoire monétaire de la France 1800–1980.* Paris: PUF.

Sauvy, Alfred, 1984, *Histoire Économique de la France entre les deux guerres.* Paris: Economica (written with the collaboration of Anita Hirsch).

Schwartz, Anna, 1986, Real and Pseudo Financial Crises, in Forrest Capie and Geoffrey E. Wood, eds., *Financial Crises and the World Banking System.* New York: Macmillan pp. 11–31.

Sicsic, Pierre, 1992, Was the Franc Poincaré Deliberately Undervalued? *Explorations in Economic History* 29: 69–92.

Sicsic, Pierre and Bertrand Villeneuve, 1993, L'afflux d'or en France de 1928 à 1934, in *Du franc Poincaré à l'écu: colloque tenu à Bercy les 3 et 4 décembre 1992, Comité pour l'histoire économique et financière de la France.* Paris: CHEFF, pp. 21–55.

Siegfried, Jules, 1906, L'alternance des crises économiques commerciales et des périodes de prospérité. *Revue des Deux Mondes*: 823–841.

Thorp, William Long, 1926, *Business Annals.* New York: US Government Printing office.

Toutain, Jean-Claude, 1987, Le produit intérieur brut de la France de 1789 à 1982. *Economies et statistiques* 15: 47–237.

Tullio, Giuseppe and Jürgen Wolters, 2003, The Objectives of French Monetary Policy during the Classical Gold Standard, 1876–1913: An Econometric Analysis of the Determinants of Banque de France's Discount Rate. *Diskussionbeiträge des Wirtschaftswissenschaft der Freien Universität Berlin* 2003: 12.

Velde, François, 2003, Government Equity and Money: John Law's System in 1720 France. Working Paper Series WP-03-31, Federal Reserve Bank of Chicago.

Velde, François. 2007, John Law's System. *American Economic Review* 97(2): 276–279.

Velde, François, 2009, Chronicle of a Deflation Unforetold. *Journal of Political Economy* 117(4): 591–634.

Vidal, Emmanuel, 1910, *History and Methods of the Paris Bourse.* Washington, DC: National Monetary Commission, Government Printing Office.

White, Eugene, 2001, Making the French Pay: The Cost and Consequences of the Napoleonic Reparations. *European Review of Economic History* 5(3): 337–365.

White, Eugene, 2007, The Crash of 1882 and the Bailout of the Paris Bourse. *Cliometrica* 1(2): 115–144.

Four Hundred Years of Central Banking in the Netherlands, 1609–2016

Gerarda Westerhuis and Jan Luiten van Zanden

7.1 Introduction

The Dutch Central Bank, as we know it today, was set up in 1814, as a result of a decision taken by King William I, who developed a comprehensive programme of economic reconstruction and institution building after acceding to the throne of the Kingdom of the United Netherlands in the same year. But the initiative was also based on a two-century experience with a kind of proto-central banking embodied by the Amsterdam Exchange Bank, established in 1609. In fact, in order to understand the history of Central Banking – and of the Swedish Riksbank in particular – the history of the Amsterdam Exchange Bank is arguably much more relevant than the history of De Nederlandsche Bank (or DNB, as the Central Bank was abbreviated to) since 1815. The Swedish Riksbank was to a large extent modelled after the Amsterdam Exchange Bank and its sister institution, the Beleenbank, and the same applies to that other 'mother of all central banks', the Bank of England of 1694.

We will therefore open this chapter with a brief discussion of the history of the Amsterdam Exchange Bank, and its proto-central bank functions. Next we will discuss the history of DNB itself, with a special focus on the first half of the 19th century when it developed into an independent central bank, largely outside the direct sphere of influence of the rather autocratic King William I.

Our approach will be to focus on the primary functions that these central banks performed. The primary aim of the Amsterdam Exchange Bank was to facilitate the payments system – its other, perhaps secondary aim was to stabilize the monetary and financial system. It also supplied credit to certain government-related institutions, but this was an unintended by-product. DNB was different from the start in the sense that its aim was to contribute to the revival of the economy after the deep crisis during the French period. But views differed about what this meant in practice, and as we will see, the king had other ideas than the bankers who were recruited to manage the institution.

In the 20th century DNB changed into a modern central bank with three important functions: monetary policy aimed at price stability, smooth functioning of the payment system and stability of the financial sector. These tasks were formally laid down in the Bank Act of 1948. The way DNB could perform these tasks changed with the increasing European integration since the 1950s. So we will see that in particular its influence on monetary policies was transferred to the European level (ESCB). The idea prevailing in the 1960s and 1970s that stability of the financial sector was best safeguarded by banks that became not too big and too powerful, was slowly loosened under pressure of increasing competition resulting from European integration and liberalization of capital markets since the 1980s. The financial crisis of 2008 showed that the remaining few large financial conglomerates endangered the stability of the Dutch financial sector. As a result, to restore confidence in the banking sector, supervision has even more been moved to Europe.

7.2 The Amsterdam Exchange Bank, 1609–1820

The years of the Revolt against the Spanish King (1572–1648) are probably the most dynamic period in the history of the Dutch economy. After 1578, when Amsterdam joined the coalition, and 1585 when the Spanish forces recaptured Antwerp, the city quickly became the central hub of international trade. It dominated, first of all, the trade with the Baltic, but increasingly all other trades as well, including commerce with the Indies which became dominated by the East India Company (VOC) set up in 1602. But trade was handicapped by the fact that in this small open economy so many different coins from abroad circulated, of which the value sometimes changed dramatically (the mid-16th century had for example seen the 'great debasement' in England). High exchange costs contributed to transaction costs, and merchants complained about the costs of acquiring high quality specie for carrying out large international transactions or for minting money for that purpose. The payments system was, in sum, highly chaotic, and merchants requested the Amsterdam city government to intervene. The Estates General tried to create some order in the chaos by introducing, in 1603, a new standard coin, the *rijksdaalder* (which would become the most important Dutch coin used in international exchange), but this was clearly not sufficient. After new requests by Amsterdam merchants, the city government set up the Amsterdam Exchange Bank in 1609, modelled after the Venetian Banco della Piazza di Rialto from 1587 (Mooij 2009).

Its aim was primarily to facilitate the payments system: merchants could deposit their coins there and receive a standard return in terms of bank money, which could be used for transactions with other merchants and others who had a bank account, such as the city government and the VOC. This was the primary service the bank supplied: it replaced costly transactions with coins or letters of exchange with giro transactions on paper. The courtage on transactions would be minimal – the exchange bank was a public institution without a profit motive (although it managed to make nice profits for the city government during much of its existence). Alternatives were suppressed: merchants were not allowed to transfer large sums in other ways, that is, via letters of exchange (the threshold was 600 guilders, or three times the annual wage of a carpenter), and private banking was not allowed. The cashiers, who had performed similar functions in the past, were prohibited (already in 1604), but this rule was in practice gradually relaxed. The bank was also supposed to hold the countervalue of the deposits in coins or bullion in its cellars, and not use it for credit, a rule to which it stuck normally. But it did lend money to the other financial institution that was set up in these years, the Amsterdamse Beleenbank of 1614, which aimed at supplying credit to those who were short of cash and did own a collateral of any kind. And it could not resist occasional claims of the city government and the related VOC to supply it with credit – operations hidden to the public, but which were highly profitable (Uittenbogaard 2009 and Van Nieuwkerk 2009a).

The strong reputation of the Exchange Bank was largely based on the fact that at any moment deposits could be withdrawn in full. In 1672, during the worst financial crisis of the 17th century, the bank established this reputation – it could indeed pay out massive sums of gold and silver in a moment of intense crisis. Exchange banks in other cities (Rotterdam, Middelburg) had been less cautious, and experienced many more problems during these years. By in principle not using its monetary reserves for supplying credit, it contributed to the stability of the monetary system. Because of the confidence in the bank, and the fact that it did not change the value of the coins it took in (which were fixed by government regulation), the value of bank money showed a substantial agio compared with the 'real' gulden that was used in daily cash transactions. This agio reflected the trust the commercial community had in bank money and became a financial instrument in the hands of the Exchange Bank: via what nowadays would be called 'open market transactions' made possible by its large reserves of silver and gold it could manipulate the bank agio and in that way isolate the internal market from large exogenous shocks (Guillard 2004). Or, as Quinn and Roberds have summarized the recent consensus about the role of the Exchange Bank, it performed three functions 'that are routinely carried out by central banks today: operating a large-value payments system, creating inconvertible money (i.e. not directly redeemable for coin), and managing the value of this money through 'open market operation' (Quinn and Roberds 2009: 44).

In the 18th century the Exchange Bank also to some extent took up the role of 'lender of last resort'. During two financial crises, in 1763 and 1773, it coordinated efforts to stabilize the financial system and to supply the market with liquidity, and in 1773 even helped to create an emergency fund, the *Beleenkamer*, to assist bankers in distress. During both crises emergency measures were so effective that the market stabilized very quickly, and only limited use was made of the new facilities created (Uittenbogaard 1996) (their signalling function was apparently already sufficient). Also in terms of long-term stability, in particular price stability (today's goal of central banking), the system developed in the initial decades of the 17th century worked well: the silver value of the guilder became stabilized (it depreciated only once in 1681 by less than 3 per cent). The exchange rate of the Dutch guilder, as a result, was very stable, in a period when many countries experienced large swings and substantial declines in the external value of their currency. Only England matched the Dutch experience in this respect. Inflation as far as it occurred was the result of real economic changes reflecting the scarcity or abundance of goods and services (including silver). Prices more or less doubled during the 190 years that the Exchange Bank was in operation, which points to an average rate of inflation of 0.37 per cent p.a. (Van Zanden 2005).

The governance of the Wisselbank was a typical example of how Dutch institutions were operating in the 'Golden Age'. The policies of the bank were carried out by a board of commissioners, composed of three to six annually appointed commissioners and chaired by a president commissioner, but they were closely monitored by the burgomasters and the city council. Not to mention the close family ties between commissioners, burgomasters and other council members, in particular during the first half of the 17th century ('t Hart 2009). Moreover, this city institution was performing functions for the local, regional and even international market, which meant that very different layers of government were also involved. Other parts of monetary policy (minting, public expenditure and the management of public debt) were the privilege of regional (Holland) and central (Estates General) state authorities, which created much room for bargaining and the need for compromise and a solution. Dehing describes a 'continuous struggle with respect to roles, responsibilities, competences and tasks between central and regional government and the city of Amsterdam. In theory, various levels of administration within the city – city council, burgomasters and bank commissioners – were pursuing the same goal. In practice it was not always easy to establish who actually pulled which strings and when, and whose influential intercession and actual decisions we have to thank for which conclusion' (Dehing 2012: 289). There was, in sum, no unified governance structure and the system showed all the features of what has been called the 'poldermodel' of Dutch politics (Prak and Van Zanden 2013).

There are perhaps two reasons for also being somewhat critical of the role the Wisselbank played in the development of the Dutch financial system. First of all, it suppressed the development of private banking – by being an efficient supplier of payment services, and by officially banning private cashiers and bankers. But once they entered the scene again – not handicapped by the official ban – this did not really result in more financial stability, as the crises of the second half of the 18th century demonstrate. The gradual development of paper money as it occurred in 18th-century England was therefore not an option for the Dutch financial system, and paper money for a long time remained an underexploited innovation (although the cashiers did make use of cashiers' notes: Jonker 1996). Moreover, it was rather conservative in the use of the large monetary reserves that were held by the bank. The Bank van Leening of 1614 initially acquired substantial support from the Wisselbank, and via this channel the Amsterdam elite in the first half of the 17th century supported a number of strategic ventures, but it abandoned this policy after 1650. Only the city of Amsterdam and the VOC continued to profit from credit supplied by the bank, but this remained a secret as the official idea was that all bank accounts were covered by the reserves of the bank. When, in the 1780s, the VOC suffered greatly as a result of the Fourth British–Dutch war, loans from the Wisselbank made it possible to keep the company afloat. But after the French took over the city in 1795 the real state of affairs became public, and confidence in the Wisselbank collapsed. Merchants withdrew their money from the bank, which continued to struggle until it was liquidated in 1821 (after the Dutch Central Bank had been set up) (Van Nieuwkerk and Van Renselaar 2009).

7.3 The Emergence of the Dutch Central Bank (DNB), 1814–1864

The recent literature on the Amsterdam Exchange Bank has tended to stress the modern central banking functions that were already performed by this early modern institution. Paradoxically, recent research on DNB has been characterized by the opposite tendency. In the older literature, the establishment of the central bank in 1814 is taken as a point of departure to analyse its evolution as a 'modern' central bank (De Jong 1967). Uittenbogaard (2014) in particular has recently questioned this approach, and stresses that the institution set up in 1814 did not 'automatically' develop into a central bank as we know it now, but that this development was contingent on choices made and policies implemented in these years. Key to understanding the evolution the new institution underwent is the context in which it was set up.

This was dramatically different from the context in which the Exchange Bank of 1609 was established. After 1807 the Dutch economy had gone through a big slump, reinforcing a process of relative decline – mainly vis-à-vis the United Kingdom – that had much older roots. Moreover, the Congress of Vienna proposed to merge the two parts of the Low Countries – the south (current Belgium) and the north (the Netherlands) – into one Kingdom, of which William I became the sovereign with almost autocratic powers. His immediate job was to revive the economy of the Northern Netherlands (the south had fared quite well under French control), and to merge the two parts of his Kingdom into one new unit. He was a highly capable administrator, with very ambitious plans for steering the economy in the desired direction. However, he desperately needed funds for realizing his great ambitions, but the state of public finances was highly problematic. Public debt was about 250 per cent of GDP of the Northern Netherlands, also because the King accepted the old debts to appease the Dutch elite, which had invested a large share of its assets in government bonds (Van Zanden and Van Riel 2004: 85–106). One of the aims of setting a central bank was to facilitate borrowing and the management of the huge public debt. Rather than serving the commercial community of Amsterdam – the purpose of the Exchange Bank – it was the interests of a newly centralized state that were behind the establishment of the new institution.

The foundation of DNB in 1814 had been prepared by debates among politicians and financial experts about the desirability of setting up a central bank, which followed the proposal by the Finance Minister Gogel of 1798 to that purpose. After the collapse of the Amsterdam Exchange Bank, the money market was characterized by recurrent shortages of money (due to trade balance deficits and high spending on warfare), a problem that had to be addressed by the new bank. It would be permitted to issue banknotes (its most important innovation), discount bills and lend on collateral of securities, commodities and specie (Uittenbogaard 2014: 52). To avoid potential government abuse, the Gogel proposal prohibited the bank from lending to any public authority. Moreover, the bank would be privately owned and controlled by its shareholders (Uittenbogaard 2014: 54). Opposition against the centralizing tendency of the bank – which would be a national institution, but located in Amsterdam – resulted in its abandonment when the political tide turned (in 1802). But the proposal was back on the agenda in 1814, after the new King assumed power. He made a number of significant changes: the government became co-owner of the bank (for 10 per cent), the King appointed the president directly (and other members of the board on the basis of choice between pairs), the government was allowed to borrow from the new bank and it became the state's cashier (Uittenbogaard 2014: 60). These changes created much more leverage for the state, and made clear that the King wanted the bank to help him raise funds for his ambitious plans for recovery and economic modernization. But this also created a problem, as the new role the bank was supposed to play jeopardized its independence within the business community of Amsterdam. Officially the aim of the bank was to facilitate and stimulate trade, but the fiscal motives the King also had created a certain tension in its architecture and operation.

That DNB was seen as an agency set up by the state, which did not immediately further the interests of the commercial elite, is also clear from its rather difficult start. It took three years to place the shares of the bank. This is a long time, but it has to be said that the capital of the bank of 5 million guilders was quite large, and its denomination of 1,000 guilders did not help to attract small capitalists. After this difficult start, the bank quickly gained the confidence of the Amsterdam commercial elite, mainly because representatives of this elite were appointed as President, secretary and other board members. Moreover, the President was appointed for life, which meant that he was quite invulnerable and could oppose, if necessary, the King. As Roland Uittenbogaard (2014) has shown convincingly, the state tried on several occasions (in 1815, 1830 and 1831) to borrow large amounts of money from DNB, but the board of the bank simply refused to comply. In 1834, in the depth of the crisis over the secession of Belgium, the bank could no longer refuse to help, but the transaction that was concluded involved a middleman and therefore meant that the bank still did not directly supply credit to the state (Uittenbogaard 2014: 89). This loan, which was raised in 1834 (when the state faced imminent bankruptcy), amounted to about 10 per cent to 15 per cent of total DNB loans, and never reached a level which would have destabilized DNB. Uittenbogaard (2014: 91) concludes that 'after repeated attempts in the first decade, the King apparently accepted that DNB was not the ideal vehicle for lending'. He moved on to create other financial institutions which he could control more completely, such as the Nederlandsche Handel Maatschappij, which acquired the monopoly on the trade with Indonesia, and out of which ABN Amro grew, as well as the Société Générale, which became the most powerful bank of the Southern Netherlands.

The management of DNB, in short, managed to keep the King at arms' length, and established a reputation for financial conservatism which was greatly appreciated by the Amsterdam elite. Yet its business developed only slowly, as its banknotes were not generally accepted and only circulated in limited networks in Amsterdam. The King wanted the bank to branch out and become a truly national bank by setting up branches in Antwerp and Brussels, but DNB simply refused to do so (with the consequence that until the secession of Belgium the branches of Société Générale played a role in facilitating transactions within (that part of) the Kingdom). After the renewal of the Charter in 1839, a similar discussion about opening up a branch in Rotterdam began, which ended in a compromise solution; DNB reached an agreement with local cashiers but did not set up a new branch.

Until the 1840s, DNB played only a limited role in facilitating the payments system. Cashiers had already in the 18th century assumed a central role in this, which was strengthened by the decline and demise of the Exchange Bank. The main problem for DNB, in taking over this role, was the limited acceptance of its banknotes by the Amsterdam community (Jonker 1996 174–175); in particular, the cashiers saw DNB as a state-led competitor threatening to take over their business. In the 1840s, a series of developments strengthened the position of DNB, however. The autocratic regime of William I was succeeded by a liberal government and constitution (definitively in 1848), which finally resolved the tension with the commercial elite. Until the 1840s, DNB had been cautious in competing with the cashiers, but could now more aggressively marginalize them. Only now did it become, also thanks to the fact that all transactions involving the government were carried out via its accounts, the central hub of the payments system. Finally, the reform of the currency system in the mid-1840s also strengthened confidence in the banknotes issued by DNB. After about 30 years it had established itself as the central hub in Amsterdam's financial system.

7.4 Towards a National Central Bank 1864–1914

By the early 1860s, DNB was still largely an Amsterdam institution, focused on the Amsterdam money market. At the same time, the Dutch economy was becoming more centralized and integrated as a result of changes that had set in during the 1830s and 1840s, such as the telegraph and railways, and increased openness to international trade. Amsterdam continued to play its role as the centre of the capital and money market, but the economy of Rotterdam was more dynamic and became an important hub of finance as well. The pressure to create a more comprehensive – perhaps even countrywide – network of branches of DNB intensified. Earlier provisions in the Bank Acts of 1814 and 1829 to open up branches in a.o. Rotterdam had been successfully ignored by the board. The new Bank Act of 1863 simply stated that before 1 January 1865, a branch in Rotterdam and 12 agencies spread over the country had to be opened. And so it happened, after which, immediately, the activities of DNB expanded rapidly. In particular, the circulation of the banknotes of DNB grew strongly after these changes (De Jong, II 1967: 313). Moreover, during the same years, the mid-1860s, a number of 'modern' banks were set up in the Netherlands, which also grew rapidly – with ups and downs, of course, due to the often rather speculative nature of these banks, and the swings in the international business cycle. This also meant that gradually DNB became a bankers' bank, with a division of labour emerging: members of the business community increasingly held their accounts with the new banks (De Jong, II 1967: 190–194).

The next major change was the move to the Gold Standard in the early 1870s, following the examples of Germany, France and other Western European countries. In 1847 silver had officially been accepted as the single basis of the currency (before 1847 bimetalism had been the official policy), but the rather sudden move to gold by (first) Germany, soon followed by France and the Scandinavian countries following the German-French war of 1871, also meant that the Netherlands had to move to gold, or face strong fluctuations in its exchange rate. The transition was completed in 1875, and was followed by a rather lengthy period of about 20 years of deflation (as the massive move to gold resulted in a sudden shrinking of the monetary base of the economy). The switch to gold was particularly problematic in the Netherlands Indies, where important trading nations (Singapore, China) remained on silver, whereas the Indonesian guilder was tied to the Dutch (gold-based) guilder. The move to gold on the other hand made it possible to further reduce the interest rate differential between British Consols and the Dutch public debt, showing the further integration of capital markets (Van Zanden and Van Riel 2004: 254–255). Debates about DNB in the final decades of the 19th century centred on the large profits made by this semi-public institution. Most shares were in private hands, and thanks to its monopoly on, for example, the issue of banknotes, the bank earned high profits and distributed high dividends (18 per cent on average during the 1860s and 1870s). The new Bank Act of 1888 substantially lowered the share of profits going to shareholders, and increased payments to the state (de Jong, III 1967: 46). But the private nature of the bank was not seriously questioned until the 1920s and 1930s.

The Dutch economy was affected by the international business cycles of the period, but DNB had only to use its standard repertoire of instruments – in particular its discount rate – to keep the currency stable and monitor the Gold Standard. The banks set up in the 1860s and 1870s became more stable, and did not require the kind of 'lender of last resort' activities that were developed in London in these years (but remember that the Amsterdam Exchange Bank had been more active in this field in the 18th century). It would take the financial crisis of the early 1920s to really involve DNB in this.

7.5 Towards a Modern Bank: 1914–1948

The period 1914 to 1948 can be characterized as a period of serious transformation. In 1914 the bank was still deeply rooted in the 19th century, operating in a national environment of stable economic and political relations and monetary links to the Gold Standard. At the end of the period, with the Bank Act of 1948, the bank was nationalized and focused mostly on public instead of private functions. The Bank Act of 1948 formed the keystone of structural developments and marked the beginning of a new era. Two wars, a banking crisis in 1920/1921 and the Great Depression of the 1930s marked a permanent rupture with the past. The bank started to combine the function of circulation bank, including monetary policies, with interference in the international payment system in the 1930s and monetary measurements in the First and Second World Wars and after 1945. Both wars involved DNB in national and international political and economic developments and policies to a greater extent than previously. During this period it started no longer to function alone but increasingly kept in touch with other institutions, persons and groups in society: the 'socialization' of DNB.

The First World War, when the Netherlands remained neutral, still necessitated more state intervention, such as regulation of the monetary system and flow of goods. Also, the state needed more support from business. For example, it was involved in the creation of the *Nederlandse Uitvoer Maatschappij* (Dutch Export Company), which controlled and monitored the international trade of the country during the First World War. During the Second World War, the bank was the most important monetary institute and, in a way, the centre of the financial exploitation of the country by the German occupiers who were allowed to pay in Reichsmarks, which DNB then had to transfer into guilders. The bank slowly degraded towards a circulation bank only (de Vries 1989).

The system of informal international cooperation of the pre-1914 period was succeeded by much more formal structures. The complex monetary problems of the interwar period – including those emanating from the Versailles Treaty – necessitated international meetings of financial experts and policy makers (Amsterdam 1919; Brussels 1920; Genova 1922). Although results were not really tangible, the last one in Genova resulted in closer cooperation between central banks in the US, the UK, France, Germany, Switzerland and the Netherlands. It formed a first step in the development towards the creation of the Bank of International Settlement (BIS) in Geneva in 1930 and towards the IMF and the World Bank after the war.

Nationally, the banking crisis of 1921–1923 was a turning point, as for the first time DNB, under considerable pressure from the Minister of Finance Colijn, played the role of lender of last resort for the banking system. It was part of the evolution of DNB becoming the 'leader of the club' of banks and emerging cooperation between DNB and the rest of the banking sector. As a result of the development of the banking sector since the 1860s, discounting by the banking sector had increased substantially, making DNB already into a banker's bank. The percentage of *disconteringen* by the banking sector of the total activity in this field by DNB increased from 52.9 per cent in 1864–1865 to 91.9 per cent in 1913–1914 (de Vries 1994: 563). As said, the banking crisis in the early 1920s pushed DNB further into her role of supervisor of the banking system. DNB helped two times to guarantee the liquidity of the banking sector, ensuring that the banking sector did not collapse. Thus, DNB supported Marx & Co Bank with almost 27 million guilders, so that the bank could be liquidated without a formal bankruptcy. For the much larger Rotterdamsche Bankvereeniging, DNB passed on a state guarantee of 60 million guilders to meet the immediate financial problems. A few small banks, however, were sacrificed in the early 1920s, without doing much harm to the system as a whole (de Vries 1989).

A few years after the banking crisis, in 1926, DNB managed to return to the Gold Standard, almost immediately after the Bank of England, and also at the old parity. There are, however, no grounds for thinking that this was a mistake, as the economy of the Netherlands expanded rapidly during the 1920s and did not seem to suffer from an overvaluation of currency (Van Zanden 1997). This changed after 1929, however, when the Gold Standard became arguably the most contentious issue in public debate. Perhaps because it had digested its financial problems successfully in the financial crisis of the early 1920s, and the banking system was in relatively good shape, there was no external pressure to leave the Gold Standard in 1931 or 1933. On the contrary, being one of the few countries with a stable currency, it attracted large inflows of capital in moments of crisis, making it difficult to leave gold. But this sticking to gold had major consequences for the domestic economy: unemployment continued to grow after 1933, and recovery was extremely weak if it existed at all. The government under the leadership of Colijn also ideologically wanted to stick to gold, and saw itself as the only remaining island of stability in an increasingly unstable world. This 'Dutch continuation of the Great Depression' lasted until September 1936, when – finally – external pressure, that is, the leaving of the Gold Standard by France and Switzerland, forced the Netherlands to abandon the Gold Standard as well (Van Zanden 1997).

The financial crisis of 1931 did have an effect on DNB, which had invested most of its resources in pound sterling (as part of the gold-exchange standard promoted by London), which suddenly lost part of its value due to the devaluation of the pound in September of that year. This despite the fact that, according to the President of DNB, even the day before the devaluation the Bank of England had guaranteed the value of DNB's holdings. The state had to step in to balance the accounts of DNB, which lost some of its former freedom; a change that would be completed by the nationalization of 1948 (de Vries 1989).

7.6 The Golden Years: 1948–1973

After the war, rebuilding the country and its economy became priority. The era 1948–1973 can be characterized as the Golden Years and a period in which the welfare state was created. The Bank Act of 1948 formed the keystone of structural developments and marked the beginning of this new era. The bank kept its limited liability form, but was nationalized, in other words ownership was transferred from private investors, mostly wealthy Dutch men from the nobility, to the Dutch state. It can be seen as a response to societal developments and also to the bank's own develop-ment. Instead of private functions, the Bank increasingly focused on public functions. Thus, an important reason for the nationalization of the bank was the idea the profits that were made belonged to the community and not to private investors. However, despite nationalization, the bank remained independent from the state and outside of democratic control. Fitting into the culture of mutual consultation of Dutch politics, the political system formulated policy goals which it delegated to the bank. The Minister of Finance was responsible for the realization of these goals, but his formal powers were limited. In practice, the Minister of Finance and President of the Bank consulted each other as equals. The bank could choose its own policy instruments. This replaced the automatic working of the Gold Standard by constantly changing policy measures (Fase 2000: 49). Only very strong Ministers of Finance – such as Pieter Lieftinck in the years of reconstruction (1945–1952) – were able to use the bank as an instrument for economic and financial policy. A *Bankraad* (Bank Council) was created which had to intervene when the minister and the bank's managing board failed to reach agreement (Fase 2000).

Although ownership and the relationship to government changed fundamentally, DNB's functions and activities showed continuity with the previous period. In this respect the Act of 1948 can be seen as institutionalization of existing practices. The Act distinguishes three important functions of the bank. First, its role as a monetary institution was enshrined as it had to bear (joint) responsibility for the stability of the value of money – the guilder. Apart from price stability, other goals were full employment, stable market conditions, equilibrium of exchange control and creation of conditions for economic growth. This implies that monetary policy was highly interwoven with general economic policy. Thus, full employment policy required active monetary policies which DNB made possible by, for example, tight regulation of bank lending and capital controls. In the period 1948–1973, the Golden Years, economic development (economic growth and low unemployment rates) was very high because of the stable monetary climate in the Netherlands, among other things.

DNB was also responsible for the smooth functioning of the Dutch payment system. This meant that it took care of the circulation of banknotes, to simplify the interbank giro payment system and to promote cross-border payments. The circulation of banknotes has increased tremendously in the period following the Second World War. Non-cash payments by bank transfer became increasingly popular during this period.

The third core activity of the bank was to ensure financial stability by supervising the financial system. At first, consultation with the banking sector happened on a voluntary basis. Later, in 1952, the Act Supervision of the Financial System (Wtk) was passed, in which supervision was legally formalized. In the years that followed, this supervisory role expanded and eventually included all financial institutions. DNB's influence was mostly tangible in the so-called *Structuurbeleid* (structural policies) aimed at keeping the banking system compartmentalized in order to prevent banks from becoming too big and too powerful, and in prudential supervision or safeguarding the solvency and liquidity of the banking sector. After the Second World War the financial sector consisted of different types of financial institutions: trading banks forming the dominant group, cooperatives, mortgage banks and savings banks. Because of the strong economic growth and the shift of liquidity to mass markets, banking services came within the reach of a much larger share of the population. A large part of the financial sector profited from this growth. As a result, a concentration process followed, which was related to increasing scale and scope in business, the creation of the European Economic Community in 1958 and the general growth of welfare in Dutch society from 1948. Larger banks were needed, with larger capital bases to service the changing financial needs of businesses and households (Uittenbogaard and Van Zanden 1999).

The bank focused on the maintenance of the existing structure with a functional separation of various financial institutions (mortgage, savings and so on), preventing banks from becoming too big and too powerful. Therefore, DNB had to give a statement of no objection in case of an intended merger, acquisition or participation (of more than 5 per cent) in another financial institution. This became an issue in 1964, when the four large commercial banks decided to merge and form two banks (ABN and AMRO). In its final approval of this move, DNB made clear that it would not approve another change towards even higher levels of concentration in the banking sector, which for a while – until 1990 – limited options for commercial banks in this respect (Uittenbogaard and Van Zanden 1999; Fase 2000).

7.7 DNB in an Increasingly International Environment: 1973-1998

The oil crisis of 1973 marked the end of the Golden Years and the beginning of a period with lower economic growth, unemployment, inflation and stagnating investments. Also, between 1971 and 1973 the Bretton Woods system with its fixed exchange rates was dismantled. After 1973, the three core functions of the bank should be seen in light of an increasingly international environment. Particularly important was the development of the Eurocurrency markets, in particular the Eurodollar market. As a result, foreign competition in the Dutch banking market increased. The implementation of the First Banking Directive in 1977 and the Second Banking Directive of 1989 stimulated international competition further. The goal of the Directives was to remove obstacles which hampered the provision of services and the establishment of branches across the borders of European Community member states. The harmonization of activities by the European Community ran parallel with the general trend of liberalization and deregulation of financial markets in the US and Western Europe. Restrictions on in- and outgoing capital movements were lifted, which led to a huge increase in capital movements worldwide. Managing the exchange rate became a central issue for DNB. Important in this respect was the decision to link the guilder to the German mark, part of the European Monetary System in 1979 (but DNB used the mark as a target already since at least 1973). The main reason for the decision was price stability and the creation of a stable link with Germany, the main export market.

Credit institutions were officially placed under the supervision of the bank in the Bank Act of 1948 and formal legislation was put in place in 1952 by the *Wet Toezicht Kredietwezen* (Wtk). In the supervision of the banking sector we see gradual changes, resulting in changes in the Wtk in 1978, in 1982 and again in 1992. Partly, these adjustments were a response to the changing market conditions: increasing use of non-cash means of payment, which made control of the money supply more difficult, and the development of cross-sectoral activities by banks ('*branche vervaging*'). Bank failures (e.g. Texeira de Mattos in the late 1960s) also contributed to the expansion of supervisory legislation. The gradual disappearance of the old segregation between commercial banks, saving banks and cooperative banks started with a crisis in the housing market in the early 1980s. Despite the *Structuurbeleid,* the bank declared that general banks were allowed to acquire mortgage banks. As a result, all independent mortgage banks disappeared and only one bank, Tilburgsche Hypotheekbank, went bankrupt in 1982. Also, most savings banks disappeared; most of them became part of bigger banking institutions.

The changes in supervision also included implementation of the consecutive European Banking Directives. Thus, the Wtk of 1992 was a result of the European integration. It lent an ear to banking supervision in the European context and the forming of financial conglomerates, as European regulation consolidated the model of universal banking (and bancassurance). As a result, in 1988, DNB allowed all financial companies to merge, and in 1990 banks and insurance companies were permitted to do so. The idea behind the deregulation was the necessity to be able to compete in the Single European Market; it was necessary for Dutch banks to increase their operating scale and extend their product portfolios. This liberalization was in sharp contrast to the 1960s and 1970s, when DNB supervision was directed towards preventing banks from becoming too big and too powerful. As a result, the Dutch banking sector changed from a highly segmented sector with numerous small and specialized banks into a very concentrated one dominated by three large banks – ABN AMRO, Rabobank and ING – all three with a diversified product portfolio and global operations (Westerhuis 2008, 2016; Westerhuis and De Jong 2015). That this implied increased vulnerability of the system as whole was a lesson learned in the 2008 crisis.

Concerning the Dutch payment system, it is interesting to note that important changes happened as well partly due to technological developments. In the course of the 1990s, DNB started to operate a fully automated interbank settlement system for large value payments (TOP), which became an integral part of the Eurozone Target system when the euro was introduced. In retail banking, new ways of electronic banking were developed, which resulted in a decrease of cash circulation and the use of cheques. Of societal relevance was the *National Betalings Circuit* (NBC) that finally, in 1997, was established after more than 20 years of consultation between DNB and the banking sector. It meant a simplification of the payment system by bank transfer (Fase 2000: 527–528).

So in this period, DNB increasingly reacted to external pressures, in particular resulting from European integration and the (perceived) increasing competition resulting from this process. DNB became less autonomous and the stability of the banking sector decreased. These developments continued after the creation of the European Monetary Union.

7.8 DNB, Europe and the Financial Crisis: 1998–Present

The creation of the Economic and Monetary Union (EMU) resulted in the end of national monetary policies, since 1983 highly dominated by Germany. Instead, European monetary policies were led by the European System of Central Banks (ESCB), created in Frankfurt in 1998 as executive institute. The change of the Bank Act of 1948 into a new one in 1998 marked this important switch of focus. The Bank Act of 1948 had served its goals for 50 years and now the objectives, tasks and activities of the bank were changed in line with the Treaty establishing the European

Community and the establishment of an ESCB. DNB came to form an integral part of the ESCB with respect to her tasks and duties. As a result, DNB has a dual function, being both part of the ESCB and an independent public body. This implies that DNB is co-responsible for the determination and implementation of the monetary policy for the euro area, and forms a link in the international payment system. At the same time, being an independent public body, DNB has to exercise the prudential supervision of financial institutions.

The president of DNB is a member of the ECB Governing Council and in that role the president can co-decide monetary policy. The Governing Council consists of the governors of all central banks of the euro area and the ECB Executive Board. Independently, this Governing Council decides what monetary policy is best for the euro area as a whole. These decisions should be independent of national and political interests. Regarding the bank's objective, it still has to maintain price stability and, without prejudice to the objective of price stability, the bank supports the general economic policies in the European Union.

In the Bank Act 1998, it is also stated that within the framework of the European System of Central Banks, DNB contributes to the performance of the following tasks (Bank Act 1998):

- to define and implement monetary policy;
- to conduct foreign exchange operations;
- to hold and manage the official foreign reserves;
- to provide for the circulation of money as far as it consists of banknotes;
- to promote the smooth operation of payment systems.

Furthermore, 'within the framework of the European System of Central Banks, the Bank contributes to the pursuit of sound policies by the competent authorities relating to the prudential supervision of banks and the stability of the financial system' (Bank Act 1998).

Another important development was the reorganization of financial supervision within the Netherlands between 2002 and 2004. Prior to the reorganization, there was a sectoral distinction with the DNB (member of ESCB) as supervisor for the banking sector, and separate supervisors for insurance and pensions (*Pensioen- en Verzekeringskamer*) and securities (*Stichting Toezicht Effectenverkeer*) respectively. Because of the emergence of financial conglomerates, the boundaries between different sectors had become blurred. Supervision changed from sectoral towards functional supervision. The Netherlands performed a pioneering role here, with the introduction of the Twin Peak model in which other European countries, such as Italy, have shown interest (DNB 2007). This supervisory model for financial markets relies on two supervisory bodies: DNB and the Authority for Financial Markets (AFM). DNB is responsible for the prudential stability of all financial institutions (micro prudential) and for the stability of the financial system (macro prudential). AFM, newly created, is responsible for conducting the business supervision of all financial firms. The securities supervisor was developed into AFM, whereas the insurance and pension supervisors were largely abolished or merged with DNB (Kremers and Schoenmaker 2010).

Thus DNB is still responsible for safeguarding financial stability in the Netherlands. Three important preconditions for financial stability are: low and stable inflation, secure payments, and sound and healthy financial institutions. However, the recent financial crisis of 2008 has painfully shown that it failed to guard a sound and healthy financial system. The few large financial conglomerates that emerged in the 1990s, mainly through mergers and acquisitions, had become an important part of the economy, as can be seen from the large ratio between their assets and gross domestic product. In 2007, this ratio was 194 per cent for ABN AMRO (€ 1,025b), 188 per cent for ING (€ 994b) and 108 per cent for Rabobank (€ 570b). And whereas perhaps their performance improved, stability of the system did not.

As a result of the financial crisis, banks were nationalized, had to split up or went bankrupt. Thus, already just before the crisis ABN AMRO was sold to a consortium of three banks, one of them being Fortis, the Belgian–Dutch financial. However, Fortis almost went bankrupt due to its low capital basis. In October 2008 the state announced it would take over the Dutch part of Fortis, including the former ABN AMRO's activities in the Netherlands. Only in 2015 were part of ABN AMRO's shares sold on the capital market again. At the same time, ING Group, a bank-insurer which received substantial state funds during the depth of the financial crisis (*Volkskrant* 2009), had to split up into ING Bank and insurer Nationale-Nederlanden. Only Rabobank survived the crisis relatively unharmed. The state, in close cooperation with DNB, also nationalized the bank-insurer SNS in 2013 because it could not meet its solvability requirements. Recently, this led to discussions about the role of DNB and the Minister of Finance in the nationalizations. In 2014, a commission concluded, for example, that DNB, when it granted permissions to SNS for a few acquisitions, had not recognized the risks that were involved in these acquisitions.

Because of the financial crisis governments were forced to save failing banks with taxpayers' money. Also it became clear that worldwide financial institutions were very closely interconnected, whereas at the same time there was no uniform supervision system within Europe. As a result, after the financial crisis, two important steps were taken: first, European rules and regulations on resolution were drafted, and second, central supervision became the responsibility of the ECB.

Thus, in 2014 important steps were taken towards the European Banking Union by the creation of European banking supervision. One goal of the introduction of European banking supervision was restoring confidence in the European financial sector. In other words, the European Banking Union aims to safeguard the safety and soundness of the banking sector in Europe, by fostering further financial integration and stability across Europe. The Banking Union consists of three pillars, the first of which is the SSM. The other two are a single resolution mechanism, which deals with banks that get into trouble (Single Resolution Mechanism, SRM), and a European deposit guarantee scheme (not in effect yet).

Within the first pillar, SSM, supervision of all banks in the euro area is a shared responsibility of the ECB and the various national supervisory authorities, one of which is DNB. Thus, under the new system, ECB works in tandem with national supervisory authorities. In practice this means that ECB has direct responsibility for 120 banks, which is around 85 per cent of all banking assets in the euro zone (DNB website), among them the Dutch financial institutions such as ABN AMRO, SNS Bank, Rabobank, ING Bank, BNG Bank and NWB Bank. Smaller banks remain under the supervision of DNB.

The second pillar focuses on resolution, which means in the first place that it is no longer the government that has to bail out a bank with taxpayers' money, but that shareholders and investors are responsible for bearing the cost of a failing bank. There are various tools, such as bail-in by shareholders and creditors or the sale of parts of the bank. Resolution rules also include that a bank in trouble will resolve in a controlled manner to ensure that customers keep access to payment services and savings. Moreover, it aims to prevent other banks from collapsing (see DNB website).

7.9 Conclusions

The history of central banking in the Netherlands can neatly be divided in to two periods – 200 years of 'proto-central banking' and 200 years of 'real central banking'. The Amsterdam Exchange Bank set up in 1609 was not designed as a central bank, but as an instrument to facilitate the payments system of the city. However, because it began to play such a large role in the financial and monetary development of the city and the state as a whole, and because all partners involved were keen on stabilizing the monetary system, it developed activities that are now associated with the classical central bank. This is what we have called 'proto-central banking'. Due to the power structures of the Dutch Republic, the overwhelming economic role played by Amsterdam, and the business-like approach of the bank itself, the Amsterdam Exchange Bank not only began to play a central role in international monetary system of the 17th and 18th centuries, but it also developed policies aimed at stabilizing the system, including support for banks which were under pressure from the volatility of markets (and policy mistakes). In the meantime, in Sweden and England in particular, new adaptations of the Exchange Bank further pioneered the role such an institution could play within the context of a centralized state, resulting in the development of the 'real' central banking model as it matured during the 18th and 19th centuries. In that new model, the central bank was much more intimately related to the national state, and in particular the management of its public debt.

After the decentralized polity of the Dutch Republic had given way to the centralized new Kingdom of the Netherlands, the new model of a central bank serving the central state (and in particular its King) was, in its turn, an important source of inspiration for the newly created Central Bank of 1814. DNB from the start, however, tried to keep the King and his ambitious economic policies at arm's length, as the Amsterdam economic elite distrusted his plans and power. This independence from the state arguably became the key to its long-term success. During the 20th century, DNB transformed into a modern central bank. During the Golden Years of economic growth and full employment DNB was state-owned but the state remained relatively at a distance as its formal powers were limited. After the oil crises, DNB became increasingly influenced by developments in the international and more specific European level. As a result, it became less autonomous as it had to follow European rules and practices.

The arguably most important aim of these two central banking institutions was stability of the financial and monetary system. Measured in terms of the stability of prices and exchange rates, the two central banks were relatively successful (the Dutch guilder was perhaps the most stable currency between 1600 and 2000). The financial crises of 1921 and 2008, however, hit the financial system hard (in 2008 even more so than in 1921); in both cases the state had to step in, showing the limitations of the role DNB could play. Again, in both cases DNB was unable to prevent a financial crisis – in many ways it seemed as unready to rescue the banking systems in 2008 as it was in 1921. But perhaps two major financial crises over a period of 400 years is not all that bad.

We can speculate about the underlying causes of the relative stability of the financial system. The most obvious explanation is that the Netherlands, from about 1600 onwards, was one of the richest countries in the world, and continues to be so until the present. It, for example, generated substantial surpluses on the balance of payments which were often invested abroad, but this also meant that the economy hardly ever suffered balance of payments constraints (with the exception of the years of reconstruction after 1945). The long history of sharing power – between the state (or the states in the period before 1798), and the business community and other organized interests, including the financial community – may also have played a role in stabilizing the socio-political and financial systems (Prak and Van Zanden 2013).

With the introduction of the EMU and the following centralization of central banking functions in Frankfurt, the history of central banking in the Netherlands now runs towards its end, so it seems. The recent financial crisis has strengthened European supervision even more. To restore confidence in the European financial sector, European rules and regulations on resolutions have been drafted (SRM) and central supervision has become the responsibility of the ECB (SSM). DNB always has been an important advisor of government policy and seems to be acting increasingly as an unorthodox think tank. For example, recently it advised the unions to demand larger wage increases to stimulate domestic demand and speed up economic growth – rather surprising policy advice for this traditionally rather conservative institution. It perhaps shows how DNB is searching for a new role within the Dutch polity. We cannot speculate what will happen in the long term (or even the medium long run) with the euro and the EMU; history is full of surprises and dramatic turns of events, which, perhaps one day, will bring DNB back as the monitor of Dutch monetary policy and guardian of its financial system.

References

Bank Act 1998, see: www.dnb.nl/en/about-dnb/organisation/wetten-en-regelgeving/i ndex.jsp

De Jong, A.M. *Geschiedenis van de Nederlandsche Bank.* Vol. II. Haarlem: De Nederlandsche Bank, 1967.

De Jong, A.M. *Geschiedenis van de Nederlandsche Bank.* Vol. III. Haarlem: De Nederlandsche Bank, 1967.

Dehing, Pit. *Geld in Amsterdam. Wisselbank En Wisselkoersen, 1650-1725*. Hilversum: Verloren, 2012.

DNB. 'Een structurele stap vooruit – ervaringen van DNB met het Twin Peaks-toezichtmodel', *DNB Kwartaalbericht*, juni 2007.

Fase, M.M.G. *Tussen behoud en vernieuwing. Geschiedenis van de Nederlandsche Bank 1948-1973*. Den Haag, Sdu Uitgevers, 2000.

Gillard, Lucien. *La Banque d'Amsterdam et Le Florin Européen Au Temps de La République Néerlandaise (1610-1820)*. Paris: EHESS, 2004.

Hart, Marjolein 't. 'Corporate Governance'. In *De Wisselbank. Van Stadsbank Tot Bank van de Wereld*, edited by Marius Van Nieuwkerk. Amsterdam: Sonsbeek Publishers bv, 2009.

Jonker, Joost. *Merchants, Bankers, Middlemen: The Amsterdam Money Market During the First Half of the 19th Century*. Amsterdam: NEHA, 1996.

Kremers, Jeroen and Dirk Schoenmaker. 'Twin Peaks: Experiences in the Netherlands', *LSE Financial Markets Group Paper Series*, December 2010.

Mooij, Joke. 'Banck van Wissel: Het Begin van Een Fenomeen'. In *De Wisselbank. Van Stadsbank Tot Bank van de Wereld*, edited by Marius Van Nieuwkerk, 28-37. Amsterdam: Sonsbeek Publishers bv, 2009.

Prak, M.R. and J.L. van Zanden. *Nederland En Het Poldermodel. Sociaal-Economische Geschiedenis van Nederland, 1000-2000*. Amsterdam: Bert Bakker, 2013.

Quinn, Stephen and William Roberds. 'Muntslag, Centrale Bankgeld En de Wisselbank'. In *De Wisselbank. Van Stadsbank Tot Bank van de Wereld*, edited by Marius Van Nieuwkerk, 92-107. Amsterdam: Sonsbeek Publishers bv, 2009.

Uittenbogaard, R.A. *Penningen en papieren. Waarom de Republiek geen centrale bank had*. Masters thesis, Utrecht University, 1996.

Uittenbogaard, R.A. *Kredietverlening door de wisselbank (1609-1802), In De Wisselbank. Van Stadsbank Tot Bank van de Wereld*, edited by Marius Van Nieuwkerk, 120-129. Amsterdam: Sonsbeek Publishers bv, 2009.

Uittenbogaard, Roland. *Evolution of Central Banking? De Nederlandsche Bank 1814-1852*. Dordrecht: Springer, 2014.

Uittenbogaard, Roland and Jan Luiten van Zanden. 'Expansion, Internationalization and Concentration, 1950-1990'. In *Worldwide Banking. ABN AMRO 1824-1999*, T. de Graaf a.o. (edited by) Amsterdam: ABN AMRO, 1999.

Van Nieuwkerk, Marius. 'De Monetaire Functie van de Wisselbank'. In *De Wisselbank. Van Stadsbank Tot Bank van de Wereld*, edited by Marius Van Nieuwkerk, 132-143. Amsterdam: Sonsbeek Publishers bv, 2009a.

Van Nieuwkerk, Marius. 'Van Stadsbank Tot Bank van de Wereld'. In *De Wisselbank. Van Stadsbank Tot Bank van de Wereld*, edited by Marius Van Nieuwkerk, 12-27. Amsterdam: Sonsbeek Publishers bv, 2009b.

Van Nieuwkerk, Marius and Corry Van Renselaar, eds. 'Willem I Treedt Aan, de Wisselbank Heeft Afgedaan'. In *De Wisselbank. Van Stadsbank Tot Bank van de Wereld*, 168-179. Amsterdam: Sonsbeek Publishers bv, 2009.

Van Zanden, J.L. *The Economic History of the Netherlands in the 20th Century*. London: Routledge, 1997.

Van Zanden, J.L. 'What Happened to the Standard of Living before the Industrial Revolution?' In *Living Standards in the Past*, edited by Robert C. Allen, T. Bengsston and M. Dribe, 173-195. Oxford: Oxford University Press, 2005.

Van Zanden, J.L. and A. Van Riel. *The Strictures of Inheritance. the Dutch Economy in the Nineteenth Century.* Princeton: Princeton University Press, 2004.

Volkskrant. 'Kroes akkoord met staatssteun ING', 18 November 2009, www.volkskrant .nl/economie/kroes-akkoord-met-staatssteun-ing~a359928/

Vries, Joh, de. *De Nederlandsche Bank van 1914–1948. Visserings tijdsvak 1914–1931.* Den Haag, 1989.

Vries, Joh, de. *De Nederlandsche Bank van 1914–1948. Trips tijdvak 1931–1948 onderbroken door de Tweede Wereldoorlog.* Den Haag, 1994.

Westerhuis, Gerarda. *Conquering the American Market. ABN AMRO, Rabobank and Nationale-Nederlanden Working in a Different Business Environment.* Amsterdam: Boom, 2008.

Westerhuis, Gerarda. 'Commercial Banking: Changing Interactions Between Banks, Markets, Industry and State'. In *The Oxford Handbook of Banking and Financial History*, Youssef Cassis, Richard S. Grossman and Catherine R. Schenk, edited by Oxford: Oxford University Press, 2016.

Westerhuis, Gerarda and Abe de Jong. *Over geld en macht. Financiering en corporate governance van het Nederlands bedrijfsleven.* Amsterdam: Boom, 2015.

8

Norges Bank 1816–2016: A History of a Small Independent Central Bank

Øyvind Eitrheim and Jan Tore Klovland*

8.1 A Monetary History in Five Parts

Norges Bank is 200 years old. Its name remains unchanged, but throughout its history Norges Bank has undergone some fundamental changes, as has the society it serves. Its core function – safeguarding a well-functioning monetary system for the nation – endures. This chapter provides a short description of Norges Bank's quest to fulfil its functions since its birth in 1816, with varying degrees of success in the face of various historical events. Some periods proved more challenging than others because of external circumstances such as war or international crises. In other periods, perhaps the bank must bear the responsibility for its failings.[1] We have structured the exposition in five parts.[2]

- *1816–1850:* Collapse and reconstruction of the monetary system. *The long promise* of resumption to convertibility of banknotes at their par silver value
- *1850–1914: Monetisation* and the rise of private deposit-taking banks

* We thank the discussant Tobias Straumann and the editors for their thoughtful comments. The views expressed are those of the authors and do not necessarily represent those of Norges Bank.

[1] In this chapter we draw heavily on recent studies of Norges Bank's history documented in Lie, Kobberrød, Thomassen and Rongved (2016), Bøhn, Eitrheim and Qvigstad (2016), Bordo, Eitrheim, Flandreau and Qvigstad (2016) and Eitrheim, Klovland and Øksendal (2016b) respectively. Regarding the 350-year history of Sveriges Riksbank, the material we present in this chapter draws on the excellent exposition of its long history by Wetterberg (2009) as well as the large empirical material which has been produced in Sveriges Riksbank's Historical Monetary and Financial Statistics project, which is documented in two edited volumes by Edvinsson, Jacobson and Waldenström (2010, 2014).

[2] The five parts and corresponding subperiods are the same as in Eitrheim, Klovland and Øksendal (2016b). These subperiods appear as shaded areas in all figures we present in this chapter.

- *1914–1940:* World War I and the *turbulent interwar years.* Postwar recession and banking crisis followed by resumption of prewar gold parity in the 1920s, and breaking out from the golden fetters in the early 1930s
- *1940–1986:* World War II and the political economy of postwar Norway; decades of tight regulation, *central planning and financial repression*
- *1986–2016: The long return to monetary stability.*

The year 1814 meant different things to Norway and Sweden. The Kiel Treaty ended the Napoleonic War in northern Europe. Norway was in transition from a tight union with Denmark to a new union with Sweden. Norway tried to exploit the political and military chaos at the end game of the Napoleonic wars to declare its independence with its 17 May 1814 Constitution. However *realpolitik* caught up with its independence aspirations. The short-lived independence was swapped with a union with Sweden, although much looser than the Swedish crown prince Carl Johan (the strongman in the royal family) had envisaged. However, the short spell of independence was not in vain. When the year 1814 ended, Norway had laid the basis for all its main nationbuilding institutions. The 17 May Constitution was renegotiated with Swedish authorities in the autumn of 1814 and with only minor adjustments it was adapted to form a loose union which linked the two countries together. Apart from a common King and a common foreign policy, Norway would have its separate government, Parliament, Supreme Court, Auditor General, and its own separate monetary system and national bank. The latter was made even clearer in the renegotiated version of the Constitution, since it stated in a new paragraph that Norway would keep its own bank and monetary system, both under parliamentary control and supervision. The political process of the formation of this bank, however, took considerable time and it was only after two years, on 14 June 1816, that the King could sanction the acts which formed the legal framework for Norges Bank and Norway's monetary system. Norges Bank is therefore still a relatively young institution relative to the Swedish Riksbank, and it has only recently passed the milestone of its first two centuries.

The name of the institution, Norges Bank, is the same but the functions of the bank have changed over the past 200 years. It started as the first and only bank in Norway in 1816. Then, as private banks entered the scene during the 19th century, Norges Bank changed and became *a* bank among other banks. At the turn of the century, Norges Bank had developed to become the nucleus in a bank-driven monetary system, a central bank. In both Norway and Sweden the 19th century was a century of monetisation and expansion of the banking system. This will be one of the themes that we will explore in this chapter. But there were also many aspects of their respective monetary systems which Norway and Sweden shared both before and after the great expansion of the banking sector. In both countries there was a strong desire after the Napoleonic wars to bring the monetary system back on firm ground, centred on banknotes redeemable in silver coins at a promised par value of speciedaler in Norway and in riksdaler in Sweden. The process of resumption became a long one in both countries. Riksdaler resumed its convertibility to silver in 1834. *The long promise* of convertibility of speciedaler, which was given in the Norges Bank Act of 1816, was soon suspended and was only fulfilled 26 years later, in 1842.

Whereas Norges Bank was granted monopoly privileges to issue banknotes in 1818, this was not granted to the Swedish Riksbank until 1903, after a substantial period where Riksbank notes circulated together with banknotes issued by a growing number of private banks. In 1873 Norway, Sweden and Denmark negotiated a plan for a Scandinavian Currency Union (SCU). In Norway this meant introducing new currency units, kroner and øre, and more generally, the introduction of the metric system. Norway joined the SCU two years later, in 1875. At the same time all three countries changed the metallic basis of their monetary system from silver to gold. This happened with minor consequences for exchange rate stability, which had been firmly established at the time of resumption to silver convertibility many decades earlier. The monetary systems of the three member states of SCU soon became more closely integrated and in 1885 Norges Bank, the Riksbank and Danmarks Nationalbank also opened mutual clearing accounts to facilitate payment settlements.

World War I was a game changer and the SCU effectively collapsed. Norway and Sweden would take very different courses. Whereas the interwar years were troublesome years everywhere, they were even more so in Norway. The 1920s were particularly bad, since Norway suffered a systemic banking crisis when a huge number of banks collapsed in the postwar depression. It took many years to overcome this banking crisis and it brought heavy burdens with it. Norges Bank became the main manager of this banking crisis in 1920–1925. This had serious consequences for its goal of gold resumption for the Norwegian krone. Whereas the Swedish krone easily had resumed its prewar gold value already in 1923, the return to the prewar gold parity in Norway was a long drawn-out process, which caused much turbulence during the years 1925–1928. Furthermore, the fall of the Norwegian krone had been much larger, aggravated by the banking crisis, and in the middle of 1924, the Norwegian kroner had only half of its prewar gold content. A rapid period of currency appreciation followed and Norway restored gold convertibility in May 1928. The goal of resuming prewar gold parities was achieved, albeit at heavy costs.

World War II gave rise to very different developments in Norway and Sweden. As an occupied country, Norway's economy entered into a severe depression whereas the neutral country, Sweden, could harvest war dividends much similar to those achieved in World War I. Thus, although Sweden came out of the war as a richer country, both countries experienced strong and persistent postwar growth. Norway's huge monetary overhang, which was created during the war by the German occupation, was gradually brought down. For the next forty years, Norges Bank practised central banking without monetary policy. Interest rates were kept permanently low and ceased to function as a rationing instrument. Instead the quantity of credit was rationed and private banks made subject to financial repression through a variety of channels. A similar regime was implemented in Sweden, with the Riksbank in a key role as coordinator of credit rationing. In Norway, the state banks were the government's primary instrument in the channelling of credit to fund investments. Industrial modernisation in export-oriented industries and housing investments were the most highly prioritised areas.

The policy change in 1986, after a decade with frequent devaluations, was the beginning of a return to monetary stability. The massive credit growth of the 1980s did not end well. The risk elements of the banks' asset portfolios had increased, and when losses emerged in 1987–1988, it turned out that the banks were severely undercapitalised. When the Norwegian banking crisis, which started in 1988, turned systemic in 1991–1992, the three largest banks were nationalised and recapitalised by the central government. The Swedish banking crises followed with a lag of a year or so. In both Norway and Sweden inflation had stabilised around 2–2.5 per cent from the early 1990s onwards, not far from the target level of inflation of the major European countries. Sweden adopted inflation targeting as its monetary policy regime already from 1993. Norway eventually adopted inflation targeting several years later, de facto from 1999 and formally from 2001.

The experiences following the global financial crisis from 2008 onwards have taught us that inflation targeting is not sufficient to guarantee monetary stability. In recent years there has been a stronger focus on financial stability and its interplay with price stability. The banks are now subject to stricter capital requirements and tighter regulations of their lending behaviour. In Norway the central bank mandate has broadened, as from 2013 it also comprises an explicit advisory role on the implementation of macro-prudential policy measures such as the level of the countercyclical capital buffer, which is now an integral part of bank capital regulations.

8.2 1816–1850: A Difficult Birth and a Long Promise

Figure 8.1 shows Norwegian and Swedish consumer price levels from 1667 onwards. From the late 1830s there is a striking similarity between the development of prices in the two countries. There are also notable differences. Whereas Norway only experienced modest inflation in the 17th century, there is significantly higher inflation in Sweden. During the Great Nordic War (1716–1719), Swedish prices showed almost fourfold increases whereas Norwegian prices increased by a modest 7 per cent. Swedish prices continued to rise on a steeper trend during most of the 18th century. During the Napoleonic War (1807–1813), however, Norwegian prices showed more than twentyfold increases, whereas Swedish prices rose somewhat less than 80 per cent.

By the end of the 18th century, Denmark-Norway had become a paper money economy. The key vehicle for this development was the establishment

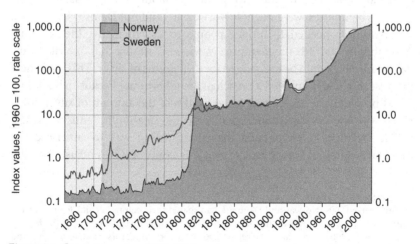

Figure 8.1 Consumer prices 1667–2016.
Source: Norges Bank HMS, Sveriges Riksbank HMFS, Grytten (2004a), Klovland (2013), Edvinsson and Söderberg (2010).

of the Courantbank in 1736. The bank soon found itself in dire straits, with notes circulating at a discount. In the last fifty years of Danish rule, notes became an important element in the circulation of means of payment and constituted the bulk of liquidity.[3] Some of the growth probably reflected increased monetisation of the economy, but the strongest source of expansion was most likely the replacement of coins by notes in the domestic circulation.[4] The massive injection of banknotes and other paper money instruments that were introduced during the war 1807–1812 triggered a massive depreciation of the Dano-Norwegian currency. The following hyperinflation caused a complete breakdown of the union's monetary system. Neither the 1813 monetary reform nor the actions taken by the 1814 constitutional assembly were sufficient to resolve the situation in Norway, but in 1816 a third attempt was made to restore the Norwegian monetary system.

8.2.1 A Difficult Birth for the Bank of Issue

When Norges Bank was established on 14 June 1816 it was born into a particularly challenging environment. The Danish-Norwegian monetary unit, the riksdaler courant, had been devalued by 90 per cent against silver in January 1813 and replaced by the riksbankdaler. One riksbankdaler was defined as 12.64 grams of fine silver. After Norway was ceded to Sweden by the Kiel Treaty in January 1814, the former viceroy of Norway, Prince Christian Frederik, decided to print 3 million riksbankdaler. These 'prince's banknotes' were the first Norwegian (and not Danish) banknotes. But trust was needed to induce people to use them. At the National Assembly in May 1814 a guarantee was issued, stating that one riksbankdaler banknote could be exchanged for 6.74 grams of silver. This was a new promise, but it also entailed a breach of an old promise because a banknote could now only be exchanged for around half the amount of silver compared with the amount promised after the devaluation in January 1813.

The Constitution stipulated that the Storting was to supervise the monetary system. History had shown this could not be entrusted to the

---

[3] Svendsen et al. (1968).

[4] In the early 1800s, Norway and Denmark had shared their common coins for more than 400 years. However, prior to the formation of the Dano-Norwegian union, in the Middle Ages 1000–1400, Norwegian sovereigns had been early initiators of state coinage and Norwegian coins soon dominated in domestic circulation. Numerous archaeological, numismatic and written sources support this finding, see e.g. Gullbekk (2009) and Skaare (1995).

King. As the Storting only convened once every third year, it delegated the responsibility to another authority. That authority would become Norges Bank. It took time to establish such a bank. The Norwegian branch of the Riksbank, the joint Danish-Norwegian bank of issue, was given the name 'Temporary Riksbank' in May 1814 and functioned as a bank of issue until Norges Bank was established.

8.2.2 Delivering the Promised Silver Value of the Banknotes Took Time

Norges Bank's main priority after its establishment in 1816 was to secure the silver value of money. On 14 June 1816, a new promise was made. The new currency unit – speciedaler – was defined as 25.28 grams of fine silver and the redemption obligation was to apply from 1 January 1819. It had been decided that ten riksbankdaler could be exchanged for one speciedaler, reducing one riksbankdaler's silver value from 6.74 grams to 2.53 grams of fine silver. The Storting recognised that the series of broken promises had to stop.

First, Norges Bank had to build up a silver reserve, which it attempted by issuing shares in the bank that were to be voluntarily paid in silver. But that did not suffice and a silver tax was imposed. The silver tax triggered civil unrest, with farmers marching on Christiania (as Oslo was called at that time). There were fears that the tax would lead to demands for a common monetary system with Sweden. The Storting decided in 1818 to postpone the fullfilment of its promise to resume silver payments.

Figure 8.2 shows the development in Norway's and Sweden's exchange rates against British pound sterling until 1850.[5] On the background of the series of previously broken promises, we regard the huge deviations between Swedish and Norwegian exchange rates in this period to be primarily due to the long and thorny road towards resumption which Norway embarked upon following the 1818 decision to postpone resumption, a road which would stretch out more than two decades before the goal was finally achieved in 1842. Also in Sweden the road towards specie payments was long and it was only in 1834 that the Riksbank resumed its legal obligation to redeem its banknotes in silver. Thus, both union partners had stated the same goal of resuming specie payments quite early after the Napoleonic wars had ended, but it took a considerable amount of time before this goal was finally achieved. And in both countries there

---

[5] Data are taken from Klovland (2004a) and Lobell (2010).

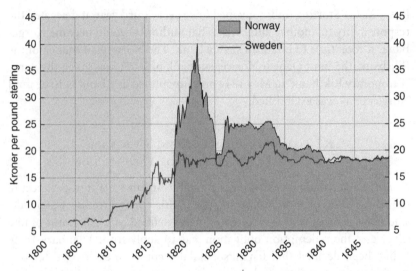

Figure 8.2 Norwegian and Swedish exchange rates against British pound sterling until 1850
Source: Norges Bank HMS, Sveriges Riksbank HMFS, Klovland (2004a), Lobell (2010).

was considerable debate on the resumption policies, in Sweden in the late 1820s (Fregert, 1999) and in Norway in the early to mid-1830s (Eitrheim, Eriksen and Sæther, 2016a).

In January 1817, Norges Bank was the only bank in the country. It received deposits, but a fee was charged for that service. Positive deposit rates were first introduced in 1842. Each regional branch set its own rate on discount lending. In earlier years people who wanted to borrow had to borrow from relatives, friends or wealthy merchants in an unregulated market. Export and import firms used banks in Copenhagen, London or Hamburg. Money was stored in chests and mattresses.

Although it was a shared ambition in both Norway and Sweden to reintroduce silver convertibility of banknotes, the resumption process turned out to be a lengthy and trouble-some process in both countries. In Norway the promise to redeem banknotes already from 1 January 1819 proved to be overly ambitious. The promise that the speciedaler would be worth 25.28 grams of silver was only delivered in 1842. The road towards convertibility in Norway was therefore a long one, but this should be seen against the background of the series of broken promises in 1813–1816. Similarly, the resumption process in Sweden took until 1834 before the dual set of riksdaler banknotes, *riksdaler banco* issued by the Riksbank and *riksdaler riksgälds* issued by the National Debt Office, resumed their fixed values in silver.

Norges Bank's head office was located in Trondhjem, far away from the government in Christiania and far away from the King in Stockholm. Bank branches were opened in Bergen and Christiania, the two largest cities in the country, and in Christianssand. In the 1830s branches were also opened in Drammen and Skien, two cities to the south-west of Christiania. In the first years, the main tasks of the bank included managing silver tax payments and handling receipts, printing and distributing banknotes and bookkeeping. When it was decided to honour the promise of exchange of a speciedaler paper note with a speciedaler silver coin in 1842, this was only feasible at Norges Bank's head office in Trondhjem, which was a long distance from the country's capital and other large cities. The exchange rate therefore varied between Norwegian cities and a holder of a speciedaler banknote in Christiania might receive, say, 2.5 per cent less silver for the note compared with a holder in Trondhjem. In 1845 Norges Bank started to honour its bank notes in silver also in Christiania, Bergen and Christianssand.

8.3 1850–1914: From a Bank among Other Banks to a Bankers' Bank

Figure 8.3 shows monetary developments in Norway and Sweden over the past 200 years. The period from 1850 to the beginning of World War I can be seen as a period of increased monetisation in both Norway and Sweden. In broad terms, Figure 8.3 reveals striking similarities as private banks enter the scene and start to manage deposits offered by the general public. The holdings of broad money (coins, notes and bank deposits) in both countries, measured in per cent of GDP, increased from below 20 per cent around 1850 to around 80 percent in 1920. This increase was primarily due to the strong expansion of the banking sector and the increased amount of money held as bank deposits. There were also differences. First, we see from Figure 8.3 (bottom) that more money was held as coins in Sweden than in Norway during the entire 19th century, although the difference gradually diminished. Second, we note that the expansion of money held as bank deposits started somewhat earlier in Norway than in Sweden. In Norway it started with rapid growth in the number of savings banks in the 1820s and 1830s. In 1848 the first commercial bank was established, and after the international financial crisis in Hamburg in 1857 many more followed. This prepared the ground for the rapid expansion of money held as bank deposits in Norway, which we see from Figure 8.3. In Sweden, on the other hand, the ratio of broad money to GDP remained at below 20 per cent until around 1870. At that time there was a rapid expansion

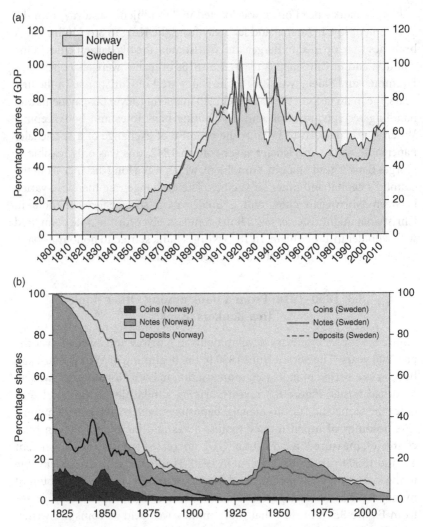

Figure 8.3 Broad money in percentage of GDP (top) and their decomposition in notes, coins and private bank deposits (bottom)
Source: Norges Bank HMS, Sveriges Riksbank HMFS, Grytten (2004b), Klovland (2004b), Edvinsson and Ögren (2014), Edvinsson (2014).

of *enskilda banks*, which soon brought the ratio of broad money to GDP up to and beyond the corresponding level in Norway.[6] These banks were

---

[6] Bordo and Jonung (1990) discuss the development of the velocity of broad money, measured as the inverse of broad money holdings in percentage of GDP, for a broad group of countries including Norway and Sweden.

also issuers of banknotes, and in contrast to Norges Bank, the Swedish Riksbank was granted monopoly rights as issuer of banknotes only after the turn of the century, from 1903 onwards. Third, we see from Figure 8.3 a rapid growth in money holdings in Norway during World War II, which was due to the German occupants who financed their war expenses in Norway by printing banknotes.

8.3.1 The Division of Responsibility between the Bank of Issue and the Government

It took a long time to establish trust in the new nation's currency – the speciedaler. Around the middle of the 19th century, fiscsal balance had been restored thanks to a period of economic growth. The government and the Storting had exercised spending restraint and managed government revenues soundly. Government debt had been repaid. The banknotes had gained trust and they were being used.

8.3.2 A Bank among Banks

The first savings bank was established in 1822, but the wave of new banks came around the middle of the century. During the 1848 financial crisis, Norges Bank was unable to meet private demand for credit at a time when demand was high. Norges Bank's silver reserves were drained and the law required that Norges Bank should hold a defined amount of silver relative to its note issuance. The government stepped in and raised loans abroad and channelled credit to the private sector.[7] The first commercial bank was founded in 1848. Norges Bank was no longer the dominant provider of credit, but a bank among other banks. A small, but first step towards a new role for Norges Bank, as a bankers' bank, took place in the autumn of 1857. A severe international crisis was triggered by overinvestment in railroad construction in the US. Norwegian importers and exporters turned to banks in Hamburg for trade credit, but to no avail. Changes in legislation prior to the crisis had loosened up the note issuing regulations, allowing Norges Bank to issue more notes on a given level of its silver reserves. This gave Norges Bank greater flexibility to deal with this new liquidity crisis than during the 1848 crisis. The bank also bolstered confidence in Norwegian bills abroad by sending substantial amounts of its silver reserves to Hamburg to back up the troubled Hamburg banks, which

---

[7] See Eitrheim, Klovland and Øksendal (2016b, chapter 4) for details.

were vital for the payments related to Norwegian foreign trade. Thus, the liquidity in the 'Norwegian' money market in Hamburg was improved.

8.3.3 From Silver to Gold and a Metric System

There had been an international movement to replace silver with gold as the standard for the monetary system, and to adopt the decimal system. In 1873, the Scandinavian countries decided to establish their own currency union based on gold, with the krone as its monetary unit. When the matter was brought up in the Storting it was decided that the gold standard should be adopted from 1 January 1874. Norway did not, however, join the Scandinavian mint union until 16 October 1875. While a speciedaler divided into 120 skillings, the krone divided into 100 øre. One speciedaler was exchanged for 4 kroner. One krone contained just above 0.4 gram of pure gold.

8.3.4 More Branches, Yet More Centralisation

In the period between 1850 and 1914, fifteen new regional Norges Bank branches were established. Many of these branches were established to remedy credit shortages in the districts. Some of them eventually exceeded their lending limits, and substantial losses were written off in 1887 and 1889. Since its beginning, Norges Bank had been a network of branches in a loose confederation. The branches were autonomous and set lending rates in their local regions.[8] As private and state banks were established, Norges Bank gradually became a bankers' bank. The need for a more professionalised central bank arose and in 1892 a new Norges Bank Act was adopted, which strengthened the head office. In 1897, the head office was moved from Trondhjem to Kristiania.[9] The Printing Works followed in 1907.

8.3.5 Norges Bank Acts as a Central Bank

Economic growth was especially strong in Kristiania through the 1890s and a homespun boom-to-bust crisis occurred at the dawn of the new century. The nucleus of the crisis was a property boom in the capital Kristiania which soon spread from real estate and related industries to banking. Good times and optimism had segued into euphoria, with a surge

---

[8] Klovland and Øksendal (2017).   [9] Christiania was spelled Kristiania from 1877.

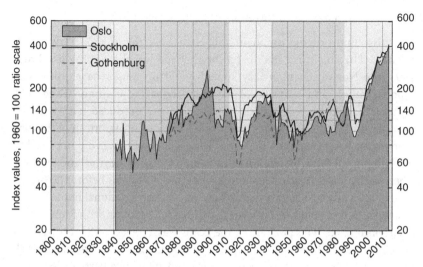

Figure 8.4 Housing prices 1819–2014
Source: Norges Bank HMS, Sveriges Riksbank HMFS, Eitrheim and Erlandsen (2004, 2005), Bohlin (2014), Söderberg et al. (2014).

in new banks. Since these banks had insufficient deposits to cover their lending, they turned to short-term market funding. These short-term funds were placed as long-term loans. In June 1899 a crisis erupted. Norges Bank had done little in advance to prevent it, but did play an active role in picking up the pieces. To 'save' the payment system, Norges Bank provided the banking system with liquidity and managed banks in crisis. Norges Bank had become the hub of the banking system – a central bank. The bank's motive for acting as a *lender of last resort* was not to save the banks, but to prevent a disruption of the payments system.[10]

Figure 8.4 shows that real house prices in the Scandinavian city of Kristiania (named Oslo from 1924) as well as in Gothenburg, and particularly in Stockholm, had trended upwards since the 1870s. The sharp peak level reached in Kristiania in 1899 was soon a distant memory when the bubble burst, and Oslo did in fact not reach the real house price level it once had in 1899 until more than a century later, in the early 2000s.[11]

[10] Eitrheim and Øksendal (2016) discuss crisis management and the interplay between monetary authoritites in Norway over two centuries.
[11] The Norwegian crisis in 1899 is one of twenty-three bubble episodes discussed in Brunnermeier and Schnabel (2016).

8.3.6 Dissolution of the Union with Sweden

The dissolution of the union in 1905 had only minor monetary consequences. The only thing that had to be changed was the coin motifs. From
1905, the Norwegian monetary system could no longer have coins with
union symbols and portraits of what had been the common King. The
symbols had to be Norwegian! New coins were produced with national
symbols. In 1906, a coin series was produced featuring a portrait of the new
Norwegian King Haakon VII.[12] The Norwegian banknotes did not need to
be changed after the dissolution of the union between Norway and Sweden.
Their design had already been overhauled in the decades before the break-
up from the union. The design emphasised Norway's national heritage, and
any features that could be associated with Norway's union with Sweden had
been eliminated. The portrait of the King was replaced with portraits of
persons who can be said to have played a major role in the fight against all
that was Swedish, Wilhelm Christie of the Independence Party in 1814 and
Peter Wessel Tordenskiold who was victorious against the Swedes at
Dynekil in 1716. These notes remained in circulation in Norway until the
end of World War II. Spending by the Germans during World War II had
then destroyed the Norwegian monetary system and the notes were replaced
in September 1945.

8.4 1914–1940: A Strong Central Bank Governor
in Turbulent Times

8.4.1 World War I

In common with the other Scandinavian countries, Norway suspended its
obligation to redeem its notes in gold within the first week of the war.
The Scandinavian currencies began to appreciate against the pound in the
autumn of 1915, but at an unequal rate. In practice this signalled the
breakdown of the Scandinavian Currency Union. Norges Bank probably
saw the suspension of gold payments as a temporary phenomenon and
acted accordingly – buying gold and thus adding to the liquidity expansion. Discount rate policy was lax, with nominal interest rates at 5 per cent
or lower and inflation rates hovering around 40 per cent per year. In the

---

[12] King Haakon VII was a Danish prince married to a British princess (Maud), the daughter
of King Edward VII and Queen Alexandra of the UK. The Norwegians thought it would
be nice to offer the throne to a British princess, thus securing some goodwill of the
process of breaking loose from the union with Sweden.

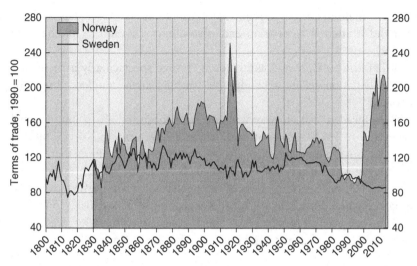

Figure 8.5 Terms of trade
Source: Norges Bank HMS, Sveriges Riksbank HMFS, Grytten (2004b), Edvinsson (2014).

two final years of World War I, the prime source of a further massive injection of base money was the domestic credit expansion of the central bank. Norges Bank was unable to withstand the demand from the government concerning the finance of fish exports to Britain and Germany during the war as purchases of provisions on government account continued up to 1920. These operations created a huge amount of krone liquidity. By 1920, the monetary base had expanded by a factor of 4–5 relative to the prewar situation, and prices had risen nearly at the same rate.

The war had brought large revenues to Norwegian export industries. Many manufacturing and mining industries had benefitted from the boom in the early war years. The shipping industry generated enormous surpluses throughout the war. Figure 8.5 shows pronounced differences in the development of the terms of trade between Norway and Sweden. Two episodes stand out, which illustrate the higher volatility in Norwegian terms of trade than the Swedish one. First, the positive shock to Norwegian terms of trade during the export boom of World War I, and, second, the more recent period when a sizable oil exporting capacity in Norway benefitted from a protracted period with high oil prices from 2000 onwards.

The financial environment of the war years was, in Norway, characterised by a speculative frenzy. Stock prices soared and the number of commercial banks increased fast, which led to a huge expansion of bank credit, often with no concern for demanding sufficient collateral. Norges

Bank took no initiatives to regulate the proliferation of speculative banks, nor did it attempt to restrain excessive money creation by the banking sector.

When the postwar restocking boom crashed spectacularly in 1920, and severe deflation set in, a nationwide banking crisis could no longer be avoided.

Both Sweden and Norway were hit by a short and sharp international recession. In 1921 GDP in Sweden fell by 8.2 per cent, in Norway by 10.1 per cent, but rebounded quickly in both countries. In this period there is also an interesting contrast between the two countries. In Sweden the wartime excesses had been less pronounced, monetary policy was turned around to a tighter stance already in 1919, and the gold parity of Swedish kronor was de facto achieved already in 1922. This is the main reason why Sweden did not experience a systemic bank crisis like the one in Norway.[13]

8.4.2 The 1920s: Banking Crisis and Gold Parity Recession

As newly appointed Chairman of Norges Bank's Board in 1920, Nicolai Rygg began by centralising its management structure. Regional branch managers were previously authorised to grant loans, but from 1920 applications for new larger loans were subject to Board approval. Between 1920 and 1925, Rygg had to concentrate time and resources on dealing with a banking sector on the brink of insolvency. Norges Bank facilitated and pressured banks to take collective responsibility. Both Norges Bank and the Ministry of Finance provided banks with liquidity and participated in recapitalisations. The problem with this policy was that it was only half-hearted and did not go all the way – the lesson of Bagehot was not adhered to – and the majority of large commercial banks succumbed to the pressure. However, with support from the provisional Public Administration Act of 1923, an orderly winding-up of banks was carried out, averting the need for immediate bankruptcy proceedings in most cases.

Beginning in the summer of 1924, monetary policy in Norway was primarily geared towards restoring the gold value of the krone to its prewar level, following the trail of Britain and Sweden. With support from the majority of the political establishment Nicolai Rygg argued adamantly for a return to gold parity. As a result of a period of contractive monetary policy, the krone was again pegged to gold on 1 May 1928 (see Figure 8.6).

---

[13] This episode is further discussed in Klovland (1998).

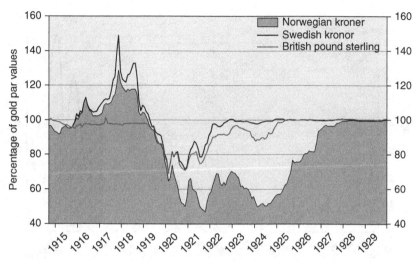

Figure 8.6 Norwegian, Swedish and British exchange rates 1914–1929, in per cent of gold par values
Source: Norges Bank HMS, Sveriges Riksbank HMFS, Klovland (2004a), Bohlin (2010).

In the middle of the 1920s the level and rate of increase in government debt became an issue of some concern. The debt accumulation had started during the war years to fund domestic purchases of provisions and imports of strategically important goods. Budget deficits continued into the 1920s. There had also been large overdrafts on government folio accounts in Norges Bank, but this was a more temporary phenomenon. These features had not been publicly known until 1925 and the disclosure ignited a heated debate.[14] Figure 8.7 shows that gross government debt as a percentage of GDP increased substantially in Norway during this period, also in comparison with Sweden, although it was still at a fairly moderate level. The figure does not include the vast sovereign funds that oil revenues have built up in Norway over the last decades. Today they are between two and three times GDP, and have made Norway a sizable net creditor internationally.

8.4.3   1930s: Breaking the Golden Fetters

In contrast to the 1920s this decade was rather uneventful with respect to central bank issues. The major event was the decision in September 1931 to follow Britain and the other Scandinavian countries off the gold standard.

[14] For a vivid discussion see Keilhau (1930).

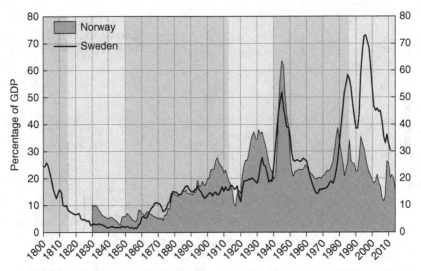

Figure 8.7 Government debt as percentage of GDP 1800–2014
Source: Norges Bank HMS, Sveriges Riksbank HMFS, Eitrheim and Fevolden (2014), Fregert and Gustavsson (2014), Grytten (2004b), Edvinsson (2014).

1931 was a troublesome year, in Norway the GDP growth was strongly negative due to the international slump as well as major labour disputes –5.3 per cent vs –3.4 per cent in Sweden. The subsequent krone depreciation strengthened the competitiveness of Norway's internationally exposed industries. After the trough of the Great Depression had been passed late in 1932, the Norwegian economy experienced solid economic growth and trade surpluses in much of the rest of the 1930s. It is well documented in the literature that the sterling bloc, Britain and Scandinavia, experienced far better economic conditions in the 1930s than many other countries, in particular the gold bloc countries.[15] With the constraints of the gold standard no longer binding the sterling bloc, countries could pursue a relatively easy monetary policy.

But why did Norway leave the hard-fought position in the gold bloc after only three and a half years? The fact that Sweden and Denmark left the gold standard may have played some role, but it was probably not the decisive argument; the days of the Scandinavian Currency Union were long gone, and to the extent that Scandinavian unity, so much favoured in principal speeches, clashed with national interests, the latter weighed more heavily.

[15] Eichengreen and Sachs (1985).

Rather, maintaining the stability of the key exchange rates was the prime goal of Norges Bank's monetary policy, as it always had been, and indeed remained up to the beginning of the 21st century.[16] The exchange rate against the pound was of vital importance to Norwegian export industries, in particular ocean shipping, for which the bulk of revenues was in sterling and the wage costs in Norwegian kroner. This was also the main argument that Norges Bank set forth in its formal address to the government to suspend the convertibility of notes for gold in 1931.[17] We believe the wording of this letter reflects the true intention of Norges Bank. Rygg later referred to the breakaway from the gold standard as the 'currency disaster of 1931'. Although maybe reluctantly, Rygg undertook the policy action to abandon gold, but it unwittingly turned out be his best move.

8.5 1940–1986: Government Bank

8.5.1 The Gold Shipment and New Board in London

On 9 April 1940, Norway was occupied by Germany. By 1938, Norges Bank had already planned how the gold reserves, which it was legally required to keep in Norway, would be secured in the event of war and occupation. The plan was implemented on the morning of 9 April 1940, and the gold shipment through Norway and onwards to England and North America kept the gold from the hands of the occupying powers. The rest of the Norwegian gold reserves and some of the Danish gold reserves had been moved to North America in 1938–1939, whereas the Swedish gold reserves remained in Stockholm. On 22 April, the Norwegian government appointed a new Board of Directors with Arnold Ræstad as Chairman. The Board accompanied the government to London. Nicolai Rygg and the leadership in Oslo continued operations in occupied Norway, while the leadership in London refused to accept the institution in Oslo. It was a de jure Norges Bank in London and in addition a de facto Norges Bank in Oslo. At the end of the war, the occupation account in Norges Bank amounted to 130 per cent of GDP. Preparations were made in both London and Oslo for an extensive liquidity withdrawal, but when it was implemented after the end of the war it had been substantially curtailed.

---

[16] The traditional and deep-rooted belief in the stability of exchange rates in Norwegian monetary policy is reviewed in Qvigstad and Skjæveland (1994), see also Eitrheim, Klovland and Øksendal (2016b).

[17] Rygg (1950, p. 441).

8.5.2 Government-controlled Monetary Policy

While in London, the government decided to place Norges Bank directly under its control. The legal act only affected the de jure Norges Bank in London. The government had no control of the de facto Norges Bank in Oslo. Wide swings in production, employment and inflation in the 1920s and 1930s had convinced the government that the economy needed to be controlled by detailed state planning. In the 1920s, Norges Bank became particularly associated with its 'gold parity policy'. Monetary policy decisions were now to be made by the government. Norges Bank became subordinated in its new role as a technical instrument in the implementation of the government's monetary, credit and foreign exchange policies.

8.5.3 Norges Bank's Return to Oslo

Norges Bank was merged back into a single institution again after the war, on 13 July 1945, and Norges Bank's main office was moved from London to Oslo. Nicolai Rygg, who had chaired the de facto institution in Oslo during the war years, was reinstated as Chairman of Norges Bank's Board of Directors. Rygg was uncomfortable with the term 'reinstated', as he felt he had held the position all along! The government decided to maintain its direct control over Norges Bank also after the war, and in 1949 the bank was nationalised.

8.5.4 Many New Tasks

The government charged Norges Bank with a host of new tasks. The bank had already expanded its work with the many bilateral clearing arrangements which had been established in the 1930s. After World War II, the tight capital control regulations required monitoring of resources and the postwar credit policy also involved substantial credit rationing which required monitoring. In 1962, the Royal Norwegian Mint was transferred from the Ministry of Finance to the bank. Not all the new tasks the bank was charged with could be seen as natural for a central bank. Many of the the tasks, however, gave Norges Bank broad and direct reach and the bank remained an important institution. Many Norges bank employees will likely consider this period as the bank's heyday.

8.5.5 System of Fixed Exchange Rates

On 15 September 1946, Norway adapted the international system of fixed exchange rates, 'Bretton Woods'. Sweden joined some years later, in 1951.

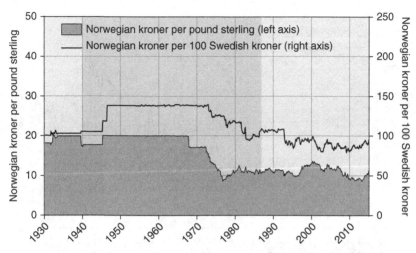

Figure 8.8 Norwegian and Swedish exchange rates 1930–2014. Norwegian kroner per pound sterling (left axis) and Norwegian kroner per 100 Swedish kroner (right axis)
Source: Norges Bank HMS, Sveriges Riksbank HMFS, Klovland (2004a), Bohlin (2010).

At that time, Swedish kronor had already appreciated substantially relative to Norwegian kroner, notably in 1945 and 1946 (see Figure 8.8). The pound sterling's exchange rate against the US dollar turned out to be far too strong and was devalued by 30 per cent in 1949. Several European countries followed suit, including Norway and Sweden.

The devaluation of the two countries' currencies increased the pressure on prices, which increased substantially both in Norway and Sweden in the late 1940s and early 1950s, also as a consequence of the Korean War. Economic policy became increasingly difficult to implement and global cooperation to maintain fixed exchange rates broke down in 1971. The government initially allowed the krone to appreciate to curb inflation but from 1976 onwards Norway and Sweden experienced a series of devaluations, for Norway a total of ten the following decade. Together with the oil price shocks of the 1970s, persistent high inflation ensued. This provides an example of the difficulty of pursuing a policy of fixed exchange rates within a system of non-market-clearing interest rates and expansive fiscal policy.

8.5.6 Rationing and Regulation

During the postwar period, the rationing of imported goods was intended to ensure that limited foreign exchange holdings were used to import goods that were needed for reconstruction. Capital movements

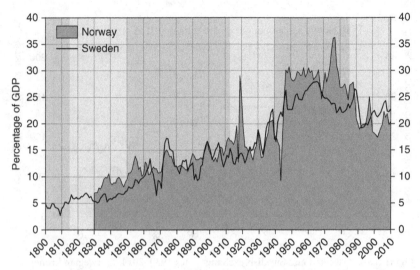

Figure 8.9 Investment in fixed capital (in percentage of GDP)
Source: Norges Bank HMS, Sveriges Riksbank HMFS, Grytten (2004b), Edvinsson (2014).

were strictly regulated. To stimulate investment, interest rates were kept low. State banks, such as the State Housing Bank and the State Educational Loan Fund, were established to secure credit for politically prioritised purposes. Restriction of private bank lending became necessary and was initially attempted through negotiations in the Cooperation Committee, which included members from Norges Bank, the Ministry of Finance, the Banking Inspectorate and private financial institutions. The Chairman of Norges Bank's Board of Directors led the negotiations. A statutory basis was introduced in 1965 for the substantial and direct regulation of lending operations of financial institutions. Monetary policy objectives and measures were drawn up by the Ministry of Finance and Norges Bank's role was that of advisor and monitor of regulatory compliance. On 9 September 1985, new legislation of Norges Bank and the monetary system came into force. The former act had been in place since 1892.

Figure 8.9 shows investment in fixed capital as a percentage of GDP. In Norway the government was committed to an industrial future centred on capital-intensive, export-oriented industries, exploitation of the hydro-electric power potential, and modernising of the important shipping sector, which had suffered large losses of tonnage during the war. Investment ratios that initially were around 15–20 per cent of GDP showed a rapid increase to around 30 per cent in the postwar era and eventually turned out to be the highest in the OECD area. This contrasts with Sweden, where investment ratios also increased, although more gradually, during the postwar era. Although Figure 8.9 reveals strong similarities between the long-run trends of the investment ratios in the two countries, the figure also illustrates how Norway and Sweden were very differently affected by the two world wars of the 20th century. During World War I, Norway's investment ratio of GDP showed a sudden increase due to large investments in the foreign shipping sector which earned enormous war dividends from high freight rates (see also Figure 8.5, which shows the development in terms of trade over the past two centuries). The contrast in investment ratios between neutral Sweden and occupied Norway during World War II is also striking.[18] In Sweden, the investment ratio continued to increase whereas in Norway it dropped sharply during the years of German occupation.[19]

Figure 8.10 shows data on short-term interest rates, set by Norges Bank and the Riksbank respectively, and government bond yields over two centuries. The broad developments over this period, both in the central bank interest rates and the government bond yields, are strikingly parallel. Norges Bank operated with somewhat higher discount rates until the middle of the 19th century. After the markets' confidence in the Norwegian speciedaler had been finally established following resumption of its convertibility into silver in 1842, the short-term interest rates of the two countries moved closely in tandem during the period of the Scandinavian Currency Union. This continued also during the interwar years. After World War II, both Norway and Sweden implemented a monetary policy regime based on low interest rates, credit rationing and financial repression. Figure 8.10 shows that Norges Bank's interest rates were maintained at a somewhat lower level than the Riksbank interest rates until the 1970s. The tightening of monetary policy in the latter half of the 1950s was notably stronger in Sweden than in Norway. The sharp increases in nominal interest rates during the 1970s and 1980s signalled the end of financial regulations.

[18] Estimates of fixed investment for Norway during World War II have been constructed by Ola H. Grytten at the Norwegian School of Economics in Bergen. These estimates will be documented in a forthcoming volume in the series Norges Bank's *Historical monetary statistics – Part III*.

[19] The German occupants invested heavily in Norway during World War II, in airfields, railroads, and in some industries. These investments are coined in concepts like 'Festung Norwegen' and the 'Atlantic Wall' along the long Norwegian coastline. But private investment fell sharply so the investment ratio declined.

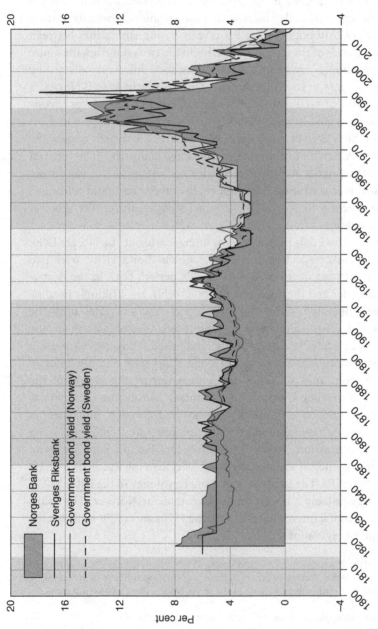

Figure 8.10 Norges Bank and Sveriges Riksbank discount rates on short-term bills and other short-term policy interest rates, government bond yields

Note: For Sweden: the Sveriges Riksbank discount rate until December 1987, from January 1987 until May 1994 the marginal interest rate on central bank liquidity reported by the Riksbank; from June 1994 onwards the rate of interest at which banks can borrow or deposit funds at the Riksbank for a period of seven days, i.e. the repo rate, which has been the Riksbank's policy rate since 1994.

Source: Norges Bank HMS, Eitrheim and Klovland (2004c, 2007).

8.5.7 Regulations Prove Ineffective and Imbalances Build Up

Regulations gradually became less effective as both capital inflows and outflows and domestic credit found new paths. This trend gathered momentum around 1980 and credit growth accelerated. Regulations were eventually abandoned and the resulting financial imbalances made both banks and borrowers very vulnerable. Oil prices fell during the winter of 1985–1986, and in May 1986 the krone was again devalued – this time by 10 per cent. The system was ripe for change.

8.6 1986–2016: The Long Return to Monetary Stability: The Interest Rate Restored as a Policy Instrument

The first period of Norges Bank's history, 'the long promise', involved twenty-six years of effort from 1816 to 1842 with a view to restore monetary stability after the Napoleonic wars. In 1986, 'the long return' back to the central bank's traditional role began. A procedure was established whereby the central bank, and not the government authorities, would set the interest rate to shore up confidence that the Norwegian krone would be kept stable against foreign currencies. The first interest rate change according to the new procedure was made on 2 December 1986.

8.6.1 Banking Crisis

To keep the krone fixed, the interest rate had to be set at a high level. Monetary policy was further supported by fiscal retrenchment. A banking industry that had long been heavily regulated was not able to cope with the wave of liberalisation. A credit boom ensued and other factors such as a drop in oil prices aggravated the situation. Large and small banks encountered problems, culminating in a banking crisis that started in 1988 and became systemic in 1991. Norges Bank's role was confined to providing liquidity loans. The Storting used taxpayer-funded capital injections to shore up the banking system. The banking crisis was resolved in 1993 when the global economy took a positive turn.

8.6.2 Inflation Targeting

In 1992, many countries, including Norway, were forced to abandon a strict fixed exchange rate policy in favour of a managed float. In August 1998 it became impossible to defend a regime that implied a fixed-rate target.

Governor Kjell Storvik set the interest rate at 8 per cent, a rate assessed as appropriate for the Norwegian economy, but lower than necessary to defend the krone exchange rate. When Svein Gjedrem assumed his position as Governor of Norges Bank in January 1999, he communicated that exchange rate stability could only be maintained over time if inflation was kept at the same level as in countries of importance to Norway. On 29 March 2001, the government adopted a new division of responsibility for economy policy. The 'fiscal policy rule' for the spending of petroleum revenues was announced and a formal inflation targeting regime was introduced.

8.6.3 International Financial Crisis

The international crisis in 2008 promptly spread to Norway. Central banks in many countries turned to unconventional measures such as large-scale purchases of private bonds. Norges Bank's main interest rate, the key policy rate, was lowered faster than implied by inflation and growth prospects. Norges Bank also contributed to alleviating the crisis by providing short-term liquidity, including US dollar liquidity to Norwegian banks. Figure 8.11 shows Norges Bank's and Sveriges Riksbank's balance as a percentage of GDP. Norges Bank's balance is shown with and without the occupation account accumulated during World War II and the oil fund from 1996 onwards. The increase in Norges Bank's balance was modest relative to the increase in the Riksbank balance in 2008–2009. The recent increase in the Riksbank balance sheet is due to its purchases of securities (quantitative easing). We note that Norges Bank's balance increased substantially during the crisis years of the 1980s, reaching a peak of close to 40 per cent of GDP in 1986.

8.6.4 Financial Stability

Figure 8.12 shows developments in money and credit in Norway over two centuries. Credit as a percentage of GDP has been growing along a rising trend since World War II. The indebtedness of the general public sector showed a local peak in 1988 prior to the above-mentioned banking crisis 1988–1993. From 1996, credit growth soon picked up again and we note that total credit to the general public, following a minor downturn after the 2008–2009 financial crisis, amounts to more than 200 per cent of GDP in 2015. Figure 8.12 also reveals some interesting aspects of money and credit developments in the long run. Whereas money and credit as a percentage of

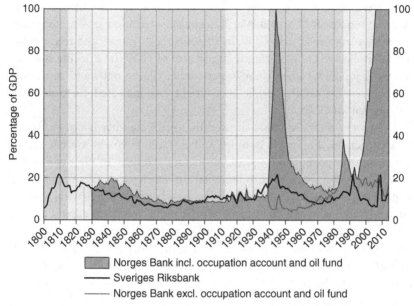

Figure 8.11 Norges Bank and Sveriges Riksbank balance (percentage of GDP)
1800–2014
Source: Norges Bank HMS, Sveriges Riksbank HMFS, Hvidsten (2013), Fregert (2014), Grytten
(2004b), Edvinsson (2014).

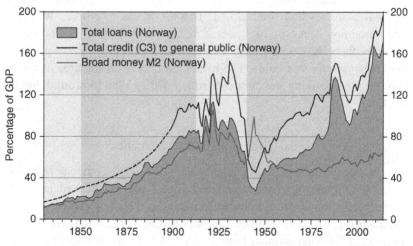

Figure 8.12 Money and credit 1830–2014
Source: Norges Bank HMS, Sveriges Riksbank HMFS, Grytten (2004b), Klovland (2004b),
Eitrheim, Gerdrup and Klovland (2004), Edvinsson and Ögren (2014), Edvinsson (2014).

GDP trended broadly together before World War II, this changed in the postwar period. Since World War II, aggregate credit has grown more than the money stock relative to GDP. In 1949, aggregate money and credit to the general public were both around 70 per cent of GDP. In 2015 the stock of money is somewhat lower than 70 per cent of GDP – notes and coins only 1.6 per cent of GDP – while total credit has increased to more than 200 per cent of GDP.

The recent financial crisis showed that price stability is not sufficient to avoid crises. Financial stability and a stable payment system are of paramount importance to uphold monetary stability. In the wake of the crisis in 2008, work was intensified to strengthen financial sector regulation. Since 2013, Norges Bank has been charged with issuing advice to the Ministry of Finance on the countercyclical capital buffer, a buffer designed to strengthen banks' resilience in a downturn and reduce the procyclicality of bank behaviour. Norges Bank had already in 1997 launched a new interbank settlement system to mitigate systemic risk in the payment system. The payment system proved to be resilient during the crisis.

8.6.5 Focus on Core Activities

Governor Hermod Skånland started the work on developing a central bank organisation with a strong focus on core tasks. In 1989, eight of the bank's regional branches had been closed. This work was intensified in 1999. The remaining domestic branches were closed in 2000–2001 and other non-core tasks were outsourced, including cash handling and the production of banknotes and coins. The bank's headcount in the area of traditional central banking was reduced from 1,300 in 1986 to around 300 in 2010.

8.6.6 Investment Management

Since its inception, Norges Bank has managed foreign exchange reserves. When the Government Pension Fund Global was established in 1990, Norges Bank was a natural choice as manager. The first capital transfer was made on 30 May 1996, in an amount of NOK 2 billion. The capital was invested in the international bond market. As the assets under management grew in value, equities and real estate were added to the portfolio. In 2016, the Fund's value had increased to NOK 7,500 billion (241 per cent of GDP).

8.7 Central Banks at a Crossroads

Norges Bank and Sveriges Riksbank are old institutions. During the course of their history they have been subject to substantial changes as they have developed into the modern type central banks we know today when these lines are being written. The financial crisis in 2008–2009 showed that all the elements of the monetary system – financial stability, a well-functioning payment system and price stability – are equally important.[20] Today central banks are at a crossroads facing a host of difficult choices to be made regarding the road ahead:[21]

- Central banks find themselves in unchartered waters today when it comes to *price stability*. Norway and Sweden have both adapted, although somewhat differently, to the international regime characterised by historically low interest rates, which have now been held for a substantial period (Figure 8.10). Long-term government bond yields are at record low levels, also in a perspective that covers two centuries. There is massive uncertainty with respect to the effects of monetary policy at these low levels.
- The strong growth in credit (Figure 8.12) and real house prices (Figure 8.4) confirms that households and firms have built up a substantial exposure to risks. If a huge negative shock to their ability to service this debt should materialise in the near future, this could easily develop into a threat to *financial stability* as well. How much should central banks and other monetary authorities do to prevent financial imbalances building up, and how should they respond if a financial crisis emerges?
- There are massive ongoing changes in payment technologies, which can be expected to exercise a great impact on the future of our *payment system*. Trust in private banks is pivotal to our monetary system today.

---

[20] Two senior central bank officials, Andrew Haldane from the Bank of England and Jan F. Qvigstad from Norges Bank, have offered their views as practitioners on these issues in Haldane and Qvigstad (2016).

[21] The book *Central banks at a crossroads. What can we learn from history*, edited by Bordo, Eitrheim, Flandreau and Qvigstad (2016), contains comprehensive material which covers different aspects of the evolution of central banks and central banking over the past two centuries, which puts the current debate about their role as guardians of monetary stability in perspective. Qvigstad (2016) discusses key principles on which to base central bank policy – recognising the importance of their credibility and ensuring accountability – illustrating these with specific cases taken from the history of Norges Bank and central banking in general.

This entails both trust in their increasingly sophisticated payment technologies and trust in banks as institutions entrusted with managing other people's money. Bank deposits could never compete with central bank money in terms of risk, but were able to do so in terms of costs.[22]

The situation is challenging both for the real economy and for the institutions that serve it, such as central banks. Insights from two centuries of monetary history witness that central banking has proved highly adaptable to changing circumstances. A central bank must be an institution with a long memory, while also being able to be light-footed and tackle new tasks. Both Norges Bank and Sveriges Riksbank have during the past thirty years regained their traditional role as guardians of the monetary system. The global financial crisis showed that the traditional understanding of this role is not sufficient to address the challenges posed by the new economy. The crisis has required unorthodox measures on the part of many central banks. The big question is: When the crisis is over, will central banks return to base or will they continue to develop unorthodox instruments and contend that this is the new orthodoxy? A smaller question concerns the immediate future for banknotes.

Bibliography

Bohlin, J. (2010). From appreciation to depreciation – the exchange rate of the Swedish krona, 1913–2008. In Edvinsson, R., T. Jacobson and D. Waldenström (eds.), *Exchange rates, prices, and wages, 1277–2008*, chapter 7, 340–411. Stockholm: Sveriges Riksbank and Ekerlids Förlag.

Bohlin, J. (2014). A price index for residential property in Göteborg, 1875–2010. In Edvinsson, R., T. Jacobson and D. Waldenström (eds.), *House prices, stock returns, national accounts, and the Riksbank balance sheet, 1620–2012*, chapter 2, 26–62. Stockholm: Sveriges Riksbank and Ekerlids Förlag.

Bøhn, H., Ø. Eitrheim and J. F. Qvigstad (2016). *Norges Bank 1816–2016. A pictorial history*. Oslo: Fagbokforlaget.

Bordo, M. D., Ø. Eitrheim, M. Flandreau and J. F. Qvigstad (eds.) (2016). *Central banks at a crossroads: What can we learn from history?* New York: Cambridge University Press.

Bordo, M. D. and L. Jonung (1990). The long-run behaviour of velocity: The institutional approach revisited. *Journal of Policy Modelling*, 12, 165–197.

Brunnermeier, M. K. and I. Schnabel (2016). Bubbles and central banks. In Bordo, M. D., Ø. Eitrheim, M. Flandreau and J. F. Qvigstad (eds.), *Central banks at a crossroads: What can we learn from history?* chapter 12. New York: Cambridge University Press.

Edvinsson, R. (2014). The Gross Domestic Product of Sweden within present borders, 1620–2012. In Edvinsson, R., T. Jacobson and D. Waldenström (eds.), *House prices,*

---

[22] Kahn, Quinn and Roberds (2016).

stock returns, national accounts, and the Riksbank balance sheet, 1620–2012, chapter 4, 101–182. Stockholm: Sveriges Riksbank and Ekerlids Förlag.

Edvinsson, R., T. Jacobson and D. Waldenström (2010). *Exchange rates, prices, and wages, 1277–2008.* Stockholm: Sveriges Riksbank and Ekerlids Förlag.

Edvinsson, R., T. Jacobson and D. Waldenström (2014). *House prices, stock returns, national accounts, and the Riksbank balance sheet, 1620–2012.* Stockholm: Sveriges Riksbank and Ekerlids Förlag.

Edvinsson, R. and A. Ögren (2014). Swedish money supply, 1620–2012. In Edvinsson, R., T. Jacobson and D. Waldenström (eds.), *House prices, stock returns, national accounts, and the Riksbank balance sheet, 1620–2012,* chapter 7, 293–338. Stockholm: Sveriges Riksbank and Ekerlids Förlag.

Edvinsson, R. and J. Söderberg (2010). The evolution of Swedish consumer prices 1290–2008. In Edvinsson, R., T. Jacobson and D. Waldenström (eds.), *Exchange rates, prices, and wages, 1277–2008,* chapter 8, 412–452. Stockholm: Sveriges Riksbank and Ekerlids Förlag.

Eichengreen, B. and J. Sachs (1985). Exchange rates and economic recovery in the 1930s. *Journal of Economic History,* 45, 925–946.

Eitrheim, Ø., I. E. Eriksen and A. Sæther (2016a). *Kampen om speciedaleren. debatten om paripolitikken 1832–1836 mellom Jacob Aall og Anton Martin Schweigaard.* Occasional Papers No. 50. Oslo. Norges Bank.

Eitrheim, Ø. and S. Erlandsen (2004). House price indices for Norway 1819–2003. In Eitrheim, Ø., J. T. Klovland and J. F. Qvigstad (eds.), *Historical Monetary Statistics for Norway 1819–2003.* Occasional Papers No. 35, chapter 9. Oslo: Norges Bank.

Eitrheim, Ø. and S. Erlandsen (2005). House price indices for Norway 1819–2003. *Scandinavian Economic History Review,* 53(3), 7–33.

Eitrheim, Ø. and M. Fevolden (2014). Norske statsfinanser 1815–2012. Data konstruert til en artikkel av Øyvind Eitrheim og Einar Lie til et bokprosjekt i regi av Finansdepartementet i anledning grunnlovsjubileet i 2014.

Eitrheim, Ø., K. Gerdrup and J. T. Klovland (2004). Credit, banking and monetary developments in Norway 1819–2003. In Eitrheim, Ø., J. T. Klovland and J. F. Qvigstad (eds.), *Historical Monetary Statistics for Norway 1819–2003.* Occasional Papers No. 35, chapter 10. Oslo: Norges Bank.

Eitrheim, Ø. and J. T. Klovland (2007). Short term interest rates in Norway 1818–2007. In Eitrheim, Ø., J. T. Klovland and J. F. Qvigstad (eds.), *Historical Monetary Statistics for Norway – Part II.* Occasional Papers No. 38, chapter 1. Oslo: Norges Bank.

Eitrheim, Ø., J. T. Klovland and L. F. Øksendal (2016b). *A monetary history of Norway 1816–2016.* Cambridge University Press.

Eitrheim, Ø. and L. F. Øksendal (2016). Crisis management and the interplay between monetary authoritites in Norway over two centuries. In *Makropolitik i kris. En vänskrift til Lars Jonung i anledning hans 70-årsdag,* chapter 12. Knut Wicksells centrum för finansvetenskap, Lunds Universitet.

Fregert, K. (1999). Ekonomporträttet: Hans Samuel Collin (1791–1833). *Ekonomisk debatt,* 27(3), 173–186.

Fregert, K. (2014). The Riksbank balance sheet, 1668–2011. In Edvinsson, R., T. Jacobson and D. Waldenström (eds.), *House prices, stock returns, national accounts, and the Riksbank balance sheet, 1620–2012,* chapter 8, 339–393. Stockholm: Sveriges Riksbank and Ekerlids Förlag.

Fregert, K. and R. Gustavsson (2014). Fiscal statistics for Sweden, 1670–2011. In Edvinsson, R., T. Jacobson and D. Waldenström (eds.), *House prices, stock returns, national accounts, and the Riksbank balance sheet, 1620–2012*, chapter 5, 183–222. Stockholm: Sveriges Riksbank and Ekerlids Förlag.

Grytten, O. H. (2004a). A consumer price index for Norway 1516–2003. In Eitrheim, Ø., J. T. Klovland and J. F. Qvigstad (eds.), *Historical monetary statistics for Norway 1819–2003*. Occasional Papers No. 35, chapter 3. Oslo: Norges Bank.

Grytten, O. H. (2004b). The gross domestic product for Norway 1830–2003. In Eitrheim, Ø., J. T. Klovland and J. F. Qvigstad (eds.), *Historical monetary statistics for Norway 1819–2003*. Occasional Papers No. 35, chapter 6. Oslo: Norges Bank.

Gullbekk, S. H. (2009). *Pengevesenets fremvekst og fall i Norge i middelalderen*. Museum Tusculanums Forlag, Københavns Universitet.

Haldane, A. and J. F. Qvigstad (2016). The evolution of central banks – a practitioner's perspective. In Bordo, M. D., Ø. Eitrheim, M. Flandreau and J. F. Qvigstad (eds.), *Central banks at a crossroads: What can we learn from history?*, chapter 15. Cambridge University Press.

Hvidsten, V. (2013). *Norges Banks balanse 1817–1945: Konsolidering av delregnskapene* [*Consolidated balance sheets*]. Staff Memo 11/2013, Norges Bank.

Kahn, C., S. Quinn and W. Roberds (2016). Central banks and payment systems: The evolving trade-off between cost and risk. In Bordo, M. D., Ø. Eitrheim, M. Flandreau and J. F. Qvigstad (eds.), *Central banks at a crossroads: What can we learn from history?*, chapter 13. Cambridge University Press.

Keilhau, W. (1930). Norway and the World War. In *Sweden, Norway, Denmark and Iceland in the World War*, 281–407. New Haven: Yale University Press.

Klovland, J. T. (1998). Monetary policy and business cycles in the interwar years: The Scandinavian experience. *European Review of Economic History*, 2, 309–344.

Klovland, J. T. (2004a). Historical exchange rate data 1819–2003. In Eitrheim, Ø., J. T. Klovland and J. F. Qvigstad (eds.), *Historical Monetary Statistics for Norway 1819–2003*. Occasional Papers No. 35, chapter 7, 289–347. Oslo: Norges Bank.

Klovland, J. T. (2004b). Monetary aggregates in Norway 1819–2003. In Eitrheim, Ø., J. T. Klovland and J. F. Qvigstad (eds.), *Historical Monetary Statistics for Norway 1819–2003*. Occasional Papers No. 35, chapter 5, 181–240. Oslo: Norges Bank.

Klovland, J. T. (2004c). Bond markets and bond yields in Norway 1820–2003. In Eitrheim, Ø., J. T. Klovland and J. F. Qvigstad (eds.), *Historical Monetary Statistics for Norway 1819–2003*. Occasional Papers No. 35, chapter 4, 99–180. Oslo: Norges Bank.

Klovland, J. T. (2013). *Contributions to a history of prices in Norway: Monthly price indices, 1777–1920*. Working paper 2013/23, Oslo: Norges Bank.

Klovland, J. T. and L. F. Øksendal (2017). The decentralized central bank: Bank rate autonomy and capital market integration in Norway, 1850–1892. *European Review of Economic History*, 21(3), 259–279.

Lie, E., J. T. Kobberrød, E. Thomassen and G. F. Rongved (2016). *Norges Bank 1816–2016*. Oslo: Fagbokforlaget.

Lobell, H. (2010). Foreign exchange rates 1804–1914. In Edvinsson, R., T. Jacobson and D. Waldenström (eds.), *Exchange rates, prices, and wages, 1277–2008*, chapter 6, 291–339. Stockholm: Sveriges Riksbank and Ekerlids Förlag.

Qvigstad, J. F. (2016). *On central banking.* New York: Cambridge University Press.

Qvigstad, J. F. and A. Skjæveland (1994). Valutakursregimer – historiske erfaringer og fremtidige utfordringer. In *Stabilitet Og Langsiktighet. Festskrift Til Hermod Skånland*, 235–271. Oslo: Aschehoug.

Rygg, N. (1950). *Norges Bank i mellomkrigstiden.* Oslo: Gyldendal.

Skaare, K. (1995). *Norges mynthistorie. Bind 1.* Oslo: Universitetsforlaget.

Söderberg, J., S. Blöndal and R. Edvinsson (2014). A price index for residential property in Stockholm, 1875–2011. In Edvinsson, R., T. Jacobson and D. Waldenström (eds.), *House prices, stock returns, national accounts, and the Riksbank balance sheet, 1620–2012*, chapter 3, 63–100. Stockholm: Sveriges Riksbank and Ekerlids Förlag.

Svendsen, K. E., S. A. Hansen, E. Olsen and E. Hofmeyer (1968). *Dansk pengehistorie.* Denmark: Danmarks Nationalbank.

Wetterberg, G. (2009). *Pengarna & makten. Riksbankens historia.* Stockholm: Sveriges Riksbank i samarbete med Atlantis.

9

The Bank of Italy, A Short History, 1893–1998

Gianni Toniolo[*]

In 1921, Montagu Norman, the long-serving Governor of the Bank of England, published a sort of manifesto outlining the main features of central banks. He stressed independence from governments, separation from commercial banks, supervision of the banking system and international cooperation (Sayers 1976, Vol. 3; Bytheway and Metzler 2016: 97–100). Norman's aim was normative rather than descriptive, to promote the convergence of the various central banks towards a single model. Unsurprisingly, his efforts were only partly successful. Institutions that were then beginning to be called central banks originated under different circumstances, and reflected idiosyncratic economic, social, political and legal traditions. Their subsequent development, while partly converging towards a single paradigm shaped by the integration of international markets and the gold standard, either maintained features reflecting specific needs of each national economy or were simply path dependent. A century later, central banks, hugely increased in number, show a good deal of common traits but are still far from being the homogeneous lot envisaged by Norman. The study of the evolution of individual central banks can shed light on national economic, institutional and political history as well as on the drivers of change of central banking at the international level.

The main idiosyncratic features of the evolution of Italian central banking reflect (i) the circumstances that brought about the political unification of the Peninsula, (ii) both the initial backwardness of the economy and the

* I am grateful to Rodney Edvinsson, Eugenio Gaiotti, Alfredo Gigliobianco, Tor Jacobson, Marco Magnani, Marcello Messori, Salvatore Rossi, Paolo Sestito, Francesco Vercelli and Daniel Waldenström for their comments on an earlier draft. I am particularly indebted to Eugene White, long-term friend, co-author, and discussant at the 2017 Riksbank Conference. The usual academic disclaimer applies.

policy efforts aimed at engineering industrialization and convergence growth, (iii) the persistence of a bank-oriented financial system, and (iv) an institutional and political environment characterized by a relatively inefficient, if pervasive, public administration.

This brief sketch of the history of the *Banca d'Italia* follows its evolution on the backdrop of the peculiar features of the Italian polity and economy.

9.1 Origins

9.1.1 The Banking System before Unification

At the time of its political unification (1861–1871),[1] with a GDP per person about 70 per cent that of Western Europe, the Italian Peninsula was a relatively backward area striving to engineer its 'modern economic growth' (Maddison 2001; Toniolo 2013).[2] Its financial system, once the most sophisticated in Europe, was equally backward. Alongside a number of small trading and financial houses, a system of savings banks was taking shape. There was no large commercial bank. The stock exchanges operating in the capital cities of the former independent states were small and poorly organized and regulated. In the South (previously the Kingdom of the Two Sicilies) two 'not-for-profit' credit institutions existed, issuing quasi-money sight-debentures. In Piedmont, Tuscany, Parma, Bologna and Venice, banks of issue had been created as public companies in the two decades prior to unification. Governments had been instrumental in promoting their birth by private capitalists, passed laws regulating the issue of bank notes, the discount operations and the composition of their balance sheets. Banks of issue turned out to be Italy's mid-nineteenth-century financial innovation. Besides underwriting the issue of government paper, they took a limited amount of deposits, and provided both short- and long-term lending to the economy.

With the Peninsula's political unification, the *Banca Nazionale nel Regno*, forerunner of the *Banca d'Italia*, emerged as the largest bank of issue, rapidly extending nationwide its branch network. It is not by chance

---

[1] The Kingdom of Italy was proclaimed in March 1861 under the Savoy monarchy (henceforth ruling over Piedmont, Liguria and Sardinia) and comprised most of today's Italy. The Venetia region was added in 1866 and the papal state (Rome) in 1871. Additional territorial gains were made as the result of the First World War.

[2] According to Maddison (2001), in 1870, Italy's GDP per person was 1,499 US dollars at 1890 purchasing power parity, as against the UK's 3,031 dollars and France's and Germany's 1,876 dollars.

that it was born in 1844 as *Banca di Genova*. Despite the city's decline from being one of sixteenth-century Europe's leading banking hubs, Genoa remained Italy's most important financial centre. In 1849, under the auspices of the Piedmontese government, a merger of *Banca di Genova* and *Banca di Torino* formed the *Banca Nazionale degli Stati Sardi*, later renamed *Banca Nazionale nel Regno d'Italia*. After the latter's acquisition of the small banks of issue of Parma, Bologna and Venice, five banks of issue were operational when the Kingdom of Italy was born in 1861. A sixth – *the Banca Romana* – was added with the acquisition of Rome in 1871. They were all privately owned and listed at the stock exchanges; unlike non-issuing banks,[3] however, the law stated limits to their operations and they were supervised by the government. Two large commercial banks were created in the wake of unification and, in the following years, a hoard of smaller ones was born. Savings banks grew in number and size and cooperative banks began to emerge. The banking system developed and diversified, while the financial market remained thin and segmented for a long time after unification.

For the first three decades of its life, the Kingdom of Italy operated with six monetary institutions. Parliament, public opinion and academics were divided on desirability of a single bank of issue but regional vested interests prevailed time and again in maintaining the status quo. It was, however, hardly an experiment in free banking, as entry was de facto blocked by formal legislation being required to create new issuing institutions. Besides setting limits to the outstanding circulation, the state kept its own representative on the boards with approval authority over relevant operations. Monetary policy was fiscally dominated for most of the thirty-odd years after unification. Convertibility was suspended during the 1866 war, in exchange for a huge loan to the government from the *Banca Nazionale*, and did not resume until 1883. Soon afterwards a swarm of bank failures prompted the government to ask the main banks of issue to bail out the ailing institutions. As a quid pro quo, it turned a blind eye to violations of the circulation limits.

9.1.2 A Severe Banking Crisis and the Birth of Banca d'Italia

The *Banca d'Italia*, the grand-child of *Banca di Genova*, was born in 1893 as the result of a banking crisis that swept away one of the banks of issue and the two largest commercial banks along with a number of mid-sized banks.

---

[3] The savings banks were also subject to government supervision.

The 1883 return to convertibility had resulted in an inflow of foreign capital, an expansion of money supply and lower interest rates. Generous credit was extended by banks to the real estate sector, which was engaged in expanding residential and commercial construction, particularly but not only in the new capital, and to manufacturing, including steel-making. As real estate prices rose, mortgage financing was assumed to be a low-risk activity.

At the end of the 1880s, a real estate crisis began. As the flow of foreign short-term credit dried up and began to reverse, banks tried to rein in credit, which was tied up in illiquid assets. Both contractors and their lenders went bust. Banks of issue were called upon to bail out smaller credit institutions. In order to do so, they expanded money supply beyond the statutory limit with the government's implicit consent. Convertibility was first de facto then officially suspended in 1893. The crisis came to a head in 1892–1993 when one of the banks of issue (*Banca Romana*) was found to be insolvent, amidst a looming social and political crisis. The government, hitherto reluctant to create a single bank of issue, moved to prompt the merger of three issuing banks (*Banca Nazionale nel Regno, Banca Nazionale Toscana* and *Banca Toscana di Credito*) into the *Banca d'Italia*, which was charged with the liquidation of *Banca Romana*. The operation was sanctioned by the Bank Act of 10 August 1893. The two southern banks of issue (*Banco di Napoli* and *Banco di Sicilia*) were allowed to survive as independent institutions but their combined circulation did not exceed 30 per cent of the total. *Banca d'Italia* began its operations on 1 January 1894.

An emergency measure, the Bank Act of 1893 did not create an appropriate institutional setting for a central bank to operate. The Bank's mission was not explicitly defined. The law set ceilings on circulation in relation to both capital and metal reserves, as well as a time limit for the absorption of the excess circulation built up during the crisis. The government retained supervision over the banks of issue, and the right to approve the appointment of the General Manager and veto power over some operations, including the setting of official discount rates. Shareholders were requested to provide fresh capital.

9.2 The Making of a Central Bank: 1894–1913

9.2.1 Cleaning Up the Balance Sheet

At the time of their merger into the *Banca d'Italia*, two of the three banks of issue were burdened with illiquid assets resulting both from their direct involvement in the real estate business and from lending of last resort during the crisis. Therefore, the initial balance sheet of Banca d'Italia was inappropriately illiquid, real estate being a large part of its assets. Moreover, the Bank was charged with the liquidation of the bankrupt Banca Romana. The Bank Act of 1893 stipulated a rigorous timeline for the disposal of illiquid assets. Shareholders, who had already suffered a substantial decline in the market value of the Bank's shares, opposed this provision, which would likely have entailed a loss of capital. A confrontation with the government followed. The new government led by Francesco Crispi, with Sidney Sonnino at the Treasury, moved rapidly to replace the General Manager Giacomo Grillo, a long-serving banker, with Giuseppe Marchiori, a civil servant and former Member of Parliament.

The new head of Banca d'Italia engineered a deal between the government and the shareholders through which the Bank became the official (monopolistic) banker of the Treasury as compensation for possible losses from the liquidation of Banca Romana. From then on, the weight of private shareholders in the management of the Bank steadily declined, with decision making progressively concentrated in the hands of the General Manger, trusted and supported both by the Treasury and the Bank's board. Successive governments consistently made the point that private interests should be subordinated to the Bank's duties towards the 'common good'. A first step was thus taken towards the creation of a 'modern' central bank fitting Norman's paradigm.

After 1897, the growth of Italy's GDP accelerated and real estate prices began to recover from the crisis levels. This enabled the Banca d'Italia to offload its illiquid assets faster than anticipated, progressively restoring the desired liquidity of its balance sheet. It would take another decade to complete the process; but by 1900, with the economy now growing faster than ever before, the short-term component of the Bank's assets reached a satisfactory level, creating conditions for flexibility in monetary policy.

9.2.2 Monetary Policy

Between 1897 and 1913, Italy's GDP grew on average by 2.4 per cent per annum, compared to 1.2 per cent in the previous thirty-odd years. The reasons for trend acceleration do not concern us here, except that it helped to produce a tacit consensus among the successive governments on time-consistent fiscal and monetary policies that steadily reduced the ratio of national debt to GDP and maintained price and exchange rate stability. This policy stance contributed to shielding the country from external monetary shocks and attracting foreign capital while at the same time reducing borrowing costs for Italian business.

In 1900, Bonaldo Stringer, a former general director of the Treasury, was appointed General Manager. He remained at the helm of the Bank (assuming the new title of Governor in 1928) until his death in 1930. A good applied economist, well connected with the business, bureaucratic, academic and political communities, he managed the transition of *Banca d'Italia* into an institution that by the late 1920s would, as we shall see, be admitted to the 'club' of central banks, with Norman's somehow reluctant approval.

In 1903–1913, the monetary authorities (Treasury and banks of issue), while not legally reintroducing convertibility, shadowed the gold standard by keeping the exchange rate within the gold points of the official parity. Monetary policy targeted the exchange rate, often buying and selling Italian consols (the *Rendita Italiana*) on the Paris Bourse. The Italian experience after 1898 shows that in the nineteenth century, monetary stability could be achieved without officially committing to the gold standard (Fratianni and Spinelli 1997; Cesarano, Cifarelli and Toniolo 2012). The legal suspension of convertibility was not lifted until 1927.

The law provided for the government's control of the main policy instruments. The amount of outstanding circulation was capped to a multiple of the reserves in specie and the Bank's capital. Changes in the policy rates required the Treasury's approval. Nevertheless, the three banks of issue progressively acquired considerable room of manoeuvre in managing the amount of the outstanding circulation, for two main reasons. First, besides the official ('normal') discount rate, 'favoured' rates applied for the trustworthiest customers. While the 'normal' rate remained fixed at 6 per cent until 1907, the 'favoured' one was reviewed every month and frequently changed. It was, therefore, the latter that became the main policy instrument. Second, after 1900, both long-term capital inflows and an increasing amount of emigrant remittances contributed to a considerable increase in gold reserves (Canovai 1911; Bonelli 1991). The room for increasing circulation, however, was managed wisely. By then a consensus existed across the political parties that, after years of weak currency and sliding external value of the lira, public interest required a stable currency.

The plurality of banks of issue did not create a problem for monetary policy management. The three banks of issue were all subject to the same limits on their outstanding circulation and the Treasury made sure that interest rates were the same for the three institutions. More important still, the size of *Banca d'Italia* made it easy for it to lead policy coordination.

Stringer stayed in constant contact with his counterpart in Naples, paying little attention to the small Sicilian bank.

The commercial bank operations of the *Banca d'Italia* did not facilitate its relations with the banking system: in this area the Bank did not fully possess the 'bank of banks' features typical of a modern central bank (Ciocca 1973). Not only was the discount market structurally small in Italy, with current account advances the preferred tool for both short- and long-term credit, but the largest banks also shied away from discounting their paper at the *Banca d'Italia* to avoid providing a competitor with valuable information about their business. Moreover, two large universal banks were created in 1894 and 1895, one of them with a substantial German capital input, filling the gap left by the two banks suspended and liquidated during the crisis of the early 1890s. *Banca Commerciale*, in particular, became a keen competitor of *Banca d'Italia* for the rediscount business of small commercial and savings banks in Northern Italy.

9.2.3 The Coming of Age of a Central Bank in the Crisis of 1907

If it may be argued that a bank of issue 'graduates' into a modern central bank when it becomes responsible for both monetary policy and the stability of the banking system, then the crisis of 1907 marks a milestone in the creation of an Italian central bank.

The first years of the new century saw substantial investment growth in the manufacturing and utilities industries and a rapid appreciation of equities. The new universal banks, *Banca Commerciale* and *Credito Italiano*, provided credit and investment-banking services such as the underwriting of new capital issues, often holding substantial amounts of industrial equity for long periods of time in their portfolios. Public finances were set on a sustainable path and the debt to GDP ratio rapidly declined, leading in 1906 to a successful voluntary conversion of the 5 per cent consols (*Rendita Italiana*) into a new 3.75 per cent *Rendita*. The Bank of Italy played a large role in designing, negotiating and providing international stand-by credit for the conversion.

In the spring of 1907, the stock market plummeted.[4] The precipitating cause was contagion from the United States and the related withdrawals of foreign capital, when the New York stock market crisis resulted in higher interest rates in London and Paris. One of the universal banks, *Società*

---

[4] For a brief overview in English of the 1907 crisis in Italy see Kindleberger (1984, pp. 143–146)

Bancaria Italiana (SBI), a weak large bank, suffered a liquidity crisis due to a maturity mismatch between assets and liabilities. The Bank of Italy moved swiftly to prevent contagion. Moral suasion was used to make the two largest universal banks bail out the ailing bank. The latter was restructured, downsized and later merged into a new institution with fresh capital. The necessary liquidity was provided by *Banca d'Italia*.

The crisis management increased the prestige of the *Banca d'Italia* in the eyes of both the government and the banking system. At the end of 1907, a law was passed allowing the Bank to hold assets denominated in foreign currencies, count them as reserves and actively operate in foreign exchange markets. It created a gold-exchange standard *ante litteram*. In the following years, up to the outbreak of the Great War, the *Banca d'Italia* operated with very substantial de facto autonomy. Its influence was felt by the exercise of moral suasion, including in the restructuring of the metal-making industry, which suffered from excess capacity. In 1911–1914, moral suasion took the form of de facto supervision by issuing operational 'instructions' to the smaller banks in order to improve their capital ratios and performance.

To summarize, in 1907 the largest Italian bank of issue acquired some of the key features of a modern central bank, setting itself above the rest of the banking system, which it proved capable of stabilizing. From then onward, it operated with a good degree of de facto autonomy, due to its success in supporting and stabilizing economic growth, a solid balance sheet, large liquid assets, and a gold reserve considerably above the legal requirements, which allowed monetary policy flexibility while at the same time maintaining the exchange rate within the gold points. What was still missing from Norman's ideal were monopoly of note issue and legal independence in setting policy rates.

9.3 Growing up During the Great War

'The 1914–18 war,' writes Sayers (1976, vol. 1: 66), 'marked the beginning of the transformation of the Bank of England from [a] public bank . . . to the central bank acknowledged as such by the Macmillan Committee of 1929-31.' The same can be said about most European central banks. It is certainly true of the *Banca d'Italia*.

When Italy was still neutral (August 1914–May 1915), several Italian banks suffered a major run on deposits. The *Banca d'Italia* prompted the government to introduce a *moratorium* on debt payments including a limit on deposit withdrawal. The banking system turned to the Bank's lending at unprecedented amounts. Setting collateralization amounts and liquidation schedules required information about each individual bank's solvency, which intermediaries were reluctant to supply, given the Bank's position as a potential competitor. Prime Minister Antonio Salandra stepped in, arguing that the protection granted to the banks with the payments moratorium and access to the rediscount window entailed a quid pro quo in the form of a disclosure obligation. In a letter to Stringher, Salandra wrote: 'Do not hesitate to obtain [information] in whatever manner, even by ordering an inspection. [Inspections] cannot be refused by banks that, though private, enjoy the exceptional privilege of moratorium which they are accused, not without some reason, of exploiting in their own interest without taking into account other interests that also deserve the government's protection.'[5] Bank supervision, informally instituted during the war, would be legislated in 1926.

As in every belligerent country, Italy's monetary policy was subordinated to the war effort, which required a swift and massive transfer of resources from the private sector to the government. A large supply of liquidity was needed for advances to the military contractors. The *Banca d'Italia* cooperated not only out of genuine patriotism but also because it believed that generous advances to the banking sector would reduce the risk of bank failures.

One of the Bank's main wartime tasks was leading the various consortia created for the issue of National Loans. Advances were made to commercial banks for subscribing to government issues that were subsequently largely placed with the public. The issue of large quantities of government debt was supposed to check inflation by absorbing the liquidity created to finance industrial production. Wartime consumer price inflation, however, ended up averaging 22 per cent per annum, slightly higher than in Germany.

The exchange rate was a constant concern to both the government and the Bank not only for its impact on the cost of purchases in Allied and neutral markets but also because of its psychological impact as a signal of the market appreciation of the likely outcome of the war. The Bank advised the government in the negotiation of foreign loans and managed the proceeds, knowing that it would be futile to try and stem the long-term depreciation of the lira but at the same time actively intervening in the

---

[5] 'Salandra to Stringher, 5 September 1914', *Archivio Centrale dello Stato, Presidenza del Consiglio, Guerra Europea*, Cartella 17, fasc. 4.

neutral markets when unfavorable military events resulted in heavy sales of lire.

Independence from the government was lost by all belligerent central banks including the *Banca d'Italia*. However, while the government set the policy goals, particularly regarding the mix of debt and monetary war financing, policy implementation was up to the Bank. The new complex tasks required technical skills that made the Bank not only a government's indispensable policy-implementer, but also its main economic advisor. More generally, positioned as it was at the crossroads of government, finance, and industry, the Bank contributed to the coordination of the war economy through soft but effective moral suasion.

The First World War was a turning point in *Banca d'Italia's* history. The loss of autonomy, particularly in monetary policy, was compensated by the acquisition of technical and administrative skills (e.g. in managing fiat money and floating government bonds) and by increased opportunities to exercise influence on the banking sector and policy-making. These gains were not lost with the return to peace, when the Bank regained its pre-war level of semi-autonomy over monetary policy.

9.4 Central Banking under Fascism

9.4.1 The Shock of Return to Peace and Another Banking Crisis

The end of the hostilities brought a swift relaxation of state control over most economic activities. Yet the war had caused both the domestic and the foreign public debt to triple, the money supply to grow fourfold, and consumer prices to rise faster than in the Allied countries, with real wages being 20 per cent lower than in 1913. Wartime low interest rates resulted in negative real rates. The exchange rate, hitherto supported by inter-Allied loans, precipitously fell as the latter were suddenly discontinued and were subject to huge fluctuations.

During the war, the reserve-currency legal ratio was formally maintained as the law stipulated that the currency issued 'on behalf of' (i.e. to finance) the government would not require metal cover. The result was a huge alteration in the composition of the Bank's balance sheet, with credits to the government making up about 73 per cent of the Bank's assets.

The restoration of normal monetary conditions was made difficult by both technical and social constraints. The government's unwillingness to authorize steep increases in the official rate meant that the Bank had to resort to soft credit rationing, by instructing its branches to be as selective as possible in the evaluation of the paper brought in for discount and to restrict advances. New deposits from the public were also rationed. The effectiveness of this policy, which in itself could bear fruit only in the medium-to-long term, was largely frustrated by social constraints. A brief post-war boom, fuelled by pent-up consumer demand and anticipated inflation, was followed by a severe slump in war-related industries and by inadequate supply of consumer goods. At the same time, a quasi-revolutionary situation was developing, which eventually fuelled the fascist reaction leading to Mussolinis's violent seizure of power in 1922. In these circumstances, it was impossible for the Bank to maintain a steady deflationary course.

The conflicting aims of monetary policy – money supply reduction and short-term support to the economy – were exacerbated by the liquidity problems of two of the largest universal banks, *Banca Italiana di Sconto*[6] (BIS) and *Banco di Roma* (BR), which were both heavily involved in long-term financing of steel-making and engineering conglomerates. The Bank was induced by the government to support these conglomerates through an ad hoc vehicle (CSVI),[7] not barred by the banking law prohibiting the discount of industrial paper not endorsed by a bank. Industrial lending was done by CSVI, which then took the paper to the Bank's discount window. As a tool to allow the rescue of both industrial concerns and, indirectly, the parent bank (BIS), CSVI was only partly successful. It could not prevent the liquidation of BIS but it spared Ansaldo, its closely connected engineering and steel-making conglomerate, from the same fate. Ansaldo survived, albeit reduced in size, as the first important industrial concern indirectly owned by the state, with the Bank's financial backing.

9.4.2 Stabilization, the Issue of Independence and the 1926 Banking Law

The official post-war dogma in Italy, as in most European countries, was that the gold standard should be restored as soon as possible. The Italian delegates to the international conferences at both Brussels and Genoa reiterated the country's commitment to a swift return to gold. Setting the parity was of course politically sensitive, as it entailed huge re-distributions among classes of citizens of the adjustment burden.

---

[6] BIS was created in 1914 from the merger of two banks one of which was the Società Bancaria Italiana, bailed out in 1907 (see above).

[7] Consorzio sovvenzioni su valori industriali (CSVI).

Mussolini's economic policies during his first years in government (1922–1925) somehow followed the pre-war liberal pattern: fiscal retrenchment, open economy and a monetary policy aimed at containing the currency's depreciation. The Finance Ministry was entrusted to Alberto de Stefani, an economics professor and moderate free trader. Stringher, who returned to head the Bank after a brief stint as minister of the Treasury, found this environment congenial to his convictions.

The seizure of dictatorial powers by Mussolini in 1925 was followed by an abrupt protectionist turn and the substitution of De Stefani with Giuseppe Volpi, a financier with business interests in the large conglomerates producing for the domestic market.

After London's return to gold, currency stabilization became the main monetary policy objective for European central banks, with Montague Norman, Bank of England Governor, trying to engineer 'stabilization loans' as part of his drive to promote central bank cooperation. However, as far as the *Banca d'Italia* was concerned, Norman was reluctant to include it in the 'club', as it did not appear to be sufficiently independent from the government. In a private conversation, Volpi himself had said to Norman: '[Independence] Stringher would never have and, indeed, he [is] much better off without'.[8] In 1926, Mussolini and Volpi decided to peg the lira to prepare for legal stabilization, directing the Bank to follow a monetary policy consistent with that aim. When Italy was asked by the *Banque Nationale de Belgique* to participate in the stabilization of the Belgian franc, again Norman objected on grounds of lack of independence prompting an interesting reply by Benjamin Strong. Independence – wrote the NY Fed Governor – cannot be judged a priori, much depending on individuals. In his opinion, Italy had made progress and Stringher could be trusted. Finally, he argued that everybody would benefit from the stabilization of the lira and it was foolish to block it in name of 'your [Norman's] conception of orthodox independence'.[9] This exchange of opinion captures the two different views of central bank independence that persist to the present day: the strict legal interpretation and the more nuanced consideration of circumstances and people leading to de facto autonomy.

As part of the stabilization process, a law was passed in 1926 which (a) gave the *Banca d'Italia* the monopoly of note issue, (b) recognized for the first time the special character of the banking business and introduced prudential regulations, and (c) entrusted *Banca d'Italia* with supervisory

---

[8] Norman to Strong 4.3.1926 Bank of England Archives, G1/307 Italy S 62.
[9] Strong to Norman 26.11.1926 Bank of England Archives, G1/307 Italy S 62.

powers. Together with international acceptance into the central banks 'club', the 1926 banking law created the institutional setting for the Bank to meet Norman's standards of a central bank. Still missing were legal autonomy in rate setting and the end of commercial bank activity (which, however, was by this time extremely limited).

Eventually, in December 1927, after a long period of successful pegging, the lira was made convertible into gold bullion. By then, Norman had at last softened his position (he reported to Strong that 'the courtship between the Bank of England and the *Banca d'Italia* is proceeding')[10] and the stabilization was supported by a stand-by credit from twenty central banks. For sheer political reasons, Mussolini imposed an overvalued parity – the so-called *Quota Novanta* (i.e. 90 lire per pound) – that Stringher was unable or unwilling to challenge, as, on the contrary, did Emile Moreau who stood up against France's Prime Minister Raymond Poincaré who also wanted an overvalued currency. In a democratic context, Moreau was aware that large segments of society opposed further deflation and supported his position, while Stringher could only accept the political diktat or leave the Bank.

Stringher died in 1930, two years after seeing his title changed from Director General to Governor. He was succeeded by Vincenzo Azzolini, a former top Treasury civil servant, who had been appointed General Manager of the Bank in 1928.

9.4.3 Monetary Policy in the Great Depression

The stabilization of the lira resulted in a net capital inflow from abroad, which significantly increased the Bank's gold and foreign exchange reserves, bringing them well above the statutory limit of 40 per cent of the outstanding circulation and short-term liabilities. However, following the 1928 rise in interest rates engineered by the US Federal Reserve, the inflow slowly petered out. In early 1929 the main European central banks raised their rediscount rates to defend the gold parity. The *Banca d'Italia* took its rate to 5.5 per cent in January and 7.0 per cent in March. The overvalued real exchange rate reduced the competitiveness of Italian products and increased the trade balance deficit. In November 1929, after the Wall Street crash, Mussolini directed Stringher to avoid reductions in the lending rate and, 'if necessary, to promptly increase it' (Cotula and Spaventa 2003: 282). However, in 1930, as the level of activity in the

---

[10] Norman to Strong 26.10.1927 Bank of England Archives, G1/307 Italy S 62.

economy rapidly decreased,[11] the rate was brought back down to 5.5 per cent, though this remained a higher level than in most other countries. The defence of the 1927 gold parity dictated the monetary policy stance, regardless of its deflationary impact.

If policy was driven by political imperatives, most economists, including some independent minds (e.g. Einaudi 1933), provided intellectual support. Throughout 1931, the exchange rate was kept within or very close to the gold points by slowly but steadily eroding the Bank's reserve ratio. After the devaluation of the pound in September 1931,[12] the defence of the parity became increasingly difficult. The Bank resorted to administrative measures to discourage conversion and the government progressively introduced controls on capital exports. When in 1933, at the London Economic Conference, Italy joined the French-led gold bloc, the convertibility of the lira was already almost nominal. From 1934 to 1935, with the preparation for the invasion of Abyssinia, the defence of the gold reserve was undertaken by controls on capital exports, clearing agreements, import duties and other administrative measures while monetary and fiscal policies were directed to finance the military build-up. The provision of the 1926 law that set a limit to the Bank's advances to the Treasury was scrapped in 1936. From then onward the *Banca d'Italia* would be legally bound to buy any amount of government bonds not subscribed by the public, opening the gates to the monetization of the debt. When in 1936 the parity of the lira was officially reduced, following the French devaluation and the end of the gold bloc, convertibility was only a legal fiction.

9.4.4 Bail-outs and Soft Nationalization of Universal Banks

In the post-war years, particularly after 1925, the two largest universal banks (*Banca Commerciale* and *Credito Italiano*) were progressively turned into industrial holdings. As private capital did not flow into the largest industrial concerns, the two banks bought large quantities of industrial equities. In 1930, with the sudden drop in both equity prices and foreign deposits, these banks' liquidity and even solvency were threatened. The government stepped in with a huge bail-out operation. In two separate deals (1930–1931), it provided the *Credito Italiano* and the *Banca Commerciale* with enough liquidity for them to continue to operate as

---

[11] In 1930, investments fell by about 30 per cent.

[12] The losses suffered by the Bank from the devaluation, which the management was accused of not foreseeing, turned the Bank and the Treasury against the gold-exchange standard prompting in the following years the conversion of reserve currencies into gold.

'ordinary' commercial banks in exchange for (a) most of their stakes in industrial and utility companies and (b) a future commitment to undertake only short-term operations. The rescue was kept a secret. It defused a banking crisis, potentially similar to those of Austria and Germany, the panic by prevanting a bank run. In order to manage the large newly acquired industrial portfolio, in 1933, the state created its own holding company, the *Istituto per la ricostruzione industriale* (IRI), which also gained control of the three largest former universal banks (Toniolo 1980; Guarino and Toniolo 1993).

Unlike in the crises of 1907 and 1921–1922, the Bank remained on the sidelines in 1931–1933 when it came to crafting and executing the bail-out and defusing of the crisis. It was however required to provide the necessary liquidity to bailout the large ailing banks.[13] The crisis, therefore, hugely impacted on the *Banca d'Italia*'s balance sheet.

9.4.5 The 1936 Bank Act

The bail-out and reorganization of the country's largest banks was crowned by the Banking Act of 1936,[14] which – with few, if significant, post-war changes – provided the legal framework for the country's central bank and banking activities until the early 1990s. The law provided for the separation of short-term credit institutions from long-term investment banks. Intermediaries defined as 'ordinary banks' were restricted to short-term lending and forbidden from holding non-financial equity. Long-term credit provision was to be performed by government-owned or -controlled institutions, authorized to issue bonds with a government guarantee.

The *Banca d'Italia* was also reformed. Its shares were delisted, with shareholders required to sell their holdings at a fixed (quite generous) price to savings banks and other government-controlled financial institutions. The Bank was transformed from a public company into a legal entity, called Institute under Public Law.[15] The Bank could no longer receive deposits from private individuals or discount paper to non-financial entities, putting an end to its commercial banking operations. All of Norman's features of a modern central bank, except legal autonomy in rate setting, were now formally met. Technically the Bank was not nationalized, but its shareholders were institutions indirectly state owned or controlled. Bank

---

[13] A huge literature on this episode exists in Italian, for more details in English see Toniolo (1995).
[14] Royal Decree-Law 12 March 1936, n. 375.   [15] Istituto di diritto pubblico.

supervision was entrusted to a newly created government body, the Inspectorate for the Defence of Savings and Credit, chaired by the Bank's Governor and almost entirely staffed by its employees.

The Bank Act of 1936 is a milestone in the history of Italy's banking system and of the *Banca d'Italia* itself. The separation of commercial and long-term banking, public ownership or control over large segments of the financial industry, and the creation of a strong supervisory body controlled by the Bank ended the system's endemic instability, which never again experienced systemic crises. At the same time, the Bank Act implicitly took stock of the inability and/or unwillingness of private capitalists to commit to long-term industrial investment and thus created investment channels through long-term lending institutions under direct or indirect state control.

9.4.6 Wartime

Italy was almost continuously at war from 1936 to 1945, first in Abyssinia, then in Spain and finally in the Second World War. Monetary policy was again directed to support the war effort. An attempt was made to limit the inflationary impact of the rapidly increasing money supply by creating the so-called 'direct capital circuit', whereby 'the authorities endeavored to channel liquidity back to the treasury' (Fratianni and Spinelli 1997: 164), by incentivizing the subscription of government securities while at the same time rationing consumption and trying to control prices. The 'circuit' was quite successful until the end of 1942, when it became increasingly difficult to channel an adequate flow of savings to the purchase of government securities. As the Axis military fortunes declined, savers were increasingly unwilling to buy Italian government bonds.

In aspects other than monetary policy, the war profoundly affected the life of the Bank. In September 1943, after the armistice between Italy and the Allied Powers, the Germans occupied Rome and immediately asked for the Bank's gold to be turned over to them. Under heavy pressure, Azzolini surrendered 117 tons of gold,[16] which was taken to German-controlled Sud Tirol (Cardarelli and Martano 2001; in English Toniolo 2005: 252–256). In 1944 Azzolini was put on trial for high treason and condemned to thirty years in jail. He was freed by a post-war amnesty and subsequently acquitted. In 1944–1945, Italy was divided into two separate states: the so-called Kingdom of the South under Allied control and the

---

[16] He was however able to save the valuable crown jewels.

Nazi-controlled Social Republic of Salò in the North. While the Bank formally remained a single legal entity, it was split into two entities each managed by a commissioner.

9.5 Rapid Growth and Financial Repression, 1945–1970s

9.5.1 Reconstruction

In December 1944, a small aircraft took Luigi Einaudi[17] to Rome from Switzerland where he had fled, fearing for his freedom in Nazi-controlled Northern Italy. He was a professor of economics of liberal, and neoclassical, orientation, and a respected columnist (including for *The Economist*). In early January he was appointed governor of the *Banca d'Italia*. At the time monetary sovereignty was shared with the Allied occupation authorities, with the Americans issuing their own legal tender, the Amlire, for the payment and supply of the troops. In two separate agreements, Einaudi managed to regain monetary sovereignty. In January 1946 the *Banca d'Italia* took upon itself the task of providing currency and credit to the occupation authorities. A year later, the American government renounced the right to receive bank notes from the Bank. By that time, inflation was rampant, but the Bank delayed taking action. It has been argued that Einaudi deliberately let inflation run in order to drastically reduce the real value of the government debt. This undocumented hypothesis is hardly consistent with Einaudi's long-held belief in monetary stability as the main defence for the small saver. Most likely, in early 1947, he did not enjoy the necessary political support for sharp monetary deflation, which, in his view, required a substantial reduction in the government's budget deficit (Gigliobianco 2006).

In 1947 Einaudi was appointed Treasury minister, while formally remaining Governor of the Bank, which was run however by Director General Donato Menichella, coming from IRI. Picked by Einaudi as his successor (he became Governor in 1948 upon Einaudi's election as President of the Republic), Menichella could not have been intellectually more different than the liberal professor, at least as far as the role of the state in the economy was concerned. He was however equally convinced of the need for stable money. In 1947, with Einaudi's strong backing from the Treasury, Menichella engineered a robust credit squeeze that drastically reduced price inflation. This policy was so successful in showing an

---

[17] What follows on Einaudi's biography is drawn from Gigliobianco (2006).

unaccustomed public the power of monetary policy, when applied with determination, that it killed inflation expectations for a long time.

The emergence of the *Banca d'Italia* as a key policy-making institution in the post-war period is due to some extent to Azzolini, who, in the 1930s, while enjoying little policy autonomy from the government, had quietly worked at strengthening the Bank's human capital, particularly by creating a research department staffed with young economists, some of whom trained abroad – rare birds in fascist Italy. As a result, the Bank emerged from the war as one of the two institutions endowed with the best human resources within the public sector (the other one was IRI). As such it was called upon to support the government in various ways, some unrelated to its monetary and supervisory tasks. Out of the limelight, Bank officials played important roles in negotiating Italy's joining the IMF and obtaining World Bank loans, as well as managing the Marshall Plan aid and grants.

In 1946 the Bank Act of 1936 was amended. The Inspectorate for the Defence of Savings and Credit was scrapped, with supervision of the financial system formally given to the *Banca d'Italia*. The setting of policy rates remained with the government on proposal of the governor.

9.5.2 Central Banking in the Golden Age

Between 1951 and 1970, Italy's real GDP grew at a yearly average of 5.6 per cent. The country's output and productivity converged to those of the more developed countries. The manufacturing base was consolidated and hugely expanded. The *Banca d'Italia* was in various ways involved in sustaining the growth process.

The pre-war (1936) financial and regulatory setting remained largely in place, but it was re-directed to growth rather than military goals. It is, therefore, not entirely possible to understand monetary policy separately from bank regulation and supervision. 'Menichella's tenure as governor was characterized by a strong defense of the Bank's autonomy, interest rate stability, and agreement with the Treasury's view on long-term growth-promoting policy' (Polsi 2001:103). By managing the issue of short-term Treasury bonds, the Bank drained and injected liquidity into the system, without moving the official policy rate, which remained unchanged throughout the 1950s. Price stability was largely assured by productivity growth and wage moderation.

In a context of 'financial repression', which prevailed in Europe and elsewhere, made possible by controls on capital exports and tight regulation of the banking sector (which also entailed an official 'bank cartel', overseen by the *Banca d'Italia* itself), the central bank could not only guarantee financial stability, but also pursue long-term allocative objectives deemed consistent with promoting economic growth in an, as yet, underdeveloped country (Battilossi 2003). The territorial spread of small banks was sustained in order to assist SMEs, in improving credit allocation with bank managers well acquainted with the local economy and in promoting the investment of savings in marginal and rural areas (Cotula and Martinez 2003: 480).

'The panoply of monetary instruments available was so ample to make it unnecessary to resort to changes in reserve requirement ratios. [Menichella] seemed to prefer moral suasion, grounded in [the Bank's] great prestige and institutional authority over the credit system, and to call upon reserve requirement ratios only when alternatives failed' (Fratianni and Spinelli 1997: 197).

Italy joined the IMF in 1947. After a relatively brief period of adjustments,[18] the exchange rate remained stable at 625 lire per dollar until August 1971. Foreign exchange stability was the main short-term goal of monetary policy and the Bank sought to increase its foreign exchange reserves even at the cost of conflicting with the Marshall Plan representative who pressed for a more expansionary stance. Italy actively participated in the European Payments Union (EPU), and slowly moved to multilateral settlements. When the Union expired and the IMF rules applied in full, the exchange rate remained remarkably stable. Before retiring, in 1960, Menichella enjoyed the *Financial Times*[19] awarding the lira the Oscar for monetary stability.

De facto independence was strengthened by, among other things, the fact that 'Einaudi and Menichella possessed remarkable personalities, technical abilities and strong ties with the domestic and international communities' (Fratianni and Spinelli 1997: 189). They were trusted by Alcide De Gasperi, the political leader of the late 1940s and early 1950s. Economic ministers, on the other hand, rotated frequently and were not always of outstanding quality.

The new governor, 46-year-old Guido Carli, belonged to a younger, less provincial generation of civil servants. He had served in government and acquired international experience and recognition, including as chairman of the EPU. Carli set out to 'modernize' the Bank's organization, by improving the internal system of incentives, increasing salaries to bring

---

[18] The last one took place in 1949, during the second sterling crisis.
[19] *Financial Times*, 11 January 1960.

them closer to the private sector's, and expanding the research department both qualitatively and quantitatively. Holders of foreign post-graduate degrees were hired in increasing numbers and leave was liberally granted to those keen on spending time at foreign or international institutions. The Bank became very active in such bodies as the BIS, the IMF, the G-10 and, later, the European Committee of Central Bank Governors.

Carli's view was broadly consistent with his predecessor's: monetary policy should aim first and foremost at sustaining the economy's real growth. On financial regulation and supervision he was, on the other hand, more conscious than Menichella that Italy's domestic financial structure should be modernized in order to better sustain investment (Polsi 2001: 114).

In 1958–1962, growth in the real economy accelerated,[20] and productive capacity was close to full utilization. Large external surpluses existed until 1962. In 1963 the economy overheated, increases in international prices fuelled domestic inflation, as did demands for higher wages easily accommodated by employers. A large external current account deficit emerged for the first time since the early 1950s. At first, unwilling to introduce deflationary policies, *Banca d'Italia* authorized the banks to increase their net external debt positions. The policy, however, backfired 'as Italian residents found it advantageous to sell securities at home and repurchase them through foreign intermediaries' (Fratianni and Spinelli 1997: 208). When the Bank realized that the policy of defending reserves by allowing banks to attract foreign funds was not working, it resorted to regulatory measures rather than to the standard tool of raising the official rate. The credit system was instructed to reduce its net external credit position. The banks responded quickly. 'The combination of the net outflow of capital and the drain of official reserves produced a sharp decline in the monetary base' (Fratianni and Spinelli 1997: 209). Interest rates rose sharply, both inflation and real output slowed and the balance of payments turned from deficit to surplus. It was the first time since 1947 that monetary policy was used to correct cyclical imbalances; it took place at the time of heated political debates, when the first contentious post-war centre-left government came to power. The Bank was criticized for delaying action and then acting too drastically. Rapid growth, however, immediately resumed, lasting to the early 1970s. As large balance of payments surpluses returned, the Bank issued regulations aimed at sterilizing the effect of

[20] Real GDP grew on average by 7 per cent p.a.

foreign capital inflows on money supply. In 1965–1968 the monetary policy target was the pegging of short-term interest rates with the aim of influencing longer-term rates and investment. This policy ended in the first half of 1969, when the Bank reverted to buying and selling short-term government securities.

9.5.3 The Troubled 1970s

Between 1968 and 1969, international interest rates rose. The so-called 'hot autumn' of student protests and trade union strikes signalled the end of wage moderation and high profits. Nominal wages doubled, CPI price inflation accelerated. 'For the first time breaks were applied to a growth process sustained by stable prices since reconstruction' (Ciocca 2007: 279). An outflow of Italian capital followed. In 1969, the official discount rate was raised for the first time in eleven years, and the Bank employed large amounts of foreign exchange reserves to defend the parity of the lira. The end of the Bretton Woods system in August 1971 increased uncertainty. In 1971–1972, monetary policy was again eased in order to sustain faltering investment; this aim was, however, frustrated as credit and liquidity rather than going to productive investments headed across the border. Government deficits increased. As the external deficit became binding, instead of changing the official monetary stance, the Bank resorted again to regulatory devices, beginning a new phase of international capital movement controls that lasted to the second half of the 1980s (Rossi 1998: 27–29).

The oil shock of 1973 resulted in higher inflation worldwide. In Italy it reached 21 per cent and remained above 12 per cent throughout 1973–1984. In 1974, facing a huge current account deficit, the government resorted to IMF support, committing to a deflationary stabilization programme. On that occasion, both the intermediate objective and monetary policy instruments underwent a significant change. A quantity target was introduced by capping the total amount of domestic credit available to the economy. The main instrument used to reach this objective could only be one of administrative nature: an upper limit was imposed on bank lending. The policy stance became very restrictive and nominal interest rates reached 12 per cent. However, two-digit inflation made *ex post* real rates negative. Inflation remained at high levels despite monetary restrictions, which proved rather ineffective for two main reasons: the explosion of government spending and full wage indexation, which created a vicious price–wage circle and made it socially and politically hard to fight inflation.

1975 was the first post-war year when GDP growth turned negative.[21] A widespread consensus emerged, including within the European Commission, that expansionary measures were needed. The government acted to stimulate exports and investments. The Bank reduced short-term rates. The expansion of domestic demand resulted in higher imports and a balance of payments deficit. The resulting turbulence in the foreign exchange market was fuelled also by a government crisis, the low level of official reserves and rumours, reported by the international press, that Italian solvency could be in doubt (Rossi 1998: 38–39). In January 1976, the exceptional measure was taken to suspend the lira's listing at the official foreign exchange market. The suspension lasted twenty days, during which reserves were increased with the proceeds of two international loans from the US and Germany. The bank rate was lifted from 6 to 12 per cent. When the foreign exchange market was reopened, the lira fell by 15 per cent. Throughout the summer, the lira remained under pressure. On top of all the administrative restrictions on foreign financial transactions, in desperation, the government introduced a 10 per cent tax on all foreign payments. In October the new government, in office with the benevolent abstention of the Communist Party, increased taxation in order to rein-in domestic demand and reduce the government deficit. Monetary policy turned restrictive, short-term real interest rates became slightly positive and monetary aggregates grew less than nominal income. The restrictive stance continued in 1978 until the balance of payments returned to equilibrium and the worse seemed to be over. Overall the rapid succession of expansionary and restrictive policies (also known as stop-and-go), which, in Italy as in other countries, characterized the 1970s, increased economic instability while doing little to sustain trend growth.

In August 1975, Carli stepped down from the Bank. After Stringher, he was the institution's longest-serving head. He was succeeded by Paolo Baffi, who had spent his entire career at the Bank.

In the 1970s, *Banca d'Italia* was once again engaged in preventing and defusing banking crises. A few long-term 'Special Credit Institutions', threatened with insolvency, were quietly bailed out and restructured. In 1974 the Bank opened a resolution procedure for the *Banca Privata Italiana*, owned by Michele Sindona, a Sicilian financier close to the Mafia. The resolution commissioner was assassinated in 1979. In 1978, the Bank inspectors reported to the Milan Court of Justice some illegal operations conducted at Roberto Calvi's *Banco Ambrosiano*. A few weeks later Baffi

---

[21] –2.1 percent over the previous year (Baffigi et al. 2013).

and Mario Sarcinelli,[22] the Bank's deputy director general responsible for bank supervision, were charged with 'wrongdoings'. It was a vicious attack on the independence of the Bank. The majority of the public opinion was outraged and expressed its solidarity to the Bank. Nevertheless, Baffi, shocked and mortified, resigned from his job in September 1979. In 1981 Baffi and Sarcinelli were acquitted in a pre-trial procedure. In the meantime, Carlo Azeglio Ciampi, the future President of the Republic in 1999–2006, had succeeded Baffi at the helm of the Bank.

The decade was one of weak governments, extreme trade union assertiveness, and social unrest exacerbated by a number of terrorist assassinations, culminating in 1978 with the kidnapping and killing of Aldo Moro, the leader of Italy's main party, the *Democrazia Cristiana*, and a former prime minister. Against this backdrop, the Italian ruling elites responded by expanding public deficit spending in order to try and accommodate the conflicting claims and vested interest, believing it to be the only way to allay at least some of the reasons for discontent. As a result, the debt to GDP ratio rose from about 30 to around 40 per cent between 1970 and 1978. Given the spending spree, this was a relatively small increase, explained by the fact that about 50 per cent of it was monetized. If there was a time, aside from the 1930s, when monetary policy was fiscally dominated, it was probably the 1970s.

Did the *Banca d'Italia* lose its independence as happened in the 1930s? The answer depends on the definition of independence. It has been suggested that in the 1970s, the Bank was politically independent but economy dependent, meaning that decision making was independent from the rather weak governments but dictated by the economic and social circumstances of the time. Carli famously argued that the Bank's refusal to print money to buy government bonds would have been a 'seditious act', resulting in the paralysis of the entire state apparatus (Gigliobianco 2006: 287). In other words, according to this interpretation, the top management of the Bank believed that the two-digit inflation was the lesser evil compared to any feasible alternative.

According to Gigliobianco (2006: 305–306), in the 1960s, the Bank had acquired a de facto government role, which saw the governor involved in actual decision making by the executive branch, so much so that in 1970 an MP for the Socialist party, a junior member in the coalition government, publicly denounced the 'hegemony' of the governor in economic policymaking. Baffi's governorship was characterized by a slow retreat of the

[22] He spent a few weeks in jail.

Bank into its established areas of responsibility, monetary policy and Bank supervision, focusing on the latter and taking major personal risks.

9.6 From the European Monetary System to the Euro

9.6.1 Regime Change in the 1980s

In 1978, Italy joined the European Monetary System (EMS), which became active in early 1979. The decision to join was highly controversial, not least within the Bank. The debate focused on whether Italy should or could afford to accept European monetary discipline. Those in favour of the EMS argued that it would force the country to adopt consistent polices, first, but not only, when it came to curbing inflation, which would otherwise be indefinitely postponed. Baffi, concerned about the weakness of the Italian economic and political system, was inclined to delay Italy's participation, fearing a failure would set back the clock on reforms he was advocating (Gigliobianco 2006: 326). The Bank nevertheless conduced the negotiations for the Treaty, obtaining for Italy a 6 per cent fluctuation margin within the European Rate Mechanism (ERM), instead of the normal 2.5 per cent.

In 1979–1980, the second oil shock resulted in another inflation hike and a slow-down in GDP growth. In July 1981, the so-called 'divorce' between the Treasury and the *Banca d'Italia* freed the latter from its residual-buyer's role of un-subscribed Treasury bills on the primary market, a major step towards full legal independence.

These three events, together with Volcker's new monetary policy stance, induced a regime change in the Bank's policy targets and instruments (Gaiotti and Angeloni 1990; Gaiotti and Rossi 2004). Monetary base and interest rate management were directed to curbing inflation. In 1981, the bank rate was raised from 16.5 to 19 per cent, and reserve requirements of the banks increased from 15.75 to 20 per cent. Real interest rates returned to positive values. In the following years, as inflation began to abate,[23] the bank rate was slowly reduced and quantitative constraints relaxed, along with administrative controls on international capital movements. The latter were finally liberalized in October 1988.

Key to curbing inflation was the exchange rate management. As Italian inflation remained higher than in the other European countries, various realignments of the lira parity within the EMR band were unavoidable.

---

[23] It fell from over 18 per cent in 1980 to 5 per cent in 1987.

It was however the Bank's policy to maintain an overvalued real exchange rate for as long as possible, to not only put a downward pressure on prices but also incentivize productivity growth.

In the second half of the 1980s, with inflation somehow under control, real GDP growth accelerated.

The 1981 'divorce' aimed at allowing the Bank larger autonomy to control inflation while at the same time stimulating the government's fiscal disipline, as it could now only rely on the market for deficit financing. The post-'divorce' regime was quite successful on the inflation front but a responsible behaviour in managing public finances did not materialize. In the 1980s, Italy's debt to GDP ratio rose from less than 50 to nearly 100 per cent. Deprived of the debt monetization free lunch, the Italian political system did not become more frugal or more willing to ask citizens to pay for growing public expenditure. With higher real interest rates, debt became more costly, as did the fiscal accommodation of sectional interests. On several occasions, Governor Ciampi expressed his concern about the unsustainable path taken by public finance. His warnings fell on deaf ears and high public debt turned out to be the poisonous legacy of the 1980s.

9.6.2 The New Banking Legislation

In 1990–1993 a new banking legislation deeply modified the institutional setting of the system that had been in place since 1936. The reform took place in multiple steps. A law of 1990 provided incentives for the transformation of savings banks into limited liability companies, paving the way to privatization. Fiscal incentives were provided for bank mergers in an effort to increase the average size of the lenders. The 1936 separation between 'ordinary' banks and those specialized in granting long-term credit allowed the two to coexist within a single banking group. In the same year, antitrust legislation was introduced, which gave the Bank of Italy antitrust regulatory authority over the financial system, questioning the long-held belief in a trade-off between competition and financial stability.

A 1991 law aimed to make equity investments more attractive in order to try and reduce the role of banks in corporate finance. It was not particularly successful; banks remained at the core of Italy's financial system, as they had been since the 1800s. In 1992, the power to modify the policy rate was assigned to the *Banca d'Italia*, which therefore acquired full legal independence on monetary policy. Finally, in 1993, the various parts of the banking legislation were revised and unified into a single new

Bank Act. Universal banking was reintroduced and prudential regulation strengthened. The Italian banking system converged towards the international standard.

9.6.3 The Crisis of the Early 1990s, Devaluations, Monetary Policy and the Euro

Throughout the second half of the 1980s and the first part of the following decade, inflation remained slightly but constantly higher than in Italy's European partners, despite the substantial success at curbing price increases. 'Complete convergence was achieved only after 1994, concurrently with a new shift in monetary policy' (Gaiotti and Rossi 2012: 30).

In the summer of 1992, the Danish people voted against the ratification of the Maastrich Treaty for the creation of a Monetary Union, signed earlier in the year. The markets were quick to recognize the project's weaknesses. Fire sales of the weakest currencies within the EMS followed. The lira was the one under heaviest pressure. The coordinated response stipulated in the 1978 Treaty did not materialize. Germany did not fully honour its commitment to buy lira. In September the Italian currency was devalued by 7 per cent, but the move did not calm the markets. Heavy selling of lira, peseta, and the British pound followed, prompting Italy and the United Kingdom to leave the exchange rate agreements (ERM). A new Italian government imposed a severe public finance squeeze, while *Banca d'Italia* raised the discount rate to 15 per cent.

Exports boomed as a result of the devaluation and, in 1994–1995, GDP grew on average by 2.5 per cent. In 1995, foreign exchange markets were again shocked by the Mexican crisis and the lira was devalued almost as much as in 1992. Inflation picked up again.

Against this backdrop, Antonio Fazio – who had succeeded Ciampi in 1993, upon his becoming prime minister – implemented a decisive monetary restriction to regain control of price inflation (Gaiotti et al. 1998). He took the unusual step of announcing the inflation rates to which the management of official interest rates would be linked. 'The effectiveness of these decisions was supported by a government-trade unions agreement that removed all forms of wage indexation and introduced the predetermination of wage increases based on the inflation objective' (Gaiotti and Secchi 2012: 20). The agreement had been reached in 1993 by Prime Minister Ciampi's government. Fiscal policy became consistent with meeting the European Monetary Union (EMU) requirement: public deficit declined from 10 per cent of GDP in 1993 to 2.7 per cent in 1998. Inflation expectations were subdued: in 1998 prices rose by only 1.8 per cent. Fazio's monetary policy was driven by his conviction that the country ran a serious risk of losing control over price inflation; it turned out, however, to be also instrumental in meeting one of the criteria for joining the EMU. Fazio himself doubted the advisability of Italy entering the EMU, and the top management of the Banca d'Italia was divided on the issue. Those against early participation in the single currency argued that the Italian economy was not competitive enough to grow under an irreversible fixed exchange rate regime. The pro-EMU camp, on the other hand, argued that joining the euro would create the political and economic incentives for necessary reforms, lacking when devaluation was the easy option. In 1998, when the political decision to participate in the EMU was made, Italy (almost) met the conditions for membership.

In December 2005,[24] Governor Fazio resigned, under heavy criticism for his handling of some bank mergers and acquisitions. A law passed at the end of that year stipulated a six-year term, renewable only once, for the governor's tenure and instituted a five-member board in charge of monetary policy and bank supervision, thus ending the 'monarchical' governance of the Bank by a life-tenured governor. In January 2006, Mario Draghi was appointed governor under the new rules. In October 2011, upon Draghi's appointment as President of the European Central Bank, Ignazio Visco took over as governor.

9.7 A 'Peculiar' Central Bank?

Going back to Lord Norman's central banking paradigm, how peculiar was the Banca d'Italia's experience?

Monetary policy broadly followed the central banking international pattern for medium-sized open economies. The exchange rate was the main target under the gold standard and in the 1920s. From the 1930s to the 1970s, Italy and most other countries were characterized by a regime often defined as 'financial repression', whereby administrative regulations were used to reach, among other objectives, price stability, by controlling the aggregate quantity of credit available to the system. The system rested on controls over international capital movements, as allowed by the Bretton Woods system. The relaxation of 'financial repression' began in the second half of the 1980s, following the timing of other countries, except Germany and the United States, the early liberalizers.

---

[24] Law 28 December 2005, n. 262.

The *Banca d'Italia* was a latecomer in gaining monopoly of note issue, which it acquired only in 1926. It also maintained commercial banking functions until 1936, much longer than its main European peers, a function that did not facilitate its regulatory and (after 1926) supervisory tasks within the banking system.

Other idiosyncratic features of Italian central banking are possibly the following: (i) a paramount focus on the growth of the real economy, which at various junctures led the Bank to directly support industrial investment and at times even to try and direct credit to specific 'strategic' sectors; (ii) given Italy's bank-oriented financial system based on universal banking, the Bank was more concerned than other central banks about avoiding banking crises, fearing the transmission to the real economy. Up to the 1930s, lending of last resort was intense and pervasive, leading also to the creation of ad hoc institutions, in close cooperation with the government. Success in this area was mixed; (iii) up to the 1980s, the Bank used administrative, rather than market, instruments in monetary policy-making more extensively than other European central banks.

The provision to the state of a large number of services other than those closely related to its statutory mission (monetary policy and stability of the banking system) stands out as a feature of *Banca d'Italia* not matched in quantity and quality by other European central banks. Besides advising the government on matters other than money and banking, the Bank was involved in drafting legislation, negotiating international economic agreements, seconding its staff to various government branches as well as to domestic and international institutions. Two of the Bank's top officials (Governor Ciampi and General manager Lamberto Dini) served as prime ministers. Various members of the Bank joined the government as cabinet ministers. The Bank's wide-ranging 'public service' activity is particularly evident in the first two decades of the twentieth century and in the second post-war, much less so during fascism.

Partly related to the above-mentioned feature is the most intriguing peculiarity of Italy's central bank, namely the prestige it enjoyed, for long spells of time, with governments, business, trade unions, even intellectuals, as well as with the public at large. In a country not endowed with a particularly efficient public administration, the *Banca d'Italia's* organization and staff stood out as being both competent and honest. The long tenure of its leaders provided an image of stability in a country where, both before 1914 and after 1945, prime ministers rotated almost once a year. The Bank, for its part, took great care in cultivating its image as one of the most trustworthy institutions, also by constant participation in the public economic policy debate. In the second part of the twentieth century its high-profile image and aura of intellectual excellence contributed to the Bank's de facto independence and to its ability to influence policy-making. One may wonder if this will also be true in the early twenty-first-century populist and anti-elite social environment.

References[25]

Battilossi, Stefano (2003), 'Capital mobility and financial repression in Italy, 1960-1990. A public finance perspective', Universidad Carlos III de Madrid W.P.

Bonelli, Franco (1991), La Banca d'Italia dal 1894 al 1913, Laterza: Roma-Bari.

Bytheway, Simon James and Mark Metzler (2016), Central Banks and Gold. How Tokyo, London and New York Shaped the Modern World, Cornell University Press: Ithaca and London.

Canovai, Tito (1911), The Banks of Issue in Italy, US Senate, National Monetary Commission, Government Printing Office: Washington, DC.

Cardarelli, Sergio and R. Martano (2001), I nazisti e l'oro della Banca d'Italia, Laterza: Roma-Bari.

Cesarano, Filippo, Giulio Cifarelli and Gianni Toniolo (2012), 'Exchange rate regimes and reserve policy: the Italian lira 1883-1911', Open Economies Review, 23(2), 253-275.

Ciocca, Pierluigi (1973), 'Note sulla politica monetaria italiana, 1900-1913', in Gianni Toniolo, ed., Lo sviluppo economico italiano 1861-1940, Laterza: Roma-Bari, pp. 241-282.

Ciocca, Pierluigi (2007), Ricchi per sempre? Una storia economica d'Italia (1796-2005), Bollati Boringhieri: Torino.

Cotula, Franco and Juan Carlos Martinez (2003), 'Stabilità e sviluppo dalla liberazione al miracolo economico', in Franco, Cotula Marcello De Cecco and Gianni Toniolo, eds., La Banca d'Italia. Sintesi della ricerca storica, 1893-1960, Laterza: Roma-Bari, pp. 415-494.

Cotula, Franco, Marcello De Cecco and Gianni Toniolo, eds. (2003), La Banca d'Italia. Sintesi della ricerca storica, 1893-1960, Laterza: Roma-Bari.

Cotula, Franco and Luigi Spaventa (2003), 'La politica monetaria tra le due guerre, 1919-1935' in Franco, Cotula Marcello De Cecco and Gianni Toniolo, eds., La Banca d'Italia. Sintesi della ricerca storica, 1893-1960, Laterza: Roma-Bari, pp. 209-310.

De Cecco, Marcello (1993), L'Italia e il sistema finanziario internazionale, 1919-1936, Laterza: Roma-Bari.

Einaudi, Luigi (1933), 'Il mio piano non è quello di Keynes', La riforma sociale, now: Luigi Einaudi (2012), Il mio piano non è quello di Keynes, Rubbettino: Soveria Mannelli.

Fratianni, Michele and Franco Spinelli (1997), A Monetary History of Italy, Cambridge University Press: New York and Cambridge.

---

[25] The bibliography in Italian is enormous. Only a few of the main works are quoted here, of which Cotula, De Cecco, and Toniolo, eds. (2003) is probably the closest approximation to a single-volume, comprehensive history of the Banca d'Italia. Preference is given, whenever available to the few existing English-language references.

Gaiotti, Eugenio and Ignazio Angeloni (1990), *Note sulla politica monetaria italiana negli anni ottanta*, Banca d'Italia: Roma.

Gaiotti, Eugenio (1998), 'The rise and fall of inflation in Italy. A comparative analysis of four different explanations', *Il Giornale degli economisti e Annali di Economia*, 57, 297–324.

Gaiotti, Eugenio and Salvatore Rossi (2004), 'Theoretical and institutional evolution in economic policy: the case of monetary regime change in Italy in the early 1980s', *Storia del Pensiero economico*, 2, 5–36.

Gaiotti, Eugenio and Alessandro Secchi (2012), 'Monetary policy and fiscal dominance in Italy from the early 1970s to the adoption of the euro: a review', *Questioni di Economia e Finanza (Occasional papers)*, n. 141, Banca d'Italia: Roma.

Gigliobianco, Alfredo (2006), *Via Nazionale. Banca d'Italia e classe dirigente. Cento anni di storia*, Donzelli: Roma.

Guarino, Giuseppe and Gianni Toniolo (1993), *La Banca d'Italia e il sistema bancario, 1919–1936*, Laterza: Roma-Bari.

Kindleberger, Charles P. (1984), *A Financial History of Western Europe*, Allen & Unwin: London.

Maddison, Angus (2001), *The World Economy. A Millennial Perspective*, OECD: Paris.

Polsi, Alessandro (2001), *Stato e Banca Centrale in Italia. Il governo della moneta e del sistema bancario dall'Ottocento a oggi*, Laterza: Roma-Bari.

Rossi, Salvatore (1998), *La politica economica italiana 1968–1998*, Laterza: Roma-Bari.

Sayers, Richard Sidney (1976), *The Bank of England, 1891–1944*, Cambridge University Press: Cambridge and New York, 3 vols.

Toniolo, Gianni (1980), *L'economia dell'Italia fascista*, Laterza: Roma-Bari.

Toniolo, Gianni (1995), 'Italian banking 1919–1936', in Charles Feinstein, ed., *Banking, Currency and Finance in Europe Between the Wars*, Clarendon Press: Oxford, pp. 296–314.

Toniolo, Gianni (2005), *Central Bank Cooperation at the Bank for International Settlements 1930–73*, Oxford University Press: Oxford.

Toniolo, Gianni (2013), 'An overview of Italy's economic growth', in ID, ed., *The Oxford Handbook of the Italian Economy since Unification*, Oxford University Press: New York and Oxford, pp. 3–36.

10

A History of the Bank of Japan, 1882–2016

Masato Shizume*

10.1 Introduction

In this chapter, we review the history of the Bank of Japan (BOJ) with a focus on the changing role of the central bank and the transformation of the national economy (Table 10.1). When Japan joined the modern world in the late 19th century as a country with a small and open economy, the Bank was created as an entity to integrate the national financial market and provide liquidity for economic growth. By the early 20th century, Japan had succeeded in joining the modern world and began pursuing its goal as an empire. Under this condition, the Bank played a pivotal role in financing wars and in stabilizing the less-disciplined national financial market. Yet during and after Japan's losing war with its main trading partners in the 1930s and 1940s, the Bank was overwhelmed by ballooning government debt and rampant inflation. When Japan re-focused its national goal on high economic growth during the 1960s and early 1970s, the Bank was revived as an engine to fuel liquidity into the national economy even without legal independence. Once the Japanese economy reached an advanced stage of development from the 1970s onward, the Bank's main task changed from providing liquidity for economic growth to stabilizing the domestic economy. In pursuing its task, the Bank has often faced trade-offs between guns and butter, stability and growth, the threat of economic backlash and the moral hazard problem. The Bank has been and still is learning from new challenges.

* The author thanks Ryoji Koike, Toshiki Jinushi, Kris James Mitchener, and Shigenori Shiratsuka for helpful comments. Earlier versions of this chapter were presented at the workshop, "Sveriges Riksbank 350 years: a central bank in a world of central banks," and a seminar at the Bank of Japan.

Table 10.1 *Chronology of developments in relation to the BOJ and Japanese economy*

Year	BOJ	Year	Japanese economy
		1859	Opening of the treaty ports
		1868	Meiji Restoration
1882	BOJ established		
1885	First BOJ notes (silver standard)		
1897	Adoption of the gold standard	1894–1895	Sino-Japanese War
		1904–1905	Russo-Japanese War
1917	Suspension of the gold standard	1914–1918	WWI
		1927	Showa Financial Crisis
1930	Return to the gold standard		
1931	Departure from the gold standard		
1942	BOJ Act of 1942	1931–1945	Asia–Pacific War
1946	Emergency Financial Measures		
1949	Amendment of the BOJ Act		
		1960	National Income-Doubling Plan
1973	Move to flexible exchange rates	1973	First oil shock
		1985	Plaza Accord
		1987	Louvre Accord
1998	BOJ Act of 1998	1997–1998	Heisei Financial Crisis

Source: See text.

10.2 Entrance to the Modern World and Establishment of the Bank

10.2.1 The Monetary System in Japan during the Pre-modern Periods (–1850s)

Japan has a long history of banking activities. During the Edo Era (1603–1867), a sophisticated market economy of sorts developed in Japan, an agrarian country that produced commodity crops widely throughout all of its territory. Taxes were levied by the *koku*, a unit of rice. Feudal lords shipped their rice to Osaka to sell to merchants in exchange for money to be used to finance their daily purchases. Seasonality in rice production forced the feudal lords to depend on commercial credits supplied by rich merchants at other times of the year. Among merchants, bills of exchange based on traded rice and claims on future rice tax to be collected by feudal lords were regarded as good collateral. Commodities from all over the country were sent to Osaka and then distributed to Edo and other sites of consumption. As commercial activities penetrated the countryside and the division of labor spread throughout the nation, some merchants began engaging in financial operations of various types. Though Japan had no formal banking system, moneychangers and other merchants formed inter-regional networks and engaged in wideranging banking activities such as deposit-taking, lending, bills of exchange, and the issuance of paper money. Moneychangers provided liquidity to the society and managed risks much in the same way as modern bankers.[1]

10.2.1.1 National Currencies in the Pre-modern Periods

From the late 7th century to the mid-10th century, the Japanese government minted copper coins modeled after Chinese ones. The coins circulated along with commodity money such as rice and cloth. A series of debasements, however, eroded credibility for the money issued by the state. In the mid-10th century, the government stopped minting on the grounds of shortages in the materials for coins, leaving commodities such as rice and cloth as Japan's only currencies.[2]

From the 12th to 16th centuries, Chinese copper coins flowed into Japan and were widely circulated within the country. During the civil war period from the late 15th through the 16th century, warlords vigorously developed gold and silver mines and began using gold and silver as money, along with rice and imported copper coins. Silver became Japan's main export good from the late 16th to early 17th centuries. Warlords in the western part of Japan were especially active in mining, minting, and exporting silver. As a result, the money in large denominations circulated in western Japan was predominantly silver.[3]

Japan entered a period of peace and political unity in the early 17th century after the civil war from the late 15th century. Under the rule of the Tokugawa Shogunate in Edo (now Tokyo), some 300 feudal lords governed territories throughout Japan until the late 19th century.

The Shogunate promoted foreign trade during the early 17th century, but later expelled the Portuguese and Spanish, imposed a ban on emigration by Japanese people, and set strict controls on foreign trade. The Shogunate pursued these policies mainly for political reasons to avoid the penetration of Christianity and to prevent potential alliances between foreign powers and the feudal lords. Only the Dutch and Chinese, who were seen as non-

---

[1] Takatsuki et al. (2017), pp. 106–43; Iwahashi (2002), pp. 459–466.
[2] Sakaehara (2002), pp. 5–39.　　[3] Sakurai (2002), pp. 42–55.

religious people, were officially allowed to trade with the government and its agents. Economic isolation made Japan a microcosm independent from the rest of the world until its treaty ports were forced open in the late 19th century.[4]

The national currency system in Japan during the Edo Era was characterized as a tri-metallic system consisting of gold, silver, and copper coin specie. The Shogunate promoted the use of gold coins as the national currency throughout the era, while allowing the use of silver and copper coins as domestic currency. Gold coins were a denominated currency based on a unit called the *ryo*, while silver coins were a currency denominated by weight based on a unit called the *monme* (the equivalent of 3.75 grams). Copper coins were a denominated currency based on the traditional unit of *mon*. The monetary units in use varied from one territory to another. The *monme* was widely used as a unit of account in the western part of Japan, including Osaka and Kyoto. The *ryo*, the gold unit, was used in the eastern part, including Edo. The *mon*, the copper unit, was used in most regions for small-denomination transactions and in some regions for large-denomination transactions, as well. While the Shogunate took control of minting and set the official exchange rates for gold, silver, and copper/iron/brass coins, the market rates fluctuated daily based on the regional balance of payments as well as the supply and demand of real money. Along with these metal forms of money, feudal lords and merchants issued paper money (clan notes and private notes) denominated in the units of the above specie. The Shogunate held back from issuing paper money until the last years of its reign.[5]

10.2.1.2 Moneychangers as Financial Institutions

Money and financial institutions promoted nationwide commercial activities throughout the Edo Era. Various types of financial activities flourished and sophisticated methods such as commodity futures emerged.

The Shogunate allowed the feudal lords to levy taxes and police the subject people in the territories. Each lord was classified by the size of his territory based on the volume of its rice harvest in a unit called the *koku*

---

[4] Toby (1991).

[5] Iwahashi (2002), pp. 431–451. After the collapse of the Tokugawa Shogunate in 1868, the new government surveyed currencies issued by the old regime that were still in circulation. According to the survey, an equivalent of 187 million yen was in circulation. Out of this sum, 88 million yen, or 47 percent, was gold coins denominated in *ryo*; 67 million yen, or 36 percent, was silver coins denominated in *ryo* (subsidiary coins of gold); 6 million yen, or 3 percent, was copper/iron/brass coins denominated in *mon*; 2 million yen, or 1 percent, was silver coins denominated in *monme*; and 25 million yen, or 13 percent, was paper money denominated in various units. The Bank of Japan (1973), pp. 152–153.

(1 *koku* = 180 liters). In return, the feudal lords were required to live in Edo every other year to express their loyalty to the Shogun. Their wives and successors, meanwhile, were required to live in Edo permanently, as hostages in effect, to deter the lords from rebelling. This system of alternate attendance (*sankin koutai*) was formalized by the Acts for Military Houses (*Buke-Shohatto*) in 1635 and lasted until the final days of the Shogunate government in the late 19th century.[6]

The alternate attendance system promoted commercial activities and the use of money, forcing the feudal lords to monetize their economic activities. The lords needed to sell their products in order to cover the expenses they incurred during the stays in Edo and on the road between Edo and their territories. The regional division of labor among warriors and commoners, meanwhile, necessitated the exchange of goods and services across regions and classes of people. Osaka was a national commercial and financial center with a rice futures market.[7]

Moneychangers engaged in a wide range of banking activities beyond currency exchange, such as accepting deposits, lending, exchange bills, and issuing paper money. They originated as merchants of various forms and operated their original businesses concurrently with banking.[8]

Japan had no central bank during the Edo Era, and the national financial market was not yet integrated. Liquidity was channeled into the economy through correspondent networks of moneychangers. Groups of moneychangers in Osaka, Kyoto, and Edo formulated guilds as hubs for the national payment networks.[9] When the feudal lords issued clan notes, they often relied upon moneychangers with expertise in reserve management.

10.2.2 Reforms after the Opening of the Treaty Ports (1860s–1880s)

After the enforced opening of the treaty ports in the 1850s, Japan began to trade internationally on a major scale. Low tariffs under the unequal treaties with major western powers forced Japanese industries to compete with foreign counterparts. After the Meiji Restoration in 1868, the new government moved to establish modern monetary and financial systems with some trial and error. In the course of events, the government introduced a multiple issuing bank system based on the US model, then supplanted it with a European style of central banking system by establishing the BOJ.[10]

---

[6] Hayami (1999), pp. 22–23.   [7] Miyamoto (1988); Schaede (1989).
[8] Sakudou (1971), pp. 105–544.   [9] Iwahashi (2002), pp. 459–464.
[10] The description below is based on Shizume and Tsurumi (2016).

10.2.2.1 Debate on Banking Systems and Establishment of National Banks

In 1868, the government introduced the *dajoukan-satsu*, a new government note based on the existing unit of account in gold (*ryo*), and abolished the use of the silver currency by weight. The *dajoukan-satsu*, the first paper money to be circulated nationwide, was initially introduced as a substitute for gold and silver coins issued under the rule of the Tokugawa Shogunate. The merchants used it as a means of payment for long-distant trades, and the feudal lords who still governed their territories used it as a reserve asset for local paper monies.[11] Yet due to massive fiscal expenditure toward the civil war and shortage of fiscal revenues, the *dajoukan-satsu* was issued in excess, which resulted in inflation.

In 1869, merchants introduced the *kawase-kaisha*, prototypes of modern commercial banks, under the leadership of the government. *Kawase-kaisha* were established in eight trading centers: Tokyo, Osaka, Kyoto, Yokohama, Kobe, Niigata, Otsu, and Tsuruga. Their primary functions were usual banking activities such as accepting deposits, extending credit, and transferring funds over long distances. They were also authorized to issue banknotes. Very soon, however, bank runs forced all of the *kawase-kaisha* except one, that in Yokohama, out of business.

In 1870, Hirobumi Ito, a high-ranking official in the Ministry of Finance (MOF) who had been sent to the United States to study American monetary and banking systems, submitted a proposal recommending the establishment of a monetary and banking system based on the gold standard with multiple issuing banks.[12] After exploring the American national banking system, Ito argued that Japan's issuing bank system should be modeled after the national banks in the United States. His reasoning was focused on the structure of the Japanese economy, which was decentralized at the time and more closely resembled the economy of the United States than it did the economies of Europe.[13]

In 1871, Kiyonari Yoshida, an MOF official who had just returned from a long stint in Europe and the United States to study their financial systems, proposed a plan for the establishment of a single issuing bank modeled after the Bank of England.[14] A sharp debate arose over the two competing plans for the new issuing bank system.

---

[11] Kobayashi (2015), pp. 323–326.

[12] The national banks in the United States were allowed to issue banknotes as privately-owned commercial banks operating under a national charter.

[13] The Bank of Japan (1982), pp. 16–18.   [14] The Bank of Japan (1982), pp. 18–19.

Ito argued: "If we introduce the U.S. system, we will be able to redeem half of the existing currency into banknotes issued by the newly established issuing companies and convert the other half into government bonds. In doing so, we will recover the credibility of the currency."[15]

Yoshida responded: "We should introduce the common method of banknote issuance in Europe by establishing an issuing company with specie reserves. By doing so, we will eventually be able to make coins and paper money convertible."

Ito criticized Yoshida's argument: "Your plan overlooks the nature of the government as an entity that can utilize the power of the private sector. It only considers the government's accounting with no thought for the progress of the people."[16]

In a sense, Ito advocated an endogenous supply of money to promote industrial development based on the banking school approach. In contrast, Yoshida emphasized stabilization through the control of money based on the currency school approach.

In 1871, the government declared that it would adopt the gold standard and introduce the yen as the new unit of account. It also issued gold coins for general use and silver coins for international trade. A year later the government issued government notes denominated in yen and proclaimed the National Bank Act of 1872. Under the Act, national banks were allowed to both engage in the usual banking activities and issue convertible notes. The establishment of private banks authorized to issue convertible notes was a compromise between Ito's and Yoshida's arguments. By law, the amount of national banknotes could not exceed 100 million yen. This was effectively an unlimited allowance for banknote issuance, given that the value of notes in circulation (including those issued by the government and former feudal lords) was currently less than 100 million yen. Yet due to strict regulations, most notably a high reserve ratio, only four national banks were established under the National Bank Act of 1872.

10.2.2.2 The Amended National Bank Act of 1876

Under amendments to the National Bank Act in 1876, the government made national banknotes inconvertible and authorized national banks to issue banknotes backed by national bonds.

The change in banking policy was prompted by a need to cope with reforms in the stipend scheme for former samurai. After the collapse of the

---

[15] Shunpo-ko Tsuisho-kai (1940), p. 527.   [16] Ministry of Finance (1905), pp. 25–26.

Tokugawa Shogunate, the government continued paying stipends to former samurai. Under fiscal reforms effected in 1876, the government stopped paying the former samurai stipends, offering coupon bonds instead. The purposes of the National Bank Act amendment were twofold: to appease the former samurai for their lost privileges by deregulating their investments through national banks, and to mobilize the capital the former samurai held as government bonds.[17] Under this arrangement, national bonds could serve as reserves for national banknote issuance. A large number of national bonds and national bank shares were floated as a result.

Ito's proposal was fully implemented at this stage. One hundred and fifty-three national banks were established from 1876 to 1879, including four re-chartered banks that had been established under the previous National Bank Act. Some banks were established by moneychangers. Others were established by merchants or former samurai.[18]

In the same year, 1876, the government chartered Mitsui Bank to go into business as Japan's first privately-owned bank not designated as a national bank (*shiritsu ginko*). Many other privately-owned banks were established in ensuing years. Though chartered to engage in the usual banking business, these privately-owned banks were prohibited from issuing banknotes.

While the origins of the national and other privately-owned banks differed, the operations of both depended on the managerial skills of moneychangers. Many other moneychangers, meanwhile, remained in the banking business without government charters. The Meiji government called these moneychangers quasi-banks.

Table 10.2 shows the number of Japanese financial institutions recognized by the government in 1881, along with their capital. A total of 149 national banks, 90 other privately-owned banks, and 369 quasi-banks were recognized. Acknowledging that it was unable to acquire sufficient information about the quasi-banks, the government advised that the quasi-bank statistics were possibly underestimated.

On average, the quasi-banks were much smaller than the national and other privately-owned banks. The capital of the national banks, other privately-owned banks, and quasi-banks averaged 295 thousand yen, 116 thousand yen, and 16 thousand yen, respectively. Even after excluding the giant Fifteenth National Bank, which had been established with funds from the

---

[17] Ministry of Finance (1905), pp. 112–113; The Bank of Japan (1982), pp. 26–28; Shizume and Tsurumi (2016).
[18] Asakura (1961).

Table 10.2 *Financial institutions as of the end of 1881*

	Number	Total capital*	Average capital*
National Banks	149	43,886	295
Excl. 15th Bank	148	26,060	176
Other privately-owned Banks	90	10,447	116
Quasi-banks	369+	5,895+	16
Total	608+	60,228+	n.a.

* thousand yen.
Source: *The Second National Statistical Abstract of the Japanese Empire*, 1884.

former feudal lords, the capital of the national banks averaged 176 thousand yen, a sum still far higher than that of the other types of financial institutions.

In response to the banking boom and in the face of rampant inflation during and after the Satsuma Rebellion of 1877, the government moved to regulate the supply of money. In the same year, Finance Minister Shigenobu Okuma proposed a cap on the banknote issuance amount by prefecture. In the next year, 1878, the National Bank Act was amended again to set an effective limit on banknote issuance. The government then introduced a regulation on the allowance of banknote issuance in each prefecture. When the total allowance for all prefectures reached a national limit of 34 million yen, the government stopped accepting requests for new bank establishments.

10.2.2.3 The Bank of Japan Act of 1882

After the Satsuma Rebellion of 1877, the government began to lean toward the establishment of a central bank as the sole issuer of convertible banknotes. In the initial phase, Finance Minister Shigenobu Okuma proposed issuing bonds in the international markets to build up specie for conversion of banknotes into specie. Another financial statesman, Masayoshi Matsukata, opposed Okuma's proposal, arguing that the issuance of foreign bonds would risk Japan's sovereignty if Japan had trouble repaying. Instead, Matsukata advocated an austerity policy toward the establishment of a central bank.[19]

In 1881, another political debate arose on the creation of a constitution. Okuma insisted on the establishment of a parliamentary system of government. Other members within the government, including Matsukata, attacked Okuma as too radical and ousted him from the Ministry. The government, meanwhile, promised to formulate a constitution based on

[19] The Bank of Japan (1982), pp. 77–106.

the more conservative Prussian constitution by 1890 and to hold a general election. Matsukata finally won a series of internal battles with Okuma and became Finance Minister in 1882. He led Japan's financial policy as Finance Minister, with some hiatuses, up to 1900, establishing the BOJ in 1882 and introducing austerity fiscal policies from the same year onwards.[20]

When Matsukata was sent to the Paris International Exposition in 1878 as the Deputy Representative from Japan, he had another mission: to study central bank systems in Europe. Initially intending to study the French system, he asked for the advice of the French Finance Minister, Léon Say. Say recommended the National Bank of Belgium (NBB) as a model for the central bank of Japan, as the bank had been recently founded (in 1850) and operated under laws and bylaws that were more clearly written than those for earlier banks such as the Bank of France. Following Say's advice, Matsukata and his subordinate studied the Belgian system extensively, as well as the system in France. The founders of the Japanese central bank and their predecessors had thus studied the monetary systems of at least Britain, France, and Belgium, as well as the United States, a nation without a central bank, before establishing the BOJ.

The NBB was a semi-public institution established to restore monetary and financial stability after a series of national financial crises. The legislation to establish it emphasized the convertibility of its banknotes and allowed liquidity provision only for short-term commercial liabilities. It operated as a private joint-stock company with commercial activities driven by the profit motive. At the same time, the NBB performed functions in the public interest such as the issuance of banknotes and operations as a government cashier. The Belgian government appointed a governor and government commissioner to run and oversee the NBB.[21]

Although political and economic conditions in Japan differed from Belgium at the onset of the BOJ, the Bank inherited the legal and institutional settings of the NBB. The Bank of Japan Act of 1882 conferred the BOJ with the status of a semi-public institution. The Bank's shares were to be owned by the private sector, and a governance mechanism was in place to ensure the Bank's accountability to shareholders. The government, meanwhile, was to appoint the governor and vice governor of the BOJ and keep the Bank's activities under its strict control. The Act stipulated that only Japanese citizens could hold shares of the Bank, and only with the permission of the Finance Minister (Articles 5 and 6). The Bank was to

---

[20] The Bank of Japan (1982), p. 107.
[21] Buyst and Maes (2008), p. 161. They review the process and purpose of the establishment of the NBB and the operation of the NBB in its early days.

engage in the businesses of: (1) discounting and buying of commercial and government bills, (2) buying and selling of gold and silver, (3) lending backed by gold or silver as collateral, (4) collecting due amounts of funds of customers with contracts, (5) accepting deposits and keeping gold, silver, and other precious metals and securities in custody, and (6) lending with overdraft contracts or with fixed term contracts on securities issued or guaranteed by the government as collaterals subject to the interest rates permitted by Finance Minister (Article 11). The Bank was to be the treasurer of the government (Article 13). The Bank was given the right to issue convertible banknotes (Article 14). The Bank was permitted to hold issued bills and checks (Article 15). The Bank was permitted to buy and sell government securities subject to the permission of the Finance Minister (Article 16). The governor of the Bank was to be appointed by the Emperor and the Vice Governor was to be appointed by the government (Article 18). Executive Directors were to be elected by the general share-holders' meeting and appointed by the Finance Minister. Auditors were to be elected by the general shareholders' meeting (Article 19). The government was to send a supervisor to the Bank's site (Article 21).[22]

10.2.2.4 National Banks and the Central Bank (1880s–1890s)

At the founding of the BOJ, Matsukata declared that the central bank was to serve as the hub of Japan's national financial and payment system, pumping in liquidity just as a heart pumps blood to the human body. He claimed that Japan suffered from insufficient liquidity. He blamed the existing national banks for driving up interest rates and hampering the national financial integration by failing to adequately cooperate with each other or adjust inter-regional surpluses and deficits of funds.[23]

The government sought to establish a financial system with a pyramid structure headed by the BOJ. It divested the national banks of their right to issue banknotes, granting that right instead to the BOJ alone. At the same time, it redeemed existing government notes in circulation.[24] The BOJ started issuing banknotes in 1885, just as Matsukata's austerity policy had reduced inflation. The first banknote issued by the BOJ was convertible to silver. Japan thus switched to the silver standard in the 1880s, dropping its

---

[22] The Bank of Japan (1986), p. 195.   [23] Matsukata (1882), p. 992.

[24] As of the end of 1881, currency in circulation totaled 196 million yen, out of which 119 million yen was government notes, 34 million yen was national banknotes, 24 million yen was bullion coins (gold/silver), and 19 million yen was subsidiary coins (silver/copper). The Bank of Japan (1986), pp. 414–415.

initial plans to adopt the gold standard from the decade before. The silver dollar (the Mexican dollar) was widely circulated in the Asia-Pacific region, and silver coins issued by Japan from the 1870s were circulated both domestically and internationally. The transformation from Japan's multiple issuing bank system to a single issuing bank system, the conversion of the previous national banks into ordinary banks, was completed by 1899.

The BOJ, however, needed time to effectively perform its functions as the central bank. The operation of the BOJ in its early days was literally "learning by doing" in a number of dimensions.

The first dimension was smoothing of the seasonality in interest rates. In theory, a central bank empowered to issue its own banknotes would be able to adjust the seasonal fluctuations in the demand for liquidity, and thus to smooth the seasonality in interest rates. Fukuda (1995), however, finds that the interest rate seasonality persists until around the end of the 19th century even as the BOJ attempted to respond in an elastic manner from the issuance of its first banknote in 1885.[25]

The second dimension was adjustment of inter-regional discrepancies in the supply and demand of liquidity. The founders of the BOJ initially expected that the correspondence network of the BOJ would work as a channel to provide liquidity nationwide. A preliminary analysis by Shizume (2017), however, shows that the correspondence network of the BOJ with other banks in the 1880s added little to the existing networks of the private banks. The BOJ built branches in the 1890s and had one headquarters and ten branches by 1900. As Ohnuki (2007) and Mitchener and Ohnuki (2007) demonstrate, the national capital market was integrated over the long run.

The third dimension was crisis management and the BOJ's role as a lender of last resort (LoLR). Matsukata Masayoshi, the founder of the BOJ, mentioned nothing about this role as an LoLR when the Bank opened in 1882, even though he had stayed in Europe after Walter Bagehot published *Lombard Street* in 1873. The BOJ changed its stance toward the financial market for the first time after facing the banking panic of 1890 in Osaka and western Japan. The Bank actively extended its lending operations by adding company stocks to eligible collaterals in ensuing years, paving the way to its LoLR function toward the end of the century.[26]

---

[25] Fukuda (1995), pp. 63–65, 71.   [26] Shizume (2017).

10.3 Guns and Butter: Wars and the Bank

10.3.1 Sino-Japanese War, Russo-Japanese War and the Gold Standard (1890s–1900s)

Japan completed its entry to the modern world by the turn of the century. It had overcome the risk of being colonized and gained recognition as an emerging economy. Japanese policymakers regarded Japan as the only Asian country with the potential to become an empire in the prevailing climate of imperialism of that time.

Under the silver standard, the Japanese economy grew at an annual rate of 3 percent over the period of 1886–1897 thanks to the depreciation of the yen against gold standard currencies (Table 10.3). A revised treaty between Japan and Great Britain in 1894 raised tariff rates and abolished Britain's consular jurisdiction and unilateral most favored nation status. The revision of unequal treaties with other western countries followed, culminating in full tariff autonomy for Japan in 1911. By this point, Japan was recognized as an emerging empire and a full member of the international community of western powers.

Yet, new challenges arose for Japan as an emerging empire. As Japan's external status improved, it faced rising costs to maintain its status and a growing trade-off between accumulating national wealth and the building of a strong army and navy. Upon joining the gold standard in 1897, Japan partly solved the trade-off by stimulating international trade and gaining easy access to the international financial market.[27] Japan was partly rewarded by its success in raising huge funds in the international market during the Russo-Japanese War.[28] At the same time, however, Japan had to compensate for the war with slower growth through contractionary monetary and fiscal policies in order to maintain the gold convertibility. The Japanese economy expanded more slowly than in the previous years on the silver standard, growing at an annual rate of only 2 percent over the period of 1898–1913 (Table 10.3). The burden of overseas war debt imposed a new constraint on the conduct of monetary and fiscal policy after the war. Japan's current account remained in the red and difficulties in financing the deficit persisted (Figure 10.1).

10.3.2 World War I Boom and the Financial Crises (1910s–1920s)

World War I (WWI) was "divine providence" for Japan.[29] Japan, distant from the battlefields of Europe and only fighting in the German territories

---

[27] Mitchener, Shizume, and Weidenmier (2010).   [28] Smethurst (2007), pp. 141–187.
[29] Metzler (2006), pp. 91–111.

Table 10.3 *Annual percent changes in output and prices (1886–1913)*

	Output (GNP)	Prices (GNP deflator)
1886–1897	3.3	4.2
1898–1913	2.2	3.8

Source: Ohkawa and Shinohara (1979), pp. 251–260.

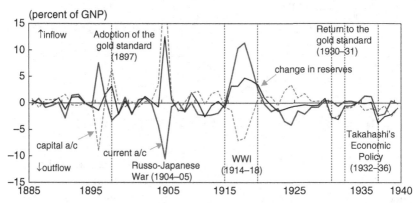

Figure 10.1 Balance of payment
Source: Yamazawa and Yamamoto (1979), pp. 220–227; Ohkawa et al. (1979), pp. 251–253.

in Asia and in the Russian Far East, grew swiftly, accumulated current account surpluses, and joined the United States as a creditor country. The balance of payments no longer restricted monetary policy.

This gave rise, however, to a new trade-off between growth and stability. Following the boom during and just after WWI, Japan suffered from economic stagnation, price deflation, and bad loan problems through the 1920s. An economic backlash and the government's attempt to maintain high economic growth even after the war created mounting bad loans among domestic commercial banks. Then, in 1923, the Great Kanto Earthquake hit the Tokyo metropolitan area and the BOJ introduced a special treatment facility for the devastated area. The BOJ's intention *ex ante* was to rescue solvent, but illiquid banks. The facility was abused *ex post*, however, by banks already in financial distress, evincing a clear moral hazard problem.

Financial panic spread nationwide in the spring of 1927 (Showa Financial Crisis). During the crisis, the BOJ functioned as an LoLR, swiftly extending its credit to combat bank runs. The crisis accelerated the long-awaited resolution of the bad loan problems and reforms of the financial

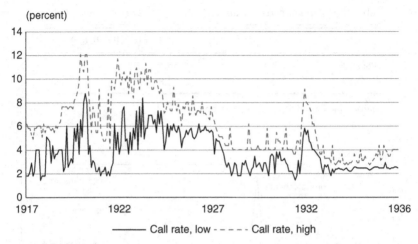

Figure 10.2 Interbank interest rates
Source: The Ministry of Finance, *Reference Book of Financial Matters*, annual editions.

system under the leadership of the government's executive branch. In 1928, the authorities introduced a new scheme for a prudential policy encouraging mergers and acquisitions, bringing in new regulations, and instituting a system of dual inspection by the MOF and the BOJ.[30]

With the steadying influence of banking reforms and public funding, financial stability was finally restored. Call rates, which had remained high between the financial panic of 1922 and Showa Financial Crisis of 1927, reflecting high-risk premia, fell substantially in the spring of 1927. This drop in rates stemmed from strong confidence in financial reforms among market participants, the disposition of the financial crisis, and the provisioning of liquidity by the BOJ secured by the government for potential losses (Figure 10.2).[31]

When financial stability was finally restored, entrenched lending by the BOJ imposed a new constraint on the operation of monetary policy. In practice, the BOJ lacked policy instruments to absorb funds from the financial markets. Most of the lending by the BOJ to the private sector after the Showa Financial Crisis of 1927 consisted of special loans. Though guaranteed by the government, the funds could not be easily removed from the financial markets. The BOJ had to bear a loss of flexibility in its monetary policy operation (Figure 10.3).[32] In response, it turned to open

[30] Shizume (2018), pp. 137–142.   [31] Shizume (2018), pp. 142–143.
[32] Shizume (2018), pp. 143–146.

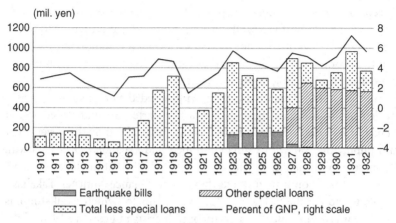

Figure 10.3 BOJ loans to the private sector
Source: The Ministry of Finance, *Reference Book for Financial Matters*, annual editions.

market operations as a new device for absorbing funds from the financial markets using government bonds as instruments.

10.3.3 The Great Depression and Departure from the Gold Standard (1930–1936)

Japan sought to restore gold convertibility, which it had suspended in 1917, following the Unites States. In January of 1930, having resolved the financial crises of the earlier decade, Japan finally returned to the gold standard. A disastrous slump and deep deflation in Japan followed, just as the Great Depression was taking hold globally.[33]

Japan stayed on the gold standard for less than two years. At the end of 1931, the veteran Finance Minister Korekiyo Takahashi led a major shift in the country's change in its macroeconomic policy. Takahashi departed from the gold standard in December 1931, initiating a drastic macroeconomic policy package including currency depreciation, fiscal stimulus, and monetary easing. Economic recovery in Japan preceded that in the United States and Europe. The Japanese economy grew at an annual rate of 6 percent during Takahashi's term in 1932–1936, with inflation contained at low levels.[34]

The BOJ supported the price of government bonds by underwriting them, selling them to financial institutions, and keeping interest rates low.

---

[33] Shizume (2012).　　[34] Shibamoto and Shizume (2014).

In return, the BOJ obtained the power to sell government securities without the permission of the MOF for each operation, and thereby to implement open market operations. By doing so the Bank planned to restore its ability to control the financial markets, something it had lost with mounting entrenched lending to private banks.[35]

But then another issue arose as Japan proceeded along its recovery path. In September of 1931, the Japanese army started an undeclared war in Manchuria in northeastern China. Though unexpected by the government and public, the war with China continued and expanded, overshadowing Japanese public finance. When convinced, in 1935, that the Japanese economy was finally on a path of steady growth, Finance Minister Takahashi negotiated to cut the military budget with plans to tighten fiscal stimulus. Then he was assassinated by a group of militarists in February 1936.

Shizume (2011) looks at the sustainability of public debt in Japan in the long run, revealing that debt sustainability was kept until 1931 and lost in and after 1932. He concludes that the loss of sustainability was mainly attributable to the loss of fiscal discipline when the international gold standard collapsed and Japan departed from the gold standard in fall–winter of 1932. Japan failed to establish a new system to govern fiscal policy, including military spending.[36] Shibamoto and Shizume (2014) also show that monetary policy during the interwar period was conducted in a manner accommodative to other economic and policy shocks.

10.3.4 The Asia-Pacific War and Financial Repression (1937–1945)

As the war extended and expanded during the 1930s and early 1940s, war finance overwhelmed monetary policy. The BOJ devoted itself to the national objective, to fight the war, under the control of the government. Japan's war with China escalated to a full scale in 1937. In December 1936, the BOJ held less than 1 billion yen in government securities and owed less than 2 billion yen of banknotes in circulation. In December 1940, a year before the outbreak of the war with the United States, the BOJ held 4 billion yen in government securities and owed 5 billion yen of banknotes in circulation. In March 1945, four months before the end of the war, the BOJ held 8 billion yen in government securities, had loaned out 14 million

---

[35] Ide (2003).

[36] Pittaluga and Seghezza (2016) argue that Japan ran unsustainable external debts even before WWI, when Japan was on gold. Japan was allowed to do so, they claim, because Britain granted Japan easy access to the international financial markets in return for Japan's protection of British economic and political interests in the Far East.

yen mainly to war industries through other banks, and owed 21 billion yen of banknotes in circulation.[37]

To suppress inflation pressures, the government and the BOJ relied on financial repression and the direct control of prices. In September 1937, the government imposed controls on international trade and long-term capital allocation. In January of 1938, it set the first Goods Mobilization Plan. In March of the same year, it passed and effectuated the National Total Mobilization Law in May, thus gaining the power to mobilize civilians for national goals. The Law became the basis of price controls and rationing on a wide variety of goods, services, employments, and wages. In April 1939, the government imposed controls on employment and wages. In October 1939, it promulgated the Prices Control Ordinance, a legislation virtually covering the prices of all goods and services. A year later, in October 1940, it promulgated the Ordinance to Regulate Banks' Allocation of Funds.[38]

As Japan's relationship with foreign countries deteriorated, the United States imposed and tightened economic sanctions against Japan. In July 1940, the United States adopted a license system for the export of scrap iron and oil. In July 1941, in response to Japan's occupation of southern French Indochina, the United States froze all Japanese assets in its territories and placed a total ban on oil shipments to Japan. The Netherlands East Indies followed suit, imposing a ban on its own oil exports to Japan. Japan depended on the United States for resources and finance, so the sanctions aggravated shortages of materials essential for the Japanese economy. After Japan went to war with the United States in December of 1941, the Japanese government formulated the Plan for the Greater East Asia Co-Prosperity Sphere. Ultimately, the plan amounted to nothing more than a pie in the sky.[39]

The Bank of Japan Act of 1882 was replaced by the Bank of Japan Act of 1942. The new Act defined the BOJ as a state entity and strengthened the government's control on the BOJ's operations. The Act of 1942 was said to have been modeled after the German Reichsbank Law enacted under the Nazi regime.[40] The convertibility clause, which had not been virtually effective since December 1931, was officially abolished at the same time. The Act of 1942 stipulated that the BOJ was to be responsible for the control of money, adjustment of finance, and reinforcement of the credit system in accordance with national policy, thereby fully utilizing the

[37] The Bank of Japan (1986), pp. 290–293.   [38] Nakamura (1999), pp. 55–77.
[39] Nakamura (1994), p. 116; Nakamura (1999), pp. 77–80.
[40] The Bank of Japan (1984), p. 478.

national economic power (Article 1). The BOJ was to devote itself entirely to achieving the national goal (Article 2). The Governor and Vice Governor were to be appointed by the government (Article 16). The Minister in charge (Finance Minister) had the authority to supervise the BOJ (Article 42). The Minister in charge was authorized to order the BOJ to take necessary actions, including changes of bylaws, if the Minister recognized it to be necessary (Article 43).[41] The Minister in charge was authorized to order financial institutions to cooperate with the BOJ if the Minister recognized it to be necessary for achieving the BOJ's goals (Article 28). The BOJ was to issue banknotes for the benefit of all public and private transactions without any limit (Article 29). The BOJ had to obtain the permission of the Minister in charge for all decisions on its discount and lending rates (Article 21). The BOJ could lend to the government without taking collateral, and apply for or underwrite government securities (Article 22). The Bank of Japan Act of 1942 was marginally revised on several occasions in ensuing decades, bit it virtually remained in effect up to 1998.

The BOJ played a pivotal role under the wartime regime. It allocated funds by rationing credit and supervised other financial institutions under the government. The war economy, however, was poorly controlled. Black markets flourished in hidden personal settings and plans for allocating materials for the total war and daily necessities failed.[42]

10.3.5 The Post-War Inflation and Reconstruction of the Economy (1945-1950s)

Japan surrendered to the allied powers and the occupation began in September 1945. The occupation lasted until the San Francisco Peace Treaty took effect in April 1952. The Japanese government was allowed to exist and formulate policies subject to the permissions of the General Headquarters of the Allied Forces (GHQ).

The Japanese economy was in disarray. A major restructuring in the deployment of human resources was badly needed. Some 2.12 million soldiers died in battle and another 300 thousand persons died in air raids. About 7.2 million troops were to be demobilized, about 4 million workers in armaments factories would lose their jobs, and 1.5 million Japanese

---

[41] The Bank of Japan (1986), pp. 210-212.
[42] According to a few witnesses, people were unable to survive without black markets. Nakamura (1994), pp. 117-122.

overseas would be repatriated. In the coal industry, the main energy source for Japan at the time, the repatriation of impressed workers from China and Korea resulted in a major energy shortage and bottleneck for economic recovery. As for physical assets, about one-fourth of the total was lost.[43]

Uncontrollable inflation broke out at around the end of the war. Though we lack reliable statistics on wartime inflation, anecdotal evidence suggests that prices soared in the black markets. Two government measures accelerated the inflation from just after Japan's surrender in August 1945 through to the end of the year: the payment of war expenses to compensate repatriated soldiers and civilians who had worked for war industries or lost their houses in air raids, and the lifting of price controls on fresh foods to promote their supply.[44] At the same time, black markets prevailed in the streets of the major cities once the war ended. The BOJ, which started collecting data on black market prices by as early as October 1945, estimated that retail prices in the black markets were 29 times higher than the official prices at the time and 92 times higher than prices from 1934 to 1936, a decade earlier (Figure 10.4).

The government took a set of Emergency Financial Measures to deal with the rampant inflation in February–March 1946. All cash had to be deposited in financial institutions, new banknotes were issued, limits were set on withdrawals, and strict government control over official prices was resumed. Inflation in black markets subsided in response, at least temporarily.[45]

Shigeru Yoshida took power in May 1946 and stayed in power until 1954, with a brief break in 1947–1948. Japan moved toward an economic recovery and a return to the international community under his leadership. His approach, known as the "Yoshida Doctrine" (though he never used those words himself), was to concentrate on the recovery and development of the economy while minimizing the burden of military spending by relying on American forces for national security. In a sense, he redefined the national goal as wealth without military power, freeing the BOJ from worries over war financing even though it was still bound to devote itself to the national goal under the Bank of Japan Act of 1942, which remained in effect.[46]

In 1947, the Yoshida Cabinet initiated the Priority Production System to boost the economy. The main idea was to concentrate physical and

---

[43] Nakamura (1994), pp. 123–124, 148.
[44] The Bank of Japan (1985), pp. 17–18; Nakamura (1994), p. 131.
[45] The Bank of Japan (1985), pp. 38–45; Nakamura (1994), pp. 149–150.
[46] Nakamura (1994), p. 175.

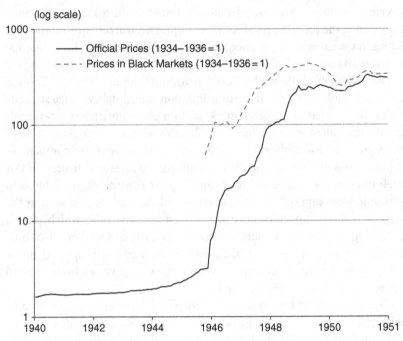

Figure 10.4 Retail prices
Source: Toyo Keizai (1954), *Price Statistics of Pre/Post-War Period*; The Bank of Japan.

financial resources to key industries such as coal and steel, resolving a bottleneck in production and igniting the whole economy. The Reconstruction Finance Bank (RFB), a government-formed bank established in January 1947 to finance key industries, floated bonds to be underwritten by the BOJ. In the same year, BOJ underwriting of public debt was banned under the newly promulgated Public Finance Act (Article 5). Technically speaking, bonds issued by the RFB were not government bonds. In effect, however, the provision of central bank credit through the RFB reignited inflation (Figure 10.4).[47]

Hisato Ichimada, the BOJ Governor for the entire Yoshida Administration (1946–1954), later recalled the difficulty of pursuing the conflicting policy goals of controlling inflation and bringing about a recovery in production at the same time.[48]

When Japan was about to reintegrate into the international community, a debate on the adjustment policy arose between hard-liners and soft-liners

---

[47] The Bank of Japan (1985), pp. 102–104, 108; Nakamura (1994), pp. 151–153.
[48] The Bank of Japan (1985), p. 60.

within the Japanese government and within the GHQ: the hard-liners insisted on containing inflation first, while the soft-liners argued for a more gradual path of balanced inflation and growth. The debate ended with the victory of the hard-liners upon the arrival of Joseph Dodge, chairman of the Bank of Detroit, as an adviser to the Supreme Commander of the GHQ in December 1948. Under the hard-line stabilization policy, the "Dodge Line," Japan (1) imposed strict controls over the national budget and taxation to eliminate the fiscal deficit, (2) limited credit extensions to curb inflation, and (3) tightened foreign trade and exchange control. Dodge, an essential believer in the free-market economy, recognized these policies as preconditions for the full re-entry of the Japanese economy into the international market under the Bretton Woods System. All of the hidden subsidies to industries and foreign trade were eliminated, along with any excess regulations not deemed to be essential as safeguards. The RFB stopped new lending in 1949 and dissolved in 1952. In April 1949, the exchange rate was set at 360 yen/ dollar. The side effect was a severe economic contraction in 1949. But then another "divine providence," the Korean War (1950–1953), helped Japan recover.[49]

Under an amendment of the Bank of Japan Act spearheaded by the GHQ in June 1949, the BOJ introduced a policy board modeled after the Federal Reserve System. The GHQ wished to enhance the independence of the BOJ's policymaking.[50] The new Act invested the policy board with the authority to decide the BOJ's discount and lending rates without approval from the Finance Minister (Articles 13 and 21). The Finance Minister, meanwhile, retained the authority to supervise the BOJ (Article 42) and to order the BOJ to take actions recognized by the Minister to be necessary, including changes of bylaws (Article 43). The provision effectively limited the legal independence of the BOJ. After the amendment, the BOJ was required to negotiate with the MOF before making any adjustment to the official discount. The board was often called "the sleeping board." These developments illustrate the relative lack of change in the policymaking process until the Act was amended in 1998.[51]

Japan concluded the San Francisco Peace Treaty in 1951 and joined the Bretton Woods System (International Monetary Fund: IMF) when the treaty came into effect the next year.

---

[49] The Bank of Japan (1985), pp. 114–115, 199–245; Nakamura (1994), pp. 155–170.
[50] The Bank of Japan (1985), pp. 267–321. [51] The Bank of Japan (1985), pp. 314–318.

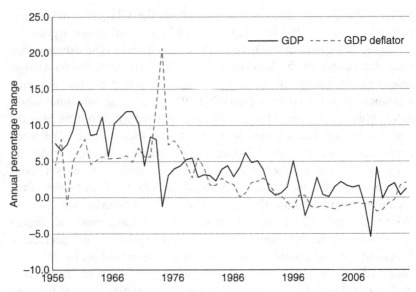

Figure 10.5 Output and prices
Source: Cabinet Office.

10.4 Japanese Miracle: Economic Growth and the Bank

10.4.1 Financing High Growth (1960s)

The Japanese economy grew at an unprecedented annual rate of 10 percent during the 1960s (Figure 10.5). In 1960, Prime Minister Hayato Ikeda, a former subordinate of Shigeru Yoshida, announced the National Income-Doubling Plan, a strategy to double Japan's real gross national product (GNP) within ten years. The plan was outpaced by reality.[52] The keys for high growth were improvements in productivity through investments to expand capacities and introduce new technologies, and growth in the demand for consumer durables supported by sustained growth of income and the emergence of the mass consumption society.[53]

The National Income-Doubling Plan assigned three roles to the public sector: to incubate the facility for growth, remove impediments to growth, and conduct appropriate fiscal and monetary policy, in order to stabilize the value of the currency, provide finance for growth, and minimize the size of the business cycles. In practice, the BOJ kept interest rates as low as

[52] Nakamura (1994), pp. 211–212.　　[53] Lincoln (1998), pp. 255–260.

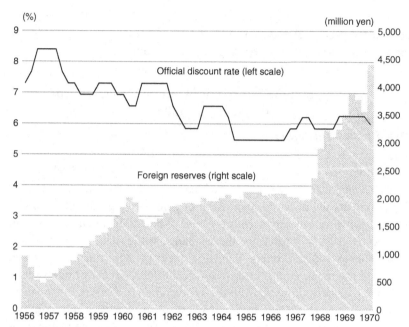

Figure 10.6 Foreign reserves and official discount rate of the BOJ
Source: Bank of Japan, *Economic Statistics Annual*, annual editions.

possible, and tightened monetary policy when the external balance deteriorated and foreign reserves fell to a certain level. As international capital movements were strictly regulated, the current account was the primary determinant of the overall balance of payments. When the boom continued and domestic demand reached a certain level, the balance of payments turned to the red, signaling that the time for monetary tightening had come (Figure 10.6).

The Japanese financial sector was heavily regulated in this period. Interest rates were virtually determined by the ordinance in accordance with changes in the official discount rate of the BOJ. The BOJ used the reserve deposit requirement ratio and "window guidance" to supplement the interest rate policy. Because interest rates were below the equilibrium, an excess demand for funds always existed. The big banks depended on borrowing from the BOJ, and the window guidance was a form of moral suasion by the BOJ to guide the credit of private banks.[54]

---

[54] Itoh et al. (2015), pp. 188–189, 193–196.

Japan became an Article 8 member of the IMF in 1964. By doing so, it committed itself to abandoning all restriction of trade accounts while still enjoying the privilege of restricting capital accounts.[55]

10.4.2 From the Developing World to the Developed World (1970s–1980s)

10.4.2.1 Two Oil Shocks

The Japanese economy had caught up with the western economies in productivity and per capita income by the early 1970s, but it also faced new challenges. In August 1971, the Nixon Administration of the United States unilaterally declared suspension of gold convertibility of the dollar to deal with its current account deficit. The Smithsonian Agreement of December 1971 pushed up the exchange value of the yen from 360 yen/dollar to 308 yen/dollar. The Agreement collapsed in the spring of 1973 and the major countries moved into a flexible exchange rate system.

Fearing negative impacts from the appreciation of the yen, the Japanese government and the BOJ responded by instituting easy fiscal and monetary policies. Meanwhile, a self-confident Kakuei Tanaka became prime minister in 1972, bringing with him a "Plan to build a New Japan." Tanaka assumed that high growth would continue over the long run and wanted to redistribute the fruits of high growth out from the Tokyo-Osaka area to rural parts of the country. Under his leadership, the Economic Planning Agency (EPA) drew up a new five-year plan forecasting 9 percent real GNP growth for 1973–1977.[56]

When the first oil shock broke out in the fall of 1973, the easy macro-economic environment sparked inflationary expectations and speculations by businesses and consumers. Labor unions demanded wage increases of more than 20 percent in 1973 and more than 30 percent only a year later, in 1974. The inflation of consumer prices rose to 12 percent in 1973 and 25 percent in 1974. The BOJ raised the official discount rate from 4.25 percent in the end of 1972 to 9 percent a year later. The Japanese economy recorded negative growth for the first time since WWII in 1974 and average annual growth of 4 percent from 1973 to 1977 (Figure 10.5).[57]

Japanese policymakers, businesses, consumers, and labor unions learned lessons from the first oil shock. At the outbreak of the second oil

---

[55] Nakamura (1994), p. 214.
[56] The Bank of Japan (1985), pp. 399–404; Lincoln (1998), pp. 260–263.
[57] The Bank of Japan (1985), pp. 420–441.

shock in 1979, they responded much more prudently and promptly than they had in the first oil shock. The BOJ quickly tightened monetary policy, businesses and consumers refrained from speculative investments, and labor unions negotiated with a more cooperative stance than before. The Japanese economy experienced lower inflation than it had during the first oil shock and suffered no major economic contraction.[58]

In the late 1970s and early 1980s, the Japanese economy grew steadily at 3–5 percent annually. Consumers favored Japanese products, both in Japan and other parts of the world. "Made in Japan" meant high-quality goods, a dramatic reversal from before. Japan continued to record a current account surplus. By as early as the 1970s, Japan was recognized as one of the great powers and its economy had grown to become the second largest in the world.

10.4.2.2 Financial Liberalization and Attempts toward International Policy Coordination (1980s)

The Japanese economy experienced a massive internationalization throughout the 1980s and 1990s. The main driving force was the country's relationship with the United States. Huge trade imbalances spurred the Reagan Administration to demand that Japan open its markets to American businesses. Whether ill-motivated or not, the Report of the Yen-Dollar Committee in 1984 bolstered a transformation of the Japanese financial system, deregulation and liberalization of financial activities, and profound changes in the operation of monetary policy. During the negotiations for the conclusion of the report, Japanese policymakers eliminated remaining regulations on international capital movement and committed to a bold and steady liberalization of interest rates on deposits, as well as bank lending. The BOJ accepted these decisions and assertively switched from monetary policy operations based on regulations and window guidance to those based on market operations. The move started in 1988 and was completed by the time the BOJ implemented a full set of reforms under the new Bank of Japan Act of 1998.[59]

During the second term of the Reagan Administration (1985–1989), the major western economies and Japan made major attempts to form internationally coordinated macroeconomic policies, including exchange rate, monetary, and fiscal policies. The Plaza Accord of September 1985 aimed to bring down the dollar through concerted interventions in foreign exchange markets in order to shift demand from Japanese to American

---

[58] Itoh et al. (2015), pp. 102–106. [59] Itoh et al. (2015), pp. 191–192.

products. The Louvre Accord of February 1987 aimed to adjust the domestic demand of major countries by coordinating monetary policies, fiscal policies, and policies for communication on exchange rates. The attempts were led by the US Secretary of the Treasury, James Baker, and the Japanese Finance Minister, Kiichi Miyazawa, and the central banks of their respective countries were deeply involved in the process. By the end of the decade, the central banks reached a broad consensus on the technical and political obstacles to effective coordination, agreeing on the benefits to be gained by "putting one's garden in order."[60]

At the high tide of these transformations, the asset price bubble emerged, expanded, and later busted. The emergence and expansion of the bubble took place when price stability seemed to be maintained. While the background of the bubble had multiple aspects, intensified bullish expectations for asset prices and the prospects of the economy played an important role. The BOJ learned a lesson: from a long-run perspective, a central bank had to conduct monetary policy focused on the stability of the financial system as well as the stability of prices.[61]

10.4.3 New Challenges (1990s–Present)

A fully revised Bank of Japan Act effectuated in 1998 stipulates the policy formation autonomy of the BOJ and requires transparency of the Bank. The purposes of the BOJ are to issue banknotes, carry out currency and monetary control, and ensure smooth settlement of funds among banks and other institutions, thereby contributing to the stability of the financial system (Article 1). The currency and monetary controls of the BOJ shall aim to achieve price stability, and thereby contribute to the sound development of the national economy (Article 2). The BOJ's autonomy regarding currency and monetary control shall be respected, while the BOJ shall endeavor to clarify to the citizens the content of its decisions and decision-making process regarding currency and monetary control (Article 3).

After the bursting of the asset price bubble, the bad loan problem shadowed the Japanese financial system and conduct of monetary policy. The prudential policy was the main responsibility of the Financial Services Agency, with some involvement of the BOJ. Meanwhile, financial

---

[60] Volcker and Gyoten (1992), pp. 228–286; Itoh et al. (2015), pp. 124–159.
[61] Okina, Shirakawa, and Shiratsuka (2001), pp. 444–445.

instability due to the bursting of the bubble and mounting non-performing assets imposed severe constraints on monetary policy.[62] The financial instability of the 1990s peaked when a number of major financial institutions failed from 1997 to 1998 (Heisei Financial Crisis). Several large securities houses and other financial institutions, including one of Japan's city banks with a nationwide branch network, collapsed in the span of a few weeks in November 1997. Meanwhile, the Asian Financial Crisis erupted in Thailand in July 1997 and spread to Korea and other countries within months, exacerbating the domestic crisis. Rumors and speculations that certain other banks were on the brink of collapse spread, compelling depositors to form long queues at those banks to withdraw their money. Then, the Long Term Credit Bank of Japan, an institution with total assets of 26 trillion yen (240 billion US dollars), ran into fundraising troubles in the summer of 1998 and was nationalized in October 1998. The BOJ played a role in containing the crisis as the LoLR on an unprecedented scale. Eventually, with help from a massive capital injection and other legislative interventions, the crisis subsided.[63]

Among central banks in the world since WWII, the BOJ was the first to hit the zero lower bound and introduce "unconventional" monetary policy measures. To deal with economic stagnation under the financial instability, the BOJ virtually hit the zero lower bound in 1995 and initiated the zero-interest rate policy (ZIRP) in 1999–2000.[64] It went on to implement the quantitative easing policy (QE) in 2001–2006 and the comprehensive monetary easing policy in 2010–2013. It then introduced the quantitative and qualitative monetary easing policy (QQE) in 2013 and the new frame-work for strengthening monetary easing by quantitative and qualitative monetary easing with yield curve control in 2016 (Figure 10.7).[65] Despite these innovations in monetary policy, growth of the money stock has remained stable and stagnant since the 1990s, suggesting that structural factors such as the decreasing and aging of the population and low investment demand of new IT industries with large network externalities may lie behind the stagnation (Figure 10.8).[66]

---

[62] Nakaso (2001).   [63] Nakaso (2001), pp. 8–16.

[64] Ueda (2005a), p. 22; Ueda (2005b), p. 3.

[65] HP of the Bank of Japan: www.boj.or.jp/en/mopo/mpmdeci/mpr_2016/index.htm/. Accessed on 26 December 2016.

[66] Shirakawa (2012). Okina and Shiratsuka (2004) argue that the downward shift in long-term economic growth in Japan was caused by multi-dimensional structural impediments to the smooth reallocation of economic resources. Baldwin and Teulings (2014) summarize discussions on secular stagnation in the global context.

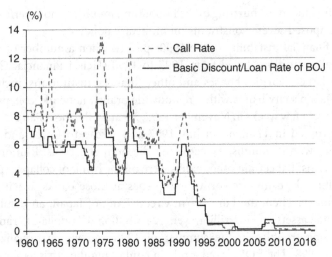

Figure 10.7 Interbank rate and lending rate of the BOJ
Source: The Bank of Japan.

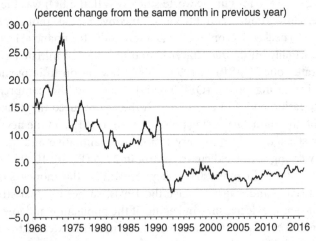

Figure 10.8 Money stock (M2)
Source: The Bank of Japan.

10.5 Conclusion

The BOJ's mandate and role within society has changed over time. When Japan joined the modern world in the late 19th century, the Bank was created as an entity to integrate the national financial market and provide liquidity for economic growth. When Japan pursued its goal as an empire in the first half of the 20th century, the Bank played a pivotal role in financing wars and in stabilizing the national financial markets. During and after Japan's losing war with its main trading partners in the 1930s and 1940s, the Bank was overwhelmed by ballooning government debt and rampant inflation. When Japan re-focused its national goal on high economic growth during the 1960s and early 1970s, the Bank was revived as an engine to fuel liquidity into the national economy. Once the Japanese economy reached an advanced stage of development from the 1970s onward, the Bank's main task changed from providing liquidity for economic growth to stabilizing the domestic economy. In pursuing this task, the Bank has often faced trade-offs between guns and butter, stability and growth, and the threat of economic backlash and the moral hazard problem. The Bank has been and still is learning from new challenges.

References

Asakura, Koukichi, Meiji Zenki Nihon Kin'yuu Kouzou Shi (History of Financial Structure in the Early Meiji Japan), Iwanami Shoten, Tokyo, 1961 (in Japanese).

Baldwin, Richard and Coen Teulings, "Introduction," Teulings, Coen and Richard Baldwin, eds., Secular Stagnation: Facts, Causes and Cures, CEPR Press, 2014, pp. 1–23. Available at: http://voxeu.org/content/secular-stagnation-facts-causes-and-cures.

Buyst, Erik and Ivo Maes, "Central Banking in Nineteenth-Century Belgium: Was the NBB a Lender of Last Resort?" Financial History Review, Vol.15, No.2, October 2008, pp.153–173.

Fukuda, Shin-ichi, "The Founding of the Bank of Japan and the Changed Behavior of Interest Rates and Inflation Rates," Journal of the Japanese and International Economies, Vol. 9, 1995, pp. 56–74.

Hayami, Akira, "Introduction: The Emergence of 'Economic Society,'" Toby, Ronald P. and Akira Hayami, eds., Emergence of Economic Society in Japan, 1600–1859, Oxford University Press, 1999, pp. 1–35.

Ide, Eisaku, "Policy Debates on Public Finance Between the Ministry of Finance and the Bank of Japan from 1930 to 1936," Monetary and Economic Studies, Vol. 33, November 2003, pp. 87–103.

Itoh, Masanao, Ryoji Koike, and Masato Shizume, "Bank of Japan's Monetary Policy in the 1980s: A View Perceived from Archived and Other Materials," Monetary and Economic Studies, Vol. 21, No.4, December 2015, pp. 97–199.

Iwahashi, Masaru, "Kinsei no kahei Shin'you" (Money and Credit in the Pre-Modern Japan), Sakurai, Eiji and Satoru Nakanishi, eds., RyuuTsuu Keizai Shi (History of the Commercial Economy), Yamakawa Shuppan Sha, Tokyo, 2002, pp. 431–469 (in Japanese).

Kobayashi, Noburu, Meiji Ishin-ki no Kahei Keizai (The Monetary Economy under the Meiji Restoration), University of Tokyo Press, Tokyo, 2015 (in Japanese).

Lincoln, Edward J., Japan: Facing Economic Maturity, Brookings Institution, Washington, DC, 1988, pp.14–68, reprinted as Chapter 9, Drysdale, Peter and Luke Gower, eds., The Japanese Economy, Part 1, Vol. II, 1998, pp. 255–301.

Makihara, Norio, Nihon Kin-Gendai Shi 2: Minken to Kenpo (The Japanese Modern and Contemporary History 2: Civil Rights and the Constitution), Iwanami Shoten, Tokyo, 2006 (in Japanese).

Matsukata, Masayoshi, "Nippon Ginko Soritsu Shishu no Setsumei" (An Explanation of the Reasons for the Establishment of the Bank of Japan), 1882, reprinted in Research Department of the Bank of Japan, ed., Nihon Kin'yu Shi Shiryo (Materials of Japanese Financial History), Vol. 4, 1958, pp. 991–1007 (in Japanese).

Metzler, Mark, Lever of Empire: The International Gold Standard and the Crisis of Liberalism in Prewar Japan, University of California Press, Berkeley and Los Angeles, California, 2006.

Ministry of Finance, Ginko Kyoku Dainiji Houkoku (The Second Report of Banking Bureau), Ministry of Finance, Tokyo, 1881 (in Japanese).

Ministry of Finance, Meiji Zaisei Shi, 13: Ginkou (Financial History of the Meiji-Era, Vol. 13: Banks), Maruzen, Tokyo, 1905 (in Japanese).

Mitchener, Kris James and Mari Ohnuki, "Capital Market Integration in Japan," Monetary and Economic Studies, Vol. 25, No. 2, November 2007, pp. 129–153.

Mitchener, Kris James, Masato Shizume, and Marc D. Weidenmier, "Why did Countries Adopt the Gold Standard? Lessons from Japan," Journal of Economic History, Vol. 70, No. 1, March 2010, pp. 27–56.

Miyamoto, Matao, Kinsei Nihon no Shijou Keizai (The Market Economy in the Pre-Modern Japan), Yuuhikaku, Tokyo, 1988 (in Japanese).

Nakamura, Takafusa, Lectures on Modern Japanese Economic History, 1926–1994, LTCB International Library Foundation, Tokyo, 1994, pp. 85–170.

Nakamura, Takafusa, "The Age of Turbulence: 1937–54," Nakamura, Takafusa and Konosuke Odaka, eds., Economic History of Japan, 1914–1955: A Dual Structure, Oxford University Press, 1999, pp. 55–110.

Nakaso, Hiroshi, "The Financial Crisis in Japan during the 1990s: How the Bank of Japan Responded and the Lessons Learnt," BIS Paper No. 6, October 2001, Bank for International Settlements, Basel.

Ohkawa, Kazushi and Miyohei Shinohara with Larry Meissner, Patterns of Japanese Economic Development: A Quantitative Appraisal, Yale University Press, New Haven, 1979.

Ohnuki, Mari, "The Bank of Japan Network and Financial Market Integration: From the Establishment of the Bank of Japan to the Early 20th Century," Monetary and Economic Studies, Vol. 25, No. 1, March 2007, pp. 95–127.

Okina, Kunio, Masaaki Shirakawa and Shigenori Shiratsuka, "The Asset Bubble and Monetary Policy: Japan's Experience in the Late 1980s and the Lessons," Monetary and Economic Studies, Special Edition, February 2001, pp.395–450.

Okina, Kunio and Shigenori Shiratsuka, "Asset Price Fluctuations, Structural Adjustments, and Sustained Economic Growth: Lessons from Japan's Experience since the Late 1980s," Monetary and Economic Studies, Special Edition, December 2004, pp. 143–167.

Pittaluga, Giovanni B. and Elena Seghezza, "How Japan Remained on the Gold Standard Despite Unsustainable External Debt," *Explorations in Economic History*, Vol. 59, January 2016, pp. 40–54.

Sakaehara, Towao, "Kehei no Hassei" (The Emergence of Money in Japan), Sakurai, Eiji and Satoru Nakanishi, eds., *RyuuTsuu Keizai Shi* (History of the Commercial Economy), Yamakawa Shuppan Sha, Tokyo, 2002, pp. 5–41 (in Japanese).

Sakudou, Youtarou, *Kinsei Houken Shakai no Kahei Kin'yuu Kouzou* (The Monetary and Financial Structure of the Pre-Modern Japanese Feudal Society), Hanawa Shobou, Tokyo, 1971 (in Japanese).

Sakurai Eiji, "Chuusei no Kahei Shin'you" (Money and Credit in the Medieval Japan), Sakurai, Eiji and Satoru Nakanishi, eds., *RyuuTsuu Keizai Shi* (History of the Commercial Economy), Yamakawa Shuppan Sha, Tokyo, 2002, pp. 42–77 (in Japanese).

Schaede, Ulrike, "Forwards and Futures in Tokugawa-Period Japan: A New Perspective on the Dojima Rice Market," *Journal of Banking and Finance*, Vol. 13, 1989, pp. 487–513.

Shibamoto, Masahiko and Masato Shizume, "Exchange Rate Adjustment, Monetary Policy and Fiscal Stimulus in Japan's Escape from the Great Depression," *Explorations in Economic History*, Vol. 53, July 2014, pp. 1–18.

Shirakawa, Masaaki, "Demographic Changes and Macroeconomic Performance: Japanese Experiences," Opening Remark at 2012 BOJ-IMES Conference, May 30, 2012, the Bank of Japan.

Shizume, Masato, "Sustainability of Public Debt: Evidence from Japan Before the Second World War," *Economic History Review*, Vol. 64, No. 4, November 2011, pp. 1113–1143.

Shizume, Masato, "The Japanese Economy during the Interwar Period: Instability in the Financial System and the Impact of the World Depression," Ögren, Anders and Lars Fredrik Øksendal, eds., *The Gold Standard Peripheries: Monetary Policy, Adjustment and Flexibility in a Global Setting*, Palgrave Macmillan, Basingstoke, 2012, pp. 211–228.

Shizume, Masato, "Banking Networks and Financial Market Integration: A Case of Japan during the Late 19th Century," mimeo, 2017.

Shizume, Masato, "Financial Crises and the Central Bank: Lessons from Japan during the 1920s," Rockoff, Hugh and Isao Suto, eds., *Coping with Financial Crises: Some Lessons from Economic History*, Springer, Verlag, 2018, pp. 131–148.

Shizume, Masato and Masayoshi Tsurumi, "Modernizing the Financial System in Japan during the 19th Century: National Banks in Japan in the Context of Free Banking," WINPEC Working Paper, No. E1607, Waseda University, September 2016.

Shunpo-ko Tsuisho-kai, *Ito Hirobumi Den* (Biography of Ito Hirobumi), 1940 (in Japanese).

Smethurst, Richard J., *From Foot Soldier to Finance Minister: Takahashi Korekiyo, Japan's Keynes*, Harvard University Press, Cambridge, ma and London, 2007.

Takatsuki, Yasuo, Shigeyuki Makihara and Masahiko Shibamoto, Shibamoto "Nougyou Kin'yuu no Mujun to Kousai Shijou no Antei" (Discrepancies in Agricultural Finance and Stable Public Finance), Fukao, Kyoji, Naofumi Nakamura, and Masayuki Nakabayashi eds., *Nihon Keizai no Rekishi 2, Kinsei* (The History of Japanese Economy, Vol. 2, The Pre-Modern Period: From the End of 16th Century to the

First Half of the 19th Century), Iwanami Shoten, Tokyo, 2017, pp. 105–147 (in Japanese).

The Bank of Japan, *Zuroku Nihon no Kahei* (The Catalogue of Japanese Currencies), Vol. 7, Tokyo, 1973 (in Japanese).

The Bank of Japan, *Nippon Ginko Hyakunen-Shi* (Bank of Japan: The First Hundred Years), Vol. 1, Tokyo, 1982 (in Japanese).

The Bank of Japan, *Nippon Ginko Hyakunen-Shi* (Bank of Japan: The First Hundred Years), Vol. 4, Tokyo, 1984 (in Japanese).

The Bank of Japan, *Nippon Ginko Hyakunen-Shi* (Bank of Japan: The First Hundred Years), Vol. 5, Tokyo, 1985 (in Japanese).

The Bank of Japan, *Nippon Ginko Hyakunen-Shi* (Bank of Japan: The First Hundred Years), Related Materials and Statistics, Tokyo, 1986 (in Japanese).

Toby, Ronald P., *State and Diplomacy in Early Modern Japan*, Stanford University Press, Stanford, CA, 1991.

Ueda, Kazuo, *Zero Kinri tono Tatakai* (A Struggle with the Zero Lower Bound), Nihon Keizai Shinbunsha, 2005a (in Japanese).

Ueda, Kazuo, "The Bank of Japan's Struggle with the Zero Lower Bound on Nominal Interest Rates: Exercises in Expectations Management," CIRJE Discussion Paper, CIRJE-F-375, September 2005b.

Volcker, Paul and Toyoo Gyoten, *Changing Fortunes: The World's Money and the Threat to American Leadership*, Crown, New York, 1992.

Yamazawa, Ippei and Yuzo Yamamoto, *Estimates of Long-Term Economic Statistics of Japan since 1868, 14, Foreign Trade and Balance of Payments*, Toyo Keizai Shinposha, Tokyo, 1979.

11

The Two Eras of Central Banking in the United States

Barry Eichengreen

11.1 Introduction

Scholars have pointed to many landmark years in the history of central banking in the United States: 1791, 1816, 1832, 1913, 1971 and 2008 are all candidates for landmark status. But I will argue that it is 1935 that most definitively separates the two distinct eras of central banking in the United States.

Before 1935, popular opposition to a powerful financial institution prompted a decentralized approach to monetary management. That opposition led to the refusal of the U.S. Congress to renew the charter of the First Bank of the United States in 1811 and to Andrew Jackson's veto of the bill to renew the charter of the Second Bank in 1832. The result was the absence of a U.S. central bank for the remainder of the 19th century and the first part of the 20th.

When the drawbacks of this approach were laid bare by crises in 1893 and 1907, the Federal Reserve System was created, but again on a decentralized basis. This approach reflected distinctive American attributes, from deep-seated distrust of "monied interests" to suspicion, bordering on hostility, between the country's South and West on the one hand and its Northeast on the other, to a strict constructionist interpretation of the Constitution that privileged the rights of the states over the federal government – attributes and attitudes that similarly shaped the debates over the First and Second Banks of the United States.

The shortcomings of this decentralized approach were then exposed by the Great Depression. In response, the Banking Act of 1935, as amended in 1942, centralized decision-making at the Board of Governors and the Federal Open Market Committee. The Federal Reserve System was still a federation of reserve banks, but it was now a federation subject to centralized decision-making in the manner of a modern central bank. This change mirrored and indeed was integral to the expanding role of the federal government initiated in response to the Depression and World War II.

11.2 Early Central Banking Experience

The birth of central banking in the United States traces back to the birth of the nation. The 13 colonies had to fight for their independence, creating a national-defense argument for a central bank to act as fiscal agent and regulate the currency. Through 1780, the Continental Congress authorized the issuance of paper currency to finance the War of Independence, resulting in inflation. In 1781 the Congress therefore chartered the Bank of North America as a private corporation, making it the first fractional-reserve limited-liability commercial bank in the new republic (and the third in the world after the Sveriges Riksbank and Bank of England). The charter required that individual investors provide $400,000 of capital. When it proved possible to raise only $70,000 in the straitened circumstances of the new republic, Superintendent of Finance Robert Morris, author of the bill chartering the Bank and proponent of a centralized institution, used the proceeds of a French government loan to subscribe the remaining shares.

The Bank of North America was modeled on the Bank of England. It was designed to do business throughout the country. Revenues accruing to the U.S. Congress would be deposited with the Bank. Its notes were redeemable in specie at par. Note issuance would be used to fund loans to the government as well as loans to private parties, including military contractors, not a few of whom had connections with the Bank's directors or were directors themselves.

The Bank of North America stabilized the finances of the new confederation and helped establish its credit with France, the Netherlands, Spain and other European countries. But since the Congress, as distinct from the states, was able to raise little revenue, it was unable to maintain the expected deposits with the Bank. There was also opposition to a bank with a privileged relationship to the government and which implicitly favored its home state, Pennsylvania. Seeing the writing on the wall, Morris converted the Bank into a Pennsylvania State-chartered corporation in 1783, repaid the government's capital, and sold a corresponding number of shares to private investors (mainly foreigners), essentially transforming the Bank of North America into a plain-vanilla commercial bank.

Morris was not alone in advocating a strong, centralized institution. Alexander Hamilton similarly advocated a Congressional charter for the Bank of North America. In 1790, as part of his campaign to rehabilitate the finances of the nation, Hamilton, now secretary of the Treasury, proposed creating a federally-chartered bank. Hamilton's bank would issue paper money, provide a repository for public funds, and act as the government's fiscal agent while also offering banking facilities for commercial transactions. Like the Bank of North America, Hamilton's vision of what came to be known as the Bank of the United States was modeled on the Bank of England, which similarly provided private as well as public banking functions.

Establishing Hamilton's bank required overcoming the opposition of Democrat-Republicans like Thomas Jefferson and James Madison, who believed in states' rights and opposed all but the most essential federal functions. Madison argued that all powers not specified in the constitution adhered to the states and, specifically, that the constitution did not authorize the federal government to charter a bank. He was an advocate of Jeffersonian democracy, that is to say, the political voice of the small farmer and landowner, and skeptical of merchants and "monied interests" who he saw as conspiring against the landowner. Jefferson, Madison, and their followers feared that a big bank would divert savings from rural areas toward urban manufacturing and mercantile interests – and, given their geographical distribution, from South to North. They feared that the creation of a central bank would undermine states' rights, leading eventually to abolition of the slave system.

Surmounting this opposition required supporters of the First Bank to agree that the Bank's charter would be limited to 20 years, setting the stage for a crisis when that charter came up for renewal in 1811. The new bank would be a private company in order to fall under the constitutional provision authorizing the federal government to incorporate businesses. The public stake would be limited to 20 percent. Notes issued by the Bank would be redeemable in specie at par, and a quarter of nongovernmental subscriptions would be paid in gold or silver. Supporters committed not to charter another federal bank and to permit states to charter as many banks as they pleased.

The First Bank was controversial throughout its two-decade-long history. Regional tensions and disagreements over states' rights remained unresolved, the only difference being that Democrats opposing the Bank were better represented in the House of Representatives in 1811 than 20 years before. The fraction of shares in the hands of foreign, mainly British, investors rose over time, heightening suspicion of the Bank. The fact that officials provided little information about the institution's financial affairs contributed to the climate of distrust. Transparency as a mechanism of accountability for an independent central bank was not yet integral, evidently, to American financial culture.

Meanwhile, there was considerable growth in the number of state-chartered banks, from 30 in 1801 to more than a hundred in 1811. Their charters dictated that these banks could do business only in individual states, creating an advantage for the Bank of the United States, which could open branches nationwide. Competition from this federally-chartered institution limited state banks' market power, forcing them to charge lower interest rates to retain market share.

State banks were also required to redeem their notes for specie on demand at par. Making that demand effective was often easier said than done, however, for noteholders at distance from the issuing institution. But the Bank of the United States, with its far-flung branch network, was in a strong position to effect this demand. Banks tempted to emit excessive numbers of notes were thus at greater risk of losing specie reserves as a result of the broad branch network and redemption capacity of the Bank of the United States.

Here we see the Bank of the United States assuming a central banking role. Its capacity to redeem was a way for the Bank to actively manage money and credit conditions, by extending the notes of other banks' varying degrees of "forbearance" (that is, by deciding whether or not to force their redemption – see Timberlake 1978, p. 10). It helped make the currency of the country "fairly sound and uniform" and "suppress[ed] the depreciated currencies of the South and West" which otherwise tended to trade at a discount relative to par (Catterall 1903, p. 114). But from a state bank perspective, it was an unwelcome intrusion and source of external pressure and competition.

Renewal of the Bank's charter was defeated by a single vote in both the House and Senate in 1810. The Bank immediately reduced its loans, creating "great business distress" in its home region (Holdsworth and Dewey 1910, p. 79). Distress deepened with the War of 1812, which the federal government financed by issuing Treasury notes and borrowing from state banks. These events culminated in 1814 in the suspension of specie payments followed by another bout of inflation. Six separate proposals to establish a Second Bank of the United States were then debated by the Congress until a bill was passed allowing the bank to open its doors on January 7, 1817.

The Second Bank resembled that of the First, with 20 percent of its capital subscribed by the government and the other 80 percent by private investors, and with a quarter of that 80 percent again to be paid in the form of specie. Just five of 25 directors were appointed by the government, reflecting this 80/20 percent split. The Bank was again required to redeem its notes in specie and maintain a stable ratio of specie to deposits.

Early management of the Second Bank was erratic. The specie/deposit ratio varied widely. The Bank's liberal provision of credit was blamed for fueling land speculation, creating asset-price inflation and then financial panic in 1819 – a panic that then worsened when the Bank proactively tightened credit and the Treasury, exercising central banking functions of its own, retired many of its recently-issued notes.

Management improved when Nicholas Biddle was appointed president of the Bank in 1823. Biddle further elaborated the institution's central banking functions, developing additional mechanisms for returning depreciated notes to country banks, thereby enhancing the uniformity of the currency. He elaborated the Bank's role as fiscal agent, providing a repository for federal revenues and transferring funds between regions. He undertook open market operations, selling government securities from the Bank's portfolio. He expanded the Bank's presence on the foreign exchange market.

This progress makes ongoing political opposition to the Bank somewhat difficult to understand. Historians like to tell this story in terms of personalities. Andrew Jackson, the populist president elected in 1828, was hostile to banks in general; as a young man Jackson had accepted worthless notes for some of his land and incurred exorbitant interest charges on some business transactions in New Orleans. Jackson and Biddle were oil and water; one was a rough-hewn country boy, the other a Princeton-educated financier. But the underlying structural disagreements were again the same: they pitted Democrats against Federalists, Southerners against Northerners, and farmers against monied interests. Distrust of the Bank's concentrated financial power manifested itself in accusations that loans were being extended to the Bank's political allies and to supportive newspaper publishers. Further complicating matters was the fact that the Bank of the United States was Philadelphia based, to the consternation of New York, the rising financial center.

Renewal became an issue in the 1832 campaign pitting the incumbent Jackson against Henry Clay. In the heat of the campaign, Congress passed a bill rechartering the Bank which Jackson vetoed on the grounds that the Bank was "subversive to the rights of the States, and dangerous to the liberties of the people ... " Jackson objected to the Bank on the grounds that foreigners were prominent among its shareholders and that domestic shareholders disproportionately resided in the Northeast.

Jackson took his victory in the1832 election as a mandate to dismantle the Bank, which he sought to do by transferring the government's deposits to private banks. When Jackson withdrew the deposits, Biddle retaliated by curtailing the Bank's loans in an echo of what had happened in 1811. Anticipating the withdrawal of federal deposits, it was prudent for him to engineer some contraction of loans so as to maintain a reasonably stable loan–deposit ratio. But in addition Biddle and his directors were angered by the veto and by the president's subsequent action; a sharp contraction of loans was a way of demonstrating the power and indispensability of their institution. The credit crunch was disruptive (Catterall 1903, p. 327). It did not help that it was superimposed on rapid inflation fueled by specie imports (silver from Mexico, gold from Europe) – see Temin (1969).

Ultimately, the Bank of the United States was converted to a Pennsylvania State-chartered bank a few weeks before its charter expired in 1836. A banking panic ensued in 1837, followed by a sharp recession. This unfortunate chain of events can be interpreted in a variety of different ways (as noted by Bordo 2012). In practice, it discredited central banking for generations to come.

11.3 Free Banking

Expiry of the Second Bank's federal charter in 1836 left no bank under federal law, so state legislatures stepped into the breech (which was precisely what the opponents of the Second Bank had in mind). Michigan in 1837 and then 17 additional states adopted free banking laws to encourage the provision of financial services. This experience is interesting as an experiment in banking in the absence of a central bank. It is also interesting in comparison with Sweden, which had its own experiment with free banking between 1830 and 1903 but in the presence of a central bank.

Free banking laws were intended to streamline regulation and simplify entry. In the preceding period, a state-government charter had to be issued before a bank could be established as a limited-liability corporation. Under so-called free banking laws, bankers were allowed to establish limited-liability corporations without obtaining government-issued charters.

This was not free-entry banking; it was entry subject to specific conditions. Opening a bank required a minimum capital subscription, which could be substantial. Banks could issue notes but were required to convert them into specie at par. They were required to hold reserves against some portion of their note emission in specie and the balance of their reserves in specific debt securities, which were lodged for safekeeping with the state banking authorities. Those bonds could be valued at par or market value, whichever was less. When the value of bonds declined significantly below the value of the liabilities they backed, the bank failed (it was closed by regulation).

The nature of the backing and the availability of information were pivotal to these arrangements. In practice, regulation of both was uneven, which accounts for the uneven nature of the results (see Dwyer 1996). Some states, New York for instance, required banks to hold relatively safe government bonds, but other states allowed banks to hold risky railway bonds (especially when there was strong pressure to develop the railways, as in Minnesota), while still others (like Michigan) allowed banks to back their notes with claims on real estate (a practice conducive to allowing those claims to be valued at inflated prices) and personal notes (which were difficult to value). These practices go a long way in explaining differences in bank-failure and depositor-recovery rates across states. They explain why banks in some states were forced to suspend specie payments while others were not.

Information provision was both a means of monitoring banks' compliance with reserve regulation and a source of market discipline. Free banks were generally required to submit reports to state banking authorities on a quarterly or annual basis and to publish them in newspapers. Commercial publications that quoted the value of the notes traded by different banks in different markets were an additional source of information. They were a reason why a bank could be penalized for excessive note emission or dubious investment practices, insofar as there might be a reluctance to accept notes quoted at a deep discount and incentives to return them to the issuing bank for redemption at par. This information was far from perfect, however. Complaints about "Wildcat Banks" – banks with questionable motives that operated out "where the wildcats roamed" – may have been exaggerated, but they were entirely without foundation.

One explanation for the defects and excesses of the system is that there was no federal institution like the First and Second Banks of the United States to exert de facto regulatory authority, which the Bank had done by using its branch system to return discounted notes to the issuing bank for redemption. The post-1836 system relied on state regulation, the competence of which varied and which was subject to race-to-the-bottom problems. (That the Swedish system was not separately structured and regulated in different regions is thus one potential explanation for why its experience differed.) There was no federal agency to engage in open market operations and manage the provision of emergency liquidity as the Second Bank had done. (That Sweden already possessed the Riksbank is thus a second potential explanation for why that country's experience with free banking was more favorable, although whether the Riksbank was cognizant of and acted on its lender-of-last-resort responsibilities in this period is disputed – see Ogren 2003 and Lakomaa 2007). Jalil (2015) points to major panics in 1837 (as noted previously), 1839, and 1857. He cautions, however, that other episodes identified as panics by Kemmerer (1910) were in fact stock market corrections or crashes that did not implicate the banking system. On balance, the incidence of banking panics in this free banking period was not obviously greater than in other periods in U.S. history, including when the country possessed a central bank.

That said, 28 years from 1837 to 1865, when the federal government put an end to free banking by imposing a prohibitive tax on state bank notes, are too short a period on which to base definitive conclusions about the efficacy of free banking and the indispensability of a central bank.

11.4 National Banking

In 1914, the establishment of a new U.S. banking institution was followed by the outbreak of a major war. In 1863, in contrast, the outbreak of a major war occasioned the establishment of a new banking arrangement. The Union government sought to finance its spending by issuing bonds and placing them with the banks. So too did the Confederate government although the enduring banking institutions were those created by the victors.

The Union established a system of federally-chartered banks known as the National Banking System. It is striking that it took an existential crisis in order for the United States to overcome deep-seated opposition to a federally-organized system. With expulsion from the Congress of its Southern members (all Democrats), Whig-Republicans favoring a centralized system were able to advance their plans. But even then there was no willingness to create a central bank as liquidity provider and lender of last resort to members. State banks were allowed to coexist alongside national banks. And national banks were prohibited from branching across state lines in yet another bow to states' rights.

National banks were required to back their notes with federal government bonds, a requirement designed to limit the kind of shady practices evident in states like Michigan and Minnesota, where real estate and personal collateral had been accepted. Critically during wartime, it created a captive market for the bonds of the Union government. Creating this market required forcing or at least encouraging state banks to seek national bank status; many did so once the government placed a prohibitive tax on note issuance by state banks in 1865. In this tax we also see the origins of the 20th-century American practice of financing bank lending by attracting deposits as opposed to issuing notes.

But requiring national banks to back or secure their notes with government bonds had unintended consequences. The supply of notes was limited by the availability of government bonds, which were in short supply. The federal government ran surpluses in the 1880s; the supply of banknotes therefore fell by more than half between 1880 and 1890. Government bonds traded at high prices, giving banks little incentive to acquire them to back the emission of additional notes when the demand for currency was high. Redemption of notes in periods of slack demand was difficult, creating a further problem of inelastic supply on the way down (Selgin and White 1994).

The National Banking Act compounded the problem of financial fragility in two additional ways. First, it discouraged banks from branching even within states where this was permitted. The shortage of government bonds made it difficult for banks interested in opening branches to furnish the latter with till cash. The absence of branching in turn made inter- and even intra-state clearing and note redemption difficult.

Second, the Act encouraged dangerous pyramiding of reserves by authorizing small ("country") banks to hold their reserves with larger ("reserve city") banks and larger banks to hold their reserves with the very largest ("central reserve city") banks in Chicago, St. Louis and, above all, New York City. It is interesting to observe how, in contrast to the beginning of the 19th century, Philadelphia no longer played much of a role, reflecting the shift in financial power to New York, while Chicago and St. Louis now did, indicating the westward shift in the country's economic center of gravity – see Cronon 1991. It is also interesting to observe how the regional organization of the reserve city system contained the seeds of Federal Reserve structure established half a century later.

Central reserve city banks, New York banks in particular, put those reserves to work by lending them to stock brokers and dealers. This was well and good when funds were flowing to the cities but became a problem when the demand for currency in the countryside spiked, causing country banks to repatriate their reserves. That repatriation precipitated the stock market crashes that attracted the attention of Kemmerer (1910). In the worst case the failure of brokers and dealers might create serious balance-sheet problems for the banks. Given the inelasticity of currency supplies, interest rates still shot up during the harvest season, when as much as 50 percent more cash was needed to pay workers and settle transactions, and to a lesser extent during the spring planting season. Sharply higher interest rates created distress among borrowers; their defaults then created problems for the banks. And given the banks' lack of geographical and economic diversification, a cluster of such defaults might lead to a wave of bank panics.

This seasonal stringency was a first consideration motivating discussions of financial reform; it was eventually embodied in the language of the Federal Reserve Act, which created a new institution "to provide an elastic currency." Panics in 1873, 1893, and 1907 and discomfort with how they were managed were the second consideration leading to the creation of the Fed.

This said, there was no straight line from the problems of the National Banking System to establishment of the Federal Reserve. There remained hostility to the idea of a federal institution with powers to manage the money supply and act as lender of last resort. One alternative would have been to supplement banknotes backed by government bonds and convertible into gold with notes backed by and convertible into silver. An experiment along these lines was the Sherman Silver Purchase Act of 1890, which instructed the Treasury to purchase 4.5 million ounces of silver a month with legal tender Treasury notes. This approach was backed by farmers and workers and opposed by "hard money" interests. It was defeated in 1896, when William Jennings Bryan campaigned for the presidency unsuccessfully on a "free silver" platform.

Another alternative was an asset-backed currency, in other words authorization for the banks to issue notes backed by commercial paper generated in the course of business transactions. This approach was supported by adherents to the Real Bills Doctrine, which counseled that credit supply should be linked to the legitimate needs of business. It was opposed by populists like Bryan who opposed all forms of nongovernmental currency. It also met with broader resistance given the country's checkered experience with private backing in the free bank era.

A third alternative was to relax restrictions on intra- and inter-state branching, reducing financial fragility and facilitating transfers of credit from where it was abundant to where it was scarce. Proposals along these lines ran up against the deeply-ingrained suspicion that branch networks would be vehicles for siphoning off the savings of farmers into the modern, industrial economy. Unit bankers also opposed branching, while reserve city banks were not unhappy with the existent correspondent system.

In the absence of more fundamental reform, ad hoc arrangements were devised to lend elasticity to the supply of credit and deal with crises. The Treasury assumed certain central banking functions, shifting its reserves from subtreasuries to national banks when more bank lending was required (Timberlake 1978). This policy developed under Leslie M. Shaw, Treasury secretary from 1902 to 1907. Shaw keyed his policies to the level of short-term interest rates, consonant with the Real Bills Doctrine. His initiatives were denounced by critics on both the Left and the Right. Shaw's policy violated the spirit of the rules-based National Banking System. It favored big central reserve city banks, more often than not those located in New York, that were recipients of Treasury transfers. Its efficacy hinged on the judgment of one man, the Treasury secretary.

There were also private efforts to address the need for crisis management. These developed out of clearinghouses created to handle interbanks in New York City and elsewhere. Starting in 1857, clearinghouses issued certificates, in effect private money, during crises. Certificates were provided against illiquid but fundamentally good collateral of member banks. The clearinghouse had the power to audit the balance sheets of its members to verify that their collateral was good. Their loan certificates, issued in small denominations, were then paid out to depositors and functioned as currency. Since certificates were the liabilities of clearinghouse members collectively, they provided depositors with insurance against the failure of their own banks, ameliorating the panic problem. And collective liability gave the members strong incentives to monitor one another's actions.

Clearinghouse cooperation peaked in the crisis of 1907 when certificates were issued in a number of different cities. But this private money was issued without legislative authority. It was of limited liquidity; clearinghouse certificates were not accepted outside the city where the clearinghouse or bank association was centered. Nor could this approach resolve the problems of banks and trust companies that were not clearinghouse members. In the 1907 crisis, the panic centered on trust companies like Knickerbocker Trust and Trust Company of America that were not members of the New York Clearinghouse.

Resolving the crisis therefore required J.P. Morgan to organize a loan to Trust Company of America. Morgan's decision to rescue Trust Company of America but to allow Knickerbocker Trust to fail may have been based on incomplete and misleading information about the condition of the latter. Morgan partner George Perkins unnecessarily aggravated the crisis with some alarming comments about Trust Company of America. Withdrawals by panicked depositors continued for two weeks; even the intervention of the country's best-known investment banker did not have the confidence-restoring capacity of the New York Clearinghouse, much less that of a government-backed central bank. And this kind of ad hoc action lacked legitimacy insofar as it was not backed by legislative authority. Evidently, outsourcing crisis resolution to an influential private banker was not politically attractive or even economically efficient.

11.5　Founding the Fed

Such was the backdrop to the decision to create the Federal Reserve System in 1913. A book could be written about this debate (and recently has – see Lowenstein 2015). For our purposes, the key factors were the inelasticity of credit supplies, the fragility of the financial system, and the ad hoc nature of crisis resolution. Dissatisfaction with prevailing arrangements was matched only by opposition to the alternatives, whether silver coinage, an asset-backed currency, or a more widely-branched banking network. By default, a central bank was the only option left standing.

Creating one required surmounting, once again, deep-seated American suspicion of Wall Street and long-standing hostility to concentrated financial power. Concretely, surmounting these obstacles represented a considerable feat of policy entrepreneurship. Among the prominent policy entrepreneurs was Paul Warburg, the German-American financier who favored a central bank along European lines to enhance the liquidity of U.S. markets but, recognizing which way the political wind was blowing, offered more limited proposals for an umbrella organization of clearinghouses.

Then there was Nelson Aldrich, senior senator from Rhode Island, who authored the Aldrich-Vreeland Act empowering banks to create local currency associations and issue, with Treasury approval, additional National Bank Notes in emergencies. The Aldrich-Vreeland Act also established a National Monetary Commission to weigh more permanent reform measures – a commission chaired by none other than Nelson Aldrich. There were the members of the Jekyl Island duck-hunting party – Aldrich, Warburg, J.P. Morgan associate Henry Davison, National City Bank president Frank Vanderlip, Harvard economics professor Piatt Andrew, and Aldrich's personal secretary Arthur Shelton, who authored a plan for a collection of local clearinghouses, overseen by a Reserve Association headquartered in Washington, D.C. and along the line's of Warburg's earlier umbrella organization.

This hybrid design – a decentralized system of regional banks but a centralized Reserve Association – encapsulated the tensions inhering in the first two decades of the Federal Reserve. The duck hunters did not agree among themselves on the optimal degree of central control. Some preferred a decentralized design, where each regional branch controlled its own policy interest rate. Others like Aldrich, seeing the problem from the perspective of Washington, D.C., preferred to centralize interest-rate policy in the hands of the Reserve Association. While the president would choose the six Reserve Association governors, the majority of Association directors under the Aldrich Plan would be chosen by banks and industrialists. Thus, whether policy would be crafted with the national interest or the narrow interests of banks and industry in mind was unclear, as was whether it would be formulated mainly in response to regional or continental conditions.

The Aldrich Plan was derailed by the Pujo Hearings and the populist backlash against the concentrated financial power which intensified with the approach of the 1912 election. But pressure to do something was intense. Carter Glass, a representative from Virginia, crafted a plan for a system of 15 to 20 regional reserve banks whose capital would be subscribed by banks in their region and would issue their own notes, replacing those of national banks. Commercial banks could obtain notes by discounting loans at their regional reserve banks, in a step toward the asset-backed-currency model of the Real Bills Doctrine. Glass, a southerner, was a champion of state's rights, echoing another important strand in U.S. financial ideology. Reflecting this, Glass designed his Reserve System as symmetrical: banks in each region would hold reserves and discount loans with their regional reserve bank, giving no special status to New York, Washington, D.C., or any other financial or political center.

The last and most consequential policy entrepreneur was Woodrow Wilson, who campaigned for the presidency on the Democratic ticket in 1912. Wilson was not opposed to centralization; he was an admirer of Hamilton and a supporter of federal government. His bug-bear was monopoly power, whether of business or banks, which he saw government as countering. A new agency of the federal government – call it "the Federal Reserve" – might be a means to this end. Thus, Wilson was attracted to Glass's plan, which he saw as a means of limiting the market power of big New York banks – although he proposed the addition of a central board of presidential appointments, equivalent to Aldrich's Reserve Association, to exercise control over the reserve banks. Reserves would be held regionally, but the institutions holding them would be subject to some degree of centralized oversight.

After much legislative wrangling, Congress agreed in 1913 to create a Federal Reserve System along Wilsonian lines. It provided for eight to 12 regional reserve banks, each with a board of directors and district members, and each with symmetrical responsibilities. There being no deficiency of demand, 12 banks were quickly established. The Act foresaw reserve bank discounts of member bank loans, ensuring more elastic provision of currency and credit than before. It established a Board of Governors in Washington, D.C., with the Treasury secretary and Comptroller of the Currency as members, to apply a yet-to-be-determined degree of central control. By 1914, the new System was up and running.

11.6 Decades of Disaster

A key provision of the Federal Reserve Act, section 14, specified that "Every Federal reserve bank shall have the power ... to establish from time to time, subject to review and determination of the Federal Reserve Board, rates of discount to be charged by the Federal Reserve Bank for each class of paper, which shall be fixed with a view of accommodating commerce and business." Three aspects are notable. First, the imprint of the Real Bills Doctrine – "with a view of accommodating commerce and business" – is clear. Second, lending, not open market operations, was the main instrument through which policy would be implemented. Third, initiative for determining its discount rate rested with the individual reserve bank, but "subject to review and determination," whatever that meant, by the Federal Reserve Board. One interpretation was that the initiative to alter their discount rates lay with the reserve banks but that the Board possessed veto power. Another was that the Board, using its power of "determination," might order a change in rates.

The Board sought to assert its authority by issuing guidelines for discount policy. In response, reserve bank governors in January 1915 established the Governors' Conference as a venue in which to assert their independence. At its second meeting, governors argued that the Federal Reserve Board had no right to limit the types of acceptances that reserve banks purchased. At the end of the year, the Governors' Conference adopted a resolution criticizing the Board. The Board's response was to demand discontinuance of the Governors' Conference, insisting that reserve bank governors could meet only when called by the Board.

In 1919, Federal Reserve Bank of New York governor Benjamin Strong announced the intention of raising his bank's discount rate, claiming that the Federal Reserve Act gave it this power. This was too much for Carter Glass, who threatened to ask the president to remove Strong for violating section 14. Glass wrote to the acting attorney general, who responded that the Board "has the right, under the powers conferred by the Federal Reserve Act, to determine what rates of discount should be charged from time to time by a Federal Reserve bank . . . " (Meltzer 2003, p. 102). While Strong deferred to the Board, he continued to challenge the validity of the decision. Aware of these sensitivities, the Board exercised its disputed power to impose discount rate changes on the reserve banks with considerable restraint.

Different reserve banks, observing different local business conditions or having different priorities, preferred discount rates at different levels. This was not entirely unreasonable; as Beckhart (1924) wrote, the "beauty of the regional plan" was that it allowed the discount rate to vary across regions "in accordance with the economic development of different parts of the country." But on other occasions the Board might instruct the banks to change their rates; the reserve banks would then put up resistance and delay. In practice, policy interest rates differed across regions for extended periods, as Cohen-Setton (2015) shows. (There is an interesting parallel with Norway between 1850 and 1892, when the different regional branches of the country's central bank kept their policy rates at different levels for extended periods, as described by Klovland and Oksendal (2015).)

Responsibility for open market operations was similarly contested, more so insofar as their importance had not been anticipated by Glass and fellow legislators. The Federal Reserve Act made no provision for coordinating security sales and purchases by reserve banks. As the utility of the instrument was discovered, the banks asserted their right to conduct such transactions independently.

In March 1923, the Federal Reserve Board issued study of open market operations. Impetus had come from the Treasury Department, which complained that haphazard open market operations by reserve banks complicated debt management operations and recommended that responsibility for such transactions should be vested with the Board. Adopt Miller, the economist on the Federal Reserve Board, tabled a proposal to this effect, but the reserve banks resisted. William Harding, governor of the Boston Fed, asserted that the Federal Reserve Act limited the Board to exercising "broad supervisory power." At most, the Board could specify the type of securities in which the reserve banks could transact but not dictate the timing or price at which those transactions took place. Miller and others disagreed (Eichengreen 1992, p.18).

The Board's response was to establish an Open Market Investment Committee comprised of five reserve bank governors "under the general supervision of the Federal Reserve Board." The five would decide on a common policy to be imposed on all 12 banks by the Board. Establishment of the OMIC was a step toward closer coordination but left unspecified the fundamental division of responsibilities between the five banks or the Board. The OMIC recommended open market purchases and sales to the reserve banks, and its recommendations were then subject to approval by the Board. But an OMIC decision to conduct open market purchases then had to be submitted to the individual reserve banks, which might decline to participate. In other words, the 1923 decisions left the reserve banks the right to opt out. Some officials asserted further that the reserve banks were also entitled to opt in – to conduct open market operations of which the Board did not approve (Chandler 1957, p. 229).

In practice, these arrangements could inhibit the conduct of expansionary open market operations. If security purchases were undertaken by a subset of reserve banks, the banks in question would see their gold cover ratios (ratios of gold to eligible liabilities and assets) decline toward the statutory minimum, forcing them to curtail their operations. The Board might attempt to compel other reserve banks to participate or to loan excess gold to their partners in the System, but those other banks might resist. D'Arista's (1994. p. 86) conclusion about the beginning of the decade, that "refusal of the majority of banks to endorse an allotment system during this period undoubtedly curtailed the amount of investments purchased," applies more widely.

A series of episodes illustrates these points. There was the famous instance in the summer of 1927 when Benjamin Strong met with Montagu Norman of the Bank of England, Hjalmar Schacht of the German Reichsbank, and Charles Rist of the Bank of France. Since 1914, the New York Fed had been the System's agent for communicating with foreign central banks. Strong was sensitive to the pressure on his counterpart and friend, Norman, from the Bank of England's ongoing gold losses resulting in part from the conversion of sterling balances by the Reichsbank and the Bank of France. The meeting, starting on July 2nd, was an attempt to find an international solution to these problems. Though Norman's idea, it was called by Strong who did not seek prior approval or notify the Board of Governors.

The upshot was a commitment by the French and German central banks to exercise restraint and by Strong to cut the New York bank's discount rate to encourage capital and gold to flow toward England. Strong took his visitors to the New York Fed and the Board of Governors to ensure that his policy became System policy. Reluctantly, the Board agreed. Other reserve banks, most prominently the Federal Reserve Bank of Chicago, did not. Its directors did not see supporting the Bank of England as a key objective of Federal Reserve policy; they were more worried about inflation and stock market speculation. (Not incidentally, Chicago had been one of the epicenters of the residential and commercial real estate bubble of the 1920s.) The Chicago bank informed the Board that it had no intention of reducing its discount rate. On September 6th, the Board voted four to three to force the Chicago Fed to cut its rate, forcing its policy on a district reserve bank for the first time in the history of the System (Meltzer 2003, p. 223).

Similarly, impetus to tighten in response to speculation on Wall Street came not from the Board but from the Chicago Fed. The bank's directors voted to increase their discount rate in January 1928; the decision was reluctantly accepted by the Board. Only two Board members in fact favored the Chicago Fed's proposal. Others worried about seeing "business penalized for the excesses in the stock market," but yielded on grounds of reserve bank autonomy (Eichengreen 1992, p. 27).

By January 1929, concern over Wall Street had spread to other reserve banks, including the New York Fed. On January 3, 1929 directors of the New York Fed voted to raise their buying rate for acceptances, but some members of the Board of Governors (Roy Young, former governor of the Federal Reserve Bank of Minneapolis, for example) dissented on the grounds that this would injure industry and trade. Young asserted that the New York Fed's action required the prior approval of the Board, which George Harrison, Strong's successor, disputed.

Next, on February 14, the directors of the New York Fed voted to increase their discount rate. When Washington instructed New York to hold off until the Board considered the matter, the directors informed the Board that they would not leave their premises on Maiden Lane until they received a response. The Board then voted to veto New York's decision, citing the adverse impact on agriculture and commerce.

Several directors of the New York Bank then threatened to resign because their powers had been usurped. One can't help but surmise that the Board was reminded of the need to exercise restraint. Finally, in August of 1929, the New York Fed was allowed to raise its discount rate.

Hindsight suggests that interest-rate policy is a blunt instrument for addressing financial risks. Better would have been to tailor discount policy to the needs of business while using regulation, what modern economists refer to as macroprudential policy and contemporaries termed direct pressure, to address financial imbalances. Part of the problem was that the System's macroprudential instruments were underdeveloped: when the Board attempted to use direct pressure to discourage lending to stock brokers and dealers, nonmember banks stepped into the breech. But another part of the problem was that the Board of Governors was reluctant to impose its will on reserve banks.

In response to the Crash, George Harrison, now governor of the New York Fed, without informing the Board of Governors or even the majority of his own directors, purchased securities to provide emergency liquidity to distressed brokers and dealers. Theory and history both suggest that Harrison's reaction was commendable. But this was not how the Board of Governors saw things. Harrison was called on the carpet. He argued that the 1923 agreement between the Board and the reserve banks empowered the latter to purchase securities for their own account. The Board asserted that open market operations were at its initiative alone. The Board threatened to veto further changes in New York's discount rate. In theory, the New York Fed might have done even more; instead it curtailed its purchases. No doubt the criticism to which Harrison and his directors were subjected was part of what prompted their volte face.

As deflation and depression deepened, pressure intensified for the Federal Reserve System to do something. In the spring of 1932, Senator Elmer Thomas, Democrat of Oklahoma, advanced legislation that would have required the Fed to print $2.4 billion of emergency banknotes backed by bonds that the government sold to the reserve banks. Fed officials concluded that conventional open market operations were the lesser evil.

But the directors of the Chicago and Boston reserve banks, seeing inflation and stock market speculation as right around the corner, hesitated to agree. As a result, the gold cover ratio of the New York Fed fell to 50 percent already in June, uncomfortably close to the 40 percent minimum perhaps. The Chicago Fed could have participated in the purchase program, transferring its excess gold to New York. But its governor, James McDougal, and its directors had been critical of New York's internationally motivated decisions in 1927. McDougal now rebuffed requests from New York for a transfer of specie, and the Board hesitated to compel him. The decision to terminate the short-lived program of expansionary open market operations in August 1932 reflected a confluence of forces, including the fact that the Congress had now adjourned for the summer recess and autumn electoral campaign. But the fact that the burden of purchases was so unevenly spread across reserve banks was undoubtedly a factor.

The final nail in the coffin was the 1933 banking crisis. Foreigners, dubious of the priorities of the incoming President, Franklin Delano Roosevelt, rushed to cash in their dollars. On March 3rd, the New York Fed asked the Chicago Fed to purchase or rediscount $400 million of its securities to raise New York's gold cover ratio. Again Chicago refused, preferring to preserve its balance sheet. Herbert Lehman, who had just succeeded FDR as governor of the State of New York, was forced to declare a statewide bank holiday on March 4th. The new president then declared a national bank holiday on March 5th, his first full day in office.

This was a profoundly unsatisfactory experience. In response, Congress adopted the 1933 Banking Act. The Open Market Policy Committee (the post-1929 successor to the Open Market Investment Committee) was renamed the Federal Open Market Committee. It was explicitly stated that "no Federal Reserve bank shall engage in open-market operations under section 14 of this Act except in accordance with regulations adopted by the Federal Reserve Board." Reserve banks purchasing or selling government securities were unambiguously required to obtain the consent of the Board. But banks could still refuse to participate in open market operations recommended by the Board. The 1933 Banking Act also prohibited officers of reserve banks from negotiating with foreign banks except with the Board's approval, in reaction against Strong's actions in 1927, when he had presented his negotiations with foreign central banks as a fait accompli.

The Banking Act of 1935 cemented these reforms. It removed the Treasury secretary and Comptroller of the Currency from the Board of Governors, lengthened the terms of the members of the Board and reorganized the FOMC, creating the modern structure of seven Board members and five reserve bank presidents. Control of open market operations was firmly vested in the FOMC. The Act authorized the Board of Governors to set reserve requirements, interest rates for deposits at member banks, and the discount rates of the individual reserve banks.

Criticism of high finance intensified as a result of the Pecora Commission Hearings on the causes of the Wall Street Crash. But given the problems of the two preceding decades, the case for a more centralized and independent Federal Reserve was overwhelming. The resulting reforms effectively inaugurated the second era of central banking in the United States.

11.7 Overview of the Second Era

In the first era, controversies centered on disputes over structure, on whether policy should be dictated by the rules of the gold standard or shaped so as to stabilize the economy-wide price level, and if policy was to be shaped then who should shape it. After the Treasury-Fed Accord in 1951, these disputes were resolved in favor of discretionary policy aimed at achieving price and economic stability. Responsibility was vested in the Federal Reserve Board and the FOMC.

The role of doctrine in this period is highlighted by Romer and Romer (2003, 2013). They show that Federal Reserve policy in the 1950s was informed by a precociously modern view of monetary policy. Board of Governors Chairman William McChesney Martin understood that, the economy having escaped the liquidity trap, monetary policy was now fully capable of pushing inflation up and down. They had a realistic view of the rate of growth and level of unemployment consistent with low and stable inflation, which they now sought to advance using open market operations. Their task was eased by the fact that the U.S. financial system was now heavily regulated, that the external environment was favorable, and that labor markets were accommodating. Political pressure was mild in a period of rapid catch-up growth, with the economy now "delivering the goods." Whatever the explanation, the results in the form of relatively low and stable inflation were favorable by the standards of before and after.

The 1960s were more problematic. Federal Reserve policy makers adopted an unrealistic view of how low unemployment could be pushed. Governors supposed that there was an exploitable long-term tradeoff between inflation and unemployment. By running the economy under high pressure of demand and accepting a higher rate of inflation, they believed that they could permanently reduce unemployment. There was political pressure to move in this direction, John F. Kennedy having campaigned in 1960 on a pledge to reduce unemployment and "get the economy moving again." In practice, additional monetary stimulus just raised inflation, with no long-term impact on the level of unemployment (in a phenomenon that became known as the Phelps-Friedman expectations-augmented Phillips Curve). The result was stop–go cycles in monetary policy. Pressure for the Fed to follow unsustainable policies intensified under the presidency of Richard Nixon, who lobbied Martin's successor, Arthur Burns, to loosen policy in support of his re-election campaign in 1972 (Abrams 2006).

The 1970s was more difficult than preceding decades, what with the collapse of the Bretton Woods System, the two oil-price shocks and the productivity slowdown. As unemployment rose, estimates of the equilibrium, or natural, rate rose with it. But although governors now had a heightened awareness of the importance of expectations, they were pessimistic about their ability to shape them. They attributed inflation to wage push and OPEC, factors largely beyond their control, and worried that price stability could be restored only at the cost of subjecting the economy to an extended period of high unemployment.

Consumer price inflation rose from the mid-single digits in 1976–78 to 11.3 percent in 1979. Conscious that the 1980 election was approaching, President Jimmy Carter replaced the ineffectual G. William Miller with a dedicated inflation fighter, Paul Volcker (formerly New York Fed president and undersecretary of the Treasury for international monetary affairs). Volcker's appointment was an acknowledgment that political interference with the conduct of monetary policy could be counterproductive. Volcker did not subscribe to the view that restrictive monetary policy was incapable of reducing inflation. Under his leadership, the FOMC raised its target for the federal funds rate to 20 percent in June 1981, bringing inflation down to 3.2 percent in 1983.

Political pressure for a more accommodating policy there still was. Farmers suffering the consequences of high interest rates drove their tractors into downtown Washington, D.C., blockading the Fed's headquarters. Contractors and construction workers sent Volcker 2 x 4 planks of wood. Sectional disputes and populist protests over monetary policy were not entirely a thing of the past, in other words. The administration of President Ronald Reagan was not exactly unresponsive to the protests, but the laissez-faire inclinations of Treasury secretary Donald Regan allowed the Fed to stay the course.

A lesson of the Volcker disinflation was that when inflation rises, the policy rate must rise *more* than proportionally to prevent real interest rates from falling and compounding the problem of excess demand. Clarida, Gali, and Gertler (2000) show that this convention was systematically pursued under Volcker and his successor, Alan Greenspan. This was in contrast to the 1960s and 1970s, when the policy rate was adjusted *less* than proportionately to inflation. This idea that the federal funds rate should respond more than proportionately to deviations of inflation from its target, with an additional adjustment for unemployment, was eventually formalized by the Stanford University economist John Taylor (1993) as the Taylor Rule.

The Taylor Rule was essentially a characterization of the policies pursued by the Federal Reserve in the 1980s and early 1990s, when it delivered satisfactory inflation and stability outcomes. But the growing prominence of the "rule" reflected discomfort with discretionary monetary policy, which might produce less satisfactory results under a less satisfactory

Fed chairman. More fundamentally, discomfort with discretionary Fed policy reflected continued unease about delegating vast powers to powerful financiers, a two-centuries-old current in American political thought.

Still another alternative, which did not assume a stable relationship between the Fed's targets and instruments, was to adopt a rule for its targets – to move to an "inflation targeting" regime like that pioneered by New Zealand starting in 1990, Canada in 1991, and then Sweden in 1993. This approach provided guideposts for not just policy but also expectations. It enhanced the central bank's ability to communicate its intentions to the public, which was valuable as an anchor for expectations and a mechanism for accountability. The disadvantage was that a formal inflation target was inflexible and arbitrary; the 2 percent target on which the pioneering adopters converged might not be optimal under all circumstances.

Given this controversy, the Fed settled for an intermediate approach where it targeted inflation, with an adjustment for the deviation of unemployment from full-employment levels, without enunciating a formal target. Support for the adoption of a formal monetary policy rule remained limited so long as monetary policy delivered satisfactory outcomes, as it appeared to do during the so-called Great Moderation from the mid-1980s to 2007. Countries that moved to formal inflation targeting earlier often did so in response to a crisis: a growth and inflation crisis in New Zealand, or the collapse of the krona's peg to the European Monetary System in Sweden. No comparable crisis afflicted the United States before 2008.

The Global Financial Crisis changed everything. It changed the Fed's objectives, making the restoration of financial stability a priority. It changed the Fed's instruments, which now included not only changes in the federal funds rate but also special-purpose vehicles with names like Maiden Lane I, II, and III used to inject funds into troubled investment banks like Bear Stearns to which the central bank was not formally permitted to lend. Those instruments included also credit easing and quantitative easing through which the Fed continued to provide liquidity to financial markets even though interest rates had already fallen to zero. The Board of Governors acknowledged that the now-distressed global banking system ran on dollar credit. In an echo of Benjamin Strong's 1927 initiative, the Fed provided dollar swap lines to the Bank of Canada, Bank of England, Swiss National Bank and Bank of Japan and, for the first time in its history, to the central banks of four emerging markets.

This response was controversial, not unlike earlier instances of crisis management in U.S. history. Some critics complained that the Fed failed to do enough. The minutes of the FOMC document the continuing preoccupation of a minority of reserve bank presidents with inflation, when it should have been clear that deflation was the real and present danger. Their preoccupation can only be understood in terms of memories of 1960s and 1970s inflation and the intellectual milieu to which they gave rise. Only in September 2012, with the announcement of QE3, the third round of quantitative easing, did the committee finally make an open-ended commitment to continue purchasing securities until deflation had been vanquished. (Earlier rounds, QE1 and QE2, had been limited in scope and duration and hence more limited in effectiveness.) There was also the fateful decision not to participate in the rescue of the investment bank Lehman Brothers in September 2008, reflecting doubts that the central bank possessed the legal authority to rescue an insolvent financial institution, and reflecting also the political criticism of the Fed's earlier rescue of Bear Stearns, motivated by the belief that such bailouts fomented moral hazard.

At a deeper level, this condemnation of the Federal Reserve for its extraordinary actions in the financial crisis reflected misgivings about the delegation of extensive powers to nonelected monetary technocrats, hostility toward big banks, and opposition to government intervention in the economy in all its manifestations – three currents in American history that can be traced back to Andrew Jackson and Nicholas Biddle. In the wake of the crisis, an awkward coalition of reformers sought to limit the Fed's ability to bail out individual financial institutions (a provision to this effect was included in the Dodd-Frank Wall Street Reform and Consumer Protection Act of 2010). Dodd-Frank also mandated that swap lines for foreign central banks be included in Government Accounting Office audits of the central bank and on the website of the Fed, ratcheting up political scrutiny.

The Fed responded to this criticism by attempting to better articulate the rationale for its actions. It sought to more systematically explain how its actions mapped into its targets. Given the breadth of its actions, it resorted to heightened transparency as a way of providing the public accountability needed to sustain its independence. The Fed adopted a formal 2 percent inflation target in 2012, a further step in the direct of transparency and clearer communication. Acknowledging that it had a responsibility for the maintenance of financial as well as price stability, it invested in a second set of tools, so-called macroprudential policies, that might be assigned to the pursuit of financial stability, allowing interest rates to be assigned to price stability. It created a Committee on Financial Stability separate from the FOMC to pursue the financial stability goal.

For the critics, none of this sufficed. They complained that the Fed, by expanding its balance sheet, was debasing the currency. They complained that near-zero interest rates encouraged risk taking, setting the stage for another financial crisis, and depressed productivity and economic growth by distorting investment decisions. Notwithstanding moves by the Fed as regulator to raise capital requirements for systematically important banks, they accused it of continuing to favor large financial institutions.

Again, the intensity of these criticisms can only be understood in terms of a history of hostility toward central banking in the United States. They prompted proposals to further limit the discretion of the FOMC by requiring it to adopt a formal interest-rate rule along the lines of the Taylor Rule or even going back to the gold standard (proposed in all seriousness by several candidates during 2016). They led to suggestions that the special nonrotating status of the president of the Federal Reserve Bank of New York on the FOMC be eliminated on the grounds that the New York bank was too close to Wall Street. They suggested that the reserve banks, on whose boards private bankers sit and who select their own leadership, be reorganized to give the Board of Governors the power to appoint and remove reserve bank presidents, a proposal that is itself a distant echo of the Banking Act of 1935.

11.8 Conclusion

Central bank decisions are always controversial. In the United States this controversy is shaped by a set of distinctive national characteristics that create enduring tensions for policy makers. There has always been a tension between rights and prerogatives of the states on the one hand and the federal government on the other, something that has prompted enduring opposition to a federal institution with wide-ranging monetary powers. Sectional divisions – whether between the North and South, agricultural and industrial regions, or the oil patch and the industrial heartland – are a fact of American life. Deep-seated suspicion of concentrated financial power with which central bankers are seen as allied is an intrinsic feature of American political culture. A significant segment of the voting public is temperamentally opposed to government expansion in all its forms and sees the central bank, as fiscal agent and financier of the government, as the agent of such expansion.

At the same time, the majority of economists, and probably the majority of Americans, would acknowledge that with time and changes in the structure of the economy the case for a modern central bank has become more compelling. Financial markets have grown more complex. Simple rules for ensuring price and economic stability without a central bank, those of the 19th-century gold standard for example, are less workable. International agreements to stabilize exchange rates like those of the Bretton Woods System have become more difficult to negotiate, much less sustain, in a multipolar world no longer dominated by a single country or group of countries. Expedients like a unilateral peg to another currency, like that adopted by Hong Kong, are not available to a country as large as the United States. And even economies like Hong Kong, which have put monetary policy on autopilot, have not been able to do away with central banking, given an expanding portfolio of responsibilities that now include microprudential supervision, macroprudential supervision, and acting as trusted advisor to the government.

Put these perspectives together and it is clear why central banking in the United States has always entailed compromise. Those compromises were evident in the hybrid public–private structure of the First and Second Banks of the United States and the decentralized nature of the Federal Reserve System. The unsatisfactory nature of those compromises was manifested in the decision to allow the charters of the First and Second Banks to lapse and then the decision in 1935 to centralize decision-making at the Federal Reserve Board. Critics continue to challenge the resulting compromise and propose further changes that have in common one characteristic, namely that they are viewed as undesirable by officials of the Federal Reserve System itself.

The legitimacy of an institution like a central bank rests ultimately on two sources. The first is "input" legitimacy: acceptance of the institution derives from the process through which decisions are reached and power is exercised. If that process gives voice to and empowers relevant stake-holders appropriately and if the interests of different parties are properly weighed, then the institution's advice and actions are more likely to be accepted. "Output" legitimacy refers to the quality of the results. If outcomes are good, then the institution is respected and agents are willing to acknowledge its authority. The extent to which it is a subject of controversy suggests that in its second century, the Federal Reserve will have to do better along both dimensions.

References

Abrams, Burton (2006), "How Richard Nixon Pressured Arthur Burns: Evidence from the Nixon Tapes," *Journal of Economic Perspectives* 20, pp. 177–188.

Beckhart, Benjamin (1924), *The Discount Policy of the Federal Reserve System*, New York: Holt.

Bordo, Michael (2012), "Could the United States have had a Better Central Bank? An Historical Counterfactual Speculation," *Journal of Macroeconomics* 34, pp. 597–607.

Catterall, Ralph (1903), *The Second Bank of the United States*, Chicago: University of Chicago Press.

Chandler, Lester (1957), *Benjamin Strong, Central Banker*, Washington, D.C.: Brookings Institution.

Clarida, Richard, Jordi Gali, and Mark Gertler (2000), "Monetary Policy Rules and Macroeconomic Stability: Evidence and Some Theory," *Quarterly Journal of Economics* 115, pp. 147–180.

Cohen-Setton, Jeremie (2015), "The Making of a Monetary Union: Evidence from U.S. Experience with Non-Uniform Discount Rates," unpublished manuscript, University of California, Berkeley (December).

Cronon, William (1991), *Nature's Metropolis: Chicago and the Great West*, New York: W.W. Norton.

D'Arista, Jane (1994), *The Evolution of U.S. Finance, Volume I: Federal Reserve Monetary Policy 1915–1935*, Armonk, New York: M.E. Sharpe.

Dwyer, Gerald Jr. (1996), "Wildcat Banking, Banking Panics, and Free Banking in the United States," *Federal Reserve Bank of Atlanta Economic Review* (December), pp. 1–20.

Eichengreen (1992), "Designing a Central Bank for Europe: A Cautionary Tale from the Early Years of the Federal Reserve System," in Matthew Canzoneri, Vittorio Grilli, and Paul Masson (eds.), *Establishing a Central Bank: Issues in Europe and Lessons from the US*, Cambridge: Cambridge University Press, pp. 13–39.

Holdsworth, John and Davis Dewey (1910), *The First and Second Banks of the United States*, Washington, D.C.: National Monetary Commission.

Jalil, Andrew (2015), "A New History of Banking Panics in the United States, 1825–1929: Construction and Implications," *American Economic Journal: Macroeconomics* 7, pp. 295–330.

Kemmerer, Edwin (1910), *Seasonal Variations in the Relative Demand for Money and Capital in the United States*, Washington, D.C.: National Monetary Commission.

Klovland, Jan Tore and Lars Oksendal (2015), "The Decentralized Central Bank: Regional Bank Rate Autonomy in Norway 1850–1892," Working Paper no. 20/2015, Oslo: Norges Bank.

Lakomaa, Erik (2007), "Free Banking in Sweden 1830–1903: Experience and Debate," *Quarterly Journal of Austrian Economics* 10, pp. 25–44.

Lowenstein, Roger (2015), *America's Bank: The Epic Struggle to Create the Federal Reserve*, New York: Penguin.

Meltzer, Allan (2003), *A History of the Federal Reserve, Volume 1: 1913–1951*, Chicago: University of Chicago Press.

Ogren, Anders (2003), "The Swedish Credit Market in Transition under the Silver and Gold Standards, 1834–1913," *Studies in Economic History* no. 2, Institute for Research in Economic History, Stockholm School of Economics.

Romer, Christina and David Romer (2003), "The Evolution of Economic Understanding and Postwar Stabilization Policy," in Federal Reserve Bank of Kansas City, *Rethinking Stabilization Policy*, Kansas City: Federal Reserve Bank of Kansas City, pp. 11–78.

Romer, Christina and David Romer (2013), "The Most Dangerous Idea in Federal Reserve History: Monetary Policy Doesn't Matter," *American Economic Review Papers and Proceedings* 103, pp. 55–60.

Selgin, George and Lawrence White (1994), "Monetary Reform and the Redemption of National Bank Notes, 1863–1913," *Business History Review* 68, pp. 205–243.

Taylor, John (1993), "Discretion versus Policy Rules in Practice," *Carnegie-Rochester Conference Series on Public Policy* 39, pp. 195–214.

Temin, Peter (1969), *The Jacksonian Economy*, New York: W.W. Norton.

Timberlake, Richard (1978), *Monetary Policy in the United States: An Intellectual and Institutional History*, Chicago: University of Chicago Press.

The Struggle of German Central Banks to Maintain Price Stability

Jakob de Haan

12.1 Introduction

During the last decades of the previous century, the *Deutsche Bundesbank* (*Bundesbank* for short) was considered very powerful. David Marsh (1992) even described the German central bank as 'the bank that rules Europe'. Also inside Germany the *Bundesbank* was considered very mighty. According to former chancellor Helmut Schmidt, the *Bundesbank* seemed like a state in the state (*Die Zeit*, 8 November, 1996: 3).

The historical experience of the *Bundesbank* pervasively informed the debate over the choice of monetary institutions in the last decades of the twentieth century (Lohmann, 1997; Issing, 2008; James, 2012). According to Fernández-Albertos (2015: 219), post-war economic developments in Germany were seen as 'a success story in which a monetary authority whose political independence was sustained by a solid institutional framework delivered credible and sound monetary policy, keeping inflation firmly under control ... The lessons from the German experience were particularly evident in the creation of a common monetary framework in Europe and the European Central Bank.'

Since the start of the European Economic and Monetary Union, the *Bundesbank* has been part of the European System of Central Banks. Its governor is part of the Governing Council of the European Central Bank, together with the six Executive Board Members of the ECB and (nowadays) 18 other governors of national central banks of the countries in the euro area. In recent years, the *Bundesbank* governor voted against several important ECB policy decisions.

I will discuss several elements of the 'success story' of the *Bundesbank*, including its (less successful) predecessor (Section 12.2), its origins (Section 12.3), its structure, mandate and independence (Section 12.4) and monetary policy strategy (Section 12.6). I will argue that the *Bundesbank*'s independence did not come automatically and that on several occasions the *Bundesbank* clashed with the German government. Often these clashes were about exchange rates (Section 12.5). Decisions about European monetary integration were in the realm of the federal government. On more than one occasion, the *Bundesbank* expressed its reservations and concerns (Section 12.7). Finally, in Section 12.8, I will discuss the *Bundesbank*'s presidents' views on European monetary policy (formally, presidents of national central banks do not represent their central bank in the ECB's Governing Council).

12.2 The *Reichsbank*

Initially, the newly established German Empire (1871) did not have a central bank. In fact, at the time Germany faced a general monetary and banking chaos due to the multiplicity of coinage systems and note-issuing banks (Flink, 1930). In 1872 there were 33 banks of issue, which were private institutions. And several of them were 'putting as many notes as possible into circulation' (NMC, 1910: 12). It was clear that in any potential panic these banks would be unable to pay out. On the initiative of the *Reichstag*, one of the chambers of the German parliament, it was decided to transform the Prussian Bank into a *Reichsbank* (Bank Act of 14 March 1875). The *Reichsbank* was given a central note-issuing role, but not a monopoly.[1]

There was a second problem at the time as Germany, which had adopted the Gold Standard in 1873, was confronted with a massive outflow of gold. The 'discussion of whether a new central bank would be needed took place in the context of actual gold losses, and a fear of even greater outflows. A central bank would, it was argued, be the best mechanism to orchestrate an appropriate response to a flow of precious metal . . . It was in the context of projecting German gold from flowing out that the phrase "guardian of the currency" was first used' (James, 1999: 7).

The governance of the *Reichsbank*, which was formally a privately owned institution, reflected its semi-public and semi-private character. The *Reichsbank* Directorate was to follow at all times the rulings and directions of the Chancellor (Marsh, 1992). The Directorate consisted of a president, a vice-president (since 1887) and six members appointed for

---

[1] Even in 1904, four other note-issuing banks were left. Banknotes were only made legal tender in 1909 (Flink, 1930).

life by the Emperor upon the nomination of the *Bundesrat* (the upper house of parliament representing the Federal States). The supervision of the *Reichsbank* was exercised through a council of curators composed of the Chancellor, who was president, and four members. The shareholders were represented in the central committee, consisting of 15 members. Three of its deputies were authorized to attend, with advisory powers, all meetings of the Directorate, and to examine the books of the bank (NMC, 1910).

The *Reichsbank* used its discount policy and its portfolio of bills as instruments in order to achieve a target for its gold holdings. In addition, it was prepared to act as lender of last resort to the German banks. James (1999: 11) therefore concludes that the 'legislative makeup of the *Reichsbank* had created a near perfect instrument for the management of a gold standard operating not on the basis of gold movements ... but through the regulation of domestic credit policy'.

Whereas in the first 20 years the *Reichsbank* had to establish its credibility as lender of last resort, after the 1890s the German banking system expanded to such an extent that it threatened the *Reichsbank's* control of the money supply. Notably after 1901, when the central bank halted some bank runs, banks used the *Reichsbank's* implicit guarantee to extend their balance sheets. However, the fundamental cause of the German hyperinflation in the 1920s was the First World War (James, 1999).

It was initially expected that this would be a short war (like the conflict of 1870–71), so that it could be fought without raising taxes; after victory, the opponents would be presented with the bill for the war (Marsh, 1992). However, when it became clear that the war would take longer, the German government still did not raise taxes enough (Holtfrerich, 1986). And when after 1916 it was no longer possible to place war loans with the public, the budget deficit had to be financed increasingly by the *Reichsbank*. Likewise, due to political instability after the war, the governments of the German Republic[2] were not able to increase taxes sufficiently to pay for the social costs of the war, social policies, and Germany's reparations payments under the Versailles Treaty (Webb, 1984).[3]

---

[2] On 9 November 1918, the German Monarchy was overthrown and the German Republic formed.

[3] As Flink (1930) points out, the total amount of reparation payments to be made by Germany was only fixed in May 1921 (at 132 billion Marks). Under those circumstances, the German government could not borrow abroad. According to Holtfrerich (1986: 167), 'the *Reichsbank* discerned an inseparable connection between the solution of the currency problem and the abatement of Reparations, and it held to this viewpoint throughout the hyperinflation period'. See also Marsh (1992: 99) and Flink (1930: 62).

The central bank accommodated the resulting public sector deficit by discounting government bills. It also continued to discount private bills. The Banking Act of May 1922 created a new *Reichsbank* on instigation of the Allies as condition for granting the Reparations moratorium proposed at the Cannes conference in January of the same year. Under the first article of the new Act, the *Reichsbank* would be independent of the government (James, 1999). However, instead of using its acquired independent position, the *Reichsbank* continued discounting government and private sector bills in ever-larger quantities (Holtfrerich, 1986). Inflation ran at 1300 per cent in 1922 (Marsh, 1992).

When at the end of 1923 the *Reichsbank* finally stopped discounting Treasury bills (its holdings of Treasury bills, which reached a high point of 190,000,000 trillion Marks in mid-November were reduced to zero by the end of the year –Marsh, 1992) inflation soon stopped.[4] According to Webb (1984: 507), the 'effectiveness of the *Reichsbank* action in eventually ending the inflation shows that its earlier passivity made the inflation possible. Whether the Directors of the *Reichsbank* are therefore to blame, however, depends on whether an earlier conversion of *Reichsbank* policy was politically possible ... an earlier attempt to force either balanced budgets on the government or a contraction on the private sector would have seriously threatened the Weimar constitutional system.'[5]

From October 1924, the new *Reichsmark* began to circulate. The conversion rate of the new currency was set at one-trillionth of a Mark (Marsh, 1992). The new Banking Law of 30 August 1924 confirmed the *Reichsbank's* independence from government; foreign representatives were given seats on the bank's new governing council (*Generalrat*), which had the power to elect the *Reichsbank* president and the other members of the Directorate. The new law formalized the new gold-exchange standard, with a commitment to exchange one 1,392 *Reichsmark* for a pound of gold (James, 1999).

---

[4] The first step towards the stabilization of the Mark was a decree (issued by the *Reichsbank* on 17 November 1923) that it would not accept any emergency money after 22 November. Emergency money was money printed by local government and large concerns. This money was needed, because the *Reichsbank* was unable to deliver enough banknotes to satisfy demand. The *Reichsbank* gave an assurance that it would redeem these emergency notes exactly as if they were its own banknotes (Schacht, 1967).

[5] Hjalmar Schacht (1967: 65–66), who replaced Rudolf von Havestein as president of the *Reichsbank* in December 1923 (against initial opposition of the *Reichsbank's* Directory), explains this passivity in similar terms: 'The legislation of 1922, which was intended to free the *Reichsbank* from the claims of the state, came to grief at the decisive moment because the *Reich* could not find any way of holding its head above the water other than by the inflationary expedient of printing banknotes.'

Forty per cent of the note issue had to be backed by gold and foreign exchange (which should not represent more than a quarter). Maintaining the gold parity implied high interest rates. According to James (1999: 25), these high levels of interest rates contributed decisively to Germany's weak economic performance during this period. However, he argues that there was no alternative, also in view of the massive fear of inflation among the population. Alternative currency systems without a nominal anchor, such as floating, 'would have produced immediate confidence problems'.

In 1927 the *Reichsbank* introduced credit constraints, believing it had no other choice, as higher policy rates would not work because it would lead to increased short-term capital inflows. According to James (1999: 28), this new policy did not change banks' behaviour. They 'continued to have very low cash reserves, and were confident that either they could obtain credit on the foreign market if needed, or that in emergency, the *Reichsbank* would not allow a major banking crisis to occur'. This was highly problematic in view of the feeble economic situation and the political uncertainty at the time (the *Reichstag* elections of September 1930 led to an increase in the number of National Socialist representatives from 12 to 128).

In 1931 a panic occurred after the failure of the Vienna-based *Osterreichische Kreditanstalt*, leading to a withdrawal of foreign capital. The new *Reichsbank* president Hans Luther (Schacht had resigned on 7 March 1930, after long-standing confrontations with the government) made it clear that banks could no longer rely on *Reichsbank* support which only made the panic worse. A general bank holiday was even needed in July 1931 after the failure of DANAT bank. During this crisis, many firms went bust and unemployment rates rose to very high levels.

After the 1931 crisis the German government imposed exchange controls, thereby in essence ending the gold-exchange standard, which made it possible for the *Reichsbank* to pursue a more expansionary policy.

In March 1933, Schacht was reappointed as president of the *Reichsbank*, replacing Luther who had resigned after Hitler had become Chancellor. According to James (1999), this was a vital move, for Hitler intended to build economic confidence in the new regime both internationally and domestically.

During the Nazi regime, the *Reichsbank* on the one hand frequently criticized the government for its fiscal policies, but on the other hand played an important role in enabling rearmament. For instance, the *Reichsbank* provided loans to the Autobahn administration. In addition, armaments were paid through the device of the MEFO bill. This was a bill drawn on the Metallurgical Research Company (MEFO).[6] Despite his initial admiration and support for Hitler, Schacht increasingly 'became convinced that, unless checked, Hitler's economic policies would lead to repeat of the 1923 trauma of inflation and ruin. Yet Schacht retained up to 1939 a naive belief that he could wield sufficient clout to persuade the Führer to switch course. Schacht's eventual failure was one of judgment. Long after he had ceased to trust Hitler, the *Reichbank's* president maintained a colossally misplaced faith in his own ability to manipulate events' (Marsh, 1992: 109–110). In January 1939, the *Reichsbank* informed Hitler about its intention not to grant the government any further credits. As a consequence, Schacht was dismissed and replaced by the Minister of Economics, Walther Funk, who remained at the helm of the central bank until the end of the Second World War.

Under the new *Reichsbank* Law of June 1939, the *Deutsche Reichsbank* – as it was now called – was brought fully under Hitler's control (Marsh, 1992). 'The *Reichsbank*, deprived of its role as "guardian of the currency" in practice simply became part of the mechanism for running the war economy' (James, 1999: 41). As the government pumped out ever-rising quantities of Treasury Bills, currency in circulation increased in tandem from RM 11 billion at the onset of the war to RM 73 billion by the time of the capitulation (James, 1999). The consequence of this was, of course, another inflation which the government (unsuccessfully in the end) tried to suppress by regulations such as a goods quota and price controls.

12.3 *Bundesbank*: Origins

It is widely believed that the *Bundesbank* has always been a very independent central bank, reflecting a strong anti-inflation sentiment among the German population.[7] However, the independence of the German central

---

[6] According to Schacht (1967: 113), 'the *Reich* guaranteed all obligations entered into by MEFO, and thus also guaranteed the MEFO bills in full. In essence all the *Reichsbank's* formal requirements were met by this scheme.' He points out though, that it was most unusual that bills could be extended over five years as was the case with MEFO bills. Furthermore, the *Reichsbank* accepted all MEFO bills at all times, irrespective of their size, number and due date, and changed them into money. The bills were discounted at a uniform rate of 4 per cent. Until 1938, some half of the MEFO bills in issue at any one time were always taken up and held by the market, and thus not presented to the *Reichsbank* for discounting. In 1938, the Reich no longer honoured the bills, as Hitler needed the money for war financing.

[7] Indeed, according to the central bank independence (CBI) measure of Cukierman, Web and Neyapti (1992), the *Bundesbank* was the most independent central bank in the world during the 1980s. On a scale from zero to one (where one reflects the highest level of

bank goes back to the preferences of the western Allied forces (notably those of the US) after the Second World War and did not reflect preferences of German politicians at the time (Neumann, 1999; Buchheim, 2001).

The Allied forces in Germany had different views about how to organize the central bank. Whereas the British initially kept the *Reichsbank* structure intact, the Americans favoured a more decentralized set-up. In 1946 Land Central Banks (LCBs) were set up in the American zone; in 1947 the French did the same in their zone. Although the LCBs were not the legal successor of the *Reichsbank*, they 'not only took over the staff and buildings as well as the furniture and equipment of the *Reichsbank* branches in their region, but also their assets and liabilities, realizable claims and holdings of *Reichsbank* notes' (Buchheim, 1999: 69). After American pressure, the British in February 1948 decided to dissolve the *Reichsbank* structure in their zone as well and to establish LCBs. Even though one of the principal tasks of the LCBs was to manage the amount of money in circulation, they did not receive the right to issue new banknotes (Buchheim, 1999).

On 1 March 1948 the *Bank deutscher Länder* (BdL) was created. The bank received the right to issue a common currency and became responsible for monetary policy, including setting policy rates and minimum reserve requirements. The Allied decree that established the BdL on 1 March 1948 required it 'to stabilize the currency and the monetary and credit systems' (Holtfrerich, 1999: 318).

In contrast to the centralized *Reichsbank* organization, the BdL had a two-tier system in which the Land Central Banks' presidents were all in the board of directors; the only other members of the board were its chairman and the president of the board of managers, whom the LCB presidents also elected. The Allied Bank Commission (ABC) became responsible for supervising the Bank and its monetary policy.

The new central bank organization made the currency reform of 1948 possible. And, according to Buchheim (1999: 62), this reform was key for economic growth to pick up: 'as there was no currency other than the *Reichsmark* which could be used to form a suitable pricing structure, the profit motive was irrelevant in the period before the currency reform'. In fact, German industrial output stagnated after the war because the 'prevailing economic conditions – economic controls, rationing, and

---

independence), it scored 0.69; for comparison: the score of the *Riksbank* at the time was 0.29. Maier and de Haan (2000) discuss the literature on the independence of the *Bundesbank*.

administrative price controls at a time of high liquidity were such that entrepreneurs could no longer realize profits'. The 1948 currency and economic reforms changed all this at a stroke.

The German governments were not represented in any of the BdL's executive bodies. This was done in order to keep the bank open to other zones (Buchheim, 1999: 76). The independence of the BdL from any political authorities (apart from the Allied Banking Commission) was also firmly anchored in the law (Buchheim, 1999: 77). And the ABC initially played a role in shaping the new central bank. For instance, it rejected the outcomes of the election results for the chairman and the president of the board of managers of the bank after which Wilhelm Vocke, a previous *Reichsbank* Directorate member, was elected as president, and Karl Bernard as chairman. Under Vocke, the BdL increasingly became a centralized system (Buchheim, 1999: 79).[8]

Although BdL decisions were subject to the explicit consent of the ABC, in practice, the latter's interference was restricted (Marsh, 1992). This is not to say that there were no conflicts (Holtfrerich, 1999). For instance, the ABC criticized the soft stance of the bank's Council against inflation in the autumn of 1948 after the currency reform, when living costs were rising dramatically at an annualized rate of almost 20 per cent. But in the end, the ABC did not veto the decision of the BdL. Berger (1997a: 435) concludes that after 1948, 'even though the ABC was still formally in charge, it remained strictly passive and helped the bank by imposing an unexpectedly unrestrictive political constraint' and shielded the BdL 'from the German authorities, which at this stage were not allowed to interfere with monetary policy'.

Under the Transition Law of 10 August 1951, the federal government took the place of the ABC as the institution permitted to participate in the Council meetings, but its veto power was drastically reduced by allowing it to only postpone the Council decisions for eight working days (Berger, 1997a). Vocke and his colleagues successfully opposed the proposal of the finance minister to replace the ABC by the federal government as the body that exercised jurisdiction over the bank. But opposition also came from several states, which sharply opposed any changes that would turn the balance towards the central government (Berger and de Haan, 1999; Stern, 1999).

---

[8] Marsh (1992: 154) writes how Vocke 'recalled with pleasure how he and his colleagues had succeeded in thwarting the Americans' decentralization plans for the new central bank. Setting up a centralized central banking system for Germany was, Vocke wrote, exactly what the Americans didn't want. "It remains a mystery . . . how we accomplished it after all".'

In the end, under the 1951 Law the central bank's independence from the German government remained intact, although the Act also stated that 'in the performance of its duties the BdL is obliged to observe and support the general economic policy of the federal government' (Buchheim, 1999: 77).

In the 1950s a tedious discussion about what eventually became the *Bundesbank* Act 1957 took place. Independence of the central bank and its structure (two-tier and decentralized vs one-tier and centralized) were key issues in this debate (Stern, 1999). The prolonged negotiations allowed the central bank to utilize the media to forge its position on price stability. One German central banker cited by Goodman states: 'From 1948, we made a very deliberate policy of getting the public on our side ... We attempted through all our publications and our speeches to explain our policies to the public and to convince them ... By explaining everything and making a very deliberate effort, we never came to a situation where a major party has ever attempted to touch our autonomy' (Goodman, 1989: 196–197).

In the end, the arrangements concerning independence in the *Bundesbank* Act of 1957 were essentially the same as in 1951. But this did not come automatically. Like at the beginning of the 1950s, the central bank and the federal government not only held different positions about how independent the central bank should be, but also disagreed about policies. At the time, the central bank followed a restrictive monetary policy also in view of the expansionary fiscal policy of the federal government, which the central bank openly criticized. When the central bank announced its intentions to further increase interest rates in March 1956, the federal government for the first time used its veto to suspend the decision for eight days (Berger, 1997b). Chancellor Adenauer (CDU) gave a speech in the *Gürzenich* hall in Cologne in which he attacked the *Bundesbank*, arguing that 'the independence of the central bank should have its limits when it ignored the policy guidelines set by the Chancellor ... However, the debate provoked by the event soon made it obvious that the public disapproved. Virtually every German newspaper, the representatives of the financial sector and even small-business interest groups took the side of the *Bundesbank* and its allies. By the end of May 1956 the Chancellor gave in and agreed to the stabilisation program as well as to the *Bundesbank*'s independent position' (Berger and de Haan, 1999: 27). According to Neumann (1999), no chancellor since Adenauer has dared to attack the German central bank in a similar fashion and to call its independence into question.[9]

---

[9] Likewise, Goodman (1992: 40) concludes: 'the BdL's ... success in maintaining price stability had won substantial praise from a society enjoying the benefits of economic

Adenauer used the changed provisions of the *Bundesbank* Act to appoint a new president. Although the old leadership was ready and willing to stay on (Marsh, 1992, p. 179), the Chancellor proposed Karl Blessing, who was at Unilever at the time and was thought to take better care of industrial interests. But Blessing hurried to assure the public that he would follow the same objectives as his predecessors. Goodman (1989) refers to this turnaround of a newly appointed *Bundesbank* Council member as the 'Thomas Becket effect' (see also Marsh, 1992: 22–23).[10]

12.4 Structure, Mandate and Independence

Like its predecessor, the *Bundesbank* had (until 2002) three main organs, i.e. the Central Bank Council, the Directorate and the Executive Boards of the Land Central Banks. However, the *Bundesbank* Act of 1957 brought about several changes, which can be seen as a compromise between supporters of a decentralized two-tier system and supporters of a centralized one-tier system (Stern, 1999). First, there was only one president of the *Bundesbank*. In addition, all (initially up to ten) members of the Directorate received voting rights in the Central Bank Council, together with the presidents of the (initially eleven) LCBs. Decisions in the Council were taken on the basis of simple majority rule; each member had one vote. The federal government could require that a decision be postponed by two weeks.

Second, the members of the Directorate were nominated by the federal government and appointed by the president of the Federal Republic for a period of normally eight years (where reappointment was possible). This term of eight years decoupled the term in office of the Directorate from the pattern of federal elections which normally are held every four years, so that it became difficult for a government to hand over the *Bundesbank* to political supporters (Kennedy, 1998).

Third, the federal government holds the capital of the *Bundesbank*. Furthermore, BdLs were turned into main offices of the *Bundesbank*. Even though they kept their names, the Land Central Banks lost their autonomous status. Before German reunification, each of the eleven states

success. This popular support, coming from much of the CDU's own constituency, proved critical in limiting the government's influence over the structure and, hence, the future policies of the central bank'.

[10] Named after Thomas à Becket, who was initially the chancellor of King Henry II, but opposed him after being appointed Archbishop of Canterbury. Indeed, the analysis of the voting behaviour of Central Bank Council members of Berger and Woitek (1997) suggests that German central bankers seldom followed the partisan beliefs of the central or state government that nominated them.

had a bank, but after reunification smaller banks were merged into larger units and one entirely new Land Central Bank (Saxony and Thuringia) was established, reducing the number of LCBs from eleven to nine on 1 November 1992.

The purpose of the *Bundesbank* was: 'to regulate the amount of money in circulation and of credit supplied to the economy, using the monetary powers conferred on it by this Act, with the aim of safeguarding the currency' (Kennedy, 1998). However, the Act's mandate for 'safeguarding the currency' left it open to whether the *Bundesbank* should stabilize the internal or external value of the DM. As will be discussed in Section 12.5, on several occasions the *Bundesbank* was forced to give in on its objective of price stability in order to maintain stable exchange rates.

The seventh amendment of the *Bundesbank* Act, which came into force on 30 April 2002, implied a drastic restructuring of the German central bank. This was the logical consequence of the transfer of monetary policy responsibility to the ECB. The former governing bodies were replaced by the eight-member Executive Board, comprising the president, the vice-president and up to six (currently four) other members. The nine Land Central Banks became Regional Offices of the *Bundesbank*. The members of the Executive Board are appointed (for a maximum of eight years) by the president of the Federal Republic of Germany. The president, the vice-president and two other members are nominated by the federal government; the other members are nominated by the *Bundesrat* in agreement with the federal government. The Executive Board meets under the chairmanship of the president or deputy president. It takes decisions by a simple majority of the votes cast. In the event of a tie, the chairman has the casting vote.

The *Bundesbank* is also involved in micro-prudential supervision. It collects the required supervisory information, but the ultimate responsibility lies here with the *Bundesanstalt für Finanzdienstleistungsaufsicht*. This arrangement takes advantage of the *Bundesbank*'s expertise but keeps it independent. Under the German constitution, any agency that takes decisions affecting specific individuals or companies, as supervisors must do, is subject to the control of ministers who are in turn responsible for their actions to parliament. Such accountability would compromise the *Bundesbank*'s independence.

Although the *Bundesbank* became much more centralized than its predecessor, even more so after German reunification, independence remained a key feature of the *Bundesbank* Act. The wording of the current law is very similar to the text of the Allied decree establishing the BdL.

Section 12 of the (revised) *Bundesbank* Act reads: 'In exercising the powers conferred on it by this Act, the *Deutsche Bundesbank* shall be independent of and not subject to instructions from the Federal Government. As far as is possible without prejudice to its tasks as part of the European System of Central Banks, it shall support the general economic policy of the Federal Government.' The 1957 version of the Act contained a similar section. But, as pointed out by Stern (1999), it is not the economic policy of the federal government as such which is to be supported but the general economic policy (that is, not each individual measure). In addition, this duty to provide support exists only 'without prejudice to the performance of its duties', i.e. to safeguard the currency.

The independence of the *Bundesbank* has also been related to the federal structure of Germany. As argued by Neumann (1999), the pluralism of nomination procedures is in accordance with the federal structure of Germany and restricts the influence of the central government. Furthermore, nominations are staggered over time to prevent a large number of Central Bank Council members being replaced in a single year, which potentially would enable political influence to be exerted.

Although the *Bundesbank* Act could have been changed at any time by a simple majority of the legislative, it was not until EMU that the law was substantially changed (apart from the changes discussed above after German reunification). This enabled the *Bundesbank* to pursue its policies aimed at price stability. However, a central bank can only pursue a stability-oriented monetary policy and remain independent if it receives sufficient public support. And indeed there is broad support among the German public for price stability and central bank independence. Helmut Schlesinger, president of the *Bundesbank* between 1991 and 1993, coined the term 'stability culture' to describe this phenomenon. After having experienced two episodes of hyperinflation, a strong aversion against inflation and a desire for monetary stability became deeply entrenched in the mind of the German people (Beyer et al., 2009).[11] But it should also be pointed out that the *Bundesbank* has actively cultivated this culture. As Neumann (1999: 304) puts it: 'If inflation is unpopular in Germany, then it is not because a substantial proportion of the population has experienced galloping inflation, but rather because those responsible at the central bank have never tired of explaining its adverse effects and

---

[11] Likewise, Issing (1993: 15) notes that: ' . . . it is no coincidence that it is the Germans, with their experience of two hyperinflations in the 20th century, who have opted for an independent central bank which is committed to price stability'.

incessantly sought to justify the particular importance of the goal of price stability and the independence of the central bank, that this priority, alone, can justify.'

At the time of the ratification of the *Bundesbank* Act, there were hardly any independent central banks in the world. Likewise, at the time the academic literature paid little attention to the appropriate institutional arrangement for a central bank. But the 'Great Inflation' of the 1970s, during which Germany had a much better inflation record than many other countries, changed all that. What kind of policies did the *Bundesbank* pursue which enabled Germany to withstand the 'Great Inflation' better than most other advanced economies and the German central bank to become 'a role model'?

12.5 External vs Internal Stability

Fixed exchange rates, free capital movements and autonomous national monetary policy constitute an impossible trinity. This increasingly became clear in the 1960s. During the Bretton Woods period, the D-Mark was revaluated vis-à-vis the US dollar on several occasions (1961, 1969 and 1971). Initially, the German central bank was opposed to the very idea of revaluing the D-Mark. For instance, Vocke, the president of the BdL declared in 1956 that the currency 'is stable, it will be kept stable, and it will certainly not be revalued!' (Marsh, 1992: 180). Although Otmar Emminger, who was in charge of international monetary affairs, disagreed, arguing that an undervalued currency would be a source of inflation, the official position of the central bank was against a revaluation. This did not change when Blessing became the *Bundesbank* president in 1958 (Holtfrerich, 1999).

In the beginning of the 1960s, Germany was wrestling both with internal and external imbalances. Inflation was rising, while current account surpluses increased. Under full convertibility of the D-Mark, it was hard to tackle both problems simultaneously, without changing the exchange rate or introducing some kind of capital control (Berger and de Haan, 1999). Ehrhard, the economics minister, was in favour of a revaluation of the D-Mark, also in view of pressure on the German currency, which the *Bundesbank* tried to relieve by easing its policies after it had tightened its policies in 1959/60.[12] Although Emminger supported the idea

---

[12] At the time, the economy was heating up rapidly and inflation was rising. However, by raising its policy rates in October 1959 and in June 1960, the *Bundesbank* also raised the

(Marsh, 1992: 182), the *Bundesbank* stuck to its position against a revaluation (Holtfrerich, 1999). However, after Chancellor Adenauer had given up his initial opposition to the idea, the German government decided on 3 March 1961 to revalue the currency by 5 per cent. In the end, the *Bundesbank* supported the decision (Berger, 1997b), although the official statement made it very clear that the initiative came from Bonn (*Bundesbank*, Monthly Report March 1961).

A similar conflict occurred in 1968/69, although the positions of the various players were somewhat different (Holtfrerich, 1999). Now the *Bundesbank* favoured a revaluation in view of the differences between inflationary developments in Germany and those abroad and the position of the balance of payments. However, Chancellor Kiesinger and, especially, the minister of finance, Franz Josef Strauß, very much opposed realignment. After the elections in September 1969,[13] the new government decided in favour of a revaluation of 9.3 per cent on 24 October 1969.

This scenario repeated itself when it became clear that the revaluation would bring only temporary relief. In April 1971 some speculative attacks occurred again, which triggered a debate on whether the D-Mark should float. A majority of the Central Bank Council (11 out of 18) supported *Bundesbank* president Klasen (who had been appointed as successor of Blessing by the new government) in his rejection of this option (Schenkluhn, 1985). However, on 9 May 1971 the government decided to temporarily let the D-Mark float in view of the pressure on the D-Mark. (The *Bundesbank* was forced in May 1971 to buy large amounts of dollars, including $1 billion in the last 40 minutes of trading on 5 May (Hetzel, 2002).) Whereas Klasen preferred the D-Mark to stick to its parity, the majority of the *Zentralbankrat* supported the view of the government in its meeting of 18/19 May (Schenkluhn, 1985).

Under the Smithsonian Agreement of 18 December 1971 there was an attempt to return to a more fixed exchange rate system, but it did not last for long. Speculative attacks in 1972 produced a new conflict between the economics minister Schiller and the *Bundesbank*. The central bank

---

interest rate differential with the US, which triggered capital imports (Berger, 1997a). Finally, the *Bundesbank* gave up its tight monetary stance in November 1960 because of its 'self-defeating' results (*Bundesbank*, Monthly Report November 1960).

[13] Interestingly, Holtfrerich (1999: 388) argues that the *Bundesbank* introduced discount rate hikes 'on 19 June (to 5 per cent) and on 10 September 1969 (to 6 per cent) in order to force the Federal Government to revalue the currency. That this occurred so shortly before the election date on 28 September ... was, given the prevailing external and internal economic dilemma, virtually a political decision by the Central Bank Council against the CDU/CSU.'

favoured capital controls, while Schiller proposed a move towards flexible exchange rates (Marsh, 1992). As the majority of the government did not support Schiller's views, he resigned. However, it soon became clear that the administrative measures taken were not effective. At the start of 1973 the dollar came under speculative attack again, forcing the *Bundesbank* to intervene very heavily. The *Bundesbank* proposed to close the foreign exchange market, but instead the government tightened capital controls. On 1 March 1973 the crisis was at its peak and the next day the foreign exchange markets were closed (von Hagen, 1999). Soon thereafter, the DM started floating against the dollar.

12.6 Monetary Policy Strategy after Bretton Woods

In a regime of a fixed exchange rate and free capital flows, money growth is endogenous. As discussed in the previous section, under the fixed exchange rate regime of Bretton Woods the *Bundesbank* increasingly faced difficulties to maintain price stability. This fundamentally changed when in March 1973 Germany let its currency float against the US dollar and the *Bundesbank* was relieved from its obligation to intervene in the exchange market.[14] After intense internal discussion (von Hagen, 1999), the *Bundesbank* decided to adopt a money targeting approach in which a formal quantitative target for money growth would provide a nominal anchor for inflation and inflation expectations.

In its Annual Report of 1973 the *Bundesbank* stated that the fight against inflation would be the principal goal of monetary policy. It was announced that 'as in 1973, in 1974 the *Bundesbank* will seek to control the central bank money stock in such a way that the volume of money and credit can expand to the extent compatible with the stability-oriented growth of the economy' (von Hagen, 1999: 424). The German central bank announced a target for the first time for the year 1975 (8 per cent). The approach to derive the money growth targets is based on the quantity identity (Deutsche Bundesbank, 1995). Taking the sum of the (maximum) rise in prices the *Bundesbank* was willing to tolerate ('unavoidable' inflation), the predicted growth in potential output, and the expected trend rate of change in velocity gives the target. In the second half of the 1970s, expected

---

[14] In reality, also after the fall of the Bretton Woods system, the *Bundesbank* had to intervene on several occasions in the foreign exchange markets due to commitments under the European Monetary System (see Section 12.6) or international attempts to coordinate policies (like the Plaza and Louvre Accords of 1985 and 1987, respectively); see Baltensperger (1999) and Goodman (1992) for details.

changes in capacity utilization were also taken into account, so that the *Bundesbank* did not yet have a medium-term orientation: 'This would have required that only expectations regarding the trend rate of growth of potential output and of the velocity of circulation be considered, while expectations regarding changes in the level of capacity utilization, or short-term deviations of the velocity of circulation from the secular trend, would have been excluded' (Neumann, 1999: 301).

Between 1975 and 1978, the target was not reached. According to von Hagen (1999), short-term employment-related goals gained prominence following the first oil price shock. But according to the *Bundesbank*, the expansionary policies were a consequence of the overestimated impact of the currency appreciation on real activity and inflation and the depth of the 1975 recession. Although money growth targets were not met, inflation came down to 2.7 per cent in 1978 (Beyer et al., 2009).

As discussed in more detail by von Hagen (1999), between 1975 and 1978 there were intense discussions within the Central Bank Council about the usefulness of monetary targeting. And frequently members had very different strategic and tactical views. As pointed out by von Hagen (1999: 425), the decision to announce a target in 1975 'was opportune for a number of reasons and thus received majority support'. These reasons included: signalling both a policy relaxation and the intention of not allowing money growth to get out of control again, making political interference more difficult, and it was consistent with the wishes of those members who favoured a steadier, more rules-based policy. However, during those years it was not obvious that the *Bundesbank* would continue this policy. According to von Hagen (1999), the creation of the EMS (see Section 12.7) exerted a strong influence in this regard. In the December 1978 Central Bank Council meeting, some members proposed to abandon monetary targeting in view of the fact that targets were missed most of the time. However, several others pointed to the wrong signal this would provide at the start of EMS. In the end it was therefore decided to announce a target for 1979. von Hagen (1999: 433) states: 'there is a certain historical irony in the fact that the introduction of new external constraints, which inevitably reduced the autonomy of the monetary authority, strengthened the hand of the proponents of monetary targeting on the Central Bank Council'.

From 1979 onwards, the target was officially set as a four-quarter target (from the fourth quarter of the previous year to the fourth quarter of the current year). More importantly, the *Bundesbank* also announced a target corridor instead of a target growth rate (Deutsche Bundesbank, 2006).

According to Baltensperger (1999: 452), 'The idea behind this corridor was that the central bank required a degree of scope with which to allow for developments that were unknown or could not be precisely foreseen at the time the targets were announced; such developments could occur on the foreign exchange and financial markets, or could involve real economic or price trends . . . the width of the corridor was meant to reflect the factors of uncertainty prevailing at the time the target was set.' After 1979, the target levels for money growth were reduced until 1985; between these years the targets were met. By subsequently reducing the monetary targets from 1979 onwards, the monetary authorities gave a clear signal that they wanted to restore price stability, but it took until the 1982 recession before inflation started to come down.[15] Inflation fell steadily from an annual average rate of 5.3 per cent in 1982 to 2.2 per cent in 1985.

Until 1984, the German central bank took the so-called 'unavoidable' rate of price rises into account in its calculation of the money growth target. According to the *Bundesbank* (1995: 80), it did so because 'price increases which have already entered into the decisions of economic agents cannot be eliminated immediately, but only step-by-step. On the other hand, this tolerated rise in prices was invariably below the current inflation rate or the forecast for the year ahead' as the bank 'did not wish to contribute to strengthening inflation expectations'. After 1984, a medium-term inflation rate of 2 per cent was assumed in calculating the money growth target. This level was considered the 'maximum inflation rate to be tolerated in the medium term'.

Until 1987 the *Bundesbank* formulated money growth targets for the central bank money stock (defined as currency in circulation plus the required minimum reserves on domestic deposits calculated at constant reserve ratios with base January 1974). Whereas currency is counted at its full weight, bank deposits are only included in accordance with their historical reserve ratios (i.e. 16.6 per cent for site deposits, 12.4 per cent

---

[15] The restrictive policy led to an open conflict with the federal government. The state secretary of finance presented the government's case for a less restrictive policy at the Central Bank Council meeting on 18 January 1979. However, after a brief discussion, the council members voted in favour of an increase in the interest rate, which the state secretary criticized in a post-meeting press conference. This led to widespread public critique and support for the *Bundesbank* (Goodman, 1992). In the same year, the government nominated Karl Otto Pöhl, who had served as state secretary of finance under Schmidt when he was minister of finance, as the new *Bundesbank* president. However, Pöhl rejected the government's call for lower interest rates. Goodman (1992: 91) thus concludes: 'Schmidt's previous relationship with Pöhl just had little apparent effect.'

for time deposits and 8.1 per cent for savings deposits), reflecting different degrees of liquidity. An important reason to focus on the central bank money stock was that it represented the *Bundesbank*'s direct contribution to money creation so that it underlined the final responsibility of the central bank for the growth of the money stock (Deutsche Bundesbank, 1995). However, from 1988 onwards, targets were announced for M3 growth. M3 is a broad money stock, but its components are assigned different weights. As pointed out by Baltensperger (1999), the background for this decision was the 'overstatement' of monetary trends based on central bank money stock due to its heavy dependence on cash balances. Due to the low level of interest rates at the time, cash balances rose sharply so that by the end of 1987, currency in circulation accounted for 52 per cent of central bank money and only 10 per cent of M3. The *Bundesbank* therefore set its targets in terms of M3 growth from 1988 onwards. Exceptionally the target for 1988 was announced without an explicit corridor ('around 5 per cent'). The calculation underlying this target was based on a growth rate of potential real output of 2–2.5 per cent, a normative inflation rate of 2 per cent and a decline in the velocity of circulation of 0.5 per cent (Baltensperger, 1999: 470).

During 1986–88, there was significant and repeated overshooting of the monetary targets set by the German central bank. According to Baltensperger (1999), external motives (restraining the appreciation of the D-Mark) and reservations about the resilience of economic growth induced the *Bundesbank* to tolerate monetary expansion above the targets set. During 1990 and 1991, the economic and political reunification of the Federal Republic and the German Democratic Republic under the State Treaty, signed on 1 July 1990, had a major impact on German monetary policy. As a consequence of the monetary union and the conversion rate between east and west German currencies set out in the Treaty, the money stock increased by about 15 per cent of west German M3 in July 1990. Money growth in 1990 was initially moderate and, for the year as a whole, on target by expanding just under 6 per cent. The target for 1991 was left unchanged at 4 to 6 per cent although it now referred to M3 for Germany as a whole and allowed, in terms of the initial level, for the jump in the money stock due to reunification (Baltensperger, 1999). However, changes in the demand for money in eastern Germany due to a move to higher interest rate deposits led to a decline in the overall growth of the German money stock. The *Bundesbank* for the first time in its history therefore changed the target corridor following the usual mid-year revision to 3 to 5 per cent. 'In doing so it explicitly emphasized that this was an expression of an unchanged basic goal, and did not imply a change in its monetary policy stance' (Baltensperger, 1999: 482). Overall the (revised) target for 1991 was virtually met. But in 1992–94 targets were not met, reflecting that the *Bundesbank* did not want to impose restrictions on the real economy and, more importantly, paid attention to exchange rate developments and the international context such as EMS turbulence (Baltensperger, 1999: 487).

For 1995 a target corridor of 4–6 per cent was set, but with M3 growth amounting to just 2.1 per cent there was substantial undershooting. For 1996 the corridor was set at 4–7 per cent in view of the instability of short-term monetary trends. At the end of 1996, the *Bundesbank* decided for the first time to extend its target horizon to two years. This decision 'reflected, on the one hand, the short-term volatility of M3 trends repeatedly identified in the previous years and thus a renewed emphasis on the medium-term nature of *Bundesbank* monetary policy. Yet in equal measure the decision was also due to the eminent "interim period" in the run up to European Monetary Union at the start of 1999' (Baltensperger, 1999: 501).

The *Bundesbank*'s policy of monetary targeting is widely considered to have been very successful, even though the targets were missed roughly half of the time. Issing et al. (2005: 50–51) argue, however, that this 'does not mean ... that the *Bundesbank* did not take monetary targets seriously. On the contrary, money growth targets were regarded as constituting the basis for a rules-oriented approach to monetary policy. Announcing a monetary target implied a commitment by the *Bundesbank* towards the public. Deviations of money growth from the target had always to be justified. Even if it is true that the reputation of the *Bundesbank* ultimately was achieved by its success in fulfilling its mandate to safeguard the stability of its currency, its final goal, current policy continuously had to be justified in the context of its pre-announced strategy. In this sense, the strategy contributed to the transparency, the accountability and the credibility of *Bundesbank*'s policy.' Furthermore, by announcing money growth targets, the *Bundesbank* tried to provide information to economic and political agents influencing expectations of inflation and make it more difficult to exert pressure on the central bank for more rapid monetary expansion (Neumann, 1999; Beyer et al., 2009). According to Baltensperger (1999: 515–517), the *Bundesbank* has 'repeatedly emphasized that it cannot conduct its policy in a vacuum and, in particular, must take account of the decisions taken by fiscal policy makers and collective wage bargainers ... A monetary policy that is strictly oriented towards price stability and is announced and anticipated accordingly is the best way of retaining the collective bargaining system within a framework consistent with price stability. The *Bundesbank* has always been acutely aware of this, and it is not least here that the advantage of a policy of preannouncing credible monetary targets lies.'

Of course, a policy of monetary targeting will only work if the long-term money demand function is stable. There is ample evidence that money demand in Germany was much more stable than in many other European countries. Fase (1998) provides an extensive overview of empirical research on the stability of money demand functions and concludes that 'money demand in Germany is relatively stable compared to other EU countries . . . The reviewed studies also indicate that the demand for broad money is generally more stable than the demand for narrow money. This finding is supportive for monetary practice in Germany, which focuses on the broad money concept . . . ' (Fase, 1998: 137).

12.7 Monetary Integration

At the end of the 1970s then French president, Valéry Giscard d'Estaing, and German chancellor, Helmut Schmidt, took the initiative for the European Monetary System (EMS). The aim of the EMS was to create a 'zone of monetary stability' in Europe. When initial negotiations about the EMS started, the *Bundesbank* was not involved; according to French president Giscard d'Estaing, because 'the *Bundesbank* President, Otmar Emminger, is unsympathetic to this plan. He does not want to be forced to sell Deutschmarks to support weak currencies, because this could encourage inflationary trends in Germany' (Bernholz, 1999: 736). Indeed, the *Bundesbank*, having in mind the difficulties it envisaged under the final years of the Bretton Woods system, was initially not very enthusiastic about these plans.[16] Later on it participated in the negotiations and according to Bernholz (1999: 758), the '*Bundesbank* was able to achieve its most important objectives, albeit with concessions on the term of the very short-term financing facility (VSTF)[17] and the volume of short-term monetary support. It regarded the adoption of the parity grid and the

[16] According to Marsh (1992), Chancellor Schmidt hinted during a visit to the *Bundesbank* that he might propose to change its independent status if it would oppose his plans.

[17] The VSTF was intended to support marginal intervention in the exchange markets and consisted of mutual credit lines among central banks to support marginal intervention. VSTF credit was both automatic and unlimited and was granted on a 45-day basis; at the request of the debtor country, it could be renewed for another three-month period (Goodman, 1992).

fixing of the bands around these parities as an important success. Even more important to the *Bundesbank* was the commitment by the chancellor and the government to agree to the suspension of the *Bundesbank's* intervention requirement if its stability-oriented monetary policy was threatened.'

The core of the EMS was the so-called Exchange Rate Mechanism (ERM). Currencies participating in the ERM were supposed to fluctuate vis-à-vis one another within a band of plus and minus 2.25 per cent around agreed-upon central rates. These central rates could be adjusted. Whenever an exchange rate reached the edge of the band, the central banks of both countries concerned were supposed to intervene on the foreign exchange market. The ERM went through a number of phases. Between 1979 and 1983 there were frequent and substantial realignments. For instance, already in September 1979 a number of currencies were devaluated vis-à-vis the D-Mark. This was a pattern to be repeated many times. Although some devaluations occurred in the second phase (1983–87), both their frequency and magnitude were substantially lower than in the previous phase. In the period 1987–92, the sequence of devaluations came to a halt. The parities and the bands of the ERM were considered to be very credible. This third phase of the ERM was also marked by new entries: the Spanish peseta in June 1989, the British pound in October 1990, and the Portuguese escudo in April 1992. During this period it looked as if exchange rates were almost fixed. However, this turned out to be illusionary. In the fourth phase of the ERM (1992–93) there was a severe currency crisis. In August 1992 the British pound fell close to the ERM floor and the Italian lira even fell below it. Eventually, the two currencies left the system. Except for the Dutch guilder, all currencies came under attack between September 1992 and August 1993. Only after the fluctuation margins were increased to 15 per cent did the foreign exchange markets become more tranquil. During the fifth phase, ERM membership broadened again as participation in the exchange rate system was one of the convergence criteria for partici-pation in the Economic and Monetary Union.

Although it was not envisaged to function like this, in practice the German D-Mark functioned as the anchor within the EMS. Schmidt and Giscard d'Estaing originally had planned that the EMS should be built around the European Currency Unit (ECU). Indeed, when it was decided to formerly set up the EMS in December 1978 the ECU was proclaimed as the central point of the new system. However, as Karl Otto Pöhl, who in his capacity as *Bundesbank* vice-president had played an important role in setting up the EMS, concludes, 'the *Bundesbank* turned the original concept [for the EMS] on its head by making the strongest currency the yardstick for the system' (Marsh, 1992: 233). As a consequence, other countries in the system had little room for manoeuvre in monetary policy making. If the German monetary authorities decided to change their interest rates, the other countries had to follow if they wanted to maintain their peg. Various countries, notably France, felt that the German-dominated ERM did not always serve their interests as the German monetary authorities, in deciding on interest rates, took into account only the economic situation in Germany so that several countries faced an interest rate which was frequently not in line with their business cycle position. This became very clear when the *Bundesbank* increased interest rates to slow down the German boom after the German reunification; at the time, the economic situation in many other EMS countries did not justify higher interest rates. As Issing (2008: 8) put it: 'The larger EMS member countries in particular were unwilling to accept a lasting necessity to act more or less in lockstep with the monetary policy of the *Bundesbank*. For the *Bundesbank*, conversely, it was not possible to pursue a monetary policy oriented towards "European objectives".'

Outside Germany, a monetary union was considered the proper answer to this problem. The political steps in this direction were based on the report of the Delors Committee – named after the chairman of this committee and then-president of the European Commission, Jacques Delors – which proposed a three-phase transition towards monetary unification. The main conclusions of the Delors Committee were incorporated in the 1992 Treaty on European Union, better known as the Maastricht Treaty, named after the Dutch city where the final negotiations took place.

Politicians in Germany, and eventually also the *Bundesbank*, supported monetary unification in Europe as well. The Bundesbank 'realized that monetary union was probably inevitable for political reasons, as many countries were not willing to accept its domination in the longer term. Its aim would therefore have to be to eliminate the weaknesses in the Delors Report, particularly as regards Stage II' (Bernholz 1999: 775–776). In a statement of February 1992 the Central Bank Council of the *Bundesbank* expressed its satisfaction that the planned institutional design for EMU, in particular the set-up of the future ECB, was largely in line with the *Bundesbank*'s recommendations. At the same time, the Council pointed out that a monetary union is 'an irrevocable joint and several community which, in the light of past experience, requires a more far-reaching association in the form of a comprehensive political union, if it is to prove durable' (Issing, 2008: 12).

The fact that the *Bundesbank* was able to strongly influence the negotiations reflected that the government needed the support of the German central bank: 'The *Bundesbank*'s involvement provided the government with the support it needed to overcome public opposition to pooling the *Deutschmark* with other European currencies. At the same time, the conditions that the *Bundesbank* demanded for its support were extensive and ongoing. The ruling coalition was able to sustain its push for monetary union by means of a dual strategy of co-opting the leadership of the *Bundesbank* and of accepting the *Bundesbank*'s positions on the details of monetary union' (Duckenfield, 1999: 95). While 'this limited the government's negotiating freedom, it also enabled it to dictate the terms of the Maastricht Treaty that related to EMU. As a result, the treaty that emerged was nearly identical to the *Bundesbank* law' (Duckenfield, 1999: 101). In the end, the government was able to obtain approval for EMU both from the *Bundestag*, where all parties except the PDS supported the project, and from the *Bundesrat*, where only Bavaria's prime minister Edmund Stoiber voted against it.

12.8 ECB Policies

The ECB's monetary policy bears some resemblance to the *Bundesbank*'s policies, although it also has some features akin to inflation targeting. Under the ECB's two-pillar strategy, the analysis of monetary factors ('monetary analysis') is paired with a broad-based non-monetary analysis of the risks to price stability in the short to medium run ('economic analysis').[18] According to the ECB (2011: 69), 'the two-pillar approach is designed to ensure that no relevant information is lost in the assessment of the risks to price stability and that appropriate attention is paid to different perspectives and the cross-checking of information in order to reach an overall judgement on the risks to price stability'. The two-pillar approach provides a 'cross-check' of the indications that stem from the shorter-term economic analysis with those from the longer-term-oriented monetary analysis (ECB, 2011).

---

[18] The 'monetary analysis' focuses on a medium- to long-term horizon. When the ECB's monetary policy strategy was introduced, the ECB Governing Council announced a quantitative 'reference value' for the annual growth rate of a broad monetary aggregate (M3). However, the ECB has always stressed that monetary policy does not react mechanically to deviations of M3 growth from the reference value. Such deviations, however, trigger increased efforts to identify and assess the underlying driving forces.

During the financial and euro crises, the ECB introduced unconventional monetary policies. Presidents of the *Bundesbank* have on several occasions expressed reservations, or even outright opposition, towards some of the unconventional monetary policies. A constant theme in these criticisms is the worry that some of these unconventional policies blur the distinction between monetary and fiscal policy and may threaten the independence of the ECB. Talking about the Securities Markets Programme (SMP), which the ECB introduced in May 2010,[19] Axel Weber (2010), who had become the *Bundesbank*'s president after the resignation of Ernst Welteke in 2004 over an expenses scandal, for instance, argues that 'There is no evidence that asset purchases have had any significant impact on average euro-area sovereign bond yields on which euro-area monetary policy must exclusively focus as its main transmission channel. But the SMP risks blurring the different responsibilities between fiscal and monetary policy. As the risks associated with the SMP outweigh its benefits, these securities purchases should now be phased out permanently as part of our non-standard policy measures.' In addition to criticizing the measure internally within the ECB Governing Council, Weber took the unusual step of making his reservations public.

Increasing discomfort with the ECB's policies and his rather isolated position eventually led to Weber's decision to withdraw his candidacy to succeed Jean-Claude Trichet as the president of the ECB and to step down as president of the German central bank ('for personal reasons'). This decision caught Chancellor Angela Merkel by surprise. After media reports that Weber was withdrawing his candidacy, Merkel invited Weber to come to Berlin. At the conclusion of the meeting, Merkel's spokesman announced that Weber was stepping down as *Bundesbank* president, effective on 30 April, a full year before his term was set to end.[20] Jens Weidmann, economic adviser to Merkel, succeeded him. As Germany did not field an alternative candidate for the ECB presidency, the European Council agreed that Mario Draghi, the governor of the *Banca d'Italia*, would become the third president of the ECB.

---

[19] Under the SMP, Eurosystem interventions were carried out in the euro-area public and private debt securities markets to ensure depth and liquidity in dysfunctional market segments and to restore the proper functioning of the monetary policy transmission mechanism. Purchases of government bonds were strictly limited to secondary markets. To ensure that liquidity conditions were not affected, all purchases were fully neutralized through liquidity-absorbing operations.

[20] Sources: www.spiegel.de/international/germany/merkel-ecb-candidate-german-central-bank-head-axel-weber-resigns-a-745083.html and www.economist.com/node/21564245 (last accessed: 28 November 2016).

In September 2011, Jürgen Stark resigned as member of the Executive Board of the ECB for 'personal reasons' nearly three years before his term expired. Stark (a former *Bundesbank* official) reportedly opposed the ECB's decision to reactivate its government bond purchase programme in August that year, as did Weidmann.[21] Deputy finance minister Jörg Asmussen succeeded Stark.

On 2 August 2012, the ECB announced a new instrument, the *Outright Monetary Transactions* (OMT), i.e. purchases of government bonds in secondary sovereign bond markets. These purchases will be limited to secondary markets, although unlike the SMP the OMT allows, in principle, for the unlimited purchase of government bonds. This step came after ECB President Draghi previously had told a conference of international investors in London in July that the ECB would do 'whatever it takes to save the euro'; these seven words had an almost instantaneous soothing effect on financial markets. A necessary condition for OMT is strict and effective conditionality attached to an appropriate European Financial Stability Facility/European Stability Mechanism programme or a precautionary programme (Enhanced Conditions Credit Line). This instrument enabled the ECB to address severe distortions in government bond markets, which originated from, in particular, unfounded fears on the part of investors of the reversibility of the euro. By signalling its readiness to intervene in government bond markets, the ECB could help, in particular, to reduce the likelihood of adverse self-fulfilling equilibria (Cour-Thiman and Winkler, 2014).

Although Draghi's initiative was welcomed by Chancellor Merkel, Weidman opposed OMT.[22] According to press reports, he was the only Governing Council member who voted against it, publicly questioning its potential effectiveness.[23] A *Bundesbank* document[24] filed to Germany's Federal Constitutional Court after the compatibility of OMT with EU and German law had been challenged, which was leaked to the German newspaper *Handelsblatt*, points to the risks of OMT for central bank independence by bringing monetary policy too close to the realm of fiscal policy.[25]

---

[21] See www.wsj.com/articles/SB10001424053111903285704576560411990091924.

[22] See www.wsj.com/articles/SB10001424053111903285704576560411990091924.

[23] See, for example, interview with *Neue Zürcher Zeitung*. Available at: www.bundesbank.de/Redaktion/DE/Interviews/2012_09_26_weidmann_nzz.html.

[24] Stellungnahme gegenüber dem Bundesverfassungsgericht zu den Verfahren mit den Az. BvR 1390/12, 2BvR 1439/12, 2BvR 1439/12, 2BvR 1824/12, 2BvE 6/12.

[25] See www.telegraph.co.uk/finance/financialcrisis/10021894/Bundesbank-declares-war-on-Mario-Draghi-bond-bail-out-at-Germanys-top-court.html (last accessed: 28 November 2016).

According to the document (p. 9), it is not the task of the central bank to guarantee the 'Zusammensetzung der Währungsunion'. The presence of redenomination risk premia is not viewed as a proper ground for unlimited monetary policy measures. In addition, Weidman argues, 'government bond purchases involve the fundamental risk of mutualising sovereign liability risks via the central bank's balance sheet. While this risk can be more or less ignored for countries with their own currency, it can be a major problem for a monetary union – especially so for one which, like the European monetary union, is not a fiscal union.'[26]

At the end of 2014 inflation in the euro area dropped below zero; since then, inflation has been persistently low. Average headline (core) inflation over the last 12 months until October 2016 amounted to 0.12 per cent (0.86 per cent), well below the ECB's aim for price stability (i.e. an inflation rate in the medium term of below but close to 2 per cent). Furthermore, market-based long-term inflation expectations became less well anchored and started drifting away from this target. In January 2015, the Governing Council of the ECB therefore decided to launch the expanded asset purchase programme (EAPP), better known as quantitative easing (QE).

Again, the *Bundesbank* was very critical. According to Weidman, 'the latest downturn in the outlook for prices and growth still leaves me unconvinced of the alleged need to use this instrument, one that I regard purely as an emergency instrument. For this will ultimately lead to a dangerous commingling of monetary and fiscal policy. Even after taking note of the latest forecast revisions, I still see a very remote risk of a deflationary spiral ... It is important to emphasise that our target is a medium-run one ... The term "medium run" ... consciously contains a certain degree of vagueness over the precise time horizon. This gives monetary policy the flexibility it needs to respond appropriately to a myriad of different types of macroeconomic shock. Monetary policy would surely be unable to cope with the expectation of always being able to guarantee an inflation rate of just under 2%, for alongside the justified desire to steer inflation back towards the 2% mark, monetary policy must also keep in mind that there are risks associated with the protracted low-interest-rate policy and the nonstandard monetary policy measures.' He also points out that his 'scepticism is not founded on what some see as chronic *Bundesbank* naysaying to a loosening of monetary policy; rather, it is the outcome of a difficult process

---

[26] See, www.bundesbank.de/Redaktion/EN/Reden/2015/2015_02_12_weidmann.html (last time accessed: 28 November 2016).

of weighing the pros and cons of QE'. As to the cons, Weitman points to the risk of mutualizing sovereign liability risks via the central bank's balance sheet.[27]

12.9 Conclusions

It was only after the foundation of a nation state in 1871 that the basis was laid for a German central bank and a national currency. The era of the Mark came to an end in the hyperinflation of 1923. The succeeding Reichsmark had an even shorter life when it was replaced by the D-Mark after the 1948 currency reform. The Allies created a new central bank system for the, at the time, not yet constitutionally established Federal Republic of Germany. In 1957, the *Bundesbank* was established as the successor of the *Bank deutscher Länder*. In 1999, the D-Mark was replaced by the euro. Since then the *Bundesbank* has remained a central bank (within the European System of Central Banks), but without its own national currency. All these changes reflect the struggle of German central banks to deliver price stability. This chapter has shown that without the consent and cooperation of the government, even a notionally independent central bank cannot maintain stable prices. Central bank independence, important as it is, does not guarantee price stability if the political circumstances are not right. This became clear in 1922. Likewise, under a totalitarian regime, the concept of central bank independence becomes meaningless. Furthermore, the exchange rate regime and international cooperation may restrict the room for manoeuvre for the central bank to maintain price stability, as this chapter has shown. Interestingly, the independence of the German central bank, which was twice imposed by foreign governments, received broad (popular and political) support in Germany during the Second World War, no doubt due to the experience in one generation of two episodes which led to the total destruction of the German currency. But it is important to note that the *Bundesbank* did not operate in a political vacuum. As Goodman (1992: 100–101) writes: 'Its independence is not written in stone; its enabling law can be changed. To maintain that independence, the *Bundesbank* has been forced to take the views of West Germany's major societal actors into account. In practice, the bank has always sought to build a coalition of supporting groups or, at a minimum, to avoid uniting too many powerful interests in

---

[27] See, www.bundesbank.de/Redaktion/EN/Reden/2016/2016_03_23_weidmann.html (last time accessed: 28 November 2016).

opposition.' It helped the *Bundesbank* to pursue policies which led to its high reputation for maintaining price stability. No wonder, therefore, that the ECB was largely modelled after the German central bank.

References

Baltensperger, E. (1999). Monetary Policy Under Conditions of Increasing Integration (1979–96). In: Deutsche Bundesbank (Ed.), *Fifty Years of the Deutsche Mark*. Oxford: Oxford University Press, pp. 439–523.

Berger, H. (1997a). The Bundesbank's Path to Independence. Evidence from the 1950s. *Public Choice*, 93, 427–453.

Berger, H. (1997b). *Konjunkturpolitik im Wirtschaftswunder: Handlungsspielräume und Verhaltensmuster von Bundesbank und Regierung in den 1950er Jahren*. Tübingen: J.C.B. Mohr (Paul Siebeck).

Berger, H. and J. de Haan (1999). A State Within the State? An Event Study on the Bundesbank (1948–1973). *Scottish Journal of Political Economy*, 46(1),17–39.

Berger, H. and U. Woitek (1997). How Opportunistic are Partisan German Central Bankers? Evidence on the Vaubel hypothesis. *European Journal of Political Economy*, 13, 807–822.

Bernholz, P. (1999). The Bundesbank and the Process of European Monetary Integration. In: Deutsche Bundesbank (Ed.), *Fifty Years of the Deutsche Mark*. Oxford: Oxford University Press, pp. 731–789.

Beyer, A., V. Gaspar, C. Gerberding and O. Issing (2009). Opting Out of the Great Inflation: German Monetary Policy after the Break Down of Bretton Woods. ECB Working Paper 1020.

Buchheim, C. (1999). The Establishment of the Bank deutscher Länder and the West German Currency Reform. In: Deutsche Bundesbank (Ed.), *Fifty Years of the Deutsche Mark*. Oxford, Oxford University Press, pp. 55–100.

Buchheim, C. (2001). Die Unabhängigkeit der Bundesbank. Folge eines amerikanischen Oktrois? *Vierteljahrshefte für Zeitgeschichte*, 49(1), 1–30.

Cour-Thiman, P. and B. Winkler (2014), The ECB's Non-standard Monetary Policy Measures. The Role of Institutional Factors and Financial Structure. European Central Bank Working Paper 1528.

Cukierman, A., S.B. Webb and B. Neyapti (1992). Measuring the Independence of Central Banks and its Effect on Policy Outcomes. *World Bank Economic Review*, 6, 353–398.

Deutsche Bundesbank (1961). Monthly Report March 1961. Frankfurt am Main: Bundesbank.

Deutsche Bundesbank (1995). *The Monetary Policy of the Bundesbank*. Frankfurt am Main: Deutsche Bundesbank.

Deutsche Bundesbank (2006). *Die Deutsche Bundesbank. Aufgabenfelder, Rechtlicher Rahmen, Geschichte*. Frankfurt am Main: Deutsche Bundesbank.

Duckenfield, M. (1999). Bundesbank-government Relations in Germany in the 1990s: From GEMU to EMU. *West European Politics*, 22(3), 87–108.

European Central Bank (2011). *The Monetary Policy of the ECB*. Frankfurt am Main: ECB.

Fase, M.M.G. (1998). *On Money and Credit in Europe. The Selected Essays of Martin M.G. Fase.* Cheltenham: Edward Elgar.

Flink, S. (1930). *The German Reichsbank and Economic Germany.* New York: Greenwood Press.

Fernández-Albertos, J. (2015). The Politics of Central Bank Independence. *Annual Review of Political Science*, 18, 217–237.

Goodman, J.B. (1989). Monetary Politics in France, Italy, and Germany. In: Guerrieri, P. and P.C. Padoan (Eds.), *The Political Economy of European Integration.* New York: Harvester Wheatsheaf.

Goodman, J.B. (1992). *Monetary Sovereignty. The Politics of Central Banking in Western Europe.* Ithaca: Cornell University Press.

Hetzel, R.L. (2002). German Monetary History in the Second Half of the Twentieth Century: From the Deutsche Mark to the Euro. Federal Reserve Bank of Richmond *Economic Quarterly*, 88(2), 29–64.

Holtfrerich, C.-L. (1986). *The German Inflation 1914–1923: Causes and Effects in International Perspective.* Berlin: Walter de Gruyter.

Holtfrerich, C. (1999). Monetary Policy under Fixed Exchange Rates (1948–70). In: Deutsche Bundesbank (Ed.), *Fifty Years of the Deutsche Mark.* Oxford: Oxford University Press, pp. 55–100.

Issing, O. (1993). Central Bank Independence and Monetary Stability. The Institute of Economic Affairs, Occasional Paper 89, London: IAE.

Issing, O. (2008). *The Birth of the Euro.* Cambridge/New York: Cambridge University Press.

Issing, O., V. Gaspar, O. Tristani and D. Vestin (2005). *Imperfect Knowledge and Monetary Policy.* The Stone Lectures in Economics. Cambridge: Cambridge University Press.

James, H. (1999). The Reichsbank 1876–1945. In: Deutsche Bundesbank (Ed.), *Fifty Years of the Deutsche Mark.* Oxford: Oxford University Press, pp. 3–53.

James, H. (2012). *Making the European Monetary Union.* Cambridge, MA: Belknap Press of Harvard University Press.

Kennedy, E. (1998). *The Bundesbank.* Washington, DC: American Institute for Contemporary German Studies.

Lohmann, S. (1997). Partisan Control of the Money Supply and Decentralized Appointment Powers. *European Journal of Political Economy*, 13, 225–246.

Maier, P. and J. de Haan (2000). How Independent is the Bundesbank Really? A Survey. In: de Haan, J. (Ed.), *The History of the Bundesbank: Lessons for the ECB.* Routledge: London, pp. 6–42.

Marsh, D. (1992). *The Bundesbank. The Bank that Rules Europe.* London: Heinemann.

National Monetary Commission (1910). *The Reichsbank 1876–1900.* 61st Congress, Second Session, Document 408.

Neumann, M.J.M. (1999). Monetary Stability: Threat and Proven Response. In: Deutsche Bundesbank (Ed.), *Fifty Years of the Deutsche Mark.* Oxford: Oxford University Press, pp. 269–306.

Schacht, H. (1967). *The Magic of Money.* London: Oldbourne.

Schenkluhn, B. (1985). *Konjunkturpolitik und Wahlen.* Bergisch Gladbach: Verlag Josef Eul.

Stern, K. (1999). The Note-issuing Bank Within the State Structure. In: Deutsche Bundesbank (Ed.), *Fifty Years of the Deutsche Mark*. Oxford: Oxford University Press, pp. 103–164.

von Hagen, J. (1999). A New Approach to Monetary Policy (1971–8). Deutsche Bundesbank (Ed.), *Fifty Years of the Deutsche Mark*. Oxford: Oxford University Press, pp. 403–438.

Weber, A.W. (2010). Monetary policy after the Crisis: A European Perspective. Keynote speech at the Shadow Open Market Committee (SOMC) symposium in New York City on 12 October 2010.

Webb, S.B. (1984). The Supply of Money and Reichsbank Financing of Government and Corporate Debt in Germany, 1919–1923. *Journal of Economic History*, 44(2), 499–507.

The People's Bank of China: From 1948 to 2016

Franklin Allen, Xian Gu, and Jun "QJ" Qian*

13.1 Introduction

With China's rising role in the global economy and markets, economists have become more interested in understanding the complexity of its financial system development and the way its central bank conducts monetary policy. China's economic performance has been impressive over the past decades, with a high GDP growth and low inflation rate. In the meantime, the financial system also experienced rapid development in the last 20 years, with the central bank steadily putting forward financial reforms. One interesting question concerns how the central bank conducts monetary policy in order to promote economic growth with a much less sophisticated financial system than in developed countries. Another is how China's monetary policy decisions help deliver a good inflation performance, while policy is not officially targeting inflation directly.

Over the last half century, the People's Bank of China (PBC henceforth) gradually changed from a mixture of a central bank and commercial bank to solely the central bank. Although the mandates of the PBC have altered slightly over the years, its monetary policy has continuously met challenges in different phases of economic development. While deeper structural reforms may be the key determinants of long-run growth, monetary policy has an important role in creating a stable macroeconomic environment that is essential for those reforms to take root.

The goal of this chapter is to provide a comprehensive review of the development of the PBC, the decision process of the PBC as well as how the

* We thank Hua Kuang from the People's Bank of China for providing valuable knowledge concerning the PBC. We are also grateful to Tor Jacobson, Yi Huang and all the participants of the Riksbank conference on central bank history for helpful comments and suggestions.

PBC communicates with market participants and coordinates with lower-level governments and other authorities. Some studies suggest that interpreting monetary policy is difficult because the PBC frequently uses a multitude of instruments ranging from required reserve ratios, to benchmark lending and deposit rates to set policy (e.g. Chen, Chow and Tillmann, 2016). In this review, we address the following questions: (1) how the PBC has performed in the last half century relative to its mandates, especially in keeping prices stable and maintaining financial stability; (2) how its monetary policy has contributed to the country's remarkable economic growth; and (3) how the PBC has promoted financial reforms to liberalize the financial system and achieve economic transition.

The remaining sections are organized as follows: In Section 13.2 we briefly review the history of China's monetary system before the establishment of the PBC in 1948. In Section 13.3, we discuss the development of the PBC since its establishment. In Section 13.4, we consider the mandates and current organizational structure of the PBC. In Section 13.5, we discuss the main functions of the PBC, including formulating and implementing monetary policies, its communications with financial markets, maintaining financial stability (especially during special episodes such as the credit crunch in 2013 and stock market crash in 2015), as well as the financial reforms that the PBC has been putting forward in recent years. Section 13.6 concludes the chapter.

13.2 Brief Overview of the History of China's Monetary System before 1948

China had long experimented with the large-scale use of paper notes as fiat money, first in the Song Dynasty (960–1279), then in the Yuan Dynasty (1286–1368) and early Ming Dynasty (1368–1644) eras. However, the government's desire for seigniorage revenue had invariably led to the overissuance of paper notes, which further resulted in high inflation or hyperinflation throughout this period. Partly due to the "currency vacuum" in early- and mid-Ming, Japanese and Spanish silver started flowing into China from the 16th century (see, e.g. Yao, 2016).

With the continuous inflow of silver, the Qing Dynasty (1644–1911) utilized a "bimetallic system," where one *tael* (or "*liang*") of un-minted silver ingot was set equal to one thousand copper coins minted by China's monetary authority. The standard copper coin ("*Zhiqian*") was by design a currency to be counted rather than weighed. Therefore, the bulky and small-denomination nature of copper cash relegated it mostly to small and local retail transactions, while silver acted as the medium for large transactions or long-distance trade. Although there was no official central bank, the Qing Dynasty had a single minting authority centered in Beijing in charge of the production of standardized copper coins, as well as provincial mints regulated by the central authority (Ma, 2012).

After the Taiping rebellion in 1850–60, the opening of China and the subsequent establishment of various treaty ports along China's coast were to bring fundamental and long-lasting changes to China's monetary and banking system through the establishment of Western merchant houses and banks that engaged in money exchange and trade finance.

At the end of the 19th century, after military defeat, the Qing Dynasty made reforms in the monetary and banking systems to accommodate the new political reality. The first major event was the establishment of the Imperial Bank of China ("*Zhongguo Tongshang Yinhang*") in 1897. This was the first Chinese modern bank. Its creation marked the beginning of a vibrant era of growth of Chinese public and private banks in the 20th century. Following that, the Bank of Communications (BComm) and the Bank of China (BOC) were established in 1908 and 1912 respectively. The second event was the establishment of a silver standard at the beginning of the 1910s although the provincial governments and treaty port authorities had already started minting silver dollars on their own in the latter half of the 19th century.

During the regional warlord era of the 1910s and 1920s, Shanghai emerged as China's financial center, with both the Bank of China and the Bank of Communications going through a process of semi-privatization that significantly weakened their ties with the central government. According to Ma (2012), the 1920s marked the "Golden Age" of modern Chinese banks, with the total capital of Chinese banks significantly increasing in this era, which led to further important changes in China's monetary system. For example, China's domestically minted silver dollars ("*Yuan Shikai*" dollar) overtook the other foreign silver dollars. In the late 1920s, banknotes and deposits as a proportion of the total money supply increased dramatically with a corresponding decline in silver and copper. At the end of the 1920s, the institutional development of the banknote exchange system led to the fast growth of banknote issuance by the Bank of China and Bank of Communications. The growth and integration of monetary and financial markets in this era of political decentralization seems to have replicated the bottom-up growth that occurred across early modern Western Europe (Rawski, 1989; Ma, 2012).

The silver standard allowed China to avoid the worst effects of the Great Depression. Soon after the establishment of the Nanjing-based Republican government of China, the central bank ("*Zhongyang Yinhang*") was established in Shanghai in 1927. The *Central Bank Rules*, released subsequently, specified its functions as a central bank such as issuing notes and managing treasury funds. In 1933, the China Peasant Bank ("*Zhongguo Nongmin Yinhang*") was established by the Nanjing-based Republican government, being one of the largest four capitalized banks in this era together with the central bank, Bank of China, and Bank of Communications.

In cooperation with the banking community in Shanghai and strenuous negotiations with the US and UK, the Nanjing government succeeded in the well-known 1935 monetary reform, which established China's first national legal tender ("*fabi*"). Only the Bank of China, the Bank of Communications, and the central bank were allowed to issue *fabi*, authorized by the government. After that, the convertibility of *fabi* was no longer tied to silver but instead was linked to a basket of major world currencies at fixed exchange rates, which marked the end of the silver standard in China. In 1937, the Japanese invasion of China launched the Nanjing government on a frantic arms program, financed primarily by printing money, which resulted in hyperinflation. The note issue multiplied nearly 300-fold from 1937 to 1945 or on average by 100 percent per year, while prices rose even faster, to nearly 1,600 times their initial level, or an average of more than 150 percent per year (Yang, 1985; Friedman, 1992). In a final desperate measure, the Republican government announced a currency reform and created the "Gold Yuan" to stabilize prices, but the reform failed. On the other hand, after the set-up of the provisional central government of the Chinese Soviet Republic in 1931, the Chinese Soviet Republic National Bank that was responsible for issuing currency was also established in the revolutionary base area. With the end of the civil war, the Communists started to establish the People's Bank of China from 1947.

13.3 The History of the PBC

China's banking system before the economic reform in the 1980s was characterized by an all-inclusive mono-bank system established in the 1950s, under which the PBC served as both a central bank and a commercial bank. In 1984, the PBC switched to being only the central bank and just kept the administrative functions of the banking system, with the status and mandates legally confirmed in 1995. In this section, we give a review of the history of the PBC since its establishment.

13.3.1 The Establishment of the PBC: 1948–1952

The People's Bank of China was established in Shijiazhuang of Hebei Province on December 1, 1948, right before the foundation of the People's Republic of China in 1949. The Bank was established by merging together the North China Bank (*"Huabei Bank"*), the North Sea Bank (*"Beihai Bank"*) and the Northwest Farmer Bank (*"Xibei Nongye Bank"*). Later in February 1949, the PBC was moved to Beijing. Hanchen Nan was appointed as the first president of the Bank. The legal tender was unified to the Renminbi ("RMB" henceforth).

After the PBC's move to Beijing, its four-level organizational system including the headquarters, regional head offices, branches and sub-branches was roughly established. The regional head offices were located at the offices of local governments, regulated directly by the headquarters in Beijing and guided by the local governments (or the local military and political committee) contemporaneously. The regional head offices were also responsible for the branches and sub-branches in their own region. By the end of 1949, four regional head offices including the East China office, the Middle South office, the Northwest office and the Southwest office, 40 provincial- or city-level branches, as well as more than 1,200 county-level sub-branches and offices were built up throughout the country.

In September 1949, the *Law of the Central People's Government of the People's Republic of China* was passed by the Chinese People's Political Consultative Conference, which brought the PBC into the organ directly under the Government Administration Council of the Central People's Government. The Law also documented that the PBC should be regulated directly by the Finance and Economic Committee and perform duties as the State Bank, responsible for issuing currency, managing treasury funds, administering financial activities, maintaining financial stability, and restoring the economy and rebuilding the country.

In 1951, the PBC asserted a claim of "positive development of credit cooperation" and started the pilot of rural credit cooperatives. By the end of 1953, more than 9,400 credit cooperatives, 20,000 credit mutual-aid cooperatives, and 3,000 credit departments of the supply-and-marketing cooperatives (*"Gongxiaoshe"*) had been built up, helping peasants solve the funding problems in production and enhancing the development of the Agricultural Cooperative Movement. In addition, the People's Insurance Company of China (PICC) was established, which constituted an integrated financial system with the BOC and BComm. In May 1952, to streamline financial institutions, the Agricultural Cooperative Bank (ACB) was incorporated into the PBC. In the same year, the Foreign Business Bureau of the PBC was merged together with the BOC; moreover, both the BComm and the insurance companies started to be regulated by the Ministry of Finance, suggesting PBC's progress to a unitary system.

13.3.2 The PBC in the Planned Economy: 1953–1977

For the large-scale economic development from 1953 to 1977, China gradually built up a highly centralized financial organizational structure and management system, as well as a top-down system of the PBC, to absorb, mobilize, centralize, and allocate credit. During these years, the PBC took the responsibilities of both managing the financial system and issuing currency.

In 1954, all the regional head offices were revoked and instead the head office in Beijing started to regulate the branches in provinces, autonomous regions, and municipalities directly, which formed a vertical management system and further strengthened the centralized system. The Agricultural Bank of China (ABC) was incorporated into the PBC as the Rural Financial Department in 1957, aiming to manage the national rural financial business. By merging together the financial institutions, the PBC became a "super bank" which undertook the dual roles of a central bank and a commercial bank. As documented by Liu (1980), it acted as the "center of cash, credit and settlement," from which currency and credit were issued, into which cash held by urban residents, and credit held by state enterprises and institutions were deposited, and through which the payments within the state sector were cleared. Under the mono-bank system during this period, the authority of currency issuance and loan decision belonged to the State Council. The banking system was not independent, and just an organ of the government (Yi, 1992).[1] The decision of money supply was subordinated to the implementation of output targets in the central plan. As most capital investment projects were financed by the budget allotments, the primary objective of the credit plan was to provide working capital to enterprises.

In 1962, to guarantee that the PBC could play an active and positive role in the national economy, the government clarified the administrative hierarchy of the PBC by documenting that the PBC head office in Beijing

---

[1] The mono-bank system of the PBC during this period is different from the first 100 years of the Riksbank, where there was no other bank. Some commercial banks such as BOC and BComm were still exerting commercial banking functions with a focus on special areas in these years.

was altered from a department directly under the State Council to an affiliated department of the State Council and the branches of the PBC were in the same hierarchy with the economic departments of local governments. In August 1977, the PBC hosted the session of the national banks, after which the *Regulation on Improving and Strengthening Banking* was released by the State Council. The Regulation officially documented that the PBC was separated from the Ministry of Finance as a top-tier unit of the State Council and that the branches of the PBC should be led directly by the head office in Beijing. At the end of 1978, the unified system of the PBC was comprehensively recovered.

13.3.3 The PBC During the Opening-up Period: 1978–2002

The objective of the economic reform and opening-up policy in 1978, according to the official documents, was to establish a socialist market-oriented economy based primarily on public ownership with planning as a guidance.[2] The reform of the banking sector was necessary to achieve this goal. The restructuring of the banking system was to give more freedom of operation and profit motives to specialized banks (commercial banks) while the macro monetary policy was controlled by the central bank (Yi, 1991).

In January 1979, the Agricultural Bank of China (ABC) was instructed to develop the rural economy. In March, the Bank of China was given the mandate to specialize in transactions related to foreign trade and investment. The State Administration of Foreign Exchange (SAFE) responsible for foreign exchange management was established in the same year. Domestic insurance business was recovered and the PICC was reestablished. In rural areas, a network of Rural Credit Cooperatives was set up under the supervision of the ABC, while Urban Credit Cooperatives (UCCs), counterparts of the RCCs in the urban areas, were also founded.

Non-bank financial intermediaries, such as the Trust and Investment Corporations (TICs) emerged and proliferated in this period as well. Correspondingly, the increasing number of financial institutions required a more centralized regulatory system as well as a comprehensive coordination mechanism. In July 1982, the State Council further emphasized that the PBC was the central bank as well as the national financial regulatory

---

[2] For instance, the *People's Daily* of October 25, 1987, published an article "Marching Along the Socialist Road with Chinese Characteristics" by Ziyang Zhao (the previous President of the Central Committee) on this.

authority under the control of the State Council. In August 1982, the Standing Committee of the National People's Congress and the State Council decided that the SAFE was separated from the BOC and further incorporated into the PBC. In late 1983, the State Council further documented the responsibilities of the PBC as the central bank and specified that the PBC started to serve as the central bank from January 1, 1984.

After the announcement of the *Interim Measures of Credit Fund Management* on February 15, 1984, the PBC started to build up the central bank system, which consisted of the first-tier branches in provinces, autonomous regions and municipalities as the local head offices, second-tier branches in prefecture-level cities, and the sub-branches in counties. All the branches and sub-branches took the responsibilities of treasury management as well as currency issuance and circulation in the districts.

However, based on the coexistence of a planned economy system and the market adjustment mechanism, the PBC was still in an early developing stage as a central bank. The main policy tool was the direct control of credit amount and currency issuance. Interference from other local government authorities largely affected the efficiency of macro control by the PBC. In addition, the PBC still granted special-purpose loans in order to support infrastructure or manufacturing sectors. As suggested by Yi (1992), the central banking system in China was at a very primitive stage, not because the central bank was not independent of the government, but because the central bank and specialized banks were not really separated. In other words, it was a mixture of a central bank system and an administrative command-driven, centrally-planned system that constituted the money supply mechanism with "Chinese characteristics."

At the end of 1993, the State Council announced the *Decision on Financial System Reform*, which further adjusted the responsibilities of the PBC as the central bank of China. The main changes included the set-up of the regulatory authorities of different financial sub-sectors (e.g. banks, non-bank financial institutions, insurance companies, and urban credit cooperatives), and the disentanglement of monetary policy from fiscal policy. From 1995, the PBC discontinued lending to the Ministry of Finance. If the Ministry of Finance planned to issue treasury bonds due to fiscal deficits, the PBC would coordinate on the timing or method of bond issuance, but would not purchase or underwrite treasury bonds or other government bonds. The policy-related activities were handed over to the three newly established policy banks: the China Development Bank (CDB), the Export-Import Bank of China (EIBC), and the Agriculture Development Bank (ADB) of China.

Afterwards, the central bank status of the PBC was legally confirmed by the passage of the *Law of the People's Republic of China on the People's Bank of China (PBC Law*, henceforth) in the Third Plenum of the Eighth National People's Congress in 1995. The Law stipulated the PBC's status, mandates, organizations, monetary policy, and financial supervision and further documented that the PBC was independent and should not be interfered with by governments during the implementation of monetary policy. The Law also announced the establishment of the Monetary Policy Committee (MPC) as the advisory council for the central bank. In April 1997, the State Council released the *Regulations on the Monetary Policy Commission of the People's Bank of China*, which stipulated that the responsibilities of the MPC were discussing monetary policies and making recommendations on the formulation or adjustment of monetary policy, the target of monetary policy, monetary policy tools, and coordination between monetary policies and other macroeconomic policies based on the defined macroeconomic target as well as the analysis of the macroeconomic situation.

13.3.4 The PBC in the Recent Years: 2003 to Date

At the end of 2003, the *Law of the People's Republic of China on the People's Bank of China (2003 Amendment)* and *the Law of the People's Republic of China on the Commercial Banks (2003 Amendment)*, which further disentangled the mandates of the PBC from those of the China Banking Regulatory Commission (CBRC), were passed by the Sixth Plenum of the Eighth National People's Congress. These laws further strengthened the PBC's mandates on the formulation and implementation of monetary policies. Since then, the PBC has no longer been responsible for the financial regulation of the banking, securities, and insurance industries, and only keeps the mandates of maintaining financial system stability and resolving systemic risks.

In the 2000s, the PBC continued to improve its organizational structure in the face of new challenges. In August 2005, the Shanghai head office was established to replace the former Shanghai branch to further improve the efficiency of decision making and the operation system of the PBC, deepen the financial market development in Shanghai, and move forward the build-up of Shanghai as an international finance center. Starting from 2008, the PBC still continues to improve the monetary policy system and strengthen the financial coordination mechanism.

13.4　The Mandates and Organization of the PBC

The status and mandates of the PBC were first legally confirmed in 1995 upon the announcement of the *PBC Law*. The amendment of the *PBC Law* in 2003 further strengthened the mandates and independence of the central bank. Overall, the PBC implements monetary policy independently without being interfered with by local governments, social organizations, and individuals under the leadership of the State Council. More specifically, the PBC has independence compared to other ministries of the State Council and local governments. For example, the PBC should not purchase and underwrite treasury bonds or other government bonds, or lend to local governments, non-bank financial institutions (unless it obtains the approval of the State Council to lend to some specific non-bank financial institutions) or any other institutions and individuals, or provide guarantees to any institutions or individuals.

According to *PBC Law (2003 Amendment)*, the mandates of the PBC include the following aspects:

(1) Drafting and enforcing relevant laws, rules and regulations that are related to its functions; (2) Formulating and implementing monetary policy in accordance with the law; (3) Issuing RMB and administering its circulation; (4) Regulating financial markets, including the interbank lending market, the interbank bond market, foreign exchange market and gold market; (5) Preventing and mitigating systemic risks to safeguard financial stability; (6) Maintaining the RMB exchange rate at an adaptive and equilibrium level; holding and managing the state foreign exchange and gold reserves; (7) Managing the State treasury as fiscal agent; (8) Making payment and settlement rules in collaboration with the relevant departments and ensuring normal operation of the payment and settlement systems; (9) Providing guidance to anti-money-laundering work in the financial sector and monitoring money-laundering-related suspicious fund movements; (10) Developing a statistics system for the financial industry and being responsible for the consolidation of financial statistics as well as the conduct of economic analysis and forecasting; (11) Administering the credit reporting industry in China and promoting the build-up of a credit information system; (12) Participating in international financial activities; (13) Engaging in financial business operations in line with the relevant rules; (14) Performing other functions prescribed by the State Council.

The People's Bank of China now consists of the PBC head office (PBCHO), the Shanghai head office, branches (including regional branches and operational offices, sub-branches in provincial capital cities;

sub-branches in quasi-provincial cities; sub-branches in prefecture-level cities; and county-level sub-branches) and some directly affiliated public institutions. The People's Bank of China head office (PBCHO) now consists of 20 departments or bureaus (Figure 13.1).

13.5 Main Functions of the PBC

As discussed above, the major responsibilities of the PBC include formulating and implementing monetary policy under the current framework, regulating the financial system and coordinating with financial institutions, and so forth. In order to improve the effectiveness of monetary policies and to develop the financial sector, the PBC has been engaging in strengthening communications with financial markets and financial reforms in recent decades. In this section, we first give a review of the monetary policy framework and tools of the PBC, and then discuss the financial reforms that the PBC has been engaging in since the 1990s.

13.5.1 Formulating and Implementing Monetary Policy

13.5.1.1 The Development of Monetary Policy Framework
During the time the PBC has served as a central bank since 1984, the framework of monetary policy has been revised and improved mainly from the direct control used previously to quantity-based adjustment, and then to price-based adjustment. Article 3 of the *PBC Law* (1995) further clarifies the monetary policy framework, by stating that "the aim of monetary policy shall be to maintain the stability of the value of the currency and thereby promote economic growth".

From 1984 to 1997 the monetary policy framework was built on the direct control of credit quotas. However, with the astonishing development of the financial system (e.g. the establishment of the stock market, interbank lending, and bond market, etc.) in the 1990s, the monetary policy framework was gradually transformed into one based on the indirect control of the amount of credit since 1998. Correspondingly, more instruments including open market operations (OMOs), deposit reserve requirement ratios, rediscount and central bank lending, as well as interest rate policies, were all used as the monetary policy instruments during this period. After the 2008 global financial crisis, liquidity in China's banking system shrank significantly because of the decrease of the trade surplus and capital inflows. In the meanwhile, active financial innovations (e.g. the rise of shadow banking) in recent years also reduced the efficiency of using

The People's Bank of China Head Office (PBCHO)	

Main Departments (or Bureaus)	**Institutions with Legal Person Status and Independent Business**

Main Departments (or Bureaus)

- ☐ General Administration Office
  (General Office of the CPC PBC Committee;
  Financial Regulatory Coordination Office)
- ☐ Legal Affairs Department
- ☐ Monetary Policy Department
- ☐ Monetary Policy Department II
- ☐ Financial Market Department
- ☐ Financial Stability Bureau
- ☐ Statistics and Analysis Department
- ☐ Accounting and Treasury Department
- ☐ Payment System Department
- ☐ Technology Department
- ☐ Currency, Gold and Silver Bureau
- ☐ State Treasury Bureau
- ☐ International Department
  (Office of Hong Kong, Macao and Taiwan Affairs)
- ☐ Internal Auditing Department
- ☐ Human Resources Department
  (Organization Division of the CPC PBC Committee)
- ☐ Research Bureau
- ☐ Credit Information System Bureau
- ☐ Anti-money Laundering Bureau
  (Security Bureau)
- ☐ Financial Consumer Protection Bureau
- ☐ Education Department of the CPC PBC Committee

Institutions with Legal Person Status and Independent Business

- ☐ China Foreign Exchange Trade System
  (National Interbank Funding Center)
- ☐ General Service Bureau
- ☐ Party School of the CPC PBC Committee
- ☐ The PBC Graduate School
- ☐ Financial News
- ☐ Credit Reference Center
- ☐ China National Clearing Center
- ☐ China Numismatic Museum
- ☐ China Center for Financial Training
- ☐ Financial Information Center
- ☐ Zhengzhou Training Institute
- ☐ China Anti-Money Laundering
  Monitoring and Analysis Center
- ☐ Centralized Purchasing Center.

Corporations directly under PBCHO

- ☐ China Banknote Printing and Minting Co.
- ☐ China Gold Coin Incorporation
- ☐ China Financial Computerization Co.
- ☐ China Financial Publishing House

Figure 13.1 The structure of the PBCHO
Source: People's Bank of China.

quantity-based instruments (e.g. OMOs) to promote economic growth. The monetary policy framework has started to emphasize the role of price-based instruments (e.g. central bank lending rates). However, as China's economy and financial system have been under a gradual transition to a more market-oriented one, both price- and quantity-based measures have been utilized simultaneously (Xie, 2004).

13.5.1.2 Monetary policy Targets and Inflation

In conducting monetary policy, the PBC has certain goals, or ultimate targets, such as price stability and stable economic growth. In trying to reach these goals, the PBC uses intermediate targets that it cannot control directly but can influence fairly predictably and that, in turn, are related to the ultimate targets the PBC is trying to achieve.

The ultimate target of China's monetary policy has evolved since the PBC started to serve as the central bank of China. In January 1986, *the Law of the People's Republic of China on Banking Regulation (Provisional Regulation)* stipulates that, "the Central bank, commercial banks and other financial institutions should implement financial policies and guidelines; other related financial services should set the target of developing the economy, stabilizing the currency and improving the socialist economic welfare," which is the earliest statement of the monetary policy target. In the *PBC Law* (1995), the monetary policy target was legally set as "stabilizing the currency so as to improve economic growth". This definition was retained in the Amendment Law of 2003. Overall, these changes have confirmed that the contribution of monetary policy to the whole economy should be based on creating a good monetary and financial environment. Mehran et al. (1996) also interpreted it as a claim by the PBC that long-term economic growth can only be realized if long-term price stability predominates; in other words, price stability should be the main target of the PBC.

Before 1986, China relied on a centrally-planned economy with no explicit intermediate targets. Similarly to the US Federal Reserve and other central banks, which employed monetary targets to stabilize inflation in the 1970s and 1980s (Goodfriend and King, 2005; Goodfriend and Prasad, 2006), China started moving to a monetary strategy anchored on intermediate targets in the late 1980s. During 1986 to 1996, the most frequently used intermediate targets in China were total credit volume and cash in circulation. However, with the fast development of the financial system in the 1990s, the credit volume held by monetary financial institutions could no longer reflect the financial condition of the whole economy. In September 1994, the PBC started to regularly release different levels of money supply indicators (M0, M1, and M2) and in 1996, the PBC formally introduced the money supply into the intermediate targets. In practice, the PBC uses M2 as the main intermediate target and in the meantime monitors M0 and M1 for reference purposes.

However, for a variable to serve as an intermediate target of monetary policy, there has to be sufficient controllability of the variable itself and a relationship with the final target of price stability. In the case of the PBC, scholars cast doubts on the controllability of the monetary aggregates, mainly through the exchange rate regime (e.g. Goldstein and Lardy,

2007) and an unstable money multiplier (e.g. Xia and Liao, 2001). The exchange rate regime, with its de facto peg of the RMB to the USD up to July 2005 and the subsequent crawling peg, led to increasing foreign exchange inflows that had to be converted into RMB and thus increased domestic money supply and inflationary pressure in China. On the other hand, the instability of the money multiplier could also lead to unpredictability of the relationship between the money base and the monetary aggregate, which could make the task of targeting the money supply more difficult.

Hence, an interesting question regarding China's monetary policy is how the relatively low level of inflation was achieved without monetary policy targeting inflation. During the periods of 1980–2016, China experienced four episodes of inflation (1979–81; 1985; 1988–89; 1992–95) and two of deflation (1998–2000; 2009): (1) in the 1980s, annual growth of money supply and GDP averaged 24.5 percent and 9.7 percent respectively, and the CPI inflation rate was recorded at an average rate of 7.6 percent; (2) in the 1990s, the average annual growth of money supply and GDP stood at 24.9 percent and 9.9 percent respectively, and average CPI inflation stood at 7.8 percent; (3) from 2000 to 2016, the CPI inflation rate was on average 2.2 percent. Xie (2004) analyzes China's monetary policy for the period of 1998–2002 and finds that within a long-term horizon, money aggregates do not affect economic growth, but do determine the inflation rate in both the short and long term. Geiger (2008) assigns the achievements in controlling inflation to a well-managed mix of price- and quantity-based monetary instruments. It is estimated that up to 24 percent of the CPI can be influenced through price controls. More recently, the administrative window guidance, which has intensified since the 2003–04 expansionary economic cycle, was crucial for successful outcomes in the absence of a well-functioning interest rate channel of monetary transmission.

13.5.1.3 The Toolkit of Monetary Policy

The PBC's conventional monetary policy instruments consist of open market operations, deposit reserve requirement ratios, central bank lending and rediscounting, controlling the interest rate, and window guidance. After the 2008 global financial crisis, new liquidity management tools were also introduced, including the Short-term Liquidity Operations (SLO), the Standing Lending Facility (SLF), Pledged Supplementary Lending (PSL), and the Medium-term Lending Facility (MLF).

13.5.1.3.1 Conventional Monetary Policy Tools

Traditionally, there are mainly three categories of policy instruments employed by the PBC: (1) quantity-based instruments, such as open market operations (OMOs) and reserve requirement ratios (RRR); (2) price-based instruments, such as interest rates on bank deposits and lending, as well as on required and excess reserves, or central bank re-financing; (3) administrative window guidance, which the PBC also uses to influence bank lending but is not directly observable. These instruments may further influence interbank market rates, which can also be affected by other market forces in the financial system.

Since 1996, OMOs have been one of the most important instruments for the PBC. The PBC conducts open market operations mainly via reverse repo and repos, purchases and sales of government bonds, and the issuance of central bank bills, regularly on Tuesdays and Thursdays, and occasionally on other weekdays based on market liquidity conditions.[3] The *Announcements of Open Market Operations* are regularly released after the operations and the *China Monetary Policy Reports* summarize the open market operations by quarter.

The deposit reserve system was introduced by the PBC in 1984, first only for exerting the central bank's function of pooling and allocating funds. At the beginning, the PBC set different reserve obligations for the different deposits with regard to their origin and the institution actually holding the reserves. In 1988, the PBC combined all different reserve requirements and set one minimum reserve requirement ratio at 13 percent. The deposit reserve ratio was reduced from 13 percent to 8 percent in 1997 (Figure 13.2). However, excess reserves have been a common problem in China. Banks, especially state-owned banks, keep excess reserves for inter-bank settlement and liquidity management (see also Allen, Gu, and Qian, 2017).

In April 2004, the PBC introduced the differentiated reserve requirement system, linking the required reserve ratio with indicators such as capital adequacy ratio or asset quality. Later, in early 2011, after the global financial crisis, the PBC further introduced a mechanism to adjust the differentiated reserve requirement on a continuous and case-by-case basis. This mechanism encouraged financial institutions to operate prudently and to regulate credit supply from a counter-cyclical perspective

---

[3] Open market operations (OMOs) are a key instrument for central banks to implement their monetary policies. For example, the Federal Reserve and the Bank of Japan conduct open market operations on a daily basis; the ECB conducts weekly refinancing operations and ad hoc fine-tuning operations in the open market.

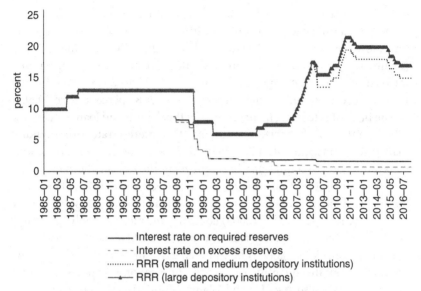

Figure 13.2 Reserve requirement ratio (RRR) and interest rates on reserves
Note: This figure plots the reserve requirement ratios (RRRs) for small/medium and
large depository institutions since 1985, as well as the interest rates on required reserves
and excess reserves since 1996. In 1988, the PBC combined all different reserve
requirements and set one minimum reserve requirement ratio at 13 percent. Before
2008's global financial crisis, the RRRs were the same for large and small/medium
depository institutions. After the crisis, the PBC first cut the RRRs for small/medium
depository institutions in order to support smaller banks. Since then, the PBC has been
employing the differentiated reserve requirement ratios.
Source: People's Bank of China.

by subjecting credit growth to the capital level in a macro-prudential
sense and by taking into consideration the systemic importance and
soundness of the financial institution as well as the stage of the business
cycle.

Central bank lending and rediscount are also important and traditional
monetary instruments in the toolkit of the PBC. After the 2008 global
financial crisis, the PBC clarified that the rediscount should be targeted to
financing demand from rural areas and small and medium-sized enterprises. In 2013, central bank liquidity loans and the Standing Lending
Facility (SLF) were introduced and then combined to provide liquidity
support to financial institutions that have complied with the requirements
of macro-prudential regulation. Given the loosened monetary policy in
2016, the ratio of the claims on depository and other financial institutions

over the total central bank assets rose to 26 percent from less than 10 percent during the period 2008 to 2015. If we do a comparison of the breakdown of central bank assets between the PBC and the US Fed (Figure 13.3), we can see that for the PBC, foreign exchange accounted for over 75 percent of the total assets from 2009 to 2015; while for the US Fed, securities held outright account for over 85 percent since 2009.

The interest rate instruments consist of the deposit and loan benchmark interest rates for financial institutions, the interest rates for liquidity management instruments (e.g., SLF, MLF, etc.), as well as the central bank lending or discount rates. In recent years, the PBC has been gradually implementing interest rate liberalization (see Section 13.5.4.2). The benefits of price-based measures have also been confirmed in some recent studies. For instance, Zhang (2009) compares the money supply (quantity) rule and interest rate (price) rule in China in a DSGE model and argues that the price rule is likely to be more effective in managing the macroeconomy than the quantity rule, with the economy experiencing less fluctuations (see also, e.g., He and Wang, 2012, 2013; Zhang, 2012).

Administrative window guidance is also one important conventional monetary policy tool of the PBC, aimed at improving credit structure. The framework for Chinese window guidance was closely modeled on the Japanese system, which had been in place for more than 40 years until its suspension in the early 1990s (Liao and Tapsoba, 2014; Itoh, Koik, and Shizume, 2015). Window guidance may take the form of meetings with commercial banks to convey the intuition of credit policy and the potential risks. In accordance with the requirement for differentiated credit policies, the PBC guides financial institutions to enhance financial support to key industries, areas and, regions, including key industrial rejuvenation programs, energy conservation and environmental protection, emerging strategic industries, and the service sector. It also provides guidance to cut back lending to high energy-consuming and polluting industries and industries with excessive capacity and restricts unauthorized lending to local government financing platforms as well as to implement a differentiated mortgage policy to promote the healthy and stable development of the property market.

13.5.1.3.2 New Liquidity Management Tools

In recent years, capital flows have been more volatile for China. In order to smooth the more frequent fluctuations in supply and demand for short-term liquidity in the banking system, from 2013 to 2014, the PBC launched several new liquidity management tools.

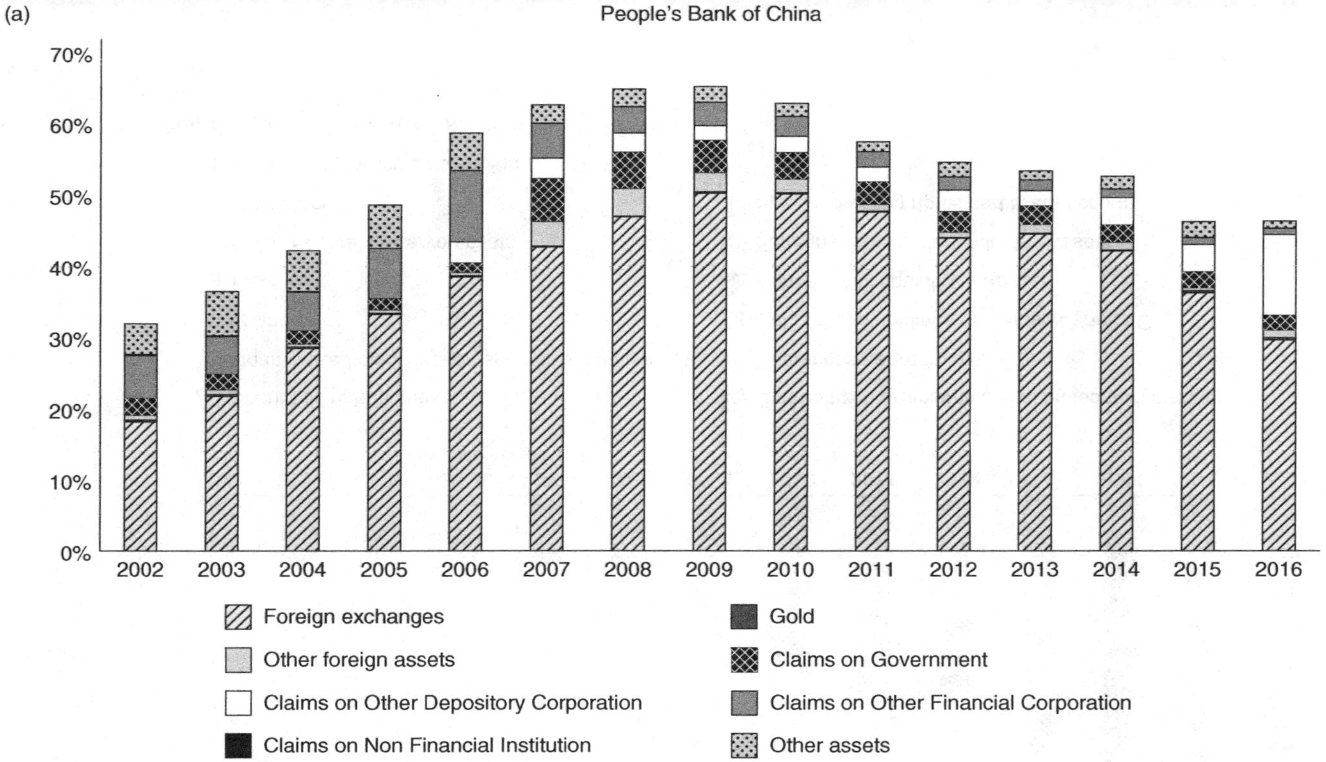

(a)

People's Bank of China

Figure 13.3 Breakdown of central bank assets: PBC vs Fed

Figure 13.3-a and 13.3-b plot the breakdown of the central bank assets of the PBC and the US Fed (scaled by the volumes of GDP) from 2002 to 2016

Figure 13.3-a Breakdown of assets (PBC)

Note: Data shown are scaled by GDP.

Source: People's Bank of China.

435

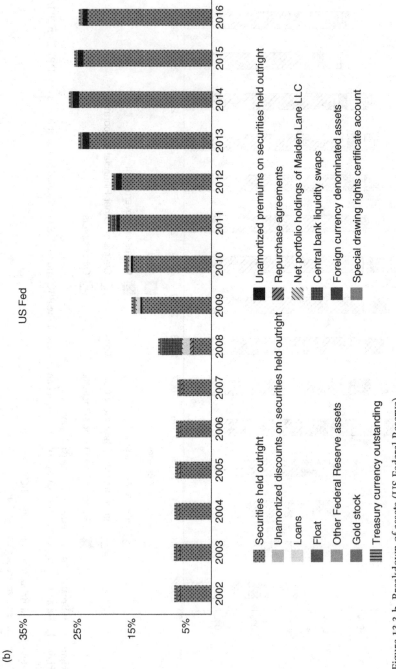

Figure 13.3-b Breakdown of assets (US Federal Reserve)
Note: Data shown are scaled by GDP.
Source: Federal Reserve Board.

The Short-term Liquidity Operations (SLOs) were introduced in early 2013, to manage the temporary liquidity fluctuations in the banking system on a discretionary basis. The SLOs are mainly repurchase operations with a maturity of less than seven days, but they can be extended if necessary (e.g. during holidays). A program similar to the ECB's Marginal Lending Facility (MLF) and the Bank of England's Operational Standing Facility (OSF), the Standing Lending Facility (SLF) was announced by the PBC in early 2013, to meet the large-scale demands for long-term liquidity of financial institutions. The maturity of the SLF is up to three months. In June 2013, the PBC conducted SLF operations in response to the liquidity crunch in the money market driven by a number of factors (see Section 13.5.3.2.1). The outstanding SLF totaled 416 billion RMB as of end-June, 2013 (Figure 13.4).

Later in April 2014, the PBC also introduced Pledged Supplementary Lending (PSL) to adjust the credit structure to promote adjustments and strengthen financial institutions' credit support to key areas and weak links in the economy, such as agriculture-related business, small and micro firms, and shanty town renovations. In September 2014, the PBC also launched the Medium-term Lending Facility (MLF), a policy instrument to provide medium-term base money to commercial banks and policy banks that comply with macro-prudential requirements.[4]

13.5.1.4 *The Decision Process of Monetary Policy*

According to the *PBC Law*, the Monetary Policy Committee is the advisory institution of the People's Bank of China in formulating monetary policy. As discussed in the previous section, it was documented in the *Regulations on the Monetary Policy Commission of the People's Bank of China* that the responsibilities of the MPC include discussing monetary policy and providing advice based on comprehensive analyses of the macroeconomic situation and targets. Currently there are 15 members of the MPC, 11 from different ministries (including the president and vice president of the PBC, the deputy secretary of the State Council, the vice chairman of the National Development and Reform Commission, the vice finance minister, the head of the State Administration of Foreign Exchange, the head of the National Bureau of Statistics, the chairman of the China Banking Regulatory Commission, the chairman of the China Securities Regulatory Commission, the chairman of the China Insurance Regulatory Commission and the president of the China Banking Association as well as three economists or experts in monetary

---

[4] For more details on the newly introduced liquidity management tools, please see also Allen et al. (2017).

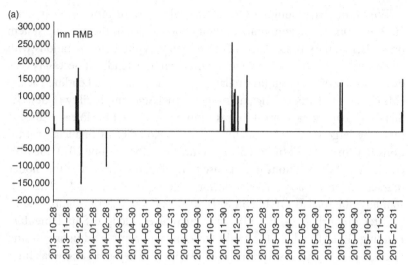

Figure 13.4 Volume of the operations of the new monetary policy instruments
Note: Figure 13.4-a and 13.4-b plot the volumes of the operations of the newly
introduced liquidity instruments since 2013. The Short-term Liquidity Operation
(SLO) is to manage the temporary liquidity fluctuations in the banking system.
The Standing Lending Facility (SLF) is to meet the large-scale demands for long-term
liquidity of financial institutions. The Pledged Supplementary Lending (PSL) is to
adjust the credit structure and the Medium-term Lending Facility (MLF) is to provide
medium-term base money to commercial banks and policy banks.
Figure 13.4-a SLOs operation volume
Source: People's Bank of China.

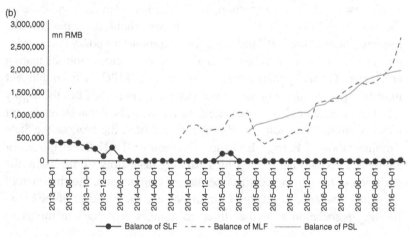

Figure 13.4-b Balance of SLF, MLF and PSL
Source: People's Bank of China.

policy). The president of the PBC served as the president of the MPC as well. Since 1999, the MPC has been hosting regular consulting conferences with academic experts.

The MPC has regular internal meetings quarterly, or, if suggested by the president or more than one-third of the committee members, it can have special meetings. From July 1997 to the end of 2014, there have been 68 regular internal meetings, and the discussions are recorded in the PBC MPC Meeting Minutes, which are submitted to the State Council. After MPC internal meetings, press releases are posted on the website of the PBC to improve transparency and guide market expectations.[5]

13.5.2 Forward Guidance and Communication with the Financial Market

The understanding of expectation guidance and central bank communications has been largely improved in the last two decades (see, e.g., Blinder, 1998; Woodford, 2001). For example, in May 1999, the FOMC of the Federal Reserve began publishing an assessment of its "bias" with respect to future changes in monetary policy in its statements. The ECB has also been fairly transparent ever since it was established in 1998. Given the zero-lower-bound constraints after the 2008 financial crisis, some central banks have experimented with forward guidance, i.e. the central banks communicate the expected future path of interest rates not as a policy commitment, but as a basis upon which to explain the policy responses based on the expected situation.

The PBC has also been engaging in improving transparency and communication with the public over the years. First, the PBC releases policy changes as well as an interpretation of the context and contents on its official website once a policy is carried out. Second, since 2001, the PBC has been publishing the *China Monetary Policy Report* quarterly, which gives a review and evaluation of the monetary policies in the previous quarter, the current macroeconomic situation and financial conditions, as well as the expectation of the macro-economy and future monetary policies. Third, the PBC has regular MPC meetings each quarter and announces a press release showing the MPC members' views on the macro-economy and monetary policies on its website after the meetings.

---

[5] For instance, the meeting press releases in 2016 can be accessed on the website of the PBC: www.pbc.gov.cn/huobizhengceersi/214481/214543/index.html. Accessed September 19, 2017.

Fourth, the president (or vice presidents) gives talks on monetary policies at different places, providing further guidance on market expectations. Moreover, when major policies are announced or sensitive financial data are released, the press secretary of the PBC will hold press conferences to address questions or interpret policies. The PBC also communicates with financial institutions and guides market expectations through window guidance (see Section 13.5.1.3.1), and monitors and supervises the inter-bank lending market, which plays a key role in the transmission of monetary policy and further affects financial markets.

13.5.3 Financial Stability

Maintaining financial stability is also one of the mandates of the PBC that the Law stipulated. After the 2008 global financial crisis, the PBC started to work on a macro-prudential management mechanism and built up the framework for monitoring and evaluating systemic risks. In this section, we will review the role and performance of the PBC in maintaining financial stability, especially during special episodes such as the credit crunch in June 2013 and the stock market crash in summer 2015.

13.5.3.1 The Framework of Maintaining Financial Stability

The modern literature on monetary policy underscores its role of fostering price stability. However, the recent events have served to emphasize the importance of its role in preserving financial stability as well (e.g. Stein, 2011). The framework of maintaining financial stability of the PBC includes, first, monitoring financial risks, as well as the development of financial markets and institutions (especially the systemically important institutions); second, analyzing the impact of changes in economic and financial environments on financial stability through an evaluation system in the central bank; third, taking measures based on the analysis results. For instance, providing liquidity support to and reorganizing illiquid financial institutions with healthy financial fundamentals as well as insolvent institutions. In the meantime, the PBC also communicates with the public on this by publishing *China Financial Stability Reports* periodically.

Since the 2008 global financial crisis, especially after China's entry into the tough development phase of "balanced transition" (the so-called phase of "the New Normal"), the ratio of non-performing loans has moved up sharply again and the shadow banking sector has been growing at a remarkable rate. Hence, it is necessary for regulators to monitor systemic risks (Chen and Zhou, 2016). The PBC has been strengthening the regulation of systemic risks through different channels. For example, it tracks the development of the macro-economy frequently, especially keeping an eye on the capability of debt repayment (household, corporate, and government sectors) and the potential risks of asset market bubbles. In the meanwhile, the PBC continuously strengthens its role on risk assessment and monitors the sub-sectors of the financial industry (commercial banking, securities, and insurance). To capture the key risks of China's financial system, a stress testing exercise was jointly conducted by the Financial Sector Assessment Program (FSAP) team and the PBC/CBRC team based on the largest 17 commercial banks in China.[6] In 2015, the PBC also started to run stress tests for the ten largest and representative securities firms (brokerage firms), of which the results are released in *China Financial Stability Reports*.

13.5.3.2 The PBC's Role During Special Episodes
The interbank lending market, the bond market, and the stock market experienced turbulence in the process of development. The PBC took a lead role in these special episodes.

13.5.3.2.1 The Credit Crunch in 2013
The credit crunch in 2013 was triggered by several factors coming together. In early May 2013, the SAFE of the PBC released an announcement to crack down on foreign exchange inflows to offset the potential shock from the Quantitative Easing (QE) exit of the Federal Reserve in the US. Hence, foreign exchange inflows dropped from an average level of 275 billion RMB during February to April, to 66.9 billion RMB in May, and further to −41.2 billion RMB in June. Moreover, the end of June is normally the time of examination (e.g. loan-to-deposit ratios, payment of reserve requirements) for banks, which further strengthened the liquidity tension.

Given the fast growth of shadow banking in terms of the issuance of wealth management products (WMPs) for medium-sized commercial banks since 2009 these banks met even more severe issues, as a large number of WMPs were due in late June. Although the large banks had excess reserves with the PBC, they refused to deploy them in the crash to help out small and medium-sized counterparts and make up for the PBC's absence from the interbank market. Therefore, the smaller shareholder banks were at risk in the short run. On June 20, the seven-day interbank

---

[6] For more details on this, please see also People's Republic of China: Financial System Stability Assessment, IMF Country Report No. 11/321: www.imf.org/external/pubs/ft/scr/2011/cr11321.pdf. Accessed September 19, 2017.

repo rate soared to 11.62 percent, the highest daily fixing since 2003, suggesting that liquidity fell sharply.

It had been widely expected by market participants that the PBC would quickly relieve the sharp rise in the interbank repo rate by injecting liquidity into the market. However, the PBC kept the market waiting until much later in the week. On June 25, the PBC finally announced that it had already extended liquidity support to some qualified financial institutions and would adjust bank liquidity properly, which largely resolved market confusion over the central bank's stance and ended the credit crunch in the interbank market.

Some anecdotal evidence showed that the PBC allowed the liquidity crunch to happen and last for several days as a warning to some domestic banks against taking too much risk on their balance sheets via excessive lending,[7] as some smaller banks tended to rely on borrowing from the short-term interbank market to finance their exposure to shadow banking activities, reflected by high-yield wealth management products. Therefore, the PBC's delay in relieving the liquidity crunch seemed to have a punitive tinge to it. In the meantime, the PBC could see around 2 trillion RMB in excess reserves, which was more than enough to meet settlement needs; therefore the liquidity shortage should not have occurred at the aggregate level.[8] As the new monetary policy instruments were introduced at the beginning of 2013, the PBC, in their *Quarterly Monetary Policy Reports*, also stated that it would further actively employ short-term tools such as the SLO and SLF to manage liquidity tensions, implicitly indicating that the liquidity crunch might be tactical.

13.5.3.2.2 Stock Market Crash in Summer 2015

Most recently, the Chinese stock market became a focal point for attention during the market run-up and crash from mid-2014 to summer 2015, which further stalled the US Federal Reserve's interest rate lift-off and created turbulence throughout global financial markets (Carpenter and Whitelaw, 2016). This large crash produced widespread panic in the market and pushed the Chinese government to implement a series of rescue policies, with the PBC playing a key role in these policies.

---

[7] For instance, a report from Barclays documented that the spike in interbank market rates is an indication of how serious policy makers are about tackling the financial imbalance in China – not least in the shadow finance system: https://wealth.barclays.com/en_ch/home/ thought-leadership/compass/compass-july-2013/china-s-liquidity-crunch.html. Accessed September 19, 2017.

[8] This is confirmed by a subsequent report by an official from the PBC: http://finance.sina .com.cn/china/jrxw/20130715/064516119954.shtml, accessed September 19, 2017.

Following 2008's global financial crisis, the Chinese stock market had been bearish until mid-2014. The CSI 300 index, which represents the broad Chinese A-share market, rose from 2,050 to a high of 5,178, then collapsed and lost 34 percent in 20 days, with 1,000 points of the index erased in one week alone. The collapse was first triggered by a regulation order from the CSRC on June 13, 2015, which banned all securities firms from providing facilities for off-market or shadow margin lending. In response, the CSI 300 index dropped from 5,221 to 4,637 from June 15 to 19, and then continuously plummeted by 7.3 percent on June 26 – 2,284 out of 2,456 listed stocks fell by 10 percent, hitting their lower bounds.

In the following days, the PBC responded to the stock market collapse with heavy interference and cooperation with other authorities. On June 26, it stepped in to stop a sell-off in the stock market, cutting the benchmark interest rate and deposit rates by 25 basis points each (to 4.85 percent and 2 percent, respectively) and the required reserve ratio (RRR) by 50 basis points. This was also the fourth time the PBC had cut lending and deposit interest rates since November 2014, and was also the first time since 2008 that it cut both interest rates and the RRR at the same time.[9] In response, the stock market rebounded a little. On June 29, the Ministry of Human Resources and Social Security and the Ministry of Finance released draft regulations for consultation, allowing pension funds managed by local governments to invest in stocks, funds, private equities, and other stock-related products. Up to 600 billion RMB (or 97 billion USD) could be channeled into China's struggling equity market.

However, there was still a mood of panic in the market, causing a strain of liquidity. Between June 29 and July 3, the CSI index lost another 13 percent in five trading days. On July 5, the CSRC announced that the PBC will "uphold market stability" by providing funds (about 41.8 billion USD or 260 billion RMB) to a state agency, the China Securities Finance (CSF), to lend money to 21 leading brokerage firms for the purpose of buying shares.[10] The PBC also announced that the CSF would receive liquidity to "hold the line" against the outbreak of systemic or regional financial risks, which suggested that the CSF was buying shares directly, using PBC money. On July 8, the CSRC banned shareholders with stakes

[9] For instance, see "People's Bank of China Cuts Interest Rates," *Wall Street Journal*, June 27, 2015: www.wsj.com/articles/peoplesbank-of-china-cuts-rates-1435397932. Accessed September 19, 2017.

[10] For more details, please see also an article from the *Financial Times* on this: www.ft.com /content/1c865eb4-22b4-11e5-bd83-71cb60e8f08c. Accessed September 19, 2017.

above 5 percent from selling shares for the next six months. On July 9, the market rebounded and the CSI 300 gained 5.8 percent. The market temporarily stabilized until August 11, when the PBC unexpectedly lowered the RMB exchange rate by almost 2 percent.

The official argument was that the Chinese stock market was not functioning properly in those months and market correction was inevitable, suggesting urgent government interventions were justified. Some recent studies have discussed the government intervention during the crash. For instance, Huang, Miao, and Wang (2016) find that the government purchase plan increased the value of rescued firms with a total net benefit of between RMB 5,697 and 6,635 billion by increasing stock demand and liquidity as well as reducing default probabilities. The Chinese stock market has been fast-growing and the rescue plans by the PBC, as well as other authorities, helped to stabilize the market during the crash, although at the cost of more uncertainty or volatility due to the trial-and-error approach in implementing rescue policies.

13.5.4 Financial Reforms

One of the enduring puzzles surrounding China's rapid growth is how it was achieved with an underdeveloped financial system. In the last two decades, China has accelerated financial reforms to liberalize the financial system, resulting in the significant development of both the financial markets and the banking system. The PBC has been involved in most of the successful reforms of financial institutions, the interest rate determination, and the RMB exchange rate regime, as well as the opening up of the capital account.

13.5.4.1 *The Reforms of Financial Institutions*

One of the most significant achievements of China's banking sector in the last decades is the partial privatization of state-owned banks. To put forward the reform, the State Council set up a leading team for the pilot of the shareholding reform of wholly state-owned banks. The office of the leading team was located in the PBC head office, responsible for studying and designing the reform scheme as well as coordinating with different participants. The aim of the privatization of state-owned banks was to improve the corporate governance structure and make state-owned banks more competitive. To achieve this goal, the PBC proposed to inject foreign reserves into these banks to improve their balance sheets in preparation for going public, and further cooperated with other ministries to study the scheme of establishing four state-owned asset management corporations to liquidate and reduce their non-performing loans (NPLs) and list the banks on the A-share and H-share markets. Till the end of 2010, all of the "Big-Five" banks (namely, the ICBC, BOC, CCB, ABC and BComm) have been listed on both A-share and H-share markets (see also, e.g., Allen et al., 2012, 2015).

13.5.4.2 *Interest Rate Liberalization*

Many central banks around the world have controlled interest rates and credit allocation in their recent history. While these restrictions were put in place to maintain financial stability and support development, they also reduced the borrowing costs of governments by imposing low interest ceilings, which may have further led to inefficient intermediation and lower growth (see, e.g., Caprio, Atiyas, and Hanson, 1994; Caprio, Hansan, and Honohan, 2001). Most central banks removed these restrictions after experiencing macroeconomic crises (Feyzioglu, Porter, and Takats, 2009). Similarly, repressed interest rates underlie structural imbalances and distortions in China's economy and, further, led to the fast growth of the shadow banking sector in recent years (Lin and Zhou, 1993; Hachem and Song, 2016; Wang et al., 2016). Interest rate liberalization is an essential part of China's price reform (He, Wang, and Yu, 2014).

Over the years, the PBC has played a key role in market-based interest rate reform, including the liberalization of interest rates in the money and bond markets as well as bank deposit and loan rates. In 1996, the PBC first removed restrictions on interbank lending rates. Later, both the at-issue yields of treasury bonds and policy banks' financial bonds were determined by market demand and supply. In January 2007, with the concerted efforts of the PBC and market members, the Shanghai Interbank Offered Rate (SHIBOR) was formally launched. Since then, the SHIBOR has been widely used in the market-based pricing of products. In April 2008, the PBC started to allow non-financial corporations to issue debt-financing instruments in the interbank bond market, based on market-based interest rates.

Deposit and lending interest rates have also been liberalized in succession in the last decade. Early in October 2004, the PBC decided to remove the upper limit of deposit and lending rates and keep only the floor rate as 90 percent of the benchmark lending rate. In July 2012, the floating bands of deposit and lending rates were adjusted, with the ceiling for deposit rates raised to 1.1 times the benchmark deposit rate, and the floor of the floating band for lending rates lowered from 90 percent to 80 percent and then to 70 percent of the benchmark lending rate. One year later, on July 20, 2013, the PBC removed the floor for the lending rate of financial institutions (with the exception of mortgage loans). In November 2014, the PBC expanded the floating band of deposit interest rates from 1.1 times the benchmark deposit rate to 1.2 times the benchmark deposit rate. On August 26, 2015, the ceiling of interest rates for time deposits beyond one year (excluding one year) was removed for financial institutions. Later, on October 24, the ceiling of interest rates for demand deposits and time deposits within one year (including one year) was removed for commercial banks and rural cooperative financial institutions, which marked the end of the interest rate controls and represented a key step in market-based interest rate reform.

As suggested by Feyzioglu, Porter, and Takats (2009), China meets several of the preconditions for successful interest rate liberalization identified by the experience of other countries (see also, e.g., He et al., 2014). Their model basically suggests that interest rate liberalization will likely result in higher interest rates, discourage marginal investment, improve the effectiveness of intermediation and monetary transmission, and enhance the financial access of underserved sectors. However, as documented by the PBC, the removal of administrative controls on interest rates does not necessarily indicate that the central bank will no longer regulate interest rates. Instead, the central bank will rely even more on market-based monetary policy tools and the transmission mechanism.

13.5.4.3 The Reforms of the Exchange Rate Regime

With the adoption of market-oriented economic system reforms and the opening-up policy since 1978, China's economy has become increasingly integrated into the world economy and its foreign exchange administration controls have been gradually eased. In the wake of the Asian financial crisis in 1997, China voluntarily narrowed the RMB exchange rate band to prevent competitive currency depreciation in the region and a worsening of the crisis. The trading band was further tightened in November 2000 and stood at about 0.01 percent fluctuation around the central parity of RMB/USD 8.277 until mid-2005, when conditions improved. On July 21, 2005, the PBC decided to change the RMB exchange rate regime and adopt a managed floating exchange rate regime based on market supply and demand with reference to a basket of currencies. The RMB/USD rate was adjusted to 8.11 at 19:00 (GMT+8)

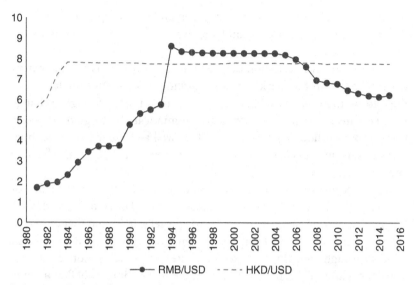

Figure 13.5 RMB and HKD exchange rate
Note: This figure plots the RMB/USD and HKD/USD exchange rate from 1980 to 2016.
Source: People's Bank of China; Hong Kong Monetary Authority.

on that day. Figure 13.5 shows the trends of the exchange rate of RMB to USD as well as HKD to USD.

Since the reform, the PBC has endeavored to improve the managed floating exchange rate regime; as a result, the flexibility of the RMB exchange rate has been greatly increased, with the currency mostly appreciating in real effective terms until recently. In June 2010, the PBC decided to further reform the RMB exchange rate regime, focusing on the role of market supply and demand with reference to a basket of currencies. After that, the RMB moved in both directions with greater flexibility. By the end of 2010, the central parity of the RMB against the USD had increased by 3 percent since the reform began. Given the larger deviation of the central parity rate from the market exchange rate – which can also sometimes last for long periods depending on market conditions – on August 11, 2015, the PBC announced that it would improve the RMB to USD central parity rate formation mechanism. This is regarded as the "2015–8–11 Exchange Rate Reform" by the financial markets. The daily quotes of the central parity that market-makers report to the China Foreign Exchange Trade System (CFETS) before the market opens should refer to the closing rate of the interbank foreign exchange market on the previous business day, and it should consider comprehensively the demand and supply conditions in the foreign exchange market and the exchange rate movements of the major currencies.[11]

However, one key question that remains unclear here is to what extent the PBC refers to the market-makers' pricing.[12] Soon after the launch of the reform, there was a short period of fluctuation in the foreign exchange market. The PBC then strengthened communications to guide expectations, provided liquidity to the market, as well as took macro-prudential measures to curb speculative trading and to prevent pro-cyclical behaviors and "herding effects" (see, e.g., Allen et al., 2017).

Some recent studies have also found evidence for the benefits of exchange rate liberalization. For instance, using a DSGE framework with Chinese characteristics, Chang, Liu, and Spiegel (2015) find that by allowing the exchange rate to float, the central bank can respond to external shocks through adjusting the exchange rate, which helps reduce external imbalances and shields the country from the adverse impact of fluctuations in foreign conditions, even though the capital account remains closed.

13.5.4.4 The Convertibility of the Capital Account

The current account in China was made convertible in 1996. Since then, the PBC (especially the SAFE affiliated with the PBC) has been promoting capital account convertibility, especially in recent years. For example, in order to invest abroad, domestic Chinese companies have to first get the approval of the investment project by the NDRC (National Development and Reform Commission) and Ministry of Commerce and then the approval of the funds transfer by the SAFE.[13] In late September 2013, the Chinese government launched the pilot enforcement of the Shanghai Free Trade Zone. Soon following that, the PBC released the guidelines to boost the Pilot Zone, with an emphasis on exploring ways to facilitate investment

---

[11] The PBC's official announcement can be found at: www.gov.cn/xinwen/2015-08/11/co ntent_2911052.htm. Shortly after the announcement, the PBC held a press conference on the 8-11 foreign exchange reform: www.gov.cn/xinwen/2015-08/11/content_2911053 .htm. Accessed September 19, 2017.

[12] The PBC did not give a clear description on to what extent it would follow the pricing by the market-makers in its announcement and press conference.

[13] The regulations on the approval of overseas investment projects by the NDRC was announced in the NDRC Order 9, 2014, with the official document available at: www .ndrc.gov.cn/zcfb/zcfbl/201404/t20140410_606600.html. Accessed September 19, 2017. The management of the overseas investments by the Ministry of Commerce was specified in the MOFComm Order 3, 2014, available at: www.mofcom.gov.cn/article/b/c/201409/ 20140900723361.shtml. Accessed September 19, 2017.

and financing remittance, promoting the convertibility of the capital account, promoting the cross-border use of RMB to allow enterprises and individuals in the Pilot Zone to use RMB price cross-border trades in a more flexible way, and deepening foreign exchange reform.

Capital account liberalization can attract more foreign capital; however, large-scale and sudden capital flows and foreign speculation significantly increase the likelihood of a twin crisis. Alessandria and Qian (2005) imply that banks can have a stronger incentive to limit the moral hazard concerning borrowers' choices of investment projects through the monitoring and designing of loan contracts following a capital account liberalization, even though the current efficiency (especially that of the state-owned banks) is relatively low. Other recent empirical studies have also found limits to the effectiveness of capital controls. For instance, Forbes, Fratzscher, and Straub (2013) argue that while capital controls may mitigate financial fragility, they are less effective for meeting macroeconomic targets. Chang et al. (2015) argue that as China's prevailing policy regime features capital controls, exchange rate targets and sterilized intervention, the optimal monetary policy involves a trade-off between sterilization costs and domestic price stability.

13.5.4.5 Discussions on the Possible Reform of Regulatory Consolidation
The institutional arrangements of financial supervisors vary by country. For example, in the US, the Federal Reserve plays a critical role in the US payments system, both as a supervisor and as a provider of whole and retail payment services; it also has substantial responsibilities of consumer protection, promoting financial stability and supervising banking organizations together with other agencies. In the Euro area, even though the ECB assumes responsibilities for monetary policy, some national central banks or other national authorities have retained substantial supervisory powers.

In the existing literature, the discussion of whether the central bank should also act as a supervisor has focused on issues of incentives and efficiency. The main case usually presented for separation is on grounds of conflict of interests (e.g. Goodhart and Schoenmaker, 1995; Bernanke, 2001). However, others argue that combining central banking and supervision in one agency could yield economies of scope. For instance, if supervisory activities gain information that is useful for carrying out monetary policy or other central bank functions, then granting some supervisory authority to the central bank may lead to better outcomes (e.g. Mishkin, 1995, 2000; Haubrich and Thomson, 2005).

In China, the current main supervisors include the PBC, the three Regulatory Commissions (CSRC, CBRC, CIRC, 3RCs henceforth) and SAFE, as well as the Ministry of Finance (as a major shareholder on behalf of the state), and the NDRC (as an economic planner). For years, there has been a substantial degree of institutional overlap and rivalry between the different supervisory authorities, which makes efficient regulation of the financial system difficult and sometimes can even block reforms. One illustration is the segmentation of Chinese bond markets, which undermined bond market development significantly.[14]

In order to strengthen the coordination among the PBC and 3RCs in the financial industry, a joint inter-ministerial meeting on financial regulation was launched by the State Council in 2013. However the mechanism didn't seem to solve the issue of separate supervision, such as how to settle disputes among authorities. A major step in this direction would be the creation of a super agency for financial regulation under the lead of the PBC, which has been discussed by both policy makers and academic researchers for years in China.[15] Recently, in the 2017 National Financial Working Conference, a State Council Financial Stability and Development Committee has been proposed, to strengthen the PBC's role in macro-prudential management and the prevention of systemic risk.[16]

13.6 Concluding Remarks

Although China is now one of the world's largest economies, how the central bank conducts monetary policy is little understood. The common perception is that the financial system in China is overwhelmingly

---

[14] There have been two separate bond markets in China, one called the interbank bond market, regulated mainly by the PBC and NDRC, and the other called the corporate bond market, regulated mainly by the CSRC and the two stock exchanges (Shanghai Stock Exchange and Shenzhen Stock Exchange). More specifically, the PBC governs bond sales and the NDRC approves bond issuance in the interbank market, mostly for state-owned and unlisted firms, and the CSRC oversees bonds in the exchange markets. For more details, please see Allen et al. (2015).

[15] For example, the PBC's website reported that both the vice president of the PBC, Gang Yi, as well as the chairman of SAFE, Gongshan Pan said that related departments have been studying the consolidation reform of the PBC and the three authorities but a concrete proposal is not clear yet. Please see: http://money.people.com.cn/bank/n1/2016/0307/c2 02331-28176498.html. Accessed September 19, 2017.

[16] According to Xinhua News, the Office of the Committee would be set up in the PBC: http://news.xinhuanet.com/fortune/2017-07/19/c_129658689.htm. Accessed September 19, 2017.

dominated by state-owned banks and that monetary policy is implemented by targeting the growth of bank credit primarily through quantity-based instruments. This chapter attempts to enhance our understanding of China's central bank system. We first review the history of the PBC as well as the history of the monetary system in China before 1948 to see how central banking was established and the PBC has evolved from the mixture of a central bank and a commercial bank to the central bank of China. The major mandates of the PBC are to formulate and implement monetary policies, guard against and eliminate financial risks, and maintain financial stability. To deal with challenges from the constantly changing internal and external environments, unlike the central banks in many advanced economies, no single policy instrument represents a good proxy of China's monetary policy and the PBC successfully combined many price-based, quantity-based, and administrative tools to help realize a relatively low inflation rate and fast economic growth as well as smooth short periods of liquidity crunches in the money market and turbulences in the stock market. Another achievement is that the PBC has been promoting financial reforms, including financial institution reforms, interest rate liberalization, and the reform of the RMB exchange rate regime actively over the past decades. This has led to the rapid development of China's financial system and may further contribute to economic growth and help balance growth in different sectors.

References

Alessandria, G. and J. Qian, 2005. Endogenous Financial Intermediation and Real Effects of Capital Account Liberalization. *Journal of International Economics*, 67: 97–128.

Allen, F., X. Gu, and J. Qian, 2017. People's Bank of China: History, Current Operations and Future Outlook. Working Paper on SSRN, https://papers.ssrn.com/sol3/papers .cfm?abstract_id=3018506. Accessed September 19, 2017.

Allen, F., J. Qian, and X. Gu, 2015. China's Financial System: Growth and Risks. *Foundations and Trends in Finance*, 9(304): 197–319.

Allen, F., J. Qian, C. Zhang, and M. Zhao, 2012, China's Financial System: Opportunities and Challenges, in *Capitalizing China*, R. Morck and J. Fan (Eds.), Chicago: University of Chicago Press, Chapter 2.

Bernanke, B., 2001. Comment, in *Prudential Supervision: What Works and What Doesn't*, Frederic Mishkin (Ed.), Chicago: University of Chicago Press, 293–297.

Blinder, A., 1998. *Central Banking in Theory and Practice*, Cambridge MA: MIT Press.

Caprio, G., I. Atiyas, and J. A. Hanson, 1994. *Financial Reforms: Theory and Experience*, Cambridge: Cambridge University Press.

Caprio, G., J. A. Hanson, and P. Honohan, 2001. Introduction and Overview: The Case for Liberalization and Some Drawbacks in Financial Liberalization, in *Financial*

Liberalization: How Far, How Fast?, G. Caprio, P. Honohan, and J. E. Stiglitz (Eds.), Cambridge: Cambridge University Press.

Carpenter J. and R. Whitelaw, 2016. The Development of China's Stock Market and Stakes for the Global Economy. NYU Stern Working Paper.

Chang, C., Z. Liu, and M. Spiegel, 2015. Capital Controls and Optimal Chinese Monetary Policy. Federal Reserve Bank of San Francisco Working Paper Series, 2012–13.

Chen, H., K. Chow, and P. Tillmann, 2016. The Effectiveness of Monetary Policy in China: Evidence from a Qual VAR. HKIMR Working Paper No. 06/2016.

Chen, X. and H. Zhou, 2016. Measuring Systemic Risk and Identifying SIFIs in Chinese Financial Sector. Tsinghua PBC School Working Paper.

Feyzioglu, T., N. Porter, and E. Takats, 2009. Interest Rate Liberalization in China. IMF Working Paper 09 171.

Forbes, K., M. Fratzscher, and R. Straub, 2013. Capital Controls and Macro Measures: What are They Good For? DIW Berlin Working Paper 1343.

Friedman, M., 1992. Franklin D. Roosevelt, Silver, and China. *Journal of Political Economy*, 100(1): 62–83.

Geiger, M., 2008. Instruments of Monetary Policy in China and Their Effectiveness: 1994–2006. UN Conference on Trade and Development Discussion Papers No. 187.

Goldstein, M. and N. Lardy, 2007. China's Exchange Rate Policy: An Overview of Some Key Issues. Peterson Institute for International Economics Working Paper.

Goodfriend, M. and R. King, 2005. The Incredible Volcker Disinflation. *Journal of Monetary Economics*, 52: 981–1016.

Goodfriend, M. and E. Prasad, 2006. A Framework for Independent Monetary Policy in China. IMF Working Paper 06/111.

Goodhart, C. and D. Schoenmaker, 1995. Should the Functions of Monetary Policy and Banking Supervision be Separated? *Oxford Economic Paper*, 47: 539–560.

Hachem, K. and Z. M. Song, 2016. Liquidity Regulation and Unintended Financial Transformation in China, NBER Working Paper No. 21880.

Haubrich, J. G. and J. B. Thomson, 2005. Umbrella Supervision and the Role of the Central Bank. Federal Reserve Bank of Cleveland, Policy Discussion Paper No. 11.

He, D. and H. Wang, 2012. The "Dual-Track" Interest Rates and the Conduct of Monetary Policy in China. *China Economic Review*, 23(4): 928–947.

He, D. and H. Wang, 2013. Monetary Policy and Bank Lending in China: Evidence from Loan-level Data. HKIMR Working Paper No. 16.

He, D., H. Wang, and X. Yu, 2014. Interest Rate Determination in China: Past, Present and Future. HKIMR Working Paper No. 04.

Huang, Y., J. Miao, and P. Wang, 2016. Saving China's Stock Market. The Graduate Institute Geneva Working Paper No. HEIDWP 09–2016.

Itoh, M., R. Koike, and M. Shizume, 2015. Bank of Japan's Monetary Policy in the 1980s: A View Perceived from Archived and Other Materials. Institute for Monetary and Economic Studies Working Paper No. 2015-E-12, Bank of Japan.

Liao, W. and S. J.-A. Tapsoba, 2014. China's Monetary Policy and Interest Rate Liberalization: Lessons from International Experiences. IMF Working Paper 14/75.

Lin, Y. and H. Zhou, 1993. Reform Financial System and Lift the Control of Interest Rates to Facilitate Long-run Economic Growth (in Chinese), *Reform*, 97–105.

Liu, H., 1980. *The Issues of the Socialist Money and Banking* (in Chinese). Beijing: The Press of Financial Economics.

Ma, D., 2012. *Money and Monetary System in China in the 19th-20th Century: An Overview.* Economic History Working Papers, 159/12. London: London School of Economics and Political Science.

Mehran, H., M. Quintyn, T. Nordmann and Laurens B., 1996. Monetary and Exchange System Reforms in China: An Experiment in Gradualism. IMF Occasional Paper No. 141, Washington, DC.

Mishkin, F., 1995. Symposium on the Monetary Transmission Mechanism. *Journal of Economic Perspectives*, 9: 3–10.

Mishkin, F., 2000. What Should Central Banks Do? *Federal Reserve Bank of St. Louis Review*, 82:1–14.

Rawski, T., 1989. *Economic Growth in Prewar China.* Berkeley: University of California Press.

Stein, J. C., 2011. Monetary Policy as Financial-stability Regulation. NBER Working Paper No. 16883.

Wang, H., H. Wang, L. Wang, and H. Zhou, 2016. Shadow Banking: China's Dual-Track Interest Rate Liberalization. PBC School of Finance Working Paper.

Woodford, M., 2001. Monetary Policy in the Information Economy, in *Economic Policy for the Information Economy.* Kansas City: Federal Reserve Bank of Kansas City, 297–330.

Xia, B. and Q. Liao, 2001. Money Supply is No Longer Suitable to Serve as Intermediary Target of China's Current Monetary Policy (in Chinese). *Journal of Economic Research*, 8: 22–43.

Xie, P., 2004. China's Monetary Policy: 1998–2002. Stanford Center for International Development Working Paper No. 217.

Yang, P., 1985. *Inflation in Old China* (in Chinese). Beijing: People's Publishing Co.

Yao, S., 2016. *China's Financial History* (in Chinese). Beijing: Higher Education Press.

Yi, G., 1991. The Monetization Process in China during the Economic Reform. *China Economic Review*, 2(1): 75–95.

Yi, G., 1992. The Money Supply Mechanism and Monetary Policy in China. *Journal of Asian Economics*, 3(2): 217–238.

Zhang, W., 2009. China's Monetary Policy: Quantity versus Price Rules. *Journal of Macroeconomics*, 31(3): 473–484.

Zhang, X., 2012. *China Monetary Policy* (in Chinese), Beijing: China Financial Press.

14

The European Central Bank

Otmar Issing*

14.1 Introduction

Among the major central banks in the world, the European Central Bank (ECB) is unique in several respects.

1. Established on 1 June 1998, it is by far the youngest central bank.
2. It was founded on the basis of an agreement between national governments. Never before in history had sovereign states ceded their responsibility for monetary policy to a supranational institution.[1]
3. This created a special, unique constellation. On one side a central bank, the ECB, responsible for a common currency, the euro, and a single monetary policy; on the other the participating nation states – today 19 – that largely retained their powers in the areas of economic and fiscal policy.
4. There is a vast cemetery of failed currencies destroyed by inflations, leading to the creation of a successor currency. The birth of the euro had a very different history. Countries or rather national currencies had to qualify by so-called convergence criteria – in the first place, low inflation – to participate in the European Monetary Union (EMU), thereby giving up their existence by being absorbed within the euro (for a comprehensive analysis, see Issing 2008).

* I am grateful for valuable comments and support by T. Jacobson, S. Kimmel, W. Modery, M. Rostagno and F. Schweikhard.

[1] The Latin Monetary Union or the Scandinavian Monetary Union in the 19th century, which are sometimes seen as a kind of predecessor, had a totally different character. The currencies of the participating countries were based on the same metal (gold and silver). A common central bank was not established. However, without a supranational authority in control of issuance these arrangements were doomed to fail. The case of Germany presents a clear case that political unification in 1871 went hand in hand with the creation of a common currency (Mark) and the establishment of a national central bank (Reichsbank in 1876).

14.2 The Rocky Road to EMU

The idea of having a single European currency had existed for a long time. A first concrete step was taken by the heads of state and government at the summit meeting in The Hague on 1 and 2 December 1969. In autumn 1970, the Werner Group, named after the then Prime Minister of Luxembourg, presented a 10-year roadmap for the establishment of an economic and monetary union.

However, in the course of the collapse of the Bretton Woods System and following turmoils in foreign exchange markets, the plan was dropped. A new, decisive step was taken in December 1978 with the agreement on the European Monetary System (EMS). The EMS turned out to become a system of fixed but adjustable exchange rates with the Deutsche Mark (DM) playing the role of the anchor currency. The dominance of the Bundesbank, de facto conducting monetary policy for 'Europe', was hardly a sustainable solution (Issing 2006). Foreign exchange crises were seen as a threat to the Single Market. And, finally, a common currency was hailed as a pacemaker to European political union as expressed already in 1950 by the French monetary expert Jacques Rueff: 'L'Europe se fera par la monnaie ou ne se fera pas.'

In 1990, the Committee of Central Bank Governors of the EU Member States unanimously approved a draft statute for a European central bank (see Tietmeyer 2005). One year earlier, the Delors Committee had proposed the creation of a monetary union in three steps. The final decision on the shape of EMU and on the starting date of 1 January 1999 was taken by the Heads of State and Government at the Maastricht summit on 9 and 10 December 1991.

14.3 The Convergence Process

The 'historical norm' for a currency area is the national territory: one country – one currency. This view was challenged by R. Mundell (1961), R.I. McKinnon (1963), and P. Kenen (1969), who analysed the criteria for an optimal currency area (OCA). Flexibility of prices and wages, and labour mobility were the main elements for identifying an economic area which would work with a common currency without coinciding with national borders. The OCA theory cannot be seen as a set of exclusive principles (Issing 2003). However, the group of 11 countries which joined the common currency in 1999 was far from being considered an optimal choice. Therefore, problems for an efficient functioning of EMU were looming from the start. Numerous economists raised concerns (Issing 2008). The direst warning was issued by M. Feldstein who went beyond economics to invoke risks of serious conflicts between the USA and Europe (Feldstein 1997).

The Maastricht Treaty stipulated that only those countries were to participate in the EMU that would fulfil some legal requirements (mainly their independence of the national central bank) and the following convergence criteria:

1. a low inflation rate;
2. sound public finances;
3. at least two years' membership in the EMS without tensions;
4. convergence of long-term nominal interest rates towards the level of (at most) the three currencies with the lowest rate in inflation.

These are all nominal variables – a fact which signals that real criteria as, e.g., formulated by the OCA theory were widely ignored. As a consequence, substantial heterogeneity was not taken seriously enough.

However, one cannot deny that some countries undertook enormous efforts to fulfil these convergence criteria. Whereas in the early 1990s substantial differences in inflation rates between the 11 countries still existed, the challenge to become part of the euro from the beginning triggered a remarkable convergence process of inflation rates to a level which was exceptionally low by historical standards (see Figure 14.1).

This holds also true for fiscal policies. The 1990s saw strong reductions in budget deficits (see Figure 14.2) albeit in some cases numbers were embellished by means of 'creative accounting'. Even before the inception of the euro, these acts set a regrettable precedent for the (non-)abidance by fiscal rules. In contrast to budget deficits, ratios for public debt to GDP diverged substantially (see Figure 14.3).

Overall, the EMU was burdened by a lack of fiscal discipline in several of its Member States. This was a bad omen for the compliance with the Stability and Growth Pact of 1997 which had been designed to monitor national fiscal policies on the European level.

An important, fundamental element of the institutional arrangement is the 'no-bail-out' clause (Article 125, Treaty on the Functioning of the European Union – TFEU) which stipulated that (in principle) the Community is not to be liable for or assume the commitments for national governments and other public entities. The same applies for Member States in relation to other governments.

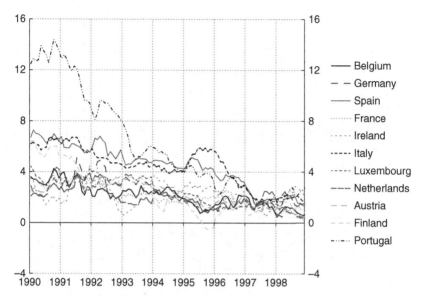

Figure 14.1 Inflation convergence 1990–1998 (annual percentage changes)
Note: Data for Belgium, Spain, France and Luxembourg are backdated with the fixed euro conversion rate used for weights provided by the ECB.
Source: Eurostat and ECB calculations.

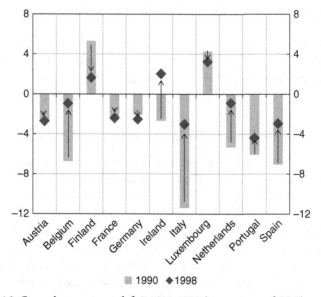

Figure 14.2 General government deficit 1990–1998 (percentages of GDP)
Note: Net lending (+) or net borrowing (-). Data for Germany for 1990 refers to West Germany. 1990 data for Spain not available, chart presents 1995 data.
Source: European Commission, Destatis, ECB calculations.

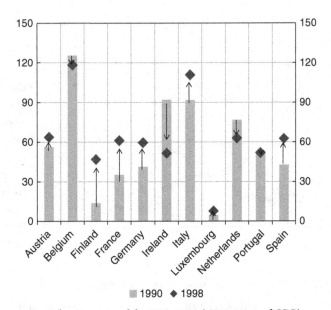

Figure 14.3 General government debt 1990–1998 (percentages of GDP)
Note: Data for Germany for 1990 refers to West Germany.
Source: European Commission and ECB.

It would not take long before fiscal policy turned out to be the 'open flank' of the EMU.

Substantial heterogeneity among countries also existed with respect to living standards. Luxembourg was on top of the league with a per-capita GDP in PPS terms, normalised to an average of 100, of 175.05, far ahead of Portugal at the end of the opposite tail (61.57) (see Table 14.1).

14.4 Birth of the Euro – a Historical Event

On 31 December 1998, the conversion rates between the euro and the individual currencies of 11 EU countries were irrevocably fixed and thus, with effect from 1 January 1999, the euro became the statutory unit of account. The conversion rates are shown in Table 14.2.

The birth of the euro marks a deep change in European monetary history. Although banknotes and coins in national currencies still circulated, they had become only representatives of the common currency, the euro. In January 2002, euro banknotes and coins replaced the national ones.

Eleven sovereign states had transferred their monetary sovereignty to a supranational institution, the ECB, and the birth of the euro implied the

Table 14.1 *Per capita GDP in purchasing power standards relative to the euro area average*

Country	Year	Per capita GDP in purchasing power standards
Euro 11	1998	100.00
Austria	1998	106.83
Belgium	1998	106.83
Finland	1998	92.11
France	1998	92.61
Germany	1998	98.50
Ireland	1998	97.66
Italy	1998	96.40
Luxembourg	1998	175.05
Netherlands	1998	103.55
Portugal	1998	61.57
Spain	1998	76.80

Note: The volume index of GDP per capita in purchasing power standards (PPS) is expressed in relation to the average for the euro area Member Countries (euro 11) set to equal 100. If the index of a country is higher than 100, this country's per capita GDP is higher than the euro area average (and vice versa). Basic figures expressed in PPS, i.e. a common currency that eliminates the difference in price levels between countries, allowing meaningful volume comparisons of GDP between countries.
Source: Eurostat.

Table 14.2 *Conversion rates*

Country	1 euro =	
Belgium	Belgian francs	40.3399
Germany	Deutsche Mark	1.95583
Spain	Spanish pesetas	166.386
France	French francs	6.55957
Ireland	Irish pounds	0.787564
Italy	Italian lire	1936.27
Luxembourg	Luxembourg francs	40.3399
Netherlands	Dutch guilders	2.20371
Austria	Austrian schillings	13.7603
Portugal	Portuguese escudos	200.482
Finland	Finish markkas	5.94573

Source: ECB (1999), 'The economic situation in the euro area at the start of Stage Three', Monthly Bulletin, January.

end for national currencies which had, in some cases, existed for much more than a hundred years. Although some national currencies had gone through periods of high inflation and currencies by reform had just kept their name, people felt a deep change at that time. The new currency was perceived as the symbol of a break in a country's history.

The decision to join the euro was deemed irrevocable. The Maastricht Treaty neither includes an option to abandon the single currency in the course of time nor a clause to expel a country from the monetary union. A national central bank and a national currency have been fundamental constituents of state formation (almost) everywhere. These elements were now transferred to a supranational institution – a transfer which deprived participating national states of important factors of sovereignty. Yet, giving up these competences did not result in the foundation of a European state, but rather meant an institutional arrangement unique in history.

The arrival of the euro had also an important impact on the international monetary system. As the currency of the second largest economic area in the world – measured by GDP – after the USA, the euro unavoidably would play a major role in international financial markets.

14.5 The ECB

The ECB is an institution of the European Union. Its foundation is based on the Maastricht Treaty. The Statute is laid down in a Protocol which is an integral part of the Treaty. Article 1:

'In accordance with Article 282 (1) of the Treaty on European Union, the European Central Bank (ECB) and the national central banks shall constitute the European System of Central Banks (ESCB). The ESCB and the national central banks of those Member States whose currency is the euro shall constitute the Eurosystem. The ESCB and the ECB shall perform their tasks and carry on their activities in accordance with the provisions of the Treaties and of this Statute.'

In the initial wording of the Maastricht Treaty, the sentence on the Eurosystem was missing. In choosing this wording, the Treaty's authors had obviously assumed that all EU members would also be members of EMU. Because this is not the case, the text of the Treaty had led to terminological confusion, since by ESCB it refers to the central banks of *all* EU Member States *and* the ECB, while at the same time in most places it refers exclusively to the central banks of those countries that actually are members of EMU (see Table 14.3). In the interest of clarity, the ECB introduced the term 'Eurosystem', comprising the ECB and the central banks of the countries belonging to EMU. In contrast, the term 'ESCB' always includes the central banks of all EU Member States. At the onset, 11 national central banks belonged to the Eurosystem. Today the number has increased to 19. The national central banks have a special character which differs from central banks in countries with a national currency. Their competences will be explained in detail.

The main tasks of the Eurosystem are laid down in Article 3:

- to define and implement the monetary policy of the Union;
- to conduct foreign exchange operations consistent with the provisions of Article 219 of that Treaty;
- to hold and manage the official foreign reserves of the Member States;
- to promote the smooth operation of payment systems and contribute to prudential supervision of credit institutions and the stability of the financial system.

Table 14.3 *The Eurosystem and the European System of Central Banks (ESCB)* [updated with current country composition]

EUROPEAN SYSTEM OF CENTRAL BANKS (ESCB)	General Council	Eurosystem	European Central Bank (ECB)	
			Governing Council	**Executive Board**
			Nationale Bank van België/Banque Nationale de Belgique	Lietuvos bankas
			Deutsche Bundesbank	Banque centrale du Luxembourg
			Eesti Pank	Central Bank of Malta
			Central Bank of Ireland	De Nederlandsche Bank
			Bank of Greece	Oesterreichische Nationalbank
			Banco de España	Banco de Portugal
			Banque de France	Banka Slovenije
			Banca d'Italia	Národná banka Slovenska
			Central Bank of Cyprus	Suomen Pankki – Finlands Bank
			Latvijas Banka	
			Bulgarian National Bank	National Bank of Romania
			Croatian National Bank	Sveriges Riksbank
			Czech National Bank	Narodowy Bank Polski
			Denmarks Nationalbank	Bank of England
			Hungarian National Bank	

Source: ECB.

Table 14.4 *ECB capital key of euro area national central banks*

National Central Bank	Capital key (%)
Nationale Bank van België/Banque Nationale de Belgique (Belgium)	2.48
Deutsche Bundesbank (Germany)	18.00
Eesti Pank (Estonia)	0.19
Central Bank of Ireland (Ireland)	1.16
Bank of Greece (Greece)	2.03
Bank of España (Spain)	8.84
Banque de France (France)	14.18
Banca d'Italia (Italy)	12.31
Central Bank of Cyprus (Cyprus)	0.15
Latvijas Banka (Latvia)	0.28
Lietuvos bankas (Lithuania)	0.41
Banque centrale du Luxembourg (Luxembourg)	0.20
Central Bank of Malta (Malta)	0.06
De Nederlandsche Bank (The Netherlands)	4.00
Oesterreichische Nationalbank (Austria)	1.96
Banco de Portugal (Portugal)	1.74
Banka Slovenije (Slovenia)	0.35
Národná banka Slovenska (Slovakia)	0.77
Suomen Pankki – Finlands Bank (Finland)	1.26
Total	70.39

Source: ECB.

In November 2014, the ECB assumed responsibility for the supervision of banks in the euro area. The Single Supervisory Mechanism (SSM) stipulates that the ECB directly oversees the 124 significant banks or banking groups. These banks hold almost 82 per cent of banking assets. Smaller banks are supposed to be supervised by their national supervisory authorities; the ECB can give instructions or possibly also become a bank's direct supervisor.

Under the SSM regulation, the ECB has also been assigned specific powers in the field of macroprudential policies. The Macroprudential Forum is composed of the Governing Council and the Supervisory Board of the ECB which is composed of the chair and vice chair, four members of the ECB and representatives of national supervisors. The Macroprudential Forum is supported by the Financial Stability Committee which comprises representatives of the ECB, national central banks and supervisory authorities. These committees in their composition are evidence of the complex structure of the Eurosystem. They provide platforms for a regular exchange of views to allow joint risk assessment and policy coordination between the ECB and national authorities.

The ECB has the monopoly on the issue of euro banknotes, that is, it has the exclusive right to authorise the issue of banknotes within the euro area (see Article 128 TFEU). Minting coins remains a right of Member States. Other provisions regulate the collection of statistical data or the external representation of the Eurosystem. The seat of the ECB is Frankfurt.

The national central banks are the sole subscribers to and holders of the capital of the ECB. The key for capital subscription reflects the respective Member States' shares in total population and GDP.

The net profit of the ECB (after deduction of contributions to a general reserve fund) shall be distributed to the shareholders in proportion to their paid-up shares.

The transfer of foreign reserve assets to the ECB is laid down in Article 30 of the Protocol: '... the ECB shall be provided by the national central banks with foreign reserve assets ...' and 'The contributions of each national central bank shall be fixed in proportion to its share in the subscribed capital of the ECB.'

14.5.1 The Single Monetary Policy

The set of tasks and their formulation reflect the special situation of the ECB as a new central bank in the context of a community of sovereign states in which responsibilities are distributed across European and national levels.

The case of monetary policy, however, is cut-and-dried: there is only one single monetary policy for the euro area, which is set in a centralised decision-making process.

The monetary policy of the ECB rests on three fundaments:

1. primacy of price stability;
2. central bank independence;
3. prohibition of monetary financing.

14.5.1.1 Primacy of Price Stability

'The primary objective of the European System of Central Banks (hereinafter referred to as ESCB) shall be to maintain price stability. Without prejudice in the objective of price stability, the ESCB shall support the general economic policies in the Union with a view to contributing to the achievement of the objectives of the Union as laid down in Article 3 of the Treaty on European Union. The ESCB shall act in accordance with the principle of an open market economy with free competition, favouring an efficient allocation of resources and in compliance with the principles set out in Article 119' (Article 127 TFEU).

Article 3 contains a long list of mainly very general goals. The most relevant ones in this context are 'balanced economic growth and price stability, a highly competitive social market economy, aiming at full employment and social progress'.

Article 119 (TFEU) is as follows:

1. 'For the purpose set out in Article 3 of the Treaty on European Union, the activities of the Member States and the Union shall include, as provided in the Treaties, the adaption of an economic policy which is based on the close coordination of Member States' economic policies, on the internal market, and on the definition of common objectives, and conducted in accordance with the principle of an open market economy with free competition.'

2. In addition, paragraph 2 of this article stipulates 'the definition and conduct of a single monetary policy and exchange-rate policy the primary objective of both of which shall be to maintain price stability ...'

3. 'These activities of the Member States and the Union shall entail compliance with the following guiding principles: stable prices, sound public finances and monetary conditions, and a sustainable balance of payments.'

These complex and partly repetitive legal prescriptions reflect the character of EMU as an institutional arrangement with one central bank and a single monetary policy on the one hand, and many Member States on the other.

The competences with regard to foreign exchange-rate policy are laid down in Article 219 (TFEU). After a complex consulting process that includes the ECB and the European Commission, the European Council can unanimously conclude formal agreements on an exchange-rate system for the euro in relation to the currencies of third states and adapt, adjust or abandon the central rates of the euro within the exchange-rate system. In the absence of such an exchange-rate system, following a similar consulting process, the European Council can formulate general orientations for exchange-rate policy. For all these cases, the decision by the European Council shall be without prejudice to the primary objective of the ESCB to maintain price stability.

So far, such actions were not taken by the Council. It is an open question to what extent the priority for price stability could be preserved if the foreign exchange rate of the euro was fixed against the currency of third states. The 'impossible triangle' of fixed exchange rate, price stability and an independent monetary policy cannot be overcome by a legal act. An initiative to submit the decision by the European Council to majority voting failed. The condition of unanimity among Member States sets a high hurdle for a decision in favour of a fixed exchange-rate regime.

14.5.1.2 Central Bank Independence

'When exercising the powers and carrying out the tasks and duties conferred upon them by the Treaties and the Statute of the ESCB and of the ECB, neither the European Central Bank, nor a national central bank, nor any member of their decision-making bodies shall seek or take instructions from Union institutions, bodies, offices or agencies and the governments of the Member States or from any other body. The Union institutions, bodies, offices or agencies and the governments of the Member States undertake to respect this principle and not to seek to influence the members of the decision-making bodies of the European Central Bank or of the national central banks in the performance of their tasks' (Article 130 TFEU).

This extensive formalisation again reflects the special character of EMU. From a legal point, the independence of the ECB/Eurosystem has the strongest fundament as it could be changed only by a unanimous decision by all governments, ratified by parliaments and in several cases supported by a referendum. The article also makes very clear that the ECB can claim 'independence' only for exercising its mandate. There have been many occasions when 'advice' or even pressure from outside was hardly in compliance with the status of independence laid down in the article.

14.5.1.3 Prohibition of Monetary Financing

'Overdraft facilities or any other type of credit facility with the European Central Bank or with the central banks of the Member States . . . in favour of Union institutions, bodies, offices or agencies, central governments, regional, local or other public authorities, other bodies governed by public law, or public undertakings of Member States shall be prohibited, as shall the purchase directly from them by the European Central Bank or national central banks of debt instruments' (Article 123 (1) TFEU).

This prohibition of monetary financing of public entities of all kinds seems to imply strong protection against pressure from outside. On the other hand, the discussion about the purchase of government bonds in the context of 'quantitative easing' has demonstrated that the distinction between direct purchases and intervention in secondary markets can become rather meaningless economically. As buying government bonds must be an option for open market operations of a central bank, their justification can be assessed by considering the intention and impact of a taken measure: a monetary policy decision is directed to influence the market in order to maintain price stability, whereas an act with the aim to support governments by lowering their financing costs would be prohibited. The cases before the European Court of Justice and the German Constitutional Court have, however, demonstrated that this distinction is not clear-cut – at least not before the court.

14.5.2 The Decision-making Bodies

The monetary policy of the ECB is based on a collective decision-making system (Articles 129 and 132 TFEU).

The Governing Council is the ECB's highest decision-making body (see Figure 14.4). It comprises the six members of the Executive Board and the governors of the national central banks which belong to the Eurosystem. The President of the EU and a member of the Commission may participate in meetings of the Governing Council, but without having the right to vote (Article 284 (1) TFEU).

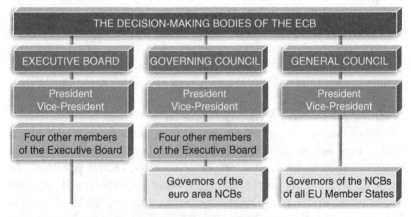

Figure 14.4 The decision-making bodies of the ECB
Source: ECB (2011), *The Monetary Policy of the ECB.*

The Governing Council and the Executive Board are chaired by the ECB President.

The main task of the Governing Council is to formulate the monetary policy of the euro area, which includes taking decisions on intermediate monetary objectives, key interest rates and the supply of reserves for banks in the Eurosystem.

The Executive Board consists of the President, the Vice-President and four other members. They are appointed by the European Council (for a period of eight years without the option of reappointment), acting by qualified majority, on a recommendation from the Council of the EU, since the Treaty of Lisbon (Article 283 (2) TFEU).

The Executive Board prepares the meetings of the Governing Council, implements monetary policy, is responsible for the current business of the ECB, and assumes certain powers delegated to it by the Governing Council.

The General Council of the ECB consists of the President and Vice-President of the ECB and the Governors of the national central banks of all EU Member States. It will exist as long as not all EU Member States have adopted the euro. The General Council has no responsibility for monetary policy. It contributes mainly to strengthening the coordination of the monetary policies of the non-euro area Member States of the EU and to the necessary preparations for irrevocably fixing the exchange rates of those EU Member States (Article 141 (2) TFEU).

Each member of the Governing Council has one vote (Article 10 (2) of the Protocol). This rule goes back to the consideration in the Committee of Central Bank Governors and expresses the principle that the members of the Governing Council are appointed in their personal capacity and as such do not act as national representatives but in full independence. In the event of a tie, the President has the casting role. (Only in special cases, e.g., concerning the capital of the ECB, votes are weighted according to capital shares of national central banks.)

As the number of members of the Governing Council increased after an amendment to Article 10.2 of the Protocol by the European Council, the Governing Council on 19 March 2009 adopted a rotation system. Under the new system the members of the Executive Board will retain permanent voting rights. Governors of national central banks will rotate in and out of voting rights after one month.

Figure 14.5 shows the rotation system for a Governing Council comprising 27 national central bank Governors. The three groups are organised according to the economic and financial weight of the countries.

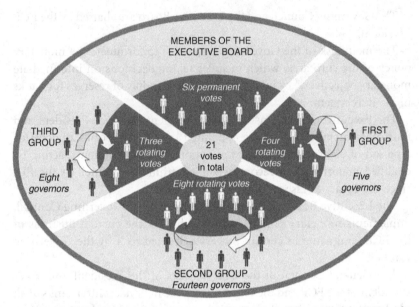

Figure 14.5 Three-group rotation system for the Governing Council of the ECB with 27 countries in the euro area
Source: ECB (2011), *The Monetary Policy of the ECB.*

While all council members will attend all meetings, only 21 members of the Governing Council will have a voting right per meeting.

14.6 The Monetary Policy Framework

14.6.1 The Two-pillar Strategy

After the establishment of the ECB, there was only little time to prepare for its new responsibility as supranational monetary policymaker. At the same time, the new central bank was confronted with an extreme degree of uncertainty: state uncertainty, parameter uncertainty and model uncertainty are common to all central banks; however, the creation of a new currency for a newly formed economic area consisting of member countries, which had been chosen only weeks before, meant an exorbitant degree of additional uncertainty in and of itself (see Issing 2005a). How was the central bank supposed to face this challenge given the sparse availability of reliable data? The intensive discussions between the responsible Board Member and experts from the ECB Directorates General Economics and Research are explained in detail in Issing et al. (2001) and ECB (1999, 2000).

In the beginning, the ECB could rely on a small but excellent staff. For additional expertise, it invited outstanding experts from other central banks and academia, and it even organised a special conference on monetary policy under uncertainty (Angeloni, Smets and Weber 2000).

The tremendous input from research combined with experience from other central banks could, however, not overcome the specific uncertainty on the transmission process of the future monetary policy for the euro area, which was likely to further evolve in response to the new monetary regime (see the Lucas critique – Lucas 1976). As a consequence, the ECB had to develop and adopt a monetary policy strategy different from those of other central banks. It could not limit itself to a specific model nor to strict rules. The strategy had to be robust at protecting against major failures.

On a proposal of the Executive Board member responsible for economics and research, the Governing Council at its meeting on 13 October 1998 resolved upon its strategy. To ensure transparency vis-à-vis the public and to demonstrate accountability, the decision was published on the same day (see ECB press release, 2014). The stability-oriented monetary policy strategy comprises these elements:

1. A quantitative definition of the primary objective of price stability, namely an annual increase in the Harmonised Index of Consumer Prices (HICP) for the euro area, of below 2 per cent. Price stability is to be maintained over the medium term.
2. A prominent role for money with a reference value for the growth of the M3 monetary aggregate set at 4 per cent in December 1998.
3. A broadly-based assessment of the outlook for future price developments which would cover all relevant information from various economic variables like wages and exchange rates, including projections.

The economic analysis comprises factors which have an immediate effect on the inflation rate, and its time horizon extends to the short-to-medium term, while the monetary analysis contains information with a focus on medium-to-longer-term risks to price stability. The monetary policy decisions are taken after cross-checking the information from the two 'pillars' (see Figure 14.6).

After extensive preparation (Issing 2003), a review of the strategy was conducted which basically confirmed the approach pursued since the start. The definition of price stability as an inflation rate below 2 per cent was confirmed. To provide a safety margin to guard against the risk of deflation, and to address the issue of a possible measurement bias in the HICP

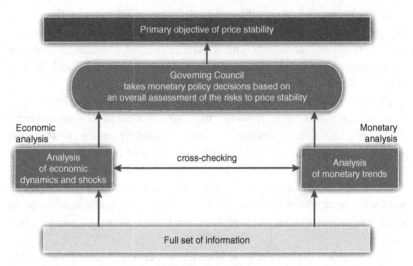

Figure 14.6 The stability-oriented monetary policy strategy of the ECB
Source: ECB (2011), *The Monetary Policy of the ECB.*

as well as the implications of inflation differentials in the euro area, the Governing Council in the pursuit of price stability would aim to maintain an inflation rate close to 2 per cent over the medium term. Moreover, the order of presentation of the economic and monetary analysis in the introductory statement of the President was changed.

Finally, it was decided no longer to conduct a review of the reference value on an annual basis.

The strategy of Inflation Targeting basically neglects the importance of money and credit (Issing 2012). The problem of such neglect became visible in the context of the financial market crisis. Further studies by the ECB (Papademos and Stark 2010) have demonstrated that the in-depth analysis of the evolution of money and credit can make a fundamental contribution to a monetary policy that takes many risks into account which are not addressed by other strategies. Recent research confirms the importance of monetary analysis in identifying risks to price stability over the medium to long term and as a means of cross-checking the signals in the economic analysis (Falagiarda and Sousa 2017).

14.6.2 The Operational Framework

The powers of a central bank, including its instruments, are usually laid down in clear legal terms. However, this is not the case for the ECB.

The Treaty contains relatively few provisions couched in relatively general terms: '. . . the ESCB (meaning the Eurosystem) shall act in accordance with the principle of an open market economy with free competition, favouring an efficient allocation of resources' (Article 2 of the Statute). The ECB shall have recourse to the national central banks to carry out operations which form part of the tasks of the ESCB (Article 12.1 of the Statute). The ECB and the national central banks may conduct open market operations as well as credit operations with credit institutions against adequate collateral (see Table 14.5).

The ECB was entitled to install a minimum reserve system (Article 19), and the Governing Council acting by a two-thirds majority may decide to resort to other instruments as well. Centralised decision-making is combined with decentralised implementation. Exploiting the latitude given by the Treaty, the ECB designed and implemented the most modern operational framework (see Table 14.5). Notable innovations include the creation of a deposit facility and the remuneration of minimum reserves (for an encompassing analysis see Mercier and Papadia 2011).

The main refinancing operation is the principal means whereby the ECB supplies the banking system with central bank money. In conducting these open market operations, the ECB could choose between fixed-rate and variable-rate tenders as well as between different methods of allotment. The two standing facilities enable credit institutions to obtain overnight liquidity or to place interest-bearing overnight deposits with the central bank. Thus, the interest rate on the marginal lending facility and on the deposit facility provide a corridor for the movements of the money-market rate. Altering the floor and the ceiling of this corridor, and widening or narrowing this corridor provide the central bank with additional room for manoeuvre.

A uniform minimum reserve ratio of 2 per cent was set for (1) all deposits with credit institutions up to an agreed maturity of two years, (2) deposits redeemable at notice of up to two years, (3) debt securities issued by credit institutions with an original maturity of up to two years and (4) money-market papers. (Since January 2012 the ratio is set at 1 per cent.) As reserve holdings are remunerated at market rates, banks have no incentive to try and evade reserve requirements. The reserve requirement has to be satisfied on an average basis over the maintenance period. This enables credit institutions to smooth the effects of fluctuations in their liquidity requirements. Under normal circumstances this arrangement strongly contributes to the stabilisation of money-market conditions. At the same time, reserve requirements create a structural demand for

Table 14.5 *Overview on Eurosystem open market operations and standing facilities*
[updated overview of open market operations and standing facilities]

Monetary policy operations	Types of transactions		Maturity	Frequency	Procedure
	Liquidity-providing	Liquidity-absorbing			
Open market operations					
Main refinancing operations	Reverse transactions	–	One week	Weekly	Standard tenders
Longer-term refinancing operations	Reverse transactions	–	Three months	Monthly	Standard tenders
Fine-tuning operations	Reverse transactions Foreign exchange swaps	Reverse transactions Collection of fixed-term deposits Foreign exchange swaps	Non-standardised	Non-regular	Quick tenders Bilateral procedures
Structural operations	Reverse transactions Outright purchases	Issuance of debt certificates Outright sales	Standardised/non-standardised –	Regular and non-regular Non-regular	Standard tenders Bilateral procedures
Standing facilities					
Marginal lending facility	Reverse transactions	–	Overnight		Access at the discretion of counterparties
Deposit facility	–	Deposits	Overnight		Access at the discretion of counterparties

Note: This procedure also applies to irregular longer-term refinancing operations with longer maturities.
Source: ECB.

central bank money 'forcing credit institutions to come to the central bank'.

This effect might prove important in the event that electronic money further gains in importance. This is an issue which is relevant for all central banks. Private electronic or digital money like Bitcoin created outside the monetary authority might increase in importance and become a major challenge for central banks (Bordo and Levin 2017). It is still an open question to what extent and with which speed digital money might crowd out central bank money. And it is even more unclear how authorities would react to this challenge – via tight regulation and/or by central banks issuing digital money themselves?

14.6.3 Accountability, Transparency, Communication

As a supranational institution, the ECB has no national counterpart. It is therefore accountable to European institutions. The ECB shall publish at least quarterly reports and the annual report on the activities of the Eurosystem shall be addressed to the European Parliament, the Council and the Commission, and also the European Council (Article 15 Protocol). The quarterly presentations by the President of the ECB to the European Parliament (Article 284.3 TFEU) is the occasion when the President explains the activities of the Eurosystem and enters into a dialogue with members of parliament.

The ECB has not only succeeded in the fulfilment of these legal obligations. In its performance on accountability it went far beyond legal requirements. As already mentioned, it published its (future) strategy ahead of the start of its monetary policy. From the beginning, after each Governing Council meeting with a monetary policy agenda, the President held a press conference, read an introductory statement, and responded to questions from a large group of journalists. It took many years before other central banks adopted this practice. The ECB published a Monthly Bulletin that was later succeeded by an Economic Bulletin when the interval between meetings was increased to (in principle) six weeks with eight meetings per year.

The Financial Stability Review provides an overview of the possible sources of risk and vulnerability to financial stability in the euro area. It is published twice a year. Other reports, for example, deal with the payments system. The ECB has established a remarkable reputation in research which is disseminated via Working Paper and Occasional Paper Series.

The ECB has also established a special relationship with academia, bank economists and the media. The yearly 'ECB and its Watchers Group' conference provides a unique forum for the interaction of leading representatives of the ECB with those groups.

Although, from the outset, the ECB published the Introductory Statement in real time, i.e. immediately after a meeting of the Governing Council, it was criticised for a lack of transparency (Buiter 1999; for a riposte see Issing 1999). The criticism essentially evolved around the decision not to publish votes.

One reason for not publishing votes was that monetary policy decisions were not taken by vote but by consensus. Consensus must not be misunderstood as unanimity. It means no more and no less than at the end of an extensive discussion in which every member of the Governing Council could express his/her view and policy preferences, the President could announce a decision. The other reason is that in a voting system in which the votes of the members were publicly revealed, in the case of the ECB their positions would inevitably be linked to their nationalities. Members act according to their personal convictions about the best single monetary policy to follow, but are collectively responsible for the decisions. In the meantime, 'Monetary Policy Accounts' are published four weeks after the meeting explaining in more detail the considerations leading to a decision. Yet, votes (and names) are not disclosed.

Like all other major central banks, the ECB has also adopted the communication tool of 'forward guidance'. After having experimented with it for some years, it is not clear why forward guidance has been referred to as a 'revolution in central bank communication' (Yellen 2012). Fortunately, the ECB has been rather cautious in applying this approach, thereby avoiding pitfalls other central banks have been confronted with (ECB 2014; Issing 2014a).

14.7 Monetary Policy, Achievements, Challenges

14.7.1 The Start

To allow a successful changeover from the monetary policies of national central banks to the new regime, on 3 December 1998, in a concerted action, all national central banks lowered their main interest rate to 3 per cent accompanied by an agreed-upon announcement from the ECB. At its meeting on 22 December, the Governing Council decided to conduct the first main refinancing operation at the fixed rate of 3 per cent on 4 January 1999. The interest rate for the marginal lending facility and the deposit facility was set at 4.5 per cent and 2 per cent, respectively. This asymmetric corridor was applied in view of market expectations of further interest rate reductions. As a transitory measure, the range between the rates on the standing facilities was restricted to 50 basis points (3.25 per cent and 2.75 per cent). This very narrow corridor was chosen to limit the possible volatility of money-market rates due to the special uncertainty around the start of the euro.

With these decisions, the Governing Council prepared the ground for a smooth transition. The single market for central bank money was established from the outset. And what is foremost striking: the changeover had no impact on financial markets whatsoever, e.g. long-term interest rates or inflation expectations. This was in strong contrast to the predictions of many sceptics about what could and would go wrong (Issing 2008). The young central bank with the small staff of the early days, and its currency, the euro, had gained credibility right from the beginning.

When the Governing Council decided on a rate cut to counter downside risks to price stability, it set a symmetrical interest rate corridor of 200 basis points with the interest rate for the main refinancing facility, the marginal lending facility, and the deposit facility reduced to 2.5 per cent, 3.5 per cent and 1.5 per cent, respectively.

It is not surprising that the ECB's innovative approach of a 'corridor system' was followed by other central banks (Mercier and Papadia 2011). Figure 14.7 shows how the ECB conducted its interest rate policy within the limits set by the rates for the two standing facilities. The ECB also adjusted the width of the corridor: it limited volatility in the market rate EONIA[2] through a narrowing of the corridor in times of increased market uncertainty. In such a situation, the central bank becomes an active intermediator in the money market. On the downside, a narrow band reduces the incentives for intermediation between banks, which should not be constrained in normal times.

14.7.2 The First Years

The early years of the ECB's monetary policy were dominated by substantial and prolonged upward price shocks (Issing 2005b). By the end of 2000, oil and import prices had risen to levels unseen since the beginning of the 1990s. While this trend reversed in 2001, food prices rose considerably on

---

[2] EONIA, the euro overnight index average, is a measure of the effective interest rate prevailing in the euro interbank overnight market.

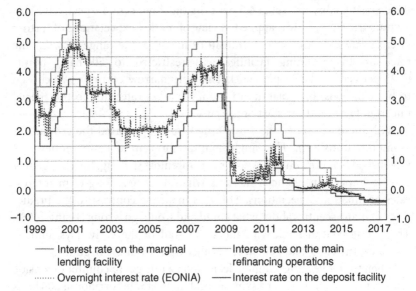

Figure 14.7 ECB interest rate policy
Source: ECB

account of livestock diseases. These were the main reasons why the year-to
-year inflation increased to more than 3 per cent in May 2001.

This was a critical challenge for the new central bank, even more so as the
exchange rate of the euro depreciated fast and substantially (Figure 14.8).

At the euro's introduction, its exchange rate against the US dollar was
1.1789 USD per euro. It reached its historic low at around 0.84 USD
in September 2000. This decline, also against other currencies of relevance,
had two negative effects for the euro area: first, it contributed to domestic
inflation via higher import prices; second, it threatened to undermine the
confidence of foreign investors in the stability of the euro. However,
mainly due to the monetary policy of the ECB which adhered to its strategy
and communicated effectively, no rise in the risk premia for euro-
denominated bonds could be observed. (In a concerted action with authorities of the USA, Japan, UK and Canada in September 2000, and again
acting alone in November, the ECB intervened in the foreign exchange
market in order to stop the decline of the euro.)

Starting in mid-1999, the ECB raised its key interest rates by a total of
225 basis points. Price pressures had gradually increased in an environment of protracted monetary expansion, a falling exchange rate, and rapid
economic growth. The minimum bid rate in the main refinancing

Figure 14.8 Euro exchange rate, 1999–2017 (EUR/USD and index)
Note: The euro real effective exchange rate represents the effective exchange rate against the main 38 trading partners. It is deflated using the CPI measure. The Euro/USD exchange rate is shown as a monthly average of daily data.
Latest observation: May 2017.
Source: ECB.

operation reached its peak of 4.75 per cent in October 2000. The ECB was especially concerned that higher import prices might cause second-round effects via wages, domestic prices and increased longer-term inflation expectations.

Although HICP inflation was still above 3 per cent, the ECB lowered its key rates by a total of 275 basis points between early 2001 and mid-2003, when the rate on the main refinancing operated had been reduced to 2 per cent. The outlook for inflation had improved and growth perspectives had declined in the context of severe shocks that hit the world economy – the terrorist attack on 11 September 2001, wars in Afghanistan and Iraq. Despite the strong expansion in M3, the monetary pillar did not suggest an alternative route for policy. Lending to the non-

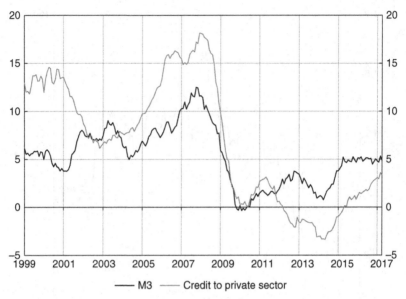

Figure 14.9 M3 growth and contribution to M3 growth from credit to private sector, 1999–2017 (annual percentage change and percentage points) [variant with *contribution* from credit growth to private sector]
Latest observation: April 2017.
Source: ECB.

financial sector continued to decline (see Figure 14.9). The high volatility in financial markets induced investors to reduce investment in risky assets and shift their capital into safer and more liquid assets included in M3. In the course of 2003, those portfolio shifts phased out and monetary dynamics calmed down. Price pressures were contained and a moderate economic recovery started. Consequently, the ECB kept its interest rates unchanged until the end of 2005.

While growth was recovering, it was only in early 2004 that inflation fell below 2 per cent. The exchange rate had risen from its historically low level.

This phase of reduced interest rates was followed by a period of raising rates by a total of 235 basis points which started in December 2005 and ended in July 2008 with a main refinancing rate of 4.25 per cent. Rapid expansion of money and credit indicated upside risks to price stability. Strong increases in oil and food prices pushed inflation to levels clearly above 2 per cent. Whereas price pressures argued in favour of a (last) rate hike on 3 July 2008, the outlook for the global economy had dramatically deteriorated, which drew strong criticism of this decision.

14.7.3 Heterogeneity across Member States

Considering the heterogeneity across member countries, the conduct of a single monetary policy raises the question 'does one size fit all?' Although inflation rates had converged substantially in the preparatory process to EMU, differentials remained.

Different inflation rates imply different real interest rates for the same nominal ECB policy rate. However, measurement should be based on inflation expectations, and the real exchange rate or competitive channel can counter-balance this divergence (Gaspar and Issing 2011). It is striking that the divergence of inflation rates in the euro area is comparable to those in another large monetary union, the US (see Figure 14.10). As it turned out, the big

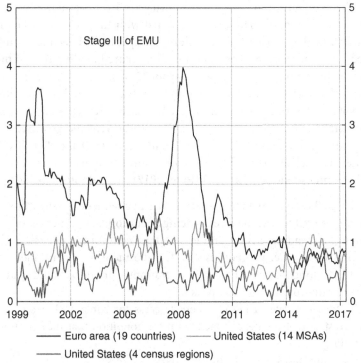

Figure 14.10 Dispersion of annual inflation in the euro area, 14 US metropolitan statistical areas (MSAs) and the four US census regions (percentage points)
Note: The dispersion is measured as unweighted standard deviation across country or region-specific inflation measures. MSAs refers to Metropolitan Statistical Areas. The four census regions are Northeast, Midwest, South, and West urban.
Latest observation: April 2017.
Source: Eurostat and US Bureau of Labor Statistics.

problem was not connected to divergence as such, but rather lay in the fact that, in the euro area, the countries with inflation rates above the average and those below remained the same over a long period, thereby accumulating competitive disadvantages and advantages, respectively.

14.7.4 Monetary Policy in Times of Financial Crises

In retrospect, the financial market crisis in early August 2007 was a warning signal for the fragility of the system. At that time, it was mainly if not exclusively interpreted as a liquidity crisis. When market liquidity dried up, the ECB acted quickly and provided practically unlimited overnight liquidity through fine-tuning operations (see ECB 2008; Trichet 2013). A number of swap lines with other central banks was established, with the main goal of overcoming a shortage in US dollar liquidity.

The deep financial market crisis erupted with the collapse of Lehman Brothers. In the aftermath of its failure, the spreads between term, unsecured interbank lending rates, and rates on secured lending rose to more than 180 basis points (Mercier and Papadia 2011).

Growth collapsed in most industrial countries, unemployment almost exploded, and price developments tended towards zero. It was the challenge for central banks (and fiscal policymakers) to prevent the great recession from turning into a great depression like in the 1930s (Fahr et al. 2011).

The ECB relied on a whole battery of measures within the existing toolbox and expanded its arsenal (Praet 2017). Notable steps include:

- The ECB reduced the main interest rates in a sequence of steps down to 0.00 per cent for the main refinancing operation, to 0.25 per cent for the marginal lending facility, and to –0.40 per cent for the deposit facility.
- Fixed-rate tender procedures with full allotment were continued.
- LTRO – longer-term refinancing operations – provided liquidity at low fixed rates for an extended period.
- TLTRO – targeted LTRO – opened access for banks to borrow at the interest rate of the deposit facility on the condition that they continued lending.
- Asset purchases program in secondary markets
  - private asset purchases
  - public asset purchases (80 bn of monthly purchases in euro are in sovereign debt markets; from initially 60 bn they were increased to 80 bn and and then reduced again to 60 bn). As a consequence of those asset purchases the ECB's balance sheet expanded dramatically (Figure 14.11).
  - collateral framework expansion (list of eligible assets).

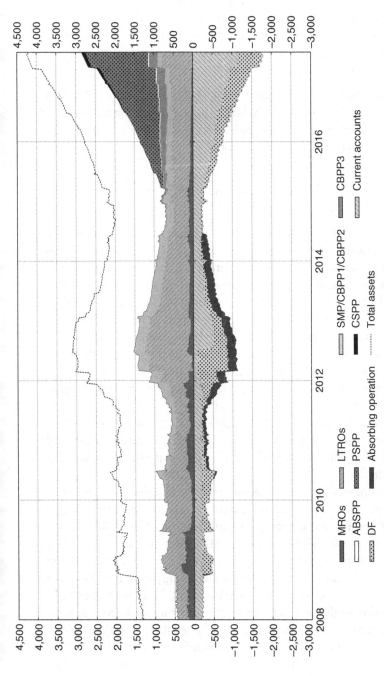

Figure 14.11 ECB balance sheet: total assets and monetary policy instruments (billion of euro)

Note: LTROs include TLRTOs.

Latest observation: 30 June 2017, except for total assets 22 June 2017.

Source: ECB.

- The announcement of OMT – Outright Monetary Transaction – by the President: 'Whatever it takes' (2 August 2012).
- The introduction of forward guidance (4 July 2013) – 'Governing Council expects the key interest rates to remain at present or lower levels for an extended period of time.'

These measures have contributed to support growth and employment via low bank lending rates (Draghi 2017). Especially in vulnerable countries, lending rates have declined, reducing the dispersion of those rates across euro area countries (see Figure 14.12).

14.7.5 Risks of Low Interest Rates

The main focus of the ECB's very expansionary monetary policy was on containing downside risks to price stability. HICP inflation approaching the zero-line raised the fear of deflation. Core inflation also reached levels below 1 per cent, but there was no indication of a downward deflationary spiral. After all, the only episode in history of such a self-accelerating process was observed in the Great Depression in the 1930s and there is no empirical evidence for a necessary negative impact of low inflation/mild deflation on economic growth (Borio and Filardo 2004). In the context of a global environment of low inflation and its impact on domestic (i.e. euro area) price developments, it might be appropriate to assess the maintenance of price stability against a longer horizon than medium term.

One might also ask why a monetary policy stance which is much more expansionary than it was at the time of the great recession should be maintained after the recovery of the economy had started to broaden and strengthen.

These arguments have to be taken seriously in light of the negative effects of an extended period of extremely low interest rates (White 2012). It is not any more appropriate to speak of adverse 'side' effects as the impact on the whole financial system becomes more and more visible. Life insurance companies, pension funds, and business pension programmes are under extreme stress stemming from this extended period of low interest rates. This environment leads to higher risk-taking also due to the fact that the ECB is a strong buyer in safe asset markets. Extremely low interest rates keep weak banks alive, which continue to extend credit to weak non-financial corporations ('zombie banks keep zombie companies alive', see Archarya, Pierret and Steffen

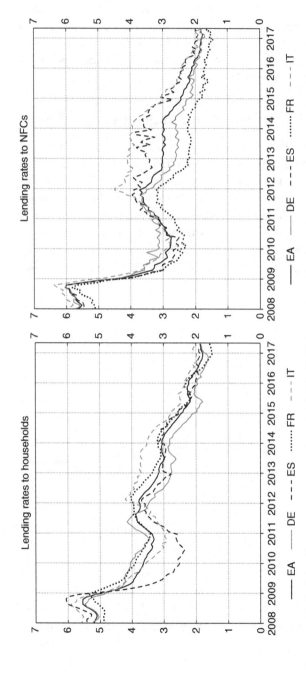

Figure 14.12 Bank lending rates – euro area countries (2008–2017) (percentages per annum)

Note: The indicator for the total cost of lending is calculated by aggregating short- and long-term rates using 24-months moving average of new business volumes.

Latest observation: April 2017.

Source: ECB.

2017). The longer the situation of low interest rates perpetuates, the more capital allocation becomes distorted, not least in the construction sector that will overexpand (Rajan 2013). This development might also have unintended redistributive effects (Brunnermeier and Sannikov 2012). The BIS is the most important voice warning against potential risks to financial stability (BIS 2016).

14.8 ECB – Success and Challenges

After a successful start, the ECB has established its reputation as a central bank that is devoted to its mandate of maintaining price stability given that inflation expectations have always been under control (see Figure 14.13). The euro is a stable currency, inflation has been kept in check and deflation – if the risk of a dangerous deflationary spiral ever existed – was avoided. In a global environment of low inflation, the ECB should not be criticised for failing its mandate of maintaining price stability when inflation, for a prolonged period, remains significantly below the target inflation of below 2 per cent.

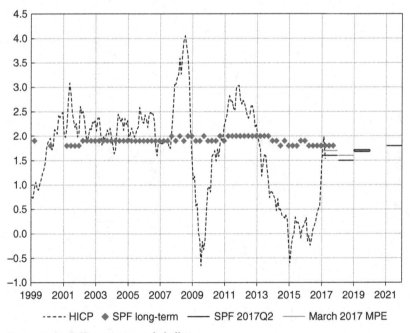

Figure 14.13 ECB – success and challenges
Source: ECB

On another note, the recent monetary policy might undermine the ECB's reputation as an independent central bank. Starting in May 2010, with substantial purchases of bonds of some governments under pressure from markets, the ECB has implicitly taken on a new role as guarantor of the maintenance of the membership of countries in the EMU, when in fact this should rather fall within the scope of responsibility of national governments (Issing 2017).

The announcement of OMT in July 2012 – 'whatever it takes' – was, on the one hand, celebrated as a kind of heroic European intervention; on the other hand, it was criticised as an act beyond the ECB's mandate. With the decision of the European Court of Justice, the case seems legally settled. However, the argument by the ECB that all actions in this direction are necessary to preserve the transmission mechanism of monetary policy is anything but convincing in economic terms.

A neutral observer argues: 'The proposal for outright monetary transactions is a transfer from countries that can borrow cheaply to countries that can't borrow cheaply. There's no point dressing it up with fancy language such as measures to improve the transmission mechanism of monetary policy. It's a straight transfer from countries that have credibility in their ability to run their public finances to countries that don't. From that perspective, it clearly violates the no-bail-out clause of the European Treaty, and it runs completely counter to this vision of the monetary union' (King 2016, p. 47).

The OMT so far remains an announcement on potential actions in future crises by buying sovereign bonds. Under its current asset purchases programme the ECB not only reduces the level of long-term interest rates in general but also keeps spreads between bonds from different countries under control (see Figure 14.14).

As a consequence, decisions of the Governing Council, especially on the purchase of government bonds, are inevitably burdened by political considerations, considerations which should have no place in an independent central bank. The effectiveness of the ECB as the 'only game in town' is a dangerous threat to the independence of the central bank.

It will be a tremendous challenge to exit from this policy and to fully assign political responsibility to the institutions it belongs to, i.e. national governments.

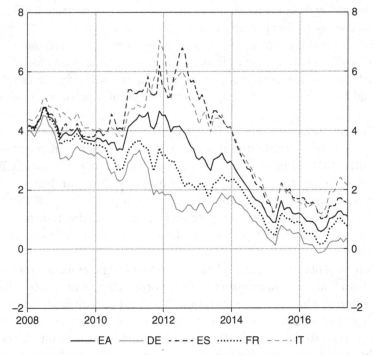

Figure 14.14 Euro area countries' long-term government bond yields (2008–2017)
(percentages per annum)
Note: Long-term government bond yields corresponds to 10-year yields. The euro area
yield is the GDP-weighted average yield across all euro area countries.
Latest observation: 8 June 2017.
Source: ECB.

References

Angeloni, I., Smets, F. and Weber, A. eds. (2000), Monetary policy-making under
    uncertainty, European Central Bank and Center for Financial Studies, Frankfurt.
Archarya, V., Pierret, D. and Steffen, S. (2017), Lender of last resort versus buyer of last
    resort – evidence from the European debt crisis, CFS, 11 April.
Bank for International Settlements (2016), 86th Annual Report, Basel, 26 June.
Bordo, M.D. and Levin, A.T. (2017), Central bank digital currency and the future of
    monetary policy, NBER Working Paper Series, Working Paper 23711, August.
Borio, C. and Filardo, A. (2004), Looking back at the international deflation record, BIS
    Working Papers, No. 152, March.
Brunnermeier, M. K. and Sannikov Y. (2012), Redistributive monetary policy, Jackson
    Hole Symposium.
Buiter, W. H. (1999), Alice in Euroland, CEPR Policy Paper Series No. 1, April.
Draghi, M. (2017), Monetary policy and the economic recovery in the euro area, Speech
    at the ECB and its Watchers XVIII Conference, Frankfurt, 6 April.

ECB (1999), The stability-oriented monetary policy strategy of the Eurosystem, Monthly Bulletin, February.

ECB (2000), The two pillars of the ECB's monetary policy strategy, Monthly Bulletin, November.

ECB (2008), The Eurosystem's open market operations during the recent period of financial market volatility, Monthly Bulletin, May.

ECB (2011), *The Monetary Policy of the ECB*, ECB, Frankfurt.

ECB (2014), The ECB's Forward Guidance, Monthly Bulletin, March.

Falagiarda, M. and Sousa, J. (2017), Forecasting euro area inflation using targeted predictors: is money coming back?, ECB Working Paper, No. 2015, February.

Fahr, S., Motto, R., Rostagno, M., Smets, F. and Tristani, O. (2011), A monetary strategy in good and bad times: lessons from the recent past, ECB Working Paper, No. 1336, May.

Feldstein, M. (1997), EMU and international conflict, *Foreign Affairs*, November/December, 60–73.

Gaspar, V., Issing O. (2011), European Central Bank and monetary policy in the euro area, *The New Palgrave Dictionary of Economics*, Online edition, S. N. Durlauf and L. W. Blume, (eds.), Palgrave Macmillan, 4 July 2017. Available at: http://www.dictionaryofeconomics.com/article?id=pde2011_M000429

Issing, O. (1999), The Eurosystem: transparent and accountable, or Willem in Euroland, *Journal of Common Market Studies*, 37:3, September, 503–519.

Issing, O. (ed.), (2003), Background studies for the ECB's evaluation of its monetary policy strategy, European Central Bank, Frankfurt, November.

Issing, O. (2005a), Monetary policy in uncharted territory, in O. Issing, V. Gaspar, O. Tristani, and D. Vestin, (eds.), *Imperfect Knowledge and Monetary Policy*, Cambridge University Press.

Issing, O. (2005b), The ECB and the euro – the first 6 years: a view from the ECB, *Journal of Policy Modelling*, June, 404–420.

Issing, O. (2006), Europe's hard fix, *International Economics and Policy*, 3: 3–4.

Issing, O. (2008), *The Birth of the Euro*, Cambridge University Press.

Issing, O. (2012), *Central Banks – Paradise Lost*, Institute for Monetary and Economic Studies, Bank of Japan, Tokyo, November.

Issing, O. (2014a), *Economic and Monetary Union in Europe*, in I. Barens, V. Caspari, B. Schefold (eds.), *Political Events and Economic Ideas*, Edward Elgar Publishing, Cheltenham.

Issing, O. (2014b), Forward guidance: a new challenge for central banks, Research Center SAFE, White Paper Series No. 16, Frankfurt.

Issing, O. (2017), Central banks – are their reputations and independence under threat from overburdening?, *International Finance*, 20:1, Spring, 92–99.

Issing, O., Gaspar, V., Angeloni, I. and Tristani, O. (2001), *Monetary Policy in the Euro Area*, Cambridge University Press.

Kenen, P. B. (1969), The optimum currency area: an eclectic view, in R. A. Mundell and A. K. Swoboda (eds.), *Monetary Problems of the International Economy*, Chicago University Press, Chicago.

King, M. A. (2016), *The End Alchemy: Money, Banking, and the Future of the Global Economy*, W.W. Norton, New York.

Lucas, R. E. (1976), Econometric policy evaluation: a critique, Carnegie-Rochester Conference Series on Public Policy 1.

McKinnon, R. I. (1963), Optimum currency areas, *American Economic Review*, 53: 4.

Mercier, P. and Papadia, F. (eds.) (2011), *The Concrete Euro*, Oxford University Press.

Mundell, R. A. (1961), A theory of optimal currency areas, *American Economic Review*, 51: 4.

Papademos, L. D. and Stark, J. (eds.) (2010), *Enhancing Monetary Analysis*, European Central Bank, Frankfurt.

Praet, P. (2017), The ECB's monetary policy: past and present, Speech at Febelfin Connect event, Brussels/Londerzeel, 16 March.

Rajan, R. (2013), A step in the dark: unconventional monetary policy after the crisis, Speech delivered at the inaugural Andrew Crockett Memorial Talk at the BIS, 23 June.

Tietmeyer, H. (2005), *Herausforderung Euro*, Hansen, München.

Trichet, J.-C. (2013), Central banking in the crisis – conceptual convergence and open questions on unconventional monetary policy, 2013 Per Jacobsson Lecture, Washington, 12 October.

White, W. (2012, Ultra easy monetary policy and the law of unintended consequences, Federal Reserve Bank of Dallas, Working Paper No. 126.

Yellen, J. L. (2012), Revolution and evolution in central bank communication, Speech at the Haas School of Business, University of California, Berkeley, 13 November.

Index

Printed in the United States
By Bookmasters